2/8/10

Dear John,

Please accept this work of mine,

You are my best director!

Yours,

Michael Bell

2/8/10

D1407561

SOA MODELING PATTERNS FOR SERVICE-ORIENTED DISCOVERY AND ANALYSIS

SOA MODELING PATTERNS FOR SERVICE-ORIENTED DISCOVERY AND ANALYSIS

MICHAEL BELL

WILEY

JOHN WILEY & SONS, INC.

Published by John Wiley & Sons, Inc., Hoboken, New Jersey.
Published simultaneously in Canada.

For general information on our other products and services, or technical support, please contact our Customer Care Department within the United States at 800-762-2974, outside the United States at 317-572-3993 or fax 317-572-4002.

Wiley also publishes its books in a variety of electronic formats. Some content that appears in print may not be available in electronic books.

For more information about Wiley products, visit our Web site at www.wiley.com.

Library of Congress Cataloging-in-Publication Data

Bell, Michael
   SOA modeling patterns for service-oriented discovery and analysis / Michael Bell.
      p.   cm.
   Includes index.
   ISBN 978-0-470-48197-4 (hardback)
   1. Web services.   2. Service-oriented architecture (Computer science)   3. Computer network architectures.   I. Title.
   TK5105.88813.B45 2010
   004.068–dc22   2009029114

Printed in the United States of America

10 9 8 7 6 5 4 3 2 1

For Agamit, Nirr, Yair, and Nitay, whose love and support carried me through this rewarding project

Service-Oriented Discovery and Analysis Patterns

Discovery and Analysis Road Map Patterns

Service Identification Patterns

Service Categorization Patterns

Contextual Analysis and Modeling Patterns

Structural Analysis and Modeling Patterns

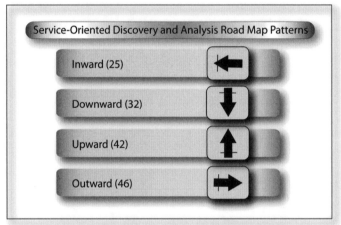

Service-Oriented Discovery and Analysis Road Map Patterns

Inward (25)

Downward (32)

Upward (42)

Outward (46)

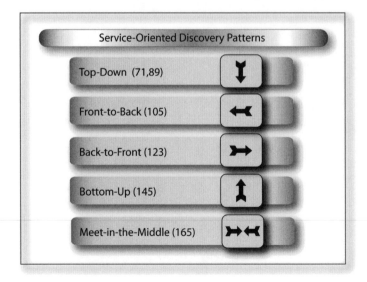

Service-Oriented Discovery Patterns

Top-Down (71,89)

Front-to-Back (105)

Back-to-Front (123)

Bottom-Up (145)

Meet-in-the-Middle (165)

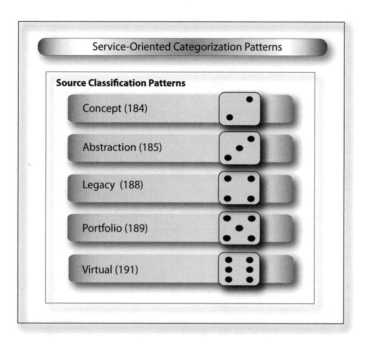

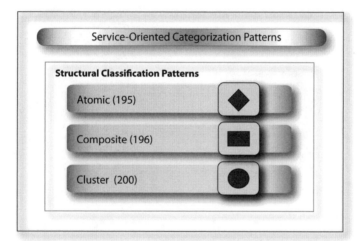

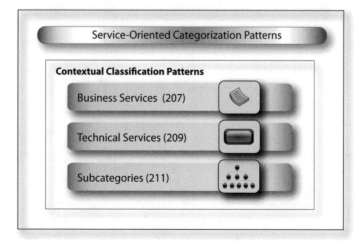

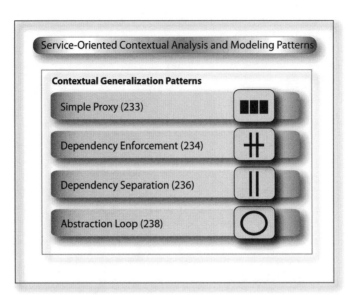

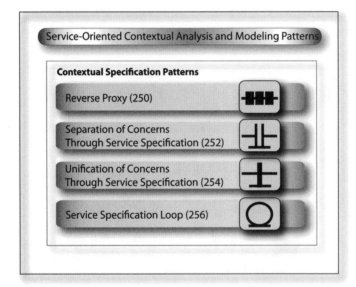

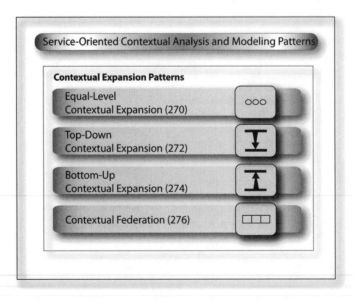

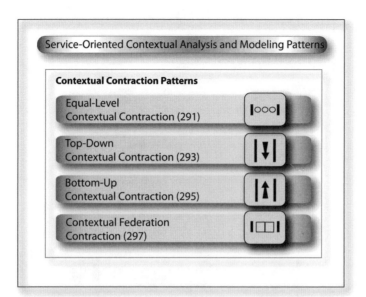

Service-Oriented Contextual Analysis and Modeling Patterns

Contextual Contraction Patterns

Equal-Level
Contextual Contraction (291)

Top-Down
Contextual Contraction (293)

Bottom-Up
Contextual Contraction (295)

Contextual Federation
Contraction (297)

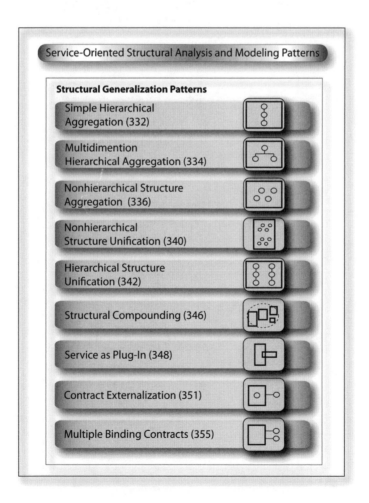

Service-Oriented Structural Analysis and Modeling Patterns

Structural Generalization Patterns

Simple Hierarchical
Aggregation (332)

Multidimention
Hierarchical Aggregation (334)

Nonhierarchical Structure
Aggregation (336)

Nonhierarchical
Structure Unification (340)

Hierarchical Structure
Unification (342)

Structural Compounding (346)

Service as Plug-In (348)

Contract Externalization (351)

Multiple Binding Contracts (355)

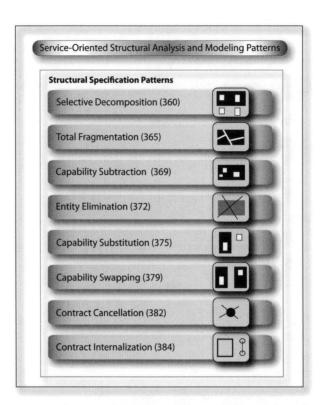

Service-Oriented Structural Analysis and Modeling Patterns

Structural Specification Patterns

Selective Decomposition (360)

Total Fragmentation (365)

Capability Subtraction (369)

Entity Elimination (372)

Capability Substitution (375)

Capability Swapping (379)

Contract Cancellation (382)

Contract Internalization (384)

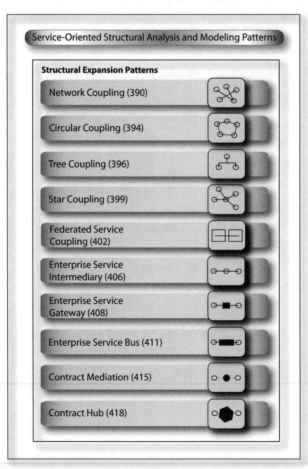

Service-Oriented Structural Analysis and Modeling Patterns

Structural Expansion Patterns

Network Coupling (390)

Circular Coupling (394)

Tree Coupling (396)

Star Coupling (399)

Federated Service Coupling (402)

Enterprise Service Intermediary (406)

Enterprise Service Gateway (408)

Enterprise Service Bus (411)

Contract Mediation (415)

Contract Hub (418)

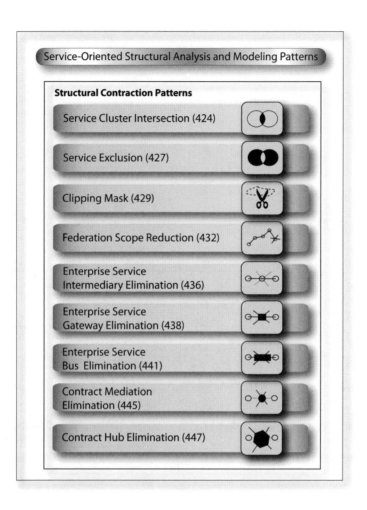

Service-Oriented Structural Analysis and Modeling Patterns

Structural Contraction Patterns

Service Cluster Intersection (424)

Service Exclusion (427)

Clipping Mask (429)

Federation Scope Reduction (432)

Enterprise Service
Intermediary Elimination (436)

Enterprise Service
Gateway Elimination (438)

Enterprise Service
Bus Elimination (441)

Contract Mediation
Elimination (445)

Contract Hub Elimination (447)

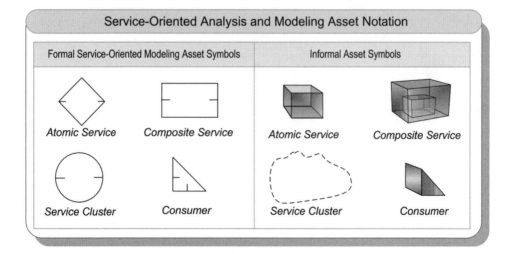

Service-Oriented Analysis and Modeling Asset Notation

Formal Service-Oriented Modeling Asset Symbols

Atomic Service   Composite Service

Service Cluster   Consumer

Informal Asset Symbols

Atomic Service   Composite Service

Service Cluster   Consumer

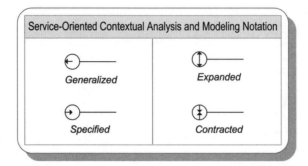

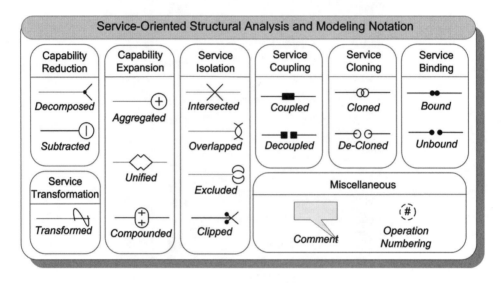

CONTENTS

Preface **xix**

Foreword **xxi**

CHAPTER 1   Introduction   **1**

What is Service-Oriented Discovery and Analysis?   2
Service-Oriented Analysis Endeavor   2
Service-Oriented Discovery Endeavor   7
Service-Oriented Discovery and Analysis Proposition   11
Driving Principles of Service-Oriented Discovery and Analysis   13
Service-Oriented Discovery and Analysis Modeling   15
Service-Oriented Discovery and Analysis Patterns   17
Summary   20

PART ONE   Service-Oriented Discovery and Analysis
Road Map Patterns   **21**

CHAPTER 2   Vertical Service Discovery and Analysis: Pursuing
Inward and Downward Road Map Patterns   **25**

Service Discovery and Analysis Inward Road Map Pattern   25
Service Discovery and Analysis Downward Road Map Pattern   32
Deliverables   38
Summary   39

CHAPTER 3   Horizontal Service Discovery and Analysis: Pursuing
Upward and Outward Road Map Patterns   **41**

Service-Oriented Discovery and Analysis Upward
Road Map Pattern   42
Service Discovery and Analysis Outward Road Map Pattern   46
Deliverables   56
Summary   56

CHAPTER 4   Service-Oriented Discovery and Analysis Best
Practices Model: Striving for Balanced Solutions   **59**

Meet-in-the-Middle Service Discovery: Balancing
the Identification Venture   59
Structural and Contextual Analysis and Modeling:
Balanced Solutions   61

Focus on Service Discovery and Analysis Cross-Cutting
Activities   62
Categorization of Services: Reality Check   64
Service-Oriented Discovery and Analysis Best
Practices Model   64
Deliverables   68
Summary   68

PART TWO   Service-Oriented Discovery Patterns   **69**

CHAPTER 5   Top-Down Business Process-Driven Service Discovery Pattern   **71**

Is Business Process Top-Down Service Discovery Practical?   71
Documenting Business Processes: Industry Standards   72
Understand Business Processes   72
Define Business Process Analysis Maturity Level   76
Study Documented Business Processes   77
Establish Service-Oriented Business Process Model   78
Discover Analysis Services   82
Deliverables   87
Summary   88

CHAPTER 6   Top-Down Attribute-Driven Service Discovery Pattern   **89**

Study Business and Technology Discovery Sources   89
Attend to the Service Discovery Process   90
Institute Core Attributes   91
Establish Attribution Model   93
Select Attributes for Service Discovery   95
Found Decision Model   97
Discover Analysis Services   100
Establish Service Taxonomy   102
Deliverables   104
Summary   104

CHAPTER 7   Front-to-Back Service Discovery Pattern   **105**

Front-to-Back Service Discovery Model   105
User Interface Control Services   106
User Interface Content Delivery Services   111
User Interface Content Rendering Services   114
User Interface Value Services   117

Front-to-Back Service Discovery Process   118
Deliverables   122
Summary   122

CHAPTER 8   Back-to-Front Service Discovery Pattern   **123**

Conceptual Data Model Perspective   123
Logical Data Model Perspective   127
Physical Data Model Perspective   139
Back-to-Front Service Discovery Process   139
Deliverables   144
Summary   144

CHAPTER 9   Bottom-Up Service Discovery Pattern   **145**

Bottom-Up Business Functionality–Driven Service Discovery   145
Bottom-Up Technology-Driven Service Discovery   152
Bottom-Up Reference Architecture–Driven Service Discovery   157
Deliverables   163
Summary   163

CHAPTER 10   Meet-in-the-Middle Service Discovery Pattern   **165**

Integration-Oriented Services   165
Common Business Services   172
Infrastructure-Oriented Services   175
Deliverables   179
Summary   180

PART THREE   Service-Oriented Categorization Patterns   **181**

CHAPTER 11   Service Source Categorization Patterns   **183**

Service Ideas and Concepts   183
Service Abstractions   185
Legacy Entities: Road-Tested Executables   188
Service Portfolio   189
Virtual Entities   191
Deliverables   191
Summary   192

CHAPTER 12   Service Structure Categorization Patterns   **193**

Service Structure Model   193
Environmental Influences on Service Structure   194
Service Structure Categorization Driving Principles   195

Atomic Service Structure: Indivisible Pattern   195
Composite Service Structure: Hierarchical Pattern   196
Service Cluster: Distributed and Federated Pattern   200
Deliverables   203
Summary   204

CHAPTER 13   Service Contextual Categorization Patterns   **205**

Contextual Classification Model: Patterns for Service
Contextual Categorization   205
Establishing Leading Service Categories   207
Service Subcategories Establishment Process   211
Deliverables   219
Summary   219

PART FOUR   Service-Oriented Contextual Analysis
             Process and Modeling Patterns   **221**

CHAPTER 14   Contextual Generalization Analysis
              Process and Modeling Patterns   **225**

Contextual Generalization Process   225
Contextual Generalization Patterns   232
Contextual Generalization Anti-Patterns   240
Deliverables   243
Summary   243

CHAPTER 15   Contextual Specification Analysis
              Process and Modeling Patterns   **245**

Contextual Specification Process   245
Contextual Specification Patterns   250
Service Specification Anti-Patterns   258
Deliverables   261
Summary   261

CHAPTER 16   Contextual Expansion Analysis Process
              and Modeling Patterns   **263**

Contextual Expansion Process   264
Contextual Expansion Levels: Organizational Zones
for Distribution of Services   265
Contextual Expansion Patterns   270
Service Contextual Expansion Anti-Patterns   278
Deliverables   281
Summary   281

CHAPTER 17   Contextual Contraction Analysis Process
and Modeling Patterns   **283**

Accommodating Demand for Contextual Contraction   283
Service Contextual Contraction Benefits   284
Service Contextual Contraction Example   285
Contextual Contraction Process   286
Contextual Contraction Patterns   290
Contextual Contraction Anti-Patterns   299
Deliverables   301
Summary   301

PART FIVE   Service-Oriented Structural Analysis
Process and Modeling Patterns   **303**

CHAPTER 18   Structural Analysis and Modeling Principles:
Introduction to Service Structural Notation
and Modeling   **305**

Structural Analysis Modeling Principles   305
Structural Modeling Notation Introduction   306
Aggregation   310
Decomposition   311
Subtraction   312
Coupling and Decoupling   313
Compounding   315
Unification   316
Transformation   318
Intersection   319
Exclusion   321
Clipping   323
Binding and Unbinding   324
Cloning and Decloning   326
Deliverables   328
Summary   329

CHAPTER 19   Structural Generalization Analysis Process
and Modeling Patterns   **331**

Aggregation Analysis: Patterns and Implementation   332
Unification Analysis: Patterns and Implementation   339
Structural Compounding Analysis: Patterns
and Implementation   345
Contract Analysis: Patterns and Implementation   351

	Deliverables	357
	Summary	357

CHAPTER 20   **Structural Specification Analysis Process and Modeling Patterns**   **359**

Decomposition Analysis: Patterns and Implementation   359
Subtraction Analysis: Patterns and Implementation   368
Refactoring Analysis: Patterns and Implementation   375
Contract Analysis: Patterns and Implementation   382
Deliverables   388
Summary   388

CHAPTER 21   **Structural Expansion Analysis Process and Modeling Patterns**   **389**

Distribution Analysis: Patterns and Implementation   390
Mediation Analysis: Patterns and Implementation   405
Contract Analysis: Patterns and Implementation   414
Deliverables   420
Summary   420

CHAPTER 22   **Structural Contraction Analysis Process and Modeling Patterns**   **423**

Distribution Reduction Analysis: Patterns and Implementation   424
Mediation Rollback Analysis: Patterns and Implementation   435
Contract Analysis: Patterns and Implementation   444
Deliverables   450
Summary   450

Index   **451**

PREFACE

One of the most challenging tasks in today's business and information technology (IT) environments is to communicate a solution to an organizational problem in a simple manner that can be easily understood by business and IT personnel alike. Is it also arduous to explain in simple words how a remedy to an enterprise concern can be applied without getting bogged down by unnecessary and confusing details that do not necessarily depict the nature of the solution. Perhaps the secret ingredient to the implementation of a successful project is people who can articulate a cure to an organizational threat in a straightforward fashion. Managers, architects, developers, analysts, and modelers should be able not only to justify their course of action but also to elaborate on the motivation behind the methodology and technologies used to meet business requirements and technical specifications.

The intrinsic difficulty in explaining a solution in plain words is related to the intricate structure of a project, which characteristically consists of various requirements, each of which must satisfy different stakeholders' imperatives. These distinct views typically represent concerns such as architecture direction and adherence to best practices, technological feasibility, implementation complexities, and even return on investment. To alleviate these challenges, *SOA Modeling Patterns for Service-Oriented Discovery and Analysis* offers a service-oriented architecture (SOA) discipline that can assist practitioners to efficiently analyze the problem domain, discover services, and propose a viable solution to an organizational concern by employing different implementation perspectives. This book also offers a simple SOA modeling language and patterns to overcome the communication barriers between business and IT professionals.

SOA Modeling Patterns for Service-Oriented Discovery and Analysis answers the most challenging questions that practitioners typically ask during the service-oriented development process:

- How should an organizational problem domain and business requirements be analyzed?
- How can practitioners separate business and technical concerns?
- How should technical specifications be inspected and verified against business requirements?
- How should a service be discovered for a software development project?
- What is the method for analyzing service's feasibility for construction and production?
- How should a service be certified for deployment and production?
- How should the SOA modeling language be employed during the service identification and examination process?
- How should the practitioner utilize the SOA modeling patterns and anti-patterns for service discovery and analysis?

The patterns provided offer road-tested analysis and discovery processes and design solutions to assist practitioners in devising an analysis proposition, a modeling artifact that helps to solve business or technological concerns. This solution proposition is also the ultimate deliverable of the service-oriented discovery and analysis discipline that is elaborated on in the book's five parts:

1. **Service-Oriented Discovery and Analysis Road Map Patterns.** This part depicts overarching milestones, goals, and guiding patterns for discovering and analyzing services. The directions and best practices described alleviate a service's internal and external architecture complexities and offer a superior solution proposition.

2. **Service-Oriented Discovery Patterns.** To assist practitioners with an effective discovery process, the patterns provided help broaden the quest for services that can aid in a solution. These repeatable service identification methods should be followed to maximize the opportunities for service discovery.

3. **Service-Oriented Categorization Patterns.** Once the services have been identified, the categorization process takes place, both to strengthen the solution and to help carve out an organizational service taxonomy to promote communication and collaboration efforts between various stakeholders.

4. **Service-Oriented Contextual Analysis Process and Modeling Patterns.** The contextual analysis process employs modeling patterns and operations to promote service reuse, architecture loose coupling, and consolidation of software assets. The term "contextual" pertains to the manipulation of service offerings, capabilities, and functionality to provide a solution.

5. **Service-Oriented Structural Analysis Process and Modeling Patterns.** Finally, the service structural perspective is subject to analysis and perfection. Here the practitioner focuses on logical and physical service formations to enhance a solution and propose an effective remedy. The modeling patterns assist with the structural manipulation of a service's internal construct as well as its surrounding environment.

FOREWORD

It's been a decade since the wild-eyed vision of service architectures first started to capture our imagination and five years since the global shift to service-oriented architecture (SOA) matured into a global industry of enabling products, methodologies, and services. The results? A mixed bag to be sure: Success stories abound of companies achieving dramatic gains in agility and efficiency; and, conversely, many companies that jumped onto the SOA bandwagon with ill-advised planning and governance produced scores of the same rigid, inflexible, and complex systems they had in the past. The time has come to step back and learn from experience, driven by the convergence of two phenomena: numerous successful case studies now available and a global economic downturn that brought a mandate to streamline the enterprise into a new kind of service delivery platform. "Enterprise 2.0" is "enterprise as a service," coupling SOA techniques with true business objectives.

Many people are surprised when they learn of the state of today's enterprise. Fifty years of automation efforts and trillions of dollars spent to extend, advance, and modernize the technology environment. And to what end? From an outside perspective, perhaps—it does seem to be working just fine. Stuff gets done, business happens, transactions flow, supply chains connect, and partners integrate. Well... yes, kind of.

What is the tariff being paid today in both cost and opportunity as a result of the current state of enterprise information technology (IT)? Looking under the hood of enterprise IT, one is reminded of Otto von Bismarck's famous quote: "The less one knows about how laws and sausage are made the better." In today's global business environment, *enterprise sausage* is made from:

- Silos of incompatible, redundant, difficult-to-integrate systems—the business equivalent of an Olympic swimmer in an iron lung.
- Core and commodity applications running on the same high-cost/low-latency infrastructure. Logic: Let's take the whole family out to Le Cirque every night and include the chicken nugget–loving children and redneck cousins who prefer pork rinds.
- Rampant overprovisioning to accommodate infrequent peak load spikes, resulting in shockingly low utilization.
- Inability to incorporate external infrastructure and third-party services, cementing rigid cost structures and stifling innovation.
- Mergers and acquisitons integration costs regularly crush expected "synergies," resulting in either outright failure or the proliferation of more silos.
- Project-based development and lack of closed-loop governance results in nonreusable services and a proliferation of unenforceable policies. That's like giving a raise to the Police Commissioner of New York City while laying off the police force.

And if that weren't enough madness for you, consider:

- *Hosting madness.* Nonstandard SKUs ensure long-term vendor lock-in, stifling creativity and creating massive opaque costs.
- *Energy madness.* Running a server in an enterprise data center for two years creates an energy cost equivalent to the price of buying the server itself. To add insult to injury: Half the servers or more are only for development and testing anyway and are barely in use most of the time.
- *Human madness.* Underutilized workforces are rampant due to silo-based application delivery and single-purpose desktops.

I could go on, but my doctor says I need to avoid stress.

So what's the prescription? If we've learned one thing in the Internet era, it's that interoperability drives efficiency. From e-mail to browsers, the impact of standards-based communications cannot be overstated. In the coming years, more companies will begin to learn from the lessons and battle scars of service-oriented architecture and service-oriented infrastructure (SOI) and how these initiatives can produce more efficient operating models. These same companies will also find that these goals must be pursued in the context of a well-designed program that aligns activities with business objectives and defines services in a process-oriented manner rather than ad hoc approach, and recognizes that security and closed-loop governance must be design-time considerations rather than afterthoughts. These are among the core lessons of the past, and today they represent the foundation for a new era of enterprise computing.

Michael Bell has been there every step of the way and is well qualified to offer the first practical guide to achieve the organizational benefits of SOA. With a common thread of "business practicality and technical feasibility" underlying each recommendation, Bell provides the missing link between architecture and results that has eluded many in the industry for years. By understanding the business motivations within an organization first and applying a transparent process of service discovery and analysis, the real benefits of service orientation can be realized. As the exuberance of the past settles into a set of basic organizational principles, these efforts can no longer be considered nice to have—they are table stakes for any organization looking to compete in the decade to come.

Eric Fuller
Founder and Chairman, SOA Software, Inc.
Founder and CEO, ServiceMesh, Inc.

CHAPTER 1

INTRODUCTION

The dust has finally settled. The computer evangelist has envisioned. The strategist has defined. The manager, architect, developer, analyst, and modeler have taken note. The enthusiasm has diminished. The exuberance has turned into a more pragmatic course of action. But what have we learned? Almost a decade has passed since the service-oriented architecture (SOA) paradigm first appeared, extending a pledge to change, repair, enhance, and promote software development best practices. Has this computing trend influenced any of our customary software implementation approaches? Has this new paradigm fostered architecture best practices that have altered the old genre of software construction methodologies? Are we better off?

Yes, the mission to build enduring, reusable, and elastic services that can withstand market volatility and be effortlessly modified to embrace technological changes has been gaining momentum. Governance and best practices have been devised. Existing off-the-shelf products already embody fundamental SOA best practices, such as software reuse, nimbleness, loose coupling, adaptability, interoperability, and consolidation. From a project management perspective, stronger ties have been established between the business institution and information technology (IT) organization. The silo implementation paradigm has been rather weakened, and cross-enterprise initiatives have been moderately increased.

For those organizations that have not been influenced by these trends, the simple advice is to start from smaller "wins." Avoid grandiose SOA plans to change the world. Promote small-size projects, incremental initiatives that over time attain final objectives. Doing this will clearly reduce implementation risks and increase productivity and improve the chances for success. But now it is time to get to work. Roll up your sleeves and embrace a positive, creative, vibrant, and contagious spirit that encourages business and IT personnel to collaborate on fulfilling organizational aims.

The service-oriented discovery and analysis discipline[1] mirrors this approach: Smaller and incremental efforts to achieving success are preferred over large-size projects that introduce perils to business execution. Take tiny steps toward devising a solution to an organizational concern that simplify rather than complicate design and architecture models, clarify rather than obscure technical specifications, and focus service construction efforts rather than blurring implementation boundaries.

The service-oriented discovery and analysis discipline can indeed guarantee success if the goals are well established and agreed upon. Therefore, begin a service-oriented architecture project on a sound foundation of analysis that not only identifies the problem domain but also assesses the feasibility of a proposed solution. Verification of the constructed services against business requirements and technological specifications is another vital contribution of the analysis process. Furthermore, start the project with the service discovery process and justify a service's existence. Persist with service identification throughout the service life cycle, and always embrace new discovery opportunities as they come along. The final artifact of this exercise is an analysis proposition that calls for service modeling activities to deliver a superior solution.

Finally, adopt a personal as well as an organizational strategy to ascertaining services, analyzing problems, and modeling solutions. Formulate an individual plan that can assist with pursuing the service-oriented discovery and analysis venture. Leverage a systematic approach for service identification, examination, and modeling. Do not overlook perhaps one of the most imperative guiding principles: Foster transparency during the discovery and analysis endeavor. The term "transparency" is about tracing and reporting on decisions that are being made during the discovery, analysis, and modeling process in terms of their business practicality and technological feasibility.

WHAT IS SERVICE-ORIENTED DISCOVERY AND ANALYSIS?

Often mentioned in one breath, the discovery and analysis of services can be separable, yet these processes share interrelated milestones and goals that unite them, forming a single service-oriented life cycle discipline. The discovery effort typically is affiliated with service identification. This is a rudimentary and continuous pursuit that yields solutions, namely services, to address an organizational concern. The analysis venture, in contrast, is a study. It is practiced independently; exercised in different phases of a service's life cycle; conducted to understand a problem domain, to ascertain and assess a solution, to verify if service capabilities meet requirements, and to authenticate service operations for production.

SERVICE-ORIENTED ANALYSIS ENDEAVOR

Among other reasons for conducting a meticulous business and technology inspection, the analysis process is chiefly a *quest for a solution* to an organizational problem that is carried out by identified services. No matter when in the life cycle of a service it is pursued, the ultimate goal of the service analysis venture is to identify the best possible remedy to a *business concern* or a *technological challenge*. Obviously, a study of a wide range of artifacts and events that are about to affect a business or have already begun to influence its performance is the driving motivation of the analysis process. However, the engagement of analysts, modelers, architects, developers, or managers in rigorous examination of the business does not necessarily take place because of immediate influences on business execution. Assessment and inspection activities can also be launched to better comprehend success, foster growth, and, most important, prevent failure of business missions.

A METICULOUS STUDY: WHAT SHOULD BE ANALYZED?   The pursuit of a solution that is presented by services to mitigate an impending problem, forecasted challenge, or already affected business or technological mission must be accompanied by a thorough analysis of business and/or technological artifacts. The two perspectives presented are the chief ingredients of almost any service-oriented analysis process. Thus the practitioner ought to focus on intrinsic questions to promote the inspection venture: What is the business or technological problem domain? What are the causes for the occurring challenge? Is a solution needed? Has a solution been proposed? How soon should remedy be applied? What aspects of the problem should be rectified? Are there any business requirements or technical specifications that offer a direction for delivering a solution? and more.

Business Perspective.   To alleviate a challenge, the search for a solution may start with the analysis of the business. This direction advocates that business artifacts should be scrupulously studied to identify the cause of a concern. The term "artifacts" pertains to affiliated business articles that can provide clues to the state of the business, its goals, missions, and imperatives. This may include business strategies and the model of business execution, business processes and related underpinning activities, and even market and customer segmentation research.

If a business solution proposition has already been issued, deliverables such as business requirements and product descriptions should be available to the analysis process. These are essential documents that embody the problems, concerns, and introduced remedies of the problem domain organization. The problem domain institution typically consists of business personnel, analysts, business architects, managers, budget experts, and executives that are assigned the duties of recommending an approach, a direction, and a solution to rectify an organizational concern.

Technological Perspective.   The service-oriented analysis endeavor should not stop short of technological capabilities' inspection if the problem domain stems from applications, services, middleware, and infrastructure discontinuity of operations that ultimately impair transaction performance. Moreover, the examination of technical properties and facilities typically conduced by the solution domain organization (often affiliated with the IT personnel) focuses on two major investigation aspects: internal construct of a software executable and its hosting environment (external landscape). The former pertains to the study of an internal application or service design. This may include understanding internal components' relationships, interaction of operations, and assessment of offered capabilities. The technical environment in which applications and services operate is the second vital ingredient of the analysis process. This is related to the architecture that drives the distribution of software assets across the organization.

Additionally, the distribution and deployment of services in the enterprise broadens the analysis efforts. This may involve the investigation of a large number of technological concerns that are related to service ecosystem integration, collaboration, configuration, and interoperability. These subjects of exploration characteristically commission architects, developers, analysts, modelers, and managers to focus on the landscape and the production environment that hosts service capabilities. Hosting responsibilities include middleware and infrastructure platforms to enable message exchange and transaction execution. Service mediation and federation are other articles for investigation that practitioners should pay close attention to.

SERVICE ANALYSIS PROCESS.   During the service-oriented development life cycle, the opportunities of conducting analysis sessions are vast. "Analysis paralysis" situations that pertain to long studies of business or technological artifacts that do not yield tangible and practical deliverables should be avoided. Moreover, excessive investigations of product artifacts, business requirements, service capabilities, environment configurations, architecture and design blueprints and deliverables alike can immensely prolong the software development life cycle.

Therefore, the rule of thumb suggests that practitioners should initiate an analysis session for each stage of a service life cycle. This is an iterative examination approach that commences during a project's inception, continues through design time, persists throughout service construction, and concludes when a service is deployed and managed in a production environment.[2] In each of these project phases, a distinct type of analysis should be launched. For example, during project inception, a practitioner should study requirements and identify the motivation for employing a service to provide a solution. Conversely, the analysis process that takes place during the service contraction addresses different concerns: It is devised both to verify if a service satisfies business or technical requirements and to guarantee high quality of operations.

Exhibit 1.1 illustrates four analysis iterations that can be conducted during a service's life span:

1. The *inception analysis* iteration characteristically takes place before a service has been proposed.
2. *Assessment analysis* is conducted after business and technical requirements propose a solution.
3. *Verification analysis* is pursued after a service has been constructed.
4. *Authentication analysis* is required before a service is deployed and persists during service operations in production.

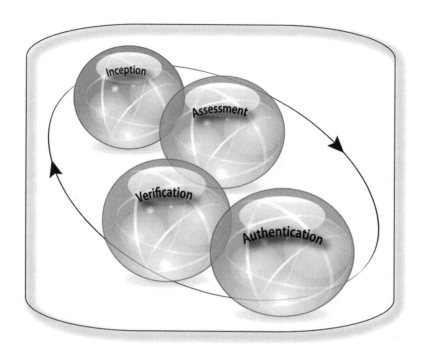

EXHIBIT 1.1   SERVICE-ORIENTED ANALYSIS ITERATIONS

The sections that follow depict an iterative process of service analysis during which an examination of a service and its hosting environment is conducted to achieve distinct analysis goals.

Inception Analysis Iteration: Analyze Prior to Service Proposition.   The analysis process that is pursued before a service has been proposed is driven by strategic imperatives that call for investigating the state of the business, tracing events that have influenced business execution, and identifying the chief concerns of an organization. This venture typically occurs before or at some point in the *inception* phase of a project, during which ideas are gathered and discussions take place to establish a firm direction for addressing problems and identifying *motivations* for instituting services. Furthermore, an analysis session that is performed before a service begins its life cycle or during its *inception* stage is typically dedicated to founding service concepts that eventually will materialize and be transformed into tangible services.

Assessment Analysis Iteration: Analyze after Service Proposition.   Once a service has been proposed and a solution is at hand, a different analysis iteration can begin. This is the time to study business requirements and learn about a software product description, features, attributes, and capabilities. However, if a technological proposition advocates creation of a service and expanding its operating environment, technical specifications should be studied and analyzed. This may include the inspection of service *design and architecture* artifacts and analysis of the introduced technological landscape. Therefore, the *assessment* of the proposed business or technical solutions should be focused on a service's feasibility to rectify an organizational concern and offer practical remedies.

Verification Analysis Iteration: Analyze after Service Construction.   Once a service has been contracted, it should be analyzed to assess the quality of its capabilities, functionality, and operations.

This service *verification* process must also confirm if the service design and architecture model meets business requirements or technical specifications. In other words, the major queries that typically should be asked during this evaluation activity are related to a service's capabilities to satisfy its corresponding consumers' necessities: "Can a service's offerings alleviate the identified business challenges?" "Does the service provide a technological solution?" "Does the service design model adhere to organizational best practices?"

Authentication Analysis Iteration: Analyze before and during Service Operations.   To ensure flawless execution of a service in a production environment, a service should be certified. This is another analysis effort that should take place before a service is ferried out to production and assumes the responsibilities that it was designated. Thus the *authentication* process should be broadened to include the inspection of internal service functionality as well as external vital aspects of service integration, collaboration, interoperability, and configuration. Furthermore, the certification of a service should not conclude with its deployment effort to a production environment. This process must persist to meet the challenges that a service might face in production, during which volatile market conditions, changes to the business mission, technological discontinuity, and disruptions to transaction processing might occur.

SERVICE ANALYSIS APPROACH.   Finally, when pursuing the service analysis process to assist with carving out a solution, adhere to a methodical approach that not only offers direction and milestones to attain, but also underlines the importance of achieving predefined goals. The quest for feasible services that can provide a satisfying remedy to an organizational concern then must be driven by an analysis *road map* that is lucid and unambiguous to analysts, architects, developers, modelers, and managers. The starting point, midpoints, and end point of the service inspection endeavor must be crystallized by employing repeatable *patterns*. These are guiding templates that are accepted by the governance body of an organization whose duties include carving out best practices and standards to streamline the analysis process.

In the sections that follow we introduce a general template for pursuing a service-oriented analysis venture.[3] This is a guiding road map that identifies the four major perspectives of service inspection process that covers vital aspects of internal and external service design and architecture. Exhibit 1.2 illustrates this concept. Note that in addition to the four recommended analysis orientations, the practitioner should adhere to the overarching organizational practices that help shape a service-oriented analysis venture:

1. Look in the Box.
2. Look out of the Box.
3. Look above the Box.
4. Look below the Box.

Look in the Box.   The solution that we are commissioned to propose is obviously executed by internal service operations. This service internal functionality embodies business and/or technical processes and is the manifestation of business requirements and technical specifications. Therefore, the practitioner should look in the "solution box" to analyze the service's internal affairs and the contribution of its capabilities to rectifying an organizational problem. While analyzing a service's internal construct, service interfaces, communication mechanisms, and binding contracts with corresponding consumers are also vital considerations that must be examined. Remember, these internal service examinations that should take place during the inception, assessment, verification, and authentication service-oriented analysis iterations should persist during a service's life cycle to perfect its operations, boost its reusability rates, and increase its performance abilities.

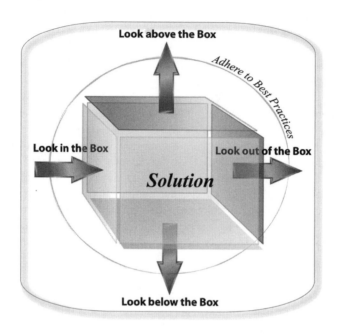

EXHIBIT 1.2 SERVICE-ORIENTED ANALYSIS ROAD MAP

Look above the Box. A practitioner should also look above the solution box to study the overarching governance standards and policies that influence service design and architecture. This analysis effort should also focus on understanding documented and undocumented business processes and exploring the manner by which they can be translated to service capabilities. To synchronize these processes and harmonize transactions, it is time to start planning an orchestration model for governing business activities across the organization. Another goal that should be attained by looking above the solution box is to get acquainted with the organizational service life cycle stages and comprehend the various transformations that a service must undergo. Among these metamorphosis activities is broadening service capabilities and functionality. This can be fulfilled by embarking on an analysis effort to help practitioners generalize and abstract services beyond their existing boundaries.

Look below the Box. The quest for a solution to an organizational concern should carry on by looking below the solution box. The term "below" identifies another perspective that must be inspected to ensure a thorough analysis process, during which the fundamental aspects of service design and architecture are scrutinized and justified. One of the leading practices that should be exercised when looking below the solution box is separation of concerns. This is an investigation effort that focuses on breaking up organizational problems into manageable units of analysis to enable loosely coupled solutions that ultimately are carried out by services.

Another important analysis activity that should take place when pursuing the below-the-box direction is the evaluation of service granularity. This exercise fosters a balanced construction of services across the organization by standardizing an allowable service size and the magnitude of their operations. In other words, striking a balance between fine-grained and coarse-grained services by limiting their growth or contraction is the art of granularity analysis. This policy eventually promotes service decomposition activities that boost reuse, nimbleness, and software elasticity.

Look out of the Box.   Finally, the out-of-the-box analysis approach engages a holistic view of a service ecosystem. This method of investigation involves a service's hosting environment and the underpinning pillars of its architecture model: service integration, interoperability, mediation, deployment, configuration, distribution, and federation. Furthermore, to better understand a service's landscape and help in carving out a message exchange and transaction model for a service provider and its corresponding consumers, the out-of-the-box direction focuses on two major scenarios of service-oriented implementation: contraction and expansion. The former identifies the necessities of an organization to minimize or limit the scope of architecture, while the latter addresses requirements for expanding service boundaries and offerings, and increasing a service's consumer base.

SERVICE-ORIENTED DISCOVERY ENDEAVOR

The quest for a solution brings us to the point of service discovery. This is the process of identifying, reusing, or collecting ideas, processes, and capabilities to alleviate an organizational concern. "Identifying" means that the practitioner discovers a solution to the problem by proposing a remedy, namely a service. The term "reusing" pertains to leveraging the functionality of an already existing service to resolve a problem. Finally, "collecting" implies that architects, analysts, developers, modelers, and managers are commissioned to devise a solution by employing a number of software entities. These may include concepts and existing legacy services and applications. Thus the software assets that are selected to participate in a solution may not be found only in a production environment: They can be in different life cycle stages, such as service conceptualization, service design and architecture, service construction, and service operations.

WHAT IS A SERVICE?   Before identifying and justifying the existence of a service, an organization must define its essence and agree on what the term "service" represents. This effort is somewhat subjective because service definitions vary from one organization to another. For some, a service is just a business function that originates from a concept. According to others, a service is merely a technical term that constitutes a physical executable that is deployed to a production environment. Therefore, lack of consensus and industry standards encourage organizations to define a service based on their necessities and business or technological imperatives.

In the context of service-oriented discovery and analysis discipline, the term "service" is a holistic definition, a universal expression that depicts any software entity that offers business or technical capabilities. This can include a wide range of "things" that can be considered services, such as a concept, business process, software component, an application, a Web service, a virtual service that operates in a virtual computing environment (such as a Cloud), a COBOL program, a database, or a middleware product. Moreover, a service that is deployed to a production environment must consist of interfaces that enable it to communicate with the outside world and meet its corresponding consumers' requirements. The binding agreement between message exchange parties is known as a contract that depicts the types of offerings a service extends to the information-requesting entities.

Remember, during the service discovery process, all discovered services are merely candidate entities that may materialize into future tangible solutions. There is no guarantee that an identified service may indeed find its way to a production environment. Therefore, the process of service discovery yields an *analysis service* that represents a temporary capability employed to offer a solution.

SERVICE DISCOVERY PROCESS.   Akin to the service analysis process that is discussed in the Service-Oriented Analysis Venture section, the service discovery effort should take place in different phases of a service life cycle.[4] This is an iterative process that commences at a service's inception, persists through service design, architecture, and construction, and continues when a

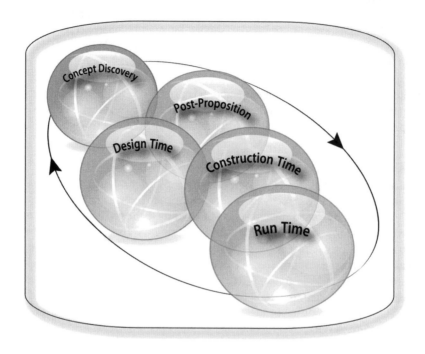

EXHIBIT 1.3 SERVICE-ORIENTED DISCOVERY ITERATIONS

service is deployed to production. This cycle of discovery can go back over the same ground if a service must undergo enhancements, redesign, or rearchitecture efforts.

Exhibit 1.3 illustrates this chain of discovery activities and identifies the five major iterations that are conducted in a service life cycle:

1. **Concept discovery** typically occurs before a solution is accepted and established, during which conceptual services are identified.
2. **Post-proposition discovery** is pursued after a solution to a problem has been proposed and adopted.
3. **Design-time discovery** is conducted during the design and architecture service life cycle phase.
4. **Construction-time discovery** obviously occurs during the construction phase of a project, during which source code is written and tested.
5. **Run-time discovery** takes place after a service has been certified and deployed to production environment.

The sections that follow elaborate on the five service discovery iterations and identify the underpinning activities that lead to identification of service capabilities.

Concept Discovery Iteration: Discover before Solution Proposition. Even before a solution has been proposed and institutionalized, the practitioner should start formalizing organizational ideas and concepts that can later serve as candidate services. This concept recognition effort is typically conducted during the service conceptualization phase, during which the problem domain is studied, remedies are discussed, resolution avenues are explored, and obviously *conceptual services* are discovered. Furthermore, the identified conceptual services typically promote a common communication language between business and IT organizations and help establish an organizational glossary that consists of concepts that can be reused across the enterprise. Finally, from a project initiation and management perspective, the service conceptualization phase also contributes to scoping a project and setting its timeline boundaries.

Post-Proposition Discovery Iteration: Discover after Solution Proposition.   The service discovery process should persist after a solution to an organizational problem has been proposed. But at this stage a different service identification approach should be applied. This new discovery iteration calls for ascertaining service capabilities and functionality that meet business requirements or technical specifications to satisfy consumers' imperatives. In other words, at this stage in a service life cycle, focus on discovery of services that are derived from business requirements and/or technical specifications. Once discovered, these offered service solutions, often referred to as candidate services, should be subject for design and architecture in the next iteration, which is discussed in the sections that follow.

Design-Time Discovery Iteration: Discover during Service Design and Architecture.   Once the candidate services have been introduced, the service design and architecture phase continues. The design venture not only focuses on firming up a service's internal composition, it is also about addressing external environment challenges, such as service integration, message exchange mechanisms, and service interoperability. During this ongoing effort, new services can be identified to complement the previous service conceptualization and service proposition efforts that are discussed in the preceding sections. These newly discovered services offer capabilities to enable a wide range of solutions, such as data transformation, mediation, security, user interface, implementation of business logic, and more.

Again, during the service design and architecture stage, the opportunities for service discovery are vast and crucial to the solution because of the technological concerns that require more attention at this stage. Finally, to document the design and architecture phase and depict the discovered services, architects, developers, analysts, modelers, and managers deliver design and architecture blueprints and modeling artifacts (also widely known as technical specifications).

Construction-Time Discovery Iteration: Discover during Service Construction.   The service construction stage again introduces ample opportunities for service discovery. This service development initiative is typically pursued by developers, architects, and technical managers by following design and architecture blueprints and adhering to organizational best practices and standards. Obviously, design artifacts are the driving aspects of service construction, but the developer may come across scenarios that call for the establishment of new services to fill in the gaps of the technical specifications that were previously delivered. To comply with enterprise best practices, again, the developer may find additional service identification opportunities. For example, to promote loose coupling standards, a bulky service should be broken up into finer-grained new services to carry out business or technical missions.

Refactoring is another development practice that characteristically introduces additional opportunities for service discovery. This is an exercise that is pursued to optimize, stylized, and modularize the source code to boost service performance and reusability factors. The developer is then commissioned not only to enhance operations and service interfaces; source code componentization is also required to group functionality in a logical manner. This effort to bundle logic into distinct executables typically leads to the identification of new services.

Run-Time Discovery Iteration: Discover after Service Deployment.   Finally, while a service operates in a production environment, additional service discovery opportunities may arise. Here the deployment and configuration of services and their adaptability to a functioning service ecosystem is road-tested. This may call for the optimization of service integration and collaboration mechanisms, enhancements to service mediation facilities, or even the improvement of a security model. This typically introduces an array of new service responsibilities and the commencement of capabilities that can fill in the gaps that are found after deployment and distribution of services.

SERVICE DISCOVERY APPROACH. The process of service discovery should be guided by organizational best practices and standards. Without a lucid governance direction, the service identification venture may take superfluous turns that typically prolong the service development effort and hinder vital deliverables that are required for service deployment to production. Therefore, a discovery method should be carved out to channel the service identification efforts and encourage practitioners to focus on the keystone solutions. Moreover, this how-to instruction manual should identify the starting point, milestones, and end point of the discovery process. The method of ascertaining new services or employing existing legacy applications to offer a remedy to an organizational concern should also elaborate on the imperative artifacts that are needed for the service discovery process. To learn more about these approaches, refer to the Service Identification Patterns section later in this chapter, and for an elaborated discussion study Chapters 5 through 10.

Exhibit 1.4 illustrates the five different paths for service discovery. These are orientations devised to facilitate efficient service identification and help practitioners to broaden the search for services that offer solution capabilities to business or technical problems. As apparent, the depicted five directions represent distinct *patterns* for service discovery (note the indicated page number that is positioned in parenthesis next to each pattern):

1. **Top Down (71,89).** This discovery approach advocates deriving new services from business processes and their underpinning activities. As an alternative, this method of service identification also calls for ascertaining conceptual services that stem from solution ideas and software product attributes.

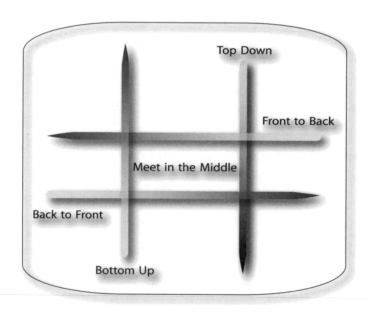

EXHIBIT 1.4 SERVICE-ORIENTED DISCOVERY PATTERNS

2. **Front-to-Back (105).** This service discovery track calls for discovering services by studying user interface deliverables, such as presentation layer logic, content rendering mechanisms, page layouts, and field validation mechanisms.

3. **Back-to-Front (123).** This service identification course takes into consideration data artifacts, such as data schemas, entity diagrams, and data structures.

4. **Bottom-Up (145).** This approach for service discovery capitalizes on existing technologies, architectures, and business processes to derive services.

5. **Meet-in-the-Middle (165).** Finally, this track for service identification shifts the focus to the environment where services operate and the various facilities that link services to each other, such as integration mechanisms, orchestration capabilities, and message exchange platforms.

SERVICE-ORIENTED DISCOVERY AND ANALYSIS PROPOSITION

The service analysis and discovery processes discussed hitherto elaborate on the approach and the road map that each effort is driven by. As the reader may recall, the analysis venture is a study, devised to explain the nature of a problem, assess a proposed solution, and certify services for production. In contrast, the discovery endeavor pinpoints new or existing services that offer capabilities to alleviate an organizational concern. These discovery and analysis initiatives take place in different stages of a service life cycle. Their yielding deliverables are distinct, yet they are interconnected because of the inherent dependency between the two processes. Therefore, the service-oriented discovery and analysis discipline as a whole combines these initiatives and calls for an analysis proposition delivery. This is a chief milestone in the service-oriented life cycle because the yielded services and their hosting environments are the enduring units of analysis for service life cycle stages.

ANALYSIS PROPOSITION.   As discussed, the final product of the service-oriented discovery and analysis is an analysis proposition. This is an *offer*, typically delivered to the business and IT organizations for study and approval. Once endorsed, these analysis findings and recommendations are utilized in the various service life cycle stages, such as conceptualization, design and architecture, construction, and operations. So what does the analysis proposition consist of? An analysis proposition does not constitute formal and final design and architecture blueprints; those are provided during the design and architecture service life cycle stage. In contrast, the analysis proposition is merely an examination of service internal and external constructs, an assessment of feasibility, and recommendations for impending service implementations.

Therefore, the chief deliverable is an analysis modeling diagram that illustrates a proposal for a solution in which services, their corresponding consumers, and their hosting environments are identified and modeled for a solution. The term "modeled" pertains to modeling efforts that are conducted by analysts, architects, modelers, developers, and managers employing an analysis modeling language and notation. Furthermore, this proposition characteristically includes *recommended* service internal and external design and architecture, such as service structures, distribution of services, integration of services, and a model for binding contracts. To read more about the modeling language and its notation, refer to the Service-Oriented Discovery and Analysis Modeling section later in this chapter and to Chapters 14 through 22.

The sections that follow depict the three major deliverables of the service-oriented discovery and analysis proposition (illustrated in Exhibit 1.5). These include the ultimate artifacts that the practitioner should consider delivering:

1. Proposing an enhanced solution
2. Proposing an alternative solution
3. Proposing a new solution

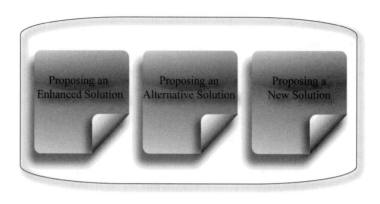

EXHIBIT 1.5   SERVICE-ORIENTED DISCOVERY AND ANALYSIS PROPOSITION DELIVERABLES

PROPOSING AN ENHANCED SOLUTION.   Obviously, an analysis proposition that is devised to enhance a solution to a problem must follow an offered remedy that is extended by business or IT personnel during a service life cycle. This pertains to four major service life span stages: inception, design and architecture, construction, and operations.

1.   In the project inception phase, the service-oriented discovery and analysis process should focus on evaluating a business or technical remedy, assess its practicality, and introduce a superior solution proposition, if appropriate. The phrase "business or technical solution" mostly pertains to business requirements or technical specifications that embody the problem domain and identify the necessary solution for implementation. From a business perspective, business requirements are fundamental artifacts that the IT organization depends on when constructing services. Technical specifications, however, are affiliated with technological and architectural capabilities of a remedy. Therefore, during the service-oriented discovery and analysis process that takes place in the project inception phase, the practitioner must examine these requirements and offer an analysis proposition if they do not fully meet organizational concerns and do not offer an adequate remedy to a problem.

2.   During the design and architecture project stage, the practitioner is commissioned to evaluate design and architecture blueprints, assess their feasibility, and propose an improved scheme. This may include internal service design and external hosting environment.

3.   The service construction phase also introduces opportunities for analysis and perfection activities. The devised tangible services and the constructed integrated environment should also be subject for optimization and improvement.

4.   When services are deployed, configured, monitored, and managed in a production environment, the opportunities for proposing enhanced service integration and collaboration models are vast. This may include improving service reusability rates, tackling interoperability challenges, and firming up message exchange routes.

PROPOSING AN ALTERNATIVE SOLUTION.   As discussed in the previous section, an analysis proposition to enhance an offered remedy can be delivered in different project life cycle stages. In contrast, an analysis proposition can be extended to explore a different avenue, an alternative solution that deviates from the original solution that was introduced in one of the project stages: inception, design and architecture, construction, or operations. The chief reasons for disagreeing with a business or technological remedy and offering an alternative proposition is typically due to misinterpretation of requirements and specifications or simply rejecting a proposed solution approach.

For example, misunderstanding of the problem domain at the project inception phase can trigger an alternate solution that is offered by the analysis proposition. Discrepancies between business requirements and architecture blueprints during the design and architecture project phase can also result in an alternative solution. Finally, inconsistencies between the constructed services and the architecture model may occur during the construction phase. This may result in disagreements about the original development direction and approach that may call for an alternative solution proposition.

PROPOSING A NEW SOLUTION.   Occasionally an analysis proposition offers a new solution that has never been proposed before. This occurs not because of misinterpretations of business requirements or noncompliance with design and architecture blueprints. An analysis proposition can be crafted because an organizational concern has not been tackled, requirements were not provided, design and architecture deliverables did not address a problem, or the development team has never been commissioned to construct the required tangible services. The responsibility of a practitioner is then to find these gaps in each of the project phases and conduct analysis and discovery sessions to tackle unaddressed issues and concerns.

DRIVING PRINCIPLES OF SERVICE-ORIENTED DISCOVERY AND ANALYSIS

The service-oriented discovery and analysis process is a repeatable discipline that offers best practices and patterns to enable practitioners identifying and inspecting a service's internal and external design and architecture. From a service-oriented analysis perspective, this venture calls for a continuous investigation and assessment of service feasibility and contribution to a business or a technological problem. This endeavor also takes place during all service life cycle stages, during which the subject for inspection differs in each step of a service's evolution. As we learned in the Service-Oriented Analysis Endeavor section, different artifacts are examined in each analysis iteration. The same applies to the service discovery process and its related iterations, when service identification opportunities vary in each service life cycle stage, as discussed in the Service-Oriented Discovery Endeavor section.

This brings us to the chief principles that should be pursued to guarantee a successful discovery and analysis effort, simplify its processes, and maximize its efficiency. The sections that follow introduce these tenets and elaborate on their contribution to the service discovery and analysis venture.

SERVICE-ORIENTED DISCOVERY AND ANALYSIS TRANSPARENCY MODEL.   Transparency is one of most intrinsic tenets of the software development life cycle initiative, and in particular it should apply to the service-oriented discovery and analysis discipline. Transparency is about the justification that practitioners must provide when making important decisions about service design, architecture, construction, deployment, or operations. In other words, every significant activity during any of the service life cycle stages should be rationalized by architects, developers, modelers, analysts, and managers. They must not only clarify the reasons that led to certain business or technical resolutions, but also indicate the cost, effort, and time of a solution implementation. Therefore, the service-oriented discovery and analysis discipline calls for the establishment of the service-oriented analysis transparency model that advocates architectural, technological, business, and operational traceability during the service life span. The term "traceability" pertains to the process of tracking the evolution of a service ecosystem and its business and technological drivers. Exhibit 1.6 illustrates these transparency components:

1. **Architectural traceability.** Architectural traceability is related to decisions that must be reported and justified in terms of design practicality, cost effectiveness, and return on investment. These must be evaluated against organizational best practices, such as software efficiency, reusability, agility, performance, elasticity, loose coupling, and interoperability.

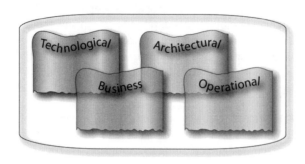

EXHIBIT 1.6   SERVICE-ORIENTED DISCOVERY AND ANALYSIS TRANS-
PARENCY MODEL

2. **Technological traceability.** This aspect of transparency is about technological decisions that must be reported and evaluated, including selection of commercial off-the-shelf (COTS) products, such as language platforms, messaging facilities, and metadata repositories. Service deployment and configuration mechanisms and service mediation and distribution techniques are other concerns that should be traced.
3. **Business traceability.** Business traceability is about identifying the business value proposition of a service, the contribution of a service hosting environment to organizational concerns, and return on investment when it comes to launching service-oriented projects. It is also about evaluating the feasibility of business strategies, practicality of business requirements, and how effective services satisfy business imperatives.
4. **Operational transparency.** This traceability aspect is related to the assessment of service operations in production. It is about the evaluation of a service's capability to interact with its consumers, exchange messages with its peer services, sustain high consumption rates, uphold high transaction volumes, and offer technological and business continuity with minimum disruption to its operations.

SERVICE MODELING: A VIRTUAL VENTURE.   "Virtual modeling of services" is a phrase that depicts the design and architecture of an intangible operating environment, simulated service processes and capabilities, and emulated service relationships with corresponding consumers. This paradigm obviously defines the manipulation of the nonphysical computing landscape that imitates a deployed production environment and the consumers it serves. The major players that participate in the design and architecture venture that takes place in a virtual service world are virtual services, consumers, networks, servers, platforms, repositories, and more. Again, this modeling environment is devised to mimic the real computing world and the transactions that are exchanged.

Therefore, service modeling is a requirement that drives the service-oriented discovery and analysis process. To virtualize a service internal structure, functionality, and its external hosting environment, leverage the proposed modeling language and notation to promote business and technological goals, solve problems, and offer efficient solutions. By modeling a proposed remedy, we not only simulate a tangible deployment landscape and its technologies and architectures, we also contribute to organizational expenditure reduction and minimize project risks. To learn more about modeling techniques, processes, and patterns that can be employed during the service-oriented discovery and analysis process, refer to Chapters 14 through 22.

PATTERNS OF IMPLEMENTATION: BEST PRACTICES AND OUT-OF-THE-BOX SOLUTIONS. During service-oriented discovery and analysis, employ the provided *patterns* for service identification and inspection. These are the best practices and predefined solutions that can reduce development cost, analysis and discovery time, and ultimately organizational expenditure. Use these repeatable templates to:

- Shape the solutions for a project or a business initiative
- Govern the overall service discovery and analysis process
- Model a virtual service environment, mimic service functionality, and simulate service integration

These patterns of design and implementation are vital to service-oriented discovery and analysis because they reduce implementation risks and introduce road-tested, out-of-the-box solutions that have been applied in similar circumstances. They are the guiding pillars of the analysis process and major contributors to shaping a service-oriented analysis proposition. An overview of the service-oriented discovery and analysis patterns is provided later in the Service-Oriented Discovery and Analysis Patterns section later in the chapter.

SERVICE-ORIENTED DISCOVERY AND ANALYSIS MODELING

An analysis proposition is articulated by an analysis proposition modeling diagram that depicts vital design perspectives of a service and its hosting environment. These views include information about *internal* service composition, such as aggregated components, service operations and interfaces, service internal boundaries, service specialties, service capabilities, and more. Service ecosystem *external* aspects, such as deployment, service coupling, contract model, distribution model, and interoperability mechanisms should also be illustrated in an analysis proposition diagram.

Furthermore, a proposed analysis solution must be presented in a formal manner, in which the design of services and their corresponding distributed environment adheres to a prescribed notation that captures relationships between services and associated consumers. This language also is devised to describe the evolution of a service and it transformation stages, starting at its inception, tracing its development phases, and depicting its maturity in production. Chapters 14–22 discuss in details modeling techniques, notations, and modeling operations.

MODELING LANGUAGE WITH TRANSPARENCY CAPABILITIES. Because analysis aspects dominate this exercise, the language that is employed to present the analysis proposition must trace decisions that are made during an analysis process. These questions include: Why should a service be decomposed? Why should a service be retired? Why should two or more services be unified? Why should a service be further abstracted? What is the driving motivation for decoupling two or more services? In which circumstances should a binding contract be established between a service and its corresponding consumers?

Furthermore, as we learned in the previous section, the service-oriented analysis and discovery transparency model also calls for an elaborated analysis proposition that traces business decisions, technological and architectural best practices and implementations, and even events during run-time in production. From a modeling perspective, these may have occurred in the past, be taking place at the present time, or be planned for the future. This analysis *traceability* approach is tuned to the time aspects of a service life cycle. That is, it describes the metamorphosis of a service since its inception, identifies its existing state, or provides an architecture plan for the future.

Exhibit 1.7 illustrates the three service-oriented discovery and analysis modeling methods, each of which presents a different state in the service life cycle: to be, as is, and used to be. These are explained in detail in the sections that follow.

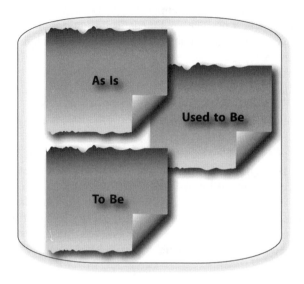

EXHIBIT 1.7   SERVICE-ORIENTED DISCOVERY AND ANALYSIS MODELING STATES

TO-BE MODELING STATE.   Nearly all of today's modeling languages offer design capabilities that reflect a futuristic state of software architecture. These languages illustrate future scenarios; some even introduce a road map for implementation. This modeling approach is focused on how a service and its hosting environment "ought to be." Thus past or current design considerations are disregarded. In other words, since the to-be modeling paradigm does not "remember" past or current service life cycle states, the only documented aspect of the service design is the future or end state of architecture formation.

The service-oriented discovery and analysis modeling venture obviously capitalizes on the to-be view. Future depiction of a solution and implementation is vital to the analysis proposition since it recommends nonexistent avenues for tackling organizational concerns.

USED-TO-BE MODELING STATE.   Unlike the to-be modeling state, which is focused just on future service architecture, the used-to-be method looks at the past. Therefore, the analysis proposition diagram depicts the past state of service design, identifies best practices that led to architectural decisions, describes technological preferences that were popular earlier in the service life span, or elucidate business strategies that influenced service design. These aspects of analysis offer a great deal of information about a service's evolution and its hosting environment, business incentives, return on investment, architecture strategies, and more.

AS-IS MODELING STATE.   The as-is modeling state that is depicted in an analysis proposition diagram illustrates the current state of a service architecture. This is an intermediate condition of the design that is clearly different from past and future planning. Thus the diagram represents a service's transformation between a selected point in the past and current implementation. This feature enables analysts, architects, managers, developers, and modelers to understand the fundamental changes that a service and its operating environment have undergone.

Such valuable information can be leveraged for learning from mistakes and errors that have occurred due to vast reasons, such as misconstrued business requirements, miscalculated capacity and consumption planning, inadequate computer resources assignment that influenced service performance, and/or unsuitable design and architecture implementations. From a return on investment perspective, the as-is modeling approach can identify the actual cost of a project that has been launched in the past. This vital information can shape future service-oriented development initiatives and serve as an essential use case study to improve future projects.

SERVICE-ORIENTED DISCOVERY AND ANALYSIS PATTERNS

By and large, patterns are intrinsic to software development disciplines since they simply offer solutions. These are proven best practices and a recommended "how to" set of remedies that can be applied to resolving problems. They are also conceived of as *repeatable methods* that have been road-tested and applied to rectify similar software development problems.

Design patterns are perhaps the most well-known guiding solutions that originated in modern computing times both to assist with understanding a problem and, most important, to offer avenues of implementation that developers and architects can employ. Moreover, these patterns are positioned to help alleviate challenges on different levels of software implementation: Some are devised to provide improved source code algorithms, others address application architectural issues, and several tackle enterprise architecture solutions.

The service-oriented discovery and analysis patterns introduce a wide range of repeatable solutions that *not only* address design and architecture challenges but also represent a new breed of patterns affiliated with the process of implementation. The processes of service identification and inspection, of discovery, of categorization, and of course of analysis and modeling can be leveraged by a practitioner to devise superior solutions to organizational concerns. These how-to best practices and policies are accompanied by what-not-to-do recommendations, often referred to as anti-patterns. Service-oriented discovery and analysis anti-patterns are also necessary to foster service reuse, consolidation, loose coupling, and business agility.

The five different discovery and analysis pattern categories that are illustrated in Exhibit 1.8 can help carve the analysis proposition that architects, developers, modelers, analysts, and

EXHIBIT 1.8   SERVICE-ORIENTED   DISCOVERY   AND   ANALYSIS PATTERNS

managers are commissioned to deliver. These constitute the recommended approaches for accomplishing the service identification and inspection venture.

DISCOVERY AND ANALYSIS ROAD MAP PATTERNS.   Governing best practices and implementation directions are imperative to service identification and inspection processes that take place during a service life cycle. Therefore, the discovery and analysis road map patterns offer orientations, overarching guiding paths[5] for ascertaining new services or engaging legacy software assets for a proposed solution. These are also repeatable analysis procedures that practitioners can employ to inspect a service's internal design or external architecture. In addition, the road map patterns set priorities and define the boundaries for service discovery and analysis activities that are practiced during a project.

The essential challenges that are addressed by the road map patterns typically are conveyed by fundamental governing questions, such as: Where do we begin with the analysis process? How do we start with service identification activities? What are the chief best practices that motivate the service discovery and analysis process? What type of inputs does the service discovery for? The answers to these questions and an elaborated plan for conducting service identification and examination are introduced in Chapters 2 through 4.

SERVICE IDENTIFICATION PATTERNS.   As the reader may remember, a model for service-oriented discovery is revealed earlier in the Service-Oriented Discovery Approach section that elaborates on the five major tracks for discovering services: Top-Down (71,89), Bottom-Up (145), Front-to-Back (105), Back-to-Front (123), and Meet-in-the-Middle (165). These service identification directions are established in Chapters 5 through 10 as formal patterns, methods of discovery that can be employed to ascertain new services or engage legacy software in a proposed solution. Furthermore, a remedy to an organizational concern typically includes services that are being developed and maintained in different life cycle stages, such as concepts, services that are being designed and constructed, or even deployed services to production. To assist with the collection of services, the introduced discovery patterns provide distinct paths for service identification. Each of these tracks guides practitioners how to inspect a diversity of project artifacts and derive services for a business or technological mission.

The patterns for service discovery also introduce methods and processes for implementation. These can be employed to maximize identification opportunities and leverage a wide range of input deliverables that can be collected to broaden the discovery venture. Consider the chief artifacts that are utilized to conduct a successful service derivation and collection initiative:

- **Business processes.** Documented and undocumented business processes, business requirements, business modeling diagrams, and business analysis documents
- **Product specifications.** An assortment of product descriptions that identify software product attributes and features
- **User interface articles.** Screen design artifacts, storyboards, page layout design requirements, and user interface scripts
- **Data and content artifacts**. Data structure specifications, data schemas, and data concepts
- **Existing technologies.** Existing technologies and technologies, such as empowering platforms, middleware, existing services, and more

SERVICE CATEGORIZATION PATTERNS.   The service categorization effort is about classifying discovered services by employing three major perspectives. The first is related to service contribution to different business and technological disciplines (also referred to as contextual contribution). This venture is chiefly about grouping services by their common specialties and the type of offerings extended to consumers. For example, a service can be affiliated with business processes that execute an equity trading order. A car insurance premium calculator is another function that can be designated to a service. From a technical perspective, content download capability or audit trail functionality can be assigned to utility services that fall under the technical category.

Second, services can be categorized by their origin, or the sources that a service stems from. For example, a service may originate from a concept found in an organizational software portfolio or even spotted in a production environment.

Third, from a structural perspective, a service can be classified by its internal formation type or external distribution method.

These categorization approaches call for the institution of patterns that can help practitioners classify a service by various aspects that define its identity. As discussed, these may be structural considerations, contextual affiliations, and even origins. To learn more about these provided service categorization patterns, refer to Chapters 11 through 13. The practitioner should leverage these methods of classification to establish an organizational taxonomy that promotes service reuse, consolidation, reduction of expenditure, and nimbleness.

CONTEXTUAL ANALYSIS AND MODELING PATTERNS.   Discussed in detail in Chapters 14 through 17, the contextual analysis and modeling patterns embody guiding principles for modeling services to offer solutions based on their semantic affiliation. The term "semantic" describes a service's association with a business or technical specialty, a field of expertise that can alleviate an organizational concern. Accounting, home insurance, and trading are examples of specialties that can drive the contextual modeling process. Therefore, the contextual modeling approach enables the manipulation of a service's functionality scope and the magnitude of its offerings in a hosting computing environment. This approach typically affects the extent of a service's capabilities and ultimately affects the dimension of its consumers' base.

To attain these goals, the contextual analysis process offers patterns to meet four different objectives for a project:

1. **Contextual generalization patterns.** A group of patterns that increase the abstraction level of a service to widen the boundary of its capabilities
2. **Contextual specification patterns.** Patterns employed to reduce service functionality and abstraction level
3. **Contextual expansion patterns.** An assortment of contextual patterns that enable the expansion of a distributed service environment
4. **Contextual contraction patterns.** A collection of patterns that assists with the contraction of a distributed service landscape and reduction of architecture scope

STRUCTURAL ANALYSIS AND MODELING PATTERNS.   In contrast to the contextual analysis and modeling patterns, which merely focus on semantic affiliations and manipulation of service functionality and capabilities, the structural patterns are devised to shape internal and external service formations to provide a superior solution. The term "structure" clearly pertains to two different aspects of service design: internal and external. The former corresponds to an internal service construct. This includes aggregation of service components, granularity level of a service, and even establishment of contracts between a service's constituents with their corresponding external consumers. The patterns that help shape service external structures, however, address different concerns: service distribution, service mediation, service federation, service integration, interoperability, and more. Consider the four different structural analysis and modeling patterns that are discussed in detail in Chapters 18 through 22:

1. **Structural generalization patterns.** Patterns that help widen a service's internal structure and as a result increase the boundary of its capabilities
2. **Structural specification patterns.** A group of patterns that trim down a service internal formation to reduce the overall scope of its operations

3. **Structural expansion patterns.** A collection of structural patterns that expand a distributed service environment and widen a deployed architecture scope
4. **Structural contraction patterns.** An assortment of structural patterns that facilitate the reduction of a distributed service landscape and contraction of architecture

SUMMARY

- The service-oriented discovery and analysis discipline consists of two major processes: service identification and analysis.
- The service-oriented analysis process is repeated in four major analysis iterations: inception, assessment, verification, and authentication.
- The discovery process calls for service identification in five different iterations: concept discovery, post-proposition, design time, construction time, and run-time.
- The analysis proposition is the final artifact of the service-oriented discovery and analysis.
- There are three major service-oriented discovery and analysis principles that should be embraced by practitioners: transparency, virtual modeling, and adoption of patterns.
- The service-oriented discovery and analysis modeling language support three major states: as-is, used-to-be, and to-be.
- The service-oriented discovery and analysis offers five pattern categories: discovery and analysis road map patterns, service identification patterns, service categorization patterns, contextual analysis and modeling patterns, and structural analysis and modeling patterns.

Notes

1. The service-oriented discovery and analysis discipline is a part of the service-oriented modeling framework (SOMF) that is featured in Michael Bell, *Service-Oriented Modeling: Service Analysis, Design, and Architecture* (Hoboken, NJ: John Wiley & Sons, 2008).

2. The service-oriented analysis process can be embedded in any existing organizational development and operations life cycle stage

3. The service-oriented analysis governing process discussed is inspired by Richard Veryard, an author on business modeling and SOA governance. Refer to Chapter 2 for a detailed discussion of his contribution.

4. The service-oriented discovery process can be incorporated in any organization development and operations life stage.

5. Start the service-oriented discovery and analysis process by studying the road map patterns offered in Chapters 2 through 4. Carving a personal and an organizational strategy should then follow.

PART ONE

SERVICE-ORIENTED DISCOVERY AND ANALYSIS ROAD MAP PATTERNS

We are now ready to start with the discovery, analysis, and modeling process of services. But where do we begin? What directions should guide us in identifying new services, analyzing their capabilities, and proposing a superior solution? What are the involved entities, and where do they originate? And finally, to what extent are these service formations influenced by the service environment that we are commissioned to inspect?

These questions are intrinsic to the service-oriented discovery and analysis discipline because they present the grassroots challenges of the software development process. Without a lucid direction and guidance, the practitioner commissioned to assess if a business solution and a proposed technological remedy will be effective may miss vital reuse and consolidation opportunities. Without a clear strategy to address the business problems that need attention, the software modeler, business architect, technical architect, developer, business analyst, technical analyst, and manager are doomed to fail.

Richard Veryard, the business and technology evangelist with the Component Based Development and Integration Forum (CBDI), has proposed a compelling model for service-based design. In an article published in 2004, Veryard introduced a new theory that outlines orientations for service design: upward, downward, inward, and sideways.[1] These design directions provide guidance and introduce discipline to the service design phase. By addressing a different concern in each of the directions, the practitioner is able to focus on a distinct set of design activities. For example, the upward direction advocates addressing business processes and orchestration. However, the sideways approach tackles interoperability challenges. Veryard's insightful paper was inspired by the work of Christopher Alexander, who is noted for his theories about the architecture of buildings.[2]

ROAD MAP FOR SERVICE-ORIENTED DISCOVERY AND ANALYSIS

When pursuing the service-oriented discovery and Analysis discipline, it is obvious that a 360-degree holistic approach mitigating a wide range of concerns is needed. Furthermore, to identify services for a small project or a large business initiative—either discovering existing or devising new entities—the rule of thumb calls for expanding the analysis efforts. The more sources of information and artifacts we examine, the richer our findings and solutions will be. Thus, influenced by Veryard's service design theory, the service-oriented discovery and analysis discipline acknowledges the importance of the different directions that can contribute to a coherent service identification and examination *road map*. These paths not only broaden the service discovery and inspection venture; they help carve a wide angle analysis proposition that can satisfy business and technological requirements.

Moreover, a service discovery and analysis road map is essential to institutionalizing a predominant method for examining a service's *internal* formation, perfecting its operations, and firming up its capabilities. A formalized direction and guidance for discovery and analysis can also be leveraged to study a service's *external* landscape,[3] examine its associations with consumers and peer services, and to propose a loosely coupled and nimble distributed environment.

ROAD MAP PATTERNS FOR SERVICE-ORIENTED DISCOVERY AND ANALYSIS

We thus introduce three different road map components of the service-oriented discovery and analysis discipline, as depicted in Exhibit P1.1. The first component consists of road map patterns, directions that foremost are devised to establish a method of service identification and inspection. Among other necessary goals, these patterns are also designed to address these challenges (note the indicated page number that is positioned in parenthesis next to each pattern):

- **Inward (25) road map pattern.** Perfect internal service offerings, study and establish business requirements and technical specifications, and firm up service capabilities and functionality.
- **Upward (42) road map pattern.** Study organizational service-oriented architecture governance, analyze business processes, and generalize a service's capabilities by widening its internal boundaries.
- **Downward (32) road map pattern.** Meticulously inspect service granularity, and assist with separation-of-concerns analysis.
- **Outward (46) road map pattern.** Organize distribution of software assets, and establish an organizational mediation model.

The second road map component calls for ensuring a rigorous service discovery and inspection process that adheres to organizational best practices. Thus the practitioner should comply

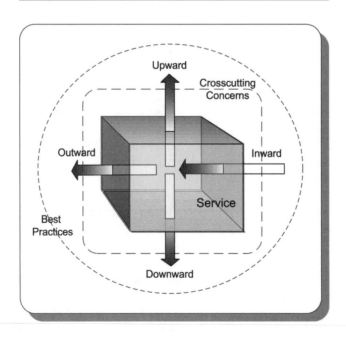

EXHIBIT P1.1 SERVICE DISCOVERY AND ANALYSIS ROAD MAP MODEL COMPONENTS

with architecture and design standards and policies during the pursuit of each individual road map pattern.

The third road map component consists of a number of *cross-cutting concerns* common to all road map patterns. These are fundamental analysis and discovery aspects that the practitioner should be aware of, such as balancing the service identification venture by ensuring that all analysis perspectives have been studied and pursuing a continuous service categorization to boost reusability rates of services.

VERTICAL AND HORIZONTAL DISCOVERY AND ANALYSIS ROAD MAP PROCESSES

The service-oriented discovery and analysis discipline not only focuses on an internal service's construct; it also addresses a wide range of service environment challenges. Therefore, an efficient discovery and analysis venture calls for both *vertical* and *horizontal* processes for identifying and inspecting services, and carving a service-oriented proposition. "Vertical" means that the scope of the discovery and analysis process is limited to a single service's capabilities, functionality, specialties, and internal structure. Conversely, the term "horizontal" advocates expanding the discovery and analysis view beyond a service domain by examining the environment where a service is hosted. This method consists of studying the execution and behavior of peer services, understanding a service's distributed environment, promoting loosely coupled architecture, and identifying new services. Therefore, Chapters 2 and 3 introduce the vertical and the horizontal discovery and analysis processes, respectively—approaches that are illustrated in Exhibit P1.2. As apparent, the vertical process leverages the *Inward* and the *Downward* activitiers and the horizontal process promotes the Upward and the Outward road map activitiers.

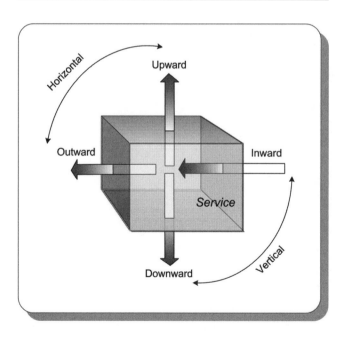

EXHIBIT P1.2   VERTICAL AND HORIZONTAL DISCOVERY AND ANALYSIS PROCESSES

Notes

1. Richard Veryard, "Business-Driven SOA #2: How Business Governs the SOA Process?" *CBDi Journal* (June 2004), pp. 1–3.

2. The process of design is discussed in Christopher Alexander, *Notes on the Synthesis of Form* (Cambridge, MA: Harvard University Press, 1964).

3. The term "service external landscape" pertains to integration, interoperability, and distribution of software assets.

CHAPTER 2

VERTICAL SERVICE DISCOVERY AND ANALYSIS
Pursuing Inward and Downward Road Map Patterns

It is time to start crafting a plan, a strategy that consists of a systematic service analysis and discovery process that focuses on a service's *internal affairs*, its internal structure, and type of offerings. The mission is to understand how business and technical imperatives drive an individual service's functionality and its capabilities. Thus it is important to study business requirements and understand technical specifications. These rudimentary analyses typically yield new services and contribute to existing service implementations.

To achieve these goals, adopt the *vertical* method that advocates utilizing the *Inward* (25) and *Downward* (32) discovery and analysis patterns. The *Inward* direction is driven by business, technical, and architectural requirements that ultimately conclude with the formation of services and the constitution of their capabilities. Thus the *Inward* method advocates studying business artifacts, such as business process modeling diagrams, market segmentation analysis documents, and product requirements. On the technological level, architecture and design blueprints and technical specifications offer technological solutions that a service is devised to provide. Perfecting the internal formation of a service is another task that should be pursued by exploiting the *Inward* discovery and analysis direction. This task pertains to designing and refactoring service operations.

The *Downward* direction, however, which is also a part of the vertical discovery and analysis process, addresses a different perspective: It promotes separation of business concerns, decomposition of services, retirement of duplicated functionality, and elimination of service capabilities. This *specification* process fosters service reuse, business agility, reduction of time to market, and increase of software elasticity. Therefore, breaking up a service into smaller and more manageable components and separating its internal processes to encourage a loose coupling design style is the chief mission of the *Downward* direction. Remember that throughout this venture that advocates the pursuit of the *Inward* (25) and *Downward* (32), the practitioner should adhere to best practices and organizational standards, as depicted by the vertical service discovery and analysis model in Exhibit 2.1.

SERVICE DISCOVERY AND ANALYSIS INWARD ROAD MAP PATTERN

The *Inward* service discovery and analysis road map pattern advocates that we rigorously inspect the service's internal affairs. Here we merely focus on an individual service and its *capabilities*.[1] "Capabilities" has become an important aspect when discussing a service's capacity to provide business or technological functionality. In technical terms, a service's capability pertains to its internal operations (also known as methods, functions, routines, etc.). These are the underpinning service processes that are so valuable to accomplishing a business or a technical task.

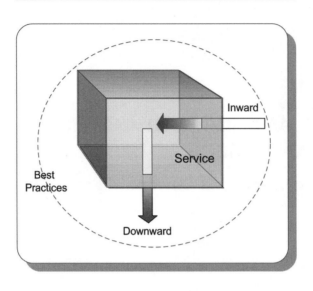

EXHIBIT 2.1   VERTICAL SERVICE DISCOVERY AND ANALYSIS MODEL

Furthermore, capabilities must be enabled by a service's internal construct. That is, by looking *inward* into a service's internal design, we must inspect its structure, the software components that make up the service, the interaction between service operations, the synchronization between its internal activities, its interfaces to the outside world, and more. This examination and identification process—the *Inward* service discovery and analysis direction —must follow a logical path that originates during a project's inception and settles during the service construction phase. Thus to understand a service's internal composition, we must follow a trail of information, from business requirements to technical specifications.

The sections that follow discuss in detail the *Inward* service discovery and analysis approach, a pattern that can be employed to assess service capabilities and compliance with business and technological requirements.

SERVICE CAPABILITIES: EVOLUTIONARY SERVICE DISCOVERY PROCESS.   Analysts, architects, software modelers, developers, and managers should be aware that service operations are not devised in a vacuum. Service functionality emanates from a large array of organizational strategy papers, requirements, and specification documents. In fact, a service's capabilities are the embodiment of its external business and technology imperatives.

Some would even argue that a service is the product of business artifacts. This implies that we start with business documents and later conclude with technical specifications. Despite this long trail of information that is needed to understand a service's internal affairs, we should be resolute about achieving the *Inward* discovery and analysis road map pattern goal: "Study the outside, but focus on the inside."

The leading source of information for understanding a service's internals is typically the business requirements that drive most projects and technological initiatives in an enterprise. Moreover, service operations, namely capabilities, constitute a chain of organizational capabilities that are formed during the service life cycle. We name this effect the *chain of service-oriented architecture (SOA) capabilities*.

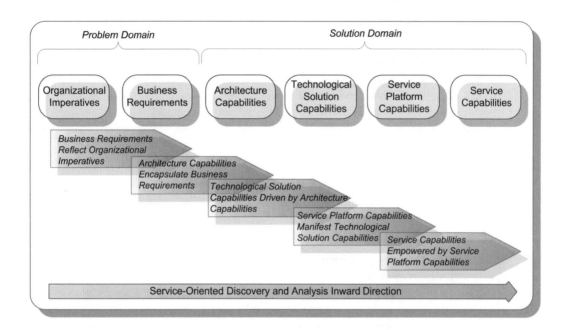

EXHIBIT 2.2   CHAIN OF SOA CAPABILITIES

Chain of SOA Capabilities.   To better comprehend this concept, let us review Exhibit 2.2. This illustration depicts six interdependent business and technological artifacts that describe the term "chain of SOA capabilities." Note the introduction of two major organizations that participate in this software product life cycle process: the Problem Domain and Solution Domain. In traditional terms, the Problem Domain is characteristically affiliated with the business unit of an organization. The technology group is associated with the Solution Domain idiom.

Problem Domain Artifacts.   The first two life cycle artifacts that are noted on the left side reside in the problem domain section: organizational imperatives and business requirements. The term "organizational imperatives" relates to organizational necessities to resolve problems that threaten the business. This may include harsh competition or even volatile market conditions. But business imperatives are not only about the dangers that an enterprise is facing. Business needs can also pertain to an organization's driving motivation to grow its revenue by developing new software products. The second term—"business requirements"— is associated with the institutionalized approach for formalizing business needs, typically by documenting the business imperatives, describing a software product, and offering a business-oriented solution.

Solution Domain Capabilities.   The remaining four chains of SOA capabilities artifacts reside in the solution domain space. They depict the process that the organization typically employs to provide technological remedies to business problems. Service capabilities—the last item in this sequence—are deeply rooted in the prior three solution domain capacities, as illustrated in Exhibit 2.2:

- **Architecture Capabilities.** These are technical architecture capabilities that encapsulate business requirements. They represent a solution that focuses on the service architectural environment, such as integration, interoperability,[2] data strategies, SOA intermediaries, service mediation, service virtualization, data virtualization, network virtualization, canonical data model, and more.

- **Technological Solution Capabilities.** These aspects identify technological solution capabilities that are driven by architecture capabilities described previously. These are service-enabling technologies, such as infrastructure, networking, load balancing and scalability facilities, disaster recovery and high-availability mechanisms, enterprise messaging frameworks, virtualization technologies, and even service configuration management.
- **Service Platform Capabilities.** These capabilities pertain to empowering technologies that enable service execution. They are service language platforms, application servers, service security facilities, service repositories, service registries, and so on.

Again, it is imperative that, during the *Inward* service discovery and analysis process, we study environmental architecture influential aspects, yet the main efforts should be focused on delving into service internal constructs and capabilities.

BUSINESS REQUIREMENTS AND TECHNICAL SPECIFICATIONS.   The *Inward* pattern approach for service discovery and analysis activities calls for starting the process by inspecting business and technological requirements and specifications. But which documents can provide the required information used to establish service capabilities and offer further opportunities for service discovery?

Indeed, some recognized software development methodologies advise a specific method to document business imperatives and technological solutions. The rule of thumb suggests, however, that each organization should develop its own documentation standards, either by adopting an exiting road-tested approach or by customizing one for internal needs.

The problem domain organization (the business institution) typically records business needs by composing a business requirements document. Subsequently, it hands the document off to the solution domain body (IT organization) that rigorously studies the business imperatives. Finally, the latter further translates the requirements into technological capabilities. These are recorded in design and architecture blueprints and technical specification documents.

Business analysts, technical analysts, business architects, technical architects, software modelers, developers, and project managers who are pursuing the *Inward* discovery and analysis pattern must study business requirements and technical specifications. These fundamental business imperatives and architecture blueprints are the essence of organizational studies and analyses that are conducted by the business and the technology groups.

There are instances, however, where a service may not originate from business requirements (as we learn in some of the service discovery chapters in Part Two). In this case, the driving motivation is purely technical, and thus the solution domain is responsible for providing the technical specifications. These are based on the solution domain organization initiatives that do not involve the business unit. Furthermore, some business units tend not to get involved in the service development life cycle. In this case, the responsibility for defining requirements falls on the shoulders of the technology organization.

BUSINESS REQUIREMENTS AND TECHNICAL SPECIFICATIONS LEAD TO SERVICE CAPABILITIES: ORGANIZATIONAL EXAMPLE.   Exhibit 2.3 exemplifies the typical contributing ingredients and the analysis processes that lead to the creation of service operations. Remember, this illustration merely depicts a scenario in which the business and technology organizations collaborate on SOA initiatives to define the problem and produce a viable solution. As noted, Service Capabilities are the final product and enduring artifact of two major organizational initiatives: Business Architecture and Technical Architecture analyses.

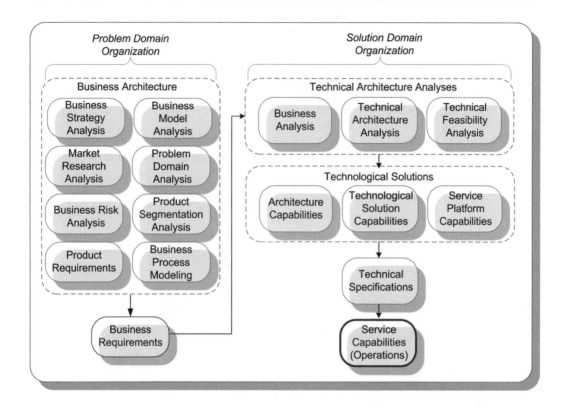

EXHIBIT 2.3   REQUIREMENTS THAT DRIVE SERVICE CAPABILITIES EXAMPLE

Problem Domain Deliverables.   We start from the problem domain organization, which performs eight different business architecture studies, yielding a final business requirements document (grouped under the Business Architecture initiative):

1. **Business Strategy Analysis.** Identification of business vision, direction, and mission
2. **Business Model Analysis.** Studying business core competence, strengths and weaknesses, and revenue-generation strategies
3. **Market Research Analysis.** Learning about business competitors, partnership opportunities, and revenue-generation prospects
4. **Problem Domain Analysis.** Inspecting business threats, assessing business risks, conducting risk mitigation approaches, learning about market events that can affect the business, studying economy indicators, and more
5. **Business Risk Analysis.** Devising a risk mitigation strategy based on possible business threats
6. **Product Segmentation Analysis.** Performing client and market studies to identify viable product development opportunities
7. **Product Requirements.** Preparing product specification documents that depict product attributes, business rules, business advantages, and business constraints
8. **Business Process Modeling.** Documenting business processes and providing business process models (typically visual diagrams)

Solution Domain Deliverables. Next, as depicted on the right-hand side of Exhibit 2.3, the technology organization conducts three major analysis studies to examine business requirements (grouped under the Technical Architecture Analyses initiative):

1. **Business Analysis.** Studying business requirements, understanding the business motivation, identifying asset reusability and consolidation opportunities; working with analysts, architects, and developers to contribute to the creation of technical specification documents
2. **Technical Architecture Analysis.** Conducting service-oriented modeling sessions that yield analysis, design, and architecture blueprints
3. **Technical Feasibility Analysis.** Assessing whether the business requirements are implementable and conducting technical risk analysis to assess implementation capabilities.

Finally, technological solutions are formalized and presented in three different views, each of which influences a service's internal implementation grouped under the Technological Solutions initiative:

1. Architectural Capabilities
2. Technological Solution Capabilities
3. Service Platform Capabilities

SERVICE COMPLIANCE AND VERIFICATION PROCESS. The *Inward* service discovery and analysis pattern addresses the compliance of service operations with business and technical imperatives. The practitioner is not exempt from inspecting how precisely a service fulfills its obligations to consumers or peer services. Exhibit 2.4 illustrates the four major compliance checkpoints that should be considered during the service verification process. These are advocated by the service discovery and analysis *Inward* pattern. If adequately followed, they contribute immensely to the quality of service capabilities.

1. **Functional Requirements.** Reflect business process modeling efforts, business activities, product functionality, and business requirements

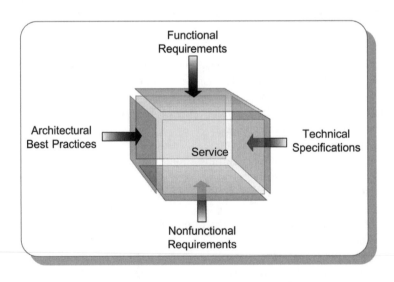

EXHIBIT 2.4 FOUR MAJOR SERVICE COMPLIANCE PERSPECTIVES

2. **Nonfunctional Requirements.** Affiliated with all aspects that are not associated with functional requirements, such as service internal security measurements, data consumption capacity, service performance, and message response time.
3. **Architectural Best Practices.** Organizational SOA standards that characteristically address service reuse and consolidation, loose coupling, software modularity, componentization, and more.
4. **Technical Specifications.** Internal service design and architecture blueprints that describe service internal structure, service contract elements, message structure, service components' interrelationship, and more.

To accomplish a useful service verification process, ask the following guiding questions:

1. Does the service capability adhere to enterprise architecture best practices?
2. Does the service construct comply with the design and architecture technical specifications?
3. Are the business process model and functional requirements being addressed adequately by service operations?
4. Are the nonfunctional prerequisites being considered and tackled?
5. Does a service contain redundant functionality that should be eliminated?
6. Does a service consist of irrelevant operations that do not contribute to its overall capability?
7. Does a service structure agree with architecture loose coupling principles?
8. Does a service capability meet the nonfunctional specifications in terms of performance, message capacity, and data consumption?
9. Can the service design accommodate high transaction volume?
10. Is the service protected? Does it comply with organizational SOA security practices?

INTERNAL SERVICE DISCOVERY AND ANALYSIS.   One of the most important aspects of a service's capability is its internal structure, which can influence the service's ability to comply with the contract that it is obligated to execute. By looking *Inward*, we are able to understand not only how a message is propagated internally among service operations; we also are capable of identifying reuse opportunities. We are not only commissioned to recommend enhancements to repair an inefficient internal process flow; we also are required to break down a service into areas of responsibilities. During this analysis process, the latter may lead to the discovery of new *internal services*.

Bundling Service Capabilities.   To accomplish internal service identification, it would be beneficial to group a service's related operations by its responsibilities. This bundling activity should be driven by association. For example, one set of operations can address the processing of customer car insurance policy enrollment. The other operation group can tackle the customer credit verification process.

When practicing this approach, consider an internal service to be a bundle of related operations—meaning that a service is defined as a software entity that consists of one or more associated capabilities. Therefore, while pursuing the service structure *Inward* analysis approach, set the focal point of the investigation on how related groups of service operations shape an internal service structure.

The method of grouping operations to constitute a service may yield valuable benefits to the service discovery process. This approach can simplify the manner in which practitioners analyze the internal structure of a service. Bear in mind, though, that this is not the only approach to identifying services. To learn more about service discovery mechanisms, refer to Chapters 5 through 10.

Internal Service Discovery Example.   Exhibit 2.5 exemplifies the internal service discovery process. The *Inward* discovery and analysis approach yields a composite service formation: the

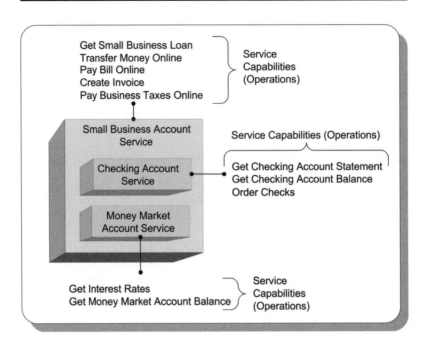

EXHIBIT 2.5   INTERNAL SERVICE DISCOVERY DRIVEN BY BUNDLED CAPABILITIES

Small Business Account Service, which encompasses two smaller services: Checking Account and Money Market Account. Note that this discovery is based on related operations that are bundled to create the corresponding services. Here the service identification process relies totally on matching related operations.

SERVICE DISCOVERY AND ANALYSIS DOWNWARD ROAD MAP PATTERN

The main charter of the *Downward* discovery and analysis activity calls for good architecture taste and an excellent sense of judgment when it comes to balancing between large and small, thin and thick, or too much versus too little. This activity pertains to the art of rationalizing service granularity levels, decomposing bulky implementations, or separating tightly coupled service capabilities. Here we are commissioned to modularize, decompose, compartmentalize, restructure, and enhance service structures to promote loose coupling service design.

Thus, the *Downward* approach is all about breaking down business concerns, business concepts, business functionalities, and service implementations into manageable, loosely coupled entities. It is also about assigning coherent responsibilities to service operations. This mission requires that we apply rules of order and aesthetics to the design of the underpinning solutions we propose.

Furthermore, the *Downward* service discovery and analysis road map pattern addresses architectural tight coupling challenges. Here the practitioner is commissioned to examine complex structural and contextual compositions of services and evaluate their contribution to the solution applied. The next list summarizes the fundamental mission of the *Downward* service discovery and analysis process:

- Fostering service componentization and modularization
- Addressing granularity levels of services

- Analyzing service structural and contextual compositions
- Simplifying complex solutions

We identify the leading activities and implementation approaches of the *Downward* pattern in the sections that follow.

SEPARATION-OF-CONCERNS ANALYSIS.   The term "separation of concerns" is traced back to the early 1970s. Edsger W. Dijkstra, a computer scientist known for his work on various programming topics, used this expression in his article "On the Role of Scientific Thought."[3] He argued that a software system is made up of multiple parts that must work simultaneously and in harmony to achieve a predefined goal. He also claimed that each of these application elements—namely concerns—must have unique functionality and contribute to the overall behavior of a system.

In recent years, the computer engineering phrase "separation of concerns" has evolved into a software design practice. In today's technical terminology, a "concern" is almost any identifiable piece of a system, such as objects, components, services, subsystems, layers, and tiers.

The chief benefits of breaking down a system into concerns are software reuse, system stability,[4] business agility, and software elasticity. These are also fundamental software development goals that should be fostered by organizational SOA best practices. Derek Greer, the software development engineer, identifies in his article "The Art of Separation of Concerns" the motivation behind this system delineation practice. He writes: "At its essence, Separation of Concerns is about order. The overall goal of Separation of Concerns is to establish a well organized system where each part fulfills a meaningful and intuitive role, while maximizing its ability to *adapt to change*. The achievement of Separation of Concerns is a goal guided more by principle than rules. Because of this, Separation of Concerns might be considered as much an art as it is a science."[5]

When practicing the *Downward* road map pattern for service discovery and analysis, it is essential to turn the focus on the core concerns that drive service identification and examination activities. It is recommended that we not only center the attention on service capabilities but that we also look at the various service components and its internal ingredients. This proposition supports the fundamental principles and best practices of the separation-of-concerns analysis:

- Loose coupling architecture
- Separation-of-service responsibilities
- Separation-of-service specialties
- Separation-of-service capabilities
- Software modularity
- Software componentization
- Component encapsulation
- Separation of business logic from technical implementation
- High cohesion of software

CONTEXTUAL SPECIFICATION ANALYSIS AND MODELING.   When pursuing *Downward* service discovery and analysis direction, a contextual specification analysis should take place—the service contextual specification process and modeling discussed in detail in Chapter 15. This effort is affiliated with the reduction of service capabilities and interfaces by breaking down a service into separate processes or even eliminating a part of its functionality. Here the practitioner is concerned merely with the semantic aspect of the service and disregards its structural or physical state. The aim of this exercise is also to narrow a service abstraction by trimming down its scope of operations. This can be attained by decreasing the spectrum of three major aspects of service specification:

1. **Functionality.** Trimming down the number of processes and activities that a service executes would evidently reduce its offerings and scope of operations.

2. **Specialty.** Decreasing the spectrum of service area of expertise would narrow the solution scale. For example, rather than designating a service with accounting duties, a service can be assigned to handle more limited accounting tasks, such as accounts payable activities.
3. **Naming.** Reduction of a service's essence and semantics is pursued by renaming a service to denote a smaller scale of duties and operational scope. This reduction of service abstraction yields a smaller functionality scope. For example, changing the name of a service from Trading Service to Equity Service would definitely indicate reduction of service offerings and the scope of its capabilities.

STRUCTURAL SPECIFICATION ANALYSIS AND MODELING.   Unlike the contextual specification process by which a service's capability scope is reduced and its overall functionality is trimmed, the structural specification analysis process addresses the inspection and modeling of service internal formations. This effort is clearly about downsizing a service by implementing the structural modeling operations that correspond to structural decomposition, retirement, substitution, or swapping service capabilities. These various structural modeling operations are discussed in Chapter 18, and the structural specification process and related patterns are elaborated on in Chapter 20.

Consider the four major analyses that are conducted during the structural specification process:

1. **Decomposition analysis.** This activity is about breaking up coarse-grained services into smaller components to avoid a tightly coupled implementation.
2. **Subtraction analysis.** The subtraction modeling operation is employed to retire a service or eliminate a part of its capabilities.
3. **Refactoring analysis.** Refactoring takes source code enhancements to increase service reusability, enhance its performance, and increase its consumer base.
4. **Contract analysis.** This process is designed to perfect contract management and binding relationship between a service and its related consumers when downsizing a service formation.

SERVICE-ORIENTED GRANULARITY ASSESSMENT.   The service discovery and analysis road map *Downward* pattern must tackle the intrinsic question that should be addressed when inspecting service capabilities: How should I size a service? At the first glance, this query may not come across as an analysis cornerstone. But the more we delve into the contribution of the service granularity assessment activity, the more we realize how central it is to the service-oriented modeling framework. As the reader may have guessed, service granularity is about service sizing. In other words, the more functions and capabilities a service offers, the more coarse-grained it is considered to be. In contrast, a service that consists of lesser components and operations is considered a fine-grained entity.

Why is service granularity analysis so critical to the service discovery and analysis process? Service sizing is not a negligible analysis effort that can be disregarded. The granularity level of a service can affect its capabilities, performance, and consumption rates in a production environment. In fact, when shaping a service's formation during the granularity analysis process, one should comply with architectural loose coupling principles. This activity must also meet the terms of asset reuse and consolidation best practices, which are often advocated by the business and technology organizations.

Service granularity can and should be measured from different perspectives, each of which represents a different view that may shape a service's construct, applicability, consumption capacity, reusability, and even abstraction levels. As explained in the sections that follow, however, there is a dependency between the granularity levels of each perspective.

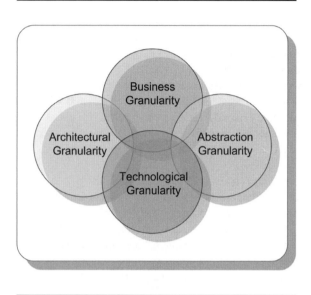

EXHIBIT 2.6　SERVICE-ORIENTED GRANULARITY ANALYSIS PERSPECTIVES

Exhibit 2.6 depicts these four major granularity dimensions that influence a service's implementation:

1. Business Granularity
2. Abstraction Granularity
3. Technological Granularity
4. Architectural Granularity

Note that these perspectives share overlapping areas, denoting dependencies between the granularity dimensions levels.

Business Granularity Perspective.　The business granularity perspective pertains to the scale of business initiatives that typically affect service granularity. These influences are associated with the *level of detail* and *magnitude* that the business organization uses to define the problem domain, propose business solutions, depict business requirements, and scale a project. The larger the business endeavor is, the more coarse-grained services can be. In contrast, a smaller business venture may derive finer-grained services. A skilled practitioner, however, can fine-tune the outcome by decomposing coarse-grained services or unifying fine-grained or ones. Consider the chief business granularity aspects that can influence a service's granularity scale:

- **Business process.** This relates to the business process granularity level of its underpinning activities. Specifically, fine-grained business processes typically lead to the construction of fine-grained services; and vice versa: Coarse-grained business processes characteristically originate coarse-grained services.
- **Business requirements.** The business granularity level perspective also represents the scope of the business requirements that are delivered to the solution domain organization. Therefore, coarse-grained services are by-products of requirements that urge large construction initiatives. Conversely, business requirements that call for small-scale projects may result in the construction of fine-grained services.

- **Project scope.** This pertains to the size of the project that is being launched, which typically is influenced by the scale of the business requirements. Large-scale business ventures yield coarse-grained services. Conversely, smaller projects that provide limited solutions, or merely introduce limited changes to exiting implementations, typically result in the construction of fine-grained services.
- **Business imperative.** Business initiatives can be measured in terms of their importance to an enterprise's survival. Strategic decisions are associated with long-term and large-scale business missions that typically yield coarse-grained services. Conversely, tactical business undertakings are regarded as short-term solutions that characteristically yield fine-grained services.

Abstraction Granularity Perspective.   "Abstraction granularity" is a term used for depicting different levels of terminologies that are associated with business or technology execution, on various importance levels. On the business end, it represents the scope of a business concept in terms of resolving business problems. For example, the household investment portfolio business idea provides a shift in a company's direction to address a wide range of investment opportunities for family members. This would be regarded as a coarse-grained business abstraction. Conversely, a fine-grained abstraction can be attributed to the individual investment portfolio concept, which attends to a narrower view of a business execution.

Similarly, technology abstractions can depict different levels of technological and architectural generalizations. The term "content aggregator engine" represents a coarse-grained abstraction that depicts a software capability to gather content for the presentation layer. In contrast, the idiom "article aggregator engine" describes a narrower software solution, and is thus regarded as a finer-grained architectural idea.

Technological Granularity Perspective.   The term "technological granularity" corresponds to the detail level and to the scope of a particular technical implementation that is devised to deliver a business solution. So what are the influencing aspects on the technical granularity perspective? Specifically, what makes a technical solution fine-grained or coarse-grained? The answers to these questions depend on the two major aspects that were described in the last two sections: business granularity and abstraction granularity. First, the scope of the business granularity perspective artifacts, such as business requirements, business process modeling, and project planning, influence the technical granularity scale. Second, business or technological abstraction levels, as described in the Abstraction Granularity Perspective section, can influence the technological granularity level immensely: coarse-grained abstractions typically lead to coarse-grained technical capabilities. In contrast, fine-grained abstractions may yield fine-grained technical remedies.

For example, the scale of a technical solution can vary. A technical cure for a business concern can address a wide range of issues or focus on limited business functionality. Imagine adding an entire line of business for the enterprise, such as small business credit card execution that may require the technical implementation of myriad business processes. This technical initiative's scope that is influenced by business requirements is regarded as a coarse-grained technological mission. Conversely, a smaller project, such as revamping a business process that already exists in a production environment calls for a fine-grained technical implementation.

Architectural Granularity Perspective.   Architectural granularity constitutes the scope of an architecture initiative in an organization. This includes two types of architecture endeavors that typically are launched before the software product construction phase takes place: business architecture and technical architecture.

The business architecture process takes precedence over any other software development life cycle discipline. It embodies all aspects of the problem domain analysis, business process modeling, and business solutions. Furthermore, a business architect typically is the person who understands the organization mission and strategy, business model, and the business execution that is driven by business processes. The person who fills this role must also be acquainted with the various enterprise products and their ability to provide business remedies. Strategic projects that encompass a wider array of business processes typically are regarded as coarse-grained business architecture solutions. However, tactical initiatives that are designed to provide a short-term cure to a painful business problem are considered to be fine-grained.

The same idea is applied to technical architecture initiatives. Technical architecture granularity is about the implementation scope of architecture. The scale of technical architecture solutions can vary: An application-level architecture, for example, addresses smaller-scale problems namely fine-grained challenges, that are affiliated with a software product's scalability, consumption and capacity planning, internal functionality, and component reuse. On the enterprise level, however, we are concerned about integration of commercial of-the-shelf (COTS) products, distribution of services, message orchestration, and enterprise architecture patterns. These are larger in magnitude coarse-grained and more complex to implement.

TOP-DOWN SERVICE DISCOVERY MODEL.   The Top-Down service discovery model introduces two essential patterns that facilitate the discovery of services: service discovery driven by business processes and attribute-driven service discovery. These methods are elaborated on in Chapters 5 and 6, respectively. The former is based on analysis of business processes and their underpinning activities. The products are services that embody the functionality of business processes and offer solutions and capabilities that meet business requirements.

The second Top-Down approach to service discovery is driven by the attribution analysis process. This method for service identification advocates that we start with extracting software product features and properties and concluding with the discovery of corresponding services that represent business and technological requirements.

Exhibit 2.7 illustrates the top-down service discovery model that should be pursued during the *Downward* service discovery and analysis direction. In the top section, note the two inputs to

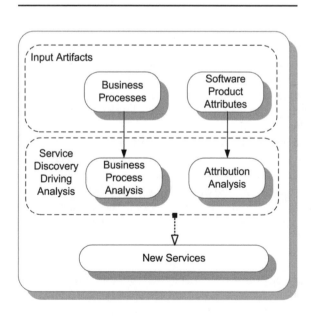

Exhibit 2.7   Top-Down Service Discovery Model

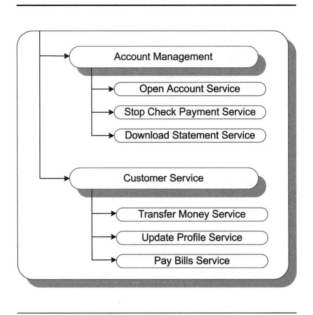

EXHIBIT 2.8   BUSINESS SERVICE TAXONOMY EXAMPLE

the service identification process: Business Processes and Software Product Attributes. The Business Processes provide analysis material for the Business Process Analysis activity. The Software Product Attributes unveils attributes and product features that are utilized during the Attribution Analysis process.

BUSINESS "SERVITIZATION" MODEL.   The efforts to identify organizational needs, break down business *responsibilities* and assign them to future services, and establish clear ownership of service execution in a production environment is the crux of the business "servitization" model. The evolutionary process of institutionalizing services also calls for compartmentalizing business concerns into manageable and understandable solutions that the technology organization can grasp. This is the nucleus of the term business "servitization." [6] In other words, servitization is simply the process of rendering business requirements into services. This activity is one of the most crucial aspects of the *Downward* road map pattern because it promotes loose coupling principles as early as possible in the service life cycle.

   Another crucial artifact of the servitization paradigm is the establishment of an organizational business *service taxonomy* by grouping services based on their responsibilities. Exhibit 2.8 exemplifies how a banking institution chose to break down its two major business occupations, denoted by the taxonomy's two entries: Account Management and Customer Service. This illustration also depicts the grouping of the subordinating services. The first three are associated with banking account activities, and the remaining three are related to customer service activities.

DELIVERABLES

Carve out an organizational vertical discovery and analysis process that offers *Inward* (25) and *Downward* (32) road map patterns. The former should focus on studying business and technological imperatives, and the latter should be employed to foster loose coupling and increase service reusability rates by pursuing service specifications activities and practicing separation of concerns best practices.

SUMMARY

- The vertical discovery and analysis process employs two distinct patterns to facilitate a service's identification, inspection, and perfection of its capabilities: *Inward* (25) and *Downward* (32) directions.
- The *Inward* (25) discovery and analysis pattern addresses design challenges of a service's internal formation, operations, and interfaces.
- The *Downward* (32) pattern offers mechanisms to promote loose coupling, increase service reusability rates, and foster business agility. This is typically achieved by specification activities that advocate service decomposition, retirement, or elimination of functionality redundancy.

Notes

1. Thomas Erl, *SOA Principles of Service Design* (Boston: Pearson, 2008), p. 14.
2. http://technet.microsoft.com/en-us/library/bb463148.aspx.
3. www.cs.utexas.edu/users/EWD/transcriptions/EWD04xx/EWD447.html.
4. www.ctrl-shift-b.com/2008/01/art-of-separation-of-concerns.html.
5. Ibid.
6. S. Vandermerwe and J. Rada, J., "Servitization of Business: Adding Value by Adding Services," *European Management Journal* 6, no. 4 (1988). pp. 314–324

CHAPTER 3

HORIZONTAL SERVICE DISCOVERY AND ANALYSIS

Pursuing Upward and Outward Road Map Patterns

Unlike the vertical service discovery and analysis process (described in Chapter 2) that advocates inspecting, modeling, and perfecting a service's internal construct, the horizontal approach to service identification and inspection focuses on the environment and the expansion or contraction of a service influence and boundaries across applications and organizations. This "big picture" perspective enables architects, developers, analysts, modelers, and managers to view a service's surroundings by shifting the attention from a service's internal capabilities and functionality to a larger spectrum of concerns.

Therefore, pursue the horizontal method for discovering, analyzing, and modeling services not only to understand the necessities of a service and its current implementation limitations and constraints but also to expand or contract its capabilities and provide greater business and technological value. Adhere to the best practices that are provided along with the two chief discovery and analysis road map patterns that facilitate these goals: *Upward* (42) and *Outward* (46). The horizontal service discovery and analysis model that is illustrated in Exhibit 3.1 identifies these two patterns and the commitment to architecture best practices and standards adherence.

To better understand architecture policies, employ the *Upward* direction. This approach would also allow expanding practitioners' business processes knowledge and domain expertise. In addition, the *Upward* direction would contribute to the Bottom-Up method of service discovery by which existing applications, services, technologies, and architectures are repurposed and reused in future projects. Furthermore, to generalize a service's functionality, capabilities, and structure and to expand its existing boundaries, the *Upward* direction offers methods and patterns for implementation.

However, the *Outward* road map direction is about expanding or contracting a service environment. This discovery and analysis approach is chiefly concerned with the distribution method of services and the manner by which they are integrated, deployed, and configured. To strengthen associations and perfect binding contracts between services and their corresponding consumers, the *Outward* direction also offers two schemes of service integration: interoperability model and mediation model.

Moreover, to enhance the service discovery process, the practitioner is commissioned to expand the scope of service identification by studying user interface artifacts and even data and repositories requirements. These would provide greater opportunities to discover new services. Finally, to facilitate the expansion or contraction of a distributed environment, the *Outward* direction provides methods for structural and contextual integration.

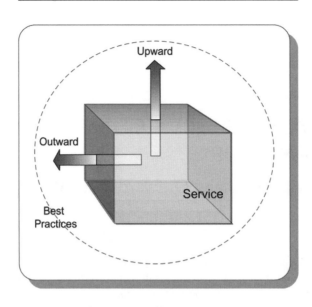

EXHIBIT 3.1   HORIZONTAL SERVICE DISCOVERY AND ANALYSIS MODEL

SERVICE-ORIENTED DISCOVERY AND ANALYSIS UPWARD ROAD MAP PATTERN

Unlike the *Inward* (25) pattern (discussed in Chapter 2) that focuses on a service's internal affairs, the *Upward* direction for service discovery and analysis consists of a larger service-oriented architecture (SOA) implementation view. The *Upward* method enables us to expand our perspective beyond an individual service construction. This approach characteristically includes an examination and study of service-oriented governance best practices, security policies, organizational software development standards, and service life cycle management. Moreover, the discovery and analysis *Upward* pattern advocates that we take a broader look at the formations of our services.

By looking *Upward*, away from an individual service's internal affairs, we observe seven major aspects that contribute immensely to the service-oriented development strategies that the organization is planning to pursue: governance, business process analysis, service orchestration, service life cycle process, Bottom-Up discovery process, contextual generalization, structural generalization, and domain expertise. Their influence on the discovery and analysis process is explained in detail in the sections that follow.

SERVICE-ORIENTED GOVERNANCE.   Service-oriented governance is the leading discipline of an SOA establishment. An SOA governance organization typically is responsible for devising service-oriented best practices and standards, establishing SOA governance policies, perfecting the SOA reference architecture, educating SOA practitioners, and more. By committing to the fundamental charter of an overseeing governance body and understanding its policies and standards, the service-oriented discovery and analysis process is bound to be aligned with the organizational business and technological direction, strategies, and business model.

For example, software consolidation is one of the most appealing imperatives for most institutions. This best practice typically leads the service-oriented discovery and analysis process to reduce service construction projects, inspect service reuse opportunities, reduce redundancy of business functionality, and even unify legacy systems.

Hence, while pursuing the service discovery and analysis *Upward* pattern, stay tuned to governance policies and standards that correspond to the service-oriented development practice. Be aware of best practices that can contribute to the service discovery and analysis process and the manner in which services should be identified and examined to help increase their quality and future stability. To learn more about the service-oriented discovery and analysis best practices model refer to Chapter 4.

BUSINESS PROCESS ANALYSIS.   The second important aspect of the *Upward* discovery and analysis road map pattern is the business process—an intrinsic force behind any enterprise business execution. Processes typically constitute the core business of an organization, and their fundamental goal is to promote the business and incur revenue.

Business processes are valuable sources for service analysis and discovery activities. As we learn in Chapter 5, the business process analysis practice is one of the most conventional methods for discovering services. A business analyst, for example, can employ a number of inspection methods: decompose a business process, bundle business activities, or even eliminate business process redundancy during a business analysis session. These examination activities often yield effective service capabilities.

Business processes are also organizational abstractions: Documented or even undocumented processes are known to be the foremost driving force and motivation behind an SOA implementation. Therefore, by moving *Upward* in the discovery and analysis ladder, we are naturally engaged in a more generalized and abstracted manner to identify new services, assess their contribution to the proposed solution, and analyze them for future production initiatives.

SERVICE-ORIENTED LIFE CYCLE PROCESS.   Remember, the *Upward* pattern for discovering and analyzing services must also be aligned with the organizational service life cycle process. It encourages staying on course with the development strategy, focusing on the service-oriented modeling process, and being aware of the big picture. This approach will simply divert the focal point from people's private agendas to organizational imperatives.

A service life cycle consists of a number of events (also known as stages), each of which contributes to a service's evolution. More specifically, the SOA practitioner transforms a service to its next life cycle state by employing one or more service-oriented modeling disciples, such as service-oriented conceptualization, service-oriented discovery and analysis, and service-oriented logical design. This evolutionary activity, in which a service commences as an idea at the inception stage and later materializes into a concrete entity, ready to be deployed and used in a production environment, is the crux of the service-oriented life cycle.

When applicable, iterate through the service discovery and analysis process in each software development life cycle stage to increase service identification opportunities.[1] This recurring process increases the quality of the discovered services and enhances the analysis proposition in each repetitive reiteration.

Exhibit 3.2 illustrates this idea. It depicts a number of staged events (Planning, Design, Construction, Quality Assurance, and Deployment) and their corresponding four iterations of service Discovery and analysis (refer to discovery and analysis iterations in Chapter 1). This arrangement is merely an example of how an organization chose to structure its internal software development life cycle process. It must be remembered, however, that each event in the life cycle affects the service discovery and analysis discipline in a different way. For example, in the planning stage, the discovery of services evolves around identification of abstractions—conceptual services—that eventually will materialize into services. Correspondingly, during the service construction, a developer may realize that a new service is required to provide different business functionality.

SERVICE-ORIENTED BOTTOM-UP DISCOVERY PROCESS.   The *Upward* road map pattern focuses on the Bottom-Up (145) pattern for identifying and inspecting services (elaborated on in Chapter 9).

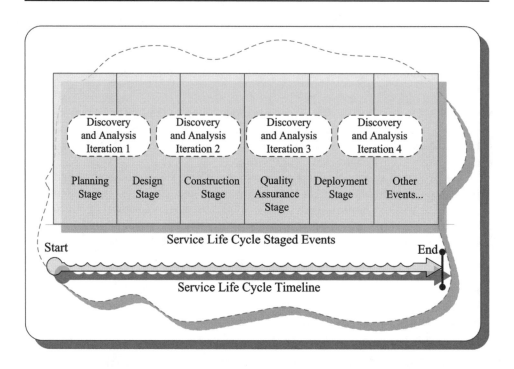

EXHIBIT 3.2   SERVICE DISCOVERY AND ANALYSIS ITERATIONS EXAMPLE

The direction is clear: We start from the lowest baseline and move up to the newly discovered services. This activity relies on existing services, legacy applications, technologies, and architectures. "Existing" means that they are already part of a production environment and have been road-tested and proven to be valuable and reliable. Moreover, the Bottom-Up process discovers new services in two ways: (1) Identifying the *gaps* between existing functionalities and those that do not exist and (2) reusing legacy software, technologies, and architectures.

Exhibit 3.3 illustrates the three major starting points that lead to the discovery of new services when pursuing the Bottom-Up approach. The existing organizational assets include the three major entities, each of which can serve as a source and input to the service discovery process:

1. **Existing Legacy Services and Applications.** This consists of analyzing the capabilities of existing services or legacy applications. The missing functionality is candidate material for instituting new services.
2. **Existing Empowering Technologies.** This consists of inspecting present deployed technologies, such as infrastructure, networking, and messaging facilities. The absence of technical services, such as infrastructure or security capabilities, characteristically offers motivation for devising new services. This can be accomplished by wrapping or transforming existing technologies.
3. **Existing Driving Architectures.** This consists of examining current operating architectures to determine how new services can bridge the architecture capability gap. For example, these can be added capabilities to address interoperability challenges between business domains or even employ broker services that can be used to transform data.

CONTEXTUAL GENERALIZATION ANALYSIS AND MODELING.   The *Upward* service discovery and analysis road map pattern suggests that a contextual generalization process should take place

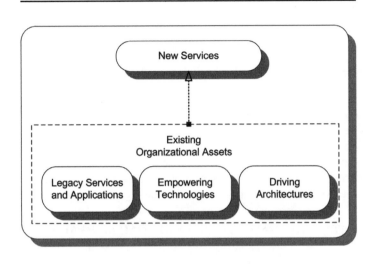

EXHIBIT 3.3   BOTTOM-UP APPROACH TO DISCOVERING SERVICES

to further explore service identification opportunities. This effort pertains to increasing a service's abstraction level and generalizing its solution scope. By broadening a service's operations spectrum and increasing its responsibilities, its corresponding consumer base will be amplified as well. This practice is discussed in detail in Chapter 14, which offers a generalization method that is accompanied by related patterns and notation to assist architects, analysts, modelers, developers, and managers to broaden the scope of the service-oriented discovery and analysis initiative.

Remember, the contextual generalization endeavor is a semantic-oriented process, not a structural effort to widen a service formation. Here the practitioner is commissioned to analyze and widen the three major contextual generalization activities that elucidate the meaning of the term "semantic-oriented":

1. **Generalizing service name.** This activity abstracts the name of a service and generalizes its essence. For example, the Accounting Service is a generalized version of the Accounts Payable Service.
2. **Generalizing service functionality.** The functionality of a service grows if it encompasses more business processes and activities.
3. **Generalizing service specialty.** This pertains to the increasing fields of expertise that a service can offer.

STRUCTURAL GENERALIZATION ANALYSIS AND MODELING.   Unlike the contextual generalization process, which is devised exclusively to broaden service processes, offerings, and abstraction level, the structural generalization effort addresses the logical and even the physical growth of a service's boundaries. This modeling exercise explores service discovery opportunities by reconciling fine-grained services, uniting service structures, or consolidating service formations. To achieve these structural generalization aims, the practitioner is commissioned to employ four major mechanisms, each of which introduces a distinct method and patterns to facilitate a structural transformation:

1. **Structural aggregation.** The process of containing child fine-grained services within a parent service
2. **Structural unification.** Merging two or more services

3. **Structural compounding.** Grouping services
4. **Service binding.** Instituting service contracts between services and their corresponding consumers

For an in-depth discussion about structural generalization analysis and modeling, refer to Chapter 19.

DOMAIN EXPERTISE.   Modelers, developers, architects, or managers are commissioned to both understand the business and be familiar with the business model and strategies of the enterprise. This is a requirement that calls for knowledge of the business condition, customer relationship, business mission, and business processes. This domain expertise is a prescription for service-oriented discovery and analysis success. It can help practitioners understand the motivation behind creating new services, identifying existing ones, or analyzing and modeling service environments.

SERVICE DISCOVERY AND ANALYSIS OUTWARD ROAD MAP PATTERN

The *Outward* pattern for service discovery and analysis focuses on the distribution of services and their empowering technologies in an interoperable computing environment. This calls for a thorough inspection of services to assess if they can collaborate on providing valuable solutions. The art of assigning business and technical responsibilities to a group of services turns out to be a complex task that must be analyzed for efficiency, reusability, performance, interoperability, and nimbleness.

The choices here are clear. We are commissioned to identify the fine line between an expanded or contracted environment, between localized or distributed technologies, and between centralized or federated architecture. We are also required to inspect the usefulness of a solution that is provided by combined capabilities of services. This means we must assess the collaborative efforts of a group of services to provide adequate remedies to organizational concerns. A detailed explanation of the *Outward* approach is provided in the sections that follow.

SERVICE-ORIENTED DISCOVERY AND ANALYSIS INTEROPERABILITY MODEL.   Interoperability simply depicts the mechanisms by which we connect the dots in a heterogeneous computing environment. "Heterogeneous" means diverse landscapes, which represent dissimilar technologies, business domains, cultures, and agendas. "Dots" are our organizational computing assets. These can be different types of services, legacy applications that are written in multiple languages and operate on a variety of platforms, hardware infrastructure, operating systems, deployment environments, and lines of business. The art of bonding enterprise entities is often referred to as *integration*; making enterprise entities "talk" to each other is the discipline of *collaboration*; and scheduling and coordinating the messages that they exchange is the practice of *orchestration*.

The service discovery and analysis *Outward* road map pattern must turn our attention to service interoperability challenges. The chief asset integration hurdles are associated with the complexity that a mixed computing environment introduces to business and information technology (IT) organizations. So the answer to the question Why should we address interoperability difficulties? is simply to leverage existing investments and retain knowledge and expertise that has been acquired over the years. Doing this can reduce expenditure and complexity inherited from old architectures that consist of mixed ingredients, such as vendor products, network protocols, data formats, servers, and monitoring tools. Thus when pursuing the *Outward* road map pattern, the practitioner should value the vast contribution of legacy assets and avoid unnecessary implementation redundancy that new service construction can pose.

Discovering and analyzing services in an interoperable computing landscape mandates that we understand its general composition, the fundamental building blocks of a typical production environment. Beyond the hardware boxes, air-conditioning pipes, and cables that provide electricity, we should also be aware of other important elements in a service ecosystem. These include

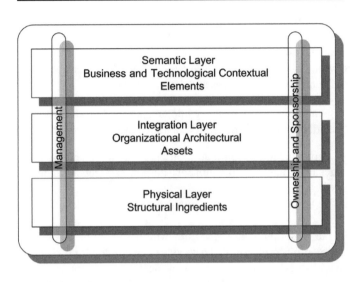

Exhibit 3.4 *Service Discovery and Analysis Interoperability Model*

financial and budgeting aspects, ownership and sponsorship, abstractions, organizational structure, and technical assets. Chapters 16, 17, 21, and 22 discuss in detail service analysis and modeling in a distributed and interoperable computing environment.

Exhibit 3.4 depicts five major components that make up the service-oriented discovery and analysis interoperability model: (1) Semantic Layer, (2) Integration Layer, (3) Physical Layer, (4) Management, and (5) Ownership and Sponsorship. A detailed explanation of these areas of concern is provided in the sections that follow.

Semantic Layer.   The interoperability semantic layer element consists of business and technological ideas that influence the construction of a heterogeneous and distributed production environment. These abstractions represent business and technological solutions. For example, premier customer service, aggressive equity investment basket, and online flea market constitute business concepts. Implementations that reflect technological abstractions, in contrast, describe service capabilities, such as business rules engine, data collection facility, or search engine pattern matcher.

From a higher level view, the semantic layer can also describe various *types* of business and technical services that operate in a production distributed environment. From a business perspective, this classification is formalized by an organizational business *taxonomy*, which is based on the various occupations in the enterprise and managed by business domains. These specialty groups within an organization are also known as lines of business that offer areas of expertise, such as claims processing, underwriting services, and loan approval. On the technological taxonomy front, types of technologies can identify the nature of an interoperability strategy, such as messaging framework, searching framework, or data access facility.

Integration Layer.   An interoperable environment heavily relies on integration capabilities that enable flawless execution of services in production. Empowering technologies and architectures (such as middleware, infrastructure, data access facilities, language platforms, and messaging frameworks) that can bridge the communication gaps between production assets are not the only facilitators that should be considered. The integration plan, architecture blueprints, technical taxonomy, canonical data model (authoritative database schema), service contracts, and an elaborated metadata model are prerequisite artifacts that enable service communication and collaboration in an interoperable computing environment as well.

The absence of these crucial artifacts would compromise the pursuit quality of the service discovery and analysis *Outward* road map pattern. Without an integration ontology that describes the relationship between organizational assets and the nature of their business contribution, it would be difficult to identify and examine services and determine their viability.

Physical Layer.   The physical aspect of every implementation introduces four major components. In their absence a functioning interoperable production environment could not exist:

1.   Integration, deployment, and configuration best practices. These organizational standards drive the packaging and incorporation of solution services and commercial off-the-shelf (COTS) products.
2.   Services and legacy applications that provide business value. databases, and metadata repositories.
3.   To connect the dots, "plumbing" facilities would also be required. The term "plumbing" pertains to the various protocols that a service must employ for message exchange and communication with its corresponding consumers across the enterprise and beyond its boundary. In addition, for software compatibility purposes, adapters and agents are used to transform protocols and data.
4.   In addition, the physical layer consists of infrastructure entities that enable transportation and transformation of messages across business boundaries. This includes network platforms, enterprise services buses (ESBs); SOA intermediaries, gateways, and hubs; and Universal Description, Discovery and Integration (UDDI) registries.

Management.   Without proper control structure and management facilities, an interoperable environment is doomed to fail. Federated service operations across lines of business or even between business partners require strong organizational support and guidance. Thus the role of management is to enable business continuity across multicultural and sociopolitical organizations in the enterprise. This is purely the art of balancing agendas of multiple interest groups and fostering best practices and standards among partnerships that share parts of this heterogeneous landscape.

Ownership and Sponsorship.   The ownership aspect of a interoperable environment is complex and raises difficulties when partnerships are formed to sponsor common services. This obstacle is even harder to overcome when software and hardware assets are distributed beyond the jurisdiction of a particular business domain. Therefore, the ownership aspect of an interoperable environment should be inspected. Here the focus should be on identifying the dominating organizations that sponsor crucial environment components, their internal structure, and the business value of their operating services in production.

SERVICE-ORIENTED DISCOVERY AND ANALYSIS MEDIATION MODEL.   In simple terms, mediation is brokering. This is the practice of intercepting messages that are being exchanged between consumers and their corresponding services. The aim is not to interfere or disrupt regular run-time operations; instead, the goal is to address major service-oriented architecture implementation objectives associated with message processing, security, policy management, and information delivery mechanisms.

The service mediation model should tackle dominating architectural concerns during the pursuit of the *Outward* road map pattern. Here we are not only required to analyze an architecture proposition and assess its feasibility, we are also encouraged to discover mediating services to enable software elasticity, expand service boundaries, extend architecture implementation across the

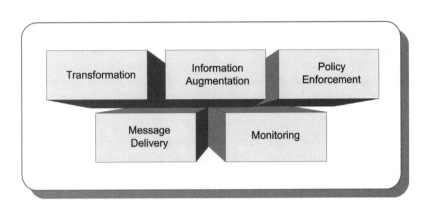

Exhibit 3.5 Service Discovery and Analysis Mediation Model

organization, and fill in the communication gaps between silo groups in the enterprise. In contrast, removing mediating services from a distributed production environment would result in contraction of an architectural implementation and reduction of service influence scope across the organization. SOA intermediaries are the most common facilities employed to fulfill these organizational business and technological imperatives. They also promote loose coupling architecture best practices. To learn more about mediation modeling and the effect of service brokers on a distributed environment refer to Chapters 16, 17, 21, and 22.

Consider the major service broker roles and their assigned responsibilities, which are illustrated in Exhibit 3.5 and discussed in detail in the sections that follow: Transformation, Information Augmentation, Policy Enforcement, Message Delivery, and Monitoring.

Transformation.   A service broker positioned between a service and a consumer often performs transformation duties. There are many types of conversions that an SOA intermediary can offer. These three are commonly used:

1. **Format conversion.** This duty pertains to conversion of data from one format to another, for example, the transformation to align different data schemas that are used for the same data source. Another common scenario addresses transformation of content that is delivered in XML format into plain text. A more strategic responsibility is to maintain an organizational canonical data model, an enterprise authoritative data schema that can be used by most lines of business.[2]
2. **Protocol conversion.** This activity is performed when communicating parties use different protocols. Consider a mainframe legacy consumer that is employing the System Network Architecture (SNA) protocol to communicate with a distributed J2EE service using TCP/IP protocol.
3. **Security model translation.** In an interoperable environment, we can often find multiple security models that are used on different hardware or employed by diverse operating systems. In cross-organizational secured environments, these schemes must be translated during a transaction to maintain security continuity. For example, consider two services: One is using the role-based access control (RBAC) model, and the other the access control list (ACL) model.

Information Augmentation.   A consumer's message that is aimed at a service end point may be intercepted by a service broker for enrichment purposes. This service intermediary can collect, unify, and compile data from various data sources to enrich the message content. Augmentation duties such as this typically are performed to offload some of the responsibilities of the participating parties in a transaction. For example, consider a service mediator that modifies an original message to include a customer's address and telephone number. Other message augmentation activities are associated with security protection that an SOA intermediary can provide, such as message content or user's credential encryption.

Policy Enforcement.   Another feature that a service broker can offer is automated management enforcements. Service security policies, for example, can be administered by third-party vendor products that offer repositories and mechanisms for applying security rules and access control policies to protect run-time activities.

Message Delivery.   Another important function that a service broker can provide is delivery mechanisms by which messages are dispatched to their destinations. These routing activities can take several forms of execution. One is intelligent routing, often called context-based routing, during which the distributed information is analyzed to determine the destination. The other routing method is based on a volume workload assessment, in which the broker determines the least busy server that the message can be forwarded to (also known as workload management).

Monitoring.   A service intermediary can provide monitoring assistance to trace compliance of service-level agreements (SLAs), detect security breaches, alert management if service security or an SLA has been compromised, offer audit trail facilities to record exceptions and events during service run-time operations, report on organizational or governmental policy noncompliant activities, and more.

FRONT-TO-BACK SERVICE DISCOVERY PROCESS.   The quest for broadening the service discovery and analysis process when pursuing the *Outward* road map pattern calls for the inspection of front-end artifacts that are characteristically associated with the presentation layer of an application. More specifically, an application that offers a graphical user interface (GUI) is a leading contender for this analysis activity. The aim here is to inspect how a user interacts with a given application and to determine what components deliver information for user display. This simple charter introduces ample opportunities for discovering services that can assist with the rendering process of content.

Funneling information to front-end user interface controls requires a set of services that can carry out data collection, matching, and rendering responsibilities. Now the service discovery *Outward* road map pattern centers on four major building blocks of the presentation layer paradigm: (1) UI Control, (2) UI Content Delivery, (3) UI Content Rendering, and (4) UI Value Persistence. These provide material for deriving service responsibilities and defining new capabilities that are associated with the user-interface domain. Exhibit 3.6 illustrates these four major inputs to the service discovery process. The Front-to-Back (105) service discovery pattern by which services can be identified and established are discussed in detail in Chapter 7.

UI Control.   The term "control" pertains to user capability to exchange information with an application via GUI widgets. These are user-interface mechanisms such as text boxes, buttons, and drop-down lists that one can employ to create, update, delete, edit, or display data. These functionalities can be further delegated to services that will be responsible for propagating the requests and submitting the actual information to back-end application processes.

UI Content Delivery.   UI content delivery mechanisms are designed to gather users' entered information and deliver it to the proper back-end application engine for further processing. These duties

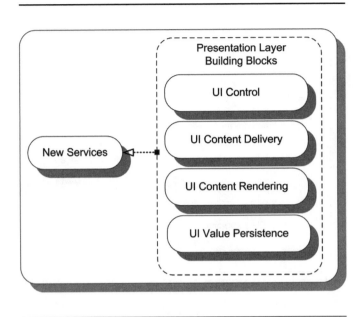

EXHIBIT 3.6   FRONT-TO-BACK SERVICE DISCOVERY MODEL

are assigned to specialized services that offer expertise in content collection from user interface facilities.

UI Content Rendering.   Rendering is the process of transforming raw content into readable and viewable information. This activity, for example, can yield processed and formatted data that constitute articles on an Internet journal, deciphered binary data that is converted to images or graphs, and digital streams that wind up as video clips. These presentation layer assets obviously must undergo a preparation process, rendering activities, before they can be viewed by users. To increase reuse of rendering functionalities, it is advisable to identify services that can efficiently carry out these tasks.

UI Value Persistence.   Specialized UI services should also facilitate the persistence of content that can be quickly accessible by a user. The term "quickly" means that this information is not necessarily saved in databases. To enable rapid retrieval of data, value persistence services can leverage memory cache mechanisms. Doing so would minimize information exchange delays and allow transaction execution that avoids time-out conditions.

BACK-TO-FRONT SERVICE DISCOVERY PROCESS.   The Back-to-Front service discovery model is another important starting point for pursuing the service identification *Outward* road map pattern. Now we focus on inspecting organizational back-end assets. Data storage is a good source of information that can provide clues to which types of services may be needed for a solution. But the practitioner should continue to inspect alternative analysis avenues in the data and information domain to tap into multiple data perspectives.

Thus the service discovery and analysis *Outward* approach advocates broadening the view beyond the narrow boundaries of the data storage and persistence field. This calls for a generic data model that encompasses a wide range of data concerns. Among the most crucial aspects are data operations that are referred to as CRUD (an acronym used to describe basic data persistence operations: create, read, update, delete). Data transportation, delivery, access, virtuality, aggregation, portability, and modeling are vital inputs to the service discovery process as well.

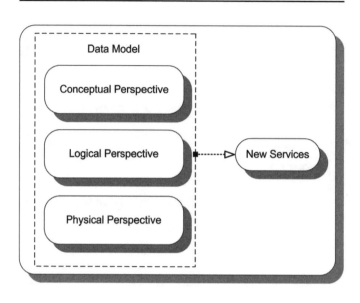

EXHIBIT 3.7   BACK-TO-FRONT SERVICE DISCOVERY MODEL

The Back-to-Front service discovery model is based on the data model dimensions that are illustrated in Exhibit 3.7. These three perspectives[3] are essential sources for the service identification process: Conceptual Perspective, Logical Perspective, and Physical Perspective. A detailed discussion that describes the Back-to-Front (105) service discovery pattern, which is based on the provided data model, can be found in Chapter 8.

Conceptual Perspective.   Data concepts are the fundamental building blocks for every data modeling and service-oriented discovery effort. Abstractions of data elements can emerge from different organizational asset sources, such as business requirements, business vocabulary, business domains, or even tracking back existing database schemas.

One of the methods that a data modeler uses to capture data concepts is to develop an abstraction model, in which data *entities* represent the "things" that describe data elements. Entities denote boundaries of concepts that shape data structures and schemas. From a data modeling perspective, entities are conceptual representations of data that identify a schematic data model of an application. For example, entities such as employee, employee profile, benefits program, and retirement package describe data types for the human resources repository. In addition, a data modeler frequently delivers entity relationship diagrams (ERDs) that illustrate the associations between abstraction entities. This artifact can play a major role in the service discovery process. It provides fundamental concepts and direction from a data perspective that should not be ignored when trying to devise effective solutions to organizational problems.

Logical Perspective.   The logical view represents the various imperatives and methods by which data is being accessed and delivered to consumers. These data processing approaches can provide motivation to discover new services that are designed to alleviate major data concerns in a distributed computing environment. Information transportation, aggregation, cleansing, transformation, searching, and virtualization are the major challenges that services can help resolve.

Furthermore, the logical perspective also identifies the relationship between the various data components and the methods by which they interact to deliver information. Data modeling artifacts, such as database schemas, ERDs, XML data tagging, and interaction diagrams, are crucial to the design of service collaboration because they provide contextual material for establishing service responsibilities and behavior.

Physical Perspective.   Analyzing storage facilities and their operations to provide processed information for applications can contribute to the discovery of services. This view calls for broadening the analysis efforts to include domains and their geographical locations, such as third-party data providers, data warehouses, virtual data facilities, and database repositories.

Here we focus on the physical means by which the data is stored, categorized, and maintained. Classifying data based on analytical, transactional, and informational categories, for example, can lead to the discovery of specialized services that are affiliated with the strategy of data distribution. Moreover, inspecting physical data storage facilities typically leads to the understanding of how data is segmented, who owns the data, and how the data is federated across organizational boundaries. This information can be further used to enhance the service discovery efforts.

CONTEXTUAL EXPANSION PROCESS AND MODELING.   Another practice that should be pursued, according to the *Outward* road map pattern, is contextual expansion analysis and modeling. This horizontal process for service identification and examination addresses the increase of a service's offerings beyond its current capacity and broadens its consumer base. This is a contextual exercise that is not initially focused on service internal affairs or on elevating its abstraction level. Here the chief concern is different: offering business and technical cross-cutting capabilities that may span applications or organizations, or even include partners. But this modeling venture is semantic. The challenges that should be alleviated are related to fundamental questions, such as: Which application or organization should share a service offerings? What are the consumers' requirements? Who are the benefiting partners? and more.

Increasing a service's influence beyond its current boundaries and sharing its offered specialties and functionality with a wider range of consumers and peer services is the chief mission of contextual expansion process and modeling. The benefits are clear: increase of service reusability, consolidation of duplicated functionality, and enhancement of communications and relationships between distributed services and consumers. The methods and patterns that can be employed to achieve these goals are discussed in detail in Chapter 16.

CONTEXTUAL CONTRACTION PROCESS AND MODELING.   Contrary to the service contextual expansion process discussed in the previous section, the contextual contraction activity is designed to achieve opposite results: Here the goal is to reduce the scope of a service's business or technical relationship with consumers and decrease its operation boundaries across a distributed environment. The focus of this exercise should *not* be on a service's internal construct. Again, this is about demoting a service by trimming down its offerings scale and reducing the magnitude of its capabilities. As a result, the service's reusability rate is reduced, the number of corresponding consumers diminishes, and the service operations are shared by fewer applications or organizations.

The motivations for practicing the service contextual contraction process are many. From a business perspective, however, the leading reasons are related to market trends, such as reduction of interested consumers, decline of market demand for products, or discontinuation and reconciliation of offered services. On the technological front, rollback of architecture initiatives, upgrading dated technologies, and cancellation of technology expansion strategies are the major reasons. Chapter 17 further elaborates on these challenges and offers methods and patterns to model the contextual contraction proposition.

STRUCTURAL EXPANSION PROCESS AND MODELING.   A practitioner pursues the structural expansion process to broaden the service architecture distribution scale across applications and organizations. This widening of service capabilities takes place in a distributed environment, in which interoperability, integration, deployment, and configurations are the chief hurdles. Thus the structural expansion exercise is about service external architecture and technology expansion factors rather than being an internal effort to dispense service capabilities. Obviously, reaching out to a larger consumer base and extending product offerings to various groups and internal silo organizations is the main motivation behind this initiative. Sharing information and interacting with external trading partners, suppliers, or service providers is another reason to embark on a structural expansion project.

The structural expansion approach involves modeling patterns that enable practitioners to describe a distributed service environment. This computing landscape is depicted by two chief deployment schemes: *centralized* and *federated* configurations that are designed to ease interoperability challenges and enhance service relationships. Moreover, the structural expansion method also offers a number of service mediation methods to enable the expansion of a distributed environment beyond its existing boundaries. These topics are discussed in detail in Chapter 21, which also provides methods of implementation and guiding patterns to follow.

STRUCTURAL CONTRACTION PROCESS AND MODELING.   *Outward* service discovery and analysis road map pattern also introduces approaches to contract a distributed environment and limit a technological and architectural expansion. Contrary to the structural expansion process, the structural contraction method advocates a rollback of architecture expansion, limiting service distribution, simplifying technological complexities, and reducing investments and expenditure in existing deployment environments.

The reduction of service deployments, configurations, and integration efforts can be achieved by limiting the roles of service intermediaries and mediation responsibilities. Modifications to the service contract model should also facilitate the structural contraction process. These challenges along with patterns and implementation approaches are discussed in detail in Chapter 22.

SERVICE-ORIENTED ORCHESTRATION: AN OVERALL WORKFLOW APPROACH.   The discussions about the *Outward* road map pattern and its contribution to proper service discovery and analysis activities brings us to the topic of *orchestration*. Orchestration is not a new SOA term. In fact, it dates back to antiquity. For a considerable number of years, it was synonymous with *system automation.* Some even believe that it was originated as early as the 1860s, when scientists such as James Clerk Maxwell, Eduard John Routh, and Adolf Hurwitz, gave birth to the control theory.[4] Their theories—which focused on mechanisms of governing engines—contributed to the control and stability of steam engines and even influenced modern aviation studies.

Thus *orchestration* is truly about controlling a production environment execution and stability, coordinating message exchange, synchronizing transactions, managing service process priorities, and monitoring business continuity. The SOA orchestration practice entails five chief requirements, each of which contributes to the overall discovery and analysis of services when pursuing the *Outward* road map pattern:

1. **Transaction management.** Planning, designing, and architecting message-exchange mechanisms between consumers and services that facilitate business execution
2. **Workflow management.** Automating business processes to eliminate the need for human intervention
3. **Service synchronization.** Coordinating service collaboration by establishing well-defined business operation schedules and time tables

4. **Administering automated business processes.** Facilitating new business requirements by applying changes to business processes and business logic
5. **Orchestration monitoring.** Supervising the automated business process in production to ensure flawless business execution and proper performance measurements

SECURITY CONCERNS FOR THE SERVICE ECOSYSTEM.   When pursuing the *Outward* road map pattern practitioners should addresses service security challenges.[5] This essential activity both guarantees operation stability and ensures business continuity. Therefore, security solutions that are devised by the technology organization should tackle a wide range of technical challenges. These remedies are designed to deal with difficulties that are intrinsic to service environments, such as interoperability, distribution of services across boundaries of business organizations, identity management, provisioning, and more.

The *Outward* road map pattern mandates that practitioners should define a proper SOA security model for the organization. "Proper" means that we adequately tackle the security gaps that need attention and steer clear of overwhelming an operating service environment with unnecessary security restrictions that typically can hamper the service's performance or limit its reusability factors. Hence, practitioners who pursue the *Outward* approach for service discovery and analysis must unearth the fine balance between "tight" and "loose" security measurements. Consider the fundamental security aspects that help define how an organization protects its services and their operations:

- **Identity management.** Interoperable computing environments often introduce difficulties when it comes to execution of transactions across organizational boundaries, such as lines of business, multiple systems, or geographically dispersed business domains. This security concern pertains to preserving the identity of the consumer who participates in message-exchange activities in a heterogeneous computing environment, such as enabling a doctor to access nationwide healthcare facilities to retrieve patients' medical information. Identity management is typically handled by assigning user roles and security access levels that are authorized across the organization, implementing single-sign-on (SSO) facilities, and employing authorization and identity management frameworks.
- **Confidentiality.** This concern is about protecting classified and sensitive information from being disclosed. The major technologies used to ensure confidentiality are various encryption mechanisms, digital certificates, and digital signatures.
- **Privacy.** Unlike confidentiality, privacy management calls for protecting individuals' information from being compromised by attackers or third-party data handlers that do not represent a person's interests. In fact, users' privacy is protected by law that requires organizations to prevent disclosure of private information. Thus institutions that own private data must classify it accordingly and apply security measures that enable data confidentiality.[6]
- **Nonrepudiation.** Nonrepudiation is a security measurement by which message-exchange parties cannot deny their participation in trading and processing the same information. In this case, the sender receives a delivery receipt, and the end point entity, the receiver, confirms the sender's identity. This security concern is critical for the verification of transaction execution and exchange of important documents that consumers and services often handle.
- **Accountability.** This security imperative requires that transactions and information exchange activities should be recorded for the purpose of auditing and paper trail analysis. Organizations often employ data-logging mechanisms that store real-time activity information, record ownership of transactions, and even trace maintenance events, such as service configuration and deployment.
- **Authorization.** Controlling users' access to organizational assets, such as applications, networks, and repositories, is the act of security authorization. Security policies and

user-provisioning practices enable proper authorization management. These typically involve security products that enable role-based access control to organizational resources, access control lists (ACLs), and more.

- **Authentication.** Authentication consists of verifying the identities of consumers, services, and applications that require access to other organizational resources. The most common method for implementing authentication verification is by passing the credentials of the parties requiring access—for instance, user identification, password, role, hardware tokens, and X.509 public keys. The latest approach advocates delivering credentials by means of message assertion techniques, such as security assertion markup language (SAML) for Web services.
- **Integrity.** This security concern ensures that unauthorized modifications to data can be detected in a timely fashion. Digital signatures, among others, are the enabling technologies that facilitate information integrity.

DELIVERABLES

Carve out an organizational horizontal service discovery and analysis process and strategies that are based on the provided *Upward* (42) and *Outward* (46) road map patterns. The *Upward* direction should be driven by instituting the keystone building blocks:

- Service-oriented governance and architecture best practices
- Business process analysis practices
- Service-oriented orchestration practices
- Service-oriented life cycle process
- Service-oriented Bottom-Up discovery process
- Contextual generalization analysis and modeling
- Structural generalization analysis and modeling

The *Outward* direction should be founded upon the vital discovery and analysis practices and models:

- Service-oriented discovery and analysis interoperability model
- Service-oriented discovery and analysis mediation model
- Front-to-Back service discovery process
- Back-to-Front service discovery process
- Contextual expansion analysis and modeling
- Contextual contraction analysis and modeling
- Structural expansion analysis and modeling
- Structural contraction analysis and modeling
- Service ecosystem security considerations

SUMMARY

- The horizontal process for service discovery and analysis is designed to expand the boundaries of a service and its hosting environment beyond their current configuration.
- The horizontal service identification and examination approach advocates employing two process implementation directions: *Upward* (42) and *Outward* (46) road map patterns.
- The *Upward* (42) road map pattern offers service generalization and Bottom-Up service discovery mechanisms. This approach also introduces organizational best practices and standards.
- The *Outward* (46) road map pattern for service discovery and analysis provides best practices and techniques to facilitate the expansion or contraction of a distributed service environment.

Notes

1. Michael Bell, *Service-Oriented Modeling: Service Analysis, Design, and Architecture* (Hoboken, NJ: John Wiley & Sons, 2008), p. 29.

2. Canonical data model can be enforced by the practice of customer data integration (CDI). For further reading, refer to http://searchdatamanagement.techtarget.com/sDefinition/0,,sid91_gci942939,00.html.

3. ANSI/X3/SPARC Study Group on Data Base Management Systems, American National Standards Institute, Bulletin of ACM SIGMOD 7, no. 2 (1975).

4. www.jstor.org/pss/112510.

5. www.ibm.com/developerworks/rational/library/4860.html.

6. http://www.rbs2.com/privacy.htm.

CHAPTER 4

SERVICE-ORIENTED DISCOVERY AND ANALYSIS BEST PRACTICES MODEL

Striving for Balanced Solutions

No matter how rigorously a service-oriented discovery and analysis discipline is pursued, the practitioner should ensure that the scope of this venture is wide and detailed enough to meet business and technical requirements. Regardless of how thoroughly a service identification and examination endeavor is being conducted, architects, developers, modelers, analysts, and managers must also promote service reuse, consolidation, and expenditure reduction. In spite of how meticulously the method of the service discovery is executed, subject matter experts must also foster a loosely coupled and simplified architecture model. These best practices should be exercised by pursuing the four major discovery and analysis discipline road map patterns that were discussed in detail in Chapters 2 and 3: *Inward* (25), *Upward* (42), *Downward* (32), and *Outward* (46).

These road map patterns of service identification, inspection, and modeling should be strongly supported and guided by a set of organizational best practices, which are policies and tenets that offer rules of implementation to mitigate the challenges in two major distinct areas of expertise: business and technology. From a business perspective, best practices should identify the driving motivation for service construction. In addition, these guiding principles should also advise what business artifacts contribute the most to the service discovery and analysis process. Technological best practices, however, are designed to alleviate different concerns: introduce an organizational integration model, address the leveraging of legacy applications, tackle service versioning issues, propose commercial off-the-shelf (COTS) products for infrastructure solutions, and more.

But perhaps one of the most important aspects of a successful discovery and analysis approach is striving for balanced solutions that can be presented to the business and information technology (IT) community for verification, approval, and certification. How can this goal be fulfilled? The sections that follow elaborate on different approaches that a practitioner should be aware of. These are activities and best practices that are typically pursued to augment, fill the gaps, and complement the service discovery venture:

MEET-IN-THE-MIDDLE SERVICE DISCOVERY: BALANCING THE IDENTIFICATION VENTURE

The vertical and horizontal processes and their affiliated road map patterns for service-oriented discovery and analysis broaden the scope of service identification by inspecting a wide range of business and technology artifacts. This study may include deliverables, such as business process modeling documents, business requirements, user-interface scripts and data entry fields, data modeling diagrams, repositories, business logic, and architecture blueprints. Each of the analyzed deliverables represents a distinct angle of a software product. To systematically and efficiently master these perspectives, the practitioner is encouraged to identify services by pursuing four different patterns for discovery: Top-Down (71,89), Bottom-Up (145), Front-to-Back (105), and Back-to-Front (123).

These four patterns for the service identification, elaborated in detail in Chapters 5 through 10, not only delve into the discovery of a single service, but they address service environment and integration concerns, such as interoperability, distribution, and federation of software assets. The presented Meet-in-the-Middle cross-cutting activity, however, is another discovery pattern that must be pursued to perfect this process. It offers an intersection point that facilitates additional opportunities to ascertain new services that otherwise would not have been found. Exhibit 4.1 illustrates these five different service identification patterns that contribute to rigorous analysis of software product requirements and artifacts to facilitate the discovery of new services or reuse of existing legacy software assets: Top-Down, Bottom-Up, Front-to-Back, Back-to-Front, and Meet-in-the-Middle.

Again, the Meet-in-the-Middle approach fills in the missing discovery gaps. These are typically capabilities that connect the dots between front-end and back-end services and applications or bridge the Bottom-Up and Top-Down patterns for discovery.

For example, the Front-to-Back approach introduces presentation layer artifacts that can be utilized to discover services, such as various widgets that a user employs to interact with the application, rendering facilities, and content searching mechanisms. However, the Back-to-Front service discovery activity relies on data repositories, data abstractions, and logical data modeling artifacts to discover services. Both approaches should "meet in the middle" to identify common services that can bridge the data-serving mechanisms on one hand and presentation activities on the other. Data Proxy, Presentation Layer Proxy, Rendering Scheduler, and Data Mapping Facility are examples of services that can be identified to serve both parties.

To read more about the service-oriented discovery patterns, refer to Chapters 5 through 10. The Meet-in-the-Middle (165) service identification pattern is discussed in detail in Chapter 10.

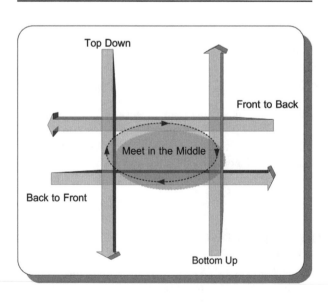

EXHIBIT 4.1 SERVICE-ORIENTED DISCOVERY PATTERNS WITH MEET-IN-THE-MIDDLE DIRECTION

STRUCTURAL AND CONTEXTUAL ANALYSIS AND MODELING: BALANCED SOLUTIONS

In Chapters 2 and 3 we learned that structural and contextual analysis and modeling is a process that calls for four different approaches that can assist with a variety of internal and external service design and architecture challenges: (1) generalization, (2) specification, (3) expansion, and (4) contraction. The reader may remember that structural modeling operations are devised to manipulate and perfect a service's internal formation and external service environment. Conversely, the contextual analysis process and its affiliated modeling activities are designed to address an increase or a decrease in a service's abstraction level and trim down or expand service offerings and functionality across the organization. By pursuing these analysis and modeling processes, a wide range of benefits typically is gained, including boosting service reusability rates, consolidating software assets, decreasing organizational expenditure, simplifying architecture complexities, discovering or retiring services, and more.

Exhibit 4.2 depicts the four processes for structural and contextual analysis and modeling that are elaborated on in Chapters 14 through 22:

1. Generalization
2. Specification
3. Expansion
4. Contraction

These four service modeling operations are designed to cover a wide solution scope that may not satisfy the scale of the requirements. How can we identify the middle ground? The middle ground represents the balanced solutions that are not too generalized, too specified, too large, too small, too fine-grained, or too coarse-grained. Is it possible to level a service implementation so

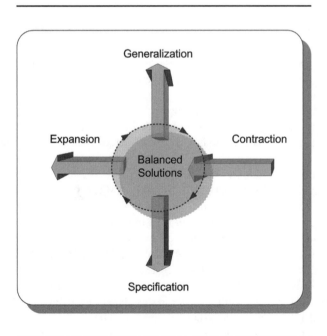

Exhibit 4.2   Structural and Contextual Analysis Operations and Modeling

that it does not step out of bounds or grow beyond the boundaries of an organizational concern? Does a service meet its business requirements or technical specifications? Does a service satisfy its corresponding consumers' requirements?

The answers to these questions can be found while pursuing a compliance process (discussed in Chapter 2 in the Service Compliance and Verification Process section) that identifies the various gaps between business requirements and technical specifications. This verification activity should also study the level of implementation granularity, which is discussed in Chapter 2 in the Service-Oriented Granularity Assessment section. Matching the scope of business requirements with technological and architectural solutions is an imperative process that should be pursued.

FOCUS ON SERVICE DISCOVERY AND ANALYSIS CROSS-CUTTING ACTIVITIES

Often referred to as *patterns*, the four service-oriented discovery and analysis road map *directions* that can guide managers, architects, analysts, modelers, and developers to carry out a service identification and examination execution strategy are the *Inward* (25), *Upward* (42), *Downward* (32), and *Outward* (46). As described in Chapters 2 and 3, the *Inward* and the *Downward* activities are pursued during the vertical service discovery and analysis process. The horizontal, however, consists of the *Upward* and *Outward* service inspection and identification directions. Each of these work flows identifies the chief concerns that one should focus on while inspecting, assessing, and discovering services.

Indeed, the practitioner should exercise a great deal of discipline, come up with balanced solutions, and concentrate on the important discovery and analysis aspects during this work. Doing so would eliminate project sidetracking, confusion, and unnecessary agendas. An important aspect to remember, though, is that we identify two major types of activities that take place during the vertical and horizontal processes: *noncontinuous* and *continuous*. Noncontinuous activities pertain to a unique activity that takes place during the pursuit of *one* of the four road map patterns. For example, studying business requirements and engaging in a service capability verification process should be pursued during the *Inward* road map direction. Conversely, separation of concerns and establishment of a service granularity model should take place when implementing the *Downward* analysis and discovery road map Direction.

The term "continuous," however, pertains to fundamental service identification and examination efforts that must *persist* during the entire service-oriented discovery and analysis phase. Therefore, the three constant and enduring *cross-cutting activities* that take place during the implementation of the *Inward, Downward, Upward,* and *Outward* activities are (1) service-oriented discovery (2) service contextual analysis and modeling and (3) service structural analysis and modeling. Again, these three activities should be conducted when pursuing each of the four road map patterns.

Exhibit 4.3 illustrates the service discovery cross-cutting model that represents an activity that persists through all four service-oriented discovery and analysis discipline road map patterns: *Upward, Outward, Downward,* and *Inward*. As apparent, during the *Upward* direction, we pursue the bottom-up service discovery. The *Outward* road map pattern consists of the Front-to-Back and Back-to-Front methods. The Top-Down service discovery approach is followed when the service identification *Downward* road map pattern is pursued. Finally, the *Inward* discovery pattern is about service Internal analysis and discovery of aggregated formations. The Meet-in-the-Middle service discovery is accomplished once all the road map directions have been followed. Refer to the Meet-in-the-Middle Service Discovery section earlier in this chapter for detailed implementation.

Exhibit 4.4 depicts the service structural and contextual analysis and modeling continuous activities that should persist during the execution of the four service-oriented discovery and analysis road map patterns. The *Upward* pattern consists of service Generalization. Service Expansion and Contraction analysis and modeling are pursued during the *Outward* direction. The *Downward*

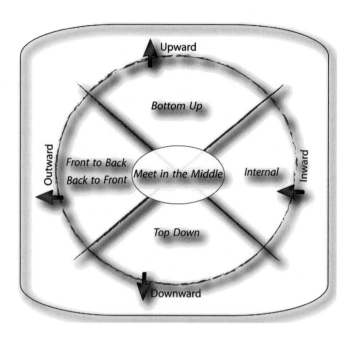

EXHIBIT 4.3   SERVICE DISCOVERY CROSS-CUTTING MODEL

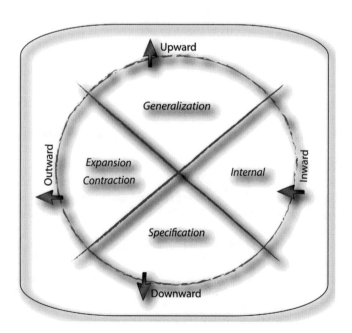

EXHIBIT 4.4   CROSS-CUTTING MODEL FOR SERVICE STRUCTURAL AND CONTEX-
TUAL ANALYSIS AND MODELING

pattern includes the service Specification analysis and modeling. Finally, the *Inward* direction is about inspecting and modeling a service's Internal contextual and structure construct.

CATEGORIZATION OF SERVICES: REALITY CHECK

Most organizations still struggle with fundamental service classification initiatives in the face of new projects or when it comes to asset portfolio management activities. What is service classification? Service categorization is the art of service typing. This process is about affiliating a service with its contribution to a problem. But it is also about arranging services in a directory structure, a taxonomy of services that identify their relationships, hierarchical associations, and collaborative capability to carry out business and technical tasks.

Remember, categorization of services should be a venture pursued before and after a project is launched. This process of classification not only contributes to the management of service inventory, but also enables reusability of software by identifying existing services that can be employed for future projects. Chapters 11 to 13 elaborate on the various service-oriented categorization mechanisms and offer a service classification strategy for business and technology challenges.

SERVICE-ORIENTED DISCOVERY AND ANALYSIS BEST PRACTICES MODEL

While pursuing the vertical and horizontal service discovery and analysis processes, managers, analysts, modelers, architects, and developers should adhere to best practices that provide guidance for the service identification, inspection, and modeling efforts. The principles and policies presented in this book can also facilitate the assessment of the proposed architectural, technological, and service capabilities solutions. These tenets tackle major analysis and discovery concerns, such as leveraging legacy implementations, understanding how various technologies can be employed to provide a solution, studying service environments, and examining potential service reuse and consolidation.

The service discovery and analysis best practices also focus on intrinsic architecture principles that foster business continuity and technological stability in production environments. In their absence a service landscape could not properly function. The most essential tenets are loose coupling, agility, asset reuse, software modularity and componentization,[1] software elasticity, interoperability, virtualization, business and architecture transparency, and traceability.

The sections that follow represent a five-component best practice model that introduces the major queries that one should ask during the process of service discovery and analysis: (1) Servitization, (2) Business Drivers, (3) Architecture Capabilities, (4) Technological Capabilities, and (5) Service Capabilities. Exhibit 4.5 illustrates these areas of concern. Note that the servitization (depicted in the center) component shares common attributes with its overlapping peers.

SERVITIZATION BEST PRACTICES.   As discussed in Chapter 2, the art of servitization is rooted in the practice of transforming business imperatives into service-oriented capabilities. It is about morphing business thoughts, ideas, and concepts into tangible solution capabilities, namely services. This process embodies a fundamental shift that idealizes the consumer-centric notion over the substance of a business product.

The term "servitization" refers to the consumption aspect of a service in terms of its capacity to satisfy its corresponding consumers. Ted Levitt identified the major impediment to the establishment of a sound organizational service concept. He wrote: "It is not surprising that, having created a successful company by making a superior product, management continues to be oriented toward the product rather than the people who consume it."[2]

Servitization best practices are the major driving force behind the service-oriented discovery and analysis activities.[3] Consider the questions that should be asked during this process:

- How can a business imperative evolve into service capabilities?
- How can business requirements be translated into service capabilities? What is the driving process?

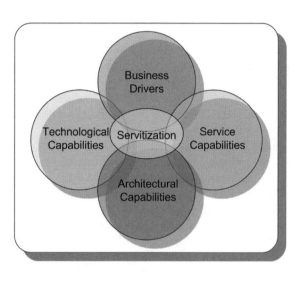

Exhibit 4.5 Service-Oriented Discovery and Analysis Best Practices Model

- What is the motivation behind service creation?
- What is the maturity model of the servitization process? Where should we start? Do we first invest in constructing services and their supporting technologies? Or do we begin with small "wins"?
- How should an organization automate business processes? Can services help?
- How do we classify services? What types of services are needed for a project?

BUSINESS DRIVERS BEST PRACTICES.   The business organization should play an important role when it comes to service-oriented projects. Business stakeholders and sponsors should take equal responsibilities in the service discovery, analysis, and modeling process; provide guidance and domain expertise, and elaborate on business strategies and requirements. These participants should also be actively engaged in the separation-of-concerns practice and in defining service capabilities.

Thus best practices should be established to enable the partnership and alignment with the technology organization. These driving principles should also elaborate on the practitioner's role and responsibilities, artifacts to deliver, timetables, road map, and milestones.[4] Consider the chief questions that business best practices should address:

- How can the business organization lead the direction of the service discovery and analysis process?
- What are the driving business artifacts that can contribute the most to the service discovery and analysis process?[5]
- Who are the business players that should be involved? What are their accountabilities and responsibilities?
- Who are the owners and sponsors of this initiative?

ARCHITECTURE CAPABILITIES BEST PRACTICES.   Service discovery and analysis best practices should offer guidance to architects, analysts, modelers, developers, and project and team managers in two major areas of architectural concern: service internal constructs and service operating environments. These architecture capabilities encompass a wide range of principles that should be addressed during a project life cycle.

Promoting service-oriented loose coupling standards requires establishing boundaries of service functionality and granularity, fostering software modularity, and encouraging componentization of service structures. These best practices should also support service reuse and consolidation, address interoperability[6] challenges, and embrace agility tenets. Furthermore, the most significant contribution should tackle the crucial involvement of legacy assets in providing a solution. This can be instrumental in leading expenditure reduction by leveraging existing knowledge, technologies, and architectures.

The typical enterprise contentious discussion "buy versus build" should be put to rest during this process. This discussion pertains to the traditional argument that favors buying COTS products over the prospect of building them in house, or vice versa. Business and IT organizations should establish a consensus among the arguing parties and apply founding principles to service-oriented projects, and product selection and evaluation activities.

Consider the chief concerns that should be addressed during the service-oriented discovery and analysis process:

- What is the organization integration model? How should services be integrated in production?
- What are the guiding principles that address leveraging legacy applications? Should there be any limitation?
- What are the fundamental requirements for employing SOA intermediaries?
- When should service mediation technologies be utilized?
- When should an organization employ an enterprise service bus (ESB)?
- What is the enterprise architecture asset federation strategy? In which circumstances should services and their platforms be federated across the organization?
- What is the motivation for using service clusters?
- What is the justification for employing composite services?
- What is the application and enterprise architecture security model?
- When should service architecture be expanded or contracted?
- What is the organization asset granularity model? What is the applied granularity matrix for service architecture?
- When should a universal description, discovery and integration (UDDI) registry be employed?
- How can an organization address interoperability issues?
- What are the recommended message transformation mechanisms?
- How should contracts be established between consumers and their corresponding services? Should contract management be centralized?
- How should organizations handle service versioning difficulties?
- How can the analysis modeling language depict service capabilities across the organization?
- What is the canonical data model that can be leveraged across the organization?
- How can data serving, access, and transformation be leveraged across that enterprise?
- What is the organization's asset virtualization model?

TECHNOLOGICAL CAPABILITIES BEST PRACTICES.   Technological capabilities best practices address the selection of mechanisms that should be used to promote business imperatives and architectural principles, which were discussed in the previous sections. These mechanisms include the empowering technologies that make services run, such as networks, metadata repositories, monitoring facilities, security policy platforms, and SOA life cycle and governance support products. Technological capabilities are also about the mechanisms that are employed to increase service scalability, enhance message delivery, and improve message orchestration.

Furthermore, technological capabilities best practices should also set standards for service performance monitoring, deployment to production, service configuration, and service-level agreement enforcement. Disaster recovery and data redundancy are other crucial elements that enable service operation stability and business continuity.

Consider the major questions that should be tackled by best practices that provide guidance during the service-oriented discovery and analysis process:

- How should product selection and evaluation be conducted?
- What are the selected COTS products that provide service infrastructure solutions?
- What are the various COTS products that can be employed to resolve data aggregation, transformation, and cleansing?
- What are the supporting service technologies and protocols? Web services description language (WSDL) based? Representational state transfer (RESTful) based? Proprietary?
- What type of COTS products should be employed to enhance service orchestration capabilities?
- What are the roles assigned to various SOA intermediaries?
- Should ESB implementation federated across the organization? Or should a centralized concept dominate the ESB implementation in the enterprise?
- What type of XML appliances should be used, and what type of message and data transformation should they handle?
- What are the specific technologies should be employed to alleviate interoperability concerns? Gateways? ESBs?
- How should service security be enforced?
- What are the guiding principles for service monitoring activities in production?
- What is the organizational disaster recovery model?
- How should services be simulated in testing environments?

SERVICE CAPABILITIES BEST PRACTICES.   To strengthen service capabilities, best practices must offer standards that practitioners can utilize for discovering and analyzing services. These principles typically are devised to facilitate the process of service identification and to establish the methods business and IT personnel employ to institute service capabilities. One of the most challenging tasks is to determine the right granularity scale of a service in the context of a project and the environment that it ought to interact with. The Service-Oriented Granularity Assessment section of Chapter 2 presented this service sizing discussion. The topic of granularity identifies the impact on a service's capacity to comply with its contracts with its corresponding consumers. For example, the granularity measurement of a service can impact performance, consumption, reusability, orchestration, and loose coupling decisions.

Consider the queries that should be addressed by the service-oriented discovery and analysis best practices:

- What is the process of service discovery?
- How can be a service analyzed for reuse?
- How should services be classified?
- What is the process for establishing service taxonomy for the organization?
- How can architects, modelers, analysts, and developers gauge service granularity? What are the driving mechanisms?
- What are the various service modeling operations that can alleviate loose coupling concerns?
- What is the process for discovering service contracts?
- When should practitioners employ virtual services?

DELIVERABLES

Devise organizational design and architecture best practices to guide practitioners with the service-oriented discovery and analysis process. These best practices should be based on the principles and the model described in the Service-Oriented Discovery and Analysis Best Practices Model section earlier in this chapter:

- Servitization best practices
- Business drivers best practices
- Architecture capabilities best practices
- Technological capabilities best practices
- Service capabilities best practices

SUMMARY

- Always strive to deliver a balanced analysis proposition that is influenced by four major guiding principles: (1) devise effective organizational best practices, (2) conduct Meet-in-the-Middle service identification activities, (3) focus on service discovery and analysis cross-cutting activities, and (4) present balanced solutions while pursing structural and contextual analysis and modeling activities.
- The service-oriented discovery and analysis best practices model consists of five distinct components: (1) servitization, (2) business drivers, (3) architecture capabilities, (4) technological capabilities, and (5) service capabilities.

Notes

1. http://blogs.windriver.com/koning/2006/09/components.html
2. Ted Levitt, *Ted Levitt on Marketing* (Boston: Harvard Business School Press, 2006), p. 207.
3. The "servitization" paradigm pertains to the process of transforming business imperatives into candidate services. This typically occurs early in the service development life cycle.
4. Organizations often employ responsibility assignment matrices (RACIs) to describe stake holders' responsibilities, roles, tasks, and deliverables for a project or a business initiative
5. Chapter 2 elaborates on the business requirements that drive the service-oriented discovery and analysis process. These business artifacts are discussed in the Business Requirements and Technical Specifications section.
6. An organizational interoperability model is discussed in Chapter 3 in the Service-Oriented Discovery and Analysis Interoperabilty Model section.

PART TWO

SERVICE-ORIENTED DISCOVERY PATTERNS

The most common questions asked during the service-oriented discovery phase are usually: What does service discovery entail? Where should we start? How should a service be discovered? What is the process of service identification? Do the ascertained services meet business or technological requirements? These questions, and others, underscore the mounting recognition that ad hoc or opportunistic approaches to identifying and establishing services for a small project or a large development initiative are not always satisfactory. The term "opportunistic" refers to the sporadic flow of ideas that arise during meetings, conference calls, or design sessions to propose solutions to an organizational concern. Despite this unmanaged solution proposition method, services can still be ascertained during the development life cycle. However, the lack of a systematic approach to discovering services may not be in line with business or technical imperatives.

The other concern that often occupies practitioners' minds is the lack of a comprehensive approach to discovering services. In other words, an unplanned service discovery venture that is not driven by a solid service identification strategy typically does not yield the right services for the project or characteristically does not satisfy the spectrum of the problem. Consider, for example, a development effort sponsored to create a Content Rendering Service for a news agency Web site. Unfortunately, the service devised to render information to a user's display merely addresses a narrow aspect of the solution. To broaden this discovery process, one should ask these questions: How should the data be delivered to the rendering service? How can data be accessed? Which software entity is designated the data formatting duty? Which service is responsible for executing business processes? How can legacy applications be utilized and be repurposed to enhance the data rendering process?

A wide-ranging service discovery process, therefore, must offer different directions to facilitate the identification and establishment of new services. This venture must consist of multiple perspectives, each of which should reveal a different business or technological exploration angle. It should also propose a *repeatable process pattern* for service discovery to avoid the reinvention of a new method for each launched project.

The term "pattern" identifies the need for a systematic method, a guiding model that offers distinct avenues that can address the scale of the problem. Furthermore, the discovery *direction* aspect is vital to any well-thought-out organizational process. This is a compass not only designed to help architects, developers, modelers, analysts, and managers locate the starting point for every service-oriented discovery effort; it also identifies the end point. The start and end points are vital to any process; however, the patterns for the service identification endeavor also set the boundaries for discovery activities.

Consider the service-oriented discovery model illustrated in Exhibit P2.1. Note that the four apparent patterns for the service identification process—Top-Down, Bottom-Up, Front-to-Back, and

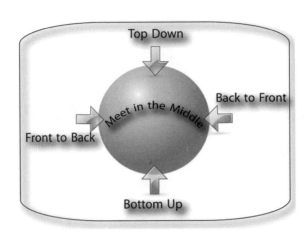

EXHIBIT P2.1   SERVICE-ORIENTED DISCOVERY PATTERNS MODEL

Back-to-Front—converge at a central point: Meet-in-the-Middle. These directions for service discovery are elaborated on in detail in Chapters 5 through 10.

- **Top-Down (71,89) service discovery pattern.** This approach advocates discovering services by two different methods: (1) analysis of documented business processes and derivation of services from the underpinning business activities and (2) extraction of software product attributes that yield new services. These two approaches to service discovery are discussed in detail in Chapters 5 and 6, respectively.
- **Bottom-Up (145) service discovery pattern.** This process addresses leveraging organizational legacy applications and services, exiting technologies, and existing architectures to provide new solutions. Refer to Chapter 9 for a detailed discussion about the Bottom-Up (145) service discovery pattern.
- **Front-to-Back (105) service discovery pattern.** The analysis of user-interface facilities yields a set of new services designed to establish and enhance application's presentation layer capabilities. This user interaction functionality typically includes, user interface (UI) features, information rendering mechanisms, user control over application functionality, information searching, content aggregation, and more. The Front-to-Back (123) service discovery pattern is elaborated on in Chapter 7.
- **Back-to-Front (123) service discovery pattern.** Enabling data access, data transformation, and data aggregation facilities are examples of service functionality that can be discovered by employing the Back-to-Front (123) discovery pattern. This topic is discussed in detail in Chapter 8.
- **Meet-in-the-Middle (165) service discovery pattern.** This service discovery venture addresses the identification of services that typically provide infrastructure, middleware, common business functionality, and integration capabilities. This process, often referred to as connecting the dots, is the intersection point for all the discussed service discovery patterns. Refer to Chapter 10 to learn more about the Meet-in-the-Middle (165) pattern.

TOP-DOWN BUSINESS PROCESS-DRIVEN SERVICE DISCOVERY PATTERN

One of the most common approaches for discovering services is the utilization of business processes that drive execution of transactions to promote the business. "Business process" is a simple term that refers to activities that an individual, an organization, an application, or a service pursues to accomplish a goal. Opening a bank account, for example, is a process that consists of a number of activities designed to enable customer banking. It is surprising to learn that most processes that an organization executes are not documented, and business automation initiatives are long overdue. The term "undocumented" means that the steps required achieving business tasks reside in people's minds; they are not recorded on paper or institutionalized for common use.

The practice of studying organizational business processes is called business process analysis. However, the method of service discovery that uses business processes to identify new services is known as the Top-Down approach. This service identification direction model is pursued since it commences with the study of enterprise business processes, continues with the discovery of business specialties, and concludes with the realization of new services.

Business process analysis is not a new practice. Many organizations have adopted methods to address two of the most vital aspects of their survival: (1) understanding how they incur revenue and (2) enhancing their business execution to meet strategic goals. These are the driving forces behind initiatives that call for analyzing and modeling business processes.

IS BUSINESS PROCESS TOP-DOWN SERVICE DISCOVERY PRACTICAL?

The business process analysis practice advocates that business analysts, modelers, architects, developers, and managers inspect documented business processes in the inception stage of each project. Analyzing processes can also be exercised outside of a particular project. Either effort requires domain expert personnel who are familiar with industry business modeling standards, business modeling languages, and tools that can facilitate the delivery of input artifacts for the Top-Down service discovery endeavor.

Without proper documentation, the Top-Down service identification effort that is driven by business processes will be a difficult task to accomplish and costly to pursue. Therefore, an organization should be first engaged in discovering and recording undocumented business processes before pursuing the Top-Down service discovery pattern. Is this preparation venture practical? The answer to this critical question must be carefully studied before an organization plans to exploit this avenue. One of the best ways to weigh the benefits against the possibility of failure is to establish a business process analysis maturity model. Doing this can help determine the magnitude of the effort, who should be involved, and what tools are required to document business processes. The level of organizational maturity is an important factor that should be considered before pursuing the Top-Down service discovery based on business process analysis artifacts. To learn more about constructing a maturity model, refer to the Define Business Process Analysis Maturity Level section later in this chapter.

DOCUMENTING BUSINESS PROCESSES: INDUSTRY STANDARDS

The art of documenting business processes is well established, and there is no shortage of industry best practices, tutorials, training, or tools that can facilitate this undertaking. A number of approaches can be used to record a business process. The most common method is to use text-based software that simply enables analysts to record processes and activities in a structured manner. A more graphical approach allows the creation of process flow diagrams and charts that depict business activities and their interaction. Another common method for describing processes and their interaction is to employ business process modeling languages. Tools and platforms for documenting business tasks are discussed in the sections that follow.

UNDERSTAND BUSINESS PROCESSES

Nothing has more influence on service formations than business processes and their underpinning activities. Indeed, there are a number of methods to identify services for construction. But when pursuing the Top-Down discovery pattern, it becomes apparent that a service embodies business functionality that affects almost every aspect of its construct. Therefore, when selecting the business process analysis approach to discovering services, we prescribe the method that advocates transforming business activities into service operations.

To help readers better understand this concept, the sections that follow not only elaborate on the structure of a business process, they also discuss operational functionality and granularity aspects. These topics also accentuate attributes that a business process and a service share.

- Business Process Structure: Service Operations Discovery Opportunities
- Business Process Flow: Influences on Service Behavior
- Business Process Granularity: Influences on Service Granularity

BUSINESS PROCESS STRUCTURE: SERVICE OPERATIONS DISCOVERY OPPORTUNITIES.   Remember, a business process must have a beginning and an end. The starting point indicates where a person, group, organization, or machine (known as *actors*) instigates a number of sequential or parallel activities. The process terminates when it achieves its clear objective. Without a lucid goal, a process may turn out to be ambiguous and useless to the service-oriented discovery process.

The other important characteristic of a process is its substance. These are the activities that make up a business process—often referred to as tasks. Activities are the fundamental building blocks and the underpinning aspects of every business process execution. The business functionality that are provided by activities typically set the boundaries of a business process and help discover service operations.

The information that is passed to a business process is known as *input*. The *output* content is the outcome of the combined activities and it is typically passed on to other business processes for further manipulation. On a grand scale, inputs and outputs of business processes constitute messages that are being exchanged between consumers and their corresponding services. As we learn in the next few sections, inputs and outputs are the fundamental building blocks of the messaging paradigm that services employ to execute transactions.

Finally, a business process must be owned by "something," either actors, such as people, groups, organizations, business domains, machines, applications, or stakeholders and sponsors.

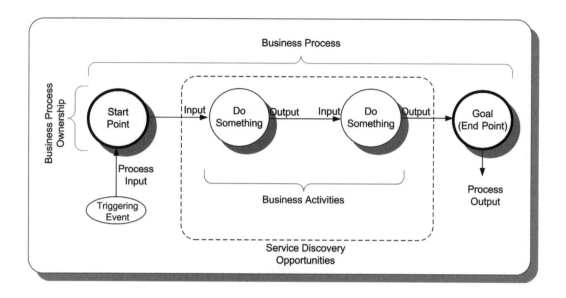

EXHIBIT 5.1   Business Process Structure and Service Discovery Opportunities

Ownership is intrinsic to every software development life cycle and in particular to service-oriented projects because of the affiliated costs and responsibilities involved.

Exhibit 5.1 exemplifies the process structure. Note the business process Start and End points and the encompassed business activities. These areas typically provide contextual material for the service discovery process. The service discovery opportunities revolve around the process activities and their inputs and outputs.

BUSINESS PROCESS FLOW: INFLUENCES ON SERVICE BEHAVIOR.   A business process would not be flexible if its underlying activities cannot operate autonomously, jointly, in sequence, simultaneously, or based on a predefined schedule. In fact, the business process modeling discipline accentuates the relationship, collaboration, and synchronization aspects of business activities. These requirements are intrinsic to discovering the future behavior of a service and even further contributing to service-oriented orchestration design, which employs messaging to exchange data.

Business process activities are typically associated with states, each of which accomplishes a part of the solution, yet collaboratively attain the final goal. This workflow of events normally is controlled by business rules that are applied to evaluate the information that is passed from one state to another.

Exhibit 5.2 illustrates the correlation between a simple flowchart that represents the capabilities of a business process and a service. Note that each activity (denoted by a square box) corresponds to a candidate service operation. The decision boxes (diamond shapes) are business rules that may be translated to service business logic, and the connectors (solid lines) may be transformed into internal data flow that a service handles. This similarity of responsibilities is shown to exemplify the common attributes that a future service may share with a business process. But as will be discussed shortly, the service identification process is not as straightforward as it may seem.

BUSINESS PROCESS GRANULARITY: INFLUENCES ON SERVICE GRANULARITY.   Can a business process be classified by its magnitude? Can we categorize a business process based on its strategic

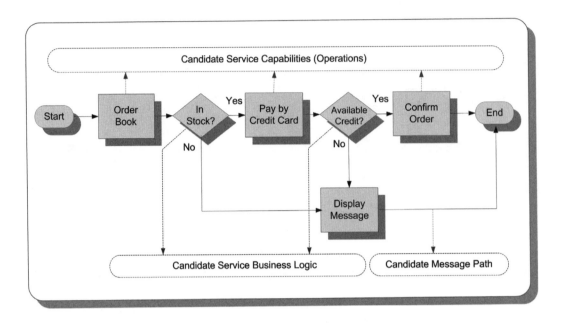

EXHIBIT 5.2   BUSINESS PROCESS FLOW INFLUENCES SERVICE BEHAVIOR

or tactical contribution to an organization? The affirmative answer points to the fact that there are a few levels of granularity that a business process can be classified as. On a personal level, for example, an individual can execute a business process by contributing some daily activities to accomplish a goal. Thus, a business process that is performed by an individual is categorized as fine-grained. On an organizational level, activities contributed to execute a business process can be attained from individuals, departments, or divisions. This collaborative effort is classified as coarse-grained business process.

As we find out later in this chapter, a business process granularity level can immensely influence a service size and the number of operations it executes. Therefore, that art of striking the right balance between the magnitude of a business process and the newly identified service or services is vital to the success of the service discovery venture. In other words, a business analyst, business architect, or a developer should consider breaking down a bulky business process or unify two or more fine-grained business processes to control the proper granularity of the derived services.

Fine-Grained Business Process.   On the personal level, professionals exercise their daily duties to reach milestones and accomplish goals that were set by management. An individual is responsible for performing tasks that are prescribed for a particular role in the organization. Therefore, a business process that is executed by an individual is classified as fine-grained business process. This means that a person's business activities contribute to a business process without involving peers or other groups in the organization. For example, an insurance underwriter is responsible for assessing the risks that are involved with issuing a particular insurance policy. Background investigation and rejection or approval of a customer application are the typical tasks, namely activities, that an underwriter performs.

Mid-Grained Business Process.   A business process that is executed by a group of people in an organization is categorized as a mid-grained granularity level. This level involves two or more individuals assigned to execute a business process by collaborating personal activities. For example, a loan processing department may consist of background investigation experts, risk assessment specialists, and customer service personnel who collaboratively execute a loan issuance business process for a customer.

Coarse-Grained Business Process.   Unlike the mid-grained business process that is comprised of a group of individuals' activities, a coarse-grained business process is comprised of activities that are contributed by departments, and divisions in the enterprise that fulfill their obligations to comply with business strategies. In other words, the charter here is different: These business activities are carried out by an institution as a whole to meet the business missions of an organization. These goals are designed, for example, to address competition challenges, increase business revenue, and provide solutions to business concerns.

Very Coarse-Grained Business Process.   Very coarse-grained business processes are executed beyond organizational boundaries: typically take place between business partners or consumers and suppliers. These processes consist of activities that involve two or more organizations performing business transactions outside their own jurisdiction.

Business Process Ownership.   As we have learned, business process granularity is really about the ownership level of the executing entity. In Exhibit 5.3, we observe four types of stewardships: (1) Individual, (2) Group, (3) Institution, and (4) Business Partners.

Again, as explained earlier in the introduction to this section, the influence of roles and the scope of a business process on service analysis, design, and later construction disciplines is vast. For example, the business process analysis may derive a coarse-grained service because of the inherit magnitude and the large amount of activities that a business process consist of. However, this undesired coarse-grained product, namely the large size of a discovered service, can be rectified by proper analysis operations that advocate decomposition of a coarse-grained business process or a bulky service after it has been discovered. For a detailed discussion about service-oriented analysis and modeling operations, see Chapters 14 through 22.

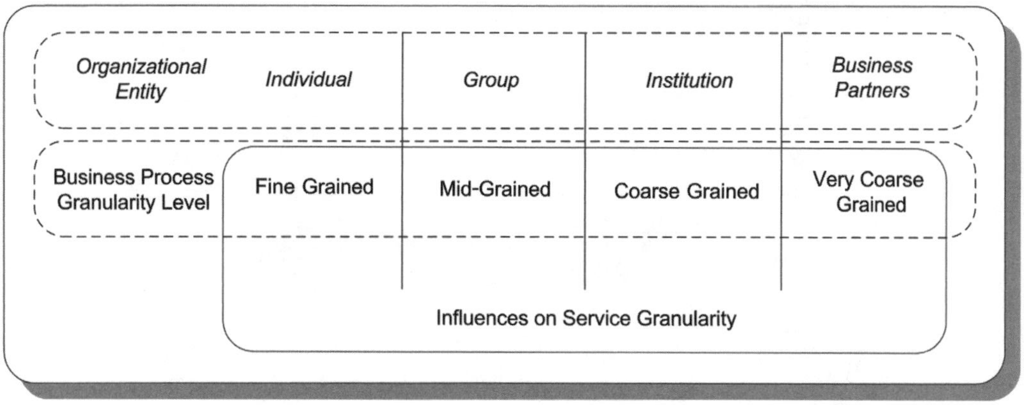

Organizational Entity	Individual	Group	Institution	Business Partners
Business Process Granularity Level	Fine Grained	Mid-Grained	Coarse Grained	Very Coarse Grained
		Influences on Service Granularity		

EXHIBIT 5.3   BUSINESS PROCESS GRANULARITY MODEL

DEFINE BUSINESS PROCESS ANALYSIS MATURITY LEVEL

If it is determined that the business process analysis approach to service discovery is worth pursuing, the next step is to identify the organizational maturity level and readiness to exercise this method. Such a model can be established simply by inspecting prior business process analysis engagements, identifying the tools that have been used to document business processes, or consulting subject experts who understand this discipline. But if this is the first initiative of its kind that the organization has undertaken, baby steps are required to embark on this initiative.

Again, to discover services that stem from business processes, a maturity model is required to determine the firm's level of expertise and competency in this field. Another parameter that can assist with weighing the organizational readiness to employ this approach is the existence of documented business processes. The absence of these artifacts would obviously classify the firm at a beginner level. However, if business processes have been documented, business process analysis best practices exist, and business process documentation and automation tools have been in use, the firm's maturity level can be conceived of as expert level. Thus let us view the proposed maturity model that is illustrated in Exhibit 5.4. To simplify this activity, three major business process analysis expertise levels are defined: Novice, Intermediate, and Expert.

NOVICE LEVEL.   A novice level indicates that the organization is not ready to embark on a business process analysis initiative. The following list describes this condition:

- Documented business processes do not exist. The organization mostly relies on undocumented procedures for business execution.
- Business process analysis has never been implemented in the firm.

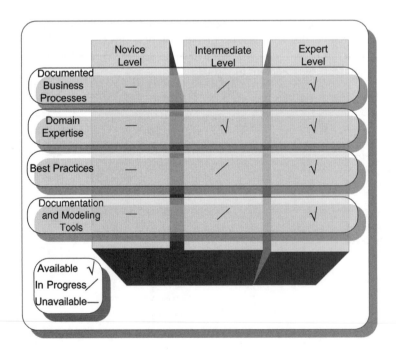

Exhibit 5.4   Business Process Analysis Maturity Model

- There are no subject matter experts who can provide valuable insights to assist with the development of an organizational business process analysis discipline.
- There are no firm-wide tools to document and model business processes.

INTERMEDIATE LEVEL.   An organization that is classified as an intermediate level can be involved in small to mid-size business process analysis initiatives. Consider the following list, which classifies the intermediate level:

- Business process documentation efforts are in progress.
- The evaluation and selection of business process modeling and documentation tools are under way.
- Organizational domain experts are capable of analyzing business processes and assisting with service discovery activities.
- Best practices and standards have been defined or are in the process of being established.

EXPERT LEVEL.   An expert-level organization is typically capable of managing large business process analysis initiatives. These initiatives can be accomplished with no major delays and a high degree of success because:

- The firm has completed the documentation of business processes. Expert charts and diagrams are available for the service discovery process.
- There are organizational best practices and standards to guide the institution of documenting business processes.
- Proficient business analysts and business architects are able to provide domain expertise for service identification efforts.
- Tools and platforms to automate and document business execution exist, including a central repository for business process information, support for business process modeling, common framework support (such as the Department of Defense architecture framework (DOAF)[1] the Zachman Framework[2]), and business process orchestration facilities.

STUDY DOCUMENTED BUSINESS PROCESSES

If the organization's business process maturity level is classified as novice, the choice is clear: Either start documenting the business processes that are affiliated with the given project, or rely on domain experts to provide a synopsis of undocumented business activities. Both approaches are not comfortable starting points. Without clearly defined business processes and their detailed activities, the service discovery effort can be hindered and fall short of success. Therefore, it is advisable to explore other approaches for service identification. These approaches are discussed in Chapters 6 through 10.

Conversely, the existence of diagrams and documentation that depict business processes indicate that the enterprise readiness level is higher. Here the starting stage is far more advanced, and the service discovery process would be shortened.

Again, we start the service discovery endeavor by studying the business processes. But where can these processes and their underpinning business activities found? Typically business processes can be recorded in business requirements. But business requirements may not be the only source for process examination. The analyst, architect, modeler, or the developer is obligated to explore additional artifacts that can provide detailed descriptions and even graphical presentations of business processes. These alternative sources can be reviewed:

- Flowchart diagrams
- Activity diagrams[3]
- Use case diagrams[4]

- State machine diagrams
- Business process model diagrams created with various commercial off-the-shelf modeling products that offer standard notations
- Documented business processes with text-based document processors[5]

ESTABLISH SERVICE-ORIENTED BUSINESS PROCESS MODEL

A service-oriented business process model is simply a framework that identifies the business processes that will participate in the Top-Down service discovery venture. The collected processes that collaboratively provide a solution to an organizational concern are now subject to analysis that ultimately yields new services.

In the context of a project, now is the time to both collect the relevant business processes that will both provide a solution to an organizational concern and clearly participate in the service discovery effort. We are thus commissioned to classify business processes according to their areas of business expertise, fields of specialties that a process contributes to. Next, this categorization endeavor will enable the establishment of business responsibilities that can be delegated later to a discovered service or even to a number of services that can carry out business missions. Exhibit 5.5 identifies the road map and the corresponding milestones required for founding a sound service-oriented business process model. These milestones are discussed in the sections that follow.

IDENTIFY BUSINESS SPECIALTIES.   Let us use a car insurance policy issuance example in which the business requirements require us to establish services that can carry out the execution of the auto insurance division. But even before discussing service identification issues, the more prioritized task would be to classify these imperatives based on business specialties—defined areas of business expertise. These business specialties can alleviate the pain of service discovery later because of the correlation between service operations and business duties.

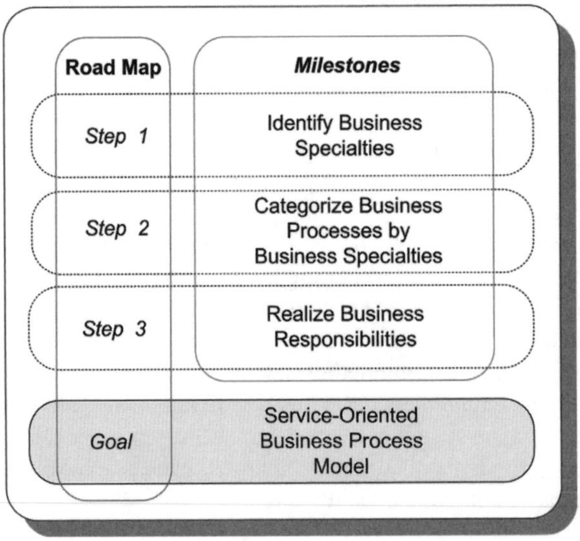

Road Map	Milestones
Step 1	Identify Business Specialties
Step 2	Categorize Business Processes by Business Specialties
Step 3	Realize Business Responsibilities
Goal	Service-Oriented Business Process Model

EXHIBIT 5.5   SERVICE-ORIENTED BUSINESS PROCESS MODEL CREATION

Obviously, the business requirements are the driving aspects of this process that lead to the discovery of business specialties. To help identify these areas of expertise, ask the following questions:

- Who are the business owners that will be sponsoring this initiative?
- What are the major duties that must be assigned to a person or a computer program that carries out these activities?
- Who will be the personnel that will execute this business mission?
- What types of skills are needed to provide these services?
- Who will be the actors?
- Are there any existing applications that already provide such functionality?

Our example starts with three major insurance business specialties: *credit verification, policy underwriting*, and *policy issuance*. Each of these disciplines typically is practiced by a group of employees, subject matter experts who both understand the car insurance industry and are able to work together to attain the final goal: issuance of an auto insurance policy.

Exhibit 5.6 exemplifies the process of business specialties discovery for the policy issuance project. The depicted three business requirements, positioned in the left column, correlate to their corresponding business specialties (on the right). As apparent, this discovery process yields three business specialties: Credit Verification, Policy Underwriting, and Policy Issuance. Note that this is merely an example that identifies a one-to-one relationship between a business requirement and its derived business specialty. There may be different instances where a number of specialties are discovered from a given requirement.

CATEGORIZE BUSINESS PROCESSES BY BUSINESS SPECIALTIES.   Next, we turn the focus to the categorization effort. This effort should be based on a business process affiliation with an area of expertise. In other words, combining processes to fulfill a duty should be accomplished in the context of a business specialty. This collection effort must take into consideration the various

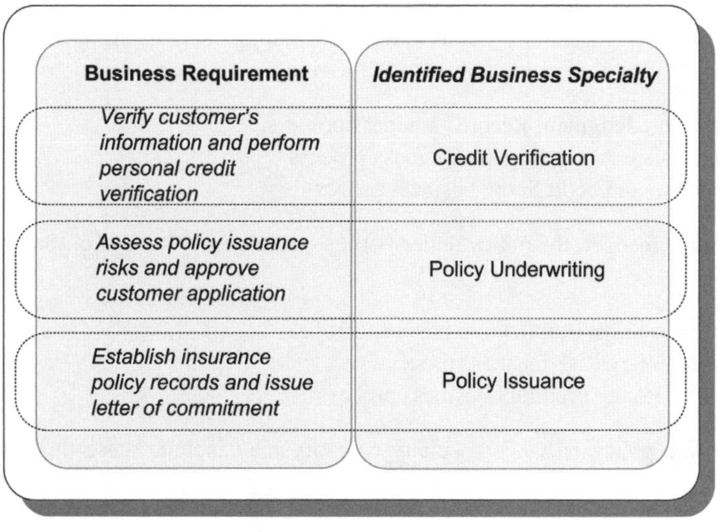

Business Requirement	Identified Business Specialty
Verify customer's information and perform personal credit verification	Credit Verification
Assess policy issuance risks and approve customer application	Policy Underwriting
Establish insurance policy records and issue letter of commitment	Policy Issuance

EXHIBIT 5.6   CORRELATION BETWEEN BUSINESS REQUIREMENTS AND BUSINESS SPECIALTIES

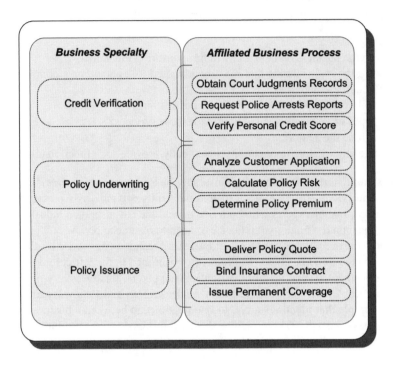

EXHIBIT 5.7   CATEGORIZATION OF BUSINESS PROCESSES EXAMPLE

stakeholders, business owners, business experts, and actors involved and also recognize the capability of each involved business process to contribute to a particular field of knowledge, namely business specialty.

We thus classify the business processes into three major categories, each of which represents an auto policy processing business specialty, as depicted in Exhibit 5.7: *Credit Verification*, *Policy Underwriting*, and *Policy Issuance*. Let us view, for example, the three affiliated business processes that collaborate to fulfill the credit confirmation mission:[6]

1. Obtain Court Judgment Records business process.
2. Request Police Arrest Reports business process.
3. Verify Personal Credit Score business process.

In the same manner, the policy underwriting specialty may consist of three related business processes:

1. Analyze Customer Application business process.
2. Calculate Policy Risk business process.
3. Determine Policy Premium business process.

Finally, the policy issuance specialty category may include these three driving business processes:

1. Deliver Policy Quote business process.
2. Bind Insurance Contract business process.
3. Issue Permanent Coverage business process.

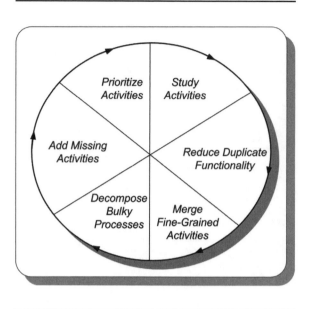

EXHIBIT 5.8   REALIZING BUSINESS RESPONSIBILITIES

REALIZE BUSINESS RESPONSIBILITIES: FIRM UP BUSINESS ACTIVITIES.   The last step is to realize business duties. The term "realize" pertains to identifying and establising the activities that a business process executes. Here the mission is simple and yet crucial to the service discovery process in terms of functionality reuse, consolidation, and prioritization: We are commissioned to study the details by delving into the functionality that each business activity proposes, eliminating unnecessary tasks, and supplementing missing responsibilities. Therefore, a business responsibility is analogous to a business activity, which is part of business process.

Consider the actions that are recommended for establishing clear and firm activities for a business process, which are also illustrated in Exhibit 5.8:

- Study business process affiliated activities.
- Reduce duplicate functionality by eliminating redundant activities that a business process possesses.
- Merge fine-grained activities.
- Decompose bulky business processes by separating activities to form smaller processes.
- Add missing activities.
- Prioritize business activities within each business process.

As depicted in Exhibit 5.9, the realization of the presented business responsibilities effort (establishment of firmed up business activities) should include three columns of related analysis information: Business Specialty, Business Process, and affiliated Business Responsibility (Business Activity). This chart is crucial to the service discovery effort because it enables us to visually inspect the future responsibilities of services. Furthermore, Exhibit 5.9 illustrates the work of analysis that was applied to firm up business activities. Note that the Calculate Risk Factor (business activity) appeared in two business processes: Calculate Policy Risk and Determine Policy Premium were consolidated by eliminating the redundant Calculate Risk Factor business activity from the

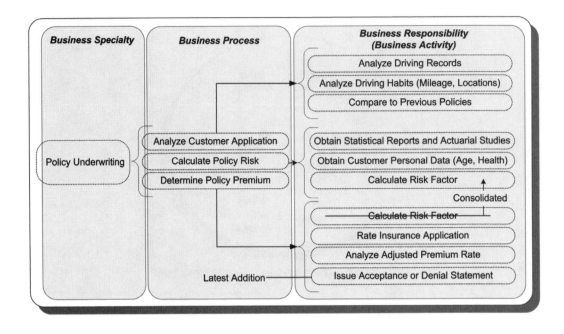

EXHIBIT 5.9   REALIZING BUSINESS RESPONSIBILITIES EXAMPLE

Determine Policy Premium business process. The other change was applied to the Determine Policy Premium business process: The Issue Acceptance or Denial Statement business activity was added.

DISCOVER ANALYSIS SERVICES

The time has arrived to identify services that stem from the business process analysis artifacts that have been produced so far. We name these findings "business propositions," as they offer direction and fundamental building blocks to the service discovery effort. Here is where the problem and the solution domain ventures meet. The business organization proposes remedies, and the solution domain further translates them into technological assets. This is also where business deliverables are being evaluated and considered for further technical analysis.

Remember that the service-oriented discovery and analysis discipline regards all the participating services in this process as *analysis services*. Thus the final outcome and the goal of discovery efforts is analysis entities that can further be inspected and modeled later on in different service-oriented life cycle stages. These contextual and structural analysis disciplines are discussed in detail in Chapters 14 through 22.

The process of service discovery is simple and straightforward. Business process analysis artifacts come in handy now. We not only study the various responsibilities of business execution, we must also define service operations and firm up a final analysis service that can be utilized later for future exploration. Consider the road map that is proposed in Exhibit 5.10. It depicts three major steps that drive the final stages of the Top-Down service identification endeavor, steps that are described in detail in the sections that follow:

1. Stop and learn the business proposition.
2. Identify service responsibilities: Discover candidate service operations.
3. Propose candidate analysis services: Bundle service capabilities.

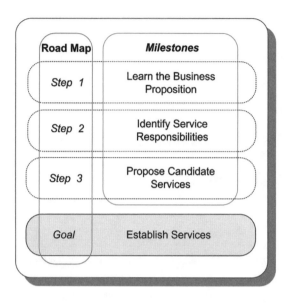

EXHIBIT 5.10   SERVICE DISCOVERY PROCESS

STOP AND LEARN THE BUSINESS PROPOSITION.   The business proposition that has been devised earlier in the business process analysis phase identifies the major *business specialties*, *business processes*, and *business activities* that are required to resolve a solution. Here, during the service discovery stage, we are commissioned to inspect these artifacts and discover opportunities for establishing new services. But remember, the rule of thumb suggests that this exercise is all about identifying business needs. The final outcome, however, may not result in the construction of a tangible service. This assertion agrees with architectural best practices that promote asset reuse across the organization. In other words, employ existing legacy applications and services rather than build new executables.

Therefore, to better understand the proposed value of a business proposition, study the delivered business process model and center the attention on these keystone items:

- Understand the project scope.
- Study business requirements.
- Study business processes.
- Get acquainted with business process modeling artifacts
- Identify business process actors.
- Learn about business responsibilities by inspecting business activities.
- Identify business stakeholders and sponsors.

Exhibit 5.11 illustrates the business process proposition example. This revised version is based on Exhibit 5.9 in the Realize Business Responsibilities section.

IDENTIFY SERVICE RESPONSIBILITIES: DISCOVER CANDIDATE SERVICE OPERATIONS.   Remember, the business proposition that included business processes and activities reflects the business view of an organization. This vital artifact typically does not attend to technological requirements. The business language that describes business responsibilities employs domain expertise vocabulary that sometimes is misunderstood by the technology organization. Therefore, the business

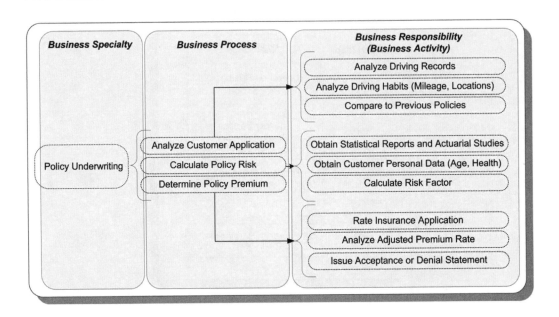

EXHIBIT 5.11 BUSINESS PROCESS PROPOSITION EXAMPLE

perspective must be interpreted to enable a smooth transformation of business to technical responsibilities. Business duties must be differentiated from service duties. Here we must both understand the intended functionality of a business activity and offer a clear technical interpretation.

Transforming Business Activities to Candidate Service Operations. The process of "converting" business activities to institute candidate service operations does not constitute an exact translation between business and technical terminology. To clarify this point, we must be clear on the difference between *business responsibilities* and *service responsibilities*. As illustrated in Exhibit 5.12, from a business perspective, a Business Responsibility is analogous to a Business Activity. However, a Service Responsibility corresponds to a Candidate Service Operation. "Candidate" means that the transformation process must go through an intermediate step until a service formation is finally confirmed.

Consider these actions that should be used to facilitate the founding of service responsibilities; these are also illustrated in Exhibit 5.13:

- **Add** service responsibilities that reflect technical implementation.
- **Combine** business activities to form fewer candidate service operations.
- **Break Down** a business activity into two or more service responsibilities.
- **Rename** business activities to accommodate technical terms.
- **"Do Not Change"** means that a particular business activity is accepted as is and there is no need for name change, breakdown, or merging with other activities.
- **Disregard** means that a business responsibility cannot be translated to a service operation.

Identify Service Responsibilities. Again, this effort should not result in the final formation of services. Here we merely identify a list of candidate service operations that will be further analyzed in the final step of the service discovery effort, which is discussed in the next section. But before

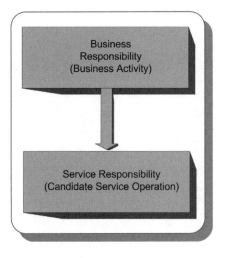

Exhibit 5.12   Transformation from Business to Service Responsibility

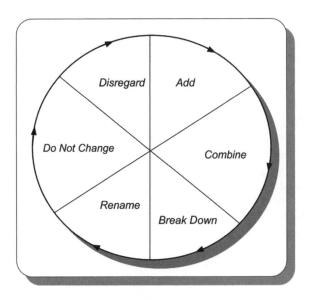

Exhibit 5.13   Actions Applied to Establishing Candidate Service Operations

moving on, let us view the example illustrated in Exhibit 5.14, which elaborates on the actions applied to establish candidate service operations.

The three panels—Business Processes, Business Responsibilities (Activities), and Service Responsibilities (Candidate Operations)—are the fundamental building blocks that facilitate the transformation of business responsibilities to service responsibilities (business activities to

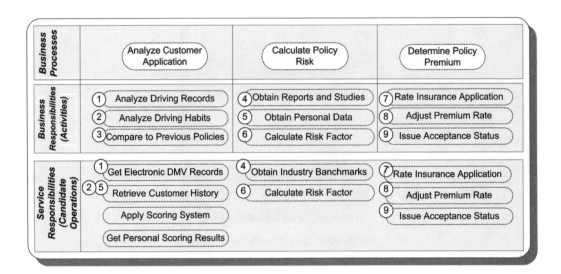

EXHIBIT 5.14   IDENTIFICATION OF SERVICE RESPONSIBILITIES EXAMPLE

candidate service operations). Here the three business processes—Analyze Customer Application, Calculate Policy Risk, and Determine Policy Premium—are displayed along with their corresponding activities. These business responsibilities are further translated into service responsibilities that do not completely resemble the originating business activities. Consider the following actions that led to these results:

- The business activity Analyze Driving Records (marked as number 1) was *renamed* Get Electronic DMV Records to better depict the technical functionality.
- The business activities Analyze Driving Habits (number 2) and Obtain Personal Data (Number 5) were *combined* into an already existing service operation (marked as numbers 2 and 5): Retrieve Customer History.
- The candidate service operations Apply Scoring System and Get Personal Scoring Results were *added* to augment missing functionality.
- Operation Numbers 4, 6, 7, 8, and 9 have not been *changed* and were accepted as candidate service operations.

DISCOVER ANALYSIS SERVICES: BUNDLING SERVICE CAPABILITIES.   Finally, we arrived at the last step, where services are discovered and realized as analysis entities. This is a simple task that requires grouping candidate service operations (service responsibilities) that were identified in the previous section into distinctive sets, each of which will then be established as a service. To attain this final goal, we must analyze candidate operation functionalities and bundle them to form analysis services. This classification process is based on candidate operation affiliation with a business duty, an execution, a milestone, or a goal that must be achieved to provide a technical solution. Remember, the purpose of this exercise is to package operations according to their contextual relationship. Structural concerns, however, should be addressed later on during the service analysis phase, which is elaborated on in Chapters 18 through 22.

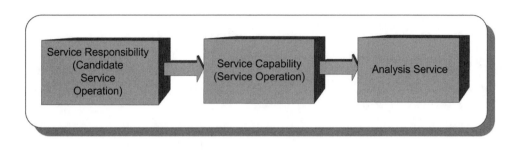

EXHIBIT 5.15   TRANSFORMATION PROCESS: FROM CANDIDATE OPERATIONS TO ANALYSIS SERVICES

To summarize this process, consider the following transformation activities that are required to establish an analysis service. These are also illustrated in Exhibit 5.15.

- Analyze service responsibilities. These are the candidate service operations that were derived earlier from business responsibilities (business activities). This step may require final adjustments, such as renaming or eliminating unnecessary operations.
- Bundle candidate operations by contextual affiliation. The conclusion of this activity yields firmed-up service operations (often referred to service capabilities).
- Recognize each discovered service operation group as an analysis service.

The art of deriving services from bundled operations must rely on individuals' expertise in the field of business analysis and service-oriented modeling. Contextual grouping or transformation of business responsibilities to service responsibilities, for example, requires domain knowledge and craftsmanship that is acquired during multiple service-oriented architecture projects. The artifact quality then depends on the practitioner's experience, creativity, and perseverance.

Exhibit 5.16 illustrates the realized services and their affiliated operations that were discovered so far. These were derived from the service responsibilities (candidate operations) that were identified in the previous section. Note that the yielded artifact includes two services: Customer Profile and Calculate Policy, each of which consists of three operations that reflect the car insurance underwriting business specialty.

Furthermore, the candidate service operation Apply Scoring System was merged with the Get Personal Scoring Results because of their identical functionality. In addition, the Obtain Industry Benchmarks candidate operation was eliminated because it was not feasible to automate this activity. And last, the Issue Acceptance Status candidate operation was eliminated as well due to its weak association with the other operations in this group. This functionality may be exported to a different service that addresses acceptance or denial responses to customers.

DELIVERABLES

To efficiently discover services that are derived from business processes and activities, establish a service-oriented discovery Top-Down model that fits the organization's development process. A number of initiatives can help accomplish this goal:

- Establish a catalog of documented business processes.
- Conduct a gap analysis study to identify the organizational business process analysis maturity level.

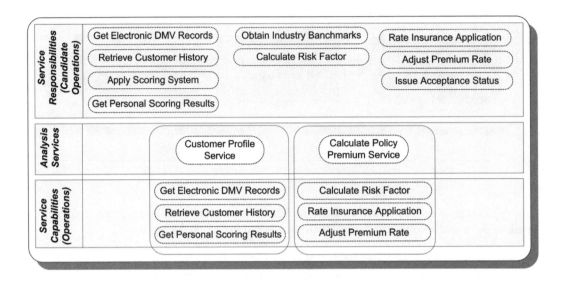

EXHIBIT 5.16 FORMING ANALYSIS SERVICES

- Found a solid business process analysis approach to enable modeling of business activities.
- Finally, develop a repeatable Top-Down service-oriented discovery pattern that can be employed for each project that calls for the development of services.

SUMMARY

- The Top-Down service discovery pattern is driven by analyzing business processes. This includes establishing business activities and deriving candidate service operations.
- Four major business process granularity scales influence service granularity levels: (1) fine-grained business process, (2) mid-grained business process, (3) coarse-grained business process, and (4) very coarse-grained business process.
- Novice level, intermediate level, and expert level are the three chief business process analysis maturity levels.
- To discover services, the practitioner should follow the four-step Top-Down service identification process:
    1. Document business processes.
    2. Study documented business processes.
    3. Establish a service-oriented business process model.
    4. Discover analysis services.

Notes

1. www.bta.mil/products/bea/html_files/dodaf.html.
2. www.zachmaninternational.com/index.php/home-article/13.
3. Russ Miles and Kim Hamilton, *Learning UML 2.0* (San Francisco: O'Reilly Media, 2006), p. 53.
4. Kurt Bittner and Ian Spence, *Use Case Modeling* (Boston: Addison-Wesley, 2002), p. 4.
5. www.ibm.com/developerworks/websphere/library/techarticles/0705_fasbinder/0705_fasbinder.html.
6. www.bls.gov/oco/ocos026.htm#nature.

CHAPTER 6

TOP-DOWN ATTRIBUTE-DRIVEN SERVICE DISCOVERY PATTERN

Unlike the service-oriented discovery model that is driven exclusively by the business process analysis discipline (discussed in Chapter 5), the Top-Down attribute-driven service discovery pattern is founded on a different study:[1] the examination of product characteristics, descriptions, features, and requirements that stem from business, technological, and architectural imperatives. Therefore, the attribution process is not driven by business functionality and activities. Here the identification of software properties contributes to the discovery of services.

The Top-Down attribute-driven service discovery pattern is conceptual by nature. In other words, this identification process is driven by an attribution model that enables practitioners to derive service abstractions that initially do not encompass business or technical processes. To firm up and finalize this effort, architects, developers, analysts, modelers, and managers are then commissioned to complete a service's detailed discovery by adding the underpinning operations and interfaces. These are the capabilities that must be established to enable communication with the outside world and maintain relationships with corresponding consumers.

Again, as the core of this service discovery approach, the attribution model is instituted to facilitate the extraction of software product properties—namely, attributes. What type of attributes would be necessary to meet the preliminary requirements for service construction? The attribution model typically is based on three major inputs, each of which represents service requirements in its own distinct view: business, technological, and architectural (discussed in the section that follows).

The final artifact of the Top-Down attribute-driven service discovery endeavor is service taxonomy. This delivery not only classifies the identified services by their contextual affiliation, it also offers a service catalog that can be used to categorize services by their type of contribution to business or technology. In addition, an organizational taxonomy characteristically promotes a common language that is comprised of a vocabulary that can be reused in future projects to boost software reusability rates.

STUDY BUSINESS AND TECHNOLOGY DISCOVERY SOURCES

The attribution process, like any other service discovery approach, requires that we rigorously study a variety of business artifacts that can facilitate the identification of product attributes and features. This does not stop with the study of business requirements alone. The range of future software descriptions can be found in a variety of organization publications and shared documents, such as problem domain, business mission, business strategy, market research and segmentation studies, and more.

But business artifacts and studies are not the only source of information that can lead to the discovery of service qualities. Technical specification papers, commercial off-the-shelf (COTS)

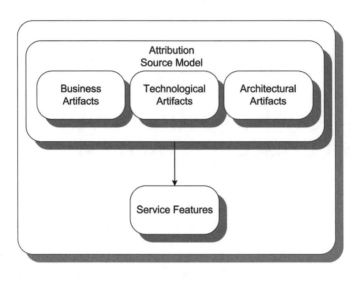

EXHIBIT 6.1   SERVICE ATTRIBUTION SOURCE MODEL

products' specifications, and nonfunctional requirements (NFR) can contribute immensely to this endeavor as well. Moreover, existing technological implementations and installations can provide discovery opportunities of service features and characteristics.

Architecture and design best practices and blueprints can also facilitate the discovery of service attributes. In fact, architecture abstractions, design patterns, and styles of implementation typically offer a wide array of study material that can be utilized to establish service behavior, structure, and operations.

The sections that follow elaborate on the process of service discovery, which utilizes extracted service features from Business, Technological, and Architectural artifacts. These attribution sources are illustrated in Exhibit 6.1. They are the three leading model components that should be analyzed to establish service attributes.

ATTEND TO THE SERVICE DISCOVERY PROCESS

The service identification process begins with the analysis of product attributes and ends with the establishment of services. This effort consists of two major goals, each of which yields vital artifacts that should be utilized in future discovery and examination activities. The first requirement is to identify analysis services. These entities are merely propositions, enduring service-oriented life cycle deliverables.

Furthermore, the service identification mission does not imply that we found new services for construction. The promise here is to foster expenditure reduction and shorten time to market by favoring use of legacy applications or services. Hence, the major benefit of pursuing the discovery process is the identification of features that are required for a solution and can be utilized to search for existing implementations to avoid redundancy of operations. If legacy entities cannot be found, obviously new services should be established.

The second objective is to devise a foundation for service taxonomy: a directory that classifies services by their business or technological affiliation. This catalog of categorized services should be utilized in future projects to promote asset reuse and consolidation.

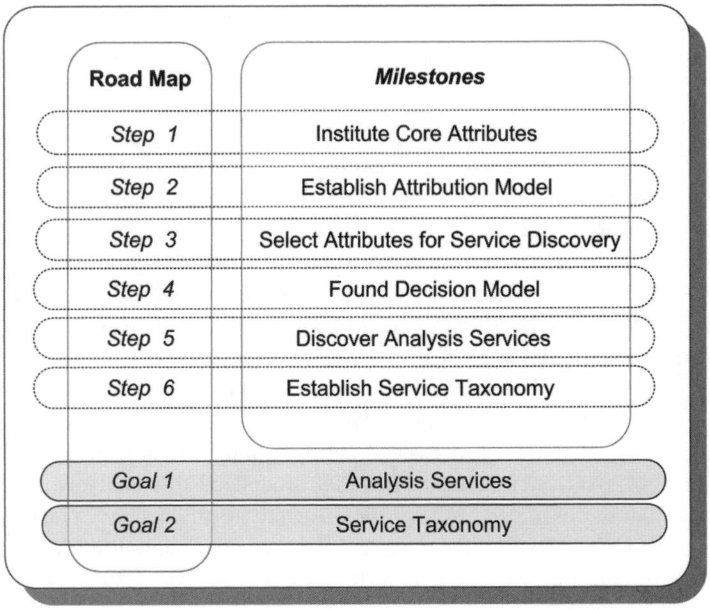

EXHIBIT 6.2   TOP-DOWN SERVICE DISCOVERY PROCESS DRIVEN BY ATTRIBUTION ANALYSIS

Consider the six steps provided for the service discovery and taxonomy institution illustrated in Exhibit 6.2. Note that the road map also depicts the two major goals that should be attained: discover Analysis Services and establish Service Taxonomy. The sections that follow elaborate in detail on each of these activities and provide a step-by-step guide for implementation.

INSTITUTE CORE ATTRIBUTES

Core attributes constitute a collection of software product descriptions and features that are usually extracted from business requirements and related technical specifications. These properties can be measured, quantified, and evaluated to facilitate the service discovery process. We call this assortment of properties *core attributes* because they are revealed in the inception state of a project. This list may be enhanced or augmented to support additional iterations of the service discovery effort. Furthermore, the attribution process, as will be explained, hinges on the quality of the identified product characteristics. Thus the collection process should be meticulous and focus on the most important capabilities that future services will offer.

CORE ATTRIBUTE COLLECTION.   An efficient service discovery effort must utilize attributes that describe distinct characteristics of a service and ultimately affect its behavior and internal structure once constructed. The behavioral aspect pertains to the unique service functionality that it will offer. The structural aspect, in contrast, is related to the service granularity and internal composition.

An attribute is not only crucial to the discovery of a service but also influences the service architecture and design. To promote high quality of services it would require conducting a thorough investigation that yields unambiguous software characteristics that precisely depict functionality and meet business requirements or technical specifications. Therefore, an effective attribute is a software product feature that specifies quantitative measurements of future service offerings and conditions, such as time constraints, weight, height, length, distance, color and Boolean values, sums of money, age, and more. For example, "term" is an attribute of a loan type that can be assigned values, such as "long," "short," or "10 months." These values are typically recognized as rules. Rules assignment is discussed later on in Define Business or Technical Discovery Rules section.

Attribute Collection and Service Discovery Example.   A home loan organization has implemented a customer enrollment application that offers three types of mortgages, each of which corresponds to a Web service: Fixed-Rate Loan Service, Adjustable-Rate Loan Service, and Balloon Loan Service. These services were discovered by identifying their features and attributes. The business requirements specify that the software product offerings should be limited to a predefined *time span* (attribute). Therefore, the fixed-rate loan is restricted to a time span of 10 to 50 years (rule), the adjustable-rate loan is limited to 30 years (rule), and the balloon mortgage should be paid within a 10- to 15-year period (rule). These collected attributes and their corresponding assigned business rules drove the discovery of the three mortgage Web services.

  As mentioned, the discovery process concluded with the identification of three services and a collection of attributes and their related rules that influenced this analysis. Exhibit 6.3 depicts the outcome. Note that the assigned values (rules) for the Term and the Points attributes are numeric; conversely, the Equal Monthly Payment and Prepayment Penalties attributes accept Boolean parameters (rules). In addition, the Adjustable Product and Interest Rates attributes are assigned alphanumeric characters (rules).

Construct an Attribution Table.   The chief questions still remain unanswered: How do we derive services from a collection of attributes? What is the process of attribute analysis? The answers to these queries are revealed in the sections that follow. The analyst, architect, modeler, developer, and manager should not determine the final services without following a systematic methodology that can facilitate the discovery of services. Refrain from taking an intuitive approach to service identification and abide by a discipline that favors analysis over guessing the outcome.

  We thus begin by constructing an attribution matrix similar to the home loan example illustrated in Exhibit 6.4. The collected attribute names should appear on the top. There is no restriction on the number of attributes that should be included for this exercise. But the rule of thumb suggests that more is better. This will expand the scope of the solution and offer a wider range of options during the analysis session that will take place later in the process. Fewer attributes can limit the analysis phase and yield noninclusive results. For the time being, omit the column of the discovered services since the service identification stage has not begun. Additionally, do not provide any values

Mortgage Offerings	Core Attributes					
Discovered Service	Equal Monthly Payments	Adjustable Product	Prepayment Penalties	Interest Rates	Term (in years)	Points (percentage of total loan)
Fixed-Rate Service	Y	N/A	Y	Fixed	10–50	1%
Adjustable Service	N	5/1	N	Adjusted	30	N/A
Balloon Service	N	N/A	N	Floating	7–10	N/A

EXHIBIT 6.3   ATTRIBUTE COLLECTION EXAMPLE TABLE

Core Attributes						
Withdrawals	Interest	Rate	Penalty	Checks	Fees	Minimum Balance

EXHIBIT 6.4   ATTRIBUTION TABLE EXAMPLE

(rules) for the various attributes yet. These fields will be filled in later during the process. So let us start with a different example.

Exhibit 6.4 exemplifies the core attributes that were extracted from business and technological artifacts that a banking institution provided. These requirements were specified to construct a software product that would offer a number of banking accounts to serve customers. The core product characteristics are described as follows:

- **Withdrawals.** What is the monthly limit on fund withdrawals?
- **Interest.** Does the account incur interest?
- **Rate.** What is the incurred rate of interest on the account?
- **Penalty.** Is a penalty applied to funds withdrawals?
- **Checks.** Can funds be withdrawn by using personal checks?
- **Fees.** Are monthly fees deducted?
- **Balance.** Does the account require a minimum balance?

ESTABLISH ATTRIBUTION MODEL

The core attributes that were discovered in the previous step are fundamental ingredients for the creation of a formalized template that can be employed to discover services. This model should not only serve as a placeholder for product features; it should also lead to the identification of service variations. The term "service variations" implies that we are allowed to combine the attributes in different ways to maximize the number of the discovered services. To better understand this concept, let us select three attributes from the core collection—penalty, interest, and rate—to form a simple *attribution model*. Remember, this process should be trouble free if the collected attributes are unambiguous and easy to understand.

Exhibit 6.5 illustrates a tree that contains three levels. Level 1 is always dedicated to the core attributes, whereas each attribute occupies a separate node: Penalty, Interest, and Rate. Next, the number of attributes in a node, in each tree descending level, is increased by 1. Therefore, Level 2 is comprised of three nodes; each combines two attributes taken from Level 1: Penalty and Interest, Penalty and Rate, and Interest and Rate. The very last level represents a converging node that includes all core attributes because we follow again the same rule: the number of attributes in a node, in each tree descending level, should be increased by 1. Therefore, Level 3 represents only one node that includes the three core attributes selected to form this model: Penalty, Interest, and Rate.

What does a four-level attribution model look like? Exhibit 6.6 illustrates this scenario. We repeat similar steps to populate the tree. Remember, the first level always includes the notes of the core attributes; each descending level increases the number of attributes in a single node by 1. The converging node, in this case depicted on Level 4, consists of all core attributes.

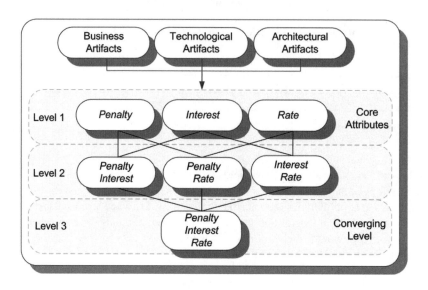

EXHIBIT 6.5   ATTRIBUTION MODEL BASED ON THREE SOFTWARE PRODUCT ATTRIBUTES

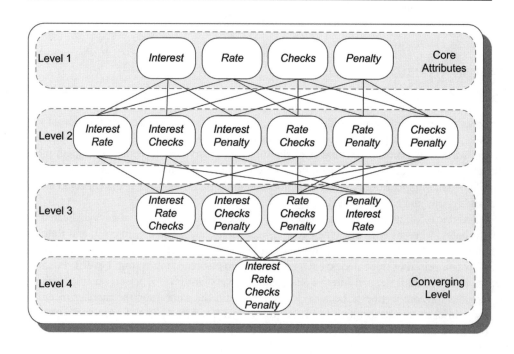

EXHIBIT 6.6   ATTRIBUTION MODEL BASED ON FOUR SOFTWARE PRODUCT ATTRIBUTES

SELECT ATTRIBUTES FOR SERVICE DISCOVERY

The time has come to select attributes that can facilitate the discovery of services. The attribution model that was created in the previous step should serve as a solid foundation for attribution analysis. But it is also a wish list that must be reexamined. Why is such a reevaluation process required? There are two major reasons to inspect core attributes.

1. As you may remember, during the establishment of the core attribute list, we were encouraged not to limit the number of extracted attributes. On the contrary, it was recommended to expand the scope of the solution by increasing the product property list.
2. This analysis effort is designed to reevaluate the core attribution in order to yield a more realistic service feature collection, acknowledging that the original core attribute assortment is merely a proposition.

Now we are required to navigate through the attribution model and select the node that contains the best attribute combination for the services that we are commissioned to build. Choosing the right service characteristics is a simple task that involves one of these three methods, which are explained in detail in the sections that follow: (1) forward attribute selection, (2) backward attribute selection, and (3) combined direction approach for attribute selection.

FORWARD ATTRIBUTE SELECTION.   It is advised to start the forward searching method at the very top of the attribution model—Level 1—and conclude at the selected node that includes the best combination of attributes that will be required for establishing services. For this exercise, view Exhibit 6.7 and find the starting point at the top. This is also the location where the core attributes

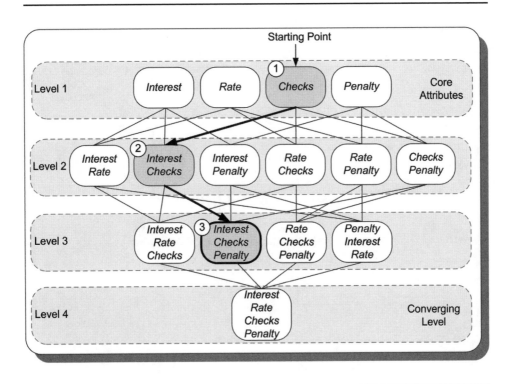

EXHIBIT 6.7   FORWARD ATTRIBUTION ANALYSIS AND COLLECTION

are positioned. The starting node (marked as 1) represents the Checks attribute. We then follow the thick arrow, moving downstream to Level 2, and passing the Interest and Checks node (marked as 2). We finally arrive to the destination node 3 (positioned on Level 3), which includes the attributes Interest, Checks, and Penalty.

Note that this simple searching approach allows for reexamination of the core entities that were provided for this activity. It is advisable to repeat this process until satisfied. Each iteration may provide a different perspective of the software product and the service characteristics that we are commissioned to discover. Thus, the final artifact may include several nodes, each of which represents a modified set of attributes version.

BACKWARD ATTRIBUTE SELECTION.　With the backward searching approach, we move the opposite direction, upstream to the desired node that contains the right combination of attributes that are needed for the service discovery stage. But where should we start from? The converging node, which is positioned at the lower level in the tree, is a good place to begin because it represents all the original core attributes. By moving up the tree structure, we evidently weed out one attribute with each decreased level. This activity is often called pruning, by which a methodological reduction yields a smaller attribute collection.

View Exhibit 6.8 to better understand this idea. Here we start at Level 4, moving up from the converging node (marked as 1 and including Interest, Rate, Checks, and Penalty attributes) to Level 3, passing node 2, which represents the Penalty, Interest, and Rate attributes. The final destination is found at node 3 (positioned on Level 2), which contains Rate and Penalty attributes.

COMBINED DIRECTION APPROACH FOR ATTRIBUTE SELECTION.　The combined attribute searching mechanism is the most practical approach because it enables multiple tree iterations to

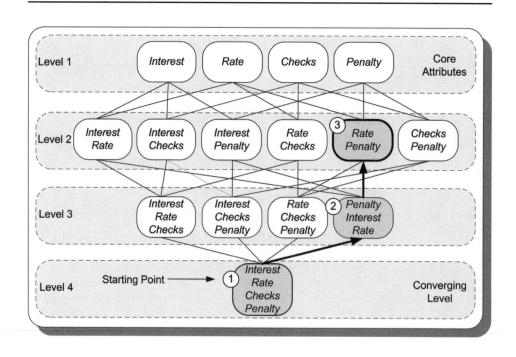

EXHIBIT 6.8　BACKWARD ATTRIBUTION ANALYSIS AND COLLECTION

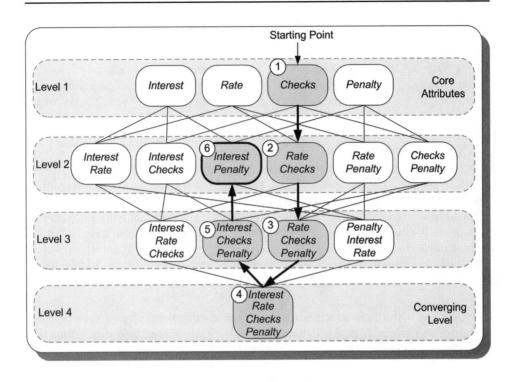

EXHIBIT 6.9 COMBINED ATTRIBUTE SEARCHING

determine the best attribute collection positioned in a node. The starting point can be at any tree level moving downstream and upstream until satisfactory results are achieved. This navigation style facilitates an elaborated analysis process, which consists of attribute deduction and addition until the ultimate group of attributes better reflects the characteristics of future services.

Exhibit 6.9 illustrates the combined direction approach for attribute selection. Here we start from node 1 (Checks), which is positioned on Level 1, descending to node 2 (Rate and Checks attributes) on Level 2. We then continue downward to Level 3 to meet node 3, which contains the attributes Rate, Checks, and Penalty. The converging node (marked as 4) that contains all core attributes (Interest, Rate, Checks, and Penalty) is our next stop; it is positioned on Level 4. Note that thus far we have increased the number of attributes by 1 with each visit to a descending level. Next, the upward process starts. We then ascend the tree to meet node 5 (Interest, Checks, and Penalty attributes) on Level 3. Finally, we visit the final destination on Level 2, selecting node 6, which contains the desired attributes: Interest and Penalty.

FOUND DECISION MODEL

A decision model is a framework that enables practitioners to identify services by assigning business or technical rules (values) to the attributes that were selected by the Forward, Backward, and Combined attribute selection methods. Moreover, establishing a decision model is a prerequisite to discovering analysis services. This process constitutes business and technological requirements and tackles two of the most fundamental aspects of software engineering: entity identity and logical behavior.

The term "entity identity" refers to the activity by which services are discovered, categorized, and evaluated according to their contribution to the business or to system architecture. More specifically, "identity" is about identifying the characteristics of a service based on its semantic affiliation. Naming a service or associating it with a certain domain, such as "Accounts Payable Service" or "Data Aggregator Service," is a way to define service individuality.

But identifying a service by its contextual affiliation is not the only contribution of the decision model. We must also define its behavior by assigning certain *rules* to its underlying functionality. These logical conditions will eventually materialize and become an integral part of service business logic that will be carried out by service operations.

BUILD A DECISION TREE STRUCTURE.   Establishing a decision model is a simple process that requires the participation of the attributes that were selected during the downward, upward, and combined searching and analysis process (discussed in the previous section). These properties are now ready to be arranged in a different format, a logical presentation that will enable service discovery later on. In computer science, the new formation is called a *decision tree*;[2] it enables the discovery of entities by applying certain rules to each attribute. The term "decision tree" was coined in 1960 to assist scientists to perform logical comparisons, identify abstractions, address uncertainties, or treat incommensurable entities (commodities that cannot be measured in the same units)

Goals to Achieve.   This new structure represents the contribution value of each participating attribute. Business or technological priorities should also be the driving motivation behind the construction of the decision tree. That is, here we should identify the importance level, in business or technological terms, of each service property by positioning each in the tree structure. Furthermore, this exercise must address the separation-of-concerns aspect by placing the selected product properties in a certain structure to encourage the discovery of diverse services. The significance of such a scheme is its promise to provide wide solution coverage, made up of different perspectives, to alleviate organizational concerns.

To summarize these objectives, consider the goals that should be achieved during this activity:

- Prioritize attributes based on business or technological significance.
- Foster separation of concerns.
- Expand the solution domain to enable the discovery of diverse services.

Adhere to the Decision Model Building Process.   We start building the decision model by utilizing the selected attribute group that was provided previously. The most important aspect to consider while constructing this tree is the *derivation direction* that will take place shortly—during the service discovery step. The guiding rule requires us to place the most significant attribute at the root of the tree while the succeeding levels host the less important service properties. This means that offspring nodes that are positioned under their parents, in the tree's hierarchical structure, are less significant in terms of business or technological perspectives. It is also essential to present the service identification logic flow by adding arrows (node "arms") that indicate the downstream discovery direction.

Exhibit 6.10 demonstrates this process. The Rate, Penalty, and Checks features are positioned on two priority levels: Level 1 and Level 2. The first level includes the Rate attribute, and the second consists of the two remaining properties: Penalty and Checks. Note that this example can be expanded to include a large number of properties, as needed. The most valuable attributes, however, should appear near the top of this structure. The banking account interest Rate is the leading concern of this software product. Penalty and Checks are second in the priority spectrum.

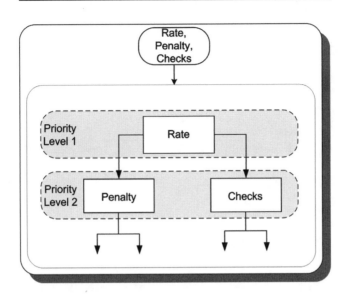

Exhibit 6.10   Decision Model Example

DEFINE BUSINESS OR TECHNICAL DISCOVERY RULES.   Before we move to the service discovery step, we are required to complete the last mission: Define discovery rules. These are the attributes' values that can influence the path that is taken to the derived services. What are the rules and how can we design effective decision mechanisms? Rules are certain conditions, measurements, number ranges, Boolean values, or any other quantitative data types that an attribute can be measured against. Consider, for example, the possible rules that can be applied to service properties:

- If age (attribute) is greater than 18 and less than 100 (rule)
- If interest rates (attribute) are greater than 6.5% (rule)
- If the distance (attribute) is longer than 2,000 miles (rule)
- If car color is red (attribute), answer should be Y or N (rule)

The process of assigning rules to attributes in the decision model is straightforward: Each node "arm" in the tree should include a rule that influences the "navigation" direction down to the leaf level. (A tree leaf is a node that does not have offspring nodes.) Exhibit 6.11 exemplifies this rule assignment activity. The Rate attribute that is positioned on Level 1 (the root node is the most important navigation aspect) signifies the bank account yearly incurring gain in percentage value. While navigating downstream, the Rate property will be measured against two value ranges: greater (navigation direction turns left) or less than 2% (direction turns right).

In the same manner, we apply different rules to offspring attributes. For example, priority Level 2 consists of Penalty and Checks. The Penalty property represents a restriction on bank account withdrawal for a certain period of time. The Checks attribute indicates whether fund withdrawals are permitted by check. These two properties are evaluated against Boolean flags: Yes or No. Note that the descending motion is determined by the answers that are applied to these queries, each of which represents a business or a technical rule.

Rules typically emanate from business requirements, product descriptions, and business process analysis artifacts. But business-affiliated rules are not the only category that can be employed.

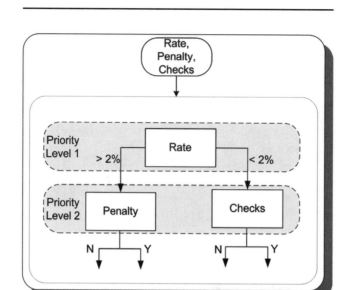

EXHIBIT 6.11 APPLYING RULES TO THE DECISION MODEL

Technical rules should be considered as well. These can include security policy rules, service orchestration rules, SOA governance rules, and even product configuration and deployment rules.

Consider the best practices that can guide the assignment of rules to attributes:

- Avoid using ambiguous rules.
- Avoid mixing rule data types, such as Boolean and number values.
- Steer clear of defining overlapping number ranges: for example, greater than 1 and less than 10, and greater than 5 and less than 15.
- Do not apply unrealistic rules, such as age greater than 150.

DISCOVER ANALYSIS SERVICES

The Top-Down service discovery that is driven by the attribution model yields service concepts. The emphasis here is on service semantic affiliations rather than the prominence of business processes (discussed in Chapter 5). The term "semantic" implies that we identify services by their affiliation to the derived attributes that were collected previously and arranged in the decision model. Obviously the rules that were assigned to the various attributes are the dominating factor in the service discovery process. Therefore, a service is identified by navigating through the nodes of the decision tree.

One of the chief goals of this exercise is to recognize a service's duties by discovering its name. This identification process will then influence the scope of a service's operations and its ability to serve its consumers. To summarize the major goals of the service discovery process, consider the driving activities:

- Identify service contextual affiliation by navigating the decision model.
- Name services according to their contextual affiliations.
- Name services based on the responsibilities that are reflected by service attributes.

SERVICE DISCOVERY PROCESS.   The discovery method is designed to identify a single service at each traversal of the decision model. Therefore, always start from the top of the tree—the root attribute—and descend down to the leaf levels. Once this goal is met, the inference process must take place to yield a service name. This approach requires that all visited attributes are evaluated against the applied rules, which influence the navigation direction.

We must repeat this identification process until all possible routes to discover services are exhausted.

When reaching the end of each downstream path, we must name a service according to the visited attributes and the rules that were applied to control the navigation. This task requires both that the participating parties understand the business and the technology behind the requirements and that they are able to determine the right service. Thus domain expertise and technical knowledge can contribute immensely to the final analysis.

Again, the goal here is to name services. The "naming" term is intrinsically about defining the scope of a service's duties and its overall functionality, which will be carried out by service operations (capabilities). Furthermore, a service's name is one of the most significant organizational vocabulary aspects. A name such as High-Return Stock Service or Fixed-Income Portfolio Service not only reveals the firm's strategy but also contributes to its communication.

To better understand this approach, inspect Exhibit 6.12, which illustrates the discovery process. This example is based on five attributes that were selected for the discovery stage: Interest, Rate, Penalty, Checks, and Fees. These attributes facilitate the identification of seven services that are positioned at different leaf levels (end nodes), each of which signifies the final stop of the seven distinct navigations.

Let us follow a single navigation path and observe the method by which a service is discovered. The path that leads to the discovery of the CD Account Service starts at the first attribute: Interest. This is the root node that is marked as 1. The Boolean value "Y" directs the navigation to the second attribute, named Rate (marked as 2). Next, the node that represents the Penalty attribute (node 3) is reached after the interest rate percentage was determined to be greater than 2. This takes us to the leaf (number 4) where a service must be defined to comply with all the attributes we have passed. This derivation process concludes with naming node 4 as the CD Account Service.

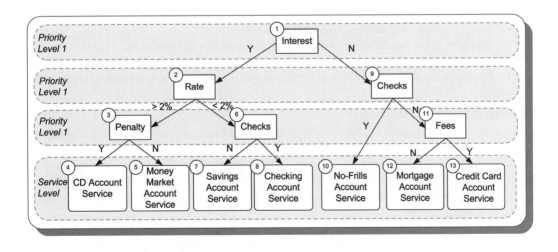

EXHIBIT 6.12   SERVICE DISCOVERY EXAMPLE

Discovered Service	Attributes				
	Interest	Rate	Penalty	Checks	Fees
CD Account	Y	>2%	Y		
Money Market Account	Y	>2%	N		
Savings Account	Y	<2%		N	
Checking Account	Y	<2%		Y	
No-Frills Account	N			Y	
Mortgage Account	N			N	N
Credit Card Account	N			N	Y

Exhibit 6.13   Service Discovery Table Example

It is advisable to create a service discovery table that encompasses the discovery process, details the various attributes and their corresponding rules that took part in this effort, and identifies the yielded services. These are illustrated in Exhibit 6.13. This document can serve multiple purposes and assist the business domain and technology organizations in understanding the various propositions represented by the diverse service findings.

ADHERE TO SERVICE DISCOVERY BEST PRACTICES.   The process of the Top-Down service discovery is driven by attributes that describe a future software product. The final artifact is analysis services that are subject to further inspection and manipulation to perfect a solution. This service identification effort should also conform to general SOA tenets, such as asset reuse, loose coupling, software consolidation, and more. But the chief objective is to separate concerns by discovering a diverse range of services, each of which embodies distinct functionality that is autonomous and loosely coupled. Consider the major best practices that can guide practitioners with the process of service discovery:

- Rely on domain expertise and technical knowledge to identify and name services.
- Always start from the root attribute level in the decision model.
- Always proceed with the navigation of the decision model downstream.
- Apply multiple iterations to cover all possible paths.
- The final destination of a single route must end at the leaf node (the attribute node that does not have offspring).
- Avoid assignment of ambiguous rules to attributes.
- A service name should also contribute to organizational vocabulary.
- The service identification process should promote enterprise language of communication.
- Employ service names to create an organizational taxonomy (discussed in the next section).

ESTABLISH SERVICE TAXONOMY

A "taxonomy" is a directory of services. It is simply a list of categorized software entities that can be established for a project or elevated to an organization level. This ontology[3] classifies services by their areas of contribution in different fields, such as business domain, architecture capabilities, technological capabilities, or service capabilities. Furthermore, taxonomy is a catalog that is arranged in a hierarchical structure that identifies the relationship of services and their collaborative solutions to organizational concerns.

SERVICE TAXONOMY CHIEF BENEFITS.   Service taxonomy can alleviate organizational communication challenges by providing a vocabulary and a terminology that can bridge the communication gaps between the business and technology organizations. This internal language is developed to institutionalize a unique jargon for the enterprise. Ultimately, it can contribute to the reusability of software assets, reduce redundancy of implemented functionalities, and decrease expenditure.

Architects, business analysts, modelers, developers, and managers can employ an organizational taxonomy to classify services based on their duties and characteristics. These categorization activities facilitate service typing that is crucial to asset portfolio management. Thus, the enterprise inventory repository of services can be cataloged based on expertise and form distinct knowledge groups, such as business services, infrastructure services, security services, communication services, data services, and more. This contextual categorization topic is discussed in detail in Chapter 13.

CREATE SERVICE TAXONOMY STRUCTURE.   Establishing service taxonomy is typically a straightforward task that requires business or technology knowledge. It is simply a categorization process by which services are classified in accordance with their fields of expertise, areas of interests, responsibilities, functionality, or even affiliation with sponsors and return on investment. Taxonomy can also be used to catalog technical assets, such as architecture types, patterns, and COTS product capabilities.

It is advisable to classify the discovered services and continue to expand on service typing after the service identification process has concluded. Doing this will enable the broadening of the solution perspective and provide a comprehensive set of remedies to future organizational concerns. The example illustrated in Exhibit 6.14 identifies three major entries in service taxonomy: CD Accounts, Money Market Accounts, and Mortgage Accounts. Each represents a corresponding service group that is specialized in a distinct field of business or technical expertise. Moreover, there is no limit on the number of categories in the structure of the taxonomy. In addition, there are no restrictions on the depth or number of levels in the service taxonomy. However, a service taxonomy

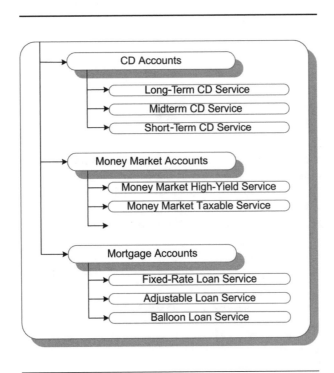

EXHIBIT 6.14   SERVICE TAXONOMY EXAMPLE

that consists of a large number of nested categories and is difficult to understand may not serve its founding purpose.

ADHERE TO SERVICE TAXONOMY FOUNDATION BEST PRACTICES.   Consider the chief best practices in establishing the service taxonomy. These should be undertaken after services have been discovered:

- Categorize services based on their contribution to the organization in various fields of expertise.
- Avoid a large number of nested classification entries.
- Simplify the service taxonomy directory by identifying the most significant categories.
- Steer clear from embedding very fine-grained services.
- Focus on service characteristics and their attributes to form the taxonomy structure.
- Do not place technical and business services under one category.
- Avoid classification of redundant functionality. This is a good time to propose consolidation of services.
- Identify further opportunities for service discovery and consolidation by inspecting the service taxonomy

DELIVERABLES

Adhere to the Top-Down discovery process that is driven by software product attribute collection and categorization. Institute an organizational repeatable service discovery process that consists of fundamental tasks that lead to the identification of new services and the founding of an enterprise service taxonomy:

- Establish an attribution model.
- Select attributes for service discovery.
- Found a decision model.
- Discover analysis services.
- Establish a service taxonomy.

SUMMARY

- The Top-Down attribute-driven service discovery process facilitates the derivation of new services by the extraction of software product attributes from business, technical, and architectural requirements.
- Analysis services and service taxonomy are the two deliverables that a practitioner ought to provide after the discovery process concludes.
- An attribution model should be established to enable the collection and classification of software product properties.
- A decision tree is employed to classify discovery rules and help discover services.

Notes

1.   An attribution model is discussed in the service-oriented modeling framework (SOMF) paradigm, featured in Michael Bell, *Service-Oriented Modeling: Service Analysis, Design, and Architecture* (Hoboken, NJ: John Wiley & Sons, 2008).

2.   Thomas H. Cormen, Charles E. Leiserson, Ronald L. Rivest, and Clifford Stein, *Introduction to Algorithms*, 2nd edition (Cambridge, MA: MIT Press, 2001), p. 166.

3.   http://msdn.microsoft.com/en-us/library/bb491121.aspx.

CHAPTER 7

FRONT-TO-BACK SERVICE DISCOVERY PATTERN

The user interface (UI) paradigm has been studied for decades. Often referred to as the presentation layer, the UI is a simple concept. Without it, software users, operators, clients, or partners would not be able to exchange information, execute automated business processes, trigger or schedule activities, and carry out transactions. In other words, without a proper interaction facility that allows one to communicate with an application's features and benefit from their capabilities, a software product is destined to fail.

To offer superior user interface solutions, the software architect, developer, modeler, analyst, and manager ought to consider three major requirements that secure a successful presentation layer implementation: (1) promote ease of *usage*, (2) allow flawless *interaction* with an application's components, and (3) enable efficient user *control* over the displayed information. These UI imperatives provide the motivation for launching a service discovery effort that begins its quest from a different direction. This new pattern of analysis process begins with user interaction concerns, explores mechanisms to *render* content, and inspects new avenues to improve control over an application's behavior. The other challenges that the Front-to-Back service discovery pattern addresses are the collection, transformation, and delivery of data to the presentation layer.

Therefore, start with the analysis of UI artifacts, such as page design, data entry validation, page navigation, and script languages. Understand the technologies behind data aggregation and content rendering. Study new avenues to enhance the performance of user display. Finally, devise new services to carry out these duties.

FRONT-TO-BACK SERVICE DISCOVERY MODEL

Recent developments in the UI field introduce different challenges: *customization* of the presentation layer and *configuration* of user preferences. Applying these modifications to the visual aspect of software—both cosmetic changes and behavior alterations—is all about enhancing UI capabilities. For example, the user can be granted authority to control aesthetic aspects of the view: colors, fonts, and shapes. From the software behavioral perspective, a consumer can personalize information by selecting areas of interest, such as favorite news, games, and financial material, as well as by filtering out (hiding) topics.

But the UI domain does not stop at a single consumer level. Due to advanced technologies, not only are customers allowed to interact with a software product, they also are permitted to *exchange information* with peers, such as product support personnel, partners, colleagues, and even social communities. This communication paradigm further evolved into a more complex architecture that enables consumers to converse simultaneously with community members. "Community" is defined as a group of people or organizations that share common interests and must interact to maintain close relationships. These may be business, political, social, and cultural interests.

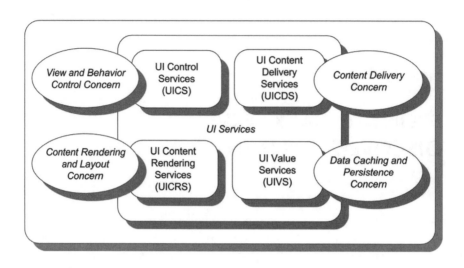

EXHIBIT 7.1   USER INTERFACE SERVICE DISCOVERY MODEL

Beyond the user control and system interaction aspects, application design efforts should also address the *delivery of content* challenges. Here the intent is to facilitate data validation, information packaging, message marshaling and structuring, message delivery, data rendering, caching data for user viewing purposes, and more.

This discussion brings us to the conclusion that specialized UI services should be devised to fill requirements in four major user-interface concerns as illustrated in Exhibit 7.1:

1. **View and Behavior Control.** User control over interface mechanisms and of presentation layer behavior (facilitated by UI Control Services)
2. **Content Delivery.** Collection, validation, transformation, marshaling, packaging, and delivery of user data (carried out by UI Content Delivery Services)
3. **Content Rendering and Layout.** Transformation of incoming data and layout of user's view to generate dynamic display interfaces (implemented by UD Content Rendering Services)
4. **Data Caching and Persistence.** Persistence of data in memory stores to enable expedient rendering operations (enabled by UI Value Services)

The correlation between the four UI concerns and their corresponding service solutions are explained in detail in the sections that follow.

USER INTERFACE CONTROL SERVICES

A user can be granted control over the presentation layer functionality on different levels. The term "control" implies that that authority is awarded to manage displayed information using, for example, graphical user interface widgets, such as submission buttons and text boxes. These features enable the interaction between consumers and application components, permit persistence of data, facilitate transactions between business partners, or permit information exchange among community members. But the term "control" is not only about managing presentation content. It can be extended to different territories, such as page navigation capabilities, preference management, and customization of view.

The opportunities to enhance user interaction mechanisms by employing services are vast. Hence, the Front-to-Back discovery charter calls for identifying services that can both address user interface control challenges and preserve content quality by proper design and architecture practices. Clearly, this effort may lead to the construction of fine-grained services because of their proximity to data entry fields and graphical widgets. Nevertheless, separation-of-concerns best practices require that we vigilantly inspect service prospects and establish a sensible balance between fine-grained and coarse-grained implementations (for more information about service granularity refer to review the Service-Oriented Granularity Assessment section in Chapter 2).

STUDY USER INTERFACE CONTROL MECHANISMS AND DUTIES.   Services that support user control of application display typically address two chief concerns: interaction control and collaboration control. The former pertains to the consumer's capability to interface with various application related components, such as back-end repositories, distributed services, and business logic implementation modules. Granting communication channels with peer users and business partners falls under the same category.

From a collaboration perspective, however, a control framework that is driven by services must provide cohesive capabilities to address the reliance between various control mechanisms that an application offers. For example, graphical user interface controls, such as buttons and checkboxes must collaborate on field and page navigation activities. Dependencies between various control capabilities should also be managed by services; for instance, influence of page display and navigation behavior on the appearance and functionality of graphical widgets.

The functionality of user interface control services (UICS) is typically classified into five major duties (illustrated in Exhibit 7.2), each of which identifies distinct capabilities that facilitate user interaction with a given application, distributed systems, or partner operations. These duties address the two major concerns that were discussed previously: interaction control and collaboration control. A detailed explanation of these rudimentary control service responsibilities are described in the sections that follow.

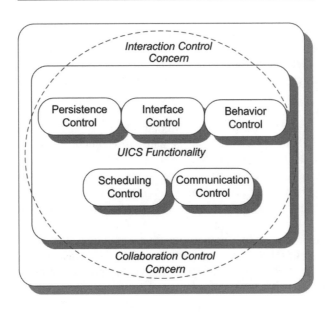

EXHIBIT 7.2   UICS FUNCTIONALITY

Persistence Control.   "Persistence control" refers to the user's ability to manipulate data by utilizing application user interfaces, such as widgets. This process is typically further delegated to data persistence services that execute four rudimentary operations: (1) create, (2) read, (3) update, and (4) delete, or CRUD services.[1] These entities should be decoupled from the user interface functionality and incorporated with the data organizational persistence layer. This will enable reuse and consolidation of similar operations across applications.

There are three major architectural implementations of the user's data persistence. The first method is coupled with the user's view layer, carried out by a "thick" client. The term "thick" pertains to a stand-alone application that is installed on a user's desktop and consists of local user interface support that also includes CRUD mechanisms. This architecture scenario is considered tightly coupled because of the functionality bundling design style.

The second architectural style utilizes CRUD services that operate behind the scenes, typically located on the server side, to carry out data persistence activities. This arrangement fits an architecture profile that supports "thin" clients. The term "thin" implies that a client program does not include major business or data persistence logic. For example, a Web browser offers user interface capabilities and typically does not directly provide CRUD activities.

The third form of persistence control is carried out by centralized CRUD operations that reside in a data access layer, a distributed software intermediary that handles data persistence. This method is designed to promote reuse across an organization and to protect the integrity of data by preventing direct access by consumers. (CRUD operations that take place in the data domain layer are discussed in detail in Chapter 8 that elaborates on the Back-to-Front (123) service discovery pattern.) The main benefit of such an intermediary is the isolation effect that enables the separation of an application from its repositories.

A major architectural consideration is security. The user capability to control CRUD functionality is typically permitted by authorization frameworks that dictate what types of operations are allowed on various presentation assets. Therefore, the role of a control service that is assigned persistence duties is to interact with provisioning and entitlement systems to both identify user credentials and verify their access and activity rights.

Finally, there are major concerns with implementations of persistence services. The chief challenge is to strike the right balance between fine-grained and coarse-grained service design. In some cases, CRUD operations that are assigned to services may fall under the anti-pattern category,[2] in which architecture impracticality outweighs the benefits. This pertains to the concern that services that handle CRUD operation typically appear to be very fine-grained. An analysis process should determine if such service implementation is feasible and adheres to organizational architecture best practices.

Interface Control.   The simplest form of user control on an application's behavior and look and feel[3] is the ability to interact with and manipulate presentation assets, such as articles, video clips, and data entry fields. As previously described, user interface controls such as widgets enable these capabilities. Therefore, the discovery of services that facilitate the communication with an application, partners, and community members may alleviate these concerns. The main challenges would be to identify the right services, establish their duties, and determine their supporting environment.

One of the most compelling propositions that can address the interaction between a user and front-end interfaces is a Service Control Framework (SCF) that is responsible for capturing and monitoring user interaction, enabling navigation, and responding to user interface events. This service facility must also address the population of displayed data either synchronously or asynchronously. "Population" pertains to placing information that is routed from servers on a user's view. This information can include controls, such as text boxes, entry fields, chat windows, and their related content. To accomplish the placement of data on a user's display, the SCF typically triggers the

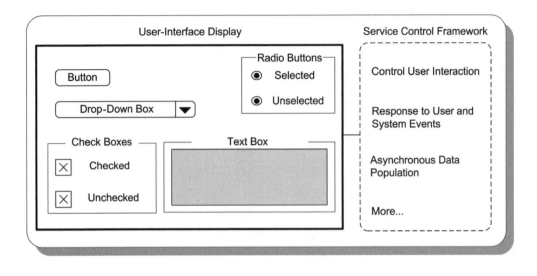

EXHIBIT 7.3   SERVICE CONTROL FRAMEWORK DUTIES

execution of different type of services: user interface content rendering services (UICRS) that are discussed in details in the User Interface Content Rendering Services section later in this chapter.

The latest technologies, such as Ajax[4] (a Web 2.0 feature), are capable of performing background asynchronous activities to allow the flow of information to the user view that is not necessarily triggered by user events. Examples include dynamic real-time geographical map downloading and navigation, updating driving directions, loading data entry fields with default values, suggesting values in search fields, and more.

To summarize the interface control duties, view Exhibit 7.3. It illustrates the user interface view (left), in which a number of widgets depict the various mechanisms that can be employed to control information and interact with an application: Button, Drop-Down Box, Radio Buttons, Check Boxes, and Text Box. Note the SCF on the right. It depicts three major features that are offered by this facility: Control User Interaction, Response to User and System Events, Asynchronous Data Population, and more.

The SCF should also address a more targeted form of user interface. This interaction paradigm is confined to small areas on a user's desktop (known as gadgets), smaller windows that are typically dedicated to special interests, such as weather, stock quotes, news, dictionaries, games, sidebars, calculators, and more. This concept is akin to the well-known Widget Engine implementation that is supported by various operating systems running on a variety of platforms.[5]

A similar concept is offered by portal applications that support portlet[6] technology (introduced by Java Specification Request [JSR] 168 specifications) empowered by application servers. This architecture adheres to loose coupling best practices that advocate separation or segmentation of an application's display and capabilities. Again, a user's screen is partitioned into smaller display areas, named portlets, each of which hosts distinct content. For example, a portlet can enable the viewing and manipulation of a company's current inventory levels, display of news, or listing of popular movies.

Finally, the SCF should also introduce a set of services designed to tackle application segmentation through the separation of the user's view. The chief responsibility here is to provide a targeted form of widget management. This concept is illustrated in Exhibit 7.4. Note that the SCF (depicted on the right) encompasses Widget Engine activities.

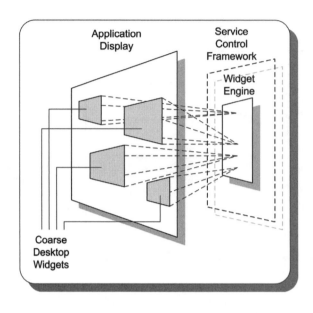

Exhibit 7.4   Service Control Framework Widget Management Duties

Behavior Control.   Application behavior can be controlled by technologies that support dynamic appearance and the manipulation of presentation assets. This would also allow users to interact with a nonstatic environment that changes according to predefined settings. Therefore, services that enable behavior control should provide two major facilities:

1.   Allow configuration of user preferences.
2.   Implement technical means designed to sustain dynamic presentation of information, dynamic content publishing, changes to user interface controls, asynchronous data persistence, communication with peer applications, and more.

The portal technology and the service control framework that were mentioned earlier exemplify the capability of dynamic presentation handling, by which targeted windows can not only change their position on the user's view but also be customized to render preferred interest items. This front-end behavior is not unique to portals. Web 2.0 technologies, for example, also provide dynamic presentation capabilities that allow asset manipulation and formatting via dynamic content publishing and management facilities.[7]

Scheduling Control.   Services that facilitate the scheduling of user events must be tuned to timetables, calendar settings, and on-demand triggering activities that are executed to accomplish business or technological tasks. For example, the need for planning bill payment agendas should be carried by scheduling control services that not only awaken sleeping processes to achieve execution goals but also communicate with partners across organizational boundaries to complete money-wiring transactions. Another example identifies the need for downloading files according to a preset timetable. These can be stock trading transaction confirmation records that can be transferred during overnight activities.

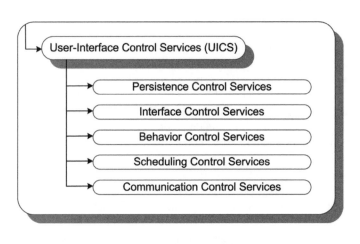

EXHIBIT 7.5   USER INTERFACE CONTROL SERVICE TAXONOMY

Communication Control.   Finally, communication control functionality is commonly carried out by specialized services that enable a user to interact with application components, professionals across departmental boundaries, business partners, and community members across the globe. A click of a button typically can trigger a set of activities that connect to software components that can understand the employed message protocols and are able to acknowledge and respond.

Communication control services specialize in message routing, operating from user interface facilities or remote locations such intermediary SOA services, proxy services, or gateway services, running on dedicated and distributed servers. These entities are also configured with routing information to enable the delivery of messages to the proper end-point interacting parties. When a large number of users and messages must be served, elaborated facilities should be planned. These are typically enterprise solutions that employ messaging frameworks across application boundaries and enterprise computing environments.

DELEGATE USER INTERFACE CONTROL DUTIES TO SERVICES.   User interface functionality should be delegated to services because of their loose coupling properties. These entities are not confined to certain areas of operations, can be distributed, and thus can be remotely configured to perform their duties. The autonomous status of a service can also facilitate the interaction with consumers and peer services across heterogeneous computing environments.

User interface facilities should be freed from auxiliary chores, such as handling communications, scheduling events, managing widgets, or providing application front-end behavior support. These responsibilities should be assigned to subject matter services for implementation. We thus propose a taxonomy of specialty services that can be employed for controlling and providing assistance to user interaction with applications. Exhibit 7.5 depicts five different groups of services that fall within the UICS category: (1) Persistence Control Services, (2) Interface Control Services, (3) Behavior Control Services, (4) Scheduling Control Services, and (5) Communication Control Services.

USER INTERFACE CONTENT DELIVERY SERVICES

The practice of collecting data from user inputs and delivering it to back-end components for further processing should be tackled by user interface content delivery services (UICDS). These entities' chief responsibility is gathering, validating, packaging, and transporting content. But their greater challenge is to facilitate the delivery of sizable material that a user may need to share with applications, colleagues, or business partners.

Complex configurations of interoperable environments that consist of diverse operating systems, networks, or language platforms call for addressing the challenge of information exchange. This is the duty of delivering content from the presentation layer to other composite and autonomous assets, such as applications, remote services, peers, and partners. The chief concern is not about the small amount of data that can be packaged in a single message. Attention should be focused on instances where clients employ their user interface to perform more complex data exchange operations to be transmitted over the network. This may include, for example, sizable transactions, messages that carry attachments, file uploading, exchange of images and videos, and more.

Remember, building a service whose responsibility is merely to collect a limited amount of input fields may be a counterproductive proposition because of the fine-grained nature of this operation. Adhering to service granularity principles that are discussed in Chapter 2 can assist with service feasibility assessment and identify the motivation behind devising services for the organization.

IDENTIFY USER INTERFACE CONTENT DELIVERY DUTIES.   Services that are responsible for delivering user interface content to remote application components and other software entities must provide technical means to overcome two major concerns: *conformity* and *transmission*. The former suggests that the user's content should be packaged according to organizational messaging format standards to guarantee flawless communication with information exchange parties. The transmission concern, however, relates to the manner by which a message is delivered. This may include intelligent services that are able to locate peer services for further processing.

Six different functionalities are imperative to any presentation layer environment that should be executed by user interface content delivery services. Their responsibilities are illustrated in Exhibit 7.6 and explained in the sections that follow.

Collection.   Collection of content from the user's view is a task that can be performed locally by a user interface facility or delegated to a remote software entity. The collection activity that is

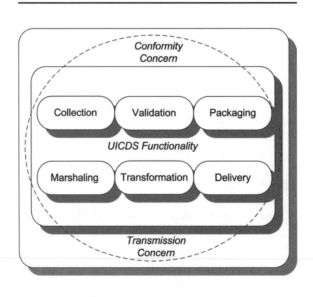

EXHIBIT 7.6   UICDS FUNCTIONALITY

performed by a remote service calls for deciphering a received message, identifying the sending party, unmarshaling the transmitted message, and further processing the information. These duties should be delegated to a collection service that can assemble the content according to a predefined and agreed-upon structure by the message exchange parties.

Presentation assets typically include diverse content formats such as text, files, videos, images, and more. The process of gathering these artifacts may involve categorization of media types and security verification. Therefore, media matching and proof of ownership must be performed by the collection service to ensure authenticity and protect the communicating parties from harm.

The collection process may turn out to be even more complex when the user's private content that is to be shared with its information exchange parties is housed in remote locations. For example, imagine personal content that is posted on multiple media storage, hard drives, hosted by third-party data providers, or is displayed on remote Web sites. This scenario may require a different treatment from the conventional method that collects user data entry fields for further distribution. When the content is dispersed in remote locations, however, the collecting service must possess a prior knowledge about various data locations and aggregate the information for further processing.

Validation.   The validation of data can be accomplished locally on the front end or remotely on a proxy server. This task of content integrity verification should take place before it is delivered to any communicating party; it includes conformity to common data schemas and formats that a project adopted, or compliance with an organizational canonical data model (authoritative data schema). Furthermore, this responsibility may go beyond validation of data entry fields or pages; here the validation service may be engaged with conformity to message size, quality of the transmitted media, identification of media types, and even permission verification of copyrighted material.

Packaging and Marshaling.   There are two dependent steps that should be pursued before a message is transmitted. over the network: packaging and marshaling. The role of packaging is simply the process of assembling user content that is gathered from different presentation layer asset locations, such as data entry fields, cache facilities, or repositories. The marshaling activity, which typically follows the packaging effort, formats the packaged content and forms a message to be transmitted over a network. In addition, the marshaling task must conform to industry standard messaging specifications that identify the format by which multiple media types, ought to be structured. The term "media" pertains to text, images, video clips and other assets that can be exchanged between consumers and their corresponding services. Web services, for example, employ the simple object access protocol (SOAP) to transmit standard messages over the Internet.

Therefore, the duty of a content delivery service is to package and marshal content for distribution. These tasks are even more complex when proprietary media formats are involved or proprietary protocols are used for message transmission. From a development point of view, typically developers are excused from marshaling messages. This feature is often offered by the language platform they use for software construction. However, for proprietary packaging and marshaling, for example, the employment of the Java architecture for XML binding (JAXB) library[8] can mitigate the nonconformance with industry standards issues.

Transformation.   User content should be transformed and prepared for packaging and marshaling if its format does not comply with predefined standards or the message receiving end excepts a proprietary message format. This responsibility should be addressed by a service designed to perform a diverse type of data conversions, cleansing, and filtering. The transformation of user interface content is called UI transformation because it involves presentation layer assets. This differs from an enterprise data transformation that is designed to process data owned by an organization rather than by individuals.

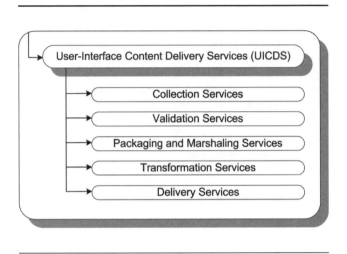

Exhibit 7.7   UICDS Taxonomy

Delivery.   Finally, the content delivery process should be handled by specialized services that are either located locally to the user desktop or remotely on distributed servers. Local delivery activities are typically associated with "thick" client technologies that consist of business logic, communication logic, and message transmission mechanisms to enable delivery of content to remote services, servers, applications, and peers. Conversely, remote content delivery may employ proxy services to handle the distribution of messages.

Other message delivery solutions to these concerns have been proposed and road-tested in recent years. Service Facade and Service Locator design patterns, for example, are institutionalized popular solutions that are embedded in many software products and libraries. With the emergence of the service technology, the task of delivering messages and matching their context with back-end business logic implementation apparently promote software asset reuse and reduction of functionality redundancy.

DELEGATE USER INTERFACE CONTENT DELIVERY DUTIES TO SERVICES.   The recognition that user interface content delivery services are viable assets to application architecture has been growing in recent years. These unique entities are designed to bridge the communication gapes between users, applications, distributed components, peers, and partners. Thus, delegate data and information delivery tasks to UICDS to better address the growing complexity of user interaction.

Exhibit 7.7 depicts service taxonomy that categorizes services by delivery capabilities: Collection, Validation, Packaging and Marshaling, Transformation, and Delivery.

USER INTERFACE CONTENT RENDERING SERVICES

"Rendering" is the process of transforming unreadable information—such as binary, delimited text, or proprietary stream media formats—into understandable structures that humans can read and view. This conversion process typically takes place before the content is placed on a user's display. The rendered assets constitute images, articles, news, video clips, advertisements, charts, diagrams, and more.

Rendering technologies fall under two major categories, each of which offers a distinct functionality that serves different purposes: *static* and *dynamic* rendering. The static approach provides solid solutions for a client program that encompasses implementation of the view locally. In other

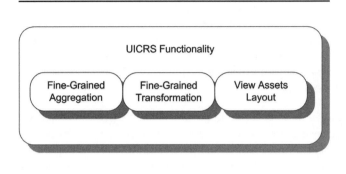

Exhibit 7.8   UICRS Functionality

words, each client program that is installed on a user's desktop also includes programming logic that renders the various assets on a local machine. This method has been employed for decades and best fits the client/server model.

Conversely, the dynamic rendering model has been used in distributed environments in which the presentation logic program is an autonomous entity, decoupled from any system, and can shared by multiple applications. This is clearly an advantage over the static approach that tightly couples the view with the client logic, requiring both to operate in the same physical location.

The dynamic view feature, for example, is offered for portal applications that employ remote rendering services as plug-ins. This technology is known as Web Services for Remote Portlets (WSRPs).[9] Moreover, the dynamic service rendering paradigm has even expanded its scope to include more advance presentation layer assets, such as remote rendering that is supported by cache facilities, virtualization of three-dimensional images, powerful animation mechanisms that are deployed on distributed grid services, and more.

STUDY UICRS MECHANISMS AND DUTIES.   User interface content rendering services (UICRS) are responsible for rendering raw data into understandable presentation assets that may be collected from various local and remote resources. The process of rendering should be loosely coupled and sharable among applications in an interoperable environment despite the differences in operating systems, hardware, networks, and language platforms.

The three main tasks that rendering services typically accomplish are Fine-Grained Aggregation, Fine-Grained Transformation, and View Assets Layout. These are illustrated in Exhibit 7.8 and explained in the sections that follow.

Fine-Grained Aggregation.   Prior to the rendering process, gathering information from a single source or multiple data locations is a necessary activity. This external data collection process is known as fine-grained aggregation because of its scope and the magnitude of the information it gathers. In other words, a rendering service should not be commissioned to undertake extreme data gathering duties because rendering services have limited data collection capabilities. These limited capabilities can affect performance and cause rendering latencies. Intensive information aggregation activities, however, should be assigned to different type of services. These are typically infrastructure entities, known as enterprise data aggregation services, that are designed to gather large loads of data distributed remotely across the enterprise.[10]

A rendering service that is designated fine-grained aggregation duties should rely mostly on enterprise-level aggregation services that specialize in remote data collection, routing data on demand to enterprise message buses (ESBs), and storage of information in cache facilities. The term "cache" relates to technologies that are able to deposit data in memory rather than on disk media. This approach of reliance on enterprise-level services to provide data would enable quick retrieval of information and accelerate the rendering process. Therefore, a rendering service's chore would be to assemble information needed merely for the presentation layer rendering process and focus on the dynamic nature of the data collection by providing real-time fine-grained aggregation to satisfy user interface display requests.

Fine-Grained Transformation.   Akin to the fine-grained aggregation process, a rendering service should not be in the business of enterprise-level data transformation. The enterprise task for massive data conversion should be assigned to enterprise-level services that specialize in data cleansing, schema mapping, data type translation, data augmentation and enrichment, data pattern machine, and more.[11] Conversely, the rendering service should focus merely on fine-grained transformation that is associated with the user's display. Therefore, the data that have been aggregated previously must undergo refinement and prepared for the presentation layer. This activity is about distilling the incoming data; this process may include conversion and mapping of data from the received version to the required format for display. Consider a number of examples that depict this effort:

- Removing unwanted characters
- Unifying data that arrives from various sources
- Converting streamed information to images and videos
- Translating binary information to character base format
- Universalizing charter sets
- Translating from one language to another

Layout View of Assets.   Laying out a page is the sole duty of the content rendering service. This effort is affiliated with the actual creation of the user interface view layer. Here the presentation assets are being formatted and arranged to fit a page for display. But this mission is not only about cosmetic construction of user controls and the visual arrangement of widgets. It must also accommodate the interaction and the behavioral aspect of individual pages and program navigation in general, including the logical layout of assets to promote ease of use and to boost user productivity.

In addition, one of the most important tasks of a rendering service is to foster content repurposing. In another words, a presentation asset can be reformatted and displayed in different view areas or placed on different pages. Think about an article, for example, that can be embedded in the News section and at the same time appear as a Technology column of an Internet newspaper.

The logical aspect can even go beyond the effort of creating a single display. It may include formations of multiple pages that can be stored in memory for fast retrieval.

Consider examples of duties that a content rendering service should assume:

- Setting default values for data entry fields
- Sizing images and videos to fit confined display areas
- Structuring text to form articles and news
- Formatting page columns
- Creating banners and menu bars
- Placing advertisements

DELEGATE CONTENT RENDERING DUTIES TO SERVICES.   Rendering activities for the user interface view should be assigned to specialized services that may operate locally on desktops or are distributed remotely across an organization for reuse purposes. Tightly coupled user view implementations that operate locally are an integral part of a single client program. This architecture is not designed for reusability because copies of executables must be installed for each client computer.

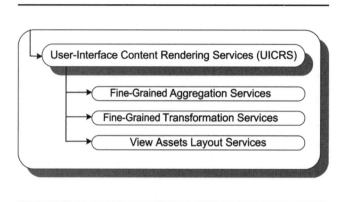

EXHIBIT 7.9 UICRS FUNCTIONALITY

Rendering activities that do not take place on the user's domain (local implementation) operate remotely—installed on a dedicated server or distributed across production environments. This configuration typically enables information rendering for a group of users who are connected to an application platform. The rendering activities occur remotely each time a user requests a page for display. This rendering technology has been improved in recent years to increase the reuse and the performance of the rendering process. Advanced rendering architectures enable sharing the view layer with other applications and services. These types of "plug-in" programs are flexible, loosely coupled, and able to offer a great deal of operational flexibility. For example, a stock market quotes panel that is rendered remotely can be displayed simultaneously on multiple users' views.

Exhibit 7.9 illustrates the three chief service types that contribute to the user interface content rendering duties: Fine-Grained Aggregation Services, Fine-Grained Transformation Services, and View Assets Layout Services.

USER INTERFACE VALUE SERVICES

The term "value service" represents a simple concept that is borrowed from the object-oriented paradigm, reminiscent of the value object idea.[12] User interface value services (UIVS) are entities that carry data that corresponds to the presentation layer. For example, presentation-layer assets such as market news, financial articles, stock portfolio, advertisements, and blogs can be delivered to the user's display by value services. In this case, these entities are responsible for both persisting financial information in memory and refreshing the content on each market event development. This noticeable correlation between value services and the content that is displayed on the user's view depends on decisions that are made by architects, modelers, analysts, and developers during design sessions. Exhibit 7.10 illustrates this concept. Note that for each section on the user's view, there is a corresponding value service; Financial Article Value Service, Market News Value Service, Stock Portfolio Value Service, and Advertisement Value Service.

As discussed, UIVS offer run-time memory-based repositories. These are cache facilities that provide rapid data withdrawal and updating mechanisms. They can be shared by multiple client programs and contain the latest version of the updated data. This is typically achieved by their embedded data persistence mechanism, which periodically refreshes the stock of information to databases according to a predefined schedule.

The Front-to-Back service discovery process advocates that we identify value services by inspecting business requirements that correspond to a user's view layouts, pages, and navigation specifications. This analysis process should influence the value service design and its

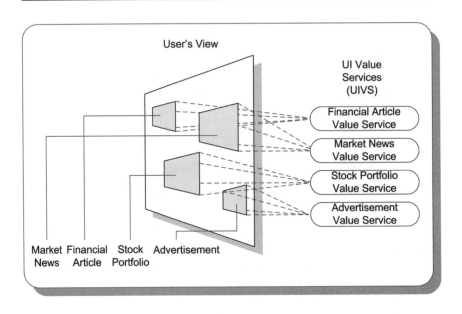

EXHIBIT 7.10   UIVS EXAMPLE

functionality, including configuration of data loads, refreshing mechanisms, and information persistence techniques.

FRONT-TO-BACK SERVICE DISCOVERY PROCESS

During most projects, user interface construction efforts are clearly driven by business requirements and technical specifications. But the underlying implementation of both the user's interaction and the behavior of the view layer are dictated by the *architectural* and *technical capabilities* that an organization can offer. These capabilities characteristically are the various existing or planned software components and infrastructure that empower the delivery of content to the user interface domain, render presentation assets, collect inputs, and allow peer-to-peer communications. Therefore, the Front-to-Back service discovery process should mostly rely on technological capabilities and yet should not disregard user interface business requirements if available. Again, the driving force behind this service identification endeavor should be technical specifications that are devised to accommodate the presentation layer and enhance user experience.

ADHERE TO THE SERVICE DISCOVERY PROCESS.   Our process then calls for three distinct activities, each of which advances the cause of service discovery.

1. We start by identifying *technical specialties* based on requirements. This typically sets the overall scope of this effort.
2. Once these areas of technical expertise have been defined, the next step is to identify service responsibilities. This activity is about discovering candidate service operations that match technical specialties.
3. The final activity firms up candidate operations that lead to the establishment of UI services. Remember that all services that are discovered in this stage should be regarded as analysis services because of their current and potential future contribution to the service-oriented analysis venture.

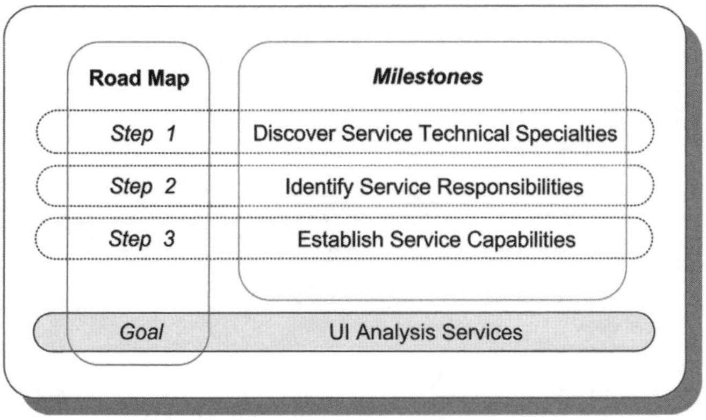

Road Map	Milestones
Step 1	Discover Service Technical Specialties
Step 2	Identify Service Responsibilities
Step 3	Establish Service Capabilities
Goal	UI Analysis Services

EXHIBIT 7.11   FRONT-TO-BACK SERVICE DISCOVERY PROCESS

Exhibit 7.11 illustrates this process. Note that the Front-to-Back service discovery approach must assist both in devising a road map for success and in defining the final goal, which obviously must lead to the foundation of analysis services.

DISCOVER SERVICE TECHNICAL SPECIALTIES.   A technical specialty is simply a field of expertise that can guide and direct architects, modelers, and developers to discover UI services for implementation. Content rendering, message marshaling, and content caching are examples of major service specialties. These are imperative cornerstone artifacts that influence and define the scope of the service discovery process.

Technical specialties clearly stem from technical specifications that can be influenced by business requirements and processes, use case documents, commercial off-the-shelf product capabilities, architectural best practices, architectural and design patterns, and more. Therefore, begin by studying the required technical abilities and various imperatives that drive this process. The rule of thumb suggests that the process of separating technology concerns to establishing specialties is a good start. Exhibit 7.12 illustrates this idea. The technical requirements Render

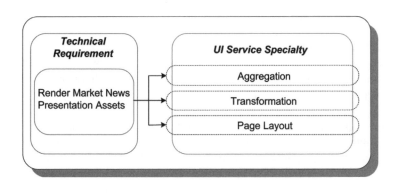

EXHIBIT 7.12   IDENTIFICATION OF UI SERVICE SPECIALTIES EXAMPLE

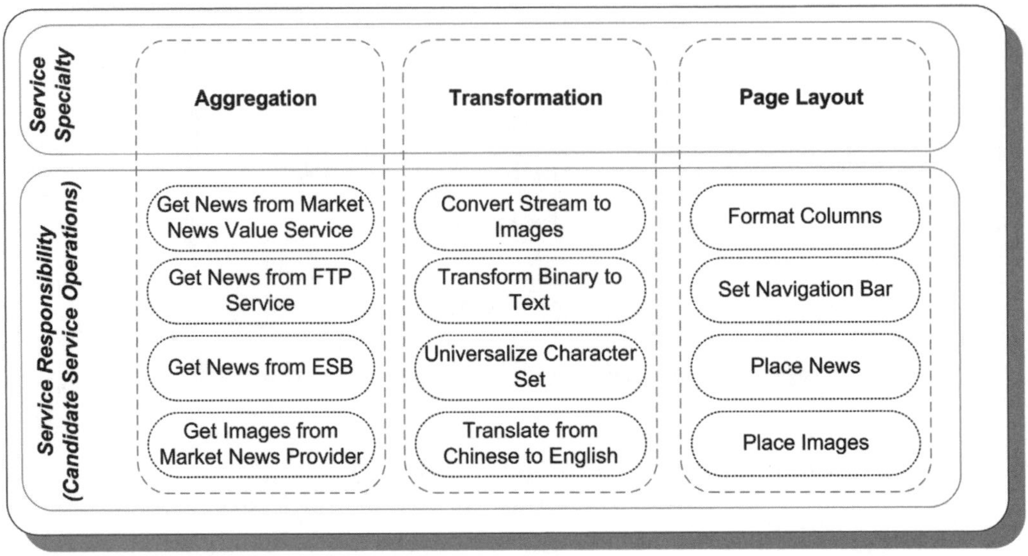

EXHIBIT 7.13   DISCOVERY OF SERVICE RESPONSIBILITIES (CANDIDATE OPERATIONS) EXAMPLE

Market News Presentation Assets lead to the discovery of three major service specialties that execute this mission: Aggregation, Transformation, and Page Layout. These discoveries define the scope of the project effort and provide clues for the identification of candidate service operations that are discussed in the next section.

IDENTIFY SERVICE RESPONSIBILITIES.   Service responsibilities are simply candidate service operations that should be founded at this stage. Therefore, for each of the previously discovered service technical specialties, list possible service operations. This process should be straightforward and rely on people's experience and knowledge in the fields of architecture, UI design, development, business analysis, and technical management. Collaborative effort of such subject matter experts can yield valuable candidate service operations that should be translated later into UI services. Exhibit 7.13 illustrates the deliverable of this initiative. Note the candidate service operations that correspond to each service specialty. These responsibilities, however, are not carved in stone and may be changed in the next step during further analysis.

DISCOVER UI SERVICES: ESTABLISH SERVICE CAPABILITIES.   The process of discovering UI services has reached its final destination, during which service responsibilities—candidate service operations—should be firmed up and verified against requirements. This activity calls for inspecting the proposed candidate operations, refining their functionality, and deriving services.

From Service Responsibilities to Service Capabilities.   The refinement process is associated with rudimentary analysis tasks that facilitate the transformation of service responsibilities (candidate service operations) to final capabilities (final service operations). Analysts, architects, modelers, and developers should apply five different analysis activities to derive final service operations:

1. **Elimination.** Purging candidate service operations if they are not directly associated with the requirements

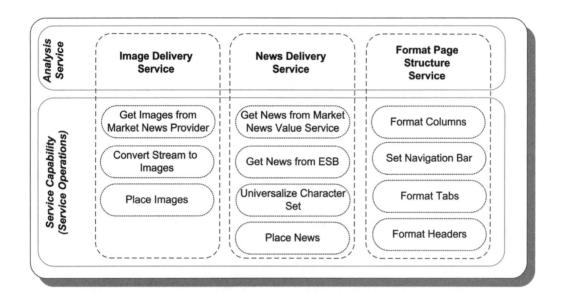

EXHIBIT 7.14   DISCOVERY OF SERVICE CAPABILITIES (FINAL OPERATIONS) EXAMPLE

2. **Merging.** Combining two or more candidate operations to reduce redundancy of functionality
3. **Renaming.** Modifying an operation name to better reflect its functionality
4. **Breaking up.** Splitting a candidate operation into two or more functionalities to decouple their activities
5. **Augmenting.** Adding functionality to compensate for missing capabilities

Discovering Analysis Services.   The discovery process requires bundling operations to form services. In other words, a service should be comprised of a group of related operations that work together to achieve a predefined goal. Furthermore, this method does not advocate that service names should be identical to the technical specialties that were discovered previously. For example, it is not expected that the transformation specialty would yield a Transformation Service.

In fact, technical specialties were formulated for the purpose of defining the scope of the discovery process and identifying fields of expertise that can provide solutions. Hence, the final set of services may possibly differ in context. However, service duties should be inline with the technical specifications and must comply with the goals that they designated to achieve. Let us inspect Exhibit 7.14, which exemplifies this process. The depicted three analysis services—Image Delivery Service, News Delivery Service, and Format Page Structure Service—were formed based on related operations that contextually agree with their corresponding responsibilities (depicted in Exhibit 7.13 that illustrates the candidate service operations). For instance, the Image Delivery Service consists of three operations that collaboratively accomplish aggregation of images, rendering, and placement on user's display.

Note the differences between candidate operations (responsibilities) defined in Exhibit 7.13 and their refined version in Exhibit 7.14. The Get News from FTP Service, Transform Binary to Text, and Translate from Chinese to English were eliminated in the course of this process. However, Format Tabs and Format Headers were added to augment service operations.

DELIVERABLES

A successful Front-to-Back service discovery effort should yield four different types of services that address UI concerns and bolster the presentation layer process. Establish a Front-to-Back service discovery pattern that is based on this service taxonomy:

1. User interface control services (UICS)
2. User interface content delivery services (UICDS)
3. User interface content rendering services (UICRS)
4. User interface value services (UIVS)

SUMMARY

- The Front-to-Back service discovery pattern advocates that the service identification effort focuses on UI mechanisms to strengthen the presentation layer.
- Four service categories are designed to carry out UI interaction and presentation activities: (1) user interface control services (UICS), (2) user interface content delivery services (UICDS), (3) user interface content rendering services (UICRS), and (4) user interface value services (UIVS).
- UI services address four different concerns: (1) view and behavior control of the presentation layer; (2) content delivery, such as data collection, validation, transformation, packaging, and delivery; (3) content rendering of transformed information; and (4) data caching and persistence, which include memory stores or disk persistence.

Notes

1. http://it.toolbox.com/blogs/the-soa-blog/soa-design-patterns-17563.
2. The term "anti-patterns" refers to impractical solutions that should be avoided during software design, architecture, and construction.
3. In software design, the term "look and feel" pertains to user interface and the presentation layer of an application.
4. http://webdesign.about.com/od/ajax/a/aa101705.htm.
5. For an example of Widget Engine, see http://widgets.yahoo.com/download/.
6. http://developers.sun.com/portalserver/reference/techart/jsr168/.
7. Ibid.
8. www.ibm.com/developerworks/webservices/library/ws-tip-jaxwsrpc2.html.
9. www.ibm.com/developerworks/library/ws-soa-progmodel5/index.html.
10. Refer to the Discover Data Access Layer Services section in Chapter 8 for more information about enterprise-level data aggregation mechanisms.
11. Refer to the Discover Data Access Layer Services section in Chapter 8 to learn more about enterprise-level data transformation duties.
12. http://java.sun.com/j2ee/patterns/ValueObject.html.

CHAPTER 8

BACK-TO-FRONT SERVICE DISCOVERY PATTERN

The Back-to-Front service discovery pattern introduces another approach to discovering and analyzing services for a project. This method of service identification represents a pattern of discovery that begins from "back-end" software assets, such as databases, data aggregators, data transformers, data searchers, and more. The incentive to start the inspection venture from exploring data repositories and their delivery facilities is rooted in one of the most vital business and technological aspects of an organization: information processing and sharing. The discovered services in this space typically are devised to standardize a *data model* across the organization and institutionalize the mechanisms that enable consumers to *access* data.

The other incurred benefits from launching the Back-to-Front service discovery endeavor are affiliated with homogenizing a *data access model* that can unify the organizational various data retrieval and manipulation methods. This leads to an additional essential topic to tackle: institution of a *canonical data model* that typically standardizes data formats across the enterprise. Moreover, the contribution of a uniformed data structure that is utilized by applications and silo organizations can enhance data integrity and security. These are imperative requirements to almost any software development initiative.

To fulfill these goals, the Back-to-Front service discovery pattern is established upon three major building blocks. These are service-oriented data model pillars that contribute to the discovery of services from different data domain points of views to enable a rigorous analysis and broaden the service identification venture: Logical Perspective, Conceptual Perspective, and Physical Perspective. This model, depicted in Exhibit 8.1, facilitates the service identification process by encouraging practitioners to inspect a wide range of data artifacts. These may include data concepts diagrams, data schemas, data flowcharts, and more.

The sections that follow elaborate on the Back-to-Front service discovery data model elements and the guiding mechanisms that can assist modelers, architects, developers, analysts, and managers with the institution of new services in the three major data discovery perspectives:

1. Conceptual data model perspective
2. Logical data model perspective
3. Physical data model perspective

CONCEPTUAL DATA MODEL PERSPECTIVE

The absence of data concepts and lack of a unified view that represents organizational data abstractions can be detrimental to most projects and operational budgets. It can also delay the *standardization* efforts of an enterprise *canonical data model*—an authoritative and agreeable schema version that modelers, architects, analysts, developers, and managers should embrace.

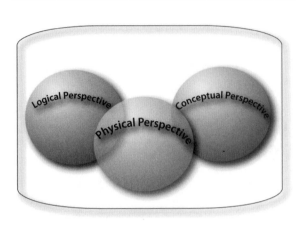

EXHIBIT 8.1   BACK-TO-FRONT SERVICE DISCOVERY DATA MODEL

Conversely, a well-established model can help carve out a joint *data strategy* to establish the scope of projects and define clear boundaries for data design initiatives.

The major contribution of data concepts to the Back-to-Front service discovery approach is the constitution of data elements. These conceptual definitions of "things" simply provide hints and motivation for constructing new services—or utilizing existing implementations—that will be designed to serve, process, transform, and distribute data to consumers. Hence, our service discovery process that depends on data assets must start with the concepts first. This also implies that a rigorous study should be dedicated to understanding the various data abstractions, their attributes, and their conceptual relationships.

IDENTIFY DATA ENTITIES: DATA CONCEPTS DRIVE SERVICE DISCOVERY.   The Back-to-Front service discovery approach employs a formal and popular data modeling discipline that was developed in 1976 by Peter Chen.[1] He introduced the entity relationship model that both leads to the discovery of data concepts and depicts data abstractions' associations. This approach proposed creating entity relationship diagrams (ERDs) that serve as fundamental artifacts for every data modeling activity.

Our starting point then begins with studying data abstractions and identifying concepts that in due course will yield services. Where do these concepts emanate from? The duty of discovering data entities typically is assigned to professionals who understand the art of data modeling and rely on business requirements, technical specifications, data requirements, and architecture blueprints for discovering data abstractions. Their deliverables also consist of elaborated diagrams that depict data entities, which eventually will be transformed to concrete collection of records in a repository. These characteristically address the question: What type of information, or things, do we store in a database?

Exhibit 8.2 illustrates four data entities that not only propose underpinning data structure conceptual elements that would ultimately influence the construction of database schemas: (1) Customer, (2) Bank Loan, (3) Loan Division, and (4) Banking Institution. These abstractions also provide the motivation for the institution of services. The provided data entities will not necessarily be directly translated to services. A refined process, a separation-of-concerns analysis, would be

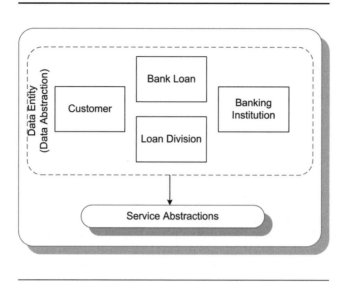

EXHIBIT 8.2   DATA ENTITIES INFLUENCE SERVICE DISCOVERY

required to further break down or even unify some of the offered entities to comply with business and technological requirements.

FORM CONTEXTUAL RELATIONSHIPS.   The discovered data entities, such as loan division and customer, must be linked to form relationships. This activity is essential to establishing associations between the data abstractions. Understanding these correlations enables data modelers and developers to link tables and relate records when the time comes to devise formalized data structures and schemas. This milestone will also endow the service discovery process with enduring abstractions that can generalize concerns and help devise efficient solutions.

Establish Service Abstraction Associations through Entity Relationship Discovery.   To form contextual relationships between data entities while demonstrating the associations between services abstractions, create a relationship matrix table akin to Exhibit 8.3. This will serve a dual purpose: (1) analyze how data concepts are affiliated to each other, and later on in the service discovery process (2) feature the links between service abstractions.

Let us start with positioning all discovered entities in the first row and also place them in the very first column. This matrix table is now ready for the relationship identification activities

	Data Entity/Service Abstraction			
	Banking Institution	**Loan Division**	**Customer**	**Bank Loan**
Bank Institution				
Loan Division				
Customer				

EXHIBIT 8.3   RELATIONSHIP MATRIX TABLE

	Data Entity/Service Abstraction			
	Banking Institution	**Loan Division**	**Customer**	**Bank Loan**
Bank Institution		Owns		
Loan Division			Serves	Offers
Customer	Banks at			

EXHIBIT 8.4   RELATIONSHIP MATRIX

that yield values (verbs) that link the horizontal and vertical data entities. Exhibit 8.4 illustrates the assignment of the relationship values that bind these entities:

- A Bank Institution (data entity) *Owns* (relationship) a Loan Division (data entity).
- A Loan Division (data entity) *Serves* (relationship) Customers (data entity).
- A Loan Division (data entity) *Offers* (relationship) Bank Loans (data entity).
- A Customer (data entity) *Banks At* (relationship) a Bank Institution (data entity).

Link Data Entities to Service Abstractions.   The time has come to demonstrate the link between data entities, and service abstractions. This effort calls for depicting the relationship between data concepts that are featured by entities and service abstractions. Remember, when it comes to discovering service abstractions, we should not commit to a straight translation between the two. Therefore, the derivation of service concepts can simply involve decomposition, unification, or even renaming data entities.

We thus utilize the ERD that is illustrated in Exhibit 8.5 for associating services with data concepts. Consider the key notation that is placed on the bottom of this diagram: The rectangle identifies a data entity, the diamond shape denotes relationships between data entities, and a round-cornered rectangle depicts a service concept. Note that a relationship symbol (diamond) is always positioned between two data entities (rectangles) and a solid line connects them. As is apparent, the Loan Division (data entity) Offers (relationship) a Bank Loan (data entity).

However, a service abstraction is always derived from a data entity (rectangle). Note that the Bank Loan data entity yields two distinct services abstractions: Fixed-Rate Loan and Adjustable Loan. The Customer (data entity) results in two service concepts: Mortgage Customer and Banking Customer, and the service concept Bank Division stems from the Loan Division data entity. Finally, the Banking Institution data entity derives two service abstractions: Private Bank and Commercial Bank. As apparent in all these examples, the link between a data entity and a service abstraction is denoted by a solid line.

Assign Entity Cardinality.   As we learned in the previous section, associations between data entities can be gauged by an assigned relationship value—usage of a noun that reveals the nature of the affiliation. For example, *owns*, *offers*, and *serves* describe the links between depicted entities. To better measure such connections, we are also required to provide a quantifier that indicates the ratio between two data entities: a number that signifies quantities or the character "N" that denotes multiplicity (any amount greater than one). Exhibit 8.6 illustrates this notation:

- One (quantifier denoted by the character "1") Banking Institution Owns one (quantifier) Loan Division.
- One (quantifier) Loan Division Serves a number (quantifier denoted by the character "N") of Customers.
- A number (quantifier) of Customers Bank at one (quantifier) Banking Institution.
- One (quantifier) Loan Division Offers a number (quantifier) of Bank Loans.

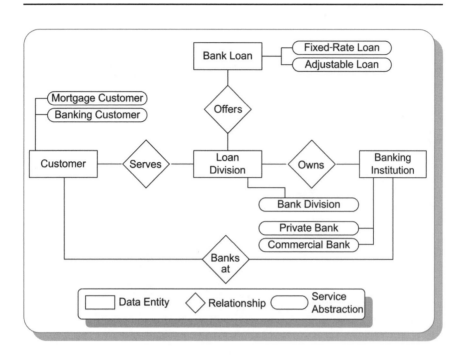

Exhibit 8.5   Entity Correlation Diagram with Service Abstractions Example

One may wonder whether the cardinality value assigned to a data entity should also pose a limit on the number of service abstractions that can be derived. On the contrary, these quantifiers should merely serve as guidance for analysis. The modeler, architect, analyst, or developer should be encouraged to break down a data entity into multiple service concepts, if appropriate, to refine the service discovery process.

IDENTIFY ATTRIBUTES: INFLUENCES ON SERVICE ATTRIBUTES.   To enhance the service discovery process, add attributes for each of the data entities that participate in this effort. This activity requires characterizing entities by simply specifying their properties. To add an attribute to a data entity, simply connect an ellipse that contains the attribute to the data entity name (contained in a rectangle) by drawing a solid line. Exhibit 8.7 depicts the various attributes that were assigned to better describe each data abstraction. Ultimately, data attributes translate to fields in a database. But they also contribute immensely to the understanding of service abstractions and the establishment of their properties. Consider for example the Loan Number, Loan Type and Rate Type attributes assigned to the Bank Loan data entity. These depictions suggest that not only is the loan division only able to offer multiple loans to consumers, it can also provide different types of mortgages.

LOGICAL DATA MODEL PERSPECTIVE

The logical perspective simply represents the various components that enable data *delivery* to consumers. This duty should be assigned to specialized service brokers that aggregate, transform, cleanse, migrate, and enable access to enterprise information. To discover these services, we must tackle two levels of data requirements: *enterprise* and *application* level. The term "enterprise level" implies that content should be available for retrieval and manipulation across multiple projects and application teams. "Application level," however, pertains to more silo implementations that are

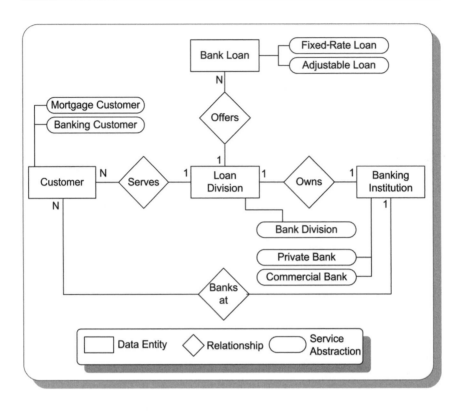

EXHIBIT 8.6   CARDINALITY ASSIGNMENT EXAMPLE

executed by smaller-scope development initiatives and are confined to a smaller organization's boundary, such as department or group. Imperatives that relate to either level should address data *accessibility* issues, *integrity*, *ownership*, *security*, and *standardization* of data formats and schemas across the enterprise.

These logical data model perspective's concerns and their solutions, which are elaborated in detail in the sections that follow, drive the Back-to-Front discovery process that yields three major service groups:

1. **Data access layer services (DALS).** These services implement four distinct functionalities: data structure standardization (establishment of a canonical data model), data persistence, data access mechanisms and security, and data mapping.
2. **Data aggregation services (DAS).** In addition to data collection duties, these services are designed to provide data searching and transformation functionality.
3. **Virtual data layer services (VDLS).** Data manipulation and processing is enabled by a virtual layer designed to reduce hardware, software, and human resources.

START WITH INSPECTION OF DATA ARCHITECTURE ARTIFACTS.   The rigorous study of data architecture artifacts can contribute immensely to the discovery of services. Pay attention to two major data requirements, as discussed in the previous section: Enterprise and application level. Start with individual applications. Study simple data modeling deliverables and understand data structures, data fields, and associated tables. Also, inspect the relationship between data entities and

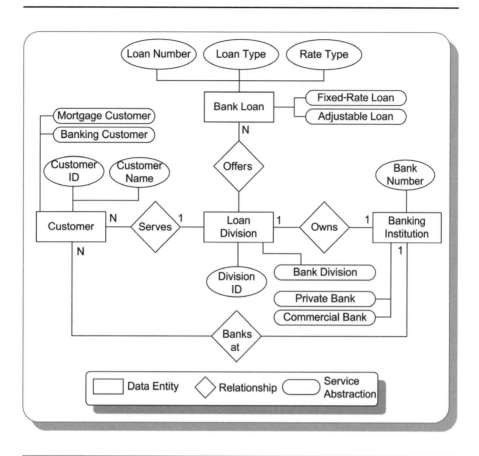

Exhibit 8.7   Attribution of Entities Influence Service Discovery Example

identify primary and foreign keys. Last, delve into database schema details and study the correlation between fields and tables.

A more advanced examination should cover the data persistence, aggregation, and transformation requirements of individual applications. Moreover, identify the required create, read, update, and delete (CRUD) operations. This will elaborate on the scope of the application's data management and functionality. In addition, study the format of data delivery structures. These can be tagged Extensible Markup Language (XML), delimited text, or more formal Web services such as Simple Object Access Protocol (SOAP) formats.

Finally, study the enterprise-level architecture requirements and available blueprints. This effort may include plans for building data access services to serve the consumer and partner communities. Additionally, understand the overall organizational data capacity and the propositions to expand data storages. Last, examine the various data sources and providers across the enterprise to encourage reuse and promote consolidation of assets.

DISCOVER DATA ACCESS LAYER SERVICES.   One of the most challenging aspects of data manipulation and persistence is the complexity that is inherently attributed to large-scale implementations. But every so often, even small-scale projects cannot be spared from convoluted architectures that lead to unreliable data persistence operations. The accumulative strain of multiple projects and technological initiatives calls for a solution for a more manageable data access mechanism that can simultaneously serve multiple applications and insure data integrity. This promise offloads the responsibility of applications to introduce proprietary solutions that are not in line with organizational data architecture standards and policies. Therefore, the discovery of DALS should provide organizational solutions to a small-scale project or a large business initiative.

Determine: Centralized or Distributed DALS?   The responsibility for serving data should be assumed by specialized services that both mediate inbound consumer messages and provide secure access to data. These entities act as proxies that deliver structured information to applications based on predefined configurations and security measurements. Such services should form a data access layer that can be reusable across an organization and hide the complexity that accompanies data retrieval, updating, or deletion operations. This data-serving brokerage functionality can be centralized or federated to benefit data persistence needs of most organizations.

The phrase "centralization of data services" means that an authoritative hub, a focal point that applications can leverage to manipulate data, is formed to control access and to protect and isolate complexities that are affiliated with persistence. Conversely, "federation of data" in an access layer entails that a number of data service groups are spread across an organization or multiple institutions. This typically reduces the pressure of high-volume requests and eliminates a single point of failure by constructing a number of data hubs that can share data-serving responsibilities.

Exhibit 8.8 illustrates these two major data architecture scenarios: centralized and federated. Note that the centralized approach (left) represents a single data access layer that is being utilized by four different applications (A1 to A4). The federated method (right), however, consists of three different data access service groups (1 to 3), each of which offers persistence facilities to eight different

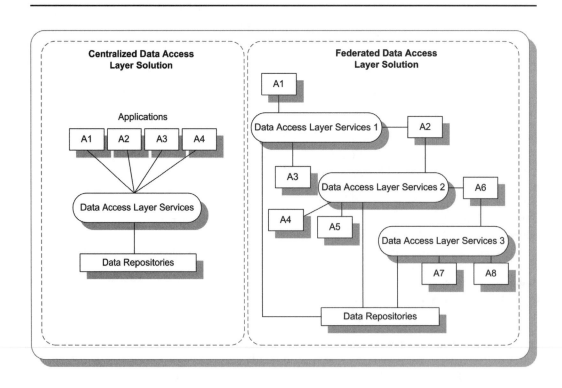

Exhibit 8.8   Centralized and Federated Data Access Layers Services

applications (A1 to A8). In the federated approach, applications A1, A2, and A3 are being served by DALS 1; A2, A4, A5, and A6 utilize DALS 2; and DALS 3 provides services to applications A6 to A8. Note that application A2 is linked to DALS 1 and 2, while application A6 is associated with DALS 2 and 3. This multiple relationship scheme is devised to ensure continuity of operations in the event of the failure of a single data access layer. In addition, each data access layer maintains message exchange associations with its corresponding Data Repositories facility.

Identify Duties of DALS.   During the Back-to-Front service discovery process, data access duties should be identified to enable better understanding of the service layer mission. Doing this will also assist modelers, architects, analysts, managers, and developers in establishing core specialties for the data-serving field. This service discovery activity is motivated by three major driving concerns, each of which is identified with a different implementation perspective: (1) organizational data persistence Standards and Policies, (2) Persistence mechanisms, and (3) Security considerations to enable data access. Exhibit 8.9 depicts these concerns and illustrates the four major DALS functionalities that are also discussed in the sections that follow:

1. Data structure standardization
2. Data persistence
3. Data mapping
4. Data access

Data Structure Standardization.   It is common that for each project launched, practitioners introduce new database schemas and data structures that are unique to their environments. These artifacts typically are upgraded and modified over time by teams that assume data ownership and responsibilities on data access and persistence. This vertical (silo) approach obviously does not benefit organizational standards and may yield duplicate data across the enterprise and produce different structures. The implications are even greater when data conversions must take place during transactions between message exchange parties.

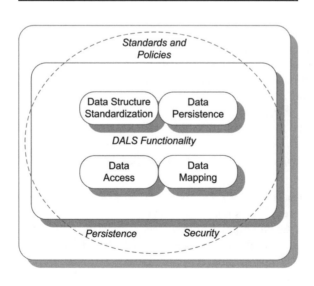

EXHIBIT 8.9   DUTIES AND IMPLEMENTATION CONCERNS OF DALS

To mitigate the inconsistencies between various data formats, the data access layer service must introduce a holistic view of information, a standardized and generalized format that can be used by various projects and applications. This data access layer is designed simply to hide the detail implementation from consumers and thus reduce the complexity affiliated with data manipulation. In addition, from an organizational standard perspective, the data persistence knowledge and expertise is kept in centralized or federated locations that can be reused by different organizations across an enterprise.

This brings us to one of the most important concerns of data structure standardization aspects: lack of an organizational *data canonical model*. The term "canonical" implies that there should be an authoritative version of data structure that people and organizations use to foster compatibility. An institutionalized and recognized data schema can also contribute to the standardization of a message format that can be utilized across an organization. The lack of such customary disciplines poses a major concern for today's production implementations. It can affect performance, increase data management expenditure, and draw down costly human and computer resources.

Data Persistence.   The most important functionalities of the data access layer and its supporting services are the four basic operations on data: (1) create, (2) read, (3) update, and (4) delete (CRUD). As the reader may remember, CRUD operations are also discussed in the Front-to-Back (105) service discovery pattern (Chapter 7) with regard to the presentation layer view. This data persistence functionality is executed within the user's domain, typically coupled with desktop programs, or distributed to a server for the benefit of multiple users. The DALS model proposes a different approach: CRUD operations can be shared among multiple applications. This idea clearly offloads and hides data operations from consumers and thus reduces the client implementation complexity level.

Additionally, on an enterprise level, CRUD operations may be implemented differently. For each of the data operations, a separate service can be dedicated to carry out the persistence task. Organizational service granularity principles, however, should guide practitioners in how to decouple or even unify these operations. Moreover, an enterprise data access service model should incorporate cache capabilities. This feature accelerates data persistence performance by providing memory storage that can rapidly read and update information.

Data Mapping.   The term "data mapping" is associated with a conversion effort that takes place to insure data format compatibility between a service and its related consumers. More specifically, this data-mapping activity is designed to bridge communication barriers between services and corresponding consumers that maintain different data schemas.

Services that provide enterprise-level data-mapping mechanisms typically operate within the data access layer and are an integral part of the data delivery component. This shared functionality is another example of organizational asset reuse capability that is designed to reduce complexity, abstract data manipulation functionality, and hide convoluted implementations from data-consuming entities. Furthermore, by centralizing or federating the ownership of data sources, consumers are excused from maintaining connections and mapping structures to various database resources.

Data Access.   The management of rights to use data resources is another important functionality of the data access services. This is not only a security implementation imperative; it is also a data isolation principle that should govern given privileges for database utilization. The permission that is granted to consumers to utilize data access services is based on three major design principles: context level access, CRUD permission, role permission.

The first principle is the context level, which is based on the information type a consumer is entitled to access. This contextual authorization can grant the rights to perform CRUD operations only on historical data, for example. Other instances would allow manipulation of transactional

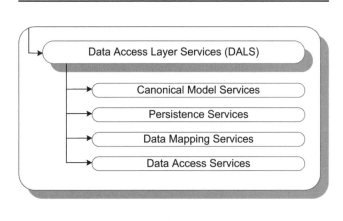

Exhibit 8.10 DALS Taxonomy

data. The second rule applies to the type of CRUD operations consumers are entitled to implement. Some, for example, would be restricted from performing data deletion; others would be prohibited from writing to a database. The third principle is associated with consumer roles and access capabilities. For example, an administrator is allowed to perform unlimited data access configurations; a loan division consumer, however, is permitted to manipulate data that are affiliated with mortgage offerings only.

Delegate DALS Duties to Services. DALS duties should be delegated to specialized services that can carry the mission of enabling access to data sources across the organization. As discussed in the previous sections, DALS offer subject matter expertise in four major fields: data structure standardization across the enterprise, CRUD facilitation and information persistence, data mapping, and access to content. These specialties are illustrated in Exhibit 8.10, which depicts a taxonomy of data access layer entities, a directory that categorizes services by their areas of contribution to the Back-to-Front discovery pattern. Thus, as illustrated, delegate data access duties to four major service groups: Canonical Model Services, Persistence Services, Data Mapping Services, and Data Access Services.

DISCOVER DATA AGGREGATION SERVICES. The term "data aggregation" refers to the act of collecting disbursed data that is made available by multiple sources, such as data repositories, third-party content providers, data warehouses, and even business partners. Once the inbound content is grouped by the collecting services, a process of merging, combining, cleansing, and refining begins. The imperative to combine information from multiple resources and process it on behalf of a consumer provides the reason for aggregating data. The term "consumer" in this context applies to applications or other type of services, such as DALS, that must employ aggregation capabilities.

Data Aggregation Services Architecture Model. A data aggregation service (DAS) acts as a proxy, located between the various content providers and consumers, to serve different types of information for diverse consuming parties and purposes. The offered content, for example, can be historical data reporting, analytical data, market news, diagrams, images and videos, and financial articles. This mediation approach that is provided by DAS typically combines data processing prior to its transmission. Data must be refined and prepared because of its initial raw condition and the different

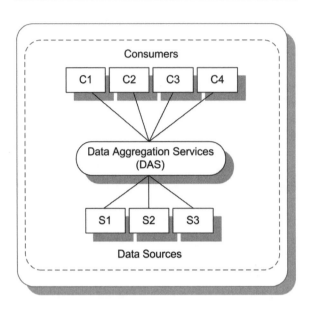

EXHIBIT 8.11   DATA AGGREGATION SERVICES ARCHITECTURE MODEL

formats in which data is being retrieved. Exhibit 8.11 exemplifies a DAS architecture model that consists of three different logical layers: Consumers, Data Aggregation Services, and Data Sources. This pattern illustrates the mediation responsibilities of the DAS.

Study Duties of DAS.   Data aggregation services are chiefly responsible for searching, retrieving, and formatting information on behalf of a consumer. These activities should be performed from *centralized* or *federated* locations. As the reader may remember, we discussed the pros and cons of the two configurations previously in the DALS section. This debate applies to the data aggregation services architecture as well. When aggregation of data takes place in interoperable and distributed environments on an enterprise level, a federated design would better satisfy technical requirements. Such a design can mitigate high-volume data-processing risks when multiple domains demand an extensive amount of information. Centralization of data collection activities, however, is an approach better suited to smaller-scale implementations where fewer applications and services are acting as data consumers.

The duties of the DAS are designed to mitigate three major architectural concerns across an organization: Interoperability challenges, compliance with Loose-Coupling best practices, and data Format Standardization. These are the motivating drivers to the three chief DAS designated functionalities, as depicted in Exhibit 8.12: Data Searching, Data collection, and Data Transformation. These functionalities are discussed in the sections that follow.

Data Searching.   Data searching is the activity that is assigned to DAS to locate the proper data source provider and insure that the found data indeed offers the correct data type that is required for retrieval. From a data locating perspective term "data type" pertains to the context of the data and not to its format. For example, a data searching activity may be focused on financial market news or on foreign affairs news. Again, the data searching task is not about data retrieval, it is merely about searching and validating data types (data collection duties are discussed in the next section).

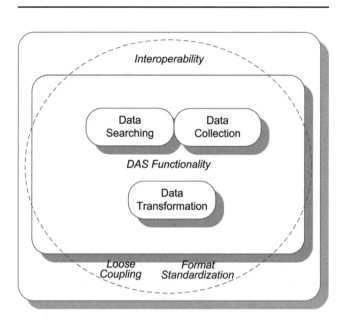

EXHIBIT 8.12   DAS DUTIES

This simple concept involves two major search approaches: *contractual* and *public*. The contractual approach is founded upon an agreement that a data source provider and DAS must obey. This accord is designed to link the parties to predefined schedule and terms of data searching. Thus, this searching process is guided by a prearranged contract that identifies the providing entity and classifies in advance the data type and quantity that will be collected. The information that is searched can be obtained by utilizing metadata tags (data descriptions, known as data about data) or even data taxonomy matching, whereby a predefined data taxonomy drives the types of data that DAS is committed to search for.

Alternatively, the public searching method is devised to search data whose location and context is unknown. In other words, there is no prior knowledge about a data provider, its origin, and the exact type of information it serves. Unknown parameters such as this introduce challenges that are typically remediated by probabilistic and fuzzy logic algorithms,[2] searching mechanisms that are driven by matching of imprecise association of information.

For environments that require business continuity and stability, the recommended approach for data searching is the contractual method. DAS implementation, therefore, should rely on steady inflow of data that was committed prior to any data retrieval activity. This would guarantee that information providers and data resources are available upon request.

Data Collection.   Data collection is an activity that is designated to DAS to collect and assemble data from various data source providers across the enterprise or even beyond its jurisdiction after the searching activity (described in the previous section) has been concluded. Therefore, this duty should not be confused with data searching tasks. Here a DAS is merely assigned to retrieve that data that has been found previously.

Data collection activities that are designed to serve a large number of consumers can be complex and typically require advanced and diverse technologies to enable the proper flow of data.

Multiple protocols and message-exchange methods may be required to enable flawless communications with information provider facilities.

Consider examples of technologies and formats that are commonly employed by DAS for data collection activities:

- Really Simple Syndication (RSS) feeds
- Binary data
- File transfer protocol (FTP)
- Object transmission
- Real-time streaming of data
- Asynchronous data exchange (employing message buses or enterprise service buses)
- Retrieval from data cache facilities
- Data collection from virtual data aggregation installations (discussed later in the Discover Virtual Data Layer Services section in the chapter)

Furthermore, relationships between the involved parties may be formed across different networks, business domains, interoperable technological environments, or even continents. This collaboration may be institutionalized by a contract, but in some cases a more informal relationship is required.

Two rudimentary bonds can be established with a data-providing facility:

1. **Restricted contract.** Parties agree on a timetable, data types, data structures, and consumption volume. These conditions are usually enforced by an automated service-level agreement.
2. **Loose contract.** A casual or noncommitting agreement in which data is voluntarily offered by a service provider.

Data Transformation.   Transformation activities are performed after the data has been searched and retrieved from various data sources and providers. Data conversion, enrichment, and cleansing is required because of the diversified data formats and types. These activities produce rudimentary and yet intensive modifications to the retrieved raw data designed to translate complex data formats, treat high volume of information, and map data types.

For example, imagine that medical patient records, retrieved by DAL, would require transformation from the received format to objects. Other instances would necessitate not only conversions of one format to another but also enrichment of the content itself. The term "enrichment" suggests that augmentation of information is needed. Such augmentation can include appending patient address and medication history. Moreover, cleansing is another important activity that takes place when the data is transformed: unwanted characters, tags, and unreadable and nonprintable information can be stripped out to prepare data for future user's view.

One of the most common methods employed to transform data is applying Extensible Style Sheet Language Transformations (XSLT).[3] This is an XML-based language utilized for converting Extensible Stylesheet Language (XSL) documents into text, HTML, or to other XML files.

Delegate DAS Duties to Services.   Delegate data searching, data collection, and date transformation duties to specialize services that are designed to offer data aggregation specialties. But before embarking on such initiative provide a service taxonomy, a directory of services categorized by their capability to offer a solution in the field of information aggregation. This taxonomy should also service a glossary of services that will enable practitioners to understand the context and the goals of the project. Moreover, when carving the DAS taxonomy, similar to Exhibit 8.13, identify the high-level service groups and drill down to specific services that can carry out data aggregation duties.

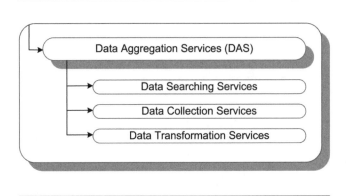

EXHIBIT 8.13   DAS TAXONOMY

DISCOVER VIRTUAL DATA LAYER SERVICES.   Data virtualization is an emerging discipline practice that is worth pursuing. Its best practices simply advocate consolidating software and hardware, by emulating physical environments. This technology has been embedded in numerous vendors' products to alleviate data integration challenges.

Substantial computing and data manipulation efforts, such as migration of data from one location to another or aggregation of information that is collected from multiple providing facilities, can be emulated by data virtualization technologies that can reduce physical implementation expenditure and resources. In fact, the promise of the data virtualization paradigm embodies architecture best practices that have been fostered for decades. These are also the cornerstone tenets of service-oriented architecture that were devised to increase reuse of computing assets and reduce human, software, and hardware expense. Thus, the duty of virtualizing data operations should be assigned to virtual data layer services (VDLS) to enhance data searching, collection, migration, and aggregation mechanisms.

VDLS Model.   Data virtualization establishes an organizational virtual computing discipline that abstracts physical data, reduces complexities, and encourages standardization of data schemas across the organization. This idea eliminates that need for physically moving or replicating substantial amounts of content that resides remotely on distributed servers to consumers' domains.

All operations on data are being performed in centralized or distributed virtual locations that are simulated to the extent they look real. For example, migration of multiple data resources would not actually yield physical movement of large data chunks from one server to another. This activity typically is achieved by creation of *views* that virtually unify and match content that is distributed to multiple business domains and production facilities. Thus, virtual data layer services should assume the responsibility for forming an organizational data mediation entity that enables a uniform view of data.

Exhibit 8.14 illustrates this VDLS model. It depicts three major layers, each of which participates in data virtualization activities.

1. The Consumer Layer (on top) consists of four consumers (C1 to C4).
2. The second layer, the Virtual Data Layer, is comprised of two major implementations: Virtual Data View and Data Service. Note that consumers C2 and C4 utilize two views each. This identifies the necessity to use more than a single data view if necessary.
3. The Data Repository and Provider Layer depicts that various sources of data offerings, such as Data Warehouse, Data Providers, and even Web services that are designed to serve data.

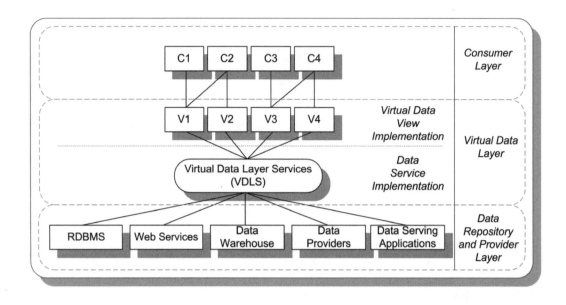

EXHIBIT 8.14   VDLS MODEL

Study VDLS Duties.   With today's technology capabilities, most of data delivery, aggregation, and manipulation can be executed by virtual data layer services. This encompasses the logical layer functionality of the data model discussed thus far in this chapter. Hence, DALS and DAS responsibilities can be virtualized by VDLS. Exhibit 8.15 outlines the data virtualization layer duties that are devised to accommodate data layer functionalities.

Functionality	Contribution
Employment of virtual data views	Creation of specialized consumers' views to enable virtual perspectives of disbursed data
Virtual data aggregation	Collection of data from multiple data sources and providers by avoiding physical data duplication
Data caching	Providing memory persistence facilities to accelerate data manipulation activities
Virtual data integration	Virtually integrate data that is retrieved from multiple resources
Canonical data model establishment	Founding of an organizational authoritative data model
Data transformation	Transformation of data structures and schemas
Message mediation	Interception of messages to ensure security and protect data integrity
Policy and security enforcements	Application of security policies to guard data
Service contract monitoring	Tracing contract breaches and data consumption allowance
Storage virtualization	Offer data storage virtualization to save on storage space facilities
Virtual data migration	Providing virtual data migration capabilities to avoid physical movement of data
Virtual data marts	Offering virtual subject matter data storage for lines of business (data marts are typically components of a data warehouse.)
Virtual data replication	Reducing needs for physical data replication across the organization

EXHIBIT 8.15   MAJOR VDLS DUTIES

Repository	Contribution
Transactional data	Transactional repositories contain data that is related to real-time message exchange information: for example, audit trails, security tracing and monitoring, storage of message content, and trading orders
Analytical data	Storage associated with historical data that can be used to generate analysis reporting for business initiatives and obtain the state of commerce, product sales, and customer orders
Knowledge base data	Knowledge base that stores product information, operating manuals, research, and engineering material about business and technology expert matters
Documentation storage	Data storage that facilitates the persistence of organizational documents for common sharing
Multimedia storage	A repository dedicated to the storage of media artifacts, such as images, videos, graphs, illustrations, diagrams, voice streams, articles, blogs, and tables
Policy data storage	A policy repository containing organizational security and management-related data, sometimes consisting of security configurations, service contracts, and service-level agreements
Metadata repositories	Catalogs that consist of data descriptions (data about data) and are useful for classifying and retrieving content and information across the enterprise
Data-mining storage	Storage of information associated with market research material, such as client and market segmentation, customer satisfaction research, and sales and promotion analysis

EXHIBIT 8.16   ORGANIZATIONAL DATA STORAGE TAXONOMY EXAMPLE

PHYSICAL DATA MODEL PERSPECTIVE

The third data model component that drives the Back-to-Front service discovery efforts identifies the physical means by which information is stored. Data repositories are not the only facilities that the physical perspective addresses. It also can include data farms, data warehouses, data marts, data grids and clusters, distributed data to geographical locations, and other data architecture production facilities that are managed by an organization or its partners.

STUDY CLASSIFICATION OF PHYSICAL DATA STORAGE.   To enable efficient discovery of services, organizational data should be classified and grouped on the foundation of an enterprise data taxonomy that identifies physical storage needs. This categorization process typically is influenced by various business domains and technology interests. For example, a small business loan division would arrange data stores according to its *transactional* or *analytical* information requirements. This classification can further yield subcategories, such as business profile, risk assessment, and credit verification databases. Consider the common enterprise data categories, a high-level data taxonomy that contributes to segmentation of information physically stored across an organization shown in Exhibit 8.16.

IDENTIFY PHYSICAL LAYER SERVICES AND THEIR DUTIES.   The service discovery process that is driven by the physical perspective is focused merely on opportunities to improve data delivery and to reduce or consolidate physical facilities by identifying motivations for service construction. But remember, this perspective does not present a virtual view. It is simply established upon the various tangible facilities that an organization owns to provide data. Therefore, the mission here is to utilize services designed to augment or save on the physical data facilities investments. Consider the major physical layer services (PLS) functionality that is depicted in Exhibit 8.17.

BACK-TO-FRONT SERVICE DISCOVERY PROCESS

The Back-to-Front service discovery process is rooted in technological capabilities. Business requirements are artifacts that should not be disregarded, but the driving aspects are obviously

Functionality	Contribution
Persistence of analytical assets	Maintaining history records and enabling access to reporting data
Reporting facilities	Providing management and technical reports
Gathering customer and market segmentation Information	Supporting data-mining storage, collecting market and client research material
Persistence of organizational multimedia assets	Managing organizational multimedia storage assets and their publications
Providing transactional data storage support	Recording transaction data, audit trail, and operation errors and exception handling information
Monitoring storage facilities	Monitoring consumption and storage capacity and handling alerts
Providing physical data replication solutions	Participating in data replication operations
Offering disaster recovery (DR) mechanisms	Mitigating DR risks and offering alternatives during downtime to ensure business continuity
Maintaining management and security policies databases	Providing storage for security policies and management for software development life cycle facilities
Collecting and maintaining knowledge research material for knowledge base storage	Supporting knowledge base systems by enabling access and retrieval of articles
Document sharing storage	Offering support for professional documentation-sharing facilities

EXHIBIT 8.17   MAJOR PLS DUTIES

technical specifications. When pursuing this venture, we must remember that every service discovery endeavor that is driven by intrinsic architectural artifacts, such as best practices and blueprints, is in fact motivated by the technological capacity of an organization. The Back-to-Front discovery approach falls into this category because data delivery services are designed to offer consumers with technical means for information searching, retrieval, data manipulation, data aggregation, data transformation, data enrichment, security, and more.

ADHERE TO THE SERVICE DISCOVERY PROCESS.   The technical path that we are about to pursue should consist of three major steps, each of which contributes to the final discovery of data delivery services. The goal and the leading road map are illustrated in Exhibit 8.18.

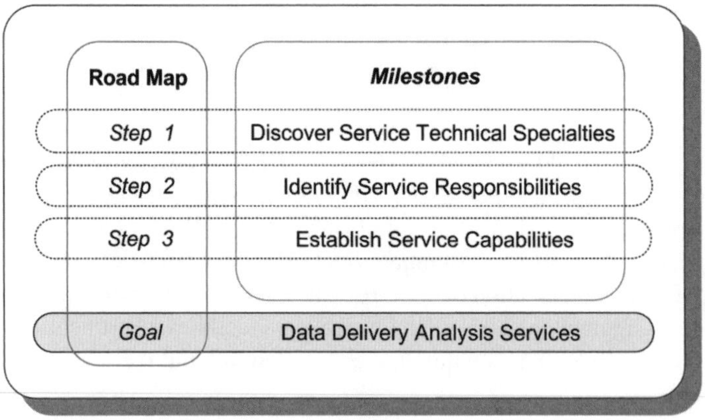

EXHIBIT 8.18   BACK-TO-FRONT SERVICE DISCOVERY PROCESS

1. **Discover Service Technical Specialties.** These are areas of data delivery expertise that services can contribute to.
2. **Identify Service Responsibilities.** As the reader may remember from previous discovery chapters, responsibilities are *candidate service operations* that have not been established.
3. **Establish Service Capabilities.** Again, capabilities are *established service operations* yielded by an analysis process.

DISCOVER DATA SERVICE TECHNICAL SPECIALTIES.   A technical specialty is a service's field of knowledge and expertise that is utilized to resolve a problem. For example, a collection of information from various data sources and providers is the art of data aggregation that only particular types of services can implement. Searching is another sort of expertise assigned to an information locator type of service capable of identifying matching data for consumers. These specialties are fundamental to the service discovery process because they help set its scope and assist with separation-of-concerns activities by encouraging detailed breakdown of requirements. (Refer to Chapter 2 for a detailed discussion about separation-of-concerns.)

What are the data model requirements that can contribute to the identification of service specialties? These are the various imperatives of the three data model perspectives discussed thus far: Conceptual, Logical, and Physical, which are illustrated in Exhibit 8.19. Note that the combined requirements yield service specialties that will be developed later into candidate service operations (also known as service responsibilities).

The data model conceptual perspective requirements are reflected in data entity diagrams that depict data abstractions as motivating sources for building services. The logical perspective's artifacts, such as database schemas and XML formats, also contribute to the discovery of specialties. Last, the physical perspective imperatives can be utilized to found service specialties that are associated with the segmentation of data sources based on business domains and data storage requirements (refer to Exhibit 8.16 for a data source taxonomy and physical data sources.)

Finally, let us view the example that is depicted in Exhibit 8.20. The technical requirement "Aggregate Customer Profile Information" derives three major data service specialties: Customer Records Searching, Customer Data Collection, and Customer Data Transformation. As previously indicated, these fields of expertise will lead to service responsibilities (candidate service operations). The discovery of responsibilities is discussed in the next section.

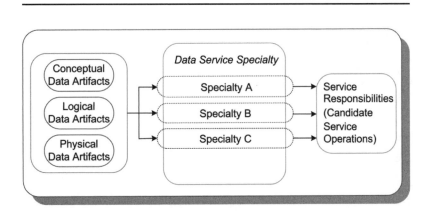

EXHIBIT 8.19   DATA SERVICE SPECIALTIES SOURCES

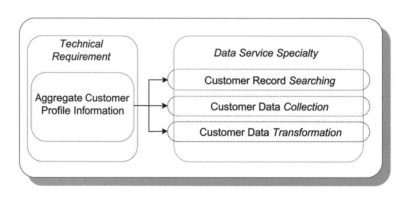

EXHIBIT 8.20   SERVICE TECHNICAL SPECIALTIES EXAMPLE

IDENTIFY SERVICE RESPONSIBILITIES.   At this stage we are commissioned to discover service responsibilities that stem from each specialty identified in the previous section. Remember, responsibilities are simply candidate service operations that are assumed at this juncture to execute future service functionality. Architects, analysts, modelers, developers, and managers should rely upon their technical expertise to accomplish this task. They should leverage analysis and whiteboard sessions for identifying future service capabilities. Exhibit 8.21 exemplifies the corresponding candidate operations that stem from the three major service technical specialties that have been established in the previous section.

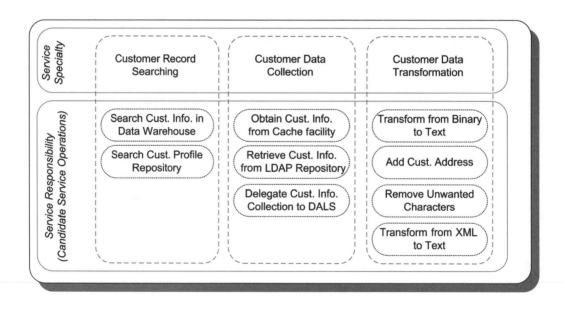

EXHIBIT 8.21   DISCOVERY-OF-SERVICE RESPONSIBILITIES EXAMPLE

DISCOVER ANALYSIS DATA SERVICES: ESTABLISH SERVICE CAPABILITIES.   The process of transforming candidate service operations (responsibilities) to final service operations (capabilities) does not necessarily have to be a complicated task. In some circumstances, however, an analysis process can last for days because of the large number of operations that must be verified and established. If the service responsibility identification effort is heading in the right direction and the findings are satisfactory, the discovery of final operations and the corresponding services should be quick.

Derive Data Service Capabilities from Service Responsibilities.   To establish final data service operations that stem from responsibilities (candidate service operations), pursue one of these activities or combine them:

- **Elimination.** Disregard a candidate operation if it is not relevant to a service's capability.
- **Merging.** Combine two or more candidate operations if their functionality is redundant.
- **Renaming.** Alter an operation's name if it does not reflect its promised functionality.
- **Breaking up.** Separate a candidate operation into two or more functionalities to ensure proper granularity.
- **Augmenting.** Add operations because of missing functionality.

Discover Data Delivery Services.   The final step of the Back-to-Front data service discovery process simply advocates that we bundle the firmed-up service operations (capabilities) into groups, each of which forms a separate service. Exhibit 8.22 illustrates this process. The three discovered services—Information Locator Service, Customer Record Aggregation Service, and Customer Record Transformation Service—are comprised of corresponding service operations that were derived from candidate operations. Remember that the final product is analysis service, as all service discovery patterns advocate in this book.

A quick comparison between Exhibits 8.21 and 8.22 reveals that there is no one-to-one correlation between candidate and final service operations. Obviously, the analysis process, to a

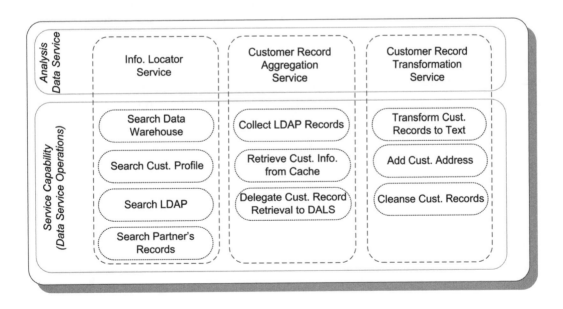

EXHIBIT 8.22   DISCOVERY-OF-SERVICE CAPABILITIES EXAMPLE

large extent, yielded dissimilar service functionality. This should be an expected outcome due to practical and technical reasons that may include reduction of redundancy, unfeasible technical tasks, or costly features that exceed the anticipated returns on investment.

Let us take a look at these Exhibits (8.21 and 8.22) and note some of most noticeable changes that were made to the candidate service operations during the establishment process of the final service operations:

- The Transform from Binary to Text and Transform from XML to Text candidate operations (in the service specialty Customer Data Transformation) were combined into a more generic format transformation functionality (in the Customer Record Transformation Service): Transform Cust. Records to Text.
- The operations Search LDAP and Search Partner's Records were added to the Info. Locator Service. This functionality was missing.
- The Search Cust. Info. in Data Warehouse (candidate service operation) was renamed to Search Data Warehouse to conform with other organizational existing implementations (in the Info. Locator Service).

DELIVERABLES

Develop an organizational data model that can be utilized for Back-to-Front service discovery efforts. The data model should consist of three major views that can broaden the service identification process. Conceptual, logical, and physical perspectives are the pillars of the data model. Each of these should offer diversified avenues and opportunities to discover new services.

SUMMARY

- The Back-to-Front service discovery pattern begins with the inspection of data artifacts, such as repositories, diagrams, and data descriptions.
- The Back-to-Front service discovery process is established upon a data model that consists of three major perspective: conceptual, logical, and physical.
- These data model perspectives contribute to the discovery of services that specialize in a wide range of fields of expertise, such as data delivery, data access, data aggregation, institution of a canonical data model, data security and privacy, and more.

Notes

1. Peter P. S. Chen, *Entity-Relationship Approach to Information Modeling And Analysis* (Rome, Italy), p. 20.
2. www.seattlerobotics.org/Encoder/mar98/fuz/fl_part1.html.
3. www.xml.com/pub/a/2002/03/27/templatexslt.html.
4. www.compositesoftware.com/solutions/data_virtualization.shtml.

CHAPTER 9

BOTTOM-UP SERVICE DISCOVERY PATTERN

To enable reuse of legacy applications and services for future implementations, the Bottom-Up service discovery pattern is devised to incorporate ready-made software solutions that have been proposed, designed, and constructed for past projects and business initiatives. It calls for a service identification process that begins with the inspection of existing software artifacts, such as source code, application components, architecture blueprints, and enabling middleware technologies. Therefore, consider the Bottom-Up service discovery effort as a vital pattern that can facilitate identification of services by starting from existing software entities that have been road tested, withstood market volatility, and endured technical challenges. Moreover, the chief goal of the Bottom-Up discovery pattern is to contribute to reduction of organizational expenditure by focusing on repurposing legacy executables, reconciling software products, and minimizing functionality redundancy.

Analysis of the software products that have been operating in production environments and the assessment of their possible contribution to a future project is a good start. It must be followed by discovering new services that can fill in the implementation gaps and offer the missing capabilities that are required to meet new business requirements and technical specifications. That is, the missing functionality should be assigned to new services that are devised to face impending challenges, increase the consumer base, and yet employ legacy applications and services.

To effectively accomplish these goals, the pursuit of Bottom-Up service discovery pattern should be driven by a service identification model that consists of three different views, as depicted in Exhibit 9.1. These three perspectives and the method of discovery are discussed in detail in the sections that follow.

1. **Legacy Software Assets:** This discovery perspective identifies existing automated business functionality and product offerings that should be utilized for a future solution. Found missing implementations are typically assigned to new services.
2. **Existing Technologies:** The existing technologies view introduces middleware and communication products that can be leveraged for solving new problems.
3. **Existing Architectures:** This perspective is another aspect that should be employed to provide new remedies to an organizational concern.[1] It can be accomplished by identifying the gaps between the end-state architecture and current reference architecture. Each of these perspectives is discussed in detail in the sections that follow.

BOTTOM-UP BUSINESS FUNCTIONALITY–DRIVEN SERVICE DISCOVERY

Rather than starting with a high-level examination of business processes and activities, as devised in the Top-Down (71) service discovery pattern (Chapter 5), the Bottom-Up service discovery method that is driven by business functionality analysis of existing software products begins from software implementations that already provide business solutions in production. This approach is founded on

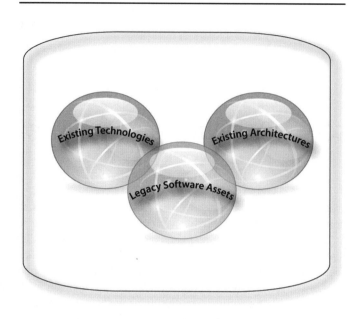

EXHIBIT 9.1 BOTTOM-UP SERVICE DISCOVERY MODEL

the notion that the inspected legacy applications and services have been road-tested and proven to have contributed to business execution.

Moreover, the chief charter of this service discovery approach calls for indentifying services by revealing functionality *gaps* in current implementations. The term "gaps" refers to software components and modules that have never been constructed and obviously are not part of the existing applications and services. To discover missing functionality, we focus on executables that have been put into action in production environments. We then start at the bottom to examine their concrete capabilities and climb up to meet unaddressed business imperatives.

This approach also advocates that we stay the course on business analysis and avoid drawing attention to technical implementations. While pursuing the process of service identification, at each step we are presented with new service opportunities. These new propositions should fill in the gaps between legacy solutions and new business requirements.

ADHERE TO THE BOTTOM-UP BUSINESS-DRIVEN SERVICE DISCOVERY PROCESS. The reader may remember that the Top-Down (71) service discovery pattern driven by business processes (Chapter 5) advocates that we start with the identification of business specialties and finally conclude with the establishment of service capabilities (firmed up operations). Conversely, here the Bottom-Up approach recommends that we take an opposite direction: The starting baseline is service capabilities (operations), moving up to found business specialties. Pursuing this reverse direction may require a number of iterations starting at the bottom and reaching high-level business imperatives. In addition, for verification purposes and firming up the findings, practitioners may find it helpful to pursue the Top-Down (71) pattern after the Bottom-Up approach has concluded.

Study the Four Steps of Service Discovery Analysis. The process of service identification that is based on the inspection of business functionality is driven by four major layers of analysis that architects, modelers, analysts, developers, and managers should pursue. These are depicted in Exhibit 9.2.

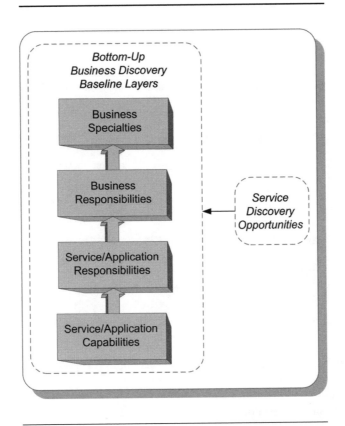

EXHIBIT 9.2   BOTTOM-UP BUSINESS-DRIVEN DISCOVERY MODEL

Each inspection level presents service discovery opportunities, starting at the concrete stage (existing software assets) and concluding with the identification of business processes and specialties. While pursuing this approach, an important point to remember is that the chief efforts should focus on identifying missing operations and ultimately discovering business processes. Doing this would enable practitioners to establish solid services that, on the low level, fill implementation gaps and, on the high level, provide business motivation.

Exhibit 9.2 details the major service discovery opportunities that are offered by the four levels of analysis: (1) Service/Application Capabilities, (2) Service/Application Responsibilities, (3) Business Responsibilities, and (4) Business Specialties. Again, these are the same steps that practitioners pursue during the Top-Down service discovery process. However, here we start from the bottom.

Understand the Service Discovery Road Map.   As discussed, Bottom-Up service discovery should focus on the identification of operations and business processes that ultimately yield services that can augment existing implementations. This process is straightforward, and each of its stages should lead to the identification of artifacts similar to those required by the Top-Down approach. For example, the identification of service responsibilities activity should yield candidate service operations. In the same manner, the establishment of business responsibilities leads to the identification of business activities and business processes.

Exhibit 9.3 depicts four major Bottom-Up steps (displayed on the left panel), each of which contributes to the service identification process. Optionally, as mentioned previously, practitioners

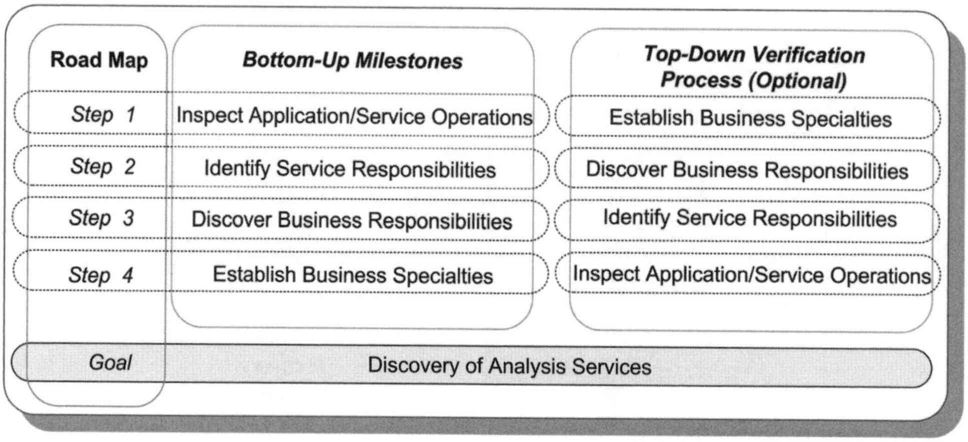

Road Map	Bottom-Up Milestones	Top-Down Verification Process (Optional)
Step 1	Inspect Application/Service Operations	Establish Business Specialties
Step 2	Identify Service Responsibilities	Discover Business Responsibilities
Step 3	Discover Business Responsibilities	Identify Service Responsibilities
Step 4	Establish Business Specialties	Inspect Application/Service Operations
Goal	Discovery of Analysis Services	

EXHIBIT 9.3   BOTTOM-UP BUSINESS FUNCTIONALITY DRIVEN SERVICE DISCOVERY PROCESS

can subsequently implement the Top-Down method (illustrated on the right) for verification purposes. These processes are also discussed in the sections that follow:

1. Start with the analysis of existing software capabilities (operations).
2. Identify service responsibilities.
3. Discover business responsibilities.
4. Establish business specialties.

START WITH ANALYSIS OF EXISTING SOFTWARE CAPABILITIES.   What is the starting point of the capability analysis endeavor? What artifacts would be required to identify unimplemented functionality that can lead to the discovery of new services? We begin simply with the examination of existing application and service capabilities. These are the operations that enable the execution of solutions to organizational problems. More specifically, these include fine-grained implementations that are carried by software routines, remote procedure calls, and methods—namely *operations*.

To facilitate a rigorous study of this material, we should simply focus on gathering and learning the artifacts that led to the existing construction of a software product. These deliverables typically can amount to myriad documents, graphical presentations, and modeling deliverables that are affiliated with prior projects and deployments to production efforts. Furthermore, one of the most important analysis sources that can shed light on existing and planned products is an organizational application and service portfolio repository. This facility can identify both software reuse and consolidation opportunities.

Exhibit 9.4 summarizes the four major capability analysis input sources and their corresponding detailed documentation: Functional Requirements, Technical Specifications, Commercial Off-the-Shelf Product Specifications, and Application and Service Portfolio Management Software. These depicted artifacts may include technical material that does necessarily apply to business functionality. However, analysts, architects, modelers, developers, and managers should focus merely on software behavior and business functionality.

While studying the compiled material of existing software functionality, identify service discovery opportunities and think about other mechanisms that can be implemented to augment the missing functionality. Obviously creating new services is a compelling remedy; however, extending

Input Sources	Documentation Details
Functional Requirements	Software behavioral diagrams and logical design documents, such as use case diagrams, flowchart diagrams, sequence diagrams, orchestration and business process modeling artifacts
Technical Specifications	Message specifications and interfaces that include input and output operation descriptions and data types
Commercial Off-the-Shelf Product Specifications	Product manuals, product architecture blueprints, flowchart and sequence diagrams, product functional specifications
Application and Service Portfolio Management Software	Profile of applications and services and description of their functionalities

EXHIBIT 9.4   MAJOR CAPABILITY ANALYSIS INPUTS

software operations can be implemented in a variety of methods. Consider three common options that organizations typically adopt to minimize the efforts to construct new services:

1. Identify opportunities to adding source code (known as wrapping) to enable compatibility with external services, applications, or any other software program. This method would augment the missing functionality by employing external executables.
2. Explore opportunities to employ off-the-shelf (read to use) adapters to expand software functionality by increasing its compatibility with other applications or services.
3. Implement the Façade pattern for message routing to employ alternative existing implementations that reside elsewhere in the enterprise.

DEFINE SERVICE RESPONSIBILITIES DRIVEN BY GAP ANALYSIS.   Organizational architecture best practices characteristically foster software reuse and consolidation by advocating utilization of existing legacy software features over development of new capabilities. This strategy calls for conducting a gap analysis study to learn more about the reuse of existing assets and their current functionality. Unfortunately, such an inspection typically reveals that there is no exact match between new business requirements and software solutions that were developed in past projects.

Therefore, the gap analysis effort is about comparing new business requirements against existing implementations. If no match is found, the next step would be to identify missing functionality and help carve out a remediation plan. The term "remediation" pertains to the mechanism that allows missing operations to be added to satisfy business imperatives. As discussed in the previous section, there are a few options to consider: wrapping existing code, employing adapters, adding facade components, or devising new services if justified.

One of the driving motivations for constructing new services to bridge the implementation gaps can be justified by defining service responsibilities—candidate service operations—for the missing functionality. This initiative is similar to the Top-Down approach. Here, however, existing operations serve as analysis material for instituting missing service responsibilities. Exhibit 9.5 illustrates this concept. Patient history and diagnosis functionalities are among the existing operations that are depicted in the Service Capability section (on the bottom). These are delivered by two services: Patient Profile Service and Patience Diagnosis Service. Displayed above is the Service Responsibility (Candidate Service Operations) panel that identifies missing doctor appointment implementation.

DISCOVER BUSINESS RESPONSIBILITIES: IDENTIFY BUSINESS ACTIVITIES AND ESTABLISH BUSINESS PROCESSES.   The reader may remember (from Chapter 5) that fine-grained business activities are regarded as business responsibilities. In addition, a group of related activities make up a business process. For example, associated activities, such as get customer name and address, get customer total investment value, and get customer household yearly income, constitute the

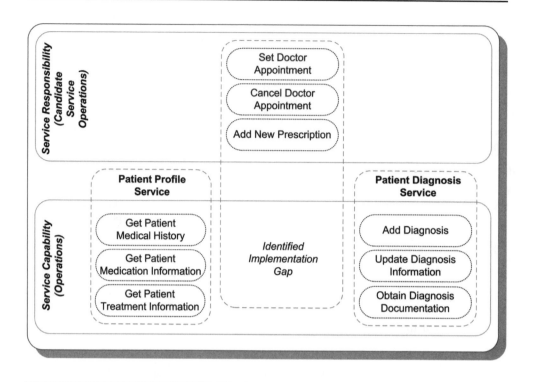

EXHIBIT 9.5 IDENTIFYING CANDIDATE SERVICE OPERATIONS EXAMPLE

customer profile business process. These business functionalities should now be identified to enable a thorough service discovery process.

One would simply argue that identifying business activities and instituting business processes at this stage would contribute little to the service identification effort. Indeed, the candidate service operations that were discovered in the previous step (featured in the last section) may provide enough clues for instituting new services. The reason for continuing with the upward analysis to discover business processes and later business specialties (discussed in the next section) is associated with two major Bottom-Up service identification aspects:

1. Enable a Top-Down process for verification of the discovered services. This is an optional action practice that can be pursued.
2. Allow more opportunities for finding services by identifying higher business abstractions—the business processes and their corresponding activities.

Now the time has come to identify business processes and their underlying activities that stem from the service responsibilities (candidate service operations) discovered in the last step. This effort requires the participation of business personnel and analysts who are able to assist with the discovery of new business processes. Exhibit 9.6 exemplifies this process, which includes three major sections: Service Responsibilities (candidate service operations that appear on bottom), Business Responsibilities (business activities that are depicted on the top), and three Business Processes columns that are made up of the business activities. Note that the illustrated business processes Manage Appointments, Manage Prescription, and Book Clinic and their corresponding enclosed activities were derived from the candidate service operations (responsibilities) that were discovered during the gap analysis in the previous section. This derivation task should be handled by skilled

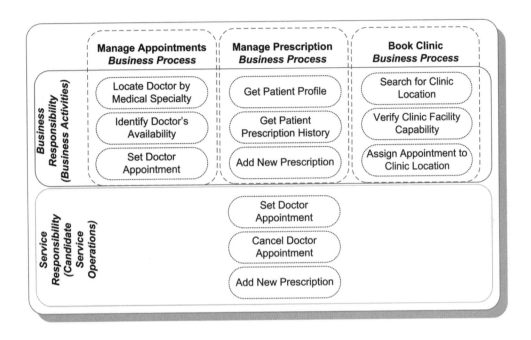

Exhibit 9.6   Identifying Business Activities and Processes Example

practitioners that on one hand are familiar with the software product, and on the other, understand the business. Note important facts about this effort:

- Group related business activities to form a business process.
- Typically there is no direct correlation between candidate service operations and business activities.
- The guiding principle suggests that the scope of business activities should be expanded to enable the discovery of more candidate service operations in future iterations. This can be achieved by pursuing the Top-Down verification process.
- The expansion of functionality introduced by the identified business activities may result in redundant or existing implementations. From an analysis standpoint, this is encouraged to enable coverage of missing operations.

CONCLUDE WITH THE DISCOVERY OF BUSINESS SPECIALTIES.   As the reader may remember, a specialty is an area of business expertise, a practice that is established both to guide practitioners to conduct the service identification process and to enable the grouping and classification of affiliated business processes. A business specialty is also a high-level abstraction of a business necessity that sets the direction of future service development. Therefore, identify a set of business specialties that corresponds to the discovered business processes discussed in the previous section. This effort is required to complete the Bottom-Up service discovery undertaking and allow future service verification that can employ the Top-Down service-oriented identification process (optional).

Exhibit 9.7 depicts two major business specialties (on top) that stem from the Business Responsibility section (on the bottom): Appointment Management and Prescription Management. Note that the Appointment Management specialty pertains to two business processes: Manage Appointments Business Process and Book Clinic Business Process. The Prescription Management specialty, however, was derived from the Manage Prescription Business Process.

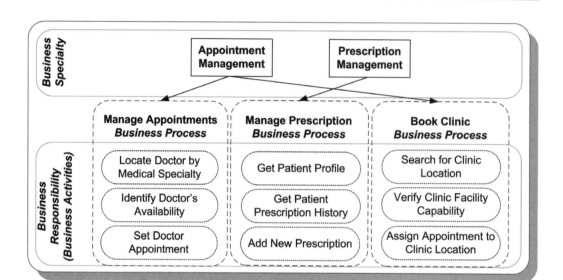

EXHIBIT 9.7   IDENTIFYING BUSINESS SPECIALTIES EXAMPLE

BOTTOM-UP TECHNOLOGY-DRIVEN SERVICE DISCOVERY

The investment in technology during years or decades provides incentives to leverage legacy implementations rather than replace them. The acquired knowledge and development expertise in a variety of supporting standards, communications, and security fields should be preserved to reduce organizational expenditure and accelerate time to market.

The Bottom-Up technology-driven service discovery approach advocates that we analyze technical capabilities of existing software. The artifacts that result are proposed services that identify gaps in technical implementations. Once constructed, these missing software features must satisfy technical specifications. In other words, the motivation for this initiative is provided by new technical requirements that call for the inspection of existing solutions before constructing new services.

We thus focus on the technology that empowers our legacy applications and services. The term "technology" does not refer to the architecture or design patterns. Here technology pertains to the mix of enabling technical ingredients used to support software operations and integration, such as protocols, network, application servers, language platforms, file formats, digital certificates, firewalls, cache facilities, configuration, security frameworks, and more. Commercial off-the-shelf products (COTS) are also regarded as technology constituents. These, for example, may offer consumer and service communication means, message routing and orchestration, and service life cycle management software packages.

ATTEND TO SERVICE DISCOVERY PROCESS.   The process of discovering services that stem from existing technologies is straightforward. It must follow a three-step methodological approach that guides architects, modelers, developers, and analysts to identify services.

1.   Start with establishing a *technology baseline model*, a foundation that identifies the currently employed technical ingredients that support exiting applications and services in production environment.
2.   Define the technical capabilities of a software product that is anchored in the baseline technology model. This would expand the scope beyond the narrow view of a particular

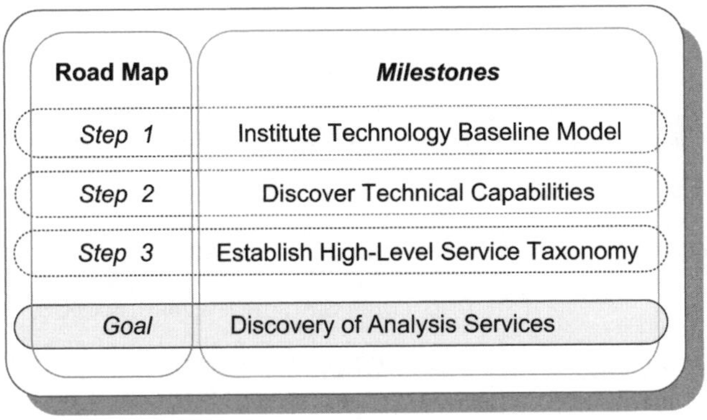

Road Map	Milestones
Step 1	Institute Technology Baseline Model
Step 2	Discover Technical Capabilities
Step 3	Establish High-Level Service Taxonomy
Goal	Discovery of Analysis Services

EXHIBIT 9.8   BOTTOM-UP TECHNOLOGY-DRIVEN SERVICE DISCOVERY PROCESS

implementation and provide an opportunity to strengthen the solution by enlarging the spectrum of service offerings.

3. Create a high-level service taxonomy that can assist with the identification of new services. This service categorization approach would enable practitioners both to arrange services based on their area of expertise and to discover the implementation gaps that should be addressed.

This brings us to the final goal: institution of analysis services that will participate in service life cycle development.

Exhibit 9.8 illustrates the Bottom-Up technology-driven service discovery process. Three steps should be pursued to identify services:

1. Institute Technology Baseline Model.
2. Discover Technical Capabilities.
3. Establish High-Level Service Taxonomy.

A detailed explanation of these activities is provided in the sections that follow.

INSTITUTE TECHNOLOGY BASELINE MODEL.   A baseline model is simply a list of existing software technologies that are utilized for supporting applications, services, or COTS products in a production environment. These are the fundamental technical ingredients of every software implementation that must flawlessly operate to ensure business continuity and demonstrate technical stability. Hence, think of a baseline model as a catalog of road tested technical mechanisms and standards without which it would be impossible to *build, deploy, and run* any software component, module, service, or application. Remember, the baseline model is not about software architecture. It is also not about fostering design patterns or styles. It is simply an inventory list of the various existing technologies that applications are built and executed upon.[2]

The technological baseline model is a necessary artifact for the service discovery process because of two major reasons: (1) it can help identify the existing technical entities that a project or an organization has been employing, and (2) it can locate the gaps between new requirements and missing technical implementations. In addition, the baseline model can represent the technical aspects that support a single project, a series of software development initiatives, or an enterprise endeavor. Each of these scopes can utilize the technical inventory list for future application development ventures.

Inventory Item	Technologies
Servers	Application Server, Web Server, Stand-Alone Server
Engines	Rules Engine, Search Engine, Data Transformation Engine
Security	Digital Certificates, Digital Signatures, Authorization, Authentication
Protocols	TCP/IP, FTP, DNS, LDAP, SMTP, POP3, MAP, RADIUS, SSH
Standards	WSDL, SOAP, XSLT, XPath, SAML, UDDI, XDI, XML, SPML

EXHIBIT 9.9   TECHNOLOGY BASELINE MODEL EXAMPLE

A software product is typically supported by a number of supporting technologies. These can be fundamental industry specifications, such as UDDI, WSDL, XSLT, or JSR 168[3] and 286.[4] Security technologies, such as digital certificates, encryption algorithms, and authorization and authentication mechanisms, can also be utilized for building and running applications and services. Exhibit 9.9 illustrates a baseline model example that represents technical ingredients of an application. Note that the Inventory column (left) consists of five major technology component categories: Servers, Engines, Security, Protocols, and Standards. Their corresponding technologies are itemized on the right.

DISCOVER TECHNOLOGICAL CAPABILITIES.   Technological capabilities are delivered by applications and services. These are the capacities of software entities that provide viable solutions to organizational concerns. A technical capability is also akin to a particular feature offered by a component, module, or service. For example, a software product's ability to transform data, convert protocols, deliver messages, search information, match data patterns, protect applications, and enable privacy of user content are all technical capabilities that should be discovered at this stage.

We are now ready to define the capabilities of our existing software product. These technical abilities should be used as analysis material to discover services (discussed in the next section). The identified services will represent the gaps, missing technical capabilities, in existing software implementations. But before moving on, consider the benefits of the technology capability identification step:

- Abstract existing technical implementation for future software reuse and expand the discovery process by generalizing technical capabilities.
- Define fields of existing technical expertise.
- Identify what type of technical functionality existing legacy software can offer.

To discover technological capabilities, simply create two sections, as depicted in Exhibit 9.10. The top panel should be dedicated to the technology baseline model discussed in the previous section. For simplification purposes, this illustration merely depicts the technology inventory Security item. Next, add a bottom panel that presents the technological capabilities. These should be derived from the baseline model and denote the various features and functionalities that

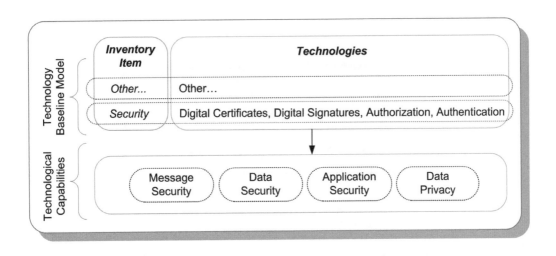

Exhibit 9.10   Discovery of Technological Capabilities Example

an existing software product can offer. Note that the Security inventory item yields four distinct technical capabilities: Message Security, Data Security, Application Security, and Data Privacy.

ESTABLISH HIGH-LEVEL SERVICE TAXONOMY.   The time has come to develop service categories that are consistent with the software technical capabilities discovered in the previous section. In other words, this step requires that we create a high-level service taxonomy that classifies services by their technical abilities. A high-level service taxonomy is a hierarchical directory that consists of service category entries. Each category identifies a group of services. This service category arrangement will enable practitioners to visually identify existing opportunities for future service discovery.

The high-level service taxonomy structure should be in accordance with particular technical areas of expertise and capacity to provide solutions. This directory formation is an intrinsic requirement that should be considered to ease the service discovery process. Architects, analysts, modelers, developers, and managers will not only be able to visualize an existing inventory of technologies but also to reuse, consolidate, and discover new services. How should such a high-level service taxonomy be created?

Start with the examination of the technological capabilities that were discovered in the previous step. Identify their functionality and prioritize their contribution to the project or to the organizational software development effort that is being launched. Each technical capability should be transformed to a high-level service category. This conversion process is depicted in Exhibit 9.11. Note that the Security Capability that is apparent in the Technological Capabilities column (left) was established as a high-level service taxonomy entry, named Security Services, shown in the High-Level Service Taxonomy column (right). This exact correlation is not mandatory but should provide guidance for constructing a high-level service taxonomy.

A refined version of Exhibit 9.11 is illustrated in Exhibit 9.12 that exemplifies the expansion process of the high-level service taxonomy. Note that we have expanded the Security Services entry to include four additional high-level service entries: Data Security Services, Message Security Services, Data Privacy Services, and Application Security Services.

DISCOVER ANALYSIS SERVICES.   The aim of the Bottom-Up technology-driven discovery is to identify gaps in implementation and devise services that satisfy new technical specifications for a

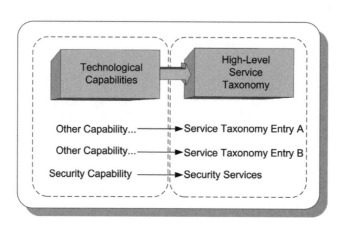

EXHIBIT 9.11   TRANSFORMATION OF TECHNOLOGICAL CAPABILITIES TO HIGH-
LEVEL SERVICE TAXONOMY

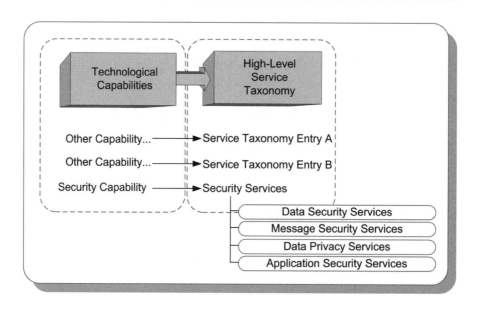

EXHIBIT 9.12   REFINED HIGH-LEVEL SERVICE TAXONOMY EXAMPLE

project or larger enterprise initiative. This goal can be achieved by expanding the high-level service taxonomy that was created earlier to incorporate newly identified services. Therefore, the various entries of the high-level service taxonomy should now be populated with new services. This process also presents the opportunity to incorporate legacy services in the same directory entries to foster software reuse and avoid redundant implementations.

To clarify this process, let us view Exhibit 9.13, which illustrates the high-level taxonomy (left) and the discovered services (right). This arrangement embodies the correlation between technical capabilities and new service capabilities. For example, the Message Security Services

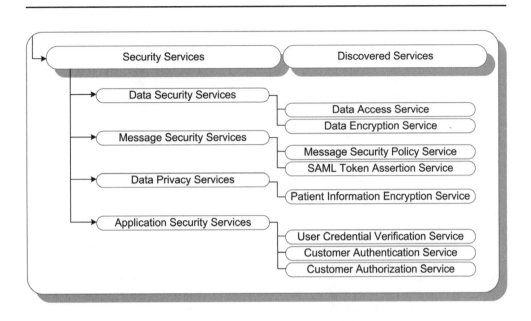

Exhibit 9.13   Service Discovery Example

high-level taxonomy entry (second entry) now contains two discovered services: Message Security Policy Service and SAML[5] Token Assertion Service.

The operations of the identified analysis services can be discovered later on based on the technical specifications provided for the project.

BOTTOM-UP REFERENCE ARCHITECTURE–DRIVEN SERVICE DISCOVERY

Service discovery driven by the analysis of architectural assets is rooted in the fundamental application or enterprise-level design best practices. These are typically devised by center of excellence or governance bodies. They are commissioned to set organizational standards for software construction, devise policies, and establish custom development methodologies. One of their most prominent deliverables that drives technological implementations, either small project or large efforts, is the *reference architecture*[6] document. This artifact is prepared during the inception phase of a software development life cycle or created for a more generic purpose, such as setting technology standards across the enterprise or carving out architectural strategies.

REFERENCE ARCHITECTURE CONTRIBUTION TO SERVICE DISCOVERY PROCESS.   The reference architecture is like an aerial map that identifies the various components and layers of architecture—technological abstractions upon which software implementations should be founded. This is not a depiction of technology capabilities that support applications and services as discussed in the Bottom-Up Technology Driven Service Discovery section. It is a binding accord that denotes common software and hardware entities that by and large offer solutions to a project or enterprise concerns. For example, reference architecture can present four layers of implementation: consumer, business, service, and operations. Each may consist of standardized COTS products, software components, specific frameworks that can be employed during projects, and even best practices for architecture implementation. Exhibit 9.14 illustrates the four layers that make up high-level

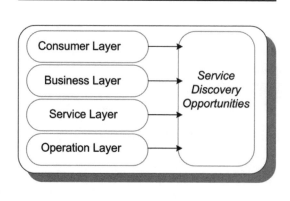

EXHIBIT 9.14 REFERENCE ARCHITECTURE MODEL EXAMPLE THAT LEADS TO SERVICE DISCOVERY

reference architecture. Note that each of these perspectives also introduces opportunities for service discovery: Consumer Layer, Business Layer, Service Layer, and Operation Layer.

Perhaps one of the most valuable contributions of reference architecture is the universal language, a vocabulary that it establishes for communication between business and technology practitioners. "Customer support messaging framework" and "booking engine" are examples of service layer components that contribute to an individual organization's terminology. This terminology can be utilized to develop an architectural asset identity and promote reuse in future projects. Services are the chief contenders to carry out this mission. Thus, the service discovery process should be driven by the various reference architecture layer formations to establish service taxonomy for a project or an enterprise strategy.

ATTEND TO THE SERVICE DISCOVERY PROCESS. Adhere to the four-step road map that drives the service discovery process. Exhibit 9.15 illustrates this effort.

1. **Establish Baseline Reference Architecture.** Start by carving out a baseline reference architecture that identifies existing layers of architectural abstractions. These should also reflect the design strategy of current software assets, COTS products, frameworks, and organizational standards.
2. **Construct Target Reference Architecture.** Focus on target reference architecture. Doing this typically involves the to-be views of future implementation. It also can represent a wish list of milestones and goals to achieve.
3. **Conduct Architecture Gap Analysis.** Conduct a gap analysis that identifies the differences between current and new architectures.
4. **Instiue Service Taxonomy.** Finally, found service taxonomy, an enduring artifact and cornerstone for future service development.

ESTABLISH BASELINE REFERENCE ARCHITECTURE. A baseline pertains to the *current state* of reference architecture.[7] It typically includes existing components, frameworks, standards, COTS products, tiers and layers, and even architectural design patterns. In addition, there are no strict reference architecture scope guidelines, meaning baseline architecture can be carved out for a particular project or enterprise scale. However, the aim normally is to set standards for the organization as a whole to bridge communication gaps between silo software implementation teams. Doing this encourages cross-enterprise technological uniformity and helps to establish service development policies.

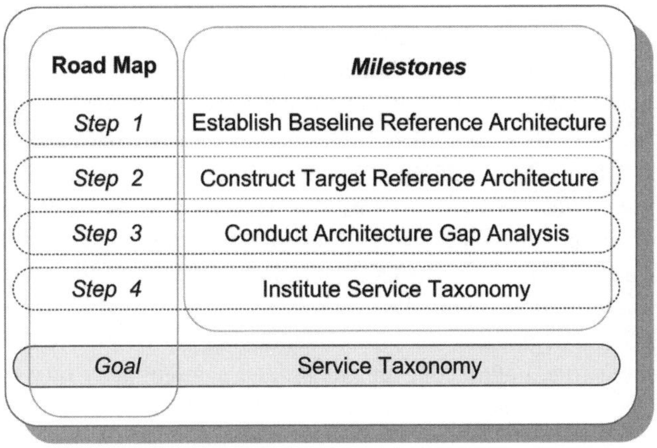

Road Map	Milestones
Step 1	Establish Baseline Reference Architecture
Step 2	Construct Target Reference Architecture
Step 3	Conduct Architecture Gap Analysis
Step 4	Institute Service Taxonomy
Goal	Service Taxonomy

EXHIBIT 9.15   SERVICE DISCOVERY PROCESS

The current state of the reference architecture should also provide an accurate map of the employed infrastructure and a means of integrating between the various layers and tiers. For example, the Business Facing Application Layer that is depicted in Exhibit 9.16 uses the Service Integration Layer for communicating with the Infrastructure Layer; note the arrows between the three entities that indicate message exchange. In the same manner, the Infrastructure Layer can utilize the Data Resource Layer by employing the Data Integration Layer. Therefore, the rule of thumb suggests that reference architecture should depict correlations between various components.

Another aspect that influences architectural relationship is the guiding principles and policies for software asset integration. These are denoted by the enclosing panel named Architecture Best Practices that should be an integral part of every softwarer development, maintenance, and operations initiative.

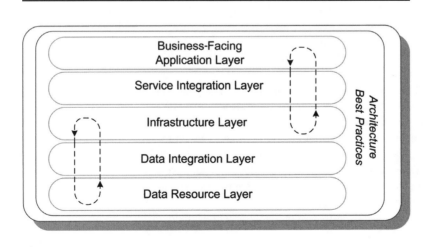

EXHIBIT 9.16   BASELINE REFERENCE ARCHITECTURE EXAMPLE

To summarize the construction process of baseline architecture, consider three major guiding principles:

1. Depict major layers and tiers of architecture.
2. Identify the correlations among architectural layers, tiers, and components.
3. Add guiding principles and standards that drive construction and integration initiatives.

CONSTRUCT TARGET REFERENCE ARCHITECTURE.   Target reference architecture is a futuristic vision and plan that identifies the major entities that will take part in a software architectural and design strategy. These ingredients, for example, constitute best practices, software integration ideas, guidelines and standards, incorporation of COTS products, communication means, and more. The overall scope of this effort can serve small-scale projects or a firm-wide spectrum. Moreover, the target architecture does not necessarily have to be identical to the baseline reference architecture. In fact, quite the opposite is true. Future concepts, ideas, and planning may vary greatly from existing schemes. These can convey a wish list or a more deterministic road map that offers remedies to organizational concerns.

Existing architecture components can even be replaced or enhanced by future mechanisms. These mechanisms typically allow target reference architecture to propose a different technological landscape or alternatives by presenting a new road map that fills in strategic gaps in implementations.

Exhibit 9.17 illustrates a target reference architecture that consists of five distinct layers: Presentation Layer, Business Logic Layer, Orchestration Layer, Infrastructure Layer, and Data Resource Layer. Each encompasses internal components. For example, the Presentation Layer includes Ajax and Portlet entities, and the Business Logic Layer incorporates two major software engines: Reservation and Flight Confirmation. Note that the Security and Monitoring and SOA Best Practices and Policies are the enclosing and cross-cutting entities that correspond to all architecture depicted layers. This enclosure articulates the need for security and standards for each target architectural development efforts. In addition, the associations between architecture layer components are identified: The arrows that connect the various components of each layer indicate their message exchange and data transmission relationship.

Consider the driving guidelines for target architecture construction:

- The target reference architecture should identify enhancements and additions to the baseline version,
- Strict correlation between baseline and target reference is not required.
- The target reference architecture should also consist of guiding best practices.
- Correlations between various architectural components that denote message exchange and data transmissions can be illustrated by connecting arrows.

CONDUCT ARCHITECTURE GAP ANALYSIS.   The gap analysis is simply a comparison between the two versions that we have constructed thus far: *baseline* and *target* reference architectures. Remember, the baseline schema represents existing architecture layers and tiers. The target, however, identifies planning and future of an end-of-state architecture. We pursue this approach to discover services that can help bridge the gap between old and new architectures.[8] If the difference between the two versions is immeasurable, the service discovery process ought to tackle a wide range of architectural concerns. Conversely, minor dissimilarities would allow a smaller spectrum of solutions to be addressed.

The gap analysis process should focus on three major differences between baseline and target reference architectures:

1. Additions to baseline reference architecture
2. Modifications to baseline reference architecture
3. Elimination of architectural layers or tiers

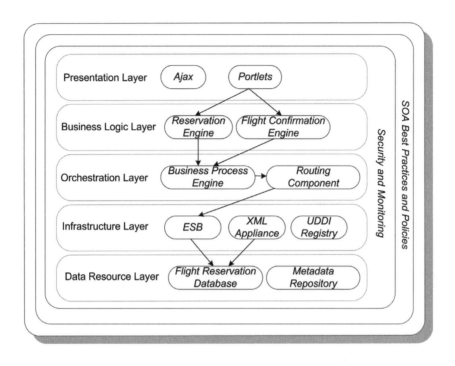

Exhibit 9.17   Target Reference Architecture Example

Obviously, additions or modifications to existing architectural assets will trigger the discovery of new services that can carry out the business or technological execution task. Elimination of layers or tiers, however, may not yield new services but potentially could trigger modifications to application or service functionality. Exhibit 9.18 exemplifies reference architecture gap analysis that involves the baseline and target schemes illustrated in Exhibits 9.16 and 9.17, respectively. Note that the Business-Facing Application Layer and Service Integration Layer, depicted in Exhibit 9.16, were removed and replaced with three different layers: Presentation Layer, Business Logic Layer, and Orchestration Layer.

INSTITUTE SERVICE TAXONOMY.   The time has arrived to found a service taxonomy from the reference architecture gap analysis conducted in the previous step. During this last stage of the Bottom-Up service discovery process, new services should be identified to bridge the baseline and target architectural propositions. Here the new software entities should be both rooted in existing solutions yet designed to carry out future missions. This process should yield service taxonomy, a directory that represents services that can increase software reuse and contribute to the consolidation of assets across the enterprise.

Exhibit 9.19 illustrates this approach. The two major entries, Business Logic Layer Services and Orchestration Layer Services, identify the reference architecture gaps, each of which consists of a group of corresponding discovered services. The former taxonomy entry represents business logic unique to the airline industry: Flight Booking Service, Flight Confirmation Service, Seat Selection Service, and Ticket Purchase Service. The second directory entry introduces services affiliated with the business orchestration layer: Workflow Manager Service, Business Rules Service, Message Routing Service, and Data Transformation Service.

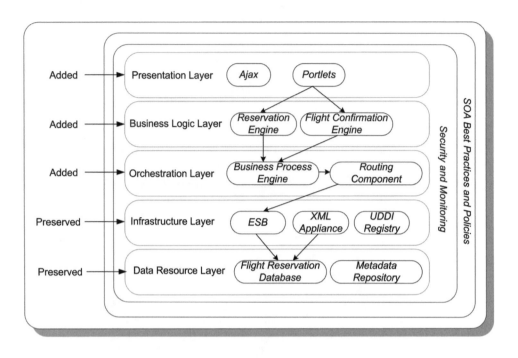

EXHIBIT 9.18   REFERENCE ARCHITECTURE GAP ANALYSIS EXAMPLE

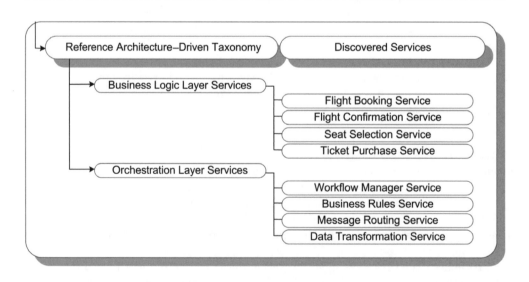

EXHIBIT 9.19   REFERENCE ARCHITECTURE–DRIVEN TAXONOMY EXAMPLE

DELIVERABLES

Carve out an efficient Bottom-Up service discovery strategy and embrace a practical process for identifying services. This approach should include three major analysis perspectives, as described in this chapter: legacy software functionality, existing technologies, and existing architectures. The Bottom-Up service discovery process should be based on three major milestones:

1. Identify missing functionality that services can execute to meet new business requirements.
2. Institute a technology baseline model to discover existing technical capabilities and drive the identification of new services.
3. Conduct an architecture gap analysis study that compares existing reference architecture components to end-state architecture imperatives. This would facilitate the discovery of new services.

SUMMARY

- The Bottom-Up service discovery approach advocates beginning the process of service identification by inspecting the contribution of legacy software to future solutions
- The Bottom-Up service discovery model consists of three major views: legacy software, existing technologies, and existing architectures.
- To identify the existing offerings and functionality of legacy software, the practitioner should employ the Bottom-Up business process analysis.
- The existing technologies perspective represents the empowering technologies used to run legacy software. These may include middleware components, messaging platforms, and application servers.
- The existing architecture view of the Bottom-Up service discovery identifies architecture concepts, best practices, and reference architecture components of current organizational software assets.

Notes

1. Mike Van Alst introduces similar approach in his Bottom-Up service discovery article: http://soamastery .blogspot.com/2007/12/service-discovery-part-1-Bottom-Up.html.
2. Some organizations refer to a baseline model as a technology stack, depicting layers of technical components that collaboratively offer solutions. This is similar to the open systems interconnection layer model or the W3C technology stack: www.w3.org/Consortium/techstack-desc.html.
3. http://jcp.org/en/jsr/detail?id=168.
4. http://developers.sun.com/portalserver/reference/techart/jsr168/#2.
5. www.oasis-open.org/committees/tc_home.php?wg_abbrev=security.
6. www.ibm.com/developerworks/rational/library/2774.html.
7. Baseline reference architecture is often referred to as baseline architecture, employing architecture patterns to communicate design decisions: http://msdn.microsoft.com/en-us/library/ms978704.aspx.
8. An interesting approach for conducting an architecture gap analysis to promote the future state of an organizational architecture is described at: http://mike2.openmethodology.org/wiki/Future-State_Logical_Architecture_ and_Gap_Analysis.

CHAPTER 10

MEET-IN-THE-MIDDLE SERVICE
DISCOVERY PATTERN

Practitioners may realize that not all technological and architectural aspects of a service ecosystem have been explored after the four distinct patterns of the service-oriented discovery process—Top-Down (71,89), Bottom-Up (145), Front-to-Back (105), and Back-to-Front (123)—have been pursued. To complete this service identification quest, architects, developers, modelers, analysts, and managers ought to identify the architectural components that are responsible for gluing together a service operating environment. The process that bridges these gaps during a service discovery venture is often referred to as connecting the dots. To connect the services that have been identified so far, a rigorous analysis process must persist. This time, however, the direction is clear: the Meet-in-the-Middle service discovery pattern simply shifts the attention to a more horizontal view of an organizational architecture. This focus is now turning to three chief areas of concern that must be addressed by specialized services: Integration Services, Common Business Services, and Infrastructure Services. Exhibit 10.1 illustrates the Meet-in-the-Middle service pattern model that consists of these services.

First, the concerns that motivate the establishment of integration-oriented services (INTOS) are *interoperability*, *distribution*, and *connectivity*. Obviously, interoperability is about bridging distributed services, enabling communication between deployed services, and introducing service mediators to process information and transform data. Other major integration challenges that should be addressed by INTOS are data integration and message integration. These challenges can be alleviated by enabling the delivery of data across the enterprise and beyond and to strengthen the message exchange model that makes execution of business transactions possible.

Second, common business services (CBS) constitute an organizational business layer, typically made up of a centralized group of services that execute business processes on behalf of distributed consumers. This configuration offers a mediation facility that is designed to both process business requests and serve business information to interested parties. In addition, such opportunity to reconcile business functionality across the enterprise also contributes to the creation of a business taxonomy, a directory of business imperatives that categorizes business services based on their specialties. This categorization of business areas of expertise immensely improves the communications between the business and IT organizations.

Finally, infrastructure-oriented services (INFOS) offer a wide range of related facilities, platforms, and capabilities. These specialized services typically are assigned infrastructure duties, such as messaging, persistence, and discovery platform functionalities. Security, mediation, virtualization, monitoring, and management capabilities are also the duties of infrastructure services.

INTEGRATION-ORIENTED SERVICES

Integration of software assets is the practice of connecting the dots. In this case, the dots are the various communicating assets, message exchange parties, consumers, and services that execute

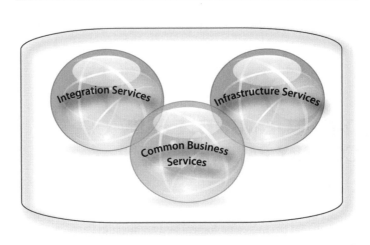

EXHIBIT 10.1   MEET-IN-THE-MIDDLE SERVICE MODEL

transactions over enterprise networks. Furthermore, integration discipline approaches for implementation call for providing an interoperability strategy for the organization. This strategy pertains to the methods and technologies employed to attain collaboration among applications, services, and consumers.[1]

Thus, the answer to the query "How do we connect our software entities?" typically is linked to the various integration methodologies that an enterprise embraces, the devised architecture that drives infrastructure design, integration best practices, and the practitioners' level of expertise. These enabling aspects should foster the use of integration-oriented services (INTOS) that are responsible for promoting collaboration and strengthening the partnership between organizational software assets.

INTEGRATION LOCALIZATION, CENTRALIZATION, AND FEDERATION.   Integration approaches vary. They characteristically depend on the environment where applications and services execute business and technical missions. In other words, the scope of connecting the dots is determined by the magnitude of the business requirements and technological specifications. In large software installations, for example, where applications rely on a mix of operating systems, networks, and protocols, integration tasks are arduous and complex. When connecting consumers and services that span multiple organizations and business partners in interoperable computing environments, the undertaking is even greater.

We thus categorize integration methods by three distinct classes, each of which represents the efforts and the various mechanisms that can achieve service collaboration: (1) localization, (2) centralization, and (3) federalization. These mechanisms not only influence the manner by which applications are able to exchange information, but they also dictate the types of technologies that should be employed. As discussed previously, the environment in which software entities communicate is also a determining integration factor that cannot be ignored.

Exhibit 10.2 illustrates this model in three different panels: Section A depicts a Localized Integration Services environment. Centralized Integration Services is shown in Section B. Section C represents a Federated Integration Services configuration. These approaches are explained in detail in the sections that follow.

Localization.   The term "localization" refers to concepts and implementation patterns for small-scale integration efforts. In other words, it refers to the method by which applications and services

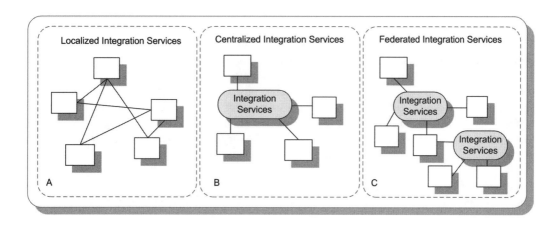

EXHIBIT 10.2 INTEGRATION METHODS

are directly connected to their consumers, to back-end data providers, to repositories, to partners, and to other resources. In addition, localization is an integration approach that fits a confined and small production environment by utilizing *point-to-point* connectivity mechanisms. This means that a service exchanges messages with its consumers with no broker interference. The same rule applies to extracting data from repositories: No intervening software parties are associated with data searching, collection, manipulation, or processing.

Furthermore, localization typically pertains to small-scale transaction execution that takes place in homogeneous computing environments where most of the software executables run on limited collections of platforms, operating systems, and networks. Here the challenges of interoperability are low and do not introduce difficulties involving software compatibility and management. Conversely, localization drawback is associated with the superfluous functionality that consumers and services must implement because of their direct connection. Unfortunately, the direct link method calls for assigning extra integration duties to services and their affiliated consumers, such as data routing, delivery, transformation, and even orchestration and coordination of message transmission.

Centralization. The term "centralization" refers a different integration approach, by which applications, services, and consumers communicate indirectly through a dedicated *hub*—a central integration facility, an intermediary tier supported by integration services. This arrangement not only enables message interception but also offers monitoring and security mechanisms to protect data transmission.

Centralizing integration is an approach typically suited to a distributed environment where language platforms, protocols, networks, and security models are disparate. This concept contributes to successful connectivity between distributed and loosely coupled software entities that must serve consumers operating in a variety of business domains and across organizations. Strengthening collaboration, for example, between a small-business loan organization and a credit verification department can be attributed to integration centralization strategies.

Remember that unlike the localization approach, discussed in the previous section, the centralization method advocates that the central integration facility (the dedicated hub) should offload integration duties from communicating consumers and related services.

Federation. Federation typically refers to geographically distributed production environments that must be bridged by integration services. These services are commissioned to achieve transaction cohesiveness and enable business continuity. The federation idea then goes one step beyond the centralization approach: Two or more central integration brokers are distributed across production facilities to ease interoperability challenges. In other words, multiple centers of integration services share control and management over mediation functionalities, such as message interception, monitoring, security, message transformation, and data aggregation.

Therefore, services that are assigned integration functionality in a federated environment should shoulder the burden of message transmission and coordination between the distributed integration centers that must collaborate. This chore of message orchestration that should be managed by federated service facilities is typically complex and often compromises the performance of data transmission. Hence, federation should be exercised in large environments where applications are dispersed across geographical regions, states, and even continents.

Choose the Right Integration Approach. When selecting the right approach for integration, consider four determining analysis factors that typically influence the discovery of supporting integration services:

1. Examine the current or planned production environment. Is it large enough in terms of number of applications, consumers, and services to justify a centralized integration landscape or a federated implementation?
2. Look at the scale of business and technical execution. Would the overall production environment's volume of transactions and messages require expansion of integration efforts beyond a point-to-point implementation (localized integration)?
3. Identify the existing technologies and infrastructure capabilities. Do these offer elaborated integration facilities that would sustain large distributions of software products?
4. Assess interoperability challenges. Do these difficulties require centralized or federated integration solutions?

STUDY INTOS MECHANISMS AND FUNCTIONALITY. The functionality of an INTOS must address interoperability challenges and offer proper connectivity capabilities to message exchange parties, such as application, services, and consumers that trade information and execute transactions. What integration scope can satisfy these enterprise imperatives? As discussed previously, not all production environments should be treated equally. The determining factors are obviously driven by the scale of business requirements and technical specifications. The rule of thumb suggests that the more dispersed and federated the environment, the better the breed of integration mechanisms an integration service must offer.

The four chief integration functionalities, illustrated in Exhibit 10.3, that INTOS characteristically offer often ensure business continuity and technical stability:

1. Business Process Integration
2. Data Integration
3. Event Integration
4. Message Integration

Note that these capabilities are based on three major concerns: (1) Interoperability, (2) Asset Distribution, and (3) Connectivity.

Business Process Integration. In a localized integration scenario where point-to-point connectivity is being exercised, the duty of business process implementation falls on message exchange parties, namely consumers and services. These software entities must not only execute business missions but also schedule, synchronize, and distribute messages. Since a local integration configuration does not necessarily support a central hub to handle business processes, it is more likely that

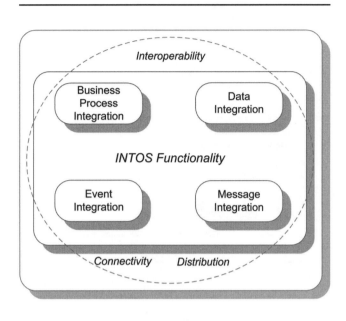

Exhibit 10.3   INTOS Functionality

business functionality implementation is duplicated across the organization. Unfortunately, business process redundancy is a common practice when it comes to such localized integration efforts. This is attributed to a lack of strategy, poor design and architecture, reduced budgets, or absence of proper motivation and technical justification.

Not all business processes should be shared with the rest of the organization. Nevertheless, most strategic and common implementations ought to be distributed to centralized or federated integration facilities. This arrangement enables business domains, applications, services, consumers, and partners to leverage the universal business process that is carried out by specialized integration services. Such a loosely coupled integration architecture also fosters consolidation of assets and thus reduces maintenance and modification costs to business logic.

Integration of business processes can be enabled by a number of frameworks, including commercial off-the-shelf (COTS) products that are supported by vendors or software libraries. These technologies offer a variety of mechanisms to integrate and execute business logic, such as enterprise message buses (ESBs), rules engines, orchestration engines, and language-specific application programming interface (API). Other mechanisms are supplied by standard pluggable architecture components that are designed to manage common and reusable business logic, such as Java business integration (JBI) based on the business integration specification referred as JSR 208.[2]

Data Integration.   As the reader may remember, the Back-to-Front service-oriented discovery, featured in Chapter 8, discusses fundamental requirements of data delivery services. These imperatives are affiliated with the means of data *delivery* to consumers, applications, services, and partners. Conversely, integration services must fulfill a different agenda: They are designed to take part in data integration architecture. The term "data integration" pertains to universal mechanisms that enable data sharing across the organization, aggregating data from a variety of sources and providers, and ensuring data integrity and format uniformity. The term "format uniformity" relates to a standardized data model, often named as canonical data model, an authoritative version of data schema that multiple consumers across an organization can agree on and comply with.

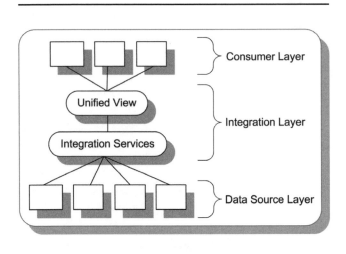

EXHIBIT 10.4   DATA SERVICE INTEGRATION MODEL

But the chief concern here is associated with the common use and repurposing of information. This means that the same data can be applied in different circumstances. Imagine, for example, that a customer profile can be utilized by the marketing and order departments of a retail institution. The former further processes the content to craft marketing strategies, while the latter leverages the information to ferry out goods to customers.

Another key challenge for integration services is to combine various data sources and present a *unified view* of information to consumers. This model is depicted in Exhibit 10.4. Note the three components that make up the integration scheme: Consumer Layer, Integration Layer, and Data Source Layer. The universal perspective is apparent at the Unified View component, which is part of the implementation of Integration Services.

Data integration is also about universalizing data access capabilities, which refers to the method by which data are commonly used and simultaneously processed by a variety of consumers. In addition, an efficient integration facility should employ data-security mechanisms to ensure the integrity of structures and schemas. Aggregation of data is another feature that integration services must offer. It can be attained by various technologies, such as virtualization layers,[3] or COTS products that enable data collection and transformation activities.

Event Integration.   It is not only business processes that can be integrated to reduce functionality redundancy. Events are also an important part of application and service execution that can be reconciled to reduce implementation overhead. What is an event? Real-time software behavior typically is influenced by environmental changes and internal occurrences that influence the logic flow of a program. These planned or unforeseen "incidents" are referred to as events that can affect the execution states of a running application or service.

External events, for example, can be the rise and fall of the stock market or particular trading equity values. Foreign exchange fluctuations or declining interest rates are other examples of outside events that can affect the execution of a monetary trading system. Conversely, internal events emerge from different sources: These can be user-interface intervention or even programming logic that monitors calculations shaped by predefined formulas.

Either internal or external real-time occurrences may take place simultaneously and even fire up other events, causing a chain of reactions that changes the behavior of a system. Hence, the greater the number of planned or unexpected incidents that an application must respond to, the more complex and resource-consuming are these operations. Migrating event management from individual implementations, such as applications, to a more centralized or even federated configuration can resolve these challenges. This can be accomplished by establishing an integration layer that consists of services that carry out the tracing and execution of events.

A growing number of technologies can facilitate the foundation of event handling and management. One of best-known approaches is Complex Event Processing (CEP).[4] This method, which is typically offered by COTS products, helps to quantify event impact and to respond accordingly to mitigate risks and provide adequate real-time solutions. Others solutions offer real-time Web services with pluggable capabilities that a developer can implement to capture and react to system events.[5]

Message Integration. Akin to the event reuse and consolidation solutions discussed in the previous section, message management introduces challenges that integration services must tackle. What are these challenges, and how should they be addressed? Handling messages that are exchanged among applications, services, and consumers requires a specialized framework solution, a hub that can resolve message synchronization, orchestration, and distribution difficulties. This mediating broker must also offer workload management capabilities, by which the volume of incoming and outgoing messages is monitored and adjusted to mitigate timeout and performance latency conditions.

Message management is not only about solving technical constraints. Orchestrating and coordinating delivery of information, driven by *business rules*, is also an essential undertaking that must be considered. This is typically achieved by evaluating message content that affects run-time delivery decisions—often called *context-based routing*. For example, a message that carries stock market news is first inspected and then routed to a trading portal. In the same manner, the content of a top business school's survey is transmitted to an education online application. This matching activity characteristically is driven by predefined business rules that can easily be altered to affect future communications and message routing paths.

Another integration functionality perspective that integration services must address when it comes to message handling is mediation. Message mediation is simply the act of intercepting messages that are exchanged between dispersed consumers, services, and applications in a distributed environment that can span lines of business and even organizations. This brokering approach resembles traffic controller responsibilities; it is akin to the Service Façade design pattern, which abstracts the relationships between services and consumers and hides their physical location and identity. What are the major benefits that message mediation implementation offers an integrated computing landscape? This indirect association approach between consumers and corresponding services typically contributes to a loose coupling design and increases reuse and consolidation of software assets. In addition, embedding message intermediaries in a production environment enriches its integration capabilities, increases business agility, and improves elasticity of software deployment. A fine balance, however, should be maintained when incorporating mediating facilities. An increased number of brokers can cause performance degradation and convolute integration efforts.

Integration-oriented services should provide solutions to reconcile message distribution and manipulation operations. These INTOS ought to offer brokering facilities that not only address technical remedies but also enable the coordination of automated business execution. Furthermore, the platforms that support message integration are widespread and common in today's production environments. They are offered by third-party vendor COTS products, such as business process modeling and orchestration technologies, ESBs, service registries, and more.

DELEGATE INTEGRATION FUNCTIONALITY TO INTOS. The functionality that is described in the previous sections should be delegated to subject matter integration services that offer various

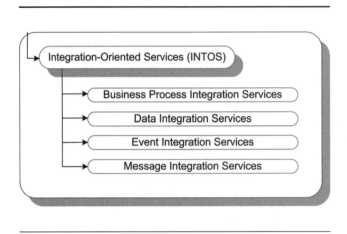

EXHIBIT 10.5   INTEGRATION-ORIENTED SERVICE TAXONOMY

integration solutions to a project or larger enterprise architecture initiative. These software capabilities should be embedded in deployment solutions and disbursed to centralized locations or federated across enterprise boundaries. This loose coupling architecture scheme clearly advocates divesting integration duties from applications and assigning them to integration framework solutions, carried by specialized services.

To begin carving out such an architectural strategy, identify a simple service taxonomy that recognizes integration functionality and satisfies business requirements and technical specifications for a project. Most important, this artifact should provide motivation for discovering future organizational integration services. Exhibit 10.5 illustrates the six different service categories for integration initiatives: (1) Business Process Integration, (2) Connectivity Integration, (3) Data Integration, (4) Message Mediation, (5) Event Integration, and (6) Message Integration. Note that this classification can be further expanded to include service subcategories.

COMMON BUSINESS SERVICES

An enterprise architecture that exposes common business resources, such as repositories and applications, to consumers can contribute immensely to the reduction of functionality redundancy and consolidation of software assets. To achieve this goal, reconciliation of business processes across the enterprise should yield a new breed of services designed to offer business execution: common business services (CBS). By grouping these entities, practitioners can form a centralized business layer that can serve multiple consumers in the enterprise and provide business value to those who reside beyond its boundaries. Remember, this arrangement is different from an application-level solution. Here, an enterprise remedy is applied to foster reuse of business services across an organization.

COMMON BUSINESS SERVICES REUSABILITY MODEL.   The idea of sharing business components, artifacts, and transactional and historical data should be exercised in environments where lines of business and partners must tap into common resources of information. For example, while the auto parts supplier queries inventory levels for replenishing storage facilities, the orders division should be able to schedule new car accessory shipments. This simple reusability model provides the motivation for ascertaining common business services to bridge the communication gaps between consumers and providers.

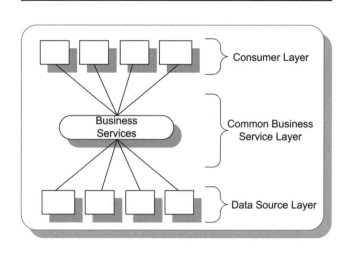

EXHIBIT 10.6   COMMON BUSINESS SERVICE LAYER MODEL

The architecture that provides such reuse capability typically is segmented by different layers of execution. Common business services clearly play a chief role in the overall design and implementation. Thus, they should be located midway, acting as intermediary entities that, on one hand, are capable of accessing data sources and, on the other, can communicate with partners and customers. This arrangement offloads business logic implementation from various applications and delegates these responsibilities to an institutionalized business layer.

Exhibit 10.6 illustrates this concept. The depicted Common Business Service Layer executes business processes on behalf of the Consumer Layer, which may consist of application, services, or partners. In addition, the Common Business Service Layer communicates with the Data Resource Layer, which may contain third-party information providers and repositories.

DELIGATE BUSINESS EXECUTION TO CBS.   Delegate business matters to CBS. Costruct a business taxonomy, a directory of business related services to boost up service reuse and establish a new language of business/IT communications. More specifically, a business taxonomy is simply a categorized directory of services classified in certain groups that identify business imperatives in an organization. This arrangement of various business functionalities should follow a certain pattern that relates services to a business function, line of business, or business occupation. Exhibit 10.7 illustrates a taxonomy that is driven by business functionality that was created for a credit card organization. Note that the six distinct business functions, carried out by business services, are grouped by their contribution to the credit card account management: (1) Application Questionnaire, (2) Background Verification, (3) Credit History, (4) Online Credit Card Payment, (5) Obtain Credit Card Statement, and (6) Dispute Charge.

Alternatively, taxonomy can provide traceability on income that a service generates for an organization. Accordingly, services can be categorized by product offerings, strategic level, and the business value they provide to consumers. This categorization can even be expanded to include incurred revenue or projected return on investment (ROI). Exhibit 10.8 depicts an ROI-driven taxonomy that classifies services according to the projected returns on investment. The Bank Reconciliation Service and General Ledger Service are grouped under the "Revenue < $1,000,000" category. However, the "Revenue > $1,000,000" class consists of two services: Accounts Payable Service and Accounts Receivable Service.

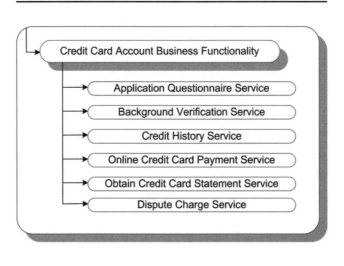

Exhibit 10.7   Business Functionality–Driven Taxonomy

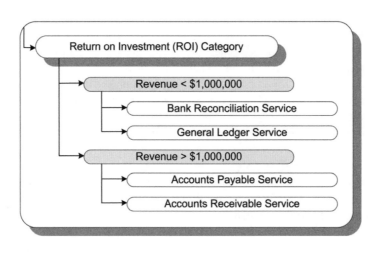

Exhibit 10.8   ROI-Driven Taxonomy

Another method that can be used for categorizing business functionality suggests arranging services by ownership and sponsorship. This affiliation with particular stakeholders in an organization is a compelling reason for classifying services by groups of interests, departments, divisions, or business domains. In fact, such a grouping approach is a common practice because of funding systems that organizations employ. More specifically, sponsors not only own business solutions, they are also responsible for development of software products and services. To better understand this classification approach, let us view Exhibit 10.9, which shows ownership categories. The depicted Home Appliance Department and Flooring Department organizations consist of corresponding funded services that execute home appliance and flooring business functionalities.

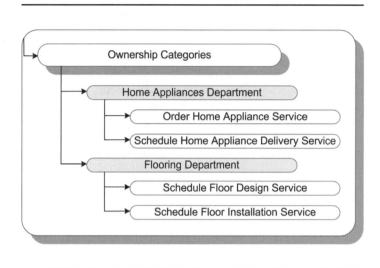

EXHIBIT 10.9   SERVICE OWNERSHIP–DRIVEN TAXONOMY

INFRASTRUCTURE-ORIENTED SERVICES

Infrastructure is the backbone of organizational architecture. Generally, it is about the technologies that provide the "plumbing," the underpinning enabling facilities that both connect and protect data, messages, applications, and services. Infrastructure is analogous to a superhighway endowed with access to enterprise data sources and business implementation; it also enables message transmission and synchronizes network traffic. Furthermore, the term "infrastructure" pertains not only to hardware that hosts applications and services; it also refers to software designed to connect message exchange parties, transform protocols and data, monitor performance and security, transmit information over networks, virtualizes operations, and more.

CONSIDER INFRASTRUCTURE-ORIENTED SERVICES.   Software entities that carry out infrastructure duties, namely INFOS, contribute to interoperability solutions, enhance communications, and security. They are typically distributed in a production environment, loosely coupled, and autonomous. Furthermore, organizations tend to purchase COTS products that offer out-of-the-box solutions to avoid home-produced infrastructure software packages.

But off-the-shelf software offerings cannot entirely satisfy enterprise technical requirements. Imagine, for example, an architectural imperative that calls for forwarding the identity of a clinical patient to a chain of healthcare facilities across the nation. This clearly would require infrastructure facilities, frameworks that are designed to fulfill the identity management task. Some proposed solutions can leverage out-of-the-box products; others would require construction of services to augment the implementation. Thus, the two flavors—vendors' products and homegrown services—can be interwoven to create an effective and customized infrastructure solution.

An organizational effort to glue production pieces together typically takes place when it comes to the employment of purchased infrastructure software. No matter how powerful and comprehensive an infrastructure vendor's product is, a customization process is always required. "Glue" pertains to the means that enable consumers and services to talk to each other in a distributed computing environment. It also refers to the ability to exchange information, execute transactions, and transform data. The "gluing" effort typically consists of three major mechanisms that can connect the dots between existing organizational software assets, such applications and services and off-the-shelf products:

1. Adopters can be developed or purchased to interconnect software entities in a production environment. An adopter both can convert messages from one format to another and is intelligent enough to transform data structures and protocols during transactions.
2. Code wrapping is another approach that developers often employ to alter existing programs and increase their compatibility with other applications and services. Here, additional software components are added or inserted to enable connectivity with the outside world.
3. Introduce proxies, which are stand-alone customized brokers that can bridge the communication gaps between various software products and consumers in the organization.

DELEGATE INFRASTRUCTURE DUTIES TO INFOS: FOUND INFRASTRUCTURE SERVICE MODEL.
The Meet-in-the-Middle service discovery method calls for the establishment of a service model that identifies the various infrastructure pillars of an organization. This model should consist of distributed, centralized or federated services designated to take part in enabling enterprise application integration.

Thus, begin with carving out a plan, an overall infrastructure implementation road map that identifies that various building blocks and their functionalities. Remember, crafting a service infrastructure strategy is a subjective matter that an organization must resolve. This effort should address particular production environment challenges and tackle existing architecture, technology, and legacy application collaboration requirements. Therefore, devise *platforms* best suited for addressing infrastructure strategies and assign these enterprise integration duties to services.

Exhibit 10.10 exemplifies this separation-of-concerns idea. The illustrated four distinct service platforms embody an organizational infrastructure proposition: Messaging Platform, Service

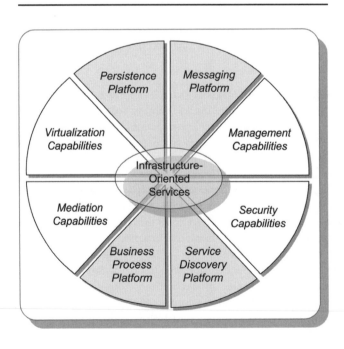

EXHIBIT 10.10 SERVICE INFRASTRUCTURE MODEL EXAMPLE

Discovery Platform, Business Process Platform, and Persistence Platform. Note that these facilities offer four different service capabilities: Management, Security, Mediation, and Virtualization. These are explained in the sections that follow.

Messaging Platform.   A messaging platform is comprised of various services that both guarantee message delivery and manage events. This is a message integration facility (also discussed previously in the Message Integration section), typically a central hub, that connects consumers, applications, services, and partners. It also enables asynchronous and synchronous communications and offers point-to-point and publish and subscribe message exchange capabilities.

Moreover, a messaging platform should conform to rudimentary message exchange patterns (MEP)[6] that describe activities and delivery paths of messages, such as *request-response* (known as in-out) or *one-way* (often referred to in-only). This standardized requirement typically is implemented in messaging platforms of COTS products, such as enterprise message buses (ESBs), the most common and the leading message management facility.

A messaging platform should not only enable connectivity and transmission of information but also offer message filtering and transformation features. The term "filtering" pertains to the ability to exclude content from the received message before it is routed to its end point. Transformation is another activity that is performed on a message to alter its structure so the receiving end can understand it.

A message platform is one of the most effective methods to enforce loose coupling architecture. It simply separates and obscures consumers from their corresponding services. In addition, a messaging facility encourages reuse by abstracting and hiding applications and their implementations yet providing a centralized point of contact that facilitates message and information sharing.

A messaging platform consists of a wide range of functionalities that typically are decoupled yet collaboratively offer a comprehensive message integration solution that can be centralized or federated across the enterprise. These duties should be delegated to INFOS that offer service management, delivery, and security capabilities, as shown in Exhibit 10.11.

Persistence Platform.   A persistence platform consists of a variety of infrastructure services that offer data processing and manipulation capabilities. Its chief duties constitute execution of create, read, update, delete (CRUD) operations by centralizing access to data sources across the organization. Furthermore, the establishment of a persistence platform also contributes to the abstraction of data structures and entities. (Data entities are discussed in Chapter 8.) This conceptual view of data fosters the institution of an enterprise canonical data model that can be reused and shared among

Messaging Platform	
INFOS Duty	**Functionality**
Message Mediation	Message transformation and enrichment, message filtering
Message Management	Metering and billing, monitoring, SLA enforcement, audit trail, exception handling, error logging, alerts and notifications
Message Security	Encryption, signature, credential assertion and passing, message audit trail
Event Management	Event triggering and scheduling, complex event processing (CEP)
Message Routing and Message Orchestration	Message orchestration, workload management, context-based routing, technical rule–based routing, business rule–based routing
Message Searching and Invocation	Asynchronous, synchronous, message searching, message binding
Message Handling Policy Management	Message routing policy, message transformation policy, mediation policy management

EXHIBIT 10.11   MESSAGING PLATFORM DUTIES AND FUNCTIONALITIES

Persistence Platform	
INFOS Duty	**Functionality**
Persistence Operations	Create, read, update, and delete (CRUD) operations
Data Access and Mediation	Access to organizational distributed repositories, data warehouses, partner information sources
Data Transformation	Data transformation, cleansing, enriching, data structure conversion, data pattern matching and merging
Data Virtualization	Abstraction of data structures, virtual aggregation, virtual data migration
Data Integrity	Data validation, data quality, data structures and types protection, canonical data model
Data Auditing and Logging	Data access traceability, data usage history tracking
Data Security and Privacy	Encryption, authorization, and authentication mechanisms
Meta Data Management	Meta-data repository management

Exhibit 10.12   Persistence Platform Duties and Functionalities

projects and business initiatives. Another benefit that an abstraction data layer offers is the ability to leverage its virtualization feature, by which data migration and aggregation can be performed without transporting physical information from one location to another.

A persistence platform should be thought of as a broker, an intermediary software asset devised to promote loosely coupled enterprise architecture. This data hub is typically created to execute data queries and process information on behalf of consumers. These mediation responsibilities also include transformation of data, such as cleansing and schema conversion. Security and privacy of content is also an important feature that persistence services provide. These features include encryption, audit trail, and logging capabilities. Exhibit 10.12 depicts these major infrastructure services functionalities.

Business Process Platform.   A business process platform consists of infrastructure services that integrate processes by centralizing the execution of business activities. This reconciliation of business logic implementation promotes reuse of software assets across the organization and fosters reduction of functionality redundancy. Furthermore, the business process platform is intrinsically a message hub whose chief responsibilities are orchestration and choreography of business execution.[7] This capability facilitates message workflow, synchronization, and scheduling of activities and coordination of transactions on behalf of consumers, applications, services, and partners.

A business process platform promotes business agility by enabling management and analysts to modify business transactions and behaviors without altering source code. This feature is characteristically built into COTS products that also offer design-time processes modeling facilities, that are driven by industry-standard business modeling languages.

Exhibit 10.13 summarizes the major functionalities of an infrastructure service that is devised to assume business process platform tasks. These capabilities include business process support, security, business event management, business process mediation, business process monitoring, and business reporting.

Service Discovery Platform.   Think about a discovery platform as an information center that points to other locations in a production environment. In fact, a service discovery facility does not host executables. It merely points to services by providing their address on a network. In addition, this platform typically consists of infrastructure services that provide three major pieces of information to software components seekers: (1) a service provider's identity, such as company name, address, and location; (2) available offerings—a taxonomy that represents service functionality; and (3) service technical descriptions, such as accessible interfaces.

Business Process Platform	
INFOS Duty	**Functionality**
Business Process Support	Business orchestration and choreography, workflow management
Business Process Mediation and Integration	Business collaboration, reconciliation of business activities
Business Event Management	Planned and random event handling, automated event monitoring and management
Business Rules	Business rules execution, dynamic rule management
Business Process Monitoring	Alerts, audit trail, SLA enforcement, business transaction monitoring, performance and consumption monitoring, revenue and billing monitoring
User Interaction	User interface and presentation layer handling
Transaction Management	Transaction execution and traceability
Business Process Security	Identity management, encryption, and document signing
Business Reporting	Analytical and transactional reporting

Exhibit 10.13   Business Process Platform Duties and Functionalities

A service discovery repository installation that enables the registry of institutions that announce their offerings on the Internet or intranets is a common infrastructure software asset employed in production. The best-known example is the Universal Description, Discovery, and Integration (UDDI)[8] facility, provided by a growing number of vendors. It is used for publishing and discovering network-based software components in a service-oriented architecture ecosystem.

From an architectural best-practices standpoint, a service discovery platform and its affiliated infrastructure services are important contributors to the loose coupling design of a service-oriented environment. A centralized or even federated discovery facility encourages reuse of distributed software components across an organization and alleviates interoperability challenges. This service publishing platform is also commonly used to categorize services based on their offered capabilities and provide a taxonomy that is often perceived as a service portfolio management facility. A service portfolio management simply identifies a service's offerings, its origin, and its capabilities to provide solution. Exhibit 10.14 outlines the four major service discovery platform capabilities that have been discussed so far.

DELIVERABLES

Craft an efficient Meet-in-the-Middle service discovery process that fits the organization deployment, infrastructure, and integration environment. Focus on the three major components of service identification: integration facilities, common business facilities, and infrastructure facilities. Each of these components should contribute to the discovery of three service categories: INOS, CBS, and INFOS

Service Discovery Platform	
INFOS Duty	**Functionality**
Searching	Identification of services by offered APIs
Business Descriptions	Business detail identification
Service Offerings	Taxonomy of services and identification of their offerings
Technical Identifications	Description of technical capability

Exhibit 10.14   Service Discovery Platform Duties and Functionalities

SUMMARY

- The Meet-in-the-Middle service discovery pattern assists with the identification of three types of services: integration-oriented services (INTOS), common business services (CBS), and infrastructure-oriented services (INFOS).
- INTOS represent a service category that provides various integration facilities, such as data integration and message integration.
- A centralized business service layer offers common business processes to distributed consumers. This business mediation configuration is called CBS.
- INFOS are an infrastructure provider group of services that offer platforms and technological capabilities to support a service ecosystem. This includes messaging, persistence, and discovery platforms. Security, mediation, virtualization, and management services are also a vital part of INFOS offerings.

Notes

1. Refer to the Service-Oriented Discovery and Analysis Interoperability Model section in Chapter 3 for a detailed discussion about organizational interoperability strategy and its corresponding layers.
2. See JBI specifications at: http://jcp.org/en/jsr/detail?id=208.
3. http://it.toolbox.com/blogs/the-soa-blog/soa-data-virtualization-and-master-data-management-14757.
4. http://complexevents.com/.
5. www.oracle.com/technology/products/event-driven-architecture/index.html.
6. http://wso2.org/library/335.
7. http://weblogs.java.net/blog/caroljmcdonald/archive/2003/10/orchestration_c.html.
8. www.oasis-open.org/committees/uddi-spec/doc/tcspecs.htm.

PART THREE

SERVICE-ORIENTED CATEGORIZATION PATTERNS

The practice of cataloging and organizing services in a distinct order that is meaningful to an organization or project is beneficial to business and technology institutions. This process is about grouping associated services by a common denominator, theme, or attribute that identifies the purpose of their existence and their contribution to related solutions. Moreover, the categorization exercise is devised not only to bring discipline to the service-oriented discovery and analysis venture but also to enable efficient service inventory management, whereby service capabilities are recognized, indexed, and registered.

There are two major driving motivations behind pursuing the service-oriented categorization process: the difficulty in selecting the right service for a solution and the challenge of reusing existing service offerings to alleviate an organizational concern. The former pertains to focusing on the problem and the mission by discovering a service that meets business or technical requirements. It relates to identifying service capabilities that can provide a remedy to a concern, verify its offered specialties, and confirm its functionality. Boosting service reusability rates is another driving motivation that encourages practitioners to embark on a service categorization effort. It entails *diversifying* service sources that can participate in providing a solution, such as employing existing legacy services, utilizing service concepts, or using virtual entities. These can contribute immensely to the reduction of organizational expenditure and decrease the service development scope.

Applying a sense of order and discipline to service inventory management can also contribute to the establishment of an organizational service *taxonomy*. The institution of a service directory fosters the utilization of a common language: A reusable glossary can be shared by silo organizations, business personnel, and development teams to boost software reuse and foster asset consolidation. Moreover, a service taxonomy can also encourage the reorganization and segmentation of a deployment environment, by which services are grouped according to their area of expertise, line of business, and even level of profitability.

A service-oriented categorization model should encourage practitioners to classify services using different perspectives. Grouping services by their specialty probably would be beneficial to business analysts who typically explore a service's ability to execute business processes. But how can architects, developers, and modelers get acquainted with a service's internal structure? What are the various service formations that can enable architects to establish a sound service ecosystem? Finally, how can managers, developers, and analysts discover new services without knowing the available organizational service inventory?

A service categorization model should also provide *patterns* for classification. These *repeatable* processes can be pursued for each launched project, architectural effort, or organizational

Exhibit P3.1 Service-Oriented Categorization Model

business initiative. But one of the most vital aspects of the service classification endeavor is the ability to broaden the spectrum of service analysis and introduce different views of a service's essence and its constitution. These views would answer the intrinsic queries regarding service internal and external architecture, capabilities, specialties, and functionalities: What is a service made of? What problem does the service resolve? In what area of expertise does the service offer solutions? Where does the service emanate from? How can the service contribute to a simplified architecture remedy? Will the service be reusable?

Exhibit P3.1 illustrates the service-oriented categorization model, which consists of three chief service classification components along with their corresponding patterns:

1. **Service Source.** This categorization component introduces patterns that enable practitioners to identify a service's origin and determine its current life cycle state.
2. **Service Structure.** This category facilitates the analysis of a service's internal formation and external integration, deployment, and configuration scheme by offering patterns for structural analysis.
3. **Service Context.** This classification component and its affiliated patterns reveal a service's functionalities, capabilities, and specialties.

The related patterns are guiding processes that enable practitioners to efficiently categorize a service's internal construct and external environment. These topics are discussed in detail in Chapters 11 through 13.

CHAPTER 11

SERVICE SOURCE
CATEGORIZATION PATTERNS

The service-oriented categorization process calls for identifying a service's origin and exploring its roots to better comprehend its characteristics, contribution to a solution, functionality scope, and offered capabilities. Moreover, by divulging the service current life cycle state, the practitioner will be able to assess its *readiness* to participate in a remedy to an organizational concern. Tracing this metamorphosis stage is essential to the service-oriented analysis activity because it allows both the thorough planning of a timely solution and the employment of diversified services in different stages of their development and operational life cycle.

What are the various sources that services can be identified with? Exhibit 11.1 illustrates the service source model, which consists of five service origins, *patterns* for categorization and discovery that can be repeated during project iterations:

1. **Concept (184).** A service concept is a formalized idea that proposes a preliminary solution to an organizational concern. It is typically discovered during the inception phase of a project.
2. **Abstraction (185).** An abstraction represents a generalized solution to various problems. Services emanate from technological, architectural, and business abstractions.
3. **Legacy (188).** Legacy entities are application and services that have been road-tested and certified to operate in a production environment.
4. **Portfolio (189).** A portfolio is a catalog of services and service concepts.
5. **Virtual (191).** Virtual entities are "intangible" and "invisible" services whose physical location, architecture, deployment, and configuration are not known to their corresponding consumers. The service capabilities, functionality, and interfaces should be the only public information that is divulged to consumers.

As the reader may have realized, the aim of the service-oriented discovery and analysis practice is, on one hand, to engage services that have been road-tested, namely legacy entities, and, on the other hand, to employ service concepts that are being formalized during the development inception phase. The notion of leveraging and combining a diversified set of services that emanate from various sources obviously contributes to reduction of functionality redundancy, reconciliation of software assets, and increase of reusability factors. The sections that follow provide a detailed explanation of each of the service source patterns and elaborate on their benefits to the service-oriented categorization process.

SERVICE IDEAS AND CONCEPTS

Organizational ideas are the first line of defense against business problems and concerns. These ideas are merely opinions that circulate among business and technology personnel and do not represent any common or formalized strategy to cure enterprise challenges. But sporadic ideas

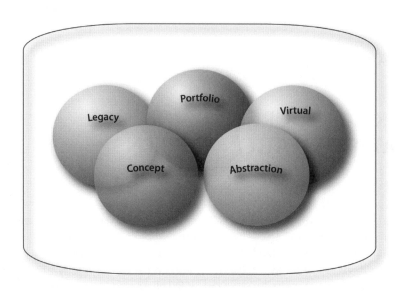

Exhibit 11.1   Service Source Patterns Model

characteristically do not yield steadfast concrete services. Thus concepts emerge next. Concepts embody business missions and constitute solutions. Moreover, the process of concept establishment typically lasts until maturity. This institutional activity results in an organizational core entity that is not tangible, yet it identifies the attributes of a candidate service that in due course will materialize and become part of a solution.

Ideas and concepts should be an integral part of the service categorization process. The driving thrust behind any classification venture are these nontangible entities that can facilitate grouping of services and the foundation of an organizational service taxonomy.

IDEAS: INFORMAL ORGANIZATIONAL ENTITIES.   Services may emanate from a diversity of ideas that are proposed to solve organizational concerns, alleviate business threats, or rectify technology challenges. Ideas are not formalized solutions and always precede requirements and specification issuance. These noninstitutionalized ideas can be thoughts that business development, architecture, business analysis, or software development teams come up with to solve problems.

Where do ideas typically originate? Meetings, workshops, conference calls, product evaluation and selection sessions, design and architecture whiteboard initiatives, and communication means such as e-mail represent *opportunistic* examples that characteristically lead to the inception of ideas. For example, the "creation of a centralized customer profile application," "moving from a personal investment portfolio approach to a more holistic household investment portfolio," and "customer focused rather than application centered" are all ideas that may materialize into concrete software executables if feasible for implementation.

CONCEPTS: FORMALIZED IDEAS.   Concepts are formalized ideas. A concept must be established first before it is published or communicated to the business or information technology (IT) organization. Unlike an idea, a concept must rely on steadfast sources of information, facts, research, and experiments before it is presented and recommended for implementation. Furthermore, the process of concept establishment typically requires substantial refinement activities that yield clear, coherent, and easy-to-understand problem-solving solutions that provide the motivations for service construction. For example, "centralized data aggregator," "data access layer," "service orchestration," and "enterprise message bus" are concepts that an organization can consider implementing.

To discover conceptual entities, refer to the best practices of the Service-Oriented Modeling Framework (SOMF); it can facilitate a meticulous analysis process during which organizational ideas are transformed into formalized service concepts. The discipline that guides practitioners to establish service concepts is called *service-oriented conceptualization,* and the deliverables are called *conceptual services.*[1]

SERVICE CONCEPTS CONTRIBUTE TO THE CATEGORIZATION PROCESS.   Again, ideas and concepts are raw sources of information that provide direction for impending service-oriented projects and business initiatives, such as software product planning, business analysis, and business process modeling. Moreover, concepts are subject to analysis prior to any service construction initiative. They serve as placeholders when modeling services for implementation. Placeholders indicate that their role in the overall service-oriented modeling process is essential because they augment the functionality missing from existing legacy applications and services.

From a service categorization perspective, concepts should be treated like any concrete service that is classified and analyzed. The fact that they are intangible should not deter practitioners from utilizing them to create a solid service taxonomy for the organization.

SERVICE ABSTRACTIONS

Unlike ideas and concepts, a service abstraction disregards the details yet preserves the common features and attributes of a concept. Namely, we typically use service abstractions to describe a general solution to a universal problem and avoid private instances that are not generic enough. Furthermore, the process of abstraction is analogous to generalization. When we remove the detailed functionality from a certain software implementation or a concept, in essence we generalize it to a higher level of understanding. For example, a Banking Account Service generalizes the services Checking Account and Savings Account. The Banking Account Service is regarded as an abstraction because it embodies the functionality of the Checking Account and Savings Account services, and yet extracts their capability details.

Service abstractions can emanate from various sources, principally from other abstractions. These can be technologies, architectures, data elements, and even business processes. Exhibit 11.2 illustrates this idea. The top panel includes four categories of software asset abstractions: Data, Architectural, Technological, and Business Processes. These are the major contributors to the layer beneath: Service Abstractions. The final artifacts are depicted on the bottom: Service Capabilities. As the reader may remember, capabilities are service operations that execute business or technical functionality.

The sections that follow describe the four chief types of abstractions that contribute to the institution of service abstractions that may result in concrete service implementations later on during the service development life cycle. In addition, these sources of influence should be reflected in an organizational taxonomy and facilitate the categorization of services:

1. Data abstractions
2. Architecture abstractions
3. Technological abstractions
4. Business processes

DATA ABSTRACTIONS.   As the reader may remember, we discussed data abstractions in the Back-to-Front (123) service discovery pattern in Chapter 8. There, a *data entity* was described as an abstracted data element that encompasses information about data structures, such as data table

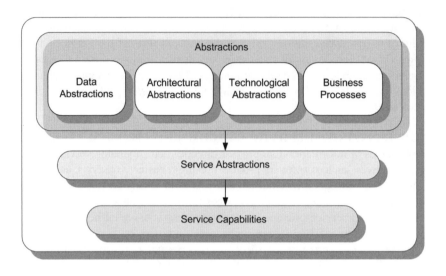

Exhibit 11.2   Software Asset Abstractions Influence Service Abstractions

columns, data types, and database schemas. This generalized notion of data contributes to the identification of service abstractions that consequently would yield a distinct breed of entities: data services. Moreover, characteristics of data abstractions provide motivation for constructing specialized data services that not only deliver content but also manipulate, transform, and enrich data during message exchange activities.

One of the major contributions of a data abstraction is the establishment of a universal generic data structure that various consumers can utilize to deliver, manipulate, or receive content. This is referred to as *canonical data model*,[2] an authoritative and reusable schema version that is sharable across an organization. A service abstraction that inherits this quality embodies such generalization properties that ultimately will be passed on to a tangible data service. Such a generalized data schema approach reduces the need for frequent updates to service contracts if data types or structures are changed by development teams.

ARCHITECTURE ABSTRACTIONS.   An architectural abstraction generalizes the underlining concepts of a software product and its operating environment. This depiction of an architectural landscape illustrates the major participating software components and their properties, and outlines their integration and collaboration scheme. The artifacts yielded by the abstraction process are typically architecture and design diagrams that depict a high-level perspective and a holistic view of current or future software assets' relationships and behavior.

Two major methods can assist with architecture generalization: usage of design patterns and layering. First, patterns represent well-established and traditional approaches for describing architectures. These patterns characteristically are devised to help resolve repeatable problems by introducing common remedies to implementation concerns. One of the most popular service-oriented architecture patterns is the Enterprise Service Bus (411), which represents a common solution to enterprise messaging challenges. The ESB pattern also embodies functionality that is related to message handling, such as message delivery, mediation, transformation, and security. Furthermore, other patterns can describe the interaction between message exchange parties and transaction handling methods, such as the Façade Service and the Locator Service. Both serve as proxies that address information delivery issues.

Second, the logical layering scheme can facilitate generalization of architectures by describing high-level composition and components of software. This is also a well-known and established approach for depicting a design scenario that can be used for analyzing distribution of software assets, separation of concerns, and decomposition of tightly coupled application and services. For example, a presentation layer consists of user-interface functionality, content rendering, and field validation activities. Another example illustrates the various activities and duties of business implementation. This is typically encompassed by the business logic layer.

Obviously, these formalized descriptions of architecture abstractions contribute to the reuse of infrastructure, applications, and services. They also provide solutions to recurring technological problems that practitioners are seeking to resolve. Thus architectural abstractions contribute to the establishment of service abstractions because of their generalized software activities, interaction, collaboration, and functionality views.

TECHNOLOGICAL ABSTRACTIONS. A technological abstraction provides a high-level perspective of a technical capability of a software product. It is chiefly associated with hiding the implementation of software and presents generalized technical aspects rather than low-level software construction details. This generalization is necessary for fostering a technical language, a communication lingo that describes technologies employing a universal terminology. Thus technological abstractions emphasize the functionality and attribute level perspective by disregarding detailed implementation of software.

For example, the technical abstraction "transport protocol" embodies any individual protocol that exists on the market, such as Java Message Service (JMS), User Datagram Protocol (UDP), XML-RPC, and Stream Control Transmission Protocol (SCTP). This generalization can also be utilized to describe a protocol functionality, such as error checking, data compression, and data transmission. "Adopter" is another generalized technical term that is associated with a software component that enables faultless message transmission between consumers and their corresponding services.

Thus, technological abstractions immensely contribute to service abstractions because of their generalization aspects. Service concepts can play a major role in universalizing technical capabilities. They can increase software reuse and introduce consolidation prospects.

BUSINESS PROCESSES. Business processes and their influence on service creation are largely discussed in Chapter 5, which elaborates on the Top-Down (71) service-oriented discovery pattern. This topic represents business processes as the chief analysis artifact that not only drives the discovery of service functionality but also influences the establishment of service operations. Therefore, think of business processes as abstractions that encompass service execution and behavior. Three major layers constitute this generalization:

1. The first obviously represents business processes.
2. The second layer consists of business activities that each business process is comprised of.
3. The derived services capabilities, also known as service operations, make up the third layer.

Exhibit 11.3 illustrates the three layers of generalization, starting at the very top where two types of business processes are depicted: Documented and Undocumented. The former pertains to processes that have been modeled and captured by various diagrams, such as workflows, flowcharts, sequence diagrams, or any business modeling language. The second type is Undocumented Processes. These are typically routines and work procedures that have never been recorded, yet practiced and executed by business personnel. The Service Abstractions section (depicted on the bottom), which is influenced by the business process layer, embodies Business Activities and their derived Service Capabilities (service operations).

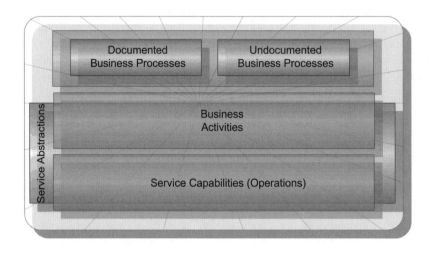

EXHIBIT 11.3   INFLUENCE OF BUSINESS ABSTRACTIONS ON SERVICE ABSTRACTIONS

ABSTRACTIONS PROMOTE SERVICE CATEGORIZATION.   As discussed in the previous sections, service abstractions can be derived from the four chief contributors to the service discovery process: data abstractions, architecture abstractions, technological abstractions, and business processes. Service abstractions contribute to software component reusability and reduction of redundant functionality. Since they generalize private instances of architecture design, or implementation, they can be used as organizational vocabulary, a language of communication to depict functionality of proposed software products and services. Abstractions can also foster development strategies by identifying a clear direction for service implementation. Therefore, it is imperative to embed service abstractions in the organizational taxonomy. They should not be disregarded; they can present a new breed of services required for a particular project or promote an architecture plan.

LEGACY ENTITIES: ROAD-TESTED EXECUTABLES

One of the most crucial aspects of the success of organizational asset reusability is leveraging legacy software for a small- or large-scale business and technological projects. Without the involvement of existing technologies, applications, services, and infrastructure entities, proposed new solutions would be costly. Furthermore, the experience and knowledge that have been accumulated in the years or decades during which legacy assets and their environment have been established may vanish.

What are the legacy assets that should be engaged in service-oriented solutions? "Legacy" refers to *existing* software components, infrastructure, consumers, applications, and services that have been road-tested in a production environment. These entities may operate within the organization's boundaries, be distributed across the enterprise, be located on partners' sites, or be executed virtually on virtual networks. (This topic is discussed further in the Virtual Entities section later in this chapter.) From a technological perspective, legacy assets may run on any language platform, such as Java, COBOL, C++, or C#.

The utilization of legacy software in new projects may pose adoption challenges and introduce integration difficulties. The root cause is typically related to the fact that these assets have been constructed to meet past demands that will not necessarily satisfy future business requirements and

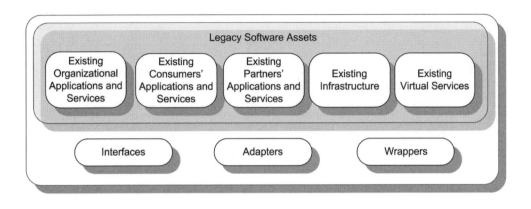

EXHIBIT 11.4   LEGACY SOFTWARE ASSETS AND ADOPTION MECHANISMS

technical specifications. With today's advanced technology solutions, this challenge can be alleviated by employing three major mechanisms:

1. Use adapters that abstract the implementation of legacy applications and services by universalizing protocols and data structures.
2. Wrap legacy software to comply with heterogeneous transmission protocols and database schemas. The term "wrap" simply pertains to source code modifications to enable communications with the outside world, such as consumers, peer applications, or services.
3. Add public interfaces that can be utilized to exchange messages with external software entities.

Exhibit 11.4 illustrates the major legacy assets that characteristically participate in service-oriented solutions: Existing Organizational Applications and Services, Existing Consumers' Application and Services, Existing Partners' Applications and Services, Existing Infrastructure, and Existing Virtual Services. In addition, note the discussed three major integration mechanisms: Interfaces, Adapter, and Wrappers.

SERVICE PORTFOLIO

A software portfolio is another source that can be utilized for identifying, typing, and categorizing services. This is simply a commercial off-the-shelf product that is offered along with a repository and graphical user-interface components that facilitate inventory management of organizational services. Furthermore, a service portfolio is also a catalog that not only profiles services according to their capabilities but also documents their life cycle stage and availability for future implementation and consumption.

The service-oriented discovery and analysis discipline advocates that a service portfolio should be examined to identify asset reuse opportunities to reduce development expenditure and accelerate time to market. Not all services that are registered in an asset portfolio are concrete. Conceptual services and service abstractions should also be part of the repository. In fact, ideas and concepts are important assets that should be recorded and utilized in future projects and product planning initiatives. Doing this obviously fosters software reusability and consolidation of applications and services. Existing legacy entities that operate in a production environment and listed in a portfolio manager are also contenders for reuse and should be considered for new projects, if appropriate.

Service Profile Information	Description
General Identification Section	
Service Name	Service name as it appears in the requirements
Service Description	General service description and its functionality
Service Type	Source, structural, and contextual types (service structural patterns are discussed in Chapter 12, contextual patterns are elaborated on in Chapter 13)
Version	Major and minor service version
Geographical Location	Physical service location (state? region? city?)
Granularity Scale	Indicate one of the following: fine grained, mid grained, or coarse grained (refer to Chapter 2 for detailed granularity specification)
Ownership and Sponsorship Section	
Business Ownership	Business organization that owns the service
Technological Ownership	Technology organization that owns the service
Sponsoring Organizations/Stakeholders	Service development and operations sponsorship
Functionality and Readiness Section	
Functionality	Description of service capabilities
Life Cycle stage/events	Current life cycle stage
Life Cycle Policy Management	Indicate if the service life cycle is managed by any COTS product
Readiness	Is the service ready for production?
Major Contractual and Service-Level Agreement Requirements Section	
Dependencies on Other Applications and Services	List of mutual dependencies of applications and services that will or already communicate with the service (include middleware and infrastructure software products, if appropriate)
Potential Number of Consumers	Indicate number of current or future consumers
Required Consumption Capabilities	Periodic consumption of messages allowed
Required Response Time	Agreed response time
Required Availability	Service's operations availability measured in hours/days units (such as 24/7)
Service Network Addressability	End point address on the network
Service Technical Description	Address of the description file, such as WSDL
Main Interfaces	List of main public interfaces that the service extends to its consumers
Major Technologies Section	
Major Protocols	List of the various protocols that services utilizes to communication with its consumers
Operating Systems	Identify which operating systems the service runs on
Language Platforms	Identify the language platforms that the service uses
Major Libraries	Indicate major libraries that are/were used to construct the service
Security and Monitoring Considerations Section	
Digital Certificates	Indicate digital certificates used
Digital Signatures	Identify digital signatures used
Encryption Mechanisms	List encryption algorithms used
Privacy Control	Elaborate on the mechanisms that enable information privacy control capabilities
Security Policy Management	Name products used for security policy enforcement
Service Provisioning Management	Indicate service provisioning and access control mechanisms
Monitoring and Alert Management	Provide a list of monitoring tools and service-level agreement enforcement technologies

Exhibit 11.5   Common Service Information Stored in Service Portfolio

What is the common information that is typically stored in a service portfolio manager? What are the parameters that profile and best describe a service in an asset repository? Exhibit 11.5 consists of six different sections that classify services and identifies their properties: (1) General Identification, (2) Ownership and Sponsorship, (3) Functionality and Readiness, (4) Major Contractual and Service-Level Agreement Requirements, (5) Major Technologies, and (6) Security and Monitoring Considerations. This information is used for discovery and analysis of legacy services and for profiling conceptual entities that consequently will materialize into tangible executables.

VIRTUAL ENTITIES

Other important sources of services that may play a major role in the distribution of software across an enterprise and beyond are virtual service facilities. These emerging technologies introduce an advanced concept of *virtualization*, by which software, hardware, and even network facilities appear to be intangible. This property implies that virtual entities are devised to provide the required functionality and solutions. However, they are not "visible," to consumers, reside in remote production environments, and in some circumstances they are offered, maintained, and supported by third-party institutions.

Therefore, the acquisition of virtual capabilities and their physical location are separable aspects that practitioners must acknowledge. In other words, a service can provide business value to consumers without revealing its actual residence, architecture structure, and design considerations. The only factual information that is exposed by a virtual service is the type of offering it extends and the interfaces it offers. This limited information typically is revealed by the binding contracts that a service maintains with its corresponding consumers.

One of the best-known paradigms supporting virtual entities is cloud computing,[3] an emerging technology that not only offers virtual service capabilities, referred to as software as a service (SaaS); it also provides infrastructure facilities, known as infrastructure as a service (IaaS). Platform as a service (PaaS) is another type of service that is extended to run executables, services, and applications.

Remember, a virtual service is not necessarily hosted by third-party vendors. An organization may choose to develop a virtual service farm located within its own boundaries. Therefore, the practitioner should be aware that the virtual notion of software does not imply that a service's location must be completely unknown. In addition, a service's physical deployment and integration should be irrelevant to its consumers' requirements. The focus, therefore, should be on understanding the offered benefits of the service virtualization approach when analyzing and categorizing services: agility, lower operations cost, scalability, reusability, performance, and security. Moreover, the practitioner should also be aware of the risks involved when employing virtual entities. Data protection, privacy of information, and business continuity are some of the perils that may sway decisions not to utilize the asset virtualization avenue.

DELIVERABLES

Carve a service source model for the organization. Include the five different service origin patterns that are identified in this chapter: (1) Concept (2) Abstraction (3) Legacy, (4) Portfolio, and (5) Virtual. Next, categorize services by their sources and the life cycle stage that they are currently at. Finally, register the services in the organization's service portfolio along with their identity information, which are listed in the six sections illustrated in Exhibit 11.5:

1. General Identification
2. Ownership and Sponsorship
3. Functionality and Readiness

   4. Major Contractual and Service-Level Agreement Requirements
   5. Major Technologies
   6. Security and Monitoring Considerations

SUMMARY

- The service origin is a fundamental component of the service-oriented categorization model that reveals a service's characteristics, its contribution to a solution, and its life cycle stage.
- Ideas and concepts, abstractions, legacy entities, software portfolio, and virtual entities are the five different sources that services can be affiliated with.

Notes

1. The Service-Oriented Modeling Framework (SOMF) introduces the service conceptualization process to discover conceptual services. Refer to Michael Bell, *Service-Oriented Modeling: Service Analysis, Design, and Architecture* (Hoboken, NJ: John Wiley & Sons, 2008), p. 69.

2. Gregor Hohpe and Bobby Woolf, *Enterprise Integration Patterns: Designing, Building, and Deploying Messaging Solutions* (Boston: Addison-Wesley, 2003), p. 355.

3. www.webguild.org/2008/07/cloud-computing-basics.php.

CHAPTER 12

SERVICE STRUCTURE CATEGORIZATION PATTERNS

The term "structure" is related to the *anatomy* of internal service composition or its external operating environment. When it comes to a service's internal analysis, a structure depicts the *modularity* of source code. This term pertains to the logical manner by which service operations are bundled and collaborate to provide a solution. Grouping operations is often referred to as source code *componentization*; it contributes to component reuse, nimbleness, and software elasticity. However, the external structure of the service environment provides a different perspective: It represents service deployment, integration, and configuration. This is the art of connecting the dots that describes how autonomous services are grouped or linked together to enable message exchange and execution of transactions.

This discussion brings us to the topic of structural categorization and the need to classify services by types of structures, also known as structural patterns. Why is this classification effort vital to the service discovery and analysis practice? Understanding design and architecture considerations and the manner by which service components are arranged, internally and externally, enables architects, developers, analysts, modelers, and managers to manipulate and perfect a service formation and its hosting environment. Manipulation of a service's structure refers to the modeling operations that are elaborated on in Chapters 18 through 22. Among other modeling capabilities, these operations are provided to couple, decompose, aggregate, federate, bind, distribute, or unify service formations to improve their internal composition or external integration.

Although the service categorization process is not about identifying service functionality, the classification of service structures can contribute to an understanding of a service's capability limitations and the scope of its operations. The most important aim, however, of the service-oriented categorization venture is to comprehend a service's formation and reveal its coupling condition (loose or tight coupling) that is dictated by a service's internal structural design or its external architecture. Therefore, the sections that follow elaborate on these vital aspects of service structural categorization and analysis. They offer a service structure model that consists of *formational patterns* to help practitioners classify a service's internal structural characteristics and external deployment attributes.

SERVICE STRUCTURE MODEL

When it comes to the identification of a service's structure and the classification of service formations, the practitioner should be aware of three chief patterns that characterize a service's internal composition or external environment configuration: (1) Atomic (195), (2) Composite (196), and (3) Cluster (200). These are the products of service design and architecture decisions that are motivated by a wide range of business and technological imperatives. Thus think of a specific service

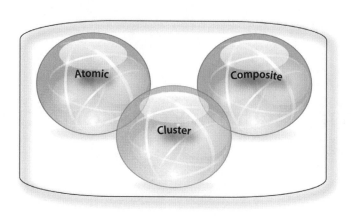

EXHIBIT 12.1 SERVICE STRUCTURE PATTERN MODEL

structure as a *pattern*, a logical arrangement of software components that is influenced by business requirements, business processes, technical specifications, service contextual affiliations, and more.

Exhibit 12.1 illustrates the three major patterns that identify distinct formations. These signature structures are discussed in detail in the sections that follow and throughout this book.

1. **Atomic (195).** Indivisible and fine-grained service formation.
2. **Composite (196).** A coarse-grained parent service that encompasses one or more finer-grained child services. This formation constitutes a hierarchical structure whose internal constituents are aggregated and hidden from the outside world.
3. **Cluster (200).** A group of distributed business and/or technological affiliated services that collaborate to provide a solution.

ENVIRONMENTAL INFLUENCES ON SERVICE STRUCTURE

In a small-scale and confined production field where technological interoperability challenges are limited, a service's internal structure must adhere to architectural simplicity and cohesiveness best practices. In other words, in a homogeneous computing environment where the distribution of software assets is not an intrinsic requirement, a service's internal formation should not be complex. Conversely, in a heterogeneous production landscape, where a mix of operating systems, networks, and language platforms must collaborate to provide solutions, a service's internal structure must accommodate the software integration and collaboration challenges.

How should a service's internal design structure accommodate a computing environment's scale and conditions? In the sections that follow, a service structure is portrayed as a by-product of its operating production environment. We will learn that composite or cluster service structures are the favorite design patterns for bridging enterprise interoperability gaps and accommodating collaboration difficulties between distributed software assets. Conversely, an atomic service structure better suits simplified design solutions for application-level architectures.

Consider the environmental influences on the service structure illustrated in Exhibit 12.2. The apparent three major service formations—atomic, composite, and cluster—are the pillars of every service-oriented project initiative. Note the two computing environments and their influences on service structure formations: Atomic Service and Composite Service typically better suit a

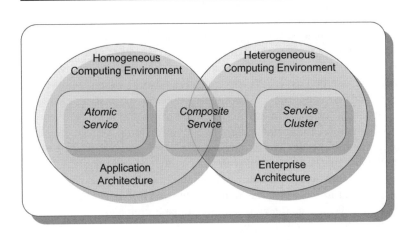

Exhibit 12.2   Environment Influences on Service Structure

Homogeneous Computing Environment, which also fall under the Application Architecture category. Conversely, Composite Service and Service Cluster are commonly found in an Heterogeneous Computing Environment and influenced by Enterprise Architecture initiatives. Moreover, as shown, a Composite Service typically plays a major role in both computing environments.

SERVICE STRUCTURE CATEGORIZATION DRIVING PRINCIPLES

Remember, as mentioned in the previous sections, a service's technical structure is greatly influenced by its operating environment and the context that motivates its formation. These influences may include business requirements, business processes, technical specifications, and design and architecture considerations to accommodate consumers' needs. Therefore, when it comes to typing and categorization of services, consider six guiding principles driven by these business and technological influences. These tenets can contribute to the analysis of a service in terms of its internal building blocks, structure, distribution, and composition of components.

1. **Atomicity.** Pertains to the indivisibility aspect of an atomic service structure. An atomicity level identifies the most fine-grained service of its type.
2. **Containment.** Identifies a composite service structure attribute, which emphasizes internal nested formations of child services.
3. **Inclusion.** Depicts a service cluster property, by which affiliated services, selected from different sources and software deployments, form a larger entity that offers a wide range of solutions.
4. **Distribution.** An architecture approach that is identified with the dispersion of software assets across the enterprise and even beyond.
5. **Hierarchy.** The foundation of a composite service internal structure.
6. **Independence.** Identifies that state of self an autonomous service.

ATOMIC SERVICE STRUCTURE: INDIVISIBLE PATTERN

An atomic structure is the most rudimentary service formation that is commonly deployed to a production environment. It is simply a fine-grained and indivisible entity that typically stays intact during the service-oriented modeling process because of practical business or technical reasons. The business considerations are vast. But one of the most compelling rationales for avoiding decomposition of a service is its limited business proposition value. The term "limited" pertains to internal operations that implement a narrow scope of the solution. The less functionality offered, the finer-grained a service is; therefore, it should be categorized as an atomic entity. This rule of thumb suggests an opposite assertion as well: A service that consists of a large number of operations and functionalities should be a candidate for decomposition during the analysis phase.

From a technical perspective, the cost may outweigh the benefits when developing, testing, deploying, monitoring, and maintaining a fine-grained atomic service. Therefore, to alleviate this challenge, it is recommended that during the service-oriented analysis phase, such an atomic formation should be aggregated or unified with other entities, if appropriate.

A fine-grained atomic service can be autonomous and loosely coupled, and deployed to a production environment to meet business requirements and technical specifications. This scheme obviously can fit a small-scale architecture solution. In larger implementations, however, an atomic service should be unified with other entities, such as composite service, service cluster, or a peer atomic service, to justify the price tag and adhere to organizational architecture best practices.[1]

COMPOSITE SERVICE STRUCTURE: HIERARCHICAL PATTERN

A structure that is referred to as *composite* constitutes an assortment of services that jointly form a dependent association.[2] These relationships are hierarchical in nature, arranged in a parent/child format. The parent is always the contained entity that typically consists of smaller, finer-grained services. A child service can also be regarded as a parent if its internal structure contains smaller services.

By observing the real world, analyzing the production environment, or inspecting the software layers that have been piling up during years and decades, we can notice composite formations that are "organically" grown or purposely designed to adhere to a hierarchical structure. For example, a legacy application that consists of internal software modules can be conceived of as a composite entity. An enterprise service bus (ESB) also exemplifies this concept: Its various software components collaboratively communicate to provide a messaging solution for an organization. But the chief aspect to remember is that a composite formation is simply comprised of one or more internal atomic or composite services. They are arranged in a hierarchical manner and work together, parent and child, to achieve a certain goal.

Now let us view a composite service structure that is depicted in Exhibit 12.3. This illustration displays three services. The Home Loan Composite Service is the outer entity, which encompasses the internal service: Fixed-Rate Loan Composite Service. This nested structure forms a hierarchical pattern that represents a parent/child relationship. Moreover, although the Fixed-Rate Loan Composite Service is an aggregated service, it also consists of its own internal finer-grained service: Loan Calculator Atomic Service. Therefore, this overall structural configuration represents two composite services and a single atomic service.

HOW IS A COMPOSITE SERVICE FORMED?   To understand how a composite service is formed, simply study the associations among its internal constituents. These relationships among services that make up a composite entity, as apparent in Exhibit 12.3, are driven by *structural considerations* or *contextual affiliations*. Structural reasons pertain to the hierarchical constitution that is formed by developers, dictated by design decisions preceding the service construction phase. They may be influenced by pragmatic architecture best practices that advocate, for example, aggregating fine-grained services to avoid unfeasible distribution.

Environmental configurations driven by production environment constraints characteristically influence the structural formation of a composite service as well. This service structure is

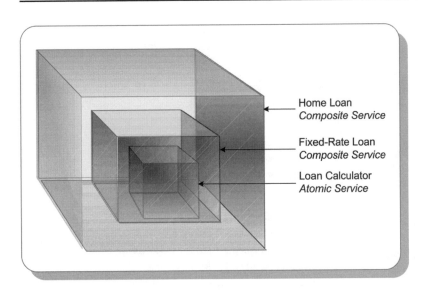

Home Loan
Composite Service

Fixed-Rate Loan
Composite Service

Loan Calculator
Atomic Service

EXHIBIT 12.3   COMPOSITE SERVICE HIERARCHICAL FORMATION PATTERN EXAMPLE

typically formed when the architect cannot tolerate an overly distributed computing landscape that consists of a growing number of fine-grained autonomous services. Thus a composite formation is created to reduce service distribution and alleviate deployment and maintenance challenges, increase their reusability rates, and even address interoperability difficulties.

From a contextual perspective, the hierarchical relationships between aggregated services are carved out based on their semantic affiliation. "Semantic" means that an aggregated service is related to its internal peers by a common business or technical field of expertise and specialties. On the business front, for example, a bond can be established between a number of small business loan services that are bundled into a composite formation to collaborate on a solution. Conversely, technical affiliations are driven by technological similarities: Links between technical services, for example, that are designed to address data transformation can be regarded as a contextual relationship that forms a composite formation.

COMPOSITE FORMATIONS LEVELS.   A composite service can be depicted in two different perspectives: application level and enterprise level. The latter term identifies and describes a composite service that operates in a distributed environment; the former addresses a service's internal structure and source code modularization.

Application-Level Composite Service.   An application-level perspective of composite formations focuses on confined and small-scale structures that originate from source code and programming modules. Here we focus on hierarchical constructs of programming language capabilities, such as service operations that can be bundled to form containing structures for analysis. In other words, operations that belong to a source code file can be grouped and transformed into internal services. This duty typically is assigned to developers charged with creating reusable and efficient code by identifying functionality reuse opportunities and striving to reduce operation redundancy.

The example that is depicted in Exhibit 12.4 clarifies this idea. The banking account source code file that represents the Banking Account Java class contains four distinct operation groups,

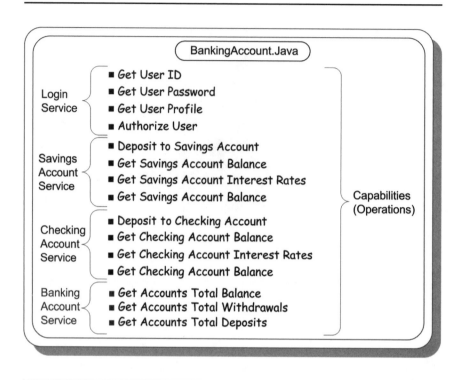

EXHIBIT 12.4   APPLICATION-LEVEL COMPOSITE FORMATION EXAMPLE

each of which constitutes a internal service: Login Service, Savings Account Service, Checking Account Service, and Banking Account Service. The latter is the most abstracted and generalized service, which is destined to contain the former services. Hence, all the services that execute these banking account activities form a composite service. The formed hierarchy is clear: The parent entity is the Banking Account Service and the containing services are regarded as its offspring.

A graphical composite view of the application-level perspective is presented in Exhibit 12.5. The containing entity Banking Account Composite Service consists of the three internal atomic services: Login Atomic Service, Savings Account Atomic Service, and Checking Account Atomic Service. Obviously, this structure can be further examined and manipulated by applying the analysis modeling operations recommended in Chapters 18 to 22. These modeling activities can assist practitioners to decompose or aggregate service formation based on architecture best practices. For example, the Login Atomic Service can be removed from the Banking Account Composite Service or aggregated into another composite service that hosts similar context-related services.

Enterprise-Level Composite Service.   An enterprise-level composite service differs from an application-level composite service. The former typically offers a wider scope of a solution. Here, the focus is on larger implementations—customarily on integration or infrastructure entities that are distributed across the organization and in some cases even beyond enterprise boundaries. Moreover, an enterprise-level composite service is a coarse-grained formation that can physically span multiple business domains or consist of virtual software components. But the distributability aspect of the enterprise version is not the major attribute that practitioners should be concerned about initially. Its composite structure is what should be thoroughly analyzed and properly designed.

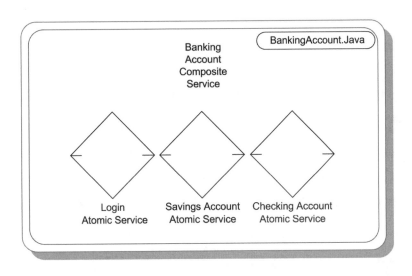

EXHIBIT 12.5 APPLICATION-LEVEL COMPOSITE VIEW EXAMPLE

This discussion calls for the analysis of one of the most essential enterprise-level composite service properties: its hierarchical structure. As discussed previously in this chapter in the introduction to Composite Service Structure section, the containing service, the outermost entity, is the dominant formation that conceptually, logically, and even physically embodies the functionality of its subordinate finer-grained services. From a conceptual point of view, the parent service must represent the concepts that its internal entities are established upon. For example, a Home+Loan Composite Service typically consists of internal services that offer different types of loans. The logical perspective calls for the hierarchical relationships between the contained loan services. Finally, the physical view represents the manner by which these services are constructed by developers. These three perspectives must be analyzed and in due time optimized for performance, reuse, and agility. Refer to Chapters 14–22 for an elaborated discussion about the service analysis and modeling process which involves these conceptual, logical, and physical perspectives.

Exhibit 12.6 illustrates an example of an enterprise-level composite service. It depicts a number of associated services, arranged in a layered structure; it is a hierarchical formation that contains aggregated services. The Business Process Engine Composite Service is the aggregating entity, which is comprised of three contained services: Business Process Management Composite Service, ESB Composite Service, and Business Process Life Cycle Composite Service. Each of these child entities are composite services themselves, since each consists of corresponding atomic services, as shown. In addition, the Monitoring Atomic Service and Alerts Atomic Service are also a part of the containing Business Process Engine Composite Service.

Note that this depiction in Exhibit 12.6 merely identifies the logical dependencies between the corresponding internal services; it disregards, for the time being, the physical implementation. In the scope of enterprise architecture, these contained entities may be physically distributed to different production environments, but their composite logical pattern does not reveal their geographical location. For example, the Business Process Engine Composite Service may be installed in one production section and provide Service Façade pattern functionality while the ESB Composite Service may operate in another.

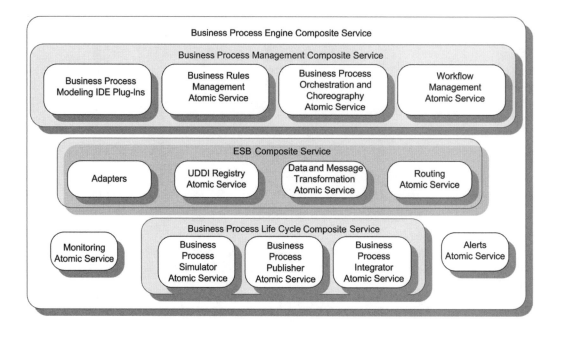

EXHIBIT 12.6 ENTERPRISE-LEVEL BUSINESS PROCESS ENGINE COMPOSITE SERVICE EXAMPLE

SERVICE CLUSTER: DISTRIBUTED AND FEDERATED PATTERN

A cluster structure is comprised of *affiliated* services—atomic and/or composite formations—that collaboratively offer solutions to business or technological concerns.[3] This scheme emphasizes distribution of software assets that are linked together to enable efficient execution of transactions and exchange of information. Furthermore, a cluster internal structure depends on architectures of existing legacy applications, services, or conceptual services that have not been implemented yet.

A cluster logical formation can constitute a large or a small service integration model. A large cluster configuration can be comprised of legacy software executables that are distributed across the boundaries of business domains, span organizations within the enterprise, or operated at partners' locations. Conversely, a practitioner may devise a different configuration that confines cluster members to a smaller environment. For example, software components or modules that are not necessarily remotely distributed across organizational boundaries can be grouped to form a local service cluster. The term "local" pertains to a smaller magnitude of the cluster structure and the limited extent of software assets distribution that may be deployed to a single production environment.

Exhibit 12.7 illustrates an accounting cluster that consists of seven distinct services. This depiction conveys *structural* and *contextual* observations. The structural aspects are denoted by the logical links (solid lines) that connect each of the services. This structural association may imply that the affiliations between the services are established because of identified message exchange paths or merely to denote a potential contract between two services. Therefore, at this stage the solid line is used simply to depict a physical association between two service cluster members.[4] In addition, the apparent loose coupling architectural style is attributed to the distribution of the services. From a contextual perspective, note the possible links, the relationships that are formed between the

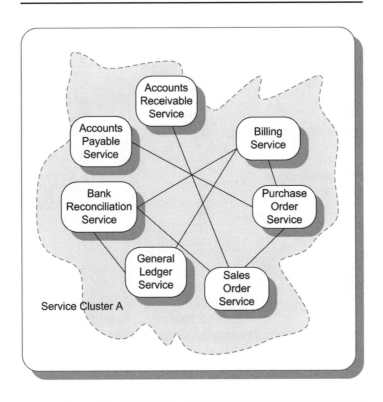

Exhibit 12.7   Accounting Service Cluster Pattern Example

cluster's members that collaboratively contribute to the delivery of an accounting solution, which involves billing, purchase order, bank reconciliation, and other fields of expertise.

PRINCIPLE OF INCLUSION.   A Service Cluster does not necessarily have to be comprised of newly deployed services or software components constructed for the purpose of instituting a logical or even a physical structure. This assertion leads to the notion that a cluster is chiefly an *abstraction*, a conceptual construct that constitutes a group of associated software assets that provide solutions. Therefore, we can conceive of a cluster as a collection of related *distributed* components that are selected from various existing or planned implementations, either applications or services, to form a virtual entity that is assembled to meet business or technological goals. This idea represents the crux of the *inclusion* principle.

Exhibit 12.8 illustrates this concept. The apparent Service Cluster A is comprised of seven services that are contributed by four sources: (1) Services B and C, which are a part of the Home Insurance Application; (2) Services E and G, which are constituents of the Car Insurance Application; and (3) Services I and J, which are affiliated with the Credit Verification Composite Service. (4) Note that the autonomous service Monitoring Atomic Service, the fourth source, is also a member of this cluster.

PRINCIPLES OF CLUSTER GRAVITY POINT.   As discussed in the previous section, a cluster consists of services that are installed locally or on disparate locations, such as across business domains

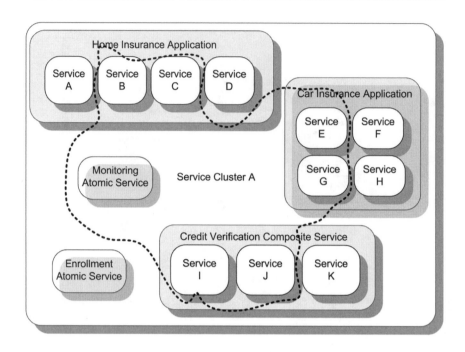

EXHIBIT 12.8 CLUSTER: INCLUSION OF SERVICES EXAMPLE

and organizations or configured on partners' remote production sites. This architecture distribution scheme does not come without perils: It increases software interoperability challenges and jeopardizes the control on scattered cluster members. To enable flawless communication between cluster constituents that operate under such software distribution configuration, a central control—a gravity point—should be assigned to one of the cluster's participating members. This assignment is designed to ensure continuity of operations and guarantee flawless execution of transactions managed by a single entity in the cluster.

In architectural terms, a gravity point can be simply a controller or Service Façade pattern that manages message inflow and outflow. This cluster member, either an atomic or composite service, is intelligent enough to direct requests to the corresponding cluster constituents and return responses to related outside consumers. Thus a gravity point is a point of contact, a liaison capable of communicating with internal cluster entities while tuned to the outside world for better collaboration and integration of message exchange. This scheme is essential to every architecture initiative that is designed to alleviate interoperability concerns and bridge the gaps between distributed assets that operate in mixed technological environments.

Exhibit 12.9 depicts the gravity point model. Service Cluster A, which provides defined boundaries for services A to H, also contains Service I, which acts as the point of contact for all cluster members. In addition, this gravity point is commissioned to communicate with outside consumers that are not an integral part of the service cluster.

A service that acts as a gravity point is designed to intercept messages on behalf of cluster members. In essence, this model of information passing prevents the outside world from directly exchanging messages with the internal cluster's participating parties. But what would the

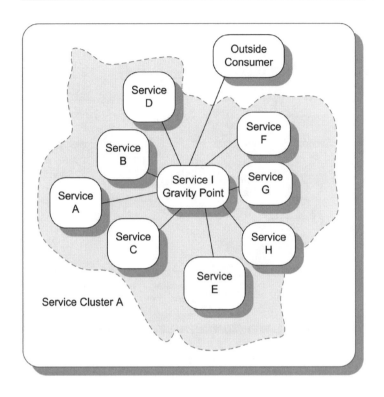

Exhibit 12.9   Cluster Gravity Point Model

consequences be if a cluster does not employ a gravity point? The alternative would be to grant access to any service that is an integral part of a cluster formation. This integration scheme would obviously boost service reuse and enhance cooperation with the surrounding environment. However, message monitoring and performance tractability capabilities may be lost if the central control provided by such service mediator is absent. In addition, security enforcement, which is a typical imperative requirement, can be compromised as well.

To resolve this conflict, a more flexible architecture can increase the feasibility of a cluster's gravity point yet still foster service reusability. This can be attained by introducing multiple gravity points within a single cluster formation, in which a number of services are assigned message mediation capabilities. Such an architectural style would obviously reduce the message load and enhance performance. Consider Exhibit 12.10, which depicts multiple gravity points within a service cluster. Services I and J are the defined gravity points for Service Cluster A. These are also the access points for outside consumers. In addition, note that Service I intercepts messages that are pointed to services A, B, C, and D. In the same manner, Service J is the contact point for services F and H.

DELIVERABLES

Devise an organizational service structural categorization process that is established on the three major formation patterns described in this chapter. Next, classify the services that are deployed to production, designed, or under contraction. This classification model should serve as a repeatable process for future structural categorization initiatives.

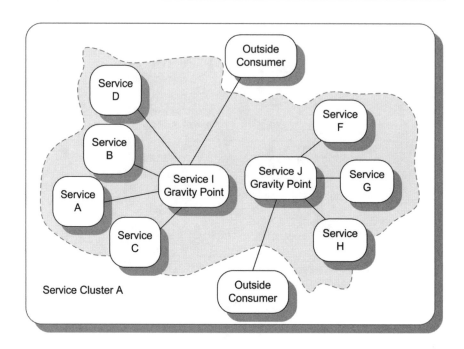

EXHIBIT 12.10   CLUSTER WITH MULTIPLE GRAVITY POINTS MODEL

SUMMARY

- The service structural categorization process addresses classification of internal and external service formations.
- The three major service structure patterns by which services can be categorized are Atomic (195), Composite (196), and Cluster (200).
- A service structure is typically influenced by business and technological requirements.
- A service hosting environment is also a determining factor that affects service formations.
- A service cluster may employ more than a single gravity point to handle outside communications on behalf of the cluster's members.

Notes

1.   To read about Atomic Service structural modeling operations and patterns, refer to Chapters 18 to 22.

2.   Chapters 18 through 22 introduce structural analysis and modeling patterns to establish and perfect composite service constructs.

3.   Refer to Chapters 18 through 22 for structural patterns and modeling mechanisms for manipulating cluster service formations.

4.   To use a more formal modeling notation, refer to Chapters 14 through 22, which introduce the employment of a modeling language for contextual and structural purposes.

CHAPTER 13

SERVICE CONTEXTUAL CATEGORIZATION PATTERNS

Unlike structural categorization discussed in Chapter 12, contextual classification is based on semantic typing of services. The term "semantic" implies that the focus of this process should be on relating a service to an area of expertise that is valuable to a solution. It also pertains to affiliating a service to a line of business and particular business functionality. From a technological perspective, a service can be associated with certain technical tasks that are vital to execution of transactions. For example, a service that executes accounts payable is typically classified as an accounting or business type of service. On the technological front, a service that is designed to handle encryption of data is characteristically categorized as a security or technical entity. These semantic relationships between services and various business or technical specialties form the crux of the contextual categorization process.

The reader may have recognized that the categorization process is about service typing. This approach assists practitioners in affiliating a service to a business or technical specialty. Therefore, classifying services by their semantic association to the type of functionality they offer contributes immensely to the establishment of an organizational service taxonomy. This catalog of service capabilities contributes to an enterprise software portfolio that fosters asset reuse and consolidation of services and ultimately minimizes duplication of functionality across the enterprise. On a project level scope, classifying services by the contribution to a solution would help focus on design and development tasks and set the right direction for the service construction efforts.

The sections that follow identify the chief components of the service contextual categorization model. These semantic contextual typing templates are referred to as *patterns of service classification*. They are devised to streamline the service categorization venture by offering a *repeatable* process and promoting a *unified* approach to grouping services based on their affiliation to business and technological occupations. Architects, developers, modelers, analysts, and managers should employ this model to enhance service-oriented analysis efforts and focus on the solution proposition for a small projects or large enterprise initiatives.

CONTEXTUAL CLASSIFICATION MODEL: PATTERNS FOR SERVICE CONTEXTUAL CATEGORIZATION

The method of contextual classification is crucial to every organization. One of the most contentious discussions taking place in today's business and technology communities is associated with service identity and classification disciplines. Often questions about how services should be classified and what the method of categorization should be help contribute to the establishment of an organizational service portfolio—a directory of software entities that classifies services based on their essence and their contribution to a project and the enterprise. In addition to promoting service reusability and reconciliation of service capabilities, the service portfolio is a vital facility that can

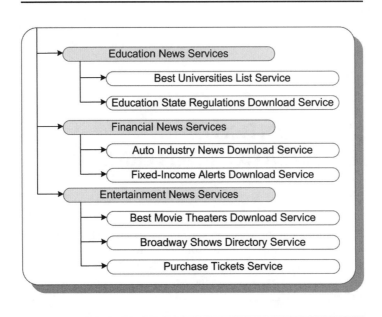

Exhibit 13.1 Institution of a Service Categorization Model Example

be employed to minimize functionality redundancy across the organization and contribute to the service discovery process.

We thus introduce three service contextual categorization patterns to facilitate the service identification process:

1. Business Services (207): A leading contextual category that identifies the contribution of a service to a business initiative.
2. Technical Services (209): A leading contextual category that associates a service with a technical solution.
3. Subcategories (211): This pattern pertains to business and technical subcategories.

The sections that follow elaborate on these leading and subordinate category classification patterns.

ESTABLISH A SERVICE CATEGORIZATION DIRECTORY.   What is the guiding method for contextual service categorization? Where should the practitioner start? How should a classification process be conducted? To establish a contextual classification model, simply devise a directory of service types. Each entry in this list of categories should represent a service specialty or capability. For example, let us view Exhibit 13.1, which illustrates three directory entries that were founded for a news agency: Education News Services, Financial News Services, and Entertainment News Services. Once the directory is established, group services under each corresponding directory entry. As apparent, the two services that are bundled under the Education News Services, for example, are the associated services Best Universities List Service and Education State Regulations Download Service.

LEADING CATEGORIES AND SUBCATEGORIES.   The service categorization model supports two levels of categories—*Leading Categories* and *Subcategories,* as depicted in Exhibit 13.2. The Leading Categories should consist of two high-level service types that are inclusive enough to encompass all the kinds of services that possibly can be found in the organization: Business Category and

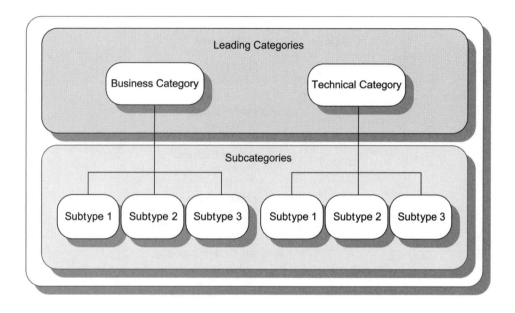

EXHIBIT 13.2 CONTEXTUAL CATEGORIZATION MODEL

Technical Category. For each of these two leading category entries, create a subcategory that includes lower corresponding classification levels. For example, under the leading Business Category, list all services associated with business specialties in the subcategories section. In the same manner continue with the technical services, each of which should be related to technological and architectural capabilities.

ESTABLISHING LEADING SERVICE CATEGORIES

As discussed in the previous section, the leading service categories are business and technical. These two classification directory starting points should be generic enough to embody the functionality and expertise of all types of services in an organization. The leading category section may include additional entries if the practitioner finds it appropriate. These may include hybrid types of services that neither belong to business nor are affiliated with the technical classification group. Remember, however, that the leading service category must be high level and generalized enough to encompass a wide range of organizational services. The sections that follow elaborate on these chief categories and the process of service classification.

BUSINESS CATEGORIZATION PROCESS.   What type of attributes must a service possess to be classified as a business entity? Is there a clear delineation between business and technical implementations? To answer these questions, one must understand the business model of the organization and the chosen strategy that drives revenue. Indeed, this assertion may sound too generic; however, to categorize a service as a business entity, we must recognize that the given answers would be associated with how we perceive the business. That is, this exercise is subjective, as the rules of classification vary for each individual organization. A general guiding principle, however, suggests that a business service is a software component that by and large executes business *processes* and performs business activities.

Exhibit 13.3   Business Categorization Process Model

A financial institution, for example, that incurs revenue by offering assistance with preparation of personal tax returns may also introduce automated means to help its customers file taxes. These capabilities can be delegated to services that embody accounting functionality and are able to execute business-related processes. Hence, services that possess such specialties should be categorized as business entities.

To help with the identification of business services, inspect their internal operations and identify their exposed public interfaces. While pursuing this activity, ask these guiding questions:

- Does the service execute business processes?
- Does the service's chief specialty attend to the business mission?
- Are most of the activities that the service performs affiliated with business implementation?
- Are the chief duties of a service related to business responsibilities?

To identify business services, a simple model for analysis and categorization is provided. The reader may be familiar with this approach since it is partly borrowed from Chapter 5, which depicts the method by which services are derived when pursuing business process analysis. Here, we utilize this approach to reveal the service's contextual affiliation. Consider the following four steps of service business categorization and verification analysis. These activities are also depicted in Exhibit 13.3. To confirm if a service is indeed a business entity, the answers to Steps 1 through 4 must be positive.

1. **Study Business Requirements.** Get acquainted with business imperatives and understand the driving motivation for the service being constructed. Have these requirements influenced the institution of the analyzed service?
2. **Identify Business Specialties.** Discover the business specialties that a service possesses. Does the service offer business expertise functionality, such as accounting, trading, insurance, or publishing?

Service Name	Business Specialty	Business Process	Service Capability (Operations)
Accounts Payable Service	Manage invoices Manage payments	Confirm invoices Print checks	Get invoice number Get customer ID Verify purchase order Integrate with Job Costing Service Print checks
Bank Reconciliation Service	Bank Account Reconciliation	Verify checking account transactions Adjust entries	Get accounts payable records Get accounts receivable records Get payroll records Get general ledger records Reconcile bank account

EXHIBIT 13.4 BUSINESS CATEGORIZATION ANALYSIS TABLE

3. **Analyze Business Processes.** Identify the business processes and the underlying business activities that a service executes. Does the service implement business processes?
4. **Inspect Service Capabilities.** Verify if the examined service operations reflect business requirements (the term "service capabilities" refers to service operations). Does the service meet business requirements?

The service categorization initiative requires a meticulous examination and verification process. It should include a thorough comparison of business requirements against service capabilities. To facilitate this task, create a verification sheet similar to Exhibit 13.4. This analysis venture should include four major inspection parameters, as illustrated in the exhibit: (1) Service Name, (2) Business Specialty, (3) Business Process, and (4) Service Capability. The Business Process column can be further broken down into business activities, if appropriate.

TECHNICAL CATEGORIZATION PROCESS.   What is a technical service? What is the process by which technical services are identified? Are technical services different from business services? These questions and similar ones are typical categorization challenges for almost any organization striving to manage its software asset portfolio efficiently. This venture is not only about establishing a universal identity for enterprise applications and services; it is also beneficial for institutionalizing ownership and sponsorship of an organization's technology arsenal. But perhaps one of the most compelling reasons to undertake such a classification initiative is to identify opportunities for software reuse across the enterprise. The technical aspect is even more crucial to organizations that desire to steer clear of duplicating existing capabilities and foster reuse of commercial off-the-shelf (COTS) products and architectures.

Again, service reusability and consolidation of technological assets are the major motivations behind this classification initiative. We are thus commissioned to discover technical identities of services by inspecting their offerings and profiling their major contribution to their operating environment. Perhaps the easiest way to classify a service as a technical entity would be to claim that "a service that is not categorized as a business entity by default it should be defined as technical." Unfortunately, this shortcut would not necessarily yield an accurate service typing assessment.

What is a technical service? A service should be categorized as a technical entity if and only if it is associated with technological or architectural capabilities. The terms technological solution capabilities and architectural capabilities is largely discussed in Chapter 2. These abilities pertain to the solution domain, the information technology organization that provides remedies to a business problem by utilizing technical means, such as language platforms, infrastructure COTS products, networks, application servers, and design and architecture best practices.

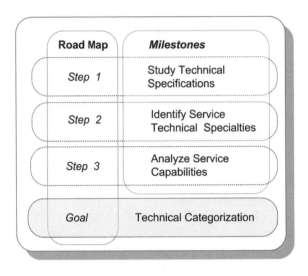

EXHIBIT 13.5   TECHNICAL CATEGORIZATION PROCESS MODEL

Indeed, the classification of a service would be arduous if business and technical properties affected operations and functionality equally. This aspect is discussed in the next section. Here, however, we merely emphasize technical aspects that are reflected by the service's internal activities and the goals it is designed to attain. Affirmative answers to the following questions typically would position a service in the technical column:

- Is the service designed to accommodate an architectural mission?
- Does the service offer a technological solution to a problem?
- Does that service functionality chiefly offer technological or architectural capabilities?
- Do the service's operations address technical solutions?
- Is the service's main specialty to provide technical remedies?

To simplify the categorization process, follow the three steps of the technical service classification and verification model. Affirmative answers to the questions presented in Steps 1 through 3 indicate that the inspected service should be categorized as a technical entity. Exhibit 13.5 illustrates this process.

1. **Study Technical Specifications.** Understand the technical specifications and the motivation that contributed to the service construction. Have these requirements driven the institution of the analyzed service?
2. **Identify Service Technical Specialties.** Does the service offer technical and architectural capabilities?
3. **Analyze Service Capabilities.** Do service operations meet technical specifications and architectural best practices?

To facilitate an efficient technical inspection and classification process, create a technical categorization analysis table, as depicted in Exhibit 13.6, consisting of three major columns: Service Name, Technical Specialty, and Service Capability. The Service Capability column should include service operations that correspond to the offered technical specialty that is apparent in the Technical Specialty column.

Service Name	Technical Specialty	Service Capability (Operations)
Identity Service	Heterogeneous identity management	Get security policy
		Get user's credentials
		Encrypt user's credentials
		Synchronize user's password
		Reset password
		Handle provisioning and deprovisioning
Download Content Service	Multimedia delivery	Download video clip
		Download article
		Download slide show
		Download images
		Download graphs

Exhibit 13.6   Technical Categorization Analysis Table

HYBRID SERVICE TYPES.   Not all services in the organization fall precisely into the business or technical categories. Hybrid types may be found as well. The hybrid class identifies services that do not distinctly match either business or technical categories. Obviously, a service design that yields such a mix of business and technical capabilities does not adhere to organizational architecture best practices. Apparent rising costs of integration, deployment, maintenance, and monitoring activities are the obvious reasons. Furthermore, such a tightly coupled implementation characteristically yields an ambiguous architecture style that must be revamped to achieve a well-integrated and loosely coupled service landscape.

From a categorization perspective, hybrid services introduce major challenges in terms of software asset reusability, consolidation, and even analysis. In addition, these entities are hard to manage, redesign, or decompose because of their intermingled and tightly coupled business and technical operations. Thus when it comes to the classification of these services, the rule of thumb is to simply create a "Hybrid" category called "Other" and tag these entities as heterogeneous implementations. Future development initiatives should address this issue by embarking on decomposition activities.

SERVICE SUBCATEGORIES ESTABLISHMENT PROCESS

The leading category level that has been discussed so far may not facilitate a useful organization service taxonomy. The depicted leading *business* and *technical* types are obviously too generic and in most circumstances would not reflect a detailed breakdown of service capabilities, functionality, or specific specialties. Therefore, to establish a viable service taxonomy, the practitioner must discover *subcategories* that can better assist with a meticulous service classification process. This calls for employment of a subcategorization effort, to ensure that services are accurately cataloged and classified based on their contribution to business and technology organizations. We thus introduce two service subcategories, each of which corresponds to its leading category: business service subcategory and technical service subcategory. These are discussed in details in the sections that follow.

BUSINESS SERVICE SUBCATEGORIES: BUSINESS TAXONOMY MODELS.   Once services are confirmed as business entities, the next step would be to arrange them based on subcategories that are useful to stakeholders, sponsors, and the development community. For example, business services can be further classified by their contribution and return on investment (ROI), strategic value, geographical distribution, business processes, or business specialty.

This catalog of services contributes to service reuse and consolidation because it helps find existing or similar implementations that can be leveraged for future projects rather than building new services. In other words, a detailed business subcategory can enable practitioners to assemble service capabilities from existing legacy applications and services based on their strengths, contribution, qualities, attributes, and specialties.

Before pursuing this analysis, establish a service subcategory model that can help arrange services in certain patterns that are acceptable to the organization. One of the most common business taxonomy structures groups services based on their contribution type, namely specialties. These may include, for example: "Hotel Reservation Services," "Ticket Purchasing Services," or "Car Rent Cancellation Services." The sections that follow elaborate on additional perspectives that can be implemented to establish a diversified business service taxonomy.

Business Specialty Subcategory Model.   As mentioned in the previous section, the most intuitive service subcategorization is to create a taxonomy based on business specialties. Obviously this would contribute to the identification of capabilities of services and even help leverage their functionality for ongoing or future projects. To achieve this goal, the specialty model can arrange services in three different directory patterns, each of which represents service capabilities from a different business perspective. The practitioner can utilize either one or all of these grouping methods:

1. **Classify services by business functionality.** Group services based on their business process affiliation.
2. **Group services by business products.** Arrange services according to their association with a business product, business requirements, or applications.
3. **Arrange services by logical layers.** Classify services by their relationship to a business solution proposition, concept, or idea.

Exhibit 13.7 illustrates the Business Specialty Subcategory along with its subordinating services. It shows three service specialty perspectives: Business Functionality, Business Product, and

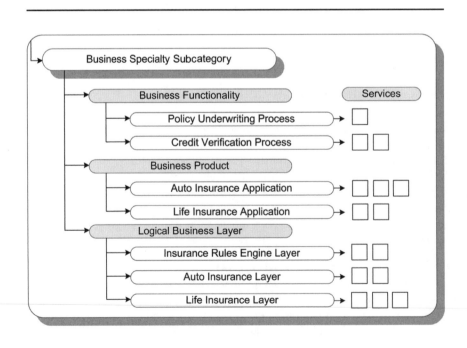

EXHIBIT 13.7   BUSINESS SPECIALTY SUBCATEGORY EXAMPLE

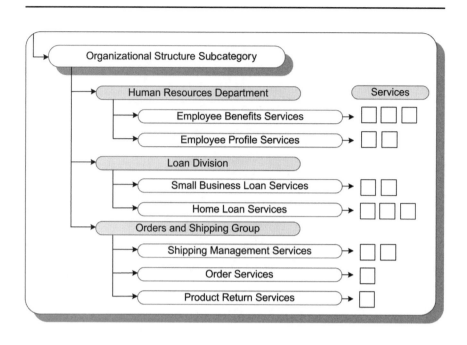

EXHIBIT **13.8**   O**RGANIZATIONAL** S**TRUCTURE** B**USINESS** S**UBCATEGORY** E**XAMPLE**

Logical Business Layer. Note that their corresponding services are depicted on the far right section under the Services title.

Organizational Structure Subcategory Model.   From a business perspective, services can also be grouped based on enterprise ownership and sponsorship. This approach groups services by stakeholder affiliation and the bodies that support and fund life cycles of services. Subcategorizing services based on organizational structure—such as divisions, departments, or lines of business—is another method that identifies services in a manner that is consistent with their contribution to business occupations or interest groups. These, for example, can be loan division, accounting department, or human resource group.

Exhibit 13.8 depicts an organizational structure subcategory that consists of customized services: Human Resources Department, Loan Division, Order and Shipping Group. Each of these supporting entities both sponsors the development of services and supports their operations in production environment. Note the Services column on the far right that consists of services that correspond to their apparent categories (on left).

Geographical Affiliation Subcategory Model.   The business structure and its management control on various internal organizations are influenced by the geographical locations of its facilities and operations. Imagine a banking institution that offers financial products, such as loans and fixed-income investment opportunities, which are distributed across states, countries, or continents. Classifying services that are installed along these geographical regions may require a different business service subcategory model. This service taxonomy must not only suit heterogeneous computing environments, it also ought to comply with local banking laws and regulations.

This subcategory model would require grouping services by centers of operations, perhaps production facilities, or even local data warehouses. Consider Exhibit 13.9, which exemplifies this model. Note that the three depicted business subordinate entries are based on the distribution of

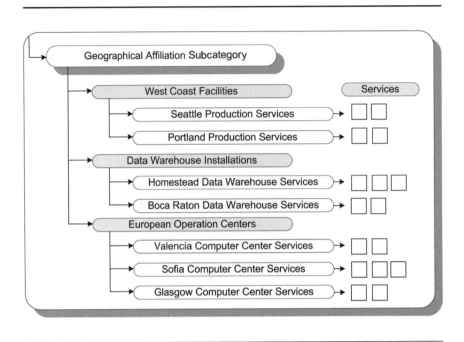

EXHIBIT 13.9   GEOGRAPHICAL AFFILIATION SERVICE BUSINESS SUBCATEGORY EXAMPLE

services across remote production facilities: West Coast Facilities, Data Warehouse Installations, and European Operation Centers. In addition, each depicted facility consists of a group of services that resides in a different geographical location. For example, the West Coast Facilities include Seattle Production Services and Portland Production Services.

Revenue and ROI Subcategory Model.   Unlike the specialty, organizational, and geographical models, the revenue-driven service taxonomy is based on the contribution value that a service offers to a business organization and its supporting stakeholders. The term "value" pertains to the revenue that is incurred during a service operation and the projected or the actual ROI. Moreover, this monetary perspective groups services not necessarily based on their functionality, consumption, or location. Rather, this arrangement helps assess the strategic merit of services and helps prioritize future funding to boost support for those whose earning goals have been met.

Exhibit 13.10 illustrates the Revenue and ROI subcategory model. The Projected Revenue and the Actual Revenue taxonomy directories identify ranges that services can be classified by. Note the Services column, on the far right, which consists of services that correspond to the projected and actual amounts. This model can be expanded to include other financial taxonomy directory entries, such as operational, maintenance, and monitoring costs.

TECHNICAL SERVICE SUBCATEGORIES: TECHNICAL TAXONOMY MODELS.   Similar to the business subcategories, the subclassification of technical services should be detailed enough to present the various service groups that offer distinct technological capabilities. Thus practitioners should craft technical taxonomy models that consist of subcategories to enable a more detailed classification. This would reveal functionalities and capabilities of services to address technological and architectural solutions.

It is imperative to view organizational technology from different perspectives because of the intrinsic complexity that accompanies almost any service integration, deployment, and

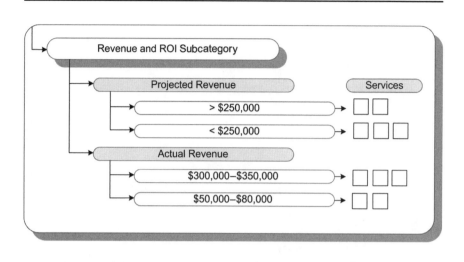

Exhibit 13.10   Revenue and ROI Service Business Subcategory Example

maintenance initiative in production. Moreover, the term "technology" typically encompasses a wide range of technical aspects by which services can be classified. These can be architecture, infrastructure, security, data delivery, platforms, and more.

Therefore, when subcategorizing technical services, concentrate on the proposed three subclassification models that would enable the various stakeholders to view capabilities and functionality of services from different perspectives. These are discussed in the sections that follow.

Technical Specialty Subcategory Model: A Map of Service Expertise.   Unlike the service business specialty that was discussed in the Business Specialties Subcategory Model section, a technical specialty identifies the service contribution to a solution in terms of architectural and technical abilities. More specifically, this subclassification approach reveals the capability of a service in a certain area of technical expertise. This may include functionality that is offered in the fields of infrastructure and messaging, data delivery and manipulation, presentation layer, information rendering and repurposing, and others. The chief aim here is to assist practitioners in accomplishing an analysis that reveals a service's strengths and weaknesses in a variety of technical subjects.

To better understand this objective, simply draw a map of service specialties that an organization can utilize for various projects and business initiatives similar to the illustration in Exhibit 13.11. This diagram should depict areas of technical expertise that are associated with the organization's architectural regions of concerns.[1] This environment should consist of services that constitute technology solutions for a project and the enterprise. The apparent five regions—Consuming Applications and Services, Consumer Integration Services, Infrastructure Services, Data Resource Integration Services, and Data Resources and Information Delivery Services—can identify service reuse opportunities and assist with carving out a service specialty subcategorization model.

Devising a map of service expertise is a good start that sets the boundary of this technical subclassification effort. This map also reflects the challenges that a project faces or organizational concerns. Next, provide a service technical specialty taxonomy that depicts the breakdown of services based on their capabilities and ability to contribute to various technological and architectural solutions. However, this detailed taxonomy does not necessarily follow the technical expertise map that has been crafted earlier. Here we should provide technical specialties that focus on a particular project or on general organizational solutions. For example, presentation layer services and

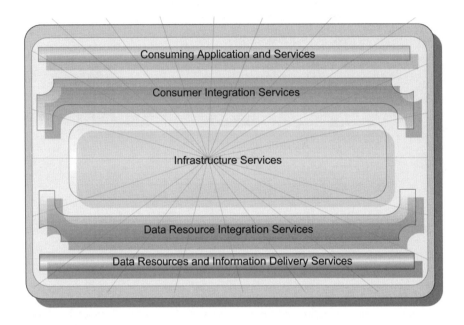

Exhibit 13.11   Map of Service Technical Expertise Example

data services. Exhibit 13.12 illustrates this concept. Note the three major specialty groups and their corresponding service groups:[2] Presentation Specialty Services, Data Specialty Services, and Infrastructure Specialty Services. This directory can be expanded to include more perspectives of organizational technologies and their related services.

Architecture Capabilities and Best Practices Subcategory Model.   Technical services can also be subcategorized according to their contribution to an architectural idea, plan, implementation, strategy, or even best practice. For example, grouping services that adhere to best practices or are designed to implement concepts can reveal different perspectives of *architectural concerns*. What is more, an architecture-driven subcategory model typically broadens the analysis view of architects, analysts, developers, modelers, and managers seeking to justify the construction of a new service or to utilize existing services. Searching for such motivation can increase the reusability of software assets and promote consolidation of services across the enterprise.

What are the architectural concerns and problems that services can rectify? These are typically challenges associated with integration, interoperability, mediation, searchability, virtualization, data aggregation, distribution, federation of software assets, and more. Services can contribute to resolving these problems by conforming to design patterns, architecture best practices, and policies. Introducing services to propose solutions to these architectural concerns can be useful to future project planning and problem-solving initiatives.

Exhibit 13.13 illustrates an architecture-driven taxonomy[3] that groups two major types of services: Mediation Services and Architecture Patterns–Driven Services. The former service group provides brokering solutions that are supported by four sorts of services: Data Transformation Services, Message Routing Services, Protocol Conversion Services, and Message Enrichment Services. The Architecture Patterns–Driven Services taxonomy entry offers services that can help implement four different architecture patterns: Composite Formation Pattern Services, Cluster Formation Pattern Services, Meta Data Mapping Pattern Services, and Service Façade Pattern Services.

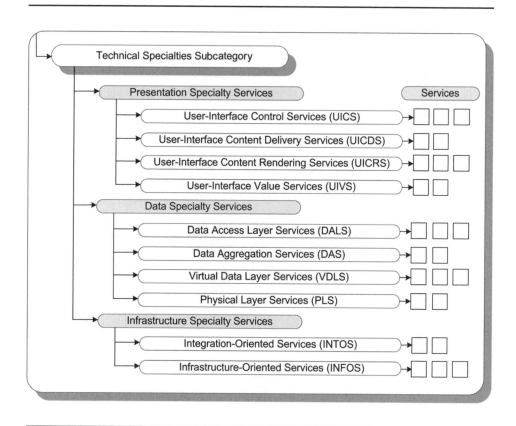

Exhibit 13.12   Technical Specialty Subcategory Example

Technological Capabilities Subcategory Model.   A subcategorization process that is based on technological capabilities calls for grouping services according to their contribution to various technologies that support and empower applications and services in production environments. Unlike the architecture taxonomy, the technological capabilities taxonomy introduces a view that is associated with *implementation mechanisms* rather than best practices, architectural concepts, or planning.

Therefore, the technological capabilities should focus on implementation concerns. For example, if an organization's major mission is to aggregate data for its consumers, then data processing, data transformation, data cleansing, and data collections should be its area of technological concerns. Thus a corresponding taxonomy should classify services that are designed to carry out these tasks. This taxonomy would reveal capabilities of services to provide solutions to projects and fulfill technological missions.

Technological concerns are also about infrastructure capabilities. These include security of data and privacy of information, monitoring and service-level agreement enforcement, policy management, integration with COTS products, and implementation and configuration of Enterprise Service Buses. Exhibit 13.14 illustrates similar technological concerns grouped by a service taxonomy that introduces two major types of services: Security Services and Infrastructure Enabling Services. The security directory consists of services that address privacy, identity, provisioning, and credential concerns. However, the infrastructure section associates services that tackle monitoring, messaging, data virtualization, and policy management challenges.

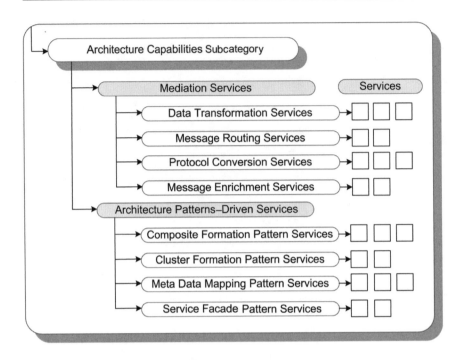

Exhibit 13.13   Architecture Capabilities Subcategory Example

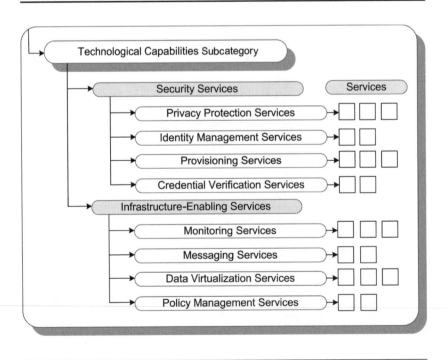

Exhibit 13.14   Technological Capabilities Subcategory Example

DELIVERABLES

Establish a service categorization model that consists of two chief classification patterns:

1. **Business and technical leading service categories.** This directory entry section should present at least two high-level service categories: business and technical services. It is possible to expand the leading category section by introducing other generic types appropriate to the service classification effort.
2. **Service subcategory.** Provide a detailed service directory with a subcategory section that corresponds to each of the leading category directory entries. Under the business type, for example, group business-oriented services. In the same manner, bundle technical services under the technical category.

SUMMARY

- Service contextual categorization is a process that addresses the classification of services based on patterns and specialties that contribute to project or organizational solutions.
- Two chief types of services are referred as leading category patterns: business and technical.
- Service subcategories are directory entries that present lower-level service classifications, each of which corresponds to a service leading category.

Notes

1. As an alternative, the practitioner can use organizational reference architecture to help establish a categorization model. The reference architecture model is discussed in Chapter 9.
2. The technical specialties and the corresponding services were initially introduced in the service discovery chapters, Chapters 5 through 10.
3. An architecture taxonomy can leverage an organizational reference architecture, as discussed in Chapter 9.

PART FOUR

SERVICE-ORIENTED CONTEXTUAL ANALYSIS PROCESS AND MODELING PATTERNS

The art of the contextual analysis and modeling process is simply to understand the essence of a service and model, modify, tune, enhance, or augment its capabilities to provide an adequate solution to a problem. This is a *modeling* endeavor designed to efficiently examine a service's purpose and shape its functionality to maximize its contribution. It is also about altering the service's influence and scope of its operations in the environment in which it operates. It is clearly about studying its offered specialties and harnessing them to provide an effective solution to an organizational concern.

The reader might have already recognized that contextual analysis is a modeling exercise that focuses on a service's specialty, the types of offerings it extends, and the spectrum of its influence in the environment in which it operates. This venture enables architects, modelers, analysts, developers, and managers to inspect service capabilities and become acquainted with the solution scope they provide. The final delivery is an analysis proposition that not only verifies the service's capabilities to satisfy business and technical imperatives but also proposes advanced solutions to boost the service's business and technical value proposition and to meet the requirements of a small project or a large business initiative.

The contextual analysis effort is about neither examination of a service's internal structure nor proposing a superior physical deployment model. Nor are tangible aspects of a service's formation and its technical configuration the goal of this exercise. Instead, focus on a service's functionality, its areas of expertise, and the scope of its operations. Understand the relationship between a service and its corresponding consumers and peer services and attend to the requirements of its consumers.

To fulfill these goals, the practitioner ought to model a virtual environment and test the assumptions that have led to the institution of a service. This modeling process should assist with the discovery of new services and contribute to the harmonization of a service ecosystem in terms of service integration, collaboration, reusability, and consolidation of redundant functionality. To help accomplish these tasks, a set of contextual analysis modeling patterns is provided. These are guiding templates, ready-to-use solutions that offer remedies for the problems they seek to resolve.

CONTEXTUAL ANALYSIS MODEL

The contextual analysis model offers a road map and milestones for service discovery and analysis implementation. It can also serve as a personal and organizational strategy—a plan for analyzing, modeling, verifying, and proposing design and architectural solutions to a project or a large business initiative. This model introduces directions and patterns for delivering analysis propositions. These

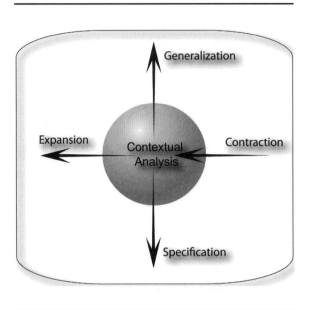

EXHIBIT P4.1   SERVICE-ORIENTED CONTEXTUAL ANALYSIS MODEL

solution styles can be easily adopted to facilitate service discovery, integration, associations, and collaboration efforts.

Remember that since this model introduces contextual analysis approaches, the focus should be on service functionality, specialty, capability, and the semantic relationship that a service establishes with its corresponding consumers. This approach may include instituting contracts, expanding or contracting service offerings throughout the organization, founding abstractions to widen the service solution scope, or trimming service capabilities. These are represented by four major analysis directions that the practitioner should consider pursuing: Generalization, Specification, Expansion, and Contraction. Exhibit P4.1 illustrates this model of analysis execution that is discussed in detail in Chapters 14 through 17.

- **Contextual generalization analysis.** This process is about generalizing service capabilities and establishing higher-level service abstractions to widen the scope of a proposed solution by employing contextual modeling patterns.
- **Contextual specification analysis.** The contextual specification analysis activity introduces methods and patterns to reduce the scope of service functionality and trim down offerings to related consumers.
- **Contextual expansion analysis.** To facilitate the growth of a distributed environment, the contextual expansion analysis process proposes mechanisms and patterns to broaden a service's influence across the organization and widen its consumer *base*.
- **Contextual contraction analysis.** Finally, modeling techniques, methods, and patterns are provided by the contextual analysis process to roll back a service expansion in a distributed environment and trim down the exposure of its operations to its related consumers.

CONTEXTUAL ANALYSIS ASSETS AND NOTATION

Finally, let us view the standard notation utilized in this part of the book. Two groups of symbols are employed to carve out an analysis proposition diagram: asset notation and modeling operation notation. These symbols depict both the services that participate in a contextual analysis diagram and the modeling operations used to discover and manipulate a service.

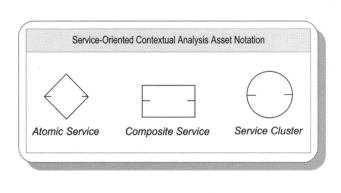

EXHIBIT P4.2   SERVICE-ORIENTED CONTEXTUAL ANALYSIS ASSET NOTATION

ASSET NOTATION.   The asset notation that is illustrated in Exhibit P4.2 consists of services that have been largely discussed in Chapter 12. These are the service-oriented modeling assets that are used to describe distinct service formations employed in an analysis proposition diagram: Atomic Service, Composite Service, and Service Cluster. Although chief attention here shifts toward the contextual aspects of service modeling, the practitioner should use these symbols to indicate the service structures that participate in a solution. Therefore, the identified service structures that are used here are treated as logical entities, not physical ones. The next summary describes each symbol.

- **Atomic Service.** An indivisible, typically fine-grained entity that is impractical to decompose into smaller services.
- **Composite Service.** A formation that consists of aggregated, child, fine-grained atomic, or other composite services.
- **Service Cluster.** A collection of related atomic or composite services that collaborates to provide solutions.

CONTEXTUAL ANALYSIS MODELING OPERATIONS NOTATION.   The modeling operations notation used to create an analysis proposition diagram is comprised of four symbols, each of which denotes a distinct activity during a contextual analysis modeling effort (illustrated in Exhibit P4.3). The next outline describes these operations.

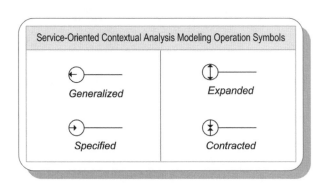

EXHIBIT P4.3   SERVICE-ORIENTED CONTEXTUAL ANALYSIS MODELING OPERATIONS SYMBOLS

- **Generalized.** The "Generalized" symbol denotes the generalization activity of a service. By pursuing this operation, the solution scope of a service widens. The final product is a new service that represents a higher abstraction level than its originator.
- **Specified.** The "Specified" symbol is used to depict the reduction of service functionality and trimmed-down capabilities. The service represents a lower abstraction level than its originator.
- **Expanded.** To illustrate the broadening of service operations and its increased exposure across the organization, the "Expanded" symbol should be employed. It would indicate the growth of a service consumer base.
- **Contracted.** The "Contracted" symbol is used when the practitioner is commissioned to reduce the boundaries of a distributed environment and narrow the consumer base of a service.

CHAPTER 14

CONTEXTUAL GENERALIZATION ANALYSIS PROCESS AND MODELING PATTERNS

Contextual generalization is simply the process of widening the *functionality* and *specialty scope* of a service by preserving its core attributes and properties. This transformation is designed to broaden a service's spectrum beyond its current dimension by increasing its *abstraction level*. It is about both amplifying its boundaries and extending its *contextual* limits by forming a new, larger service. Furthermore, recall that this typing activity should not be focused on manipulating a service's structure. Applying environmental changes, such as alteration to a service ecosystem and modification to messaging configurations, is not what this analysis is interested in. The issues are merely *semantic*, and the chief goal is service discovery through generalization activities that not only identify new entities but also depict the evolution of a service.

The reader may wonder if the relationship formed between the original service and its abstracted services calls for the construction of a composite structure. Do the resulting products discovered during the contextual generalization process lead to the construction of a specific service formation? The answer to this question is not necessarily affirmative. In fact, this venture is, by and large, not about physical aggregation of services and certainly not about manipulation of service structures. Here the intention is to discover new services and identify *semantic* affiliations between the core service and its abstracted formation.[1]

Service-oriented analysis operations that tackle structural manipulation of entities address different concerns. The service relationships that are identified here by the contextual generalization process, however, can influence a service's internal physical structure and its associations with external autonomous and distributed services. These physical modifications to service structure are discussed in Chapters 18 through 22, which elaborate on service-oriented structural analysis patterns that are employed to alter a service's physical formation.

CONTEXTUAL GENERALIZATION PROCESS

The sections that follow answer the three chief questions that can guide practitioners to contextually generalize a service: What are the contextual properties of a service? What are the aspects that should be generalized? How can a service's contextual boundary be generalized? There are three major contributing factors to contextual generalization of a service: service naming, service functionality, and service specialty. These semantic characteristics drive the generalization process and influence service logical or physical structures later on during the service-oriented structural analysis phase (discussed in Chapters 18 through 22) and construction. Therefore, when generalizing a service context, stay aware of these fundamental attributes that define a service's essence and its offerings.

GENERALIZING SERVICE NAMES.   One of the most important aspects of the contextual generalization process is naming a discovered service. The new service's name must embody the *meaning* of the originating core service. The term "meaning" pertains to the essence of the service. Ask the following questions to ascertain the originating service context:

- What is the service's chief specialty and field of expertise?
- What types of solutions does the service offer?
- What is the service's main functionality?

A generalized service name should then reflect the answers to these questions and even elevate the originating service abstraction level.

For example, let us begin with the core entity Fixed-Rate Mortgage Service. This name implies that the service's specialty is in the field of offering home loans to real estate buyers. The type of loan is also a known property: fixed rate. The contextual generalized version of this service should elevate its abstraction level to a higher degree, yielding Mortgage Service. Note that the new service preserves the context of the core service.

GENERALIZING SERVICE FUNCTIONALITY. Service functionality represents the business or technical processes that a service executes. A business process is comprised of underpinning business activities that are carried out by service operations. This implementation is the major contributor to the contextual generalization process. The credit verification process, for example, is the generalized version of the insurance credit verification process. The insurance underwriting process is another generalized product that originates from the car insurance underwriting process.

A service's technical processes contribute to service contextual generalization in the same manner. These are the underpinning activities that reflect a service's technical functionality. For example, the generalization of the compress audit trail file process, which consists of technical activities, simply yields the compress file process.

GENERALIZING SERVICE SPECIALTY. A specialty typically identifies a service's field of expertise. This is an area of business or technical discipline that a service was designed to contribute to. Trading, accounting, credit verification, small business loan application processing, and movie downloader are examples of service specialties. These are subjects for contextual generalization because they identify the chief "professional occupation" of a service and contribute to the understanding of service capabilities. The specialty loan application processing, for example, is the generalized product of the small business loan application processing. In the same manner, consider the multimedia downloader as the generalized version of the core specialty movie downloader.

CONTEXTUAL GENERALIZATION EXAMPLE. To better understand this simple concept, let us view Exhibit 14.1, which represents the idea of contextual generalization. Disregard for the time being the structural aspect of a service and think of the depicted entities as contexts (i.e., semantic abstractions that can be manipulated to form universal entities).

The Fixed-Income Analysis Service (far left in the exhibit) forms the Portfolio Analysis Service that constitutes a higher level of abstraction. The last item in the chain, the Financial Analysis Toolbox Service, is generalized from the Portfolio Analysis Service. Note that the more the context widens, the larger are its semantic boundaries. This effect not only increases its spectrum of influence but also raises its capability to address a wider range of organizational concerns. In addition, the common attributes that are preserved during the generalization process—indicated in the upper left corner—are Investment Instruments and Financial Analysis. These are never lost despite this transformation.

BENEFITS AND OPPORTUNITIES. The contextual generalization process consists of service analysis activities and patterns designed to increase semantic reuse. In other words, the more we climb up the ladder of abstractions, the more we incur asset consolidation opportunities. The more we universalize a service's context, the larger is the scope of the solution. The more we generalize its

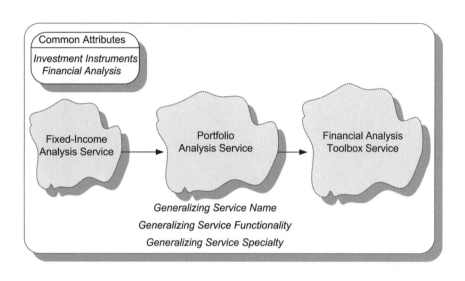

EXHIBIT 14.1 CONTEXTUAL GENERALIZATION EXAMPLE

perspective, the less complex is its implementation. Therefore, the chief aim of this exercise is to augment the knowledge of a service by increasing its contextual peripheries. This effort typically yields a service that consists of more operations offering more significant capabilities.

Furthermore, the introduced patterns of the contextual generalization are designed to guide practitioners with the abstraction process, discover new services, and form relationships and dependencies between the originating core services and their descendants. These associations can be further refined and later utilized to construct atomic and composite services, and service clusters.

The generalization process of a service's context does not always yield benefits. This activity can also result in oversized coarse-grained entities that would be costly to develop, deploy, and support. Hence, practitioners should strike a fine balance between overgeneralization of service context and undersized entities that offer negligible business or technological value.

START WITH CORE KNOWLEDGE: DEFINE "GROUND ZERO."   The contextual generalization process is straightforward and requires domain and technical expertise. Domain expertise is necessary if a service is classified as a business entity. It can help a practitioner comprehend the business responsibility of a service and facilitate the abstraction process. Generalizing a technical service, however, calls for the involvement of a subject matter expert who understands its technical capabilities and who is able to abstract its functionality.

Begin with the identification of the smallest unit of knowledge, the service that constitutes "ground zero" for this effort. In other words, start with the service that embodies the least functionality and whose semantic scope appears as narrow as possible. Choose a service that can be generalized over one that is already abstracted. Meticulously select the service that represents the first level of abstraction rather than the one that may not be feasible to generalize.

The ground zero service is not necessarily an Atomic (195) pattern. The generalization starting point can also be a composite or service cluster. It all depends on the milestones and the goals of this process. Most important to consider is that the rule of thumb calls for moving up toward a more generalized entity that may result in a universal solution that can offer a wider remedy to a concern.

Finally, before charting generalization solutions for a project or a larger initiative, study the three major asset symbols that represent the Atomic (195), Composite (196), and Service

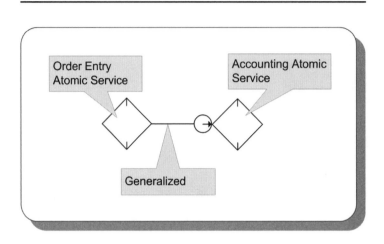

EXHIBIT 14.2   CONTEXTUAL GENERALIZATION OF AN ATOMIC SERVICE EXAMPLE

Cluster (200) patterns. In addition, the generalization notation should be utilized to express the abstraction process. Luckily, only one simple symbol can help accomplish this task—named "Generalized."

GENERALIZING ATOMIC SERVICES.   Let us start from a simple example where the involved services are fine-grained atomic formations, depicted in Exhibit 14.2. The Order Entry Atomic Service represents a smaller unit of an accounting solution. This generalization process yields an Accounting Atomic Service that opens up the opportunity for creating additional accounting types of services, such as Accounts Payable and Accounts Receivable. Note that the "Generalized" symbol is utilized here to convey abstraction. The arrow that is surrounded by a circle should always be pointed at the generalized product. In this case, the Accounting Atomic Service is the resulting abstraction.

For small-scale implementations, an Atomic (195) pattern is a good starting point. In addition, start from an atomic formation when the magnitude of the solution is small and fine-grained services are feasible propositions.[2]

Remember, if the core service is an atomic formation, it does not inevitably mean that its yielding abstraction must be a more complex structure pattern, such as a Composite (196) or Cluster (200). This is merely a semantic exercise that accentuates contextual associations between the core entity and its resulting abstraction. However, as a result of this contextual generalization effort, practitioners may recommend service structure modification to accommodate the expected functionality growth. As we will notice later, the increase in service scope and contextual boundary may motivate architects, modelers, and developers to consider altering a service's physical formation. But as stated, this is not the focus of our mission now. Deferring such decisions to later stages in the service-oriented analysis process can benefit design and architecture outcomes. (Refer to Chapters 18 through 22 on structural analysis patterns and modeling.)

GENERALIZING COMPOSITE SERVICES.   A composite service can also be involved in a business or technological contextual generalization process. A Composite (196) pattern is a hierarchical formation that semantically encompasses smaller services. Therefore, the contextual generalization activity conceives of composite structures as nested containers of knowledge where the outer entity typically acquires its expertise from its internal services. Furthermore, from a generalization perspective, the dominating service, the entity with which we begin the abstraction process from, is the outer aggregating service. The containing child services are not subject for generalization.

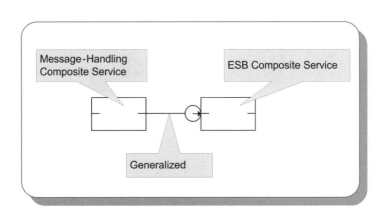

EXHIBIT 14.3 CONTEXTUAL GENERALIZATION COMPOSITE SERVICE FORMATION EXAMPLE

Contextual Generalization of a Composite Service Example. Exhibit 14.3 demonstrates a contextual generalization activity in which a technical composite service is abstracted to form a more universal solution to a messaging problem. The Message Handling Composite Service is the core entity that derives a larger abstraction: ESB (Enterprise Message Bus) Composite Service. As mentioned previously, each of these participating formations embodies functionality that is carried out by their corresponding internal services. In addition, note that this generalization process is driven by technological abstractions of services and not necessarily their technical structures. Indeed, an ESB also constitutes a middleware product that is characteristically positioned between a service provider and related consumers, yet this architectural aspect is disregarded for the time being.

Benefits of Composite Service Contextual Generalization Process. Obviously, in comparison to an atomic formation, a composite service can cover a wider range of solutions because its initial contextual boundary is greater. Therefore, when a composite service is the originating entity, the ground zero of a contextual generalization activity, it yields even larger abstractions, representing services that offer larger solution boundaries. From a business perspective, this is a crucial benefit because of the ability to include more business processes, business rules, business specialties, and business functionality.

In regard to the contextual generalization of technical services, composite services can be universalized to simplify architectural and technological complexities and extend their capability scope. In multifaceted and heterogeneous computing environments, composite formations are useful because they can be generalized, for example, to bridge interoperability gaps.[3] To understand this idea let us view again Exhibit 14.3. The resulting contextual generalization product ESB Composite Service originated from the Message-Handling Composite Service. This abstraction will enable us to delegate additional functionality to the ESB Composite Service, such as message routing capabilities, message transformation, and even orchestration features.

Another undisputed advantage of the generalization process is recognized when abstracting architecture capabilities. These include concepts and software assets that facilitate integration and collaboration of applications, consumers, services, and commercial off-the-shelf products. Thus, generalized composite services that present architectural interests typically contribute to the organizational communication language, a vocabulary created to foster reusability of software assets across the enterprise.

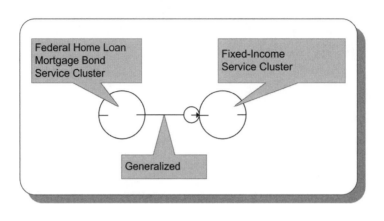

EXHIBIT 14.4 CONTEXTUAL GENERALIZATION SERVICE CLUSTER FORMATION EXAMPLE

GENERALIZING SERVICE CLUSTERS.   Unlike with atomic and composite services, the incentive for generalizing a cluster formation is rooted in its intrinsic capability to *increase* its knowledge and expertise by tapping into various resources across the organization, such as applications, common services, and even partners' domains. That is, from a semantic perspective, conceive of a service cluster as a collection of services, each of which is designated an area of specialty that contributes to a range of solutions. Since a cluster is comprised of related services, the contextual generalization activity would yield a cluster abstraction whose magnitude and boundaries are bound to grow. It is not the physical size that we referred to: A service cluster abstraction is created to encompass more business or technical functionality. Subsequently, this contextual generalization process later may provide motivation to increase the physical structure of a cluster.[4]

Generalization of a Service Cluster Example.   Let us view Exhibit 14.4 illustrating a generalization activity, starting at the ground zero Federal Home Loan Mortgage Bond Service Cluster and resulting in the Fixed-Income Service Cluster abstraction. This activity constitutes a cluster transformation that yields a much larger entity that not only embodies mortgage bonds functionality; it also has the potential to include future services that offer fixed-income instruments. This semantic generalization is a necessary step that should be taken to promote reusability of software assets distributed across the organization yet participate and collaborate to provide solutions for new projects or business initiatives.

Remember the newly created Fixed-Income Service Cluster is obviously an abstraction that may have been elicited from an existing implementation or derived from an idea or other smaller abstraction. Either concrete or intangible ground zero entities can be utilized to generate a higher-level generalization.

Benefits of Service Cluster Contextual Generalization Process.   Contextual generalization achieves increase of contextual boundary by abstracting functionality and processes of an existing service cluster. As you may remember, the generalized entity is the one that grows; the core cluster remains untouched. This conceptual transformation typically increases the number of participating service members in the generalized cluster version. To accommodate such service solution growth, the practitioner should tap the enterprise service inventory portfolio. This would increase the reusability factor of services and strengthen the federation and collaboration between lines of business.

Imagine, for example, an accounting software package that offers various services, such as Accounts Payable Service, General Ledger Service, and Accounts Receivable Service. Each of these is a distributed entity that is a part of a remote application while also being a member of an accounting cluster. Since the contextual generalization process is conceptual in essence, adding more functionality to this service cluster would be a matter of finding the right services and updating design and architecture artifacts, such as diagrams and documents.

From a business perspective, the cluster generalization venture fosters inclusion of different lines of business in the organization. This would encourage the collaboration of various stakeholders to participate in enterprise-wide service development initiatives, contribute their expertise and knowledge, and strengthen the solutions they propose. Such integration of resources across various domains typically yields effective service-oriented architecture strategies and enhances communications between participating parties.

On the technological front, the generalization of service clusters that contributes to abstraction of architectures and technologies characteristically spurs collaboration between various information technology implementation groups. This usually results in new strategies that address mechanisms to reduce interoperability challenges in a mixture of networks, operating systems, language platforms, and hardware.

GENERALIZING MIXED SERVICE FORMATIONS. It is more likely that generalization activities would yield a larger service formation that is attributed to expanding the functionality scope and operation boundaries of an originating service. Therefore, it is conceivable that the resulting abstracted service structure would exceed the magnitude of the core service and as result transform it into a different service structure.[5]

For example, a generalized atomic service is bound to morph into a composite formation if the design justifies this conversion. It is the practitioner's responsibility to suggest such an approach to accommodate the abstraction process. In the same manner, the generalization of a Composite service may yield a service cluster. Again, the architect, developer, modeler, and analyst should recommend this transformation during design and architecture sessions.

Let us take a look at a generalization process depicted in Exhibit 14.5. This abstraction scenario begins at a core service (ground zero) yet yields a different service structure. Here the Inventory Control Atomic Service is transformed to its generalized version: Small Business Composite Service. In the same manner, the generalization activity that is illustrated in Exhibit 14.6 produces the Car Parts Service Cluster that is the abstracted version of its core service: Mufflers and Exhaust

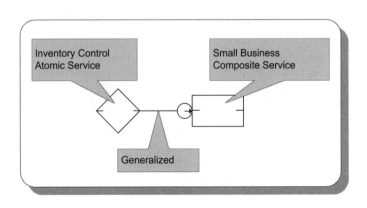

EXHIBIT 14.5 ATOMIC-TO-COMPOSITE CONTEXTUAL GENERALIZATION EXAMPLE

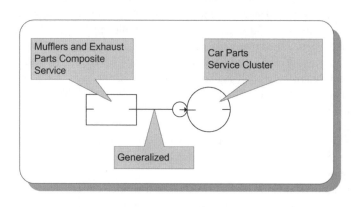

EXHIBIT 14.6   COMPOSITE-TO-CLUSTER CONTEXTUAL GENERALIZATION EXAMPLE

Parts Composite Service. Each example embodies a fundamental shift of the service formation that should be seriously considered when designing and architecting solutions.

CONTEXTUAL GENERALIZATION PATTERNS

Service contextual generalization patterns are simply templates designed to assist architects, modelers, analysts, and developers to abstract services based on predefined methods that formulate solutions. These styles are useful when practitioners are seeking to maximize service reusability, enhance design decisions, and identify relationships and dependencies between the abstracted services. Therefore, think of generalization patterns as out-of-box remedies that can be applied to address similar problems in different circumstances. These styles not only constitute repeatable solutions to problems, they also allow practitioners to focus on resolutions rather than spending their valuable time reinventing service generalization methods.

Before applying a contextual generalization pattern, follow the three simple and logical steps that can assist with the abstraction of services:

1. **Define the problem that requires a solution.** Is it a business concern? Is it a technological issue? Does the problem require a wide range of solutions? What is the scope of the requirements?
2. **Identify the motivation for contextually generalizing a service.** Should a service be generalized to expand its functionality? Would a broader solution solve the problem? Would the service abstraction be capable of providing an adequate remedy? Would widening the service's contextual scope help augment its capabilities?
3. **Inspect the solution that is offered by a contextual generalization pattern.** Can the offered pattern solution be applied to the problem? Would the outcome of using the pattern address the business or technological concerns?

The sections that follow introduce four major contextual generalization patterns that offer repeatable solutions to service abstraction efforts. Each of these styles should be applied when the initial service offerings do not satisfy business requirements or technical specifications and must be expanded to accommodate the broadened concerns.

1. Simple Proxy (233)
2. Dependency Enforcement (234)
3. Dependency Separation (236)
4. Abstraction Loop (238)

SIMPLE PROXY PATTERN.   The Simple Proxy pattern[6] advocates that the service generalization process be accomplished by employing an intermediate service hub, a proxy that moderates the transformation of the abstraction process. Furthermore, an abstracted proxy service does not represent the end result of a generalization effort, yet it is a crucial step that mediates the *evolution* of a service because it typically is positioned between the originating core service and the final abstraction. For example, imagine a cluster named Customer-Support Service that is generalized from a core atomic entity that offers customer profile information—Customer Profile Service. This steep transition between the very small to the very large abstraction calls for devising a proxy that sits between the two to temper this transition.

Problem.   A disproportional contextual generalization takes place when the differences between the core service's abstraction level and its generalized entity are vast. The term "disproportional" pertains to major differences in terms of service functionality, processes, and capabilities magnitude. That is, the final product offers a much larger solution scope and range of operations than its originator. This situation typically yields an unbalanced deployment environment that consists of both very fine-grained and extremely coarse-grained services.

Solution.   The Simple Proxy pattern introduces an extra step for generalization, one that is essential to improving abstraction logic, avoiding incoherent service transformation, and maintaining a consistent service evolution. One of the most important reasons for introducing proxy abstractions is to maintain the right balance between fine-grained and coarse-grained service implementations in terms of their size, number of operations, and scope of service capabilities. In other words, the Simple Proxy pattern ensures that an architecture model includes services that fit a predefined and acceptable organizational granularity scale. Too fine-grained or too coarse-grained services should be reexamined to adhere to architecture best practices.

EXAMPLE.   Exhibit 14.7 depicts a generalization process that utilizes a proxy: the Professional Liability Insurance Composite Service. It links the Personal Liability Insurance Atomic Service to the General Liability Insurance Service Cluster. This contextual generalization activity encourages a temperate service evolution that originates at an atomic formation and concludes with a service cluster. Note the employment of the "Generalized" symbol that denotes the abstraction elevation between each pair of services.

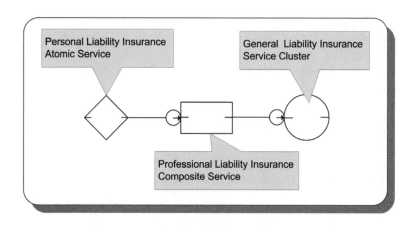

EXHIBIT 14.7   SIMPLE PROXY PATTERN EXAMPLE

Pattern Identification	
Name	Simple Proxy Pattern
Category	Contextual Generalization Analysis

Problems, Solutions, and Implementations	
Problem	The difference between the core service's abstraction level and its yielding generalized version is vast. The yielding product consists of far more operations and processes, and offers a far larger solution scope.
Solution	Introduce a proxy service that moderates the generalization process by gradually abstracting the core service's capabilities.
Applicability	Applies to a service generalization process that is bound to include multiple levels of abstraction.
Method	The contextual generalization process should employ a proxy service positioned between the originating entity and its generalized final product. Each elevated abstraction level should be supported by an intervening service that moderates the abstraction effort.
Benefits	1. Moderating the service generalization process.
	2. Controlling evolution of services through mediation.
	3. Fostering proper service granularity scaling.
Risks	Excessive usage of proxy services may affect execution performance once this proposition has been accepted and implemented.
Notation	Employ the "Generalized" symbol.

EXHIBIT 14.8 SIMPLE PROXY PATTERN SUMMARY TABLE

Synopsis. The Simple Proxy pattern addresses the contextual generalization of a service by introducing an intermediary step to moderate its transformation. The mediating role can be designated to a single proxy software entity or to multiple services, each of which represents a higher abstraction level than its successor in the chain. The final product then is the one that is the most abstracted and generalized. Consider Exhibit 14.8, which summarizes these service-typing challenges and outlines the solution, method of implementation, benefits, and risks attributed to the employment of the Simple Proxy pattern.

DEPENDENCY ENFORCEMENT PATTERN. The Dependency Enforcement pattern provides a contextual coupling solution. The term "contextual coupling" means that two or more core services, so-called ground zeros, are involved in a parallel generalization effort that converges into one final abstracted service. This simple notion of reconciliation results in a bundled structure that embodies the core functionality and attributes of the originating services. Remember, the aim here is to establish a larger abstraction that acquires its knowledge and expertise from the context and field of expertise of the originating services. This does not necessarily imply that the Dependency Enforcement pattern dictates unification or aggregation of services. But it certainly provides such motivation for future design and architecture decisions.[7]

Problem. The practice of design and construction of a fine-grained service should be reevaluated. This entity, which is limited in capability scope, typically does not offer an adequate range of solutions to satisfy business or technical requirements. Furthermore, an abstraction derived from a single service may not fully alleviate an organization concern.

Solution. To broaden the spectrum of a solution and increase contextual capabilities of an individual service, simply join its offerings and areas of expertise with other related services. This can

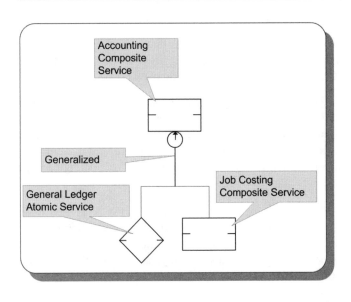

EXHIBIT 14.9   DEPENDENCY ENFORCEMENT PATTERN

Pattern Identification	
Name	Dependency Enforcement Pattern
Category	Contextual Generalization Analysis

Problems, Solutions, and Implementations	
Problem	An abstraction that is derived from a single core service may not offer an adequate solution that corresponds to the scope of the problem.
Solution	The generalized service should embody abstractions that originate at two or more single core services.
Applicability	Typically applies to fine-grained services that do not fully meet business requirements or technical specifications.
Method	The generalization approach consists of two steps: (1) Identify fine-grained services that can participate in proving a solution; (2) the final product of the generalization effort should embody the capabilities and specialties of participating services.
Benefits	1. Expand the scope of an offered solution by merging abstractions of multiple core services.
	2. Establish logical dependencies between abstractions.
	3. Encourage contextual coupling and merging of fine-grained services.
	4. Foster functionality reconciliation and reduction of operation redundancies.
	5. Promote reuse of future concrete services.
	6. Provide motivation for aggregation and unification during design time.
Risks	The final generalized product may become a tightly coupled and coarse-grained service once implemented.
Notation	Employ the "Generalized" symbol.

EXHIBIT 14.10   DEPENDENCY ENFORCEMENT PATTERN SUMMARY TABLE

be achieved by abstracting multiple core services and merging their capabilities. Consider the two rudimentary guiding steps to facilitate the contextual generalization process:

1. Identify two or more fine-grained services that can contribute to a solution.
2. The generalization process should yield a single abstracted product that embodies the processes and areas of expertise of these participating services.

Example. Let us view Exhibit 14.9, which illustrates a contextual generalization process. The General Ledger Atomic Service and the Job Costing Composite Service are the core services that participate in the generalization activity. The dependency that is established between these entities results in a greater abstraction: the Accounting Composite Service that embodies their contexts and functionalities. The motivation for establishing a universal accounting package that offers various accounting modules, implemented by services, is shown here.

Synopsis. Remember, the contextual generalization process is devised to expand an individual service's capabilities by boosting its expertise and functionality spectrum. This scope increase pertains only to its contextual aspects, ignoring its structural constraints. Exhibit 14.10 summarizes this goal by outlining the problem, solution, applicability, method, benefits, and risks of the Dependency Enforcement pattern utilization.

DEPENDENCY SEPARATION PATTERN. In comparison to Dependency Enforcement (234) pattern, the Dependency Separation pattern yields opposite results: Here the aim is to separate a service into two or more abstractions, each of which will offer a generalized and distinguished functionality view. In other words, this contextual decomposition style not only splits a service into distinct entities, it also generalizes their solutions. The final products are abstracted services, each of which can represent business processes of different lines of business and applications, or generalized technical specialties. Thus the major benefit of this pattern is obviously to enhance the separation-of-concerns activities and, at the same time, foster assets reuse.[8] Furthermore, the Dependency Separation pattern motivates practitioners to adhere to loose coupling architecture best practices once a service materializes and is transformed into a concrete implementation.

Problem. The problem that motivates practitioners to employ the Dependency Separation pattern represents a combination of three chief challenges that must be tackled during the contextual generation process.

1. The core service is too bulky and requires separation of its functionality into two or more capability groups.
2. The service offers too many areas of expertise that should be broken up to boost its reusability factor.
3. These fields of service specialties are not generalized enough and thus must be further abstracted to further foster reuse of operations.

Solution. To alleviate these challenges, the analyst, architect, developer, modeler, and manager should analyze the service contextual scope and proceed with its separation into two or more service abstractions, each of which should lead to the establishment of a new service which ultimately will include more operations and extended capabilities in its own field of expertise. Consider the chief steps that should be implemented to fulfill this generalization goal:

- Analyze the core service's processes and overall capabilities. Is the service too coarse grained? Does its offered expertise exceed the scope of requirements?
- Separate the core service into two or more entities, each of which generalizes its original offerings to establish higher abstractions that address different business or technical concerns.

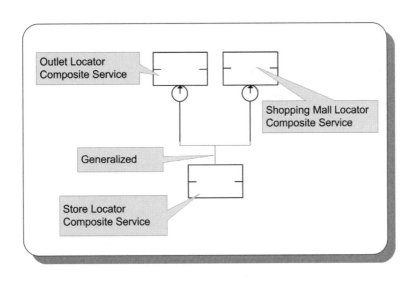

EXHIBIT 14.11 DEPENDENCY SEPARATION STYLE

Example. Exhibit 14.11 illustrates the Dependency Separation pattern example. The Store Locator Composite Service is contextually decomposed into two different abstractions, each of which represents a different store lookup perspective: the Outlet Locator Composite Service and the Shopping Mall Locator Composite Service. These generalized perspectives not only embed the notion of store-searching capabilities, they also represent a different business view. Note that the core service Store Locator Composite Service yields two composite formations. These, however, are larger in

Pattern Identification	
Name	Dependency Separation Pattern
Category	Contextual Generalization Analysis
Problems, Solutions, and Implementations	
Problem	1. A service is too bulky. 2. Service specialties are tightly coupled, each of which must be generalized to meet requirements. 3. Offered service specialties are not generalized enough to foster reuse.
Solution	Discern service functionality into two or more higher-level abstractions to promote reusability of capabilities and separate its tightly coupled specialties.
Applicability	Applies to a coarse-grained service whose contextual properties must be generalized to foster service reuse.
Method	Consider two steps when employing the Dependency Separation pattern: (1) Analyze the core service capability scope and its specialty range; (2) two or more generalized services should emanate from the originating service, each of which represents a higher abstraction level.
Benefits	1. Facilitate the separation of concerns process. 2. Foster service reuse. 3. Promote decoupling of service specialties. 4. Assist with service contextual decomposition. 5. Promote loose coupling architecture implementation.
Risks	Excessive separation of the core service may lead to fine-grained services once constructed.
Notation	Employ the "Generalized" symbol.

EXHIBIT 14.12 DEPENDENCY SEPARATION PATTERN SUMMARY TABLE

scope and operations. In addition, to fulfill this aim, the "Generalized" symbol is utilized to denote the Contextual Generalization process.

Synopsis.   The Dependency Separation pattern is designed to assist practitioners with the separation-of-concerns process, by which a core service is broken up into two or more higher-level abstractions. These generalized entities can lead to reusable services that offer broader functionality scope each in its specialty field. Exhibit 14.12 outlines this goal and presents the problem, solution, applicability, method, benefits, and risks attributed to the utilization of the Dependency Separation pattern.

ABSTRACTION LOOP PATTERN.   The Abstraction Loop pattern promotes a simple contextual generalization purpose; it combines the previous two patterns into one: the Dependency Separation (236) pattern and the Dependency Enforcement (234) pattern. This process is straightforward: Begin with a core service, generalize it into two or more distinct entities, and finally merge the entities into one service.

The reader may wonder why the converging effort takes place after separating a service. What is to be gained by starting the generalization process from a single service and concluding with a single one as well? The answer lies in the capability of the Abstraction Loop pattern to split a core service into various abstractions, discover new services, and later unite these derived generalizations into a higher-level abstraction product. This inclusion characteristic can later promote the establishment of service relationships between aggregated child services that reside in a composite formation based on the hierarchy that the generalization process created or even identify associations between service cluster members.

Problem.   The chief problem is affiliated with lack of organizational best practices that can guide practitioners to establish two major service formations: composite and cluster. First, the lack of a systematic process that can facilitate the establishment of a hierarchy among services to help form a composite structure is perhaps one of the greatest contributors to an unstable service environment and an inconsistent service design style. Second, an organizational deficiency of a method that can bind services together to found a service group, namely a cluster, is another challenge that can lead to disarrayed architecture model. The term "disarray" pertains to unclear relationship between services that make up a composite service or a service cluster. The absence of these best practices obviously can later yield incoherent relationships between composite formation's aggregated services, unclear associations between service cluster members, and even vague affiliations between autonomous services. As a final result, these challenges can affect the quality of process orchestration and service transaction modeling.

Solution.   To resolve these vital challenges, employ the Abstraction Loop pattern to enable a logical modeling process. Remember, the chief aim here is to establish rational associations between services and identifying service groups by employing the contextual generalization method. Consider the three chief steps to fulfill these tasks:

1. Identify a core service from which the contextual generalization process can originate.
2. Derive service abstractions that each can be supported by a new service.
3. Unite all resulting generalizations into a holistic entity that embodies its originators' functionalities and capabilities.

Example.   Exhibit 14.13 illustrates the employment of the Abstraction Loop pattern. This set of activities starts at the core entity Municipal Bonds Lookup Atomic Service. The inclusion process begins here too. The generalization activity occurs on two fronts by creating the Bonds Lookup

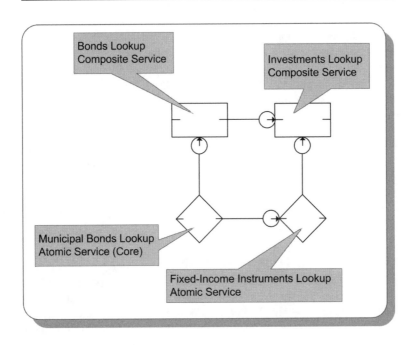

EXHIBIT 14.13   ABSTRACTION LOOP PATTERN EXAMPLE

Pattern Identification	
Name	Abstraction Loop Pattern
Category	Contextual Generalization Analysis
Problems, Solutions, and Implementations	
Problem	Lack of a modeling method for establishing service associations and hierarchies influences service orchestration and transaction quality.
Solution	Employ the Abstraction Loop pattern to firm up the process of service relationship establishment.
Applicability	Applies to development environments that require a systematic approach for establishing service relationships.
Method	Consists of major three steps: (1) Identify the originating service; (2) derive two or more service abstractions; (3) unite the generalized entities into a holistic service abstraction that embodies the functionality and capabilities of its originators.
Benefits	1. Discovering associated services that are derived by the generalization activity.
	2. Identifying potential relationships between aggregated services that are a part of a composite formation.
	3. Ascertaining contextual affiliation of services that are members of a service cluster.
	4. Promoting inclusion of service practices by discovering common functionalities.
Risks	The most generalized entity in the chain may lead to the creation of an inefficient and bulky service.
Notation	Employ the "Generalized" symbol.

EXHIBIT 14.14   ABSTRACTION LOOP PATTERN SUMMARY TABLE

Composite Service and the Fixed-Income Instruments Lookup Atomic Service. Finally, these services are converged into the newly abstracted formation, the Investment Lookup Composite Service. Note that the created generalization circle encompasses a related group of services that not only share functionality; they also create a hierarchy that is attributed to their abstraction level.

One would argue that Exhibit 14.13 actually depicts a composite formation, in which the Investments Lookup Composite Service is the parent service that encompasses its originator services. This assertion can indeed materialize when finalizing an analysis proposition. However, at this stage, focus on the contextual affiliation of service rather than on their physical structures.

Synopsis.   The Abstraction Loop pattern should be employed to found relationships between aggregated services that reside in a composite formation. The pattern can also be utilized to form associations between service cluster members. Again, this process should be focused on their relationships and disregard by the time being the structural aspects. These benefits are further outlined in Exhibit 14.14, which also identifies the problem, method of implementation, risks, and solutions affiliated with the utilization of the Abstraction Loop pattern.

CONTEXTUAL GENERALIZATION ANTI-PATTERNS

Governance and implementation best practices provide the driving principles for service-oriented development. Without clear guidance and established design and architecture policies, milestones and goals would be difficult to attain. The process of founding best practices does not necessarily yield prescription documents or development manuals. Just as generalization patterns subscribe to best breed of service design and construction methods, anti-patterns simply convey what not to do. In other words, anti-patterns point to impractical practices, unfeasible approaches, and unrealistic methods of service implementation. In the context of service contextual generalization, anti-patterns simply suggest that certain abstraction methods should not be pursued because of their ineffectiveness or their negligible contribution to the process. Just "do not do!"

The sections that follow introduce four anti-patterns that advocate avoidance of unpractical service contextual generalization approaches by illustrating paradoxical or inefficient styles of implementations:

1. Double Standard (240)
2. Round-Trip (241)
3. Steep Boundary Reduction (241)
4. Extreme Generalization (242)

DOUBLE STANDARD ANTI-PATTERN: AVOID SELF-GENERALIZATION.   The Double Standard anti-pattern suggests that a service cannot be a product of itself; in other words, avoid self-generalization. When generalizing a core service, the resulting product should be a newly created service. This rule should comply with the promise of contextual generalization method that advocates that a service abstraction is the outcome of the generalized core service.

Why is self-generalization not recommended? There are two chief reasons to avoid such a modeling style: *analysis traceability* and *service discoverability*. First, The term "traceability" pertains to transparency of the service development life cycle process. This is about tracing and preserving the activities that lead to design and architecture artifacts and decisions. Therefore, during the contextual generalization effort, the practitioner ought to track the transformation and document the evolution of a service. This includes recording a service's states and the various formations that a service morphs into. Furthermore, these newly created services may play significant roles in establishing service structures, establishing containment schemes, or cluster formations. Therefore, avoid self-generalization by promoting the creation of new services to increase the traceability of the analysis and modeling process.

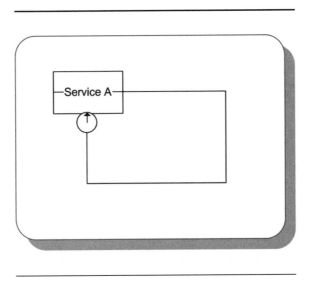

Exhibit 14.15 Double Standard Anti-Pattern

The second reason for avoiding the self-generalization is associated with the service discovery effort. This pertains to the practice of discovering new services and the associated best practices designed to promote a loosely coupled architecture model, increase reusability rates, discourage tightly coupled design, and foster business agility. This can be attained by delegating solution responsibilities to multiple services rather than employing a single service to provide a wide range of solutions.

Exhibit 14.15 depicts the Double Standard anti-pattern idea. Service A is self-generalized and therefore it does not yield a new abstraction. Note that the "Generalized" symbol points to the core service itself.

ROUND-TRIP ANTI-PATTERN: AVOID CIRCULAR GENERALIZATION. The Round-Trip anti-pattern completes a generalization circle that includes two or more services and ends with the very core service from which it begins. This is a paradoxical solution because a service cannot be the generalization product of itself. From a software development perspective, this conflict can yield ambiguous implementations and obviously be impractical for deployment to production. Furthermore, a contextual generalization that traces back to the core service should be avoided because the final product must be a completely different entity that represents a higher level of abstraction.

Exhibit 14.16 illustrates the Round-Trip anti-pattern. As discussed, this scenario begins with Service A, continues with Services B, C, and D, and concludes at the starting point A. In simple generalization cases, typically it is easy to spot such a conflict. In larger implementations, however, where the chain of generalization is longer, tracing such a condition would be difficult. Thus, adhere to the rule of thumb that suggests that if a loop ends where it starts, there may be a problem.

STEEP BOUNDARY REDUCTION ANTI-PATTERN: AVOID REDUCTION OF SERVICE FUNCTIONALITY BOUNDARY. The Steep Boundary Reduction anti-pattern simply warns practitioners against a generalization outcome that achieves an opposite result: reduction in a service's functionality boundary and operations' scope. In other words, the Steep Boundary Reduction anti-pattern depicts an unfeasible scenario in which the core service's context is larger than its abstraction. This circumstance can be avoided by reevaluating the generalization process and ensuring that the final

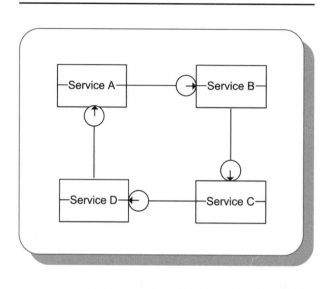

EXHIBIT 14.16   ROUND-TRIP ANTI-PATTERN

product complies with the simple rule of the contextual generalization practice: The emanating service should always embody the functionality of its originators.

Assuming that an atomic service formation is contextually smaller (from a functionality and operations perspective) than a service cluster, Exhibit 14.17 demonstrates the Steep Boundary Reduction anti-pattern and its undesired result. The core Service Cluster A originates the Atomic Service A. Remember that Service Cluster A aggregates a group of affiliated services, some of which may be atomic and others composite. But even if their functionality size may be limited, their contextual boundary should be larger than the yielding atomic service.

EXTREME GENERALIZATION ANTI-PATTERN: MODERATE ABSTRACTION LEVELS.   The Extreme Generalization anti-pattern introduces an impractical scenario that depicts a generalization product that contextually is much larger than its originating core service. That is, the abstracted service grew disproportionally during the generalization process. To better understand this occurrence, let us

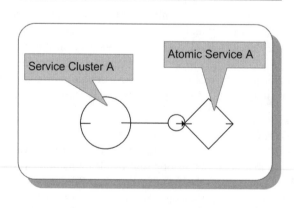

EXHIBIT 14.17   STEEP BOUNDARY REDUCTION ANTI-PATTERN

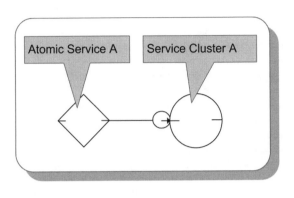

EXHIBIT 14.18   EXTREME GENERALIZATION ANTI-PATTERN

view Exhibit 14.18 and again assume that an atomic service formation is contextually smaller (from a functionality and operations perspective) than a service cluster. The exhibit illustrates a generalization activity that starts off with an atomic service named Atomic Service A and produces Service Cluster A. This transition from an atomic formation to a service cluster may be an unachievable goal once the service is analyzed and designed for construction.

Again, the major impediment would be to justify such an extreme contextual transition. The justification for generalizing an Atomic (195) pattern and turning it into a Cluster (200) pattern would be negligible. To resolve this undesirable effect, utilize the generalization method that is offered by the Simple Proxy (233) pattern, discussed earlier, to include an intermediary step for such service transformation. With the proxy solution, a core service would be moderately generalized by introducing multiple abstraction levels, each of which would be presented by a newly discovered service. This approach would moderate extreme contextual increments and provide solid motivation for implementation.

DELIVERABLES

The architect, developer, analyst, modeler, and manager should be responsible for delivering a contextual generalization diagram (as depicted in modeling examples of this chapter) that rationalizes the associations between the newly created services, identifies service abstractions, and illustrates the service contextual generalization typing process.

SUMMARY

- The sole objective of the contextual generalization process is to broaden a service's capabilities by generalizing its duties and widening the scope of its operations. This goal can be achieved by deriving higher-level abstractions that in time would be transformed into concrete services.
- Service abstraction is about generalizing service names, service functionality, and service specialty.
- The contextual essence of atomic, composite, and cluster formations can be generalized to broaden their scope of capabilities.
- The introduced contextual generalization patterns are devised to address reusability challenges, create loosely coupled assets, found proxy layers to increase software agility, and ascertain new services.
- The contextual generalization anti-patterns introduce a collection of best practices that should be applied when employing the contextual generalization patterns.

Notes

1. This analysis is influenced by the semantic generalization study and the research on elements of a language that took place in the 1820s. Refer to www.encyclopedia.com/topic/semantics.aspx.

2. Avoid generalization of coarse-grained services because of their already broadened functionality scope.

3. Refer to the Enterprise-Level Composite Service section in Chapter 12 to learn about two types of composite formations: application level and enterprise level.

4. To read more about expanding structural aspects of a service cluster, refer to Chapter 21.

5. It is important to remember that the contextual generalization is a semantic exercise that may influence service structural modeling decisions, as described in Chapters 18 to 22.

6. Similar to the Proxy pattern depicted by Erich Gamma, Richard Helm, Ralph Johnson, and John Vlissides, *Design Patterns: Elements of Reusable Object-Oriented Software* (Boston: Addison-Wesley, 1994), p. 207. However, the Simple Proxy (233) pattern involves a service provider, a consumer, and an intermediary proxy service. Remember, these are contextual affiliations that depict semantic layers, not physical implementations.

7. The Dependency Enforcement (234) pattern can be later interpreted into a physical coupling or unification of services. This pattern, however, merely suggests a conceptual coupling before a concrete implementation takes place.

8. The Dependency Separation (236) pattern introduces an opportunity for physical consolidation. This approach, however, is conceptual and suggests future service decomposition.

CHAPTER 15

CONTEXTUAL SPECIFICATION ANALYSIS PROCESS AND MODELING PATTERNS

Contextual specification is the process of reducing the abstraction level of a service. This "degeneralization" activity both narrows service functionality boundaries and decreases the scope of operations.[1] Furthermore, the specification method is designed to trim the capacity of a service and limit its responsibilities by downsizing its contextual aspects. Reduction of contextual aspects means that the service will offer a smaller part of the solution and thus alleviate a narrower portion of the problem. Creating a new service and avoiding applying changes to the originating entity, the core service, would be the preferred specification method.

Remember, the contextual specification process is not about service decomposition and certainly not about breaking down software assets. Here the chief concern is simply the reduction of a service abstraction level to smaller manageable units, each of which is created to *partially* preserve attributes of the originating core service. The term "reduction" pertains to three major aspects of specification: service naming, functionality, and specialty. Understand these three influencing factors on a service's contextual scope can affect service design and architecture considerations and have implications for future production environments.

CONTEXTUAL SPECIFICATION PROCESS

The contextual specification of a service is driven by three major contributing factors:

1. The service name that embodies its essence (i.e., the reason that it was originated, its general offerings, and the solution that it proposes)
2. The functionality and operations that a service is designed to provide
3. The area of expertise to which a service can contribute

Once the scope of these three major contextual ingredients has been reduced, the resulting product will introduce contracted capabilities yet still conserve the fundamental properties of its originating service. Therefore, architects, analysts, developers, modelers, and managers who utilize the service specification method should examine the fundamental semantic properties of a service to enable its efficient scope reduction.

DEGENERALIZING A SERVICE NAME. A new service should preserve some of the properties of the core entity—the originating service is more abstract in nature and encompasses a wider range of solutions. One of these attributes that should be passed from the originator to the resulting product is the name that undergoes transformation as well. This evolutionary process calls for narrowing the scope of operations and responsibilities by reduction of a service's essence and semantics—namely, assigning a new name that conveys this change. For example, the Retirement Planner Calculator Service name is the specified product of the Financial Calculator Service. The Portfolio Management

Calculator Service name identifies another contextually reduced instance of the Financial Calculator Service.

DEGENERALIZING SERVICE FUNCTIONALITY.   Degeneralizing service functionality calls for trimming down service abilities. This process is all about identifying the core service's business or technical processes and delegating part of its underpinning activities to a newly created entity. The reduction of service implementation is reflected here by simply filtering out functionality that ultimately will decrease service operations. This elimination approach typically yields a smaller service that executes a narrower range of activities. The business insurance claims functionality exemplifies contextual specification of the small-business insurance process. The latter may encompass a wider range of small-business insurance activities, such as small-business insurance underwriting tasks and small-business insurance application processing.

DEGENERALIZING SERVICE SPECIALTY.   Akin to the reduction of its responsibilities and operations, discussed in the previous section, a service's offered specialty can be trimmed down as well. The term "specialty" pertains to the inimitable area of knowledge that a service contributes to. This can include expertise in insurance property risk assessment, execution of fixed-income bond purchasing, and even transformation of data capabilities. These business and technical fields of proficiency are the subject of degeneralization when contextually specifying service capabilities. The resulting product is obviously limited in domain (business) or technical knowledge, transforming the core service into a smaller one and, in some circumstances, is less significant to a solution. Remember, this is not about reduction of service efficiency or capacity to attain consumption goals; the aim here is simply to decrease the range of a service's main occupation.

CONTEXTUAL SPECIFICATION EXAMPLE: REDUCTION OF KNOWLEDGE, PROCESS, AND RESPONSIBILITIES.   Let us take a look at a simple example that illustrates a contextual specification scenario, in which a core service, the most generalized entity, derives lower levels of abstractions. This process is depicted in Exhibit 15.1. The Book Shipping Atomic Service, on the far right, embodies the capabilities of its descending entity: Fiction Book Shipping Atomic Service. But the process does not stop here. It continues with the commencement of the last service in the chain: the Commercial Fiction Book Shipping Atomic Service. Note that this contextual specification effort introduces a three-step reduction in the abstraction level of each descending service. The first one in the succession is also the most generalized entity, and the last represents the lowest abstraction

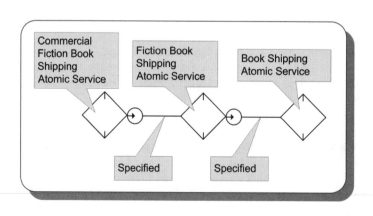

EXHIBIT 15.1 CONTEXTUAL SPECIFICATION EXAMPLE

level in the chain. In addition, to denote this service evolution, the "Specified" modeling symbol is employed in both contextual specification instances.

CONTEXTUAL SPECIFICATION MAJOR BENEFITS.   One of the most palpable benefits of the contextual specification process is the ability to *separate concerns* [2] through the reduction of a service's abstraction level. In other words, by trimming a service's functionality and limiting its scope, one can analyze its fundamental components—the pieces that typically make up a service. This semantic analysis activity enables practitioners to understand the service's root processes and the essence of its contribution to business and technology.

Again, this process is not about service decomposition or breaking the service up into smaller units. The contextual specification accentuates reduction in service scope because its current constitution is *too generalized*. Remember, the contextual specification exercise is all about analysis that is tailored to find the best remedy to an organizational problem. Among other goals, the abstraction reduction imperative aim is also to avoid the establishment of an impractical service that is too bulky, too coarse-grained, and too cumbersome to manage and employ. To fulfill this vital task, a process of analysis is needed to reduce a service's capabilities and specialties by employing the contextual specification method. Thus, use this specification approach to create various services that correspond to different granularity levels and to assess their individual capability to resolve the problem. The practitioner may decide later, however, to select the proper service that can be employed for the project, utilize all derived services to create hierarchical formations, or even to establish service groups. Either of these remedies would help meet requirements and provide an adequate solution to concerns.

The decrease of a service's scope and functionality would not necessarily reduce its reusability factor. A too-generalized service abstraction may not promote reuse either. The challenge is to find the right balance between the generalization and the specification aspects of a service. Doing so fosters service reusability and influences design, architecture, and contraction decisions.

WHERE SHOULD THE SPECIFICATION PROCESS BEGIN?   A too-generalized service that would not be practical to implement is a good candidate for contextual specification. The term "too-generalized" pertains to a service that represents a high level of abstraction and consists of business or technical processes that do not necessarily focus on a particular problem. This term classifies a service as a coarse-grained construct that is characteristically subject to reduction. Therefore, start trimming capabilities and degeneralizing the abstraction level of a service that is contextually too large to handle, whose solution is ineffective, and that may pose development and maintenance challenges during its life cycle. The aim of this exercise is to reduce complexity and increase the lucidity of service capabilities.

SPECIFICATION OF ATOMIC SERVICE.   An atomic service is designed to address a narrow scope of the problem. Thus, its abstraction level is considered moderately low. Its contribution to business or technology could become negligible if its capabilities are trimmed further. Therefore, the contextual specification process that starts with an atomic service can be a challenging task because of the limited reduction spectrum that its construct allows. In other words, further abstraction levels reduction of an atomic service will result in a more fine-grained service that may not be practical to employ for resolving a problem. To avoid a result that cannot be put into practice, it is beneficial to assess the outcome of such activity in terms of service granularity and future influences on service reuse and effectiveness. Namely, steer clear of specification activities that produce impractical services.

Exhibit 15.2 illustrates a contextual specification process that involves the Mainstream Fiction Book Orders Atomic Service. This entity also serves as the starting point for the process. The resulting entity, the Literary Fiction Book Orders Atomic Service, embodies a subset of its originator's attributes and processes. Note that the Mainstream Fiction Book Orders service may

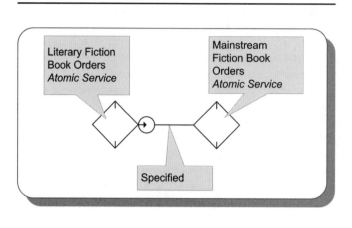

EXHIBIT 15.2 ATOMIC SERVICE SPECIFICATION EXAMPLE

consist of other subcategory functionalities that can be specified as well (not shown in the exhibit), such as ordering commercial fiction books.

SPECIFICATION OF COMPOSITE SERVICE. The reader may remember from Chapter 12 that composite services can be classified into two major perspectives: application-level and enterprise-level. A composite formation that operates in the former's domain typically is designed to address confined concerns that are naturally affiliated with reuse of software in a well-defined boundary of an application. Conversely, the enterprise-level composite service is designed to meet the demands of cross-organizational boundaries in distributed computing environments. Both are hierarchical by nature. That is, a composite service consists of internal child services that collaborate to attain a practical solution.

A contextual specification process that involves a composite service should address functionality and abstraction-level reduction by limiting the capabilities of its aggregated internal services. One of the fundamental challenges that typically arises from such activity is associated with the hierarchical formation, the composite construct of the service that naturally imposes *dependencies* between the internal services that it encompasses. As a result of the specification process, the rendered product, the contextually specified entity, may consist of fewer aggregated services that tackle a narrower range of the problem. This is akin to peeling off layers of the core service to accommodate a reduction of its functionality. This dependency between the internal aggregated services should be thoroughly inspected to avoid a fundamental change in the composite hierarchy and its core attributes. Remember, although the specification process results in a reduction of the overall composite service functionality the final product must retain its core attributes.

Exhibit 15.3 illustrates a contextual specification process that starts at the Magazine Order Composite Service. This reduction of functionality yields a lower level of abstraction that is represented by two atomic services: Scholarly Magazine Order Atomic Service and Utility Magazine Order Atomic Service. Note that the Magazine Order Composite Service may consist of more types of magazines, such as narrative or interview. It is important to note that a core composite service, the originating entity, can yield more than one specified service, as illustrated in the exhibit. However, the rendered entities must continue to share the core attributes of the originating composite service, such as magazine publication and magazine order capabilities.

SPECIFYING A SERVICE CLUSTER. A service cluster is also a subject for degeneralization. The complex distributed aspect of a cluster and the mounting number of relationships that may be

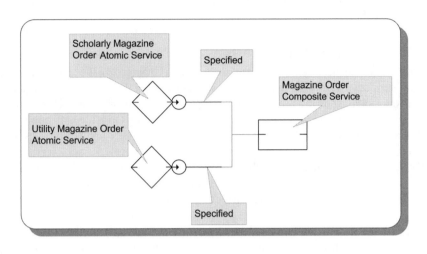

EXHIBIT 15.3   COMPOSITE SERVICE SPECIFICATION EXAMPLE

established between its collaborating members are the driving forces and motivation behind the contextual specification process. In other words, an extremely generalized and diversified cluster that does not provide a clear solution is a preferred candidate for reduction of functionality and, most important, streamlining its operations. Furthermore, an overgeneralized cluster typically consists of services that form complex internal relationships that are difficult to operate and maintain. Decreasing scope, sharpening the goals that a cluster ought to attain, and reducing a complex cluster formation should be the practitioner's major objectives.

Exhibit 15.4 illustrates a contextual specification process that emanates from the core service Tree Packaging and Shipping Service Cluster. The Deciduous Tree Shipping Composite Service represents a subset of the originator's functionality. This reduction in scope of service capability characterizes the nature of the specification effort. Note that this activity can yield three other

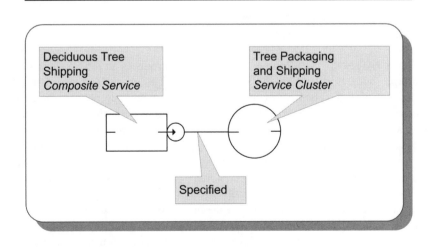

EXHIBIT 15.4   SERVICE CLUSTER CONTEXTUAL SPECIFICATION EXAMPLE

ordering processes, such as shipping cedar, conifer, evergreen, willow, and maple trees. These are not shown in the exhibit.

CONTEXTUAL SPECIFICATION PATTERNS

Similar to the contextual generalization effort (discussed in Chapter 14), the contextual specification process should utilize patterns not only to save time and shorten the service analysis and discovery phase but also to solve recurring problems with a predefined set of solutions. This remedy toolbox introduces specification patterns, styles that can guide practitioners to efficiently apply reduction in a service's operational scope. As a result, the service's functionality and capabilities are trimmed down to meet business or technical requirements, discover new services, and lower the abstraction level of the core services. Furthermore, think of the contextual specification patterns as templates, molds that can assist with both separation-of-software concerns and foster the loose coupling of service components. This guidance should have an enduring influence on future service-oriented development, deployment, and operations in production environments.

Consider the simple preliminary steps to perform before applying the contextual specification patterns. These will help practitioners to discover the motivation behind the use of any pattern and identify the expected results.

- **Analyze the problem domain.** What is the problem that needs solving? Is it a business proposition? Technical issue? Do the requirements mandate reductions of functionality?
- **Identify the motivation for service specification.** Is the core service too generic? Should the service's capability be reduced? Do the service's operations have an unclear agenda and goals?
- **Examine the solution that is provided by the specification pattern.** What would be the outcome of utilizing a specific contextual specification pattern? Will the process yield new services? Will this activity foster a loosely coupled architectural environment?

The sections that follow elaborate on four chief contextual specification patterns that foster service reuse, functionality consolidation, reduction of redundant operations, and separation of concerns as well as loose coupling best practices:

1. Reverse Proxy (250)
2. Separation of Concerns through Service Specification (252)
3. Unification of Concerns through Service Specification (254)
4. Service Specification Loop (256)

REVERSE PROXY PATTERN.   The Reverse Proxy pattern introduces an intermediate stage between the core service—subject to contextual specification activity—and its trimmed-down version. To moderate the reduction in functionality and capabilities, a mediating service should be injected between these two entities. Thus, this pattern should be employed when the originating service is proportionally larger than its final rendered entity.[3] Moreover, remember that the employment of a contextual specification pattern should not only ease the way to finding a solution, it is also designed to ascertain new services. Although the proxy service is not regarded as the final artifact of the specification venture, it should be considered a new service discovered during this exploration effort. It is important to note that the specification process is not limited to instituting a single proxy. Multiple proxies can be inserted between a core services and its final derived service abstraction.

Another important aspect of the proxy idea is promoting the proportional reduction of a service's abstraction without compromising the preservation of its properties. In other words, the proxy service represents a notch below its originator in terms of functionality to avoid a radical reduction of capabilities.

Problem. Obviously, a bulky service, a coarse-grained entity, is the right candidate for the contextual specification process. But this degeneralization effort can introduce design and architecture challenges when the scope of capabilities gap between the originating service and its derived product is too wide. In other words, the abstraction level of the rendered specified service is disproportionally lower than its originator. This typically leads to the creation of an unbalanced service ecosystem that consists of services that are both too fine-grained and too coarse-grained.

Solution. To reduce service capabilities gradually during the contextual specification process, introduce a mediating service, a proxy that preserves some of its originator's capabilities. The final product should clearly present the lower abstraction level in this chain of functionality reduction. Consider the three chief steps that should be pursued when employing the Reverse Proxy pattern:

1. Identify the candidate core service that should participate in the contextual specification process.
2. Insert a single or multiple proxy services between the core service and its final degeneralized product.
3. Verify that a gradual reduction in service functionality has been applied to the specification process and that each discovered service in the chain indeed represents a lower level of abstraction.

Example. To better comprehend this concept, let us view Exhibit 15.5, which illustrates a contextual specification process that utilizes the proxy Property and Liability Home Insurance Composite Service. It plays the role of a mediator positioned between the originating entity Home Owner's Insurance Service Cluster and the yielding artifact "Dwelling" Insurance Atomic Service. Note that this descending ladder both reduces the responsibility of each derived service in the chain and influences its formation: First, the service cluster is downsized to a composite service. The final product is further trimmed down to an atomic entity.

Synopsis. The Reverse Proxy pattern is designed to address radical reduction of functionality and extreme specification results. This pattern typically is employed to mitigate the risk of deploying services that are too far high or far low on the organizational granularity scale. These challenges are

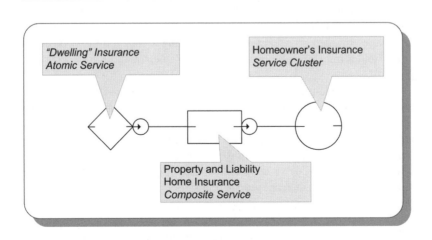

EXHIBIT 15.5 REVERSE PROXY PATTERN EXAMPLE

Pattern Identification	
Name	Reverse Proxy Pattern
Category	Contextual Specification Analysis

Problems, Solutions, and Implementations	
Problem	The specified product abstraction level is far lower than its originating service.
Solution	Moderate reduction of the service degeneralization process.
Applicability	Applies to bulky and coarse-grained services that must be contextually decomposed.
Method	Take three steps to employ the Reverse Proxy pattern: (1) Identify the core service for contextual specification; (2) insert a proxy service or multiple proxies between the core service and its final degeneralized product; (3) verify that a gradual reduction in service functionality has been applied to the specification process.
Benefits	1. Moderating the service abstraction reduction process and avoiding a radical decrease of service capabilities.
	2. Controlling evolution of services through mediation.
	3. Fostering loose coupling best practices.
	4. Discovery of new services.
Risks	Excessive use of proxy services may impact message exchange performance.
Notation	Employ the "Specified" symbol.

EXHIBIT 15.6 REVERSE PROXY PATTERN SUMMARY TABLE

outlined in Exhibit 15.6, which that also summarizes the problem, solution, applicability, method, benefits, and risks involved when employing the Reverse Proxy pattern.

SEPARATION OF CONCERNS THROUGH SERVICE SPECIFICATION PATTERN. The Separation of Concerns through Service Specification pattern is designed to contextually divide a service into two or more entities, each of which will offer a lower level of abstraction and distinguished functionality. In other words, this contextual decomposition style not only splits a service into distinct operation groups, it also reduces the solution scope for each derived service. The final products are abstracted services, each of which may represent limited scope of business processes or reduced technical capabilities. If the functionality of derived services can completely address the organizational concern, it is possible to eliminate the originating service. This should be the sheer responsibility of the practitioner that is commissioned to weight the benefits against advantages of such elimination.

The major benefit of this pattern is obviously to enhance separation-of-concerns activities and foster assets reuse. Furthermore, the Separation of Concerns through Service Specification pattern motivates practitioners to adhere to loose coupling architecture best practices once a service is developed and is transformed into a concrete implementation.[4]

Problem. An overly coarse-grained service imposes design and development challenges because of its internal wide scope of solutions that it offers. A service that possesses such design constraint is clearly hard to integrate, deploy, maintain, and monitor in a production environment. But perhaps one of the greatest challenges is to increase the reusability factor of a service if its offered specialties are tightly coupled to the extent that is hard to separate and reuse. Remember that a service specialty is a field of expertise to which a service is capable of contributing. Therefore, tightly coupled specialties must be separated to increase service reusability and foster a loosely coupled architecture environment.

Solution. The solution to these problems should not only address breaking up a coarse-grained service that encompasses a large number of operations and interfaces but also separating its core specialties into more manageable units. This contextual decomposition obviously must take place

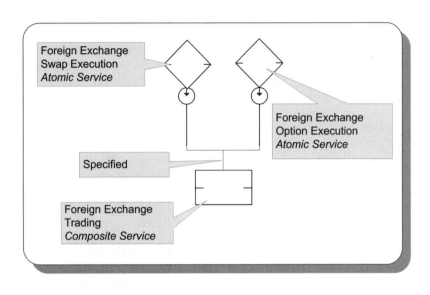

EXHIBIT 15.7   SEPARATION OF CONCERNS THROUGH SERVICE SPECIFICATION PATTERN

Pattern Identification	
Name	Separation of Concerns through Service Specification Pattern
Category	Contextual Specification Analysis
Problems, Solutions, and Implementations	
Problem	An overly coarse-grained service introduces integration, deployment, and maintenance difficulties because of its tightly coupled implementation and offered mix of specialties.
Solution	The service should be broken up into lower levels of abstraction and distinct areas of expertise.
Applicability	Applies to oversized service that must be contextually decomposed.
Method	Pursue two main steps to achieve the contextual decomposition goal: (1) Identify the proper candidate for contextual specification; (2) separate the core service into distinct areas of expertise.
Benefits	1. Enable separation-of-concerns analysis.
	2. Foster service reuse.
	3. Increase software isolation.
	4. Assist with service contextual decomposition.
	5. Promote loose coupling architecture implementation.
Risks	Excessive contextual specification activities may yield impractical fine-grained services.
Notation	Employ the "Specified" symbol.

EXHIBIT 15.8   SEPARATION OF CONCERNS THROUGH SERVICE SPECIFICATION PATTERN SUMMARY TABLE

when a service is too coarse grained and the prospect of its efficient integration with peer services and consumers, deployment, and maintenance in production is challenged. To accomplish these goals, consider the two chief steps that should be pursued when employing the Separation of Concerns through Service Specification pattern:

1. Identify the candidate core service for the contextual specification process.
2. Separate service operations and interfaces by creating lower-level abstractions that are represented by finer-grained services.

Example.   Exhibit 15.7 illustrates the Separation of Concerns through Service Specification pattern example. The Foreign Exchange Trading Composite Service is contextually decomposed into two different entities, each of which represents a lower-level abstraction of the foreign exchange perspective: the Foreign Exchange Swap Execution Atomic Service and the Foreign Exchange Option Execution Atomic Service. These separated and specified perspectives not only introduce a detailed implementation of the core service but also represent a different perspective. Note the utilization of the "Specified" modeling symbol to denote reduction of functionality and filtering of expertise.

Synopsis.   The Separation of Concerns through Service Specification pattern is designed to guide practitioners to contextually analyze and decompose bulky services that introduce design and operational challenges during their life cycle. This approach also advocates separating a service's specialties into distinct areas of expertise to increase their reusability level and foster a loosely coupled production environment. These challenges are outlined in Exhibit 15.8, which also identifies the problem, solution, applicability, method, benefits, and risks involved with the employment of the Separation of Concerns through Service Specification pattern.

UNIFICATION OF CONCERNS THROUGH SERVICE SPECIFICATION PATTERN.   Unlike the Separation of Concerns through Service Specification (252) pattern, the Unification of Concerns through Service Specification pattern is about contextually coupling two or more core abstractions to create a consolidated entity. This new rendered service represents a lower abstraction level that typically embodies a subset of the originators' attributes and capabilities.

This simple idea of extracting parts of functionalities of services and combining them into a unified implementation both promotes consolidation of functionalities and enhances service reusability. Furthermore, this process not only enables practitioners to find commonalities among services that share mutual interests and processes, it also encourages future merging of service capabilities by creating a new dedicated service to handle this distinct functionality. Again, this union does not entirely combine whole services, nor is the rendered service larger than any of its individual originators. Here we are simply commissioned to cherry-pick functionality that can be merged to create a new business or technical executable.[5]

Problem.   Unrelated operations and interfaces that a service encompasses typically introduce challenges with integration, management, design and architecture, deployment, and monitoring. Thus, a service that is comprised of such a mix of contextual properties must be streamlined to simplify its internal design and alleviate the risk of architecture complexities.

Solution.   Create a service that consists of imported operations and interfaces that were extracted from various core services. This contextual separation should take place when the transported capabilities do not belong or should be separated from the original core services. The final product then typically represents a lower level of abstraction that contains functionality that may serve its originators. Consider the two major steps that should be pursued when employing this pattern:

1. Identify operations and interfaces that are candidates for extraction. These capabilities should be found in two or more services.
2. Export these operations and interfaces to a newly created service that represents a lower level of abstraction.

Example.   Exhibit 15.9 illustrates the Unification of Concerns through Service Specification pattern. The originating entities, Fixed-Income Trading Composite Service and Foreign Exchange Trading Composite Service, are the contributors to the institution of the Order Routing Atomic Service. This functionality selection and reduction in service responsibility contributes to the establishment of a lower abstraction designed to implement a subset of the processes of the combined

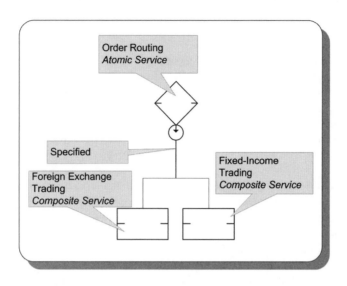

Exhibit 15.9   Unification of Concerns through Service Specification
Pattern

Pattern Identification	
Name	Unification of Concerns through Service Specification Pattern
Category	Contextual Specification Analysis
Problems, Solutions, and Implementations	
Problem	Two or more services consist of contextually unrelated operations and interfaces.
Solution	Extract these service capabilities and transport them into a newly created service that also represents a lower level of abstraction.
Applicability	Applies to services that encompass unrelated functionality that must be exported to streamline their design.
Method	To pursue the contextual specification process, attend to the two major steps: (1) Select candidate operations and interfaces that are a part of various core services; (2) create a new service that consists of the imported capabilities.
Benefits	1. Fostering consolidation of service functionalities.
	2. Encouraging contextual coupling by merging common functionalities.
	3. Promoting functionality reconciliation and reduction of operation redundancies.
	4. Supporting reuse of future service implementation.
	5. Providing motivation for service decomposition during design time.
	6. Encouraging loose coupling architecture best practices.
Risks	The contextually specified product may include unrelated operations if the imported capabilities are not carefully examined.
Notation	Employ the "Specified" symbol.

Exhibit 15.10   Unification of Concerns through Service Specification Pattern Summary Table

and originating trading services. Therefore, although the rendered product is regarded as a *part of* trading functionality and specialty, its reduced operational scope also implies that its abstraction level was trimmed down to a lower level.

Synopsis.   Remember that the Unification of Concerns through Service Specification pattern calls for a selective collection of operations and interfaces from various services and combines them into a newly created service. This responsibility reduction is designed to streamline the operations of the originating services and separate their unrelated capabilities by exporting them to a new service. Exhibit 15.10 outlines these challenges and summarizes the solution, method of implementation, and benefits related to the pursuit of the Unification Of Concerns through Service Specification pattern.

SERVICE SPECIFICATION LOOP PATTERN.   To understand the Service Specification Loop pattern, imagine a circle formed by services that begins at the main entity and spawns two or more services. These descendants then close the ring by merging into the final rendered service. This pattern depicts a service transformation through reduction of scope, limitation of execution boundary, and trimmed-down capabilities. In other words, the Service Specification Loop pattern is a common scenario in which a core service, the most generalized entity in the chain, derives lower levels of service abstractions. As mentioned, this contextual typing leads to a converged product that is regarded as the most specified item in the loop.

The chief benefit of such a scheme is the establishment of relationships that tie services of the same type to a mutual cause. The root motivation to tie these entities by their contextual association is to establish a group of affiliated functionalities that can offer a powerful solution to organizational concerns. In addition, doing this can encourage practitioners to create service clusters that not only consist of related distributed members but also provide interoperability solutions. A composite service, a hierarchical formation, can also be considered for design and construction because of the carved relationship that are found between the discovered lower level service abstractions.

Problem.   The lack of an institutional modeling process that can guide the establishment of relationships between services and identify common implementations is the core problem that motivates the pursuit of the Service Specification Loop pattern. Furthermore, the inability to relate services and integrate their individual offerings to resolve a common organizational concern is a major challenge that should be addressed. Another challenge that calls for a solution is a dearth of best practices to guide architects, modelers, analysts, developers, and managers to construct composite formations based on hierarchical affiliation between aggregated entities. Standards that can assist with service clusters design should also be devised by architecture policies.

Solution.   To alleviate these design, architecture, implementation, and maintenance challenges, employ the contextual specification process to found relationships between the derived services. This method of responsibility reduction and degeneralization of a core service not only guides practitioners to discover new services but also promotes a loosely coupled paradigm in a production environment. Consider the two simple steps for pursuing this solution:

1.   Identify a core service that can derive two or more services that represent lower level of abstractions.
2.   Merge these derived services into a final product. The resulting service should represent the lowest abstraction level in the chain.

Example.   Exhibit 15.11 illustrates the Service Specification Loop pattern. The Tax Return Service Cluster is the most generalized item that originates two lower-level service abstractions: Exempt Tax Return Composite Service and Individual Tax Return Composite Service. These entities are merged

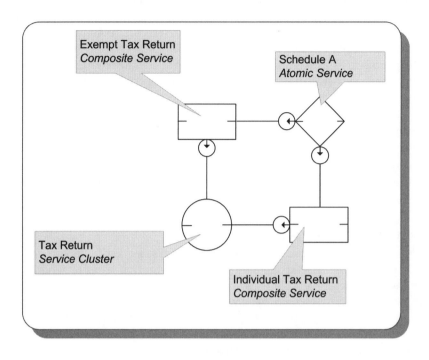

EXHIBIT 15.11   SERVICE SPECIFICATION LOOP PATTERN EXAMPLE

Pattern Identification	
Name	Service Specification Loop Pattern
Category	Contextual Specification Analysis

Problems, Solutions, and Implementations	
Problem	Lack of modeling best practices that can assist practitioners to establish hierarchical and nonhierarchical service associations hampers service integration and orchestration initiatives.
Solution	Employ the contextual specification approach to create proper relationships between services.
Applicability	Applies to development environments that are seeking to employ a systematic approach for instituting service relationships.
Method	Pursue the two major steps to establish proper relationships between services: (1) Identify a candidate core service that can derive two or more lower-level abstractions represented by services; (2) merge these derived products into a final service that represents the lowest level of abstraction in the chain.
Benefits	1. Discovering services by utilizing the contextual specification process. 2. Ascertaining service groups. 3. Identifying motivations for establishing service clusters and composite services. 4. Promoting loose coupling best practices. 5. Fostering separation-of-concerns best practices.
Risks	A succession of specification activities may produce a too fine-grained service.
Notation	Employ the "Specified" symbol.

EXHIBIT 15.12   SERVICE SPECIFICATION LOOP PATTERN SUMMARY TABLE

into the Schedule A Atomic Service. To readers who are not familiar with the term "Schedule A," it is worth mentioning that both the exempt and individual tax returns must also include the Schedule A form designed to collect itemized deductions. The Schedule A Atomic Service is not only designated the responsibility to automate this task; it also represents the common functionality of the originating services. Note that this specification method not only encourages the formation of relationships between the rendered services, it also offers a sense of order by creating a hierarchical formation that results in the most specified entity in the loop.

Synopsis.   The Service Specification Loop pattern is devised to address the discovery of new services and ascertaining service associations. This identification approach can involve autonomous services, aggregated services contained in a composite formation, or even service cluster members. These challenges are outlined in Exhibit 15.12, which also identifies the problem, solution, applicability, method, benefits, and risks affiliated with the Service Specification Loop pattern.

SERVICE SPECIFICATION ANTI-PATTERNS

Patterns, as discussed earlier, typically are best practices that guide practitioners to successfully employ the contextual specification approach to reduce abstraction levels of services, trim down their functionality, and scale back their scope of operations. These are simply templates that are ready-to-use, out-of-the-box solutions for implementation. Conversely, anti-patterns are a set of what-not-to-do standards. They warn against impractical utilization of the service contextual specification method. They also advocate against creating conflicting conditions and yielding paradoxical products that will be unfeasible to construct and implement.

Imagine, for example, a contextual specification activity that yields a service whose abstraction level is greater than that of its originator. How can the practitioner steer clear of such circumstances? Or consider, for instance, a radical reduction of functionality that takes place when a service cluster yields an atomic service. Should this be avoided? Should we allow such a drastic reduction of service scope?

The sections that follow depict four major contextual specification anti-patterns that answer these questions. They elaborate on common scenarios that practitioners should avoid:

1. Self-Specification (258)
2. Circular Specification (259)
3. Contextual Specification Conflict (259)
4. Extreme Specification (260)

SELF-SPECIFICATION ANTI-PATTERN.   The Self-Specification anti-pattern advocates that a core service must yield a lower level of abstraction by creating a *new* service. That is, a service cannot be a specified product of itself. Therefore, the specification process must always identify a new service whose scope of operation is more limited and reduced in capabilities. Moreover, the practitioner should conceive of the contextual specification process as a depiction of a service's evolution, whereas the newly discovered service carries on some of the core service's attributes. Thus, modifications to the originating entity should be avoided, yet selected functionality should be passed on to its descendants.

The Self-Specification anti-pattern also cautions against erasing a service's identity by modifying its core properties and capabilities. This best practice advocates that the specification process should be employed to promote transparency by preserving a service's intermediate life cycle stages. In other words, the originating service should always stay intact to enable better design and architecture traceability. This calls for introducing new services that can efficiently address some of the concerns.

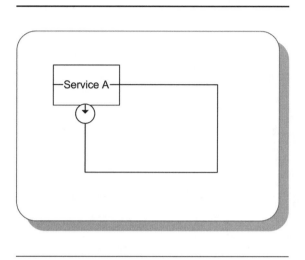

Exhibit 15.13 Self-Specification Anti-Pattern

Exhibit 15.13 illustrates the Self-Specification anti-pattern process. As is apparent, Service A reduces its own abstraction level, functionality, and capabilities without passing its attributes and part of its operations to a lower level of abstraction, namely to a new service.

CIRCULAR SPECIFICATION ANTI-PATTERN. A series of contextual service specifications that involves a chain of descending services cannot start and end at the same service. This scenario is paradoxical because a service cannot become its own specified product. To better understand this situation, think about a core service—the starting point of a contextual specification activity—that is unusually generalized and highly abstracted, and thus requires a series of reductions in scope. The functionalities of its descendants will be gradually trimmed down as the specification activity progresses. By the end of this process, the very last discovered service—the smallest abstraction in the chain—closes the circle by converging with the starting point. In other words, the specified product of the last service in this loop is the very first service that this process emanated from. Should such a situation be allowed? The answer to this question is definitely no.

To better comprehend this scenario, let us view Exhibit 15.14 depicting a Circular Specification anti-pattern process, during which Service B emanates from Service A. Next, Service C is derived from Service B. The process continues with the discovery of Service D. Finally, Service A is the specification product of Service D. Since Service A is the originating service in the chain, it would be irrational to conclude that Service A is also the specification product of itself.

CONTEXTUAL SPECIFICATION CONFLICT ANTI-PATTERN. Remember, all discovered services during the specification process always should possess less functionality, and their scope of operation should be reduced. Accordingly, their abstraction level should be lower as the specification activity progresses. The Contextual Specification Conflict anti-pattern cautions against taking the opposite route: Imagine that a contextual specification process yields a service that represents a higher abstraction level than its originator. In other words, the elicited service turns out to be more generalized than its creator. This situation should be avoided because of the conflict that it represents.

This simple best practice is illustrated in Exhibit 15.15, which depicts an originating service and its contextually specified product: Atomic Service A and Service Cluster A, respectively. Note that the core service is an atomic entity that yields a service cluster formation. This transition

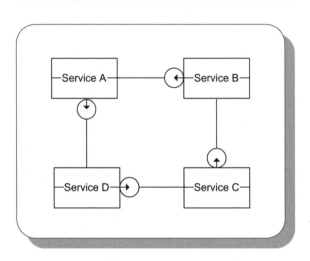

EXHIBIT 15.14 CIRCULAR SPECIFICATION ANTI-PATTERN

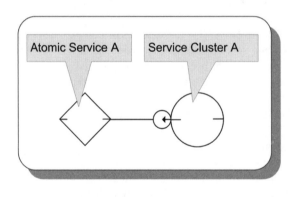

EXHIBIT 15.15 CONTEXTUAL SPECIFICATION CONFLICT ANTI-
PATTERN EXAMPLE

generates a much larger construct that consists of associated service members that jointly form a cluster. Note that this assertion is based on the assumption that a service cluster is contextually larger than an atomic service. To avoid this situation, simply compare the originating service's capabilities and operational scope to its newly discovered service's process boundaries and determine if the outcome is similar to the conflict that is presented by this pattern.

EXTREME SPECIFICATION ANTI-PATTERN. Finally, the last anti-pattern in this series represents an "extreme" transformation of a core service. The term "extreme" pertains to the process of contextual specification that leads to the discovery of a new service that is proportionally much smaller in scope than its originator in terms of operations boundaries, capability, and functionality. View, for example, Exhibit 15.16. It introduces the Extreme Specification anti-pattern, which involves two

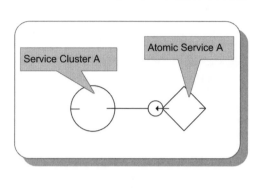

EXHIBIT 15.16   EXTREME SPECIFICATION ANTI-PATTERN

different service formations: the core service named Service Cluster A and its derived entity Atomic Service A.

This radical transformation from a service cluster to an atomic construct should be alarming to the practitioner because of the immoderate reduction in scope and functionality. More specifically, a cluster formation encompasses two or more business and/or technical affiliated services that can address a wide range of problems. The specification process that trims down such a complex and large entity must be restrained by some mechanisms to avoid a disproportional reduction in the service abstraction level.

To circumvent similar circumstances, employ the Reverse Proxy (250) pattern. This method should be employed to moderate the transition from a high-level to a low-level abstraction, from a core service that is bound to address a wide range of solutions to an entity whose responsibilities are drastically reduced, from an originating service that is delegated a wide functionality scope to a rendered product that is devised to handle a very small portion of the solution.

DELIVERABLES

This chapter introduces contextual specification diagrams that propose reduction of a service's capability scope and the contextual decomposition of a coarse-grained service. Prepare such a diagram to depict the service-oriented analysis process and the identified new services. Adhere to the best practices, and employ the various patterns that are elaborated on in this chapter.

SUMMARY

- The contextual specification process is devised to assist architects, modelers, developers, analysts, and managers to reduce the scope of a core service by decreasing its capabilities spectrum and produce a new service that represents a lower abstraction level.
- The participating assets in the contextual specification effort are atomic, composite, and cluster formations that should be conceived of as conceptual entities. Their physical structure should not be the focus of this analysis venture.
- The contextual specification patterns foster service reuse, functionality consolidation, reduction of duplicate operations, and separation of concerns as well as loose coupling best practices.
- The contextual specification anti-pattern is a collection of best practices and policies that guide practitioners with the application of the contextual specification patterns.

Notes

1. The contextual specification process is a semantic specification of service capabilities that introduces reduction of a service's abstraction level rather than a structural manipulation to limit service granularity level.

2. Refer to the Separation of Concerns Analysis section in Chapter 2.

3. Note that a proxy service introduced by the Reverse Proxy (250) pattern is devised to moderate the contextual reduction of a service. Conversely, Chapter 14 introduces the Simple Proxy (233) pattern to moderate the increase in service abstraction.

4. The Separation of Concerns through Service Specification (252) pattern typically yields decomposition of service structures. However, this pattern is merely conceptual and accentuates the separation of service functionality, operations, and even specialties.

5. This contextual unification typically motivates practitioners to unify service structures during the structural analysis process depicted in Chapter 14. However, the unification of concerns through service specification is a contextual exercise, a conceptual act that proposes service structural changes in the future.

CHAPTER 16

CONTEXTUAL EXPANSION ANALYSIS PROCESS AND MODELING PATTERNS

Unlike the service contextual generalization process that addresses the increase of service abstraction levels (discussed in Chapter 14), contextual expansion is simply about extending the territorial aspects of a service to increase its reusability factor and sharing capabilities. The term "territorial" does not necessarily pertain to physical landscapes or concrete boundaries of an enterprise or governance entity. This contextual exercise is a virtual expansion that calls for the *growth* of a service's *offerings* and *influence* beyond its current spectrum to increase and diversify the range of its consumer base. Remember, this contextual growth of a service starts from internal service capabilities and expands beyond the service semantic boundary, spanning across local or enterprise landscapes.

For example, a service can be expanded from a small component to provide solutions to an application's module, from a module to an application's tier, from a single application to multiple applications, from a group of systems to a line of business implementations, from a single business domain to multiple domains, and from cross-organizational operations to serve third-party vendors and partners. Again, this expansion is about broadening the offering power of a service to provide increased solutions to organizational needs by *cross-cutting* business[1] or technological concerns. It is also about widening a service's capabilities horizontally to span multiple integration efforts within the organization and even beyond its boundaries.

Imagine, for example, a Client Profile Service developed for the marketing department that enables the retrieval of customer information, such as shopping behavior, address, and household income. This implementation can be shared by other organizational entities: the accounts receivable application, shipping department, and the orders division. But since the original Client Profile Service implementation was devised to provide only marketing solutions, an expansion of its *contextual influence* will be required. This may call for service redesign, rearchitecture, and redeployment efforts to accommodate the new business or technical platforms. Remember, the adoption of the service by other organizational entities would not necessarily require modification to the service's specialties. Client information retrieval capabilities and service expertise would not be subject to alteration either.

Recall that the contextual expansion activity always yields a new service that stems from a core service. Therefore, this process introduces a design and architecture dilemma that should be resolved: Should a core service that has been expanded to provide business or technical support to a larger consumer base be eliminated or retired? The answer to this question depends on the defined goals of the modeling initiative that an organization conducts. Obviously, if the aim is to increase reusability of software assets and reduce expenditure, no multiple instances of a single service should be retained in a production environment. Thus, the expanded version should become the "true" operational version, and the originating service should be retired. Conversely, multiple instances of a service should be maintained in a large federated or distributed computing landscape, as we learn in the sections that follow. In addition, environments that require replication of functionality, such as disaster recovery, would also motivate practitioners to retain duplicate capabilities to ensure continuity of operations in production.

CONTEXTUAL EXPANSION PROCESS

What are the major service transformation aspects that should be considered when pursuing the contextual expansion process? What type of changes should a service undergo to accommodate demand for growth and territorial influence? Consider the eight chief service contextual expansion requirements that should be pursued to address the expansion of services across consumer boundaries, application modules, tiers, lines of business, and third-party partners and vendors.

1. **Solution repurposing.** Expand service solutions to enable applications and organizations to share the same set of functionality.
2. **Service contract spectrum.** Modify the service contract to meet increasing demands by a growing number of applications, organizations, consumers, and partners.
3. **Diversified consumers.** Provide solutions to the mix of consumers that represent different lines of businesses and organizations.
4. **Information repurposing.** Modify the initial purpose of content retrieval to meet more diversified service consumption needs.
5. **Cross-cutting concerns.** Provide comparable solutions to business and technology concerns.
6. **Service adoptability and agility.** Enhance service capability to quickly provide solutions to other business or technical concerns.
7. **Integration.** Identify the needs for new service integration capabilities.
8. **Interoperability.** Address interoperability challenges triggered by contextual expansion.

SERVICE CONTEXTUAL EXPANSION BENEFITS.   The contextual expansion of a service is driven by a number of motivating aspects, each of which offers architectural, design, and management benefits. Perhaps one of the most essential advantages is *semantic reconciliation*. The phrase "semantic reconciliation" relates to consolidation of ideas, the unification of concepts that typically fosters reduction of service construction efforts, and the decline of functionality redundancy.[2]

Consider, for example, a number of employee records software implementations that organizations launch across their lines of business and domains. Each of these deployed services provides employee information to different audiences and for different purposes, such as the human resources department, employee benefits center, and employee training facilities organization. The expansion of a single service to accommodate these diverse needs across the enterprise can reduce expenditure and maintenance cost. Expanding an existing service's influence and enhancing its capabilities to adapt to changes, to offer functionality to a diverse group of consumers, and to close communication gaps between business domains by offering cross-cutting capabilities can increase reuse and agility. This notion of consolidation and encouraging the reduction of service duplication is the main promise of the semantic reconciliation benefit.

The other substantial benefit of the service expansion is *contextual integration,* which typically answers the chief questions associated with service collaboration: What software assets should be integrated? What are their common responsibilities? How can services be federated across an organization to provide solutions? What are the common business processes that should be integrated or reconciled? What are the common and comparable technological concepts that should be consolidated?

Finally, alleviating *communication challenges* across an organization and beyond its boundaries is another benefit that the contextual expansion process introduces. This includes enhancing collaboration between business domains that share common business processes and implementation components. In addition, closer commerce relationships with vendors, suppliers, and partners can be attained by expanding the contextual notion of services.

SERVICE CONTEXTUAL EXPANSION EXAMPLE.   To better understand the service contextual expansion process, consider Exhibit 16.1, which exemplifies this idea. The core service (far left) Customer Profile Composite Service is being contextually expanded beyond the *Application Component* domain. The resulting product (far right) identifies the transition to the *Application Tier* zone. This transformation extends a service's growth and influence beyond its original creation. Raising a service's visibility beyond its inception state obviously increases its reusability and spurs the motivation for asset consolidation.

The reader may wonder what the status of an expanded service should be after its offerings are enhanced to accommodate its new dimension. Should it be eliminated, suspended, or simply demoted? The answer to this question is obviously in the hands of the architects, analysts, modelers, developers, and managers who devised this scheme. The rule of thumb suggests retiring the core service once its successor is capable of serving a larger consumer audience and its solutions are repurposed. But this decision should be carefully considered and revisited after studying the service environment and its consumers' requirements.

Note the three major contextual expansion diagram components illustrated in Exhibit 16.1. First, utilize the formal service notation that identifies the type of services that participate in this venture: atomic, composite, and/or service cluster. Second, employ the "Expanded" symbol to denote the contextual expansion effort. Third, identify the service expansion zones and cross-domains where a service transformation takes place. In this exhibit, a type of swim lane diagram[3] depicts the two subsets of a service evolution and their corresponding application sectors: Customer Records Application Component and Customer Records Application Tier. The more expanded the service, the more sections this diagram should have.

CONTEXTUAL EXPANSION LEVELS: ORGANIZATIONAL ZONES FOR DISTRIBUTION OF SERVICES

The contextual expansion of a service is conceptual by nature. The physical aspects of service integration and interoperability issues should not be the concerns that drive this process. Here we

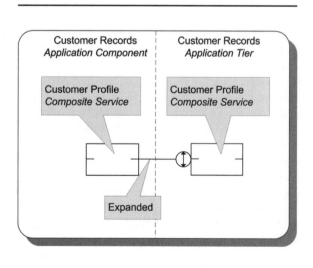

EXHIBIT 16.1   CONTEXTUAL EXPANSION EXAMPLE

take a *horizontal* approach to asset reuse, by which an overarching plan is carved out to solve cross-cutting concerns, similar problems that may involve neighboring lines of business, related domains, and trading partners.

This expansion method advocates that we should not be bogged down by the generalization of service abstraction levels, as described in Chapter 14. An attempt to boost service functionality and operations in the belief that this scheme may better serve other organizations in the enterprise should not be exercised either. The preferred direction would be to expand a service beyond its current charter to facilitate the needs of a more diversified consumer base and enhance its adaptability capacity for the benefit of other applications and organizations.

Again, this process is *not* about elevating a service's abstraction levels and generalizing its functionality. Here we are commissioned to enhance service *elasticity* to enable business and technological integration with other zones in the organization. The term "zone" pertains to the areas of expansion where a service can fit in and offer valuable solutions on larger scale of operations. To better understand this mission, consider three major expansion levels, each requiring a different degree of service implementation complexity and introducing a distinct set of integration difficulties yet necessitating comparable functionality and specialty. The sections that follow elaborate on these three levels of contextual expansion.

Level 1: Application-level contextual expansion
Level 2: Enterprise-level contextual expansion
Level 3: Partner-level contextual expansion

LEVEL 1: APPLICATION-LEVEL CONTEXTUAL EXPANSION.   Level 1 indentifies service requirements for an *application's scope level*. This includes *local* implementation of services that enable the execution of processes and message exchange with a limited range of consumers. The term "local" identifies *departmental* rather than cross-organizational software requirements that span lines of business boundaries. Furthermore, Level 1 is typically confined to needs of applications, and the expansion of a service takes place within an application boundary. This contextual expansion may consist of efforts, such as enlarging the scope of a service's offerings to various modules that an application is comprised of, application tiers, or even a collection of local applications that may have a need for a common service.

According to this model, service offerings may be expanded from an application's component to serve an assortment of modules. A service may grow from an application module to accommodate the needs of an isolated tier or a number of loosely coupled tiers. A service may be expanded from facilitating a small-scale application to providing common specialties to a group of local applications. Level 1 encompasses all these ranges, but not beyond these boundaries.

Remember, the contextual expansion activity is about depicting service growth in terms of its semantic level rather than offering a structural analysis of the resulting product. Exhibit 16.2 illustrates the contextual expansion process that expands the Life Insurance Policy Processing Composite Service from an application tier level (named Life Insurance Policy Application Tier) to a larger departmental entity: the Life Insurance Policy Processing Center Department. The depicted service growth takes place locally within a department boundary.

This contextual expansion obviously would spur initiatives to upgrade the composite formation to a service cluster, accommodate its new consumer base, and enable larger consumption rates. Note that this cross-boundary service typing not only advocates promotion of service capabilities, it also calls for expanding the service formation from its initial composite construct to a larger entity: service cluster. But this structural promotion should not be the chief concern at this stage. The practitioner, however, should recommend structural growth when the structural analysis process takes place. (Refer to Chapters 18 through 22 for structural analysis and modeling topics.)

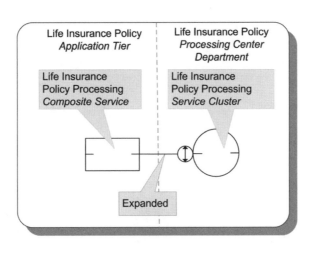

EXHIBIT 16.2 LEVEL 1 CONTEXTUAL EXPANSION EXAMPLE

LEVEL 2: ENTERPRISE-LEVEL CONTEXTUAL EXPANSION. Unlike the contextual expansion represented by Level 1, Level 2 exceeds the service departmental scope to satisfy cross-organizational business and technological integration requirements and to alleviate technological and business interoperability[4] challenges. The term "integration" does not pertain to physical integration of concrete software assets. Here we refer to integration from a *conceptual* perspective: a plan or a new strategy that can improve the collaboration and orchestration of processes. Such service expansion typically contributes to consolidation of functionality across domains and lines of business in the enterprise. This enterprise-level contextual expansion may include expanding service responsibility to accommodate automation of business processes across departments, divisions, and specialty groups that offer unique professional expertise to the subject they support.

Moreover, promoting a product executed by a service across the enterprise, such as Store Locations Lookup or Account Lookup, is one of the main benefits of the contextual expansion process. Broadening a service's conceptual aspect contributes to both the creation of a common organizational language and the development of a vocabulary that can enhance collaboration and communications across the enterprise. The discovery of business and technology cross-cutting concerns that organizations share is another contribution of contextual expansion.

Exhibit 16.3 depicts an enterprise-level (Level 2) contextual expansion initiative since a service visibility is raised to accommodate cross-organizational concerns. As apparent, the Live Media Download Facility Atomic Service that originally was created for the Video Recording Department is transformed to a Live Media Download Facility Composite Service. This process was designed to expand the service's offerings to the consumers of the Movie Production Entertainment Division. Note that the essence of the service has not changed, and its main specialty is preserved during this conversion. In fact, this contextual transition does call for the development of new service operations and specialties to accommodate the new environment. Therefore, this exercise is about repurposing the solution: reworking the service's contract scope, enhancing service adaptability to attend to a larger and more diversified consumer base, and discovering business and technology cross-cutting concerns.

LEVEL 3: PARTNER-LEVEL CONTEXTUAL EXPANSION. The Level 3 contextual expansion of a service typically takes place between an enterprise and its partners in commerce. These external entities

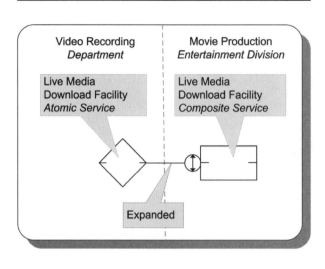

EXHIBIT 16.3   LEVEL 2 CONTEXTUAL EXPANSION EXAMPLE

may include vendors, suppliers, service providers, contractors, and other institutions that depend on the enterprise offerings. To enhance the communications channels with the outside world, the service's territorial boundaries can be expanded beyond its current organizational influence. This scope characteristically includes information exchange with external parties that rely on crucial interorganizational business transactions. For example, a retailer that buys goods from importers and manufacturers may be required to expand a few responsibilities of its internal services to enable the ordering of merchandise from its suppliers. This *promotion of commerce* is enabled by expanding the boundaries of a service to meet Level 3 requirements.

Akin to Level 2, the contextual expansion at Level 3 must address integration challenges between an enterprise and its outside consumers or service providers. Not only must the service contract be redesigned to enable efficient integration, a plan should also be carved out to accommodate interoperability challenges. Remember, the Level 3 contextual expansion is not about the physical revamping or relocation of a service; it is more about virtual integration, a conceptual proposition that offers solutions. The physical implementation should follow the contextual expansion analysis proposition. Thus, the contextual expansion paradigm provides answers to the vital questions: What service offerings and interfaces must be exposed to transaction partners to meet business requirements? What business processes are involved? What should the new contract terms be?

Exhibit 16.4 depicts contextual expansion of a service to accommodate interorganization transaction needs. This effort involves the Merchandise Orders Composite Service that is promoted to Level 3 rank. This process will both serve the Toys Retail Division and the Toys Manufacturer Company (zones pictured on top). Note that despite broadening of the Merchandise Orders Composite Service's responsibilities, the resulting product still maintains its composite formation.

MULTILEVEL SERVICE EXPANSION.   Finally, the multilevel contextual service expansion depicts the promotion of a service from the lowest rank: Level 1. This trend continues to meet vital requirements of Level 2. Finally, the service's responsibilities are expanded to attend to the necessities of the consumer community affiliated with Level 3. Indeed, this transition is rather steep and would require major planning initiatives to attain the final goal. But the benefiting communities—consumers

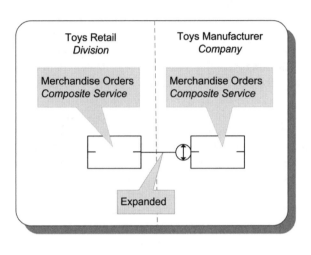

EXHIBIT 16.4   LEVEL 3 CONTEXTUAL EXPANSION EXAMPLE

or providers—will be vast, and the return on investment could potentially exceed the initial forecast.

The transformation of a service from its departmental state, where the number of consuming parties is quite often limited in size, to a universal entity that facilitates interorganizational transactions can benefit a wide range of consumers. Not only will the service's user base grow, more diversified partners will join this venture to profit from the offered business promotion. To better understand this concept, view Exhibit 16.5, which depicts such a service transition. Note that the three zones of expansion: Health Records Department, Healthcare Management Division, and Healthcare Practitioners Company. These are now benefiting from the expansion of the Doctor Appointment Record Persistence Composite Service.

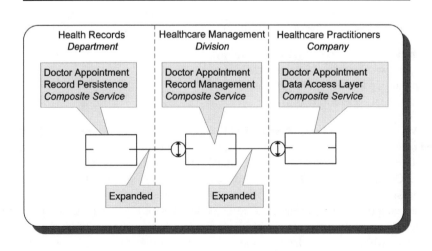

EXHIBIT 16.5   MULTILEVEL SERVICE EXPANSION EXAMPLE

CONTEXTUAL EXPANSION PATTERNS

Remember, as mentioned previously, the contextual expansion process is all about a virtual proposition, an analysis process devised to facilitate efficient service discovery and to foster design and architecture best practices to widen service consumer base. This approach is extended to advance a service's valuable contribution to a project or to vital organization initiatives.

To promote this cause, the contextual expansion patterns offer best practices and replicable solutions designed to transform service operations *beyond* their current utilization capacity. This influence broadening process pertains to expansion of service capabilities to meet requirements of a more diversified group of consumers, to address cross-organizational asset reusability, and even to strengthen collaboration with third-party providers. These partners may be consulting firms, manufacturers, and suppliers. Furthermore, contextual expansion patterns can also contribute to the consolidation of services and a reduction of overlapping business processes or technical implementations.

The central stage that patterns play in the service-oriented discovery and analysis phase often leads to the identification of federated formations or centralized service configurations that may materialize later during the service construction phase. Thus, the contextual expansion practice and its analysis patterns are designed to offer motivation for federating services across the enterprise or simply devise service centralization remedies. Both approaches are elaborated on in the sections that follow.

Before applying any of the contextual expansion patterns, consider three simple steps to ensure proper utilization:

1. **Study the problem domain.** Do business or technical requirements call for expanding service offerings to cross-organizational entities? Do they mandate promoting service capabilities to meet a wider consumer base? Is the business expanding its product line? Does the business intend to cut down its offerings to clients?
2. **Identify the motivation for utilizing a contextual expansion pattern.** Is reusability of software the reason for using a contextual expansion pattern? Is consolidation of business processes the motivation? Do collaborations with business partners need improvement?
3. **Inspect the solution that is offered by a contextual expansion pattern.** Can the offered solution be applied to the problem that we are trying to resolve? Would the contextual expansion pattern utilization address business or technological concerns?

The sections that follow elaborate on four different contextual expansion patterns that can assist practitioners to extend service capabilities and functionality across the organization:

1. Equal-Level Contextual Expansion (270)
2. Top-Down Contextual Expansion (272)
3. Bottom-Up Contextual Expansion (274)
4. Contextual Federation (276)

EQUAL-LEVEL CONTEXTUAL EXPANSION PATTERN.   The levels of service expansion are largely discussed previously in the Service Contextual Expansion Benefits section. The reader may remember that a level is simply a zone of organizational operations to which a service contributes. The Equal-Level Contextual Expansion pattern advocates expanding service offerings in the same contextual expansion level without crossing the level's boundaries.

For example, the expansion of a core service that originated in Level 1 is confined to local applications and departmental scope of operations. In the same manner, the service expansion that occurs within the boundaries of Level 2 consists of the transition that a service undergoes to accommodate cross-organizational requirements. These may be business or technical imperatives demanded by multiple departments, lines of business, business domains, and even divisions.

Finally, the Equal-Level Contextual Expansion pattern implemented in Level 3 pertains to enabling transactions with outside parties, such as partners, vendors, manufacturers, and suppliers.

Problem. Each contextual expansion level introduces challenges of its own. Planning and justifying the extension of service offerings that cross multiple contextual expansion levels requires rigorous analysis and justification, and a coherent strategy to increase service reusability rates and foster consolidation of capabilities. The enormous challenge of bridging the communications gaps, integrating with multiple organizational zones, accommodating interoperability requirements, and maintaining a service whose offerings span multiple applications is a major concern to enterprise architecture organizations.

Solution. To alleviate these concerns, the Equal-Level Contextual Expansion pattern advocates promoting service capabilities in a single contextual expansion level. The integration and deployment of services in a given contextual expansion zone must be planned and structured. This solution must include several ingredients that identify a particular level's requirements. Generally, the magnitude of the service expansion effort should be classified and assessed before it is pursued. Consider these analysis considerations that can guide service expansion in a single contextual expansion level:

- Understand consumers' requirements pertaining to a particular contextual expansion level. Consider the demand for business processes, functionality, and service specialty.
- Learn about imperative consumption levels and contract necessities. What operations and interfaces are required to satisfy contract conditions?
- Study integration strategies and technologies that are utilized in a targeted contextual expansion level.
- Identify infrastructure, middleware, and platforms to which a service can be deployed.
- Assess risks and carve out a mitigation plan to avoid service expansion failure.

Example. Exhibit 16.6 illustrates the Equal-Level Contextual Expansion pattern that involves the core entity General Ledger Composite Service. This virtual promotion of a service's influence takes place in three different zones of operations: Accounts Payable Department, Accounts Receivable

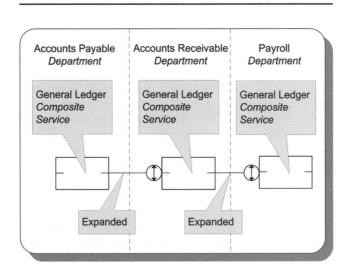

EXHIBIT 16.6 EQUAL-LEVEL CONTEXTUAL EXPANSION PATTERN EXAMPLE

Pattern Identification	
Name	Equal-Level Contextual Expansion Pattern
Category	Contextual Expansion Analysis

Problems, Solutions, and Implementations	
Problem	Expanding service offerings across multiple contextual expansion levels can be architecturally complex and costly from an integration perspective.
Solution	Advocate the expansion of service capabilities within a single contextual expansion level rather than embarking on complex integration initiatives that span multiple levels.
Applicability	Applies to a production environment that supports single or multiple contextual expansion levels for services.
Method	Study business and requirements, identify technological specifications, and conduct risk analysis to justify service expansion within a single contextual expansion level.
Benefits	1. Encourages analysis to satisfy a particular consumer base.
	2. Identifying service reuse and consolidation opportunities within a particular contextual expansion level.
	3. Encourages to develop organizational best practices that address service expansion in a single contextual expansion level.
Risks	Guiding principles for a production environment that does not have a clear delineation between contextual expansion levels may not be valuable.
Notation	Employ the "Expanded" symbol.

Exhibit 16.7   Equal-Level Contextual Expansion Pattern Summary Table

Department, and Payroll Department. Note that the service's contextual expansion activity takes place in the operational boundaries of Level 2 (known as enterprise-level contextual expansion). Furthermore, since this process involved three different services—the core service and its two expanded virtual versions—the practitioner should determine if the additional service instances should be maintained or if they should be unified to promote asset reuse.

Synopsis.   The practitioner must be aware of various difficulties when expanding service boundaries to satisfy the demands of a particular group of consumers. The Equal-Level Contextual Expansion pattern introduces a set of best practices and guidelines for extending service offerings within a single contextual expansion level to increase reusability rates and foster consolidation of software assets. Exhibit 16.7 outlines the challenges, solution, implementation methods, applicability, and risks affiliated with the employment of the Equal-Level Contextual Expansion pattern.

TOP-DOWN CONTEXTUAL EXPANSION PATTERN.   The Top-Down Contextual Expansion pattern suggests that a service's offering should be expanded beyond the boundary of a single level and that the originating position should always be the higher level, moving downward to a lower level. For example, a service that meets the requirements of consumers in Level 2 should be expanded to attend to business or technical necessities of Level 1 as well. In the same manner, a service that initially originated in Level 3 should be adapted by consumers affiliated with Level 2.

Problem.   In many circumstances, designing a service to offer business or technological capabilities to a single contextual expansion level may not be practical. A few factors must be considered before pursuing such approach. Low service reusability rates and high development, maintenance, and monitoring costs are typical of a service that offers capabilities to a single contextual expansion level.

Solution.   The Top-Down Contextual Expansion pattern emphasizes the need for including lower-level organizational zones to both increase software reuse and minimize costs related to service adaptation, maintenance, and monitoring. For example, a service that was designed to support Level 2 consumers (enterprise-level) could be easily adapted to meet application-level requirements associated with service expansion Level 1. Recall that application-level requirements are associated with services that operate locally, may offer common functionality to application modules and tiers, or provide value to two or more departmental applications.

Therefore, a service that was originally devised to support cross-organizational requirements (Level 2) can be effortlessly transformed to carry out operations related to local applications and departments (Level 1). In other words, this is a feasible proposition because the service was initially architected to support a larger consumer base and sustain higher consumption rates.

Consider the chief analysis initiatives that should be accomplished before employing the Top-Down Contextual Expansion pattern:

- Study the business requirements of all involved contextual expansion levels (Levels 1 to 3). This should include the various consumers' demands for business processes, functionalities, and service specialties.
- Conduct a gap analysis study to identify the missing functionality and capability that a certain contextual expansion level is lacking. Use this information to modify service contracts with the corresponding new consumers.
- Understand technologies and integration strategies utilized in each of the involved contextual expansion levels. This should include infrastructure, middleware, and platforms that will enable communications with the expanded service capabilities.
- Assess risks and carve out a mitigation strategy to avoid service expansion failure.

Example.   Exhibit 16.8 depicts the Top-Down Contextual Expansion pattern implementation. The two organizational zones, the SUV Parts Department and the Car Parts Division, are the environments that the Car Parts Inventory Composite Service is devised to support. Note that the proposed solution calls for expanding the core service that was originated at the Car Parts Division (affiliated

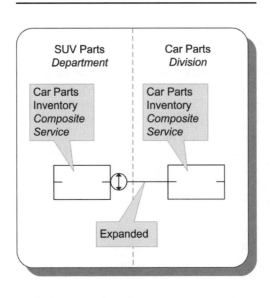

EXHIBIT 16.8   TOP-DOWN CONTEXTUAL EXPANSION
PATTERN EXAMPLE

Pattern Identification	
Name	Top-Down Contextual Expansion Pattern
Category	Contextual Expansion Analysis

Problems, Solutions, and Implementations	
Problem	Low reusability rates and high development and maintenance costs are typical of a service that offers capabilities to a single contextual expansion level.
Solution	Employ a service that has been designed to serve a higher contextual expansion level to share its capabilities with consumers that are affiliated with lower levels.
Applicability	Applies to distributed service environment where lower contextual expansion levels can utilize a service that has been designed for a higher contextual expansion level.
Method	Analyze business and technical requirements demanded by consumers affiliated with all involved contextual expansion levels; conduct a gap analysis to identify the missing operations and interfaces; and assess risks and offer a mitigation strategy for service offerings expansion.
Benefits	1. Reducing service integration costs.
	2. Minimizing modification to service design, architecture, and construction.
	3. Increase of software reuse across organizational boundaries.
Risks	Integration efforts may be complex and costly.
Notation	Employ the "Expanded" symbol.

Exhibit 16.9 Top-Down Contextual Expansion Pattern Summary Table

with enterprise level, Level 2) to also meet the consuming requirements of the SUV Parts Department (affiliated with application level, Level 1). This top-down expansion approach would obviously require alterations to enable the transformation, yet these modifications typically are negligible.

Synopsis. The Top-Down Contextual Expansion pattern offers best practices and a solution to increase service reuse and decrease maintainability efforts. The provided solution advocates employing a service that was initially designed for a consumer base affiliated with a higher contextual expansion level organizational zone. The contextual expansion then is exercised to include lower level organizational zones. Exhibit 16.9 outlines these challenges and summarizes the solution, method of implementation, benefits, and risks that are related to the employment of the Top-Down Contextual Expansion pattern.

BOTTOM-UP CONTEXTUAL EXPANSION PATTERN. The Bottom-Up Contextual Expansion pattern simply addresses the requirements for extending service offerings to higher-level contextual expansion zones. For example, consider service capabilities originally devised to support a single application's tier in Level 1, now expanded to also address the business and technological concerns of larger groups of consumers that are associated with Level 2 (enterprise-level). Once implemented, this virtual bottom-up contextual transition typically introduces integration and interoperability challenges. These difficulties arise because the core service that is now a candidate for expansion was designed to tackle local solutions. But the benefits may outweigh the efforts because the core service is subject for modifications that will contribute to its reusability rates and meet requirements of a larger consumer base.

Problem. A service that offers solutions to a single contextual expansion zone may be underutilized, and its development and maintenance cost may outweigh the benefits of its implementation.

Solution. The Bottom-Up Contextual Expansion pattern advocates increasing service influence by extending its business or technical offerings to a higher-level contextual expansion zone. This would require adjustments and modification to service contracts, and enhancing the performance of service operations and interfaces. Integration efforts and investment in broadening service functionality will also be required to meet requirements of new consumers. Consider the chief analysis initiatives to ensure successful employment of the Bottom-Up Contextual Expansion pattern:

- Review the business requirements and technical specifications of the involved contextual expansion levels. This should include demands for processes, functionalities, and specialties.
- Conduct a gap analysis study to identify the functionality that the higher contextual expansion level is lacking. Add the necessary capability to service contracts with the new related consumers.
- Study the technologies and integration strategies that are utilized in higher contextual expansion zone.
- Assess risks and carve out a mitigation strategy to avoid service expansion failure.

Example.   Consider the example depicted in Exhibit 16.10. The illustrated Bottom-Up Contextual Expansion pattern represents a service promotion activity that originates at the Loan Organization. This proposal advocates expanding the usage of the Loan Calculator Composite Service beyond its organizational boundaries for the benefit of Internet users. The practitioner should strive to increase the reusability of software by avoiding multiple instances of the Loan Calculator Composite Service. This should be accomplished simply by enhancing the core service to support larger consumer groups.

Synopsis.   The Bottom-Up Contextual Expansion pattern should be utilized when service offerings provided to a lower contextual expansion zone are being considered for expansion to a higher-level zone. Doing this would increase service reuse and justify the cost of its development, maintenance, and operations. Exhibit 16.11 outlines the problem, solution, applicability, method, benefits, and risks that are affiliated with the employment of the Bottom-Up Contextual Expansion pattern.

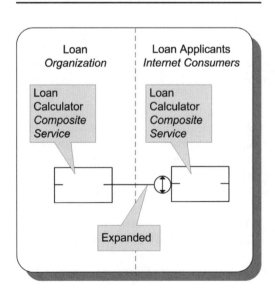

EXHIBIT 16.10   BOTTOM-UP CONTEXTUAL EXPANSION PATTERN EXAMPLE

Pattern Identification	
Name	Bottom-Up Contextual Expansion Pattern
Category	Contextual Expansion Analysis
Problems, Solutions, and Implementations	
Problem	A service that offers business functionality to a single contextual expansion zone is underutilized and requires high development and maintenance costs.
Solution	Extend offerings of a service that has been design to serve a lower contextual expansion zone to consumers affiliated with a higher contextual expansion level to boost its reusability rates and reduce maintenance costs.
Applicability	Applies to distributed service environment that higher contextual expansion levels can utilize a service that has been designed for a lower contextual expansion zone.
Method	Analyze business and technical requirements that are demanded by consumers affiliated with the targeted contextual expansion level; conduct a gap analysis to identify the missing operations and interfaces; and assess risks and offer mitigation strategy for service offerings expansion.
Benefits	1. Introducing the opportunity to expand a service beyond its current operational level to promote organizational software reuse.
	2. Reducing silo service operations in the enterprise by exposing their interfaces to a larger user group.
	3. Encouraging the discovery of business and technology cross-cutting concerns by moving up the ladder of responsibilities.
Risks	Integration efforts may be complex and costly.
Notation	Employ the "Expanded" symbol

EXHIBIT 16.11 BOTTOM-UP CONTEXTUAL EXPANSION PATTERN SUMMARY TABLE

CONTEXTUAL FEDERATION PATTERN. The Contextual Federation pattern essentially advocates resolving interoperability and distribution of software assets challenges by abandoning the service centralization paradigm that offers an organizational focal point access to business and technical processes. Conversely, the approach the service federation model offers is to clone a service and distribute its instances across the enterprise to enable various organizations to share information and execute transactions. This method typically enables consumer diversification and widening its base. Furthermore, the Contextual Federation pattern not only delivers consistent information to consumers, it also bridges the communication gaps between silo organizations. From the technological perspective, this pattern can alleviate interoperability challenges when a service is bound to expand its offerings.

Problem. Two major problems typically motivate practitioners to employ the Contextual Federation pattern: impromptu duplicated software installations across the organization and enterprise centralization of services. First, software reuse is an essential architectural best practice that organizations should be most resolute about. The sporadic and unplanned "copy-and-paste" approach toward implementation, by which source code is duplicated to be used in multiple applications or services, typically results in unnecessary consequences, such as duplication of functionality across the enterprise and increase of cost and maintenance. This practice promotes lack of conformity with enterprise software development standards. The second challenge that must be addressed is the lack of operation stability of the service centralization model with large distributed environments. This approach typically becomes a message exchange bottleneck and contributes to degradation of performance.

Solution. The software reusability best practice should not be practiced at all costs. There are justifiable circumstances where service functionality must be duplicated to advance architecture and design goals. However "organically grown," unplanned distributions of replicated services should not be practiced, as explained previously in the Problem section. One of the most common scenarios that necessitate a planned and organized duplication of service capabilities is in large and distributed environments. Therefore, service functionality replication typically comes to pass when software products or systems must communicate and collaborate across regions, states, and even continents.

Consider, for example, five similar international foreign-exchange service instances that are distributed to five different continents. Each service instance must not only enable trading of currency in its deployed continent but also must communicate with its peer instances across the globe. Real-time currency values should also be exchanged among the five service instances to support price consistency across them. This architecture distribution style is known as federation since the participating service instances are design to offer similar functionality, yet operate remotely and in harmony

Furthermore, consider another example that can utilize the Contextual Federation pattern: It can be employed to design and build disaster recovery (DR) sites. The DR solution ensures business continuity and restoration of an application and its repositories in case of a catastrophe. Therefore, DR installations must replicate the software and hardware assets of a production environment to enable quick revival of operations. This duplication of functionality is necessary to ensure flawless functionality of applications and services.

Example. The illustration depicted in Exhibit 16.12 exemplifies a contextual expansion that promotes a federated design by involving four different shoe departments, distributed to different country regions: Western, Eastern, Northern, and Southern. The apparent federated Shoe Orders Atomic services must both enable real-time entries of customer orders and post instant updates to the shoe manufacturer's inventory repository. This collaborative interaction among the four different service instances justifies this contextual expansion style.

Synopsis. Remember, the Contextual Federation pattern is devised to virtually plan a distributed environment that consists of chained service instances that offer identical functionality. This contextual expansion uses cloned services to break organizational silo implementations and make

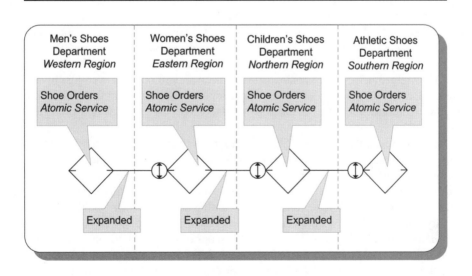

EXHIBIT 16.12 CONTEXTUAL FEDERATION PATTERN EXAMPLE

Pattern Identification	
Name	Contextual Federation Pattern
Category	Contextual Expansion Analysis

Problems, Solutions, and Implementations	
Problem	A centralized service configuration is not a viable solution to facilitate a large distributed environment. Performance degradation and message bottlenecks are the main challenges
Solution	Establish a service federation that can be harnessed to transport information and bridge communication gaps between silo applications and organizations.
Applicability	Applies to a large distributed service environment that spans multiple applications, organizations, and partners.
Method	A federated installation consists of service instances that are cloned to carry on transaction and share information. The distribution of these entities can span multiple production environments and organization boundaries.
Benefits	1. Proposing an interoperability solution for large distributed architecture model.
	2. Enhancing transmission and sharing of information across an organization's geographical and management structures.
	3. Improving communications between lines of business.
	4. Enabling a Hub-and-Spoke architecture style that is executed by services.
	5. Facilitating replication of software assets to ensure business continuity.
Risks	Distribution of service instances typically increase service management and monitoring cost.
Notation	Employ the "Expanded" symbol.

EXHIBIT 16.13　CONTEXTUAL FEDERATION PATTERN SUMMARY TABLE

information available to remote consumers. The problem, solution, applicability, method, benefits, and risks of the Contextual Federation pattern implementation are outlined in Exhibit 16.13.

SERVICE CONTEXTUAL EXPANSION ANTI-PATTERNS

Contextual expansion anti-patterns simply advise practitioners which practices should be avoided during service expansion activities. If followed, these recommendations can contribute to the increase of service reusability and enhance reconciliation of redundant processes across the organization. Furthermore, one of the most common misuses of the contextual expansion approach is broadening a service's consumer base by creating multiple copies of a single service. This impractical action typically leads to duplication in functionality and amplification of service integration complexities. Thus remember: Service contextual expansion should not be driven just by consumers' immediate priorities. The process of broadening a service's offerings and the decision to enhance its adaption capabilities should be dictated by architectural best practices and strategies to avoid unnecessary costs.

Other misuses of this service analysis discipline are associated with confusion between service contextual generalization and contextual expansion. A simple principle to remember is that the generalization process yields a new service abstraction whose functionality and scope of its proposed solutions may be altered to meet new requirements. For example, the Job Cost Service may yield a more generalized version named Accounting Service, which would include additional functionality and specialties, such as accounts receivable and accounts payable. The contextual expansion activity, however, typically preserves that scope of service functionality and service name, yet it is designed to attend to more diversified consumer entities that represent different fields of interests, departments, divisions, lines of business, or external institutions. In this case, the Job Cost Service would probably retain its name across all expansion levels.

The sections that follow elaborate on the four chief service contextual expansion anti-patterns that address activities to avoid.

1. Service Cloning (279)
2. Expansion through Generalization (280)
3. Expansion through Specification (280)
4. Excessive Contextual Expansion (281)

SERVICE CLONING ANTI-PATTERN: AVOID FUNCTIONALITY REDUNDANCY WHEN POSSIBLE.
The Service Cloning anti-pattern warns against excessive duplication of service functionality or Service Cloning. There is no defense against source code "copy-and-paste" activities that are pursued in the name of "saving time." Furthermore, duplicating business or technical functionality by creating multiple service instances promises to increase organizational expenditure and maintenance costs carries the risk of performance degradation.

There are circumstances, however, where cloning a service would promote design and architecture goals. These were discussed previously in the Contextual Federation pattern (276). Service federation is one of the instances where practitioners may consider service expansion by distributing service functionality across large production environments by employing service instances. Replication of software and disaster recovery implementations are other examples that mandate duplication of services.

Exhibit 16.14 illustrates the Service Cloning anti-pattern. The apparent duplication of functionality that is promoted by the expansion of the Customer Profile Composite Service takes place in the Equity Trading Department zone. Typically this scenario should be avoided to increase service reuse and encourage reconciliation of processes across the organization.

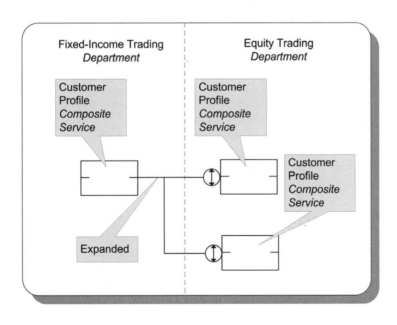

EXHIBIT 16.14 SERVICE CLONING ANTI-PATTERN EXAMPLE

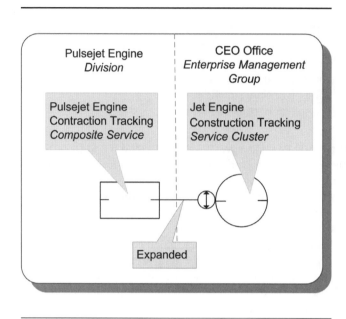

EXHIBIT 16.15   EXPANSION THROUGH GENERALIZATION ANTI-PATTERN

EXPANSION THROUGH GENERALIZATION ANTI-PATTERN: AVOID GENERALIZATION.   The service contextual expansion effort is *not* about elevating service abstraction levels that typically increase the scope of service expertise and areas of specialty. Therefore, avoid service generalization when promoting service offerings through the expansion method. If the aim is to rename a service and alter its identity, modify the nature of its capabilities, substantially broaden its expertise field, or add operations designed to widen or modify the solution scope, then use the contextual generalization approach discussed in Chapter 14. Therefore, employ the contextual expansion analysis approach to advance software reuse by increasing a service's consumer spectrum. This measure is preferred over performing surgical modifications to a service's essence and disregarding the motivation that drove its creation in the first place.

Exhibit 16.15 depicts a misuse of the contextual expansion analysis method. The scenario is in essence a generalization case, where the core service Pulsejet Engine Construction Tracking Composite Service is generalized, yielding a higher abstraction level entity: Jet Engine Contraction Tracking Service Cluster. The latter offers to the Chief Executive Officer's Office reports on construction monitoring and project tracking of diverse jet engines that the company manufactures, such as Motorjets, Turbojet, Low-Bypass Turbofan, High-Bypass Turbofan, and Ramjet.

EXPANSION THROUGH SPECIFICATION ANTI-PATTERN: AVOID SPECIFICATION.   Not only should service contextual Expansion through Generalization be avoided, but expansion through contextual specification should not be practiced. Remember, the service contextual specification process, discussed in Chapter 15, is a method of reducing the service abstraction level by filtering out some of its functionality and narrowing the scope of its capabilities. In other words, specification is about limiting a service's area of expertise. In this case, the rendered product is an entity that relinquishes some of its offerings. But the service expansion process does not call for trimming business or technical capabilities. On the contrary, service operations should retain their expertise and their offered functionalities. Contextual expansion is indeed about increasing reusability of software by preserving the initial service offerings and increasing the consumer range.

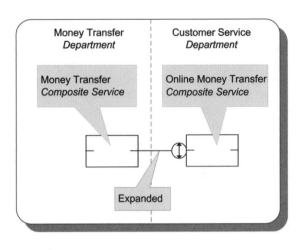

EXHIBIT 16.16   EXPANSION THROUGH SPECIFICATION ANTI-PATTERN
EXAMPLE

Exhibit 16.16 depicts misuse of the contextual expansion activity: The Money Transfer Composite Service, in essence, was contextually specified rather than contextual expanded, reduced from a higher-generalization level to a lower-abstraction rank. Although it was formerly designed to offer diverse funds relocation transactions, such as payout services and mobile money-transfer services, apparently its resulting product's capability, the Online Money Transfer Composite Service's functionality, was trimmed down to support only one type of transaction.

EXCESSIVE CONTEXTUAL EXPANSION ANTI-PATTERN.   The Excessive Contextual Expansion anti-pattern warns against needless promotion of service offerings to organizational zones. The term "needless promotion" pertains to distribution of service capabilities that will never be leveraged or where the cost for implementation outweighs the benefits. Moreover, the federation or centralization of service operations to serve an excessive number of consumers may not be practical as well because of design and implementation constraints. Therefore, the service expansion limits must be rigorously examined to achieve a rational analysis proposition that will yield a balanced design and architectural blueprint.

DELIVERABLES

A contextual expansion diagram, as illustrated in the modeling examples presented in this chapter, should be delivered to depict the mechanisms and the method of integration implementation for promoting service reuse and consolidation of software assets. This artifact should identify the contextual expansion zones that service capabilities should be extended to. In addition, employ the contextual expansion modeling patterns and anti-patterns to enforce style and effective solution to the analysis proposition deliverable.

SUMMARY
- The contextual expansion process is about enhancing service reusability and fostering consolidation of software assets in a distributed environment. This is a virtual modeling venture, a semantic exercise that involves planning and a clear strategy to promote service offering across the organization by expanding its consumer base.

- There are three organizational zones for distribution of services: application-level (Level 1), enterprise-level (Level 2), and partner-level (Level 3).
  - Level 1 hosts services the contribute to small-scale and local departmental applications.
  - Level 2 is assigned to services offerings that span multiple organizations, departments, or divisions.
  - Level 3 accommodates services that contribute to the communication between an enterprise and its related partners, such as contractors, suppliers, and trading institutions.
- The introduced contextual expansion patterns address interoperability, reusability, asset consolidation, efficiency, and performance challenges.

Notes

1. From an implementation perspective, cross-cutting business concerns is a paradigm that has been introduced by aspect-oriented programming (AOP) to promote loose coupling and modularity of software components.

2. The term "semantic reconciliation" also refers to reduction of duplicated service capabilities and functionality across an organization by merging autonomous services that operate across the enterprise. Therefore, the term "reconciliation" should not be confused with structural unification of services; it is merely a proposition to reconcile redundant service operations.

3. www.agilemodeling.com/style/activityDiagram.htm#Swimlanes.

4. The term "business interoperability" typically depicts interaction between two or more organizations, each of which adheres to distinct business models and implements different business processes, yet they must collaborate to exchange transactions. Similar interpretation is provided by Péter Bernus and Mark S. Fox, *Knowledge Sharing in the Integrated Enterprise* (New York: Springer, 2005), p. 306.

CHAPTER 17

CONTEXTUAL CONTRACTION ANALYSIS PROCESS AND MODELING PATTERNS

Contextual contraction is the process of reducing a service's offerings due to lack of interest in its continued business or technological value proposition. This is simply about rolling back a service's operations, reducing its reusability rates, and, as a result, trimming its consumer scope. The exposure of the service to departments, divisions, or enterprise partners diminishes as well.[1] A decline in market demand, outdated technologies, and rising maintenance costs are the chief drivers for the contextual contraction effort. Recall that this activity is not a physical cutback of service inventories; nor is the implementation a major subject to modification. The contextual activity of this operation is conceptual by nature, and the final artifact should serve as an analysis proposition that can be utilized in future design, architecture, and construction initiatives. This is a modeling exercise that takes place on paper, ahead of any tangible manipulation of a service's structure or alteration of its environment.[2]

Indeed, planning the reduction of a service's involvement in the execution of organizational missions will clearly affect its reusability factor because of its shrinking exposure to enterprise applications, organizations, or partners. But here software reuse is not the major goal. Two chief drivers can motivate architects, modelers, analysts, developers, or managers to pursue the contextual contraction route: *business and technological considerations*. First, from a business perspective, the reasons can be vast. Business downsizing or changes to business missions, strategies, processes, and requirements are clearly chief causes. These may include modifications to existing lines of products or adaption of new revenue-generating channels that are influenced by consumer demand and market competition over legacy implementations.

Second, architectural and technological changes also contributes to the motivation for service contraction. As mentioned, among these aspects are trends in the computer technology field that typically introduce more efficient and productive developments designed to replace or augment existing implementations. But perhaps one of the chief incentives for narrowing an expanded architectural landscape is to simplify complex technological environments. These are *overconceptualized architectures* that introduce overly disseminated component and service deployments. The term "overconceptualized" indicates that the initial design would yield a distributed software asset environment that is arduous to manage, monitor, and maintain. Transaction performance degradation can also be attributed to a service ecosystem comprised of unnecessary intermediaries or proxies that intercept messages at various message exchange stages.

ACCOMMODATING DEMAND FOR CONTEXTUAL CONTRACTION

The service contextual contraction approach introduces a few aspects designed to reduce business or technical functionality across an organization. This cutback may not necessarily call for the elimination of certain service capabilities. It is simply designed to limit architectural and technological *concepts* that may lead to tangible solutions. Reducing service intermediaries and proxies that greatly contribute to the expansion of service offerings exemplifies a contraction scenario. Decreasing the scope of a service federated environment is another aspect that typically contributes to the *decline of software distribution* across an organization.

Again, the contextual contraction is obviously a transformation process that calls not only for limiting service expansion but also for committing to a smaller implementation. This proposed transition is not only about the removal of proxies and mediating entities; it also involves subscribing to smaller-scale solutions devised to meet narrower consumer requirements. Furthermore, like the contextual expansion (discussed in Chapter 16), this service evolution is not designed to alter the specialties offered by a service. Rather, preserving a service's capabilities on a smaller scale is the chief goal.

What type of changes should a service undergo to accommodate demand for contraction? How can the reduction of service offerings be addressed across an organization? Consider the chief aspects that contribute to the service contextual contraction process that can yield a tangible alteration to a service's essence and its environment. These may include discontinuing service operations on a few functionality levels, such as application, across departments, divisions, lines of business, and even business partners.

To accommodate a contextual contraction process, consider the chief aspects that drive the reduction of a service's influence across organization boundaries and beyond:

- **Selection of consumers.** Providing solutions to a selected group of consumers in lieu of extending service offerings to a diversified consumer profile.
- **Solution scope reduction.** Reducing service solution scope to a limited number of organizations across or beyond the enterprise.
- **Service contract spectrum.** Altering a service's contract to meet limited demands for its business or technical offerings.
- **Consumption repurposing.** Modifying service consumption needs according to reduced consumer demand.
- **Cross-cutting concerns.** Trimming cross-cutting business and technology solution propositions to organizations that share common concerns.
- **Service adaptability.** Limiting computing resources, development budgets, and maintenance efforts to meet requirements of smaller-scale service environment.
- **Service integration.** Alleviating service integration challenges by simplifying relationships and collaborations between services to enable reduction of service implementations.
- **Interoperability.** Limiting service interoperability implementation across the enterprise.

SERVICE CONTEXTUAL CONTRACTION BENEFITS

The contextual contraction paradigm subscribes to a simple principle: a virtual reduction of service influence across the enterprise. The term "virtual reduction" pertains to a plan, a proposition that identifies the need to narrow the consumer's spectrum to which a service contributes business or technical value. This process, also known as *semantic contraction*, identifies the business functionality that can be removed from various applications, organization processes, and partners' transactions to enable contraction of service operations. Furthermore, this contraction activity focuses on selecting the type of context that can be eradicated to minimize and optimize an implementation, without compromising the overall business mission and execution. This effort limiting the involvement of a service across organizational initiatives typically simplifies integration implementations, deployments, monitoring, and maintenance. Again, the contextual contraction is not about removing functionality from a service itself; this effort merely suggests limiting or reducing service contracts with its existing consumers.

Furthermore, on the service collaboration front, the semantic integration aspect of a service, known as *contextual integration*, is clearly one of the most challenging concerns that practitioners

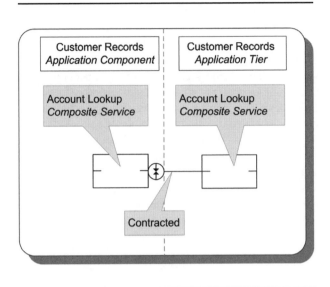

EXHIBIT 17.1   CONTEXTUAL CONTRACTION EXAMPLE

must address. This challenge is attributed to the intricate nature of service orchestration, message exchange, and transaction synchronization. Thus, to simplify a complex environment, the contextual contraction effort ought to tackle two chief problems: distribution reduction of software assets and untangling unnecessary relationships between services and their corresponding consumers. This reorganization effort typically contributes to the optimization and perfection of a service's environment, reconstruction and enactment of service deployment, and reinstitution and improvement of service/consumer associations. Moreover, on the service orchestration front, this reorganization would enable architects, modelers, analysts, and developers to reexamine and enhance the message exchange paths between services and their corresponding consumers to achieve better performance and reduce design inefficiencies.

SERVICE CONTEXTUAL CONTRACTION EXAMPLE

To better understand this simple concept of service contextual contraction, let us view the example presented in Exhibit 17.1. The apparent Customer Records Application Tier and the Customer Records Application Component share the Account Lookup Composite Service functionality. The process of contraction is performed by scaling back the service offerings for the Application Tier and reinstituting the Application Component version. In other words, this process calls for *disengagement* of the Account Lookup Composite Service from the Application Tier's consumers. Recall that the contextual contraction effort is about a proposition, a virtual introduction to a solution that calls for elimination of functionality from one or more implementations, either on an application level or across an organization.

Note that the contextual contraction process is articulated by the "Contracted" symbol that points toward the Application Component section of the diagram. It denotes the direction of the contraction process. That is, the Application Tier section will no longer utilize the Account Lookup Composite Service. In addition, scaling back service operations will not necessarily yield a more fine-grained service. In most cases, the service physical structure will stay intact and will not be altered to accommodate the newly reduced consumption goals. This scenario is similar to the one illustrated in Exhibit 17.1, in which the service contraction does not affect its composite formation.

CONTEXTUAL CONTRACTION PROCESS

The service contextual contraction process can be applied to three different environments: application-level, enterprise-level, and partner-level. These environments are sections of an organization that differ in their scope of operations, business process spectrum, and technological boundaries. In addition, each of these enterprise sectors supports distinct corresponding consumers, who are provided with various solution scales to alleviate their concerns. As we will learn in the sections that follow, an application-level environment level is confined to a departmental boundary. In other words, a service offering is extended to a limited number of consumers, and the offered solutions are not necessarily distributed across the organization. Thus, we call this environment level *local implementation*. For example, the equity trading department may support specialized services that promote stock ordering transactions, such as Stock Ordering Service and Symbol Routing Service that will not necessarily be distributed across the enterprise.

An enterprise-level environment is more complex by nature because it must maintain strong communication and collaboration protocols across organizations, such as lines of business, divisions, and multiple departments. Therefore, this landscape should sponsor a different breed of services. These services ought to be distributed and even federated across the organization to maintain high reusability factors. For example, the Universal Client Profile Service and the Vendor List Service are entities that can be utilized by multiple applications, divisions, and departments.

The third environment level, the partner-level, pertains to the business ties that the enterprise maintains with the outside world, including vendors, manufacturers, trading partners, and suppliers. This landscape introduces integration and security challenges that practitioners must address.

The sections that follow elaborate on the methods and process that should be utilized to perform service contextual contraction activities. These differ in scope and approach at each environment level:

> Level 1: Application-level contextual contraction
> Level 2: Enterprise-level contraction
> Level 3: Partner-level contextual contraction

LEVEL 1: APPLICATION-LEVEL CONTEXTUAL CONTRACTION.   As discussed, Level 1 defines departmental boundaries that confine the contraction of service operations to a local implementation. The term "local" typically denotes a small-scale deployment of an application or a group of services that execute business or technical processes on behalf of a single organization. Furthermore, the spectrum of a departmental operation characteristically supports a smaller consumer scale in lieu of diverse interest groups that subscribe to high-volume consumption needs. Therefore, Level 1 identifies requirements that *neither* call for highly distributed computing landscapes nor demand solutions to address challenging interoperability concerns.

The term "application-level" also signifies a limited service environment that is confined to an application structure, such as tiers, components, modules, or even involving two or more applications. Remember, however, that the contraction process that is regarded as Level 1 does not cross the boundaries of an organization. In addition, this service contraction process calls for reducing the exposure of a service or hiding its implementation from consumers who no longer require its offerings within its local confined boundaries.

From a business perspective, this software isolation is usually necessary because of modifications to functionality and requirements of business products. Alterations to business process and market trends can also motivate the reduction or even elimination of service consumption needs. On the architectural and technological level, contextual contraction of a service can be proposed to scale back a complex implementation, revamp an intricate deployment, or replace a service with advanced technologies.

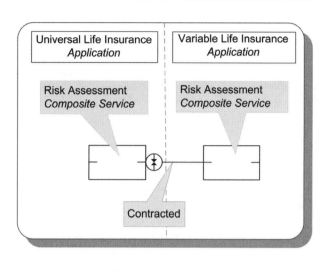

EXHIBIT 17.2   LEVEL 1 CONTEXTUAL CONTRACTION EXAMPLE

Exhibit 17.2 tells the story of an organization that is determined to eliminate its Variable Life Insurance product yet maintain its Universal Life Insurance offerings. These offerings are supported by the Variable Life Insurance Application and Universal Life Insurance Application, respectively. Thus, the service contextual contraction proposition calls for the discontinuation of the Risk Assessment Composite Service offerings to the Variable Life Insurance consumers. Note that this transformation process yields a service that is confined to the boundary of the Universal Life Insurance Application.

LEVEL 2: ENTERPRISE-LEVEL CONTRACTION.   The Level 2 environment supports a more diversified consumer base. This landscape involves service operation boundaries that span multiple business domains, lines of business, or organizations that share common business cross-cutting and technology concerns. These enterprise entities are typically structured as departments, divisions, or groups of interests that collaborate to promote the business across the enterprise.

The contraction process that takes place in a Level 2 environment obviously must involve multiple organizations and address untangling communication and collaboration activities that have been established and strengthened during months or years. The contextual contraction activity also calls for reversing previous integration efforts between distributed software assets such as applications and services. Thus, the reduction of a service's influence and the elimination of its involvement with sections of the business should be carefully planned. This planning entails a meticulous analysis of existing dependencies between various lines of business in the face of imminent service contraction efforts.

Why would the practitioner embark on a contextual contraction effort in Level 2? What are the motivating aspects that drive the discontinuation of service offerings to some business sections? The answers to these questions are rooted in business and technological reasons that typically induce the reduction of business initiatives or architectural contraction. One of the chief business reasons calling for the decrease of business activities or a rollback of business processes is the elimination of lines of business and specialties that are no longer required because of market trends or lack of demand for certain products.

Other business events that can influence decisions to limit or reduce distribution of services are fundamental changes in business and management structures, such as reorganizations, shifting or

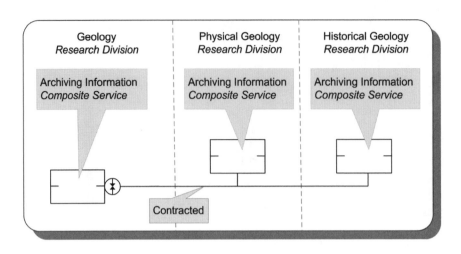

Exhibit 17.3   Level 2 Contextual Contraction Example

replacement of key executives, or alterations to the chain of organizational command. Such changes may trigger modifications to existing products and applications and even the elimination or unification of lines of business, departments, and divisions. In addition, the consolidation of business processes is a common practice when two or more organizations merge. Mergers typically spur the discontinuation of services and reduction in consumer scope.

From an architectural and technological perspective, the pursuit of contextual contraction activities is influenced by a large array of integration concerns and interoperability constraints. The main ones are associated with overly distributed environments and the desire to simplify production environments. The contraction effort of a service ecosystem is also ascribed to the reevaluation of architectural concepts and the examination of their implementation in light of software performance degradation or inefficiencies of transaction execution. Another reason for service technical contextual contraction is the reduction of federated implementations across an organization. In other words, decreasing a service's distribution across an enterprise and eliminating members of a federated service can also trigger a technological contraction that minimizes the scope of software distribution.

Exhibit 17.3 illustrates a contextual contraction process that spans three different divisions (takes place in Level 2): Geology Research Division, Physical Geology Research Division, and Historical Geology Research Division. This activity calls for rolling back Archiving Information Composite Service involvement with operations of two research divisions—Physical Geology Research Division and Historical Geology Research Division—because of business reconciliation initiatives in the enterprise. This action depicts the reduction of service offerings that ultimately would lead to discontinuation of archiving operations to these divisions. The resulting product is the Archiving Information Composite Service that will exclusively serve the Geology Research Division.

LEVEL 3: PARTNER-LEVEL CONTEXTUAL CONTRACTION.   The environment that is presented by Level 3 depicts the relationships that an enterprise maintains with its outside partners. These partners can include a variety of suppliers, manufacturers, consulting companies, information providers, client institutions, and other external message exchange parties. This collaboration was initially established to promote the business by strengthening alliances with institutions that are dominant contributors to the enterprise's strategies, mission, and revenue generation. These interfaces with

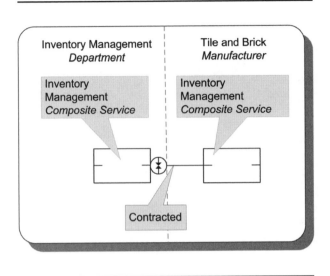

EXHIBIT 17.4   LEVEL 3 CONTEXTUAL CONTRACTION EXAMPLE

the outside world are also known as business to business (B2B), typically enabled by services that carry out transaction and information exchange activities.

The contextual contraction effort that takes place in the commerce environment of Level 3 is pursued to reduce the collaboration with the outside world, such as business partners and suppliers. But before taking this step, we must consider a wide range of business and technological constraints that are established because of existing interorganizational relationships. From a semantic perspective, however, the service contraction venture is about an analysis proposition, a virtual solution that is not tightly affiliated with the physical deployment of services. The emphasis here should be on a plan that devises contraction activities or reduction of service offerings that promote the optimization of business or technological processes. The term "optimization" pertains to the improvement of transaction efficiency among message exchange parties, removal of duplicate functionalities, or total disengagement form business partners. This is all about the concepts that drive an architectural downsizing.

Why should a Level 3 service environment be downsized? What are the chief motivating aspects that encourage practitioners to scale back an architectural scheme? The answers to these questions are characteristically affiliated with business and technological reasons. The most critical issues are related to the discontinuation of relationships with partners. This discontinuation may be attributed to eliminating the inbound or outbound flow of certain goods and products, halting manufacturing orders, or simply cutting ties with partners that no longer contribute to the enterprise.

Exhibit 17.4 illustrates a contextual contraction process that takes place between the Inventory Management Department of an organization and the Tile and Brick Manufacturer. Both utilize the Inventory Management Composite Service. The contraction analysis proposition calls for the discontinuation of this collaboration between the two entities. The Inventory Management Composite Service's visibility will be reduced yet will continue to operate on a lower capacity to provide inventory calculations and order-level reporting to the rest of the Inventory Management Department.

MULTILEVEL SERVICE CONTEXTUAL CONTRACTION.   The contraction of a service's capacity and its offered functionality can span all the environment levels discussed so far. This contextual contraction process may take place within a departmental level (Level 1), cross lines of business and

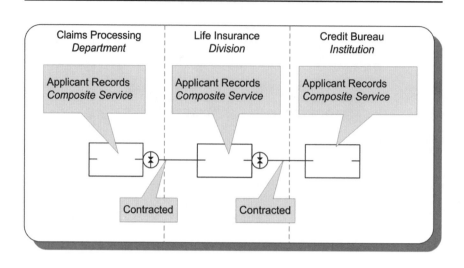

EXHIBIT 17.5   MULTILEVEL CONTEXTUAL CONTRACTION EXAMPLE

domains (Level 2), and even reach beyond enterprise boundaries to disengage partners and third-party institution consumers (Level 3). Rolling back such an operation typically calls for a major business and technological undertaking that involves multiple applications and services. This roll-back may affect architectural and technical decisions and influence concepts that have been established to craft existing implementations.

To justify such a reduction of a service's offerings, a contextual contraction process should yield a conceptual blueprint that elaborates on the execution steps and the involved entities. This architectural contraction process should also depict the transformation of a service, starting at the core services and identifying their corresponding end states, namely the final product.

Exhibit 17.5 illustrates this road map. Note the contraction process that spans three environment levels: Claims Processing Department (Level 1), Life Insurance Division (Level 2), and Credit Bureau Institution (Level 3). In addition, it is apparent that the Life Insurance Division is an intermediary environment that is positioned between the Claims Processing Department and the Credit Bureau Institution. Here the contextual contraction process calls for disengagement of the Applicant Records Composite Service from the Credit Bureau Institution. Therefore, the Life Insurance Division role as a mediator is not required anymore. This contraction activity finally settles with the confinement of the applicant to the Claims Processing Department.

CONTEXTUAL CONTRACTION PATTERNS

The contextual contraction patterns offer best practices and methods for analysis and promote service-oriented discovery approaches. These repeatable solution templates are designed to help practitioners both to institutionalize the examination process of services and boost opportunities for service identification. The provided contextual contraction patterns also offer styles for service functionality consolidation and foster software reuse by reducing overlapping business and technical processes. This simple concept of service contraction influences the scope of application architecture and enterprise architecture by reconciling impracticable service implementations.

Remember, the contextual contraction process is all about the introduction of an analysis proposition, a conceptual solution that addresses the contraction of a service and its environment to simplify complexities. This venture should neither address physical implementation of services nor offer tangible and structural remedies to an organizational concern. Therefore, the proposed patterns can guide practitioners to form a virtual service environment that ultimately will yield tangible deliverables later on in the service life cycle process. For structural manipulations of services discussion, refer to Chapters 18 through 22.

Before applying any of the contextual contraction patterns, consider simple steps that can help ease the service contraction process:

- **Study the problem domain.** Do business requirements or technical specifications call for reduction of service responsibilities across organizational entities? Is there any justification for narrowing the consumers' scope? Does the business organization plan to discontinue one or more product lines? Should relationships with one or more business partners be terminated?
- **Identify the motivation for utilizing a contextual contraction pattern.** Is boosting reusability of services the reason for using a contextual contraction pattern? Is consolidation of service operations the driving motivation? Does the current state of an application or computing environment call for narrowing the architectural scope?
- **Inspect the solution that is offered by a contextual contraction pattern.** Can the offered remedy help alleviate business or technological concerns? Would the contextual contraction pattern tackle introduce viable solutions?

The sections that follow propose answers to these questions. They introduce four chief patterns that represent distinct perspectives and offer corresponding solutions.

1. Equal-Level Contextual Contraction (291)
2. Top-Down Contextual Contraction (293)
3. Bottom-Up Contextual Contraction (295)
4. Contextual Federation Contraction (297)

EQUAL-LEVEL CONTEXTUAL CONTRACTION PATTERN. The Equal-Level Contextual Contraction pattern addresses concerns that are associated with the reduction of service offerings only in one of the environment levels (Level 1, Level 2, or Level 3) that have been defined earlier in Contextual Contraction Process section. In other words, this style tackles the issues that are limited to service contraction activities confined to a single environment level without crossing boundaries. In addition, the reduction of service's influence and operations—typical to a particular level—should focus on two major aspects that mitigate the risks of a service's disengagement from its corresponding consumers: (1) minimizing the negative business and technical impact on consumers, and (2) reducing perils that are associated with rolling back service deployments.

For example, the service contextual contraction that takes place in Level 1, the application-level view, deals with application-level challenges. It may include removal of offerings from an application tier level and in exchange strengthening the application component level. In contrast, service contraction that occurs exclusively in an environment associated with Level 2 addresses untangling integration and disengagement from consumers' affairs across organizational boundaries. This step typically pertains to minimizing distributed environments and reducing architectural complexity across the enterprise. Finally, a Level 3 service contraction is different from Level 1 and Level 2. It is related to the discontinuation of partner relationships and restructuring the B2B architecture.

Problem. A contextual contraction process that takes place across two or the three environment levels is a complex proposition that should be reevaluated and perhaps avoided in certain circumstances. Not only have the dependencies of consumers on services across the environments imposed risks to the contraction activity, but interoperability challenges must be addressed ahead of an impending contraction effort.

Solution.   The reader might realize that the array of issues that should be addressed in each environment level is different because of the unique characteristics of architectures, technologies, and the business processes that each executes. Thus, the Equal-Level Contextual Contraction pattern calls for a smooth transitioning out of duty of the services unique to each individual level. This is proposed to avoid the challenges that may arise when pursuing contraction activities across multiple levels. Filling the vacuum created due to the contraction process should also be addressed, if appropriate. This relates to the replacement of functionality that was trimmed by the contextual contraction activity or compensating for loss of capabilities. Consider the four recommended steps to employ when utilizing the Equal-Level Contextual Contraction pattern:

1. Conduct a thorough study to identify the unique consumers' requirements that are associated with a specific environment level. Understand individual level's boundaries and its driving business motivations.
2. Study the technological and architectural constraints affiliated with the targeted environment level.
3. Propose a contextual contraction road map that consists of milestones and goals.
4. Introduce a risk assessment and a mitigation plan to avoid interruption to business execution and technical continuity.

Example.   Exhibit 17.6 depicts the Equal-Level Contextual Contraction pattern process that proposes the discontinuation of the Rebates Calculator Composite Service in two distinct departments (in a Level 2 environment): Gold Card Services Department and Platinum Card Services Department. Recall that the contextual contraction process neither accentuates physical service deployments nor does it focus on structural formations of services. This exercise is merely about a virtual proposition, a conceptual scheme that recommends the reduction of service roles and responsibilities in the contraction process. Therefore, focus on the service contextual reduction influence rather

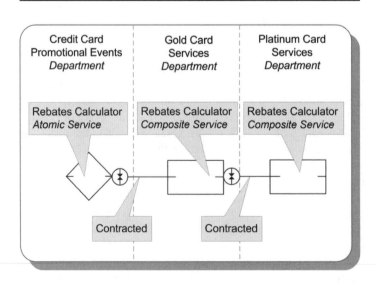

EXHIBIT 17.6   EQUAL-LEVEL CONTEXTUAL CONTRACTION PATTERN EXAMPLE

Pattern Identification	
Name	Equal-Level Contextual Contraction Pattern
Category	Contextual Contraction Analysis

Problems, Solutions, and Implementations	
Problem	A contextual contraction process that takes place across environment levels is complex.
Solution	Focus on reduction of service boundaries and offerings in a single environment level.
Applicability	Applies to a complex and large distributed environment.
Method	Analyze the specific environment in which the contextual contraction is about to take place; study related architectural and technological constraints; propose a contraction road map; and assess the involved risks.
Benefits	1. Identifying architectural contraction considerations and challenges that are unique to each environment level.
	2. Discovering distinct environment level characteristics that pertain to corresponding consumer requirements.
	3. Reducing complexities associated with a particular environment level.
	4. Assisting practitioners to isolate architectural concerns and simplify their solutions in lieu of applying remedies on a grand scale, attempting to resolve cross-environment level problems.
Risks	The contraction process that takes place in a single environment level may not be generic enough to offer a holistic organizational solution.
Notation	Employ the "Contracted" symbol.

Exhibit 17.7   Equal-Level Contextual Contraction Pattern Summary Table

than on structural modeling. Concentrate on the semantic aspect of the contraction activity rather than on the physical deployment.

Synopsis.   Remember, the Equal-Level Contextual Contraction pattern advocates that the reduction of a service's offerings should be conducted in a single environment level rather than tackling a larger contraction initiative. This pattern also calls for dissecting the distributed environment into smaller sections to enable an efficient and rigorous analysis by concentrating on an individual environment level. Exhibit 17.7 summarizes the problem, solution, applicability, method, benefits, and risks of this pattern.

TOP-DOWN CONTEXTUAL CONTRACTION PATTERN.   The Top-Down Contextual Contraction pattern calls for the reduction or removal of service offerings that take place across environment levels. The guiding principle of this pattern suggests that the originating entity, the service where the contraction process starts from, should be associated with the higher-level environment that is subject to elimination. Consider, for example, a service contraction activity that spans environments Level 1 and Level 2. In this particular case, the starting contraction point originates at Level 2 and concludes at Level 1. Likewise, when the Top-Down Contextual Contraction pattern involves environments Level 2 and Level 3, the originating service should be a part of Level 3. If the contraction process occurs on all three levels, obviously the sequence of contraction would be: Level 3, Level 2, and down to Level 1.[3]

Problem.   A number of motivating concerns urge the employment of the Top-Down Contextual Contraction pattern, which advocates retaining service offerings to lower environment levels and disallowing utilization of a service to higher levels. This activity is proposed to avoid the complexities involved with making a service available to higher-environment levels, such as complex architecture and integration models, risk of increased integration costs, and interoperability challenges.

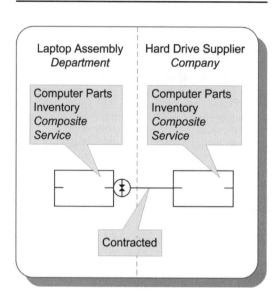

EXHIBIT 17.8   TOP-DOWN (LEVEL 3 AND LEVEL 1) CONTEXTUAL
CONTRACTION PATTERN EXAMPLE

Solution.   A contraction process that starts at a high-level environment and reaches lower levels is called *service localization.* This significant shift of service offerings assignment implies that the practitioner chooses first to address higher complexity levels by removing service functionality from an environment that is more integrated, potentially heterogeneous, and largely distributed or federated. Furthermore, this assertion also identifies the need to narrow the architectural scope by minimizing consumer diversification. This pattern promotes localization of services, reduction of consumption volumes, and simplification of complex operations. Consider the three steps to pursue when employing the Top-Down Contextual Contraction pattern:

1. Analyze the environments levels that are involved in the contextual contraction process in terms of consumers' functionality dependency and business and technological constraints.
2. Propose a road map for the contraction that prioritizes the reduction of capability boundaries. The sequence of implementation should also be scheduled.
3. Provide a risk assessment and mitigation plan to avoid interruption to business and technical execution.

Example.   Exhibit 17.8 illustrates the Top-Down Contextual Contraction pattern that involves the Laptop Assembly Department and the Hard Drive Supplier Company. The contextual contraction occurs in Level 3 (partner-level), where an internal organization maintains a transaction relationship with a hard drive supplier. This collaboration is bound to conclude with the discontinuation of hard drive inventory replenishment. Furthermore, the depicted contraction process reduces the boundary of Computer Parts Inventory Composite Service to a departmental level by abandoning the B2B notion. This would obviously lead to reduction of consumer scope, and thus service consumption demand will dwindle. The Computer Parts Inventory Composite Service will not necessarily retire. It will continue to serve local inventory management requirements (Level 1, application-level), yet its external involvement with the outside world will diminish.

Pattern Identification	
Name	Top-Down Contextual Contraction Pattern
Category	Contextual Contraction Analysis
Problems, Solutions, and Implementations	
Problem	Higher environment levels that utilize a service typically introduce complex architectures, interoperability challenges, and high operations, monitoring, and maintenance costs.
Solution	Employ the Top-Down Contextual Contraction pattern to propose narrowing service offerings by limiting contracts with consumers that are related to higher environment levels.
Applicability	Applies to a large distributed landscape that consists of multiple environment levels.
Method	Analyze the environment levels involved in the contextual contraction process; propose an implementation road map; conduct risk analysis; and offer a mitigation plan to avoid business and technical discontinuity.
Benefits	1. Minimizing architectural complexities and narrowing architecture scope by eliminating service functionality from higher-level environments.
	2. Reducing integration costs.
	3. Simplifying service operations by localizing deployments and shifting the burden to lower-level environments.
Risks	Blocking access to higher-level environments may reduce service reusability rates.
Notation	Employ the "Contracted" symbol.

Exhibit 17.9 Top-Down Contextual Contraction Pattern Summary Table

Synopsis. The Top-Down Contextual Contraction pattern is simply about retaining service offerings for lower environment levels and blocking access to service capabilities for higher levels. This simple concept is summarized in Exhibit 17.9, which also outlines the problem, solution, applicability, method, benefits, and risks.

BOTTOM-UP CONTEXTUAL CONTRACTION PATTERN. The Bottom-Up Contextual Contraction process is about proposing the transformation of service capabilities to accommodate a larger and more diversified consumer base. It would definitely boost a service's reusability rates and increase its visibility across the organization. Unlike the top-down approach, the bottom-up method advocates starting the reduction of the service offerings process from lower-level environments and continuing toward the higher levels. For example, a service contraction activity that involves Level 1 and Level 2 should start from the lower environment Level 1. In the same manner, when Level 2 and Level 3 are part of the service contraction effort, start with environment Level 2 and conclude with Level 3. This also applies to cases that include the three possible environment levels: Begin with Level 1, continue with Level 2, and end with Level 3.[4]

Problem. As discussed, the Bottom-Up Contextual Contraction pattern advocates eliminating silo service implementation in lower environment levels and transforming its functionality to serve higher levels. The motivating aspects of such a proposal are rooted in a number of concerns that my be addressed, such as boosting service reusability rates, increasing service visibility, and enabling a more diversified group of consumers to utilize service offerings. Breaking silo service implementations that are confined to local environments is also a vital improvement that must be addressed.

Solution. The Bottom-Up Contextual Contraction pattern calls for *delocalization* of service operations. The concept of delocalization pertains to shifting service functionality from the application-level or departmental deployments toward a universal architecture designed to break up silo implementations. When discontinuing service operations in the lower levels first, in essence, practitioners choose to migrate a service's offerings from a limited edition to a more centralized or federated version that provides horizontal business and technological value to the enterprise. But this approach does not come without the risk of compromising integration simplicity. Indeed, the reusability of a service will increase when it is designed to satisfy higher-level consumption rates and provide value to a more diversified crowd of consumers. The integration and collaboration scheme that is required to accommodate this service contraction pattern, however, is bound to develop complex deployment styles that typically are difficult to monitor and maintain.

To accommodate service delocalization and increase service reusability rates, consider this three-step implementation approach:

1. Study the environment levels that are involved in the contextual contraction process. Understand consumers' demands for business functionality, and analyze technological barriers and challenges.
2. Propose a plan for service contraction. Prioritize the reduction of functionality, and offer an inclusive road map for implementation that includes milestones and goals.
3. Introduce a risk assessment and mitigation plan to avoid interruption to business and technical execution.

Example.   Exhibit 17.10 illustrates a Bottom-Up Contextual Contraction process that takes place between Level 2 (enterprise-level) and Level 1 (application-level). The depicted contraction involves the Small Business Loan Application and Loans Division. This activity results in the elimination of Loan Processing Atomic Service offerings from a departmental level and shifting its capabilities to serve a cross-organizational configuration that will more likely increase service reusability and expose it to a wider range of consumers. Remember, the depicted contextual contraction is about elimination of local implementation that is conveyed by the delocalization term discussed earlier.

Synopsis.   The Bottom-Up Contextual Contraction pattern addresses the increase of service reusability rates and organizational visibility. It would clearly amplify and diversify the service consumer base. In addition, this pattern advocates breaking up silo operations by shifting service offerings toward a more centralized configuration and eliminating its functionality in lower levels.

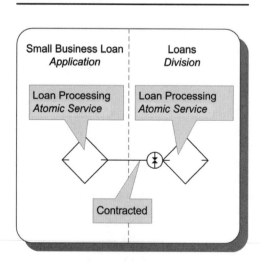

EXHIBIT 17.10   BOTTOM-UP CONTEXTUAL CONTRACTION
PATTERN EXAMPLE

Pattern Identification	
Name	Bottom-Up Contextual Contraction Pattern
Category	Contextual Contraction Analysis
Problems, Solutions, and Implementations	
Problem	1. Low service reusability rates.
	2. Service is not exposed to a wide range of consumers.
	3. Service operations confined to silo environment.
Solution	Utilize the Bottom-Up Contextual Contraction pattern to raise the availability of service offerings to a wider consumer audience and eliminate local service implementation.
Applicability	Applies to a large distributed environment that consists of different environment levels.
Method	Analyze the lower- and upper-level environments; propose a clear road map that consists of milestones and goals; conduct risk analysis; and offer a mitigation plan to avoid business disruptions.
Benefits	1. Increasing reusability factors of services.
	2. Offering solutions to a wider consumer audience.
	3. Centralizing service operations.
	4. Enabling higher service consumption rates.
	5. Minimizing silo service operations.
Risks	Compromising integration and architecture simplicity.
Notation	Employ the "Contracted" symbol.

Exhibit 17.11   Bottom-Up Contextual Contraction Pattern Summary Table

These challenges are outlined in Exhibit 17.11, which also summarizes the problem, solution, applicability, method, benefits, and risks related to the utilization of the Bottom-Up Contextual Contraction pattern.

CONTEXTUAL FEDERATION CONTRACTION PATTERN.   As the reader may remember, the federation notion that was introduced in Chapter 16 calls for devising a distributed environment in which services are cloned, "replicated" to promote an architectural goal. These disseminated and chained service instances are essential components of a design because they both act as hubs, proxies that are responsible for passing messages and information[5] to their remote consumers, and introduce an alternative to the centralized computing notion. The term "centralization" implies that a service acts as a universal intersection point for message exchange and transaction processing. The federated approach, in contrast, embodies a different architectural strategy that is best suited for heterogeneous computing environments or widely spread and diversified consumer groups, each of which represents a distinct set of business and technological requirements.

The Contextual Federation contraction pattern addresses the rollback of a service instance that is distributed across the organization. Rolling back service operations means disengagement of a service instance from a line of business, department, division, or an application. Thus, this contextual contraction process is about removing a service from the chained set of services that constitutes a federation. Unlinking a service also implies that the boundaries of a distributed service capabilities are narrowed.[6]

Problem.   Business and technological concerns typically motivate practitioners to employ the Contextual Federation Contraction pattern. From a business perspective, the reasons can be numerous. One of the most compelling for service operations contraction is lack of business interest and the diminishing value proposition that a service offers. The reasons for employing the contextual contraction approach can include elimination of products, reduction of client offerings, loss of business and revenue, or business alteration to business model and strategies. Technological concerns can also motivate to reduce the federation of services across an organization. These concerns can include architecture complexities, dated software products, performance degradation, scalability issues, and oversized and saturated distributed environment.

Solution.   The Contextual Federation Contraction pattern advocates that the reduction or elimination of a service federation should be performed in logical steps, moderately rolling back service deployments with utmost caution to avoid business disruptions. Naturally, this chain of service environment contraction starts with the elimination of services that are no longer viable to business or the technology organizations. Thus, to ensure business and technical continuity, the practitioner should study the dependencies of the federated formation members and identify the impact and risks associated with this effort.

Remember, the Contextual Federation contraction pattern is about neither the physical retirement of services nor eliminating service operations. This approach merely calls for a meticulous analysis of a federated environment, inspection of the involved services, identification of service dependencies, and assessment of the service value proposition to the business and corresponding consumers. Rolling back service distribution and federation is the outcome of this venture. This exercise also calls for analyzing the business processes that are naturally distributed and executed by the various federated service members, again, to ensure flawless business execution.

Adhere to three major guiding steps when pursuing the Contextual Federation contraction pattern:

1. Analyze the federated service environment. This step should include studying the requirements of the various consumers who utilize the federated service architecture.
2. Provide a detailed road map that consists of milestones, goals, schedules, and sequence of service contractions.
3. Conduct a risk analysis and mitigation study to avoid disruption to business and technical execution continuity.

Example.   Exhibit 17.12 illustrates the Contextual Federation Contraction pattern. The decision to reduce the scope of a book publishing organization's architecture calls for rolling back the distribution of the Author Royalties Atomic Service. Thus this process begins at the Book Distribution

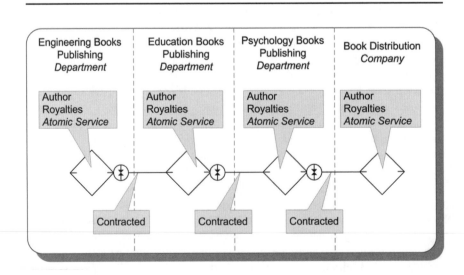

EXHIBIT 17.12   CONTEXTUAL FEDERATION CONTRACTION PATTERN EXAMPLE

Pattern Identification	
Name	Contextual Federation Contraction Pattern
Category	Contextual Contraction Analysis

Problems, Solutions, and Implementations	
Problem	1. An oversized distributed environment contributes to architectural complexity.
Solution	A contextual contraction process should take place to discontinue service offerings to selected consumers in a federated service configuration.
Applicability	Applies to a distributed environment that employs service federations.
Method	The method of the contextual contraction process includes rigorous analysis, planning a gradual reduction of services that participate in a federation; and assessment of involved risks.
Benefits	1. Introducing a step-by-step plan for rolling back a federated service environment. 2. Identifying challenges associated with the contraction of a highly distributed architectural environment. 3. Proposing a low-risk reduction of federated service offerings across organizations while ensuring flawless execution of business processes.
Risks	Contraction of service influences and offerings across the organization may introduce business and technological interruptions.
Notation	Employ the "Contracted" symbol.

EXHIBIT 17.13   CONTEXTUAL FEDERATION CONTRACTION PATTERN SUMMARY TABLE

Company (far right) and spans three organizational departments: Psychology Books Publishing Department, Education Books Publishing Department, and Engineering Books Publishing Department. The latter is the organization that will continue to leverage the Author Royalties Atomic Service's offerings. Note that the practitioner who proposed this approach also identified the exact order by which the contextual contraction process should take place. This proposition required a meticulous analysis activity during which the Author Royalties Atomic Service was examined to ensure risk reduction and flawless business continuity.

Synopsis.   A federation represents service instances that are assigned to widen business or technical capability boundaries. It can span multiple organizations in the enterprise and even include business partners. The Contextual Federation Contraction pattern is about *reduction* of these service influences and their affiliated offerings to consumers who operated in large distributed environment. Exhibit 17.13 outlines the core problem and summarizes the problem, solution, applicability, method, benefits, and risks associated with the utilization of the Contextual Federation Contraction pattern.

CONTEXTUAL CONTRACTION ANTI-PATTERNS

One of the most undesirable affects of the contextual contraction effort is reduction of service reuse. This can affect consumption requirements on a limited organizational scale, within an application boundary, or on a larger scope—cross-organizational entities and partners' collaborations. Either of these environment levels can be severely affected and have lasting and irreversible technological and financial repercussions. Therefore, proceed with service contraction activities only after meticulously investigating of service relationships, studying architectural components' dependencies, and examining existing service integration capabilities.

The sections that follow elaborate on the three major service contextual contraction anti-patterns and the best practices that can be applied during the service contraction process:

1. Unordered Contextual Contraction (300)
2. Unjustified Contextual Contraction (300)
3. Extreme Federated Service Contraction (300)

UNORDERED CONTEXTUAL CONTRACTION ANTI-PATTERN. Contracting an architectural environment and reducing service implementations across the organization, or applying this reduction logic within a single application, must be performed with the utmost care. One of the most vital aspects of such an executable rollback is the *logical order* by which software assets are removed or scaled back. Therefore, while embarking on the contextual contraction analysis effort, practitioners must focus on the dependencies that a service has established with its consumers and counterparts. The term "dependency" pertains to business and technological influences that can affect business continuity and the flawless execution of services in production environments if modifications to service distribution and deployment are planned.

From a business perspective, an unordered sequence of service detachment from a certain environment and its consumers can disrupt the transmission of messages and execution of transactions due to dependencies of existing business processes. The succession of business activities and their orchestration should also be meticulously examined to avoid information delivery disruption. Furthermore, the vacuum that is formed because of the service contraction effort should be compensated for or filled with proper processes in a logical manner. This aspect should also be inspected to reduce business risks caused by the service contraction order.

Architectural and technological dependencies introduce other concerns that should be taken into consideration when decreasing a service environment. One of the most vital aspects of architectural contraction is the sequence by which integrated software assets are separated or retired. Thus, a complex integration scheme must be studied before reducing the architecture's scope. This analysis should include identification of message exchange patterns between a service and its corresponding consumers. In addition, the contextual contraction proposition should offer alternative consumption solutions in case a service will be disengaged from certain consumers. These architectural and technological substitutes should also be applied in a logical sequence to avoid disruption of operations.

UNJUSTIFIED CONTEXTUAL CONTRACTION ANTI-PATTERN. The Unjustified Contextual Contraction anti-pattern counsels against reducing service offerings that will neither benefit the business organization nor enhance the architectural or technological implementations. The proposition to eliminate or scale back service operations, reduce consumption volumes, and discontinue relationships with consumers and partners should be thoroughly examined before executed. Once the contraction proposition has been implemented, reversal of the physical contraction activities is typically costly and would require substantial investments to undo the negative impact on business and technology. Consider the four major concerns that should be fully inspected before launching a service contextual contraction:

1. Decreasing service reuse across application components, lines of business, and partners.
2. Applying alternatives to compensate for a service's contraction may outweigh the benefits.
3. Contraction of an architecture can increase tightly coupled software formations and minimize the establishment of a loosely coupled computing environment.
4. Contraction can reduce the scope of service distribution and harm the efforts to promote software elasticity.

EXTREME FEDERATED SERVICE CONTRACTION ANTI-PATTERN. The Extreme Federated Service Contraction anti-pattern warns against an excessive rollback of service instances that are part of a federated deployment. This extreme reduction in service operations ultimately leads to a tightly coupled implementation because of the drastic architecture collapse. In addition, the pressure on a contracted architecture can increase due to fewer services that must maintain the same transaction processing volume. Not only must the remaining services in the federated environment chain fill in the formed gaps; they also must continue to support a wide spectrum of consumer demand.

However, this effort is well justified if the contraction of service functionality activity is launched due to a reduction in service consumption and lack of consumer interest.

DELIVERABLES

Carve out a contextual contraction diagram similar to the examples provided in this chapter. This artifact should reflect a modeling proposition that identifies the agenda of a service contraction endeavor. Environment Levels 1, 2, and 3 should be embedded in the diagram to denote the direction and the strategy of service capability reduction. In addition, employ the "Contracted" modeling symbol to indicate service environment scale-down or decrease of service federation scope.

SUMMARY

- The contextual contraction process is a virtual exercise that addresses the reduction of a service's capability scope and the scale-back of service functionality across an organization. Trimming down the distribution of services is the chief charter of this process. The contraction requirements typically are attributed to business model and strategy alterations, which may include lack of demand for products or management reorganization. On the technological front, the optimization of architectural model, technology upgrades, and service integration enhancements are the major contributors to the service contraction venture.
- The contextual contraction patterns offer best practices and methods for analysis and promote service-oriented discovery approaches. Consider the chief benefits of these modeling styles:
  - Institutionalize the examination process of services.
  - Boost opportunities for service identification.
  - Improve the process of service functionality consolidation and reconciliation of capabilities.
  - Foster software reuse.
  - Promote minimization of silo service operations.

Notes

1. Note that contextual contraction is about the reduction of a service's offerings in the environment in which it operates, unlike contextual specification, which is devised to reduce a service's abstraction level.
2. For service structural analysis and modeling, refer to Chapters 18 through 22.
3. Remember that the Top-Down Contextual Contraction (293) pattern advocates removing functionality and service offerings from a higher-level environment. In other words, this scope reduction of a service's influence is designed to trim down the spectrum of the consuming parties.
4. Another goal of the Bottom-Up Contextual Contraction (295) pattern is to break organizational silos by reconciling functionality. This consolidation of service offerings typically starts with local implementations to universalize consumption patterns.
5. A service federation is commonly used to pass security credentials and consumer identities in an interoperable computing environment. The federated identity concept is affiliated with such functionality: http://msdn.microsoft.com/en-us/architecture/cc836393.aspx.
6. The Contextual Federation Contraction (297) pattern typically encourages structural contraction of a service federation. Refer to the Federation Scope Reduction pattern section in Chapter 22 to learn more about the methods of structural implementation.

PART FIVE

SERVICE-ORIENTED STRUCTURAL ANALYSIS PROCESS AND MODELING PATTERNS

The service structural analysis process is a *modeling* practice that offers best practices and patterns to manipulate a service formation and enhance, tune, or alter its structure to maximize its performance, balance its granularity level, and increase its reusability factor. This exercise is merely about examining a service construct and identifying avenues to improve its *internal* design and *external* deployment model. After inspecting and enhancing a service's internal components, one cannot underestimate the external distribution and configuration of a service, which are also vital to the success of the structural analysis venture. Again, this analysis and modeling venture should focus on two chief views: internal service structure and its underpinning components, and the external perspective which is about service integration, configuration, and deployment that take place in a distributed computing environment.

Although the structural analysis and modeling practice is greatly influenced by the contextual aspects of a service, such as service naming, service functionality and specialty, and a range of capabilities, the structural manipulation of a service is focused purely on logical or physical arrangement of internal and external software components to provide the best possible solutions. The term "arrangement" pertains to the modeling operations devised to transform a service and its environment into a more feasible landscape to perfect the offered remedies to organizational concerns. These modeling tools, introduced in Chapter 18, include a formal structural notation that consists of symbols to use when carving out an analysis proposition.

The structural analysis and modeling process offers solutions to overcome challenges in terms of service reuse, interoperability, and collaboration between a service and its corresponding consumers. The chief questions that an architect, developer, modeler, analyst, or manager ought to ask during this effort are affiliated with the nature of modeling tasks that should be applied to a changing service environment. For example: What type of modeling operations should be utilized when business requirements call for a reduction of service offerings? How can an internal service structure be reduced to meet technical specifications? What mechanisms should be employed to enable the expansion of a service ecosystem? and How can a distributed environment be contracted? The answers to these questions and others alike are provided by the structural analysis model in the chapters that follow.

One of the most essential benefits of the structural analysis and modeling practice is clearly to boost the reusability rates of a service by manipulating its internal components and external environment. Consolidation of service formations, identification of new services, and perfection of service contracts are also major contributions of the structural analysis and modeling process. To fulfill these objectives, the practitioner ought to be engaged in four different forms of structural

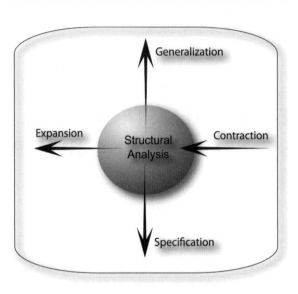

EXHIBIT P5.1   SERVICE-ORIENTED STRUCTURAL ANALYSIS MODEL

analysis and modeling, each of which introduces a different perspective of a service and its affiliated hosting landscape: Generalization, Specification, Expansion, and Contraction. (This model is
illustrated in Exhibit P5.1.) These structural views offer analysis processes, modeling mechanisms,
and patterns to accelerate carving out a structural analysis proposition.

1. **Structural Generalization.** This process is designed to broaden a service's internal structure by employing aggregation, unification, and compounding modeling techniques. These
   operations are applied on a service's internal structure to consolidate fine-grained services
   and increase service capabilities.
2. **Structural Specification.** This examination and modeling of service internal formation
   utilizes decomposition, subtraction, and refactoring means to break up a coarse-grained
   service and avoid tightly coupled design conditions.
3. **Structural Expansion.** To facilitate the increase of architectural scope and expand a distributed service environment, this process introduces distribution and mediation mechanisms and patterns.
4. **Structural Contraction.** Finally, structural modeling operations are devised to limit service
   expansion in a distributed environment and to downsize architecture deployment.

CHAPTER 18

STRUCTURAL ANALYSIS AND MODELING PRINCIPLES
Introduction to Service Structural Notation and Modeling

Structural analysis and modeling is a process pursued by architects, modelers, analysts, developers, and managers to describe a service's *internal formation* or an *external distributed computing environment* that consists of deployed services. These structural aspects are depicted by the relationships established between the services and their corresponding consumers, instituted binding contracts, and service coupling styles that "glue" a distributed environment together. The chief driving principles of the structural analysis and modeling are to improve service reusability rates, seek software consolidation opportunities, foster business agility, enable software elasticity, and encourage a loosely coupled distributed landscape. These benefits typically promote superior service structural configuration, deployment, and integration solutions for organizational concerns.

The structural analysis and modeling practice also offers a communication language that is employed to carve out an analysis proposition that depicts the structural foundation of a service. Here the practitioner looks at a service's internal and external construct and applies modeling operations to better satisfy business or technical requirements. Among other influences, this modeling process is also driven by the contextual aspects of a service that are described in detail in Chapters 14 to 17 on contextual analysis. As the reader will recall, these contextual forces pertain to a service's functionality, specialty, relationships with peers and consumers, and boundaries within the environment it operates.

The concluding artifact of the structural analysis modeling endeavor is an analysis proposition delivered in a formal modeling diagram that utilizes a notation to describe and document the various structural modeling *operations* that are applied on modeling *assets*. The sections that follow provide detailed explanation of the toolbox capabilities offered to practitioners to assist in delivering valuable analysis artifacts.

STRUCTURAL ANALYSIS MODELING PRINCIPLES

A service structural analysis and modeling effort should be driven by three chief perspectives: *process*, *time*, and *transparency*. These modeling characteristics typically influence practitioners' decisions when it comes to carving out a strategy for service structural configuration, deployment, and integration. The driving modeling process perspective describes a service progression and development during a service-oriented life cycle. It typically illustrates how a service changes during its life span. The time perspective, however, answers the question: When has the service been altered, created, or retired? When have design and architecture decisions made? This information is significant to the architecture strategy, financial planning, and budgeting. Last, the transparency perspective of the modeling effort is associated with the justification and motivation for creating a service, making architectural decisions, modifying service functionality, or eliminating service capabilities.

PROCESS DRIVEN: ILLUSTRATE SERVICE EVOLUTION.   During the structural modeling effort, the practitioner must communicate the modeling process to the business and information technology communities. This modeling process reporting pertains to the descriptions of service *transformation* from one structure to another. Service evolution is another vital aspect that should be documented to explain the different steps and their *sequence* that led to constitution of service current state. For example, during its life span, a service may structurally morph from an atomic formation to a composite structure. This process should be broken down by distinct activities and sequences to illustrate the service metamorphosis.

TIME-SENSITIVE DRIVEN: DEPICT SERVICE STATE.   The time attribute of a structural modeling process is vital to understanding a service's internal structure in each of the service-oriented life cycle phases. This aspect typically answers these questions: What was the structural composition of a service? What is its current design scheme? and What is the proposition for its future architecture? This essential information also pertains to the external environment composition of a service ecosystem in terms of service and consumer integration, collaboration, and relationship.

TRANSPARENCY DRIVEN: JUSTIFY AND DEFEND.   The transparency attribute of a service structural modeling process is related to the justification and rationale of a certain operation that is applied on a service or on its hosting environment.[1] To comply with the organizational transparency policy, ask the guiding questions before altering a service formation: Why are we decomposing a service? Why the consolidation of two or more services is essential? What are the benefits of retiring a service?

At any given time during the service structural modeling venture, the practitioner should be ready to justify and defend the direction that is followed from three different perspectives:

1. **Architectural traceability.** The architectural best practices that drive structural modification to a service typically are related to boosting reusability, fostering a loosely coupled architecture environment, expanding or narrowing service capability scope, simplifying service integration and relationship complexities, and more.
2. **Technological traceability.** Technological reasons that can influence the structural formation of a service or the composition of its environment can be integration with commercial off-the-shelf products, service deployment and configuration aspects, and more.
3. **Business traceability.** The reasons for applying a modeling operation on a service structure can also emanate from business requirements. The business value proposition of a service and its return on investment are also crucial determining factors that can influence service formation or its operating environment.

STRUCTURAL MODELING NOTATION INTRODUCTION

A service-oriented modeling diagram consists of two major building blocks: modeling *assets* and *modeling* operations. Without these ingredients, it would be impossible to depict a modeling process, an analysis activity, and introduce an analysis proposition that offers a solution to an organizational problem. Modeling assets describe the service structures that participate in a service-oriented modeling diagram. Modeling operations, however, are modeling activities. These are logical steps that the practitioner applies to analyze services and manipulate their structures to achieve the best possible solution proposition.

Modeling assets and modeling operations correspond to modeling symbols that can be employed to depict an analysis process and a solution to a problem. These two symbol categories are discussed in detail in the sections that follow.

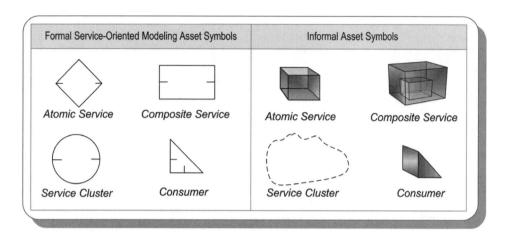

EXHIBIT 18.1   SERVICE-ORIENTED MODELING ASSETS NOTATION

MODELING ASSETS AND CORRESPONDING NOTATION.   In the context of structural analysis, modeling assets are the service formations introduced in Chapter 12 and discussed thereafter. These entities represent software compositions, patterns used when modeling a service ecosystem: Atomic (195), Composite (196), and Cluster (200). In addition, a consumer entity is added to this group to generalize the notion of a service requester. This may include a service that also acts as a consumer, an application that utilizes service offerings, or a remote partner. Furthermore, to prepare a practical analysis proposition diagram for a project or a larger business initiative, these structures are subject to manipulation and transformation. The operations that are being applied on these modeling assets may alter their core identity, modify their internal construct, augment their capabilities, or preserve and enhance their operations' signatures.

Consider the summary of service and consumer structures that typically are used in the modeling diagrams introduced in the chapters that follow:

- **Atomic service.** An indivisible formation that includes processes, operations, and interfaces.
- **Composite service.** A coarse-grained hierarchical structure that consists of smaller, finer-grained child services, such as atomic or other composite services.
- **Service cluster.** Represents a collection of distributed atomic or composite services.
- **Consumer.** A generalized symbol that identifies a consuming entity, such as a service that is also a consumer, an application, or a remote partner.

Each of the service structures and consumers involved in a modeling venture is presented by a *formal* and an *informal* [2] symbol illustrated in Exhibit 18.1. The formal notation is apparent in the Formal Service-Oriented Modeling Asset Symbols view (far left). The informal symbols appear in the Informal Asset Symbols view (far right).

MODELING OPERATIONS AND CORRESPONDING NOTATION.   A modeling operation is a service-oriented modeling activity designed to help architects, modelers, developers, analysts, and managers manipulate a service internal structure and its external environment. These actions contribute to a broad spectrum of objectives. From an internal architecture perspective, for example, an operation can help enhance a service formation, increase its reusability factor, or even improve its

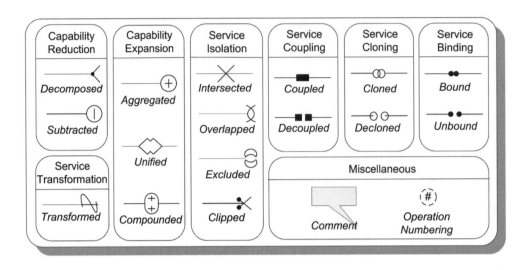

Exhibit 18.2   Service-Oriented Modeling Notation

performance. Modeling operations can also be utilized to address a service's external relationships. These may include coupling distributed services to strengthen their collaboration, binding services and corresponding consumers to contracts, forming service groups to reinforce solutions, and more.

Remember, the structural modeling operations are devised merely to influence service internal and external structures. However, a service's business or technical contextual affiliation is a major contributor to its structure manipulation and to the environment in which it operates. A service formation then will be influenced by its specialty, the type of process it executes, the line of business it supports, and the relationships that it maintains with its corresponding consumers and peer services. Refer to the contextual analysis discussions in Chapters 14-17 to understand how contextual modeling affect structural modeling.

Exhibit 18.2 illustrates the 18 symbols that can be used to carve out an analysis proposition diagram and introduce a solution to an organizational problem. Each of the symbols corresponds to a modeling operation that can shape a modeling diagram outcome and its proposed remedies to an arising enterprise concern. Moreover, the symbols are grouped into eight distinct categories, each of which tackles different aspects of the modeling process: Capability Reduction, Service Transformation, Capability Expansion, Service Isolation, Service Coupling, Service Cloning, Service Binding, and Miscellaneous.

Before moving to the detailed depiction of each symbol and its related operation, consider a summary of each of the eight symbol categories and their corresponding modeling operations. These modeling operation groups are discussed in the sections that follow.

Capability Reduction.   The capability reduction symbol group consists of two modeling operations that can be employed to break down a service into smaller finer-grained services and totally or partially retire a service.

1. **Decomposed.** This symbol is utilized to depict the scope reduction of a service by breaking it up into smaller and finer-grained services.
2. **Subtracted.** The subtracted symbol is designed to identify service retirement and discontinuation of service capabilities.

Service Transformation.   The service transformation group consists of the transformed modeling symbol, which depicts the transformation of one service structure to another. For example, this modeling operation enables the practitioner to convert an atomic service structure to a composite formation.

Capability Expansion.   The capability expansion category consists of three structural modeling operations, each of which is represented by a unique symbol employed to depict service capability augmentation, unify services, and group services.

1. **Aggregated.** The aggregated symbol represents a modeling operation that depicts containment of a service within a larger and coarse-grained service formation.
2. **Unified.** This modeling symbol illustrates the merging activity of two services.
3. **Compounded.** This symbol denotes the grouping of two or more services.

Service Isolation.   The service isolation symbol category represents four distinct modeling operations that can be utilized to separate one or more services from their affiliated group. This structural detachment enables the practitioner to reduce functionality redundancy, identify common services in a distributed environment, or simply isolate services to provide new solutions to arising problems.

1. **Intersected.** This symbol enables practitioners to superimpose clusters and create overlapping regions.
2. **Overlapped.** The overlapped symbol targets a region, created by two or more overlaid clusters, that consists of common services.
3. **Excluded.** This symbol targets the services that are *not* positioned in the overlapped region created by two or more superimposed clusters.
4. **Clipped.** The clipped symbol represents a modeling operation that enables the isolation of a service group deployed in a distributed environment with no clustering support.

Service Coupling.   The service coupling symbol group consists of two modeling symbols that depict the relationship between two services. This association is a rudimentary mechanism that can help practitioners identify service and consumer dependencies.

1. **Coupled.** The coupled symbol identifies an association between two services.
2. **Decoupled.** This symbol depicts the discontinuation of a relationship between two services.

Service Cloning.   The service cloning symbol group consists of a modeling operation that depicts the establishment of a service instance created from an originating service. The other modeling operation can reverse this process to individualize each instance that has been created.

- **Cloned.** Enables the creation of service instances that originate from a core service.
- **Decloned.** The decloned modeling symbol is utilized to denote the reversal of service cloning by converting each instance to a stand-alone and autonomous service.

Service Binding.   The service binding symbol category consists of modeling operations that enable the institution or the discontinuation of service and consumer contracts.

- **Bound.** The bound symbol represents a modeling operation that enables the founding of a contract between a service provider and its related consumer.
- **Unbound.** This symbol is employed to denote the discontinuation of a contract that binds a service and its corresponding consumers.

Miscellaneous.   The miscellaneous group consists of two symbols that do not depict any particular operation. They are provided for documentation purposes.

1. **Comment.** A place-holder for inserting practitioners' remarks.
2. **Operation Numbering**: Modeling operations can be numbered to depict the sequence of activities that is provided by an analysis proposition.

AGGREGATION

The aggregation modeling operation is employed to expand a service's capabilities when the solution scope is too narrow or its structure is too fine-grained. This process can be fulfilled simply by inserting source code to extend capability boundaries or by aggregating a finer-grained service in the hosting service formation. The participating entities in this spectrum-broadening effort can be an atomic formation, a composite structure, or a group of services—a service cluster. To achieve this modeling goal, employ the "Aggregated" symbol, which facilitates the aggregation process.

MODELING EXAMPLE.   Exhibit 18.3 depicts the process of aggregation in two different perspectives: 3D View (far right) and the Service-Oriented Modeling Formal Diagram View (far left).[3] The visual containment is apparent in the 3D View, which involves parent composite service CO-1 and its aggregated atomic service A-1 (service A-1 resides within service CO-1 space). In the formal modeling diagram, the "Aggregated" symbol is used to denote this kind of hierarchical relationship. Note that the symbol's plus sign is pointed to the containing entity: composite service CO-1.

MODELING BEST PRACTICES.   Consider the set of rules that should be applied when employing the "Aggregated" symbol:

- The aggregation operation can be applied to Atomic (195), Composite (196), and Cluster (200) service patterns.
- A finer-grained service should be aggregated into a coarse-grained service.

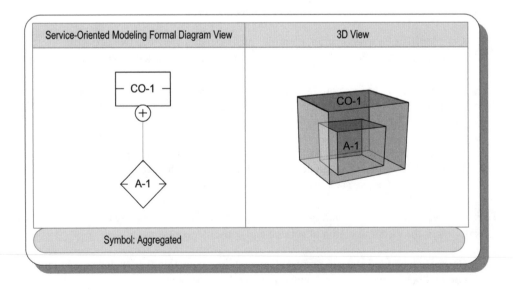

EXHIBIT 18.3   AGGREGATION OPERATION EXAMPLE

- An atomic formation that aggregates a child service must be transformed into a composite service. Employ the "Transformed" symbol discussed in the Transformation section.

RELATED MODELING PATTERNS.   To read more about the utilization of the "Aggregated" symbol and the patterns that employ aggregation operations, refer to Chapter 19 and the three related patterns that are discussed:

1. Simple Hierarchical Aggregation (332)
2. Multidimension Hierarchical Aggregation (334)
3. Nonhierarchical Structure Aggregation (336)

DECOMPOSITION

The decomposition operation typically is applied on a bulky and coarse-grained service that should be broken up into finer-grained services to increase its reusability rate, ease maintenance challenges, boost its performance, and foster a loosely coupled architecture. This process also simplifies architectural complexities and promotes business agility. Remember, this modeling operation is employed to separate tightly coupled services, and thus they should continue to operate independently after the decomposition activity occurs. To accomplish a decomposition task, utilize the "Decomposed" symbol to denote the separation of an entity into two or more services.

MODELING EXAMPLE.   Exhibit 18.4 illustrates a decomposition scenario in two apparent perspectives: 3D View (far right) and Service-Oriented Formal Modeling Diagram View (far left). The former depicts a composite service before the decomposition operation took place (in the upper window, named "Before") and after the separation has occurred (in the lower window, named "After"). The "Decomposed" symbol is employed in the formal modeling diagram (on left). In this view, atomic service A-1 is separated from its containing parent composite service CO-1.

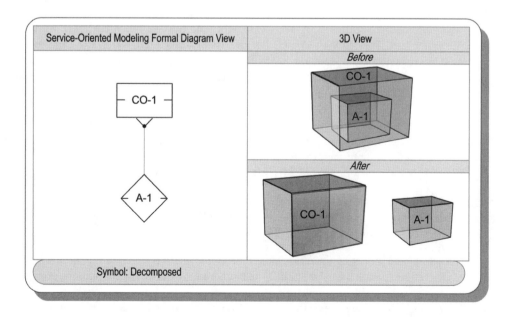

EXHIBIT 18.4   DECOMPOSITION OPERATION EXAMPLE

MODELING BEST PRACTICES.   Consider a set of modeling best practices that should be adhered to when using the decomposition operation:

- After a decomposition activity takes place, all separated services become autonomous entities that are structurally independent of each other.
- Composite and cluster service formations are structures that can be decomposed into smaller finer-grained entities. It is impractical, however, to break up an atomic fine-grained service into smaller services.
- A composite service should be transformed into an atomic entity if all of its aggregated internal services were extracted.

RELATED MODELING PATTERNS.   To learn about the decomposition process and its various application methods, refer to the patterns that employ the "Decomposed" modeling symbol in Chapter 20.

- Selective Decomposition (360)
- Total Fragmentation (365)
- Capability-Swapping (379)

SUBTRACTION

The subtraction modeling operation is used when service retirement or discontinuation of service capabilities is essential. This elimination process can be motivated by a variety of organizational necessities dictated by business requirements or technical specifications. The most compelling reasons that lead to the permanent removal of a service from a production environment are reduction in its reusability rates, a dwindling number of consumers, or a decrease in incurred revenue. To accomplish this task, employ the "Subtracted" modeling symbol to denote the demise of a service. The subtraction operation is typically a costly proposition because of the efforts required to untie the relationships between the removed service and its corresponding consumers. This may involve alteration to contracts, messaging frameworks, and infrastructure.

MODELING EXAMPLE.   Exhibit 18.5 exemplifies the subtraction modeling operation that is apparent in two different perspectives: 3D View (far right) and Service-Oriented Modeling Formal Diagram View (far left). The 3D View depicts the process of service removal in two different windows, titled "Before" and "After." Obviously, the former, which appears on top, illustrates the state of composite service CO-1 and atomic service A-2 before the subtraction has taken place. The latter depicts the final results after the elimination of services A-1 and A-2. Note that atomic service A-1 was aggregated in service CO-1.

However, the formal modeling diagram view (on left) illustrates this process by employing the "Subtracted" modeling symbol. Here atomic service A-1 has been removed from composite service CO-1 and retired. Note that a self-elimination activity is performed on atomic A-2. This activity depicts a total removal of a service from a production environment.

MODELING BEST PRACTICES.   Consider the set of modeling best practices that apply to the subtraction operation and the manner by which services should be retired and removed from a production environment or an analysis proposition diagram.

- The subtraction modeling operation should be employed to denote retirement of a service.
- A subtraction operation can be applied on autonomous entities, such as atomic, composite, and cluster structures.
- Subtraction can be used to extract a service from a composite formation or a service cluster and at the same time discontinue its operations.
- It is possible to subtract individual operations from an atomic service.

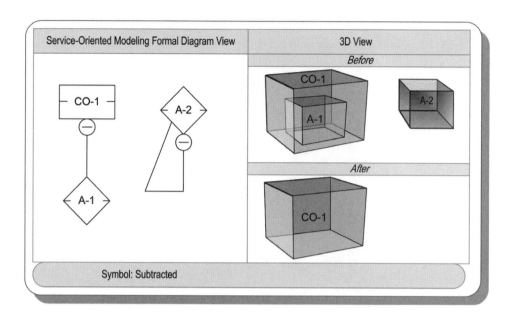

EXHIBIT 18.5   SUBTRACTION OPERATION EXAMPLE

RELATED MODELING PATTERNS.   The employment of the subtraction operation is essential to the reduction of service capabilities and the decrease of a proposed solution. To learn more about this service scope manipulation and the process of subtraction analysis, refer to the related modeling patterns discussed in detail in Chapter 20:

- Capability Subtraction (369)
- Entity Elimination (372)
- Capability Substitution (375)

COUPLING AND DECOUPLING

To carve out the right strategy for handling message delivery and orchestration, establishing message routes between services and their affiliated consumers, and founding a proper contract model that binds services to their corresponding peers or consumers, the coupling modeling operation is introduced. This service linking activity can help practitioners propose a solution that establishes associations among distributed software entities. The connectivity that influences service affiliations is a vital modeling task that employs the "Coupled" symbol in an analysis proposition diagram. In contrast, the "Decoupled" sign should be utilized when the intention is to untie the links between a service and its consuming party. Finally, remember that the coupling and decoupling modeling operations are rudimentary activities that convey a future communication scheme and, most important, identify the state of dependencies between message exchange parties.

MODELING EXAMPLE.   Exhibit 18.6 exemplifies the mutual dependencies of two services: the composite service CO-1 and atomic service A-1. This simple modeling operation is illustrated in two different perspectives: 3D View and Service-Oriented Modeling Formal Diagram View. The former consists of two windows, titled "Before" and "After." Evidently, they depict the state of the services before the coupled operation occurred and after. In the formal modeling diagram (on left),

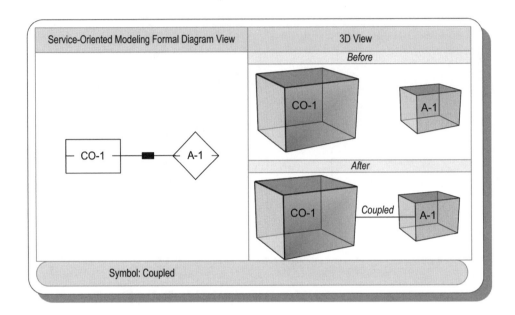

EXHIBIT 18.6   SERVICE COUPLING OPERATION EXAMPLE

the "Coupled" symbol is utilized to denote the association between the participating services in this endeavor: composite service CO-1 and its peer, atomic service A-1.

Exhibit 18.7, however, exemplifies the decoupling modeling operation. The 3D View (far right) again illustrates the state of service dependencies before the decoupled operation has taken place and after the relationship between composite service CO-1 and atomic service A-1 is discontinued. As apparent, the "Decoupled" modeling symbol is employed only in the formal modeling diagram view (far left).

MODELING BEST PRACTICES.   Remember, coupling a service to its peer or related consumer means establishing dependencies. Conversely, decoupling implies ceasing the ties between two service-oriented entities. Consider the guiding rules for implementing these modeling operations:

- The coupling and decoupling operations should involve autonomous service structures.
- Only two services should be coupled to each other.
- Only two services should be decoupled from each other.
- A service or a consumer can be simultaneously coupled to one or more services or consumers. The same rule applies to the decoupling operation.

RELATED MODELING PATTERNS.   The coupling modeling operation is employed extensively when broadening an organizational architecture scope and expanding a distributed environment. The related patterns that elaborate on coupling techniques and the process of implementation can be found in Chapter 21. To learn more about advanced modeling mechanisms that employ the "coupled" symbol, refer to the patterns that follow:

- Network Coupling (390)
- Circular Coupling (394)
- Tree Coupling (396)

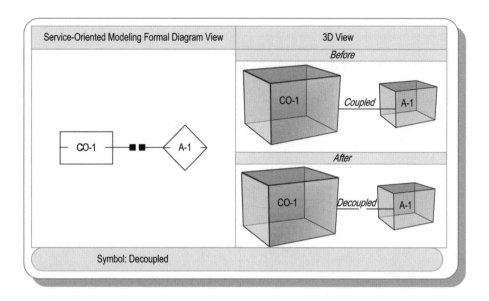

EXHIBIT 18.7 SERVICE DECOUPLING OPERATION EXAMPLE

- Star Coupling (399)
- Federated Service Coupling (402)
- Enterprise Service Intermediary (406)
- Enterprise Service Bus (411)

However, the decoupling modeling operation is employed when organizational best practices call for the reduction of architecture scope and the contraction of a distributed environment. Refer to Chapter 22 for mechanisms that facilitate the fulfillment of these goals, and study the following patterns, which employ decoupling of services from their related consumers:

- Federation Scope Reduction (432)
- Enterprise Service Intermediary Elimination (436)
- Enterprise Service Gateway Elimination (438)
- Enterprise Service Bus Elimination (441)

COMPOUNDING

Rather than assigning a broad range of responsibilities to a single service, a small collection of services that characteristically resides in close proximity is given mutual goals and shared duties to provide solutions to problems that arise. This tiny assortment of autonomous services is configured to work together toward achieving a mutual goal, such as exchange information to facilitate execution of transactions in a distributed environment. But this compounding operation should not be confused with clustering. Indeed, a service cluster resembles a compounded formation. A cluster, however, is a larger constitution that consists of service members that are remotely distributed, each of which may belong to other service structures or applications.

Employ the compounding modeling operation to augment a service's capabilities and extend its functionality through the addition of peer satellite services that should be positioned close by to reduce maintenance cost, architecture complexity, and integration challenges.

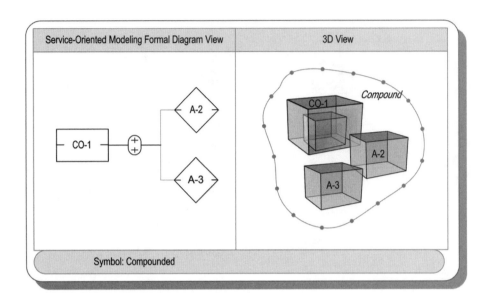

EXHIBIT 18.8   COMPOUNDING OPERATION EXAMPLE

MODELING EXAMPLE.   The modeling example illustrated in Exhibit 18.8 illustrates a compound service formation in two different perspectives: the 3D View (far right) and the Service-Oriented Modeling Formal Diagram View (far left). They depict the service grouping process by including three services: composite service CO-1, atomic service A-2, and atomic service A-3. Note that in the formal modeling diagram view, the "Compounded" symbol is employed to denote the relationships between the compound group members.

MODELING BEST PRACTICES.   A compound formation enables practitioners to strengthen a service solution and augment its capability by employing peer services to share its growing responsibilities. Doing this typically fosters loosely coupled architecture. Consider three modeling rules that contribute to these best practices:

1.   Position compound service members in close proximity to each other.
2.   A service that is a part of a compound formation is an autonomous service.
3.   Atomic and composite services can be part of a compound entity.

RELATED MODELING PATTERNS.   The structural generalization of services discussed in Chapter 19 further elaborates on the compounding process and the modeling techniques that facilitate the creation of service compound formations. The following related modeling patterns introduce approaches that can be employed to extend service capability and the scope of its operations:

- Structural Compounding (346)
- Service as Plug-In (348)

UNIFICATION

The structural unification operation is devised to merge two services into one entity. This process can be accomplished by combining operations and interfaces, yielding a service that embodies their

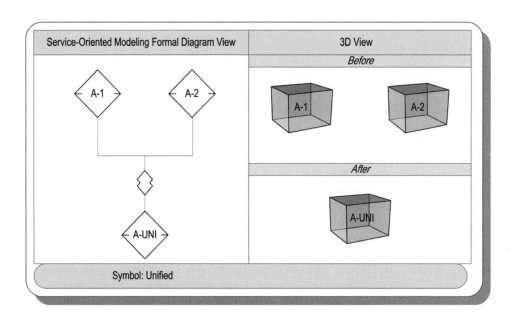

EXHIBIT 18.9 SERVICE UNIFICATION OPERATION EXAMPLE

functionalities and capabilities. The motivation for such a union is obviously rooted in architecture best practices that advocate uniting related fine-grained services that offer a narrow scope of a solution to an organizational concern. The term "related" pertains to the contextual affiliation of the services and specialty that associates them with the same line of business, occupation, consumer requirement, or technical task. Typically the reversal of this unification process is impractical since the participating services lose their identity and their structure is altered to accommodate the merger. Although the task here is to structurally unify two or more services, the contextual influence is obviously noticeable.

The unification modeling operation also offers asset consolidation opportunities to facilitate the extension of a service's boundaries beyond its current operational limits. To depict this process, employ the "Unified" symbol to denote the merger between services in an analysis proposition diagram. Chapter 19 further elaborates on the mechanisms and process for employing the unification operation.

MODELING EXAMPLE. Exhibit 18.9 illustrates the process of service unification in two different perspectives: the 3D View and the Service-Oriented Modeling Formal Diagram View. The former consists of two merging stages named "Before" and "After." In the first state, the merging process starts with the two autonomous formations, atomic service A-1 and atomic service A-2. After these two entities have been united, the result is the service structure atomic service A-UNI. Note that in the formal modeling diagram view (far left), the "Unified" symbol is used to denote the merger between atomic services A-1 and A-2. Again, similar to the result shown in the 3D panel, the rendered service is atomic service A-UNI.

MODELING BEST PRACTICES. When applying the unification modeling operation, it is imperative to follow a systematic approach that yields a final artifact that embodies the functionalities and capabilities of the involved services. Analyze internal dependencies and external relationships with consumers and peer services of complex formations before merging activities. The term "complex" applies to composite or hierarchical structures that aggregate smaller finer-grained services. Service clusters fall into the same category because of their distributed service model. Consider this guidance to assist practitioners with unification activities:

- Atomic, composite, and service cluster formations can be candidates for unification analysis.
- Atomic formations are the least complex structures to unify.
- It is recommended to unify similar service structures. That is, merge an atomic service with another atomic service, a composite service with another composite service, or a service cluster with another service cluster. Avoid unifying a mix of service structures.
- When a unification process involves two or more composite services, start with the first composite service by merging its internal aggregated child atomic services. The same process should persist for each of the involved composite services.
- It is impractical to merge a service cluster with other cluster formations if it consists of a large number of service members.

RELATED MODELING PATTERNS.   The unification operation is discussed further in detail in Chapter 19. It introduces the process of merging services, methods of implementation, and two related patterns that address the consolidation of service-oriented entities with structural differences:

- Hierarchical Structure Unification (342)
- Nonhierarchical Structure Unification (340)

TRANSFORMATION

The transformation modeling operation depicts a service's structural conversion from one state to another by employing the "Transformed" symbol. This process takes place after a composite or atomic service structure is modified by the aggregation, subtraction, or decomposition analysis operations. More specifically, an atomic service is transformed to a composite service after it aggregates a finer-grained service. However, an "empty" composite service whose internal services were extracted by employing the decomposition or the subtraction modeling operations should be transformed into an atomic service. In both scenarios, the practitioner must denote the fundamental change of a service's formation in the analysis proposition diagram.

When it comes to the modeling process of a service cluster structure, remember that an "empty" cluster formation that does not contain internal service members should be eliminated. Thus, no transformation modeling operations should be applied in this case.

MODELING EXAMPLE.   To depict the service transformation process, the practitioner should number the sequence of the modeling operations and stages, as illustrated in the Service-Oriented Modeling Formal Diagram View (far left) and the 3D View (far right) in Exhibit 18.10. Note that in the formal modeling diagram, the "Decomposed" symbol is employed in step 1 to depict the separation of atomic service A-1 from its containing composite service CO-1. In the second step, the "Transformed" symbol is used (marked as 2) to denote a conversion from a composite formation to an atomic structure; this process finally yields an atomic service named A-CO-1. The 3D View does not indicate the sequence of events but illustrates the state of the composite service CO-1 before the transformation process had begun and after it is completed.

MODELING BEST PRACTICES.   During the service-oriented modeling process, the practitioner is commissioned to depict and record modeling activities. As described in Chapter 1, this fundamental requirement of the as-is modeling principle applies during the course of service transformation. In

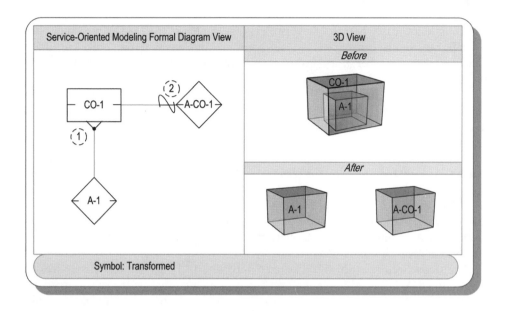

EXHIBIT 18.10 SERVICE TRANSFORMATION OPERATION EXAMPLE

other words, when a service is transformed, architects, modelers, developers, analysts, and managers must denote the service's structure conversion by identifying the various steps leading up to the results. Consider the four best practices that offer modeling guidance when employing the transformation operation:

1. An atomic and a composite service can be transformed by utilizing the "Transformed" modeling symbol.
2. An atomic service should be transformed to a composite service if it aggregates finer-grained services.
3. A composite service whose all internal child services have been extracted should be transformed into an atomic service.
4. A service cluster should not transformed into any other formation.

RELATED MODELING PATTERNS.   The modeling patterns that are listed next elaborate on transformation process and the various methods of implementation. These approaches employ the "Transformed" symbol when hierarchical and nonhierarchical service structures are involved.

- Nonhierarchical Structure Aggregation (336)
- Hierarchical Structure Unification (342)
- Total Fragmentation (365)

INTERSECTION

Identification of common services and discovery of redundant functionality across a distributed service environment is one of the most fundamental asset reuse best practices. To increase reusability rates of services and reduce duplicate business and technical processes, employ the intersection modeling operation. This method requires establishing clusters that group services according to their area of specialties and affiliation to a line of business, organization, or consumer base.

For example, the Fixed-Income Trading Service cluster and the Equity Trading Service cluster are two formations that gather subject matter expert services to promote the trading business. To find common functionality between these two clusters, simply overlay the entities to discover services that possess similar capabilities. In other words, this modeling exercise is like creating a Venn diagram that yields a number of regions for analysis purposes. The overlapping sections obviously share common attributes.

The practitioner can achieve a similar effect by employing the "Intersected" symbol to denote intersection between two or more service clusters. To discover common services or redundant functionality, utilize the "Overlapped" modeling symbol to depict the services that reside in the overlapping regions.

MODELING EXAMPLE.   The two examples that follow illustrate these intersection modeling concepts. The intersection operation is depicted in Exhibit 18.11, where the two participating service clusters CL-1 and CL-2 that appear in the 3D View and the Service-Oriented Modeling Formal Diagram View clearly intersect, yielding an overlapping region that consists of two services. Note that in the formal modeling diagram (far left), the "Intersected" symbol is employed to denote the relationship between the two clusters.

The second example, which is illustrated in Exhibit 18.12, emphasizes the services (atomic services A-1 and A-2) that reside in the overlapping region created by the superimposed service clusters CL-1 and CL-2. The term "emphasizes" pertains to the attention that must be shifted to these discovered common assets. These are now subject to analysis and future planning. Note the use of the "Overlapped" symbol (in additional to the "Intersected" symbol), which identifies services A-1 and A-2 as occupants of the overlapping region. This representation of the modeling operation is apparent in the formal modeling diagram (far left).

MODELING BEST PRACTICES.   Remember, the "Intersected" and the "Overlapped" modeling symbols should be employed during service cluster analysis operations. To accommodate this inspection and the associated modeling efforts, the practitioner must establish two or more clusters, each of

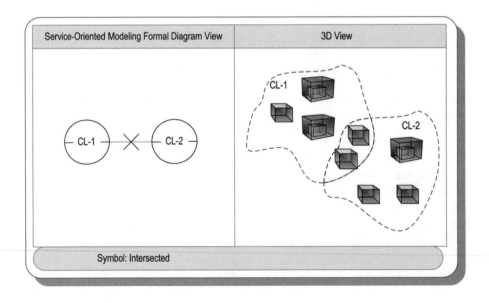

EXHIBIT 18.11   SERVICE CLUSTER INTERSECTION OPERATION EXAMPLE

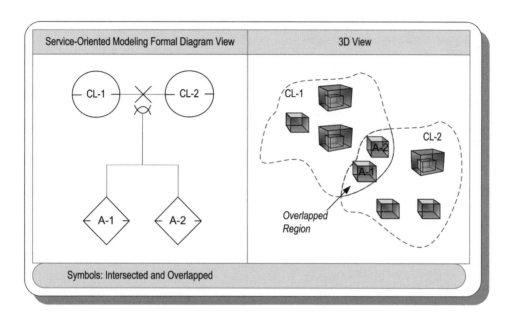

EXHIBIT 18.12 OVERLAPPING OPERATION EXAMPLE

which should represent an organizational occupation, line of business, or specialty. Once the overlapping regions are discovered, further analysis is required to determine the outlook of the identified common functionality offered by services. Consider the rudimentary affiliated guiding rules that can help alleviate these challenges:

- Employ the intersection operation to depict the structural intersection between two or more clusters.
- Employ the "Overlapped" symbol to discover common regions between two or more superimposed service clusters.
- The services that reside in the common regions typically share identical attributes, functionality, and capabilities.
- The service structures that reside in the overlapped regions can be atomic or composite formations.
- The services that do not occupy the intersected areas should not be the focus of analysis activities.

RELATED MODELING PATTERNS. The employment of the intersection and the overlapping modeling operations is discussed in detail in Chapter 22, which further elaborates on the process and methods of identifying common functionality and discovering asset consolidation opportunities. These are exemplified by two leading patterns:

1. Service Cluster Intersection (424)
2. Service Exclusion (427)

EXCLUSION

Unlike the overlapping modeling operation, the exclusion method focuses on the analysis of services that reside in the regions that do not overlap. Here the practitioner should intersect two or more

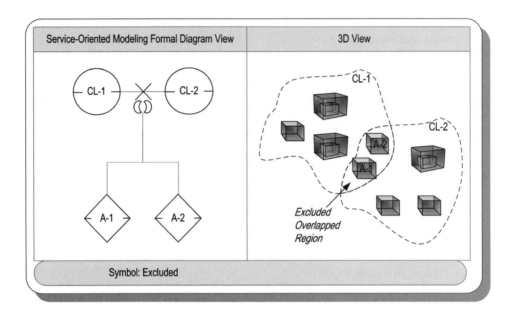

Exhibit 18.13   Service Exclusion Operation Example

service clusters to discover the uncommon functionality and discard the shared service attributes and capabilities. Therefore, utilize the two modeling symbols "Intersected" and "Excluded," which enable architects, modelers, analysts, developers, and managers to focus their attention on the services in surrounding sections. Furthermore, the exclusion modeling activity typically is employed during the contraction of architecture and the scope reduction of a distributed environment. This method of isolation analysis enables practitioners to concentrate on the range of services unique to their supporting environment by disregarding their commonalities.

MODELING EXAMPLE.   To exclude the atomic services A-1 and A-2, which reside in the common overlapping area of the intersected clusters CL-1 and CL-2, employ the "Intersected" and "Excluded" modeling symbols. This is illustrated in the Service-Oriented Modeling Formal Diagram View (far left) in Exhibit 18.13. Note that the overlapped region that is visible in the 3D View also identifies atomic services A-1 and A-2 as the secondary interest to this analysis activity since they reside in the excluded overlapping region.

MODELING BEST PRACTICES.   Remember, the exclusion modeling operation is designed to isolate the services that are not positioned in the overlapping regions of two or more superimposed cluster formations. Thus, unlike the "Overlapped" symbol, the employment of the "Excluded" modeling sign implies that the services positioned in the intersected regions are not the focus of analysis. Three guidelines further elaborate on these principles:

1. To identify uncommon services, employ the cluster intersection to isolate the services that reside in the overlapping sections by using the "Excluded" modeling symbol.
2. The overlapping regions of intersected service clusters typically consist of atomic and/or composite services.
3. The exclusion modeling operation enables practitioners to focus on the nonoverlapping regions of two or more intersected service clusters.

RELATED MODELING PATTERNS.   To read more about service exclusion, refer to the Service Exclusion (427) pattern discussed in Chapter 22, which elaborates on Service Exclusion methods and the process of service separation in a distributed environment.

CLIPPING

Anther method that can assist practitioners in isolating services without the utilization of intersected service cluster formations is the service clipping modeling operation. This approach enables one to select distributed services that reside in various deployment environments to participate in analysis and modeling sessions. These chosen entities can be part of a service cluster, aggregated in composite formations, or just autonomous services that operate independently across the organization. Furthermore, the clipping modeling operation allows the selection of services from a diversified resource pool by initially disregarding their contextual and structural dependencies. Doing this would enable practitioners to provide a solution that consists of legacy software assets actually designed to solve past and unrelated organizational concerns.[4] The clipping modeling operation can also be used to select concepts and ideas that have not been materialized and transformed into services.

MODELING EXAMPLE.   To better understand the clipping operation concept, view Exhibit 18.14, which illustrates a simple modeling process involving services selected from three different environments. These are composite service CO-1 (part of the service cluster CL-1), an autonomous atomic service A-1, and atomic service A-3, aggregated in composite service CO-2. Note that the 3D View (far right) depicts the services that have not been selected as well; in the Service-Oriented Modeling Formal Diagram View, the unselected entities are not shown. However, the latter perspective employs the "Clipped" symbol to identify the sources and their corresponding extracted services.

MODELING BEST PRACTICES.   The clipping modeling operation is designed to isolate services from their existing environments to solve problems that arise. This service selection should be

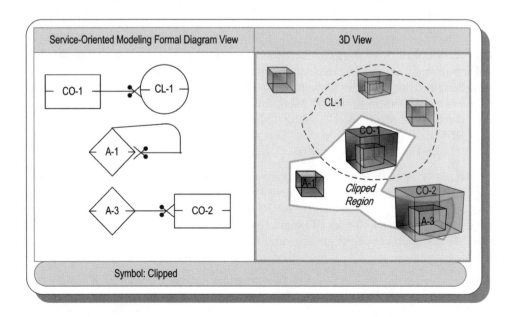

EXHIBIT 18.14   SERVICE CLIPPING OPERATION EXAMPLE

pursued by initially disregarding structural dependencies on other distributed formations or contextual affiliations with lines of business, organizations, and applications. In addition, by ignoring the existing service associations with stakeholders, sponsors, or hosting environments, the organizational silo execution model can be broadened to accommodate enterprise solutions. Consider the three best practices that can facilitate overcoming these challenges:

1. The clipping modeling operation can be employed to extract atomic and composite services that reside in a service cluster or a composite structure.
2. The clipping operation can also be used to isolate a service cluster, a composite service, or an atomic service from its distributed environment.
3. The clipping process typically yields an isolated group of services selected to participate in a new solution despite their contribution to past or existing organizational concerns.

RELATED MODELING PATTERNS.   The Clipping Mask (429) pattern discussed in Chapter 22 further elaborates on implementation methods and the process of service isolation that does not require cluster formations to define common and uncommon regions.

BINDING AND UNBINDING

Unlike the coupling modeling operation, the binding operation is about formally linking a service consumer to a service provider. This affiliation indicates that a service is committed to expose interfaces and accommodate affiliated consumers' requirements. These requirements include consumption necessities, type of functionalities, and scope of capabilities. Moreover, an established contract typically involves the creation of artifacts that bind a service to its related consumers, such as policy definitions, schema definitions, and description language definitions. To establish a contractual relationship between message exchange parties in a modeling diagram, employ the "Bound" symbol. This association can be later untied by utilizing the "Unbound" symbol.

Remember, a contract can be instituted between two peer services or between a service and its related consumers. A more loosely coupled contract management can be proposed by employing a centralized contract facility to enable the expansion of a distributed environment. Organizational architecture scope can also be broadened by employing a mediating service that typically is positioned between a consumer and its corresponding service.

MODELING EXAMPLE.   To bind a contract between a service and a consumer, employ the "Bound" symbol shown in the Service-Oriented Modeling Formal Diagram View (far left) in Exhibit 18.15. This simple illustration identifies a contract association between composite service CO-1 and the related consumer CONS-1. In the 3D View, this relationship is depicted again by utilizing the informal notation. To untie this relationship founded between composite service CO-1 and consumers CONS-1, employ the "Unbound" symbol, as shown in Exhibit 18.16 in the Service-Oriented Modeling Formal Diagram View (far left).

MODELING BEST PRACTICES.   The best practices outline is devised to assist practitioners with binding and unbinding contracts between service providers and related consumers. Remember that the "Bound" modeling symbol denotes the establishment of a formal relationship between message exchange parties, while the "Unbound" sign is employed to indicate the discontinuation of associations. Six best practices depict guiding rules for service and consumer binding and unbinding modeling operations:

1. To formalize the affiliation between a service and its related consumer, a binding contract should be established.
2. Use the "Bound" modeling symbol to identify a contractual relationship between a service and a related consumer.
3. Employ the "Unbound" modeling symbol to denote the discontinuation of a contract between a service and its corresponding consumer.

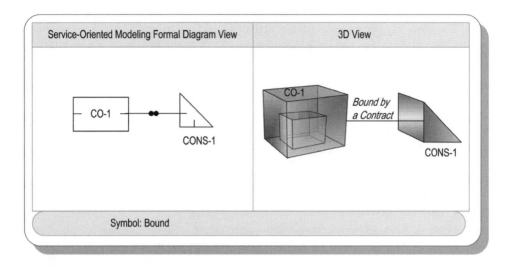

EXHIBIT 18.15 CONTRACT BINDING OPERATION EXAMPLE

4. A service can maintain multiple binding contracts with its corresponding consumers. (Refer to the Multiple Binding Contracts (355) pattern in Chapter 19 for implementation methods.)
5. An aggregated service that is part of a larger composite formation should not maintain contracts with external services. This relationship institution should be delegated to the containing parent entity. (Refer to the Contract Externalization (351) pattern in Chapter 19 for process and implementation details.)
6. A service cluster member should utilize a cluster gravity point to maintain contracts on its behalf. (Chapter 12 elaborates on the cluster gravity point concept.)

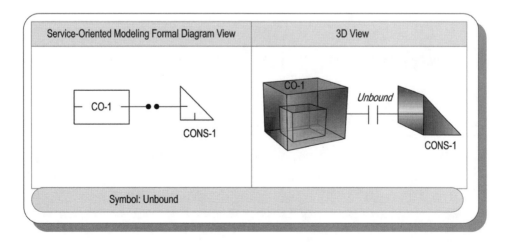

EXHIBIT 18.16 CONTRACT UNBINDING OPERATION EXAMPLE

RELATED MODELING PATTERNS.   Chapters 19 through 22 elaborate on contract binding and un-binding and discuss the methods and the process for formally associating a service with its related consumer. The modeling patterns can guide practitioners on how to bind and unbind contracts during the four structural analysis phases: generalization, specification, expansion, and contraction.

- Contract Mediation (415)
- Contract Hub (418)
- Contract Externalization (351)
- Multiple Binding Contracts (355)
- Contract Internalization (384)
- Contract Mediation Elimination (445)
- Contract Hub Elimination (447)
- Contract Cancellation (382)

CLONING AND DECLONING

The service cloning modeling operation is employed to create identical instances of a core service. This activity yields duplicate service capabilities that can be used in two types of configurations: local and distributed environments. The term "local" refers to the deployment of multiple service instances on a stand-alone server (often called vertical scaling) or installed on multiple servers (horizontal scaling) to ensure system execution stability and avoid a single point of failure. When an enterprise consists of distributed software that spans multiple organizations, lines of business, or applications, service clones can be used to form a federated computing environment that makes information available across silo implementations.

Disaster recovery sites can also utilize instances of services to ensure business continuity and avoid technical execution interruption. This option typically is configured to duplicate the original service functionality running in a production environment.

To denote a cloning activity in a modeling diagram, use the "Cloned" symbol. The "Decloned" sign should be employed to indicate when a service instance transforms into an independent entity. In other words, the decloning operation individualizes a service and permits modifications to its operations, alterations to its capabilities, and changes to its functionality.

MODELING EXAMPLE.   Exhibit 18.17 illustrates the cloning modeling process that is captured in perspectives: 3D View and the Service-Oriented Modeling Formal Diagram View. This activity

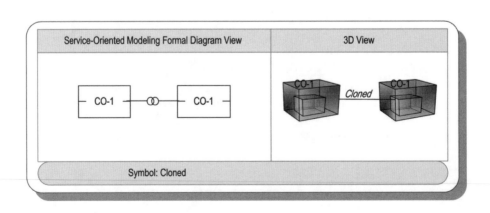

Exhibit 18.17   Service Cloning Operations Example

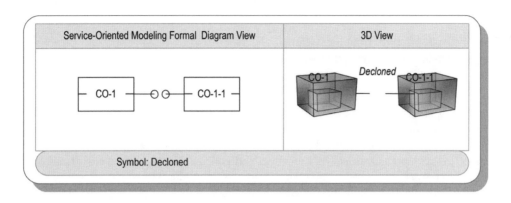

Service-Oriented Modeling Formal Diagram View	3D View
CO-1 ──◯◯── CO-1-1	Decloned
Symbol: Decloned	

EXHIBIT 18.18   SERVICE DECLONING OPERATIONS EXAMPLE

involves the core composite service CO-1, which yields a duplicated version of itself (also named CO-1). Note the utilization of the "Cloned" symbol depicted in the formal modeling diagram (far left).

The decloning modeling operation is illustrated in Exhibit 18.18. The composite service CO-1 is separated from its duplicated instance, which is renamed CO-1-1. Note the employment of the "Decloned" symbol in the formal modeling diagram (far left).

MODELING BEST PRACTICES.   Remember that the chief use of the cloning modeling operation is to depict the distribution and the deployment of service instances. These duplicate capabilities are devised to ensure continuity of operations and carry vital information across the enterprise, spanning multiple applications, departments, divisions, and even partners. Consider the five guiding best practices that elaborate on fundamental service cloning rules:

1. Employ the "Cloned" symbol to depict the creation of a service instance that originates from a core service. Assign identical names to all established instances.
2. Utilize the "Decloned" symbol to denote the separation of a core service from its instances. Each duplicated service should become an autonomous service and be assigned a unique name.
3. The cloning modeling operation can be used to describe a disaster recovery environment that requires duplicated functionality.
4. The cloning approach can be employed to depict a federated service environment in which service instances are linked to share vital information with silo organizations and applications.
5. The cloning method can also be leveraged to ensure business and technical continuity by scaling service instances on a single server (vertical scaling) or on multiple servers (horizontal scaling). This deployed duplicate functionality is designed to avoid a single point of failure in an architecture model.

RELATED MODELING PATTERNS.   In the context of modeling patterns paradigm, the cloning operation is employed to depict the expansion of a distributed environment and the broadening of the scope of an organizational architecture. When the time comes to optimize a distributed computing landscape and contract the deployment of an architecture model, the decloning operation should be utilized to trim down a federated service configuration. Refer to the two patterns that discuss service federation in Chapters 21 and 22:

- Federated Service Coupling (402)
- Federation Scope Reduction (432)

DELIVERABLES

The examples in this chapter are service-oriented analysis proposition diagrams that exemplify the utilization of various structural operations that can be applied to alter a service formation and its hosting environment. These structural modeling activities are also pursued to discover new services by complying with organizational best practices and policies. The guiding standards may include fostering a loosely coupled service landscape, boosting service reusability rates, encouraging service consolidation to reduce functionality redundancy across the organization, and more.

To be able to offer an efficient analysis proposition, employ these modeling operations and adhere to their corresponding best practices. In the section that follows, analysis proposition diagrams are discussed. Utilize these artifacts to submit a consistent solution proposition for a project or a larger organizational initiative.

SERVICE ANALYSIS PROPOSITION DIAGRAMS.   Obviously, an analysis proposition diagram can incorporate a combination of structural operations, a more complex configuration that illustrates the sequence of modeling events and the service evolution process. To help explain how the practitioner can combine various structural operations to achieve a modeling goal, refer to the chapters that follow and the detailed modeling patterns they offer. Furthermore, an analysis proposition should not necessarily be presented by a single diagram. A number of modeling views can be presented by individual diagrams, each of which can depict a distinct perspective of the solution.

Consider the chief diagram types that can collaboratively present a remedy to an organizational concern:

- **Internal service composition diagram.** This structural analysis proposition diagram should illustrate the internal manipulation of a service formation that can be accomplished using one or more modeling operations, such as aggregation, unification, compounding, decomposition, and subtraction.
- **Contract binding diagram.** This diagram should depict the contract binding between a service and its corresponding consumers in a distributed architecture environment. It may include institution of contracts in an expanded or contracted service ecosystem.
- **Service coupling diagram.** The service coupling diagram describes the rudimentary relationships between services and their related consumers in a distributed architecture environment. It may include the depiction of service distribution mechanisms, such as circular coupling, tree coupling, network coupling, star coupling, and federation coupling (discussed in Chapter 21). The service coupling diagram can also describe an architecture state and a distributed environment from two different perspectives:
  1. **Service environment expansion view.** This view is about broadening the distribution of services and employing mediation service facilities, such as service proxies, gateways, and enterprise service bus, to expand an architecture spectrum.
  2. **Service environment contraction view.** This perspective should describe the mechanisms that facilitate the scope reduction of a distributed environment and the contraction of an architecture scope.

RELATED MODELING ANALYSES AND CORRESPONDING PATTERNS.   Exhibit 18.19 details the analysis proposition diagrams and their related structural analysis process. The corresponding chapters are also listed.

Analysis Proposition Diagram Name	Related Structural Analysis Process	Related Chapters
Internal Service Composition Diagram	Aggregation analysis, unification analysis, structural compounding analysis, contract analysis	Chapter 19
	Decomposition analysis, subtraction analysis, refactoring analysis, contract analysis	Chapter 20
Contract Binding Diagram	Contract analyses	Chapters 19–22
Service Coupling Diagram	Distribution analysis, mediation analysis, contract analysis	Chapter 21
	Distribution reduction analysis, mediation rollback analysis, contract analysis	Chapter 22

EXHIBIT 18.19   MODELING DIAGRAMS AND RELATED STRUCTURAL ANALYSES

SUMMARY

- The structural analysis modeling process is driven by three chief aspects: process, time, and transparency.
- An organization should adopt three major structural analysis modeling transparency policies: architectural traceability, technological traceability, and business traceability.
- A structural modeling notation consists of asset and operations symbols.
- The service structures that participate in a modeling venture are Atomic (195), Composite (196), and Cluster (200) patterns.
- The structural modeling process consists of eight operation groups:
  1. Capability reduction
  2. Service transformation
  3. Capability expansion
  4. Service isolation
  5. Service coupling
  6. Service cloning
  7. Service binding
  8. Miscellaneous

Notes

1. Recall that this transparency principle applies to structural manipulation of services. A more generalized transparency model is discussed in Chapter 1, in the Service-Oriented Discovery and Analysis Transparency Model section.

2. The informal notation is a 3D representation of the formal modeling notation used to ease the study of the service structural modeling process.

3. First-time readers should study the informal 3D (typically shown on the far right panel) presentation before inspecting the formal modeling notation (usually appears on the left panel).

4. The clipping modeling operation is analogous to the clipping mask activity provided by graphical design packages to create isolated regions for drawing and artistic manipulations. This approach enables the artist to select a region on the artwork canvas and apply changes without affecting the surrounding areas.

CHAPTER 19

STRUCTURAL GENERALIZATION ANALYSIS PROCESS AND MODELING PATTERNS

The structural generalization process introduces methods and implementation techniques that practitioners can employ to broaden a service's internal logical and physical boundaries. This broadening exercise is about increasing the service's *size* by widening its formation utilizing the three chief modeling operations that enable this transformation: service *aggregation*, *unification*, and *compounding*. Although the structural generalization analysis and modeling process is influenced by the contextual aspects of a service, the chief goal here is to focus on widening its structural boundaries. The contextual ingredients, such as types of offerings, service specialty, and service functionality, should not be the focus of the generalization venture.[1] Furthermore, practitioners who are engaged in structural generalization activities should disregard the service type and its contribution to business or technical aspects of the solution. These service categories are semantic by nature and should not be manipulated during the structural generalization process.

The motivation behind the structural generalization process is associated mainly with business requirements and technical specifications. These are extended by the business and information technology organization because of a variety of concerns that must be addressed and rectified. Among these vital issues that are required attention are new projects that are designed to launch new applications, modifications and enhancements to existing technologies, and revamping architectures. These initiatives typically spur design, architecture, and development of services to meet business and technological aims.

To fulfill the structural generalization goals, employ the facilitating mechanisms that enable widening service boundaries and contribute to efforts to manipulate service internal structures. Techniques employ the structural modeling operations (discussed in Chapter 18) are elaborated in the sections that follow. The introduced analyses, processes, and modeling patterns are the tools that enable practitioners to carve an analysis proposition that adheres to organizational best practices. This chapter then introduces four methods and affiliated modeling patterns that can assist practitioners with broadening service boundaries and its capabilities:

1. **Aggregation analysis.** The aggregation analysis process is devised to guide practitioners to broaden a service's dimensions by augmenting its capabilities with finer-grained services that are inserted to its internal structure.
2. **Unification analysis.** The unification analysis effort is proposed to merge fine-grained services. This venture typically improves service reusability rates, reduce unnecessary expenditure, and help consolidate software assets.
3. **Compounding analysis.** Structural Compounding analysis is pursued to identify opportunities for service partnership that is employed to offer collaborative solutions. This effort is designed to augment a service's capabilities by employing peer services.

4. Contract analysis. The contract analysis process enables practitioners to reevaluate, assess, enhance, and reestablish contracts between a service that its internal structure is broadening and its corresponding growing consumer's base.

AGGREGATION ANALYSIS: PATTERNS AND IMPLEMENTATION

The aggregation analysis process simply enables architects, modelers, analysts, developers, and managers to enrich an atomic or composite service or service cluster functionality by widening the scope of their proposed solutions and enhancing their capabilities. These goals can be achieved by aggregating one or more fine-grained services into a larger and coarse-grained service formation. Ultimately, relationships should be established between the internal services to create internal message exchange routes and information delivery mechanisms.

Remember, this aggregation process is merely a *structural manipulation* of service internal components. Namely, here our goal is to insert or inject a software entity into an existing and larger service. The *containment* aspect of this operation should be the main focus of this exercise. Consider, for example, aggregating the fine-grained New York Municipal Bond Service into the coarse-grained Fixed-Income Trading Service. This act not only enhances the Fixed-Income Trading Service capability, but it also widens its scope of operations. The contextual aspect, however, should not *dominate* this effort. In other words, practitioners should not be concerned about a particular type of a service, its business affiliation, or its technological abstraction. Business processes and even the conceptual connotation of a particular product should be ignored as well. Refer to the provided contextual analysis and modeling patterns that are discussed in Chapters 14 through 17.

Another mission that is affiliated with the aggregation analysis discipline is to examine a service's internal components and assess its overall capabilities to satisfy business and technological requirements. This inspection process should focus on streamlining internal service relationships and improving the overall architecture. The granularity scale of a service should also be inspected to ensure that the structural aggregation operation did not produce an overly coarse-grained service.

STRUCTURAL AGGREGATION PATTERNS AND ANTI-PATTERNS.   The service aggregation patterns that are introduced in this section are fundamental analysis and reusable templates designed to resolve service structural inefficiencies. Adapt the proposed best practices that can promote asset reuse and consolidation in the enterprise, and help stabilize and stylize service internal structures. Furthermore, the proposed aggregation anti-patterns are devised to introduce best practices for service aggregation activities. These are a set of rules that should be followed to strengthen the relationship between internal service constituents and help ascertain service interfaces.

SIMPLE HIERARCHICAL AGGREGATION PATTERN.   The Simple Hierarchical Aggregation pattern represents a hierarchical formation of nested services that are bundled together in a parent/child style. A parent service, the outermost containing entity, typically dominates the overall internal structure, influences internal message routing and delegation, and shapes the interfaces of the child services. In contrast, child services are characteristically finer-grained, hidden from the outside world's access, and collaborate to execute business or technical missions. This general aggregated scheme that accentuates hierarchical service formation mainly involves composite and atomic services.

Problem.   Why is there a need to create hierarchical compositions? The answer to this question is rooted in the impracticality of deploying and maintaining fine-grained services that contribute negligible business and technology value. Moreover, these software assets, scattered in a deployment environment, are usually not used to their maximum capacity. They operate independently and maintain unstructured relationship with their corresponding consumers or peer services. This is related to the manner by which services are associated to each other and the logical affiliation that they must maintain to exchange messages.

Solution.   Hierarchical formations introduce a formalized design structure that architects, developers, modelers, analysts, and managers can understand and control. This simple service grouping concept ultimately yields a coarse-grained composite construct that internalizes scattered finer-grained services, such as an atomic or smaller composite service, to increase the scope of a solution. In addition, enforcing internal service collaboration helps widen the spectrum of remedies to organizational problems.

How can a hierarchical software asset contribute to business executions? Hierarchical formations of this nature are designed to increase composite service execution and performance stability[2] and to reduce maintenance costs. In other words, bundling service operations typically increases operational reliability and enhances interactions and collaboration between internal services. Furthermore, shielding the exposure of internal services to external consumers is a common software development practice for hiding or isolating functionality. This method is not employed to protect the integrity of service operations but to apply order and implementation disciplines to software construction.

Example.   Exhibit 19.1 demonstrates how to insert a service at a certain level in a hierarchy and establish parent/child dependencies. This approach is depicted in two views: 3D View (far right) and Formal Service-Oriented Modeling Formal Diagram View (far left). The 3D visual version identifies three services that collaborate on executing a solution. They form a hierarchical structure, in which service C-1 (composite) is the outer service that contains service C-2. The latter is a composite service as well that consists of atomic service A-1.

The apparent formal diagram (far left) illustrates the same structure arrangement by employing the "Aggregated" symbol. Again, atomic service A-1 is contained in composite service C-2, and the latter is a part of C-1. Note that the architectural traceability aspect of this operation (on the bottom) indicates that services A-1 and C-2 are too fine-grained and thus require aggregation.

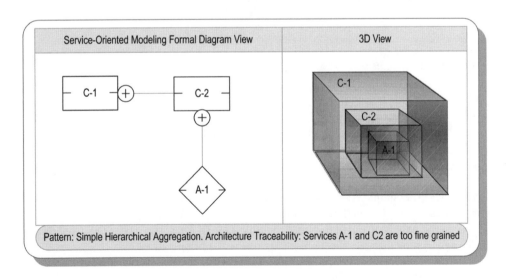

Exhibit 19.1   Simple Hierarchical Aggregation Pattern

Pattern Identification	
Name	Simple Hierarchical Aggregation Pattern
Category	Structural Generalization Analysis
Problems, Solutions, and Implementations	
Problem	1. Low service reusability rate.
	2. Service is too fine grained.
	3. Environment consists of unmanaged scattered services.
	4. Solution scope is too narrow.
	5. Unclear relationship between associated services.
Solution	Create a hierarchical composite formation that institutes lucid relationships between parent and child services.
Applicability	1. Apply to reconcile an overly distributed service environment.
	2. Employ to bundle scattered services into a more tightly coupled service formation.
	3. Establish hierarchical structure to strengthen and stylize service relationships.
Method	The most coarse-gained entity, the parent service, should consist of one or more fine-grained child services.
Benefits	1. Enhancing software stability.
	2. Promoting asset consolidation.
	3. Boosting service reuse.
	4. Isolating software implementation.
Risks	Excessive aggregation activities may contribute to a tightly coupled service formation.
Notation	Use the "Aggregated" symbol.

Exhibit 19.2   Simple Hierarchical Aggregation Pattern Summary

Anti-Pattern Name	Best Practice
Extreme Aggregation	Avoid complex and excessive aggregation that can affect service performance and reusability factors.
Service Containment Rule	A service that consists of one or more smaller fine-grained services (either atomic or composite) should always be regarded as a composite service.
Service Granularity Rule	The outermost service in a hierarchical formation should always be conceived of as the coarsest-grained entity in the structure. Its subordinate services, however, form finer-grained constructs.
Excessive Level Count	A hierarchical formation should not contain a large number of levels.

Exhibit 19.3   Simple Hierarchical Aggregation Anti-Patterns

Synopsis.   The Simple Hierarchical Aggregation pattern advocates aggregating a fine-grained child service in a larger parent service to increase the solution scope of the parent service and its reusability factor. Exhibit 19.2 further outlines the challenges, solutions, and implementation principles that drive and motivate this effort. In addition, note the references to the related patterns that offer similar solutions to comparable problems.

Anti-Patterns.   The Simple Hierarchical Aggregation anti-patterns are a set of rules and best practices that advise managers, architects, modelers, analysts, and developers about implementation techniques that should be *avoided* (outlined in Exhibit 19.3). These are devised to avoid the misuse of service aggregation that can affect reuse or performance of operations.

MULTIDIMENSION HIERARCHICAL AGGREGATION PATTERN.   The Multidimension Hierarchical Aggregation pattern proposes to expand the overall service functionality and its offered solution by adding internal child services. But this insertion should not affect the depth of the service hierarchy.

This implies that the chain of parent and subordinate services should not be increased. Instead, a fine-grained service should be added to broaden a specific level in the construct. In other words, unlike the Simple Hierarchical Aggregation pattern (332), here the rule of injecting services is loosened: More than one child service can be related to a parent.

For example, the child services Savings Account Service, Checking Account Service, and Credit Card Account Service, positioned on the same hierarchy level, can be encompassed within the parent Banking Account Service. This activity would not only increase the operation's scope of the composite formation but would also affirm order and structure in increasingly complex structures.

Problem. Hierarchical service formations introduce tightly coupled structures that in some circumstances may negatively affect service operations, performance, monitoring, and maintenance. This is attributed to the special relationship that is established between a parent and child entity because of the *vertical* manner in which messages are internally delegated and routed. The term "vertical" implies that this process typically is confined to an internal top-down (parent to child) or bottom-up (child to parent) message exchange direction. This narrowing effect is shaped by the structure that imposes *limitations on the spectrum of a solution* and clearly limits the number of services that can take part in a hierarchical formation.

Solution. Widen the vertical scope of a service hierarchy and achieve a more horizontal remedy to a problem by positioning more than one child service on a single hierarchy level. In other words, the internal design permits a parent service to maintain relationships with multiple children. Moreover, broadening the base of a hierarchical formation would guarantee a more diversified service population whose internal relationships are highly structured and organized.

Example. Exhibit 19.4 illustrates the Multidimension Hierarchical Aggregation pattern. The two apparent perspectives: 3D View (far right) and the Service-Oriented Modeling Formal Diagram View (far left) depict a structural generalization model that broadens the scope of the solution by placing the C-2 and C-3 composite services on the same hierarchical level. Remember, this process

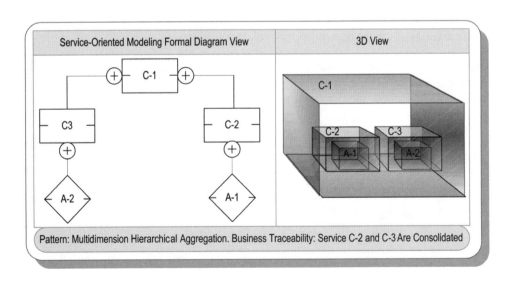

Exhibit 19.4 Multidimension Hierarchical Aggregation Pattern

Pattern Identification	
Name	Multidimension Hierarchical Aggregation Pattern
Category	Structural Generalization Analysis

Problems, Solutions, and Implementations	
Problem	1. The hierarchical service formation is too tightly coupled. 2. The hierarchical service structure limits the scope of the solution.
Solution	Create a composite entity that allows a single parent service to encompass more than one child service.
Applicability	Apply when a composite service's solution proposition does not satisfy the scope of the requirements.
Method	A hierarchical structure level should consist of two or more finer-grained child services that are associated to a single parent service.
Benefits	1. Broaden the solution scope of a composite service. 2. Assert order and structure to internal service formation.
Risks	Excessive positioning of aggregated services on the same level may introduce a complex composite service internal design.
Notation	Use the "Aggregated" symbol.

EXHIBIT 19.5   MULTIDIMENSION HIERARCHICAL AGGREGATION PATTERN SUMMARY

merely adds children to the same parent service to increase the parent service capability. Moreover, this activity is about widening the solution scope of the parent service by manipulating the structural aspect of the general service formation. Note, the aggregated child services C-2 and C-3 are composite services as well, aggregating the finer-grained atomic services A-1 and A-2, respectively. In addition, the performed aggregation operations are accomplished by employing the "Aggregated" symbol in the formal modeling diagram view.

Synopsis.   The Multidimension Hierarchical Aggregation pattern advocates the placement of more than one child service on a hierarchy level. This pattern would widen the solution scope of the overall composite formation and in particular widen the scope of the parent service operations. Exhibit 19.5 provides identification information and problems, solutions, and implementation principles that correspond to the Multidimension Hierarchical Aggregation pattern. This summary also outlines the major benefits and risks of this pattern and possible applications.

Anti-Patterns.   The anti-patterns that are depicted in Exhibit 19.6 introduce rules and guiding principles that practitioners should be receptive to when employing the Multidimension Hierarchical Aggregation pattern. These anti-patterns are affiliated to excessive service aggregation activities or to complex service relationships.

Anti-Pattern Name	Best Practice
Complex Aggregation	Steer clear of complex hierarchical service formations that are populated with a large number of nested services.
Overloaded Hierarchy Level	Avoid positioning a large number of child services on a single hierarchy level.
Ambiguous Aggregation	Circumvent complex service relationships: A child service should be affiliated with a single parent service.

EXHIBIT 19.6   MULTIDIMENSION HIERARCHICAL AGGREGATION ANTI-PATTERNS

NONHIERARCHICAL STRUCTURE AGGREGATION PATTERN.   Unlike the Simple Hierarchical Aggregation pattern (332), the Nonhierarchical Structure Aggregation pattern addresses the insertion process of a fine-grained service into a service formation that does not necessarily maintain internal parent/child type of relationships. These two major structures are atomic and service clusters. The reader may remember that it would be impractical to break down an atomic formation into smaller services. But from an aggregation process perspective, a practitioner can augment an atomic service by inserting other services into its internal structure. This activity would obviously transform an atomic structure into a composite formation.

A service cluster is also subject to aggregation analysis. Recall that cluster members are simply business or technology-affiliated entities that collaborate to achieve a goal and interface to propose a solution to a problem. In addition, a cluster does not maintain hierarchical relationships between its internal constituents. These associations are based merely on contextual links between the containing services, such as common service specialties, business functionality, or even technical capabilities. Therefore, the Nonhierarchical Structure Aggregation pattern tackles the injection of a service into an existing cluster formation by avoiding the need to establish parent/child relationships.

Problem.   A given service environment consists of nonhierarchical service structures that offer limited capabilities and provide a narrow solution scope. How can their offerings' scope be broadened? Would adding more operations to their existing implementation would meet business requirements or technical specifications?

Solution.   To broaden the capabilities and extend the solution spectrum of a service that does not maintain an internal hierarchical structure, employ the Nonhierarchical Structure Aggregation pattern that addresses the mechanisms of injecting child services by simply expanding an existing parent service structure. The solution to the challenges is fairly simple:

1. Utilize the aggregation modeling operation to augment service capabilities and solution scope.
2. If the aggregation process involves an atomic structure, identify the various relationships between the injected services and establish parent/child associations. In other words, the aggregation process transforms an atomic service to a composite service. In addition, when founding links between internal parents and child services, consider their granularity scale. Obviously coarse-grained services should be placed higher in the hierarchy while finer-grained should be located on lower levels.
3. If the involved structure is a service cluster conduct a meticulous analysis to identify dependencies of cluster members on other applications and services. This analysis should provide solid information that can be utilized to institute new service relationships and found proper contracts to accommodate the aggregated entities. Remember that a cluster formation is not hierarchical and thus the aggregation modeling activity merely broadens its solution boundary.

Example.   Exhibit 19.7 illustrates the aggregation process that involves the containing cluster CL-1 and the aggregated entities CO-2 (composite service that consists of atomic service A-1), and atomic services A-2 and A-3. This activity emphasizes the need for establishing new service contracts and instituting message routes to connect the distributed assets that take part in the cluster activities. Note the usage of the "Aggregated" symbol that denotes containment of services CO-2, A-2, and A-3 within the nonhierarchical structure of cluster CL-1. In addition, from a business traceability perspective, it is indicated (on the bottom) that this process took place because cluster CL-1 offers limited capabilities.

Synopsis.   The Nonhierarchical Structure Aggregation pattern should be employed to enrich service capabilities and broaden its remedy scope. This process pertains to a service formation that does not maintain or entirely support an internal hierarchical design. An atomic service and a service cluster fall under this category. Exhibit 19.8 summarizes the key factors that should motivate

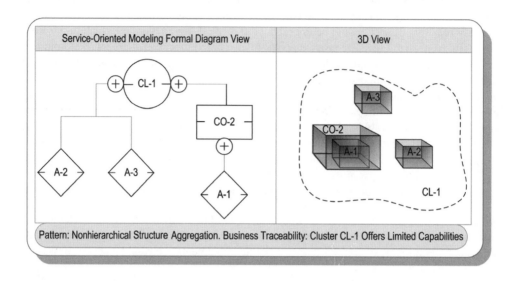

EXHIBIT 19.7   NONHIERARCHICAL STRUCTURE AGGREGATION PATTERN

practitioners to employ the Nonhierarchical Structure Aggregation pattern. The problem, solution, applicability, method, benefits, and risks are also provided for future reference.

Anti-Patterns.   Exhibit 19.9 introduces anti-patterns that identify the various risks that practitioners should be aware of when employing the Nonhierarchical Structure Aggregation pattern. These are affiliated with the integration of the newly aggregated services and their relationships with the existing entities. Attend to the introduced best practices and avoid unnecessary implementation perils that ultimately can affect performance and attainability of services.

Pattern Identification	
Name	Nonhierarchical Structure Aggregation Pattern
Category	Structural Generalization Analysis
Problems, Solutions, and Implementations	
Problem	A service environment consists of nonhierarchical service structures, such as atomic and cluster, that offer limited capabilities and provide a narrow solution scope.
Solution	Augment atomic service and service cluster capabilities by injecting services and functionality into their existing structures.
Applicability	1. Apply to fine-grained atomic services that require business or technical augmentation.
	2. Utilize this pattern when a solution scope of a service cluster is too narrow.
Method	The Nonhierarchical Structure Aggregation pattern addresses three major aspects of implementation: (1) inserting a service into an existing one; (2) reinstituting internal relationship to accommodate the augmentation; (3) altering internal message delegation and path.
Benefits	1. Broadening the solution scope of an atomic service and service cluster.
	2. Widening atomic service and service cluster capabilities.
Risks	Excessive usage can yield oversized, tightly coupled, and very coarse-grained services that will be hard to maintain and support.
Notation	Use the "Aggregated" and the "Transformed" symbols.

EXHIBIT 19.8   NONHIERARCHICAL STRUCTURE AGGREGATION PATTERN SUMMARY

Anti-Pattern Name	Best Practice
Oversized Cluster	Avoid excessive aggregation that typically leads to a large cluster size that eventually introduces management and performance challenges.
Untransformed Atomic Service	An atomic service should be transformed into a composite entity if it aggregates at least one service.
Disarrayed Associations	The establishment of internal service relationship to ensure clear associations and stable internal message activities should follow an aggregation modeling operation.

Exhibit 19.9   Nonhierarchical Structure Aggregation Anti-Patterns

UNIFICATION ANALYSIS: PATTERNS AND IMPLEMENTATION

The service unification analysis and modeling process addresses the fundamental concern of software viability to the business and technology organizations. More specifically, it is about the consolidation of service operations and interfaces and reconciliation of functionality that is duplicated across applications or other services. But this effort does not focus only on reducing overlapping software implementations. This activity is also about reevaluating and rescaling service granularity and identifying opportunities for merging fine-grained entities.

One of the most crucial aspects to remember is that the service unification task should not be based on service contextual aspects. That is, this venture merely accentuates the structural manipulation of services that leads to the consolidation of service identities and creation of a new formation that embodies its originators' capabilities, yet maintains its own identity. Merging atomic, composite, or cluster structures are the core operations of this exercise. For example, if the Client Home Address Atomic Service is unified with the Client Work Address Atomic Service, the product is clearly a coarser-grained entity, and structurally larger than each of its originators. Again, service names, concepts, and abstraction levels should not drive this process, however, influence structural modeling activities.

The service unification analysis effort should be concerned about two major asset consolidation perspectives: enterprise-level and application-level. The former focuses on examination of autonomous or distributed services and whether they are candidates for unification. The selected assets for unification on the enterprise level typically consume a considerable amount of computer resources and require substantial operational budgets, yet in most circumstances the benefits outweigh the cost when it comes to consolidation of software.

From an application-level perspective, an architect, analyst, or developer should employ the unification process if the service-oriented analysis effort concludes that there is no particular reason to maintain separate executables or redundant processes. This activity is often a part of refactoring, during which service redesign and rearchitecture takes place to determine how to optimize source code and algorithms.

STRUCTURAL UNIFICATION PATTERNS AND ANTI-PATTERNS.   The sections that follow represent fundamental patterns and best practices designed to guide practitioners how to merge services. This simple concept of unification is part of the service-oriented analysis process that is employed not only for analyzing the current state of a service's structure and its granularity scale but also to promote opportunities for software consolidation. In addition, source code redesign and architecture reevaluation initiatives can change the state of a service by uniting it with its peers. This typically alters its structural identity and yields a new formation devised to address a larger scope of the problem.

What structures can take part in this unification activity? All service formations that have been discussed so far can participate in this process: composite and atomic services, and service clusters. The consolidation of these entities, however, would require different methods and treatments because of their distinct internal constitution. We thus distinguish between *hierarchical* and *nonhierarchical* unification, each of which introduces different levels of difficulties and methods of implementation.

NONHIERARCHICAL STRUCTURE UNIFICATION PATTERN.   The Nonhierarchical Structure Unification pattern is devised to merge services that in their current state do not maintain or entirely support an internal hierarchy of aggregated services. Remember, this unification activity should not be confused with aggregation. This structural modeling unification operation merges a service structure with a peer service formation to the extent that the involved parties lose their individual identity.

Moreover, one of the simplest forms of unification activities takes place when a candidate service for the reconciliation process does *not* consist of complex internal structures. Here the term "complex" refers to hierarchical formations that are shaped by parent/child relationships. An atomic service and a service cluster are regarded as nonhierarchical entities, and thus are the best contenders for the unification effort. An atomic service is made up of operations and interfaces that are relatively easier to merge with other services. Similar process simplicity applies to a cluster entity. Indeed, a cluster formation may contain composite services. Merging a cluster with its counterparts, however, would require simply increasing the boundaries of the unified cluster to form a new periphery and establishing new relationships between the unified services.

Problem.   The problem that is addressed by the Nonhierarchical Structure Unification pattern pertains to ad hoc, unplanned, or organically grown fine-grained atomic service and small scale service cluster that clearly do not justify the invested resources and budgets allocated to support their operations. Reconciling business process redundancy and duplication of functionality is another important reason for merging service structures.

Furthermore, balancing the granularity levels of a service structure is another compelling cause for merging it with its peers. "Balancing granularity" means that a service formation should be structurally proportioned when it comes to its size and the amount of operations that it offers. Very fine-grained service structures characteristically do not add substantial value to large production environments. They should be unified with other formations that share common capabilities and functionalities to increase reusability rates and boost consumers' interests.

Solution.   If the service-oriented analysis findings justify software asset consolidation, the solution would be to unify a service with its counterparts. Furthermore, the reasons that are indicated in the Problem section should be compelling enough to proceed with nonhierarchical structure merging. Two classes of services that fall under this category, as discussed earlier: Nonhierarchical service formations are atomic services or service clusters. Both do not maintain internal layers of execution between parent and child entities. But the method of unification varies.

Remember, in the Unification section in Chapter 18, the recommendation is to not to unify a mix of service structures during the merging activities. In other words, this best practice advocates to unify the same type of service formations. For example, an atomic service should be united with another atomic service. The same rule applies to service cluster unification. Consider two paths of service consolidation. We start first with merging atomic services and conclude with service clusters:

- Examine the atomic services that are candidates for unification. Study their functionality, capabilities, and interfaces.
- As a part of the inspection effort, identify the granularity level of each service that will be involved in the unification process.
- Since the identity of the participating services ought to be merged during the unification activity, merely focus on consolidating their operations by removing redundant processes. Common interfaces should also be combined to eliminate duplication of functionality.

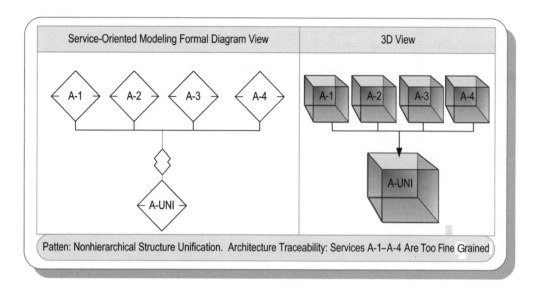

EXHIBIT 19.10   NONHIERARCHICAL STRUCTURE UNIFICATION PATTERN EXAMPLE

With service clusters the process of unification is different:

- Examine the various service clusters that take part in the unification process.
- Study the overall capabilities of each merged cluster and understand the relationship of cluster members, message path and delivery mechanisms, and their binding contracts.
- Eliminate redundant functionality by unifying or retiring cluster member services.
- The merging process must establish new service relationships. This establishment pertains to founding and configuring message orchestration mechanisms, instituting mediation services, and updating enterprise service buses.

Example.   Exhibit 19.10 illustrates a simple unification process that involves four different atomic services: A-1, A-2, A-3, and A-4. This scenario is presented by two different views: 3D View (far right) and Service-Oriented Modeling Formal Diagram View (far left). The "Unified" symbol is utilized to depict this consolidation activity in the formal diagram. Note that it also points to the entity that unifies all services: atomic service A-UNI. In addition, the architecture aspect that motivates this action is indicated on the bottom: From a design traceability point of view, the decision to bond these services is attributed to their fine-grained granularity.

Synopsis.   The Nonhierarchical Structure Unification pattern addresses the merging challenges of service formations. These candidate service structures for unification are nonhierarchical formations. Consider summary Exhibit 19.11, which depicts the Nonhierarchical Structure Unification pattern profile that identifies the problem, solution, applicability, method, benefits, and risks. This synopsis is similar to the Hierarchical Structure Unification (342) pattern elaborated on in the section that follows. Many similarities can be found between these two patterns, especially the described problems and proposed solutions. The unification methods, however, vary because of their distinct service structure formations.

Pattern Identification	
Name	Nonhierarchical Structure Unification Pattern
Category	Structural Generalization

Problems, Solutions, and Implementations	
Problem	1. Service is too fine-grained.
	2. Operations and portfolio management costs outweigh the benefits.
	3. Contribution to solution is limited.
	4. Functionality redundancy detected among services.
Solution	Consolidate services by reconciling functionality commonalities, reducing process redundancy, and eliminating identities.
Applicability	1. Apply when consolidation of atomic service or service cluster is required (nonhierarchical structures).
	2. Employ when identity of services can be merged.
	3. Use to refactor source code.
	4. Utilize for rearchitecture and redesign initiatives.
Method	Remove boundaries from the unified services by reconciling their common operations and merging their redundant interfaces.
Benefits	Promotion of software asset consolidation.
Risks	1. It would be impractical to reverse a unification process.
	2. The product of a unification activity may turn out to be too coarse grained.
Notation	Use the "Unified" symbol.

EXHIBIT 19.11   NONHIERARCHICAL STRUCTURE UNIFICATION SUMMARY TABLE

Anti-Patterns.   Consider the anti-patterns and best practices that are devised to guide practitioners to utilize the Nonhierarchical Unification pattern. These are fundamental rules, depicted in Exhibit 19.12, that dictate the best way to achieve the process of service unification.

Anti-Pattern Name	Best Practice
Unification as Aggregation	The unification modeling operation merges service structures and is not devised to aggregate service formations.
Excessive Unification	Avoid excessive unification activities that yield bulky and very coarse-grained entities.
Mixed Unification	Unification of dissimilar service structures, such as service cluster and atomic service, should be avoided.

EXHIBIT 19.12   NONHIERARCHICAL UNIFICATION ANTI-PATTERNS

HIERARCHICAL STRUCTURE UNIFICATION PATTERN.   The Hierarchical Structure Unification pattern addresses the process and the method for merging services whose internal structures are layered and follow a systematic parent/child model. The chief questions that are being answered here are: How can a practitioner unify two or more composite services? What are the steps necessary to accomplish consolidation of hierarchies? How can tightly coupled service formations be reconciled? The answers to these queries are provided by the Hierarchical Structure Unification pattern that advocates a three-step incremental and methodical approach to unifying complex structures: First, the motivation for asset consolidation should be introduced. Second, a meticulous analysis of the composite structure should be conducted. Finally, service modeling steps should drive the solution.

Problem.   The answers to the question: "Why are we required to unify services?" are straightforward: A too fine-grained service should be consolidated with a service alike because it does not offer substantial contribution to the business or technology. In addition, a service should be a candidate for unification because its reusability rates are low and its consumer base diminishes. Finally, a service should be united with its peers because of luck of funding to support its operations, maintenance, and monitoring.

Solution.   The proposition to unify assets that cannot stand on their own is somehow perilous. Is there any guarantee that a coarse-grained service that is made up of former fine-grained services can be more valuable to the organization? Is there any assurance that a merger between two or more services will yield an entity that is less costly to the enterprise? Is there any promise that the service unification process will produce a software executable that is less complex than its predecessor(s)?

There is a tendency to unify services with the anticipation that a drastic alteration of their structure can repair their design, architecture, and construction deficiencies. This assertion is not always justified. Therefore, the unification process must begin with a scrupulous analysis effort that identifies the benefits and disadvantages of service consolidation. This step is even more relevant when it comes to merging composite services that are comprised of nested service levels.

The yielding entity should not only embody the identity of its originators, it should also offer comparable capabilities. In addition, it is highly recommended that a consolidation process that involves fine-grained hierarchical structures should be merged and transformed into an Atomic service to simplify the artifact. Consider the following Hierarchical Structure Unification steps that involve two or more composite services:

1. Separate internal services by employing the "Decomposed" symbol.
2. Transform composite to atomic structures if they do not consist of any internal service by using the "Transformed" symbol.
3. Consolidate all derived atomic services by utilizing the "Unified" symbol.

Example.   Exhibit 19.13 represents two views of the Hierarchical Structure Unification pattern: 3D View (on top) and Service-Oriented Modeling Formal Diagram View (on bottom). The former depicts a unification process that involves the two composite services CO-1 and CO-2. These are unified into the atomic service A-UNI.

The bottom view introduces the formal modeling perspective. Seven simple steps involve the unification of composite services CO-1 and CO-2:

1. Atomic services A-1 and A-2 are decomposed from their corresponding parent CO-1 by using the "Decomposed" symbol.
2. Since CO-1 is now empty. Therefore it is transformed to atomic service A-UNI by utilizing the "Transformed" symbol.
3. The decomposed atomic services A-1 and A-2 are unified with atomic service A-UNI (continues to carry its name) by utilizing the "Unified" symbol.
4. Atomic service A-3 is decomposed from composite service CO-2 (note the "Decomposed" symbol used for this activity).
5. Since CO-2 is now empty, it is transformed to atomic service A-CO2 by utilizing the "Transformed" symbol.
6. Atomic service A-3 is unified with atomic service A-CO2 (continues to carry its name) by employing the "Unified" symbol.
7. Finally, atomic service A-CO2 is unified with atomic service A-UNI by using the "Unified" symbol. A-UNI continues to carry its original name.

Synopsis.   The Hierarchical Structure Unification pattern addresses merging operations between fine-grained composite services. Exhibit 19.14 identifies that key features of the pattern. The top

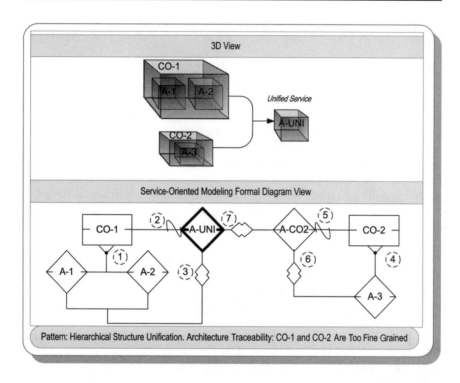

EXHIBIT 19.13   HIERARCHICAL STRUCTURE UNIFICATION PATTERN EXAMPLE

Pattern Identification	
Name	Hierarchical Structure Unification Pattern
Category	Structural Generalization

Problems, Solutions, and Implementations	
Problem	1. Service is too fine-grained.
	2. Service is comprised of internal complex hierarchical structure.
	3. Operations and portfolio management costs outweigh the benefits.
	3. Contribution to solution is limited.
	4. Functionality redundancy is detected.
Solution	Consolidate services by simplifying their hierarchical internal structures, reconciling functionality commonalities, reducing process redundancy, and merging identities.
Applicability	1. Apply when consolidation of composite fine-grained services is required (services with hierarchical structures).
	2. Employ when service identities can be merged.
	3. Use to refactor source code.
	4. Utilize for rearchitecture and redesign initiatives.
Method	Simplifying services' hierarchical structures by decomposing their encompassed child services, eliminating their common operations, and merging their redundant interfaces.
Benefits	1. Service granularity alignment.
	2. Reduction of design and architecture complexities.
	3. Promotion of software asset consolidation.
Risks	1. It would be impractical to reverse a unification process.
	2. The yielding product of a unification activity may turn out to be too coarse-grained.
Notation	Use the "Unified," "Decomposed," and "Transformed" symbols.

EXHIBIT 19.14   HIERARCHICAL STRUCTURE UNIFICATION SUMMARY TABLE

Anti-Pattern Name	Best Practice
Impractical Unification Product	The yielding unification product should be an atomic service that embodies its originators' functionality and identities.
Excessive Unification	Avoid excessive unification activities that yield bulky and very coarse-grained entities.
Improper Unification Order	Internal services should first be decomposed from the parent service before any unification activity.
Empty Composite Service	A composite service whose internal services were removed should be transformed to an atomic service. That is, a composite service should never be empty.

Exhibit 19.15   Hierarchical Structure Unification Anti-Patterns

section (Pattern Identification) introduces this pattern and its specialty. Note that the unification process falls under the Structural Generalization category because the unified product increases its solution capabilities. In addition, the bottom section specifies the problem, solution, applicability, method, benefits, and risks involved when using the Hierarchical Structure Unification pattern.

Anti-Patterns.   The Hierarchical Structure Unification anti-patterns offer fundamental best practices when the unification process of complex structures takes place. These are depicted in Exhibit 19.15. Remember, this structural generalization approach typically engages fine-grained composite services that must be first decomposed and transformed to atomic services. The final product should be an atomic service larger than its originating service yet its design is simpler.

STRUCTURAL COMPOUNDING ANALYSIS: PATTERNS AND IMPLEMENTATION

Another form of structural generalization is service compounding. This is simply a method that guides practitioners how to extend a service's offerings and capabilities by linking it to its peer services. This grouping concept is introduced to foster a service partnership rather than creating a self-sufficient and very coarse-grained service that is difficult to operate and support. The term "partnership" implies that a group of services are responsible for accomplishing a mutual goal by collaborating on message exchange and transaction execution. But this form of cooperation should not be confused with service clustering. In contrast, a cluster formation is comprised of distributed services that usually operate across applications and organization. Structural compounding, though, is a modest version of clustering, by which two or more services are structurally positioned in close proximity. This coalition is designed simply to extend and strengthen a proposed solution.

The neighboring relationships that are founded between a compounded service formation members are to better structure a deployment environment and offer a sense of order to the integration of software entities. Think about a service compound as a group of related entities that share mutual goals yet are structurally connected to simplify service construction efforts, integration ventures, deployment efforts, and maintenance initiatives. This bundling activity is influenced by the context of the involved services. The term "context" in that regard pertains to business or technical associations, such as an accounting, trading, banking, or insurance service.

One of the most crucial aspects of the service compounding process is the ability to offload responsibilities from an individual service by complementing its capabilities with offerings of external adjacent services that collaborate to meet business requirements and technical specifications.

STRUCTURAL COMPOUNDING PATTERNS AND ANTI-PATTERNS.   The Structural Compounding process introduces patterns and anti-patterns that offer service structural analysis best practices designed to help architects, modelers, developers, analysts, and managers to discover, inspect, and model services efficiently. The patterns presented in the sections that follow elaborate on the process of service compounding, service augmentation, and service capability extension. However, the anti-pattern section discusses the misuse of the compounding activity and the best practices to which the practitioner should adhere.

STRUCTURAL COMPOUNDING PATTERN.   The Structural Compounding pattern addresses the method and process for creating a service group. This straightforward concept of gathering services to tackle a problem and to offer a bolder solution, *without altering* the internal structure of each particular participant service, is the art of compounding. Recall that such an assembly effort creates a new collaborative boundary of execution that includes two or more services. But the final product should *not* be regarded as a service cluster because its members are not distributed, yet they are adjacent. This service neighboring scheme is merely devised to institute a group of services that are structurally bonded by their relationships and contextual connotation. It is all about increasing the solution power to alleviate organizational concerns by employing structural compounding means.

Although the most important aspect of the Structural Compounding pattern is the emphasis on structural arrangements, the contextual aspect is a vital influencing motivation. For example, imagine a group of three services that are assembled to contribute to the doctor appointments automation process of a healthcare division: Patient Diagnosis Service, Doctor Appointments Service, and Appointment Verification Service. Indeed, their apparent contextual affiliation links them to achieve a mutual goal. But beyond their conceptual association, the structural aspect requires the attention of architects, modelers, analysts, developers, and managers.

Problem.   There are two chief concerns that drive the motivation for employing the Structural Compounding pattern: Service granularity and unstructured deployment environment. First, a service boundary should be extended based on architecture and design best practice guidelines. That is, expanding the scope of a service solution should comply with an organizational structural policy that the architect, modeler, analyst, developer, and manager should be aware of and attend to. The term "boundary" here pertains to the volume of operations, business or technical processes, and interfaces that a service is allowed to execute. It is also about the upper limit to which a service can grow without compromising service quality. In other words, service granularity principles should not be ignored. As the reader may already know, exceeding the boundary of a service can form a bulky and very coarse-grained entity that typically introduces management nightmares and contributes to performance degradation because of structural inefficiencies.

Second, two other significant problems that often emerge during a service development life cycle are unstructured deployment environments and disorderly service management. These are caused by the inability to classify services based on their contribution to the organization. This service grouping and categorization effort should be driven by proper design. But lack of such best practices yield disarrayed service installations that do not follow logical architecture schemes. Unstructured integration environments that are hard to control and monitor are typically the result of poor design practices. Lack of logical architecture disciplines and the inability to clearly define relationships between services and their corresponding consumers are also attributed to undefined collaboration principles that drive message exchange and delivery paths.

Solution.   One of the chief reasons that practitioners should utilize the Structural Compounding pattern is to enable the growth of a solution's scope by grouping services to carry out a mutual mission. This approach is about augmentation of a service's capabilities by enhancing its collaboration with its external peer services rather than growing from the inside. Moreover, the risk of exceeding structural limits promotes the simple concept of compounding that plainly enables practitioners grouping services to widen the solution spectrum.

A compound arrangement may include atomic or composite services that are "attached" to each other to promote their agendas. In addition, as mentioned previously, this exercise is about enforcing an order and design aesthetic to enhance the logical aspect of service partnership. To fulfill this alliance fundamental design and architecture steps should be considered, such as involving associated services in executing transactions, establishing robust message exchange mechanisms, and instituting contracts to support this collaboration.

Example.   Exhibit 19.16 illustrates the Structural Compounding pattern that represents two different perspectives: the 3D View (far right) and the Service-Oriented Modeling Formal Diagram View (far left). This scenario involves three services that are grouped to provide a collaborative solution to a problem. These entities include the two composite services CO-1 and CO-2 and the atomic service A-4. Note the use of the "Compounded" symbol in the formal diagram view. It denotes the grouping of the three services that form a compound relationship. In addition, the "Aggregated" symbol is utilized to describe the internal structures of the composite services CO-1 and CO-2. The former aggregates atomic services A-2 and A-3, and the latter consists of only one atomic service, A-1.

Synopsis.   Exhibit 19.17 identifies the major Structural Compounding pattern problems and solutions. As indicated, the driving challenge is extending a service's capabilities beyond its current structural boundary. To exceed this limit, the solution supports service compounding, by which a group of services are harnessed to support a collaborative remedy to the problem. This approach also advocates avoiding changes to a service's internal operations by augmenting its operations with external resources.

Anti-Patterns.   The Structural Compounding anti-patterns are designed to alert practitioners about misuse and impractical implementations that can lead to performance degradation and ambiguous

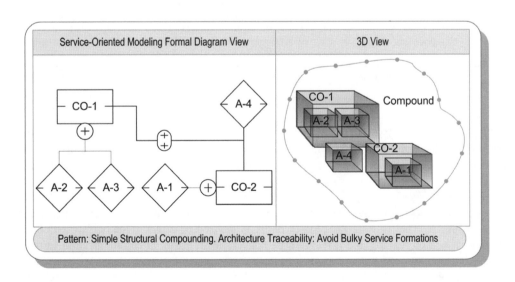

EXHIBIT 19.16   STRUCTURAL COMPOUNDING PATTERN EXAMPLE

Pattern Identification	
Name	Structural Compounding Pattern
Category	Structural Generalization

Problems, Solutions, and Implementations	
Problem	1. The solution that is offered by a service requires structural augmentation.
	2. The service capability boundary has been maximized and cannot be extended to provide additional solutions.
Solution	1. Enlarge the boundary of a solution by compounding two or more services.
	2. Bond two or more services' structures to form a group of service executions.
Applicability	1. Apply structural compounding to form groups of services to enable contextual affiliation.
	2. Employ when a service has reached its growth limits in terms of its granularity scale, yet it requires structural augmentation.
Method	Assemble a group of services to provide a solution without adding operations to any of the participating entities. This structural compounding process may require the establishment of new relationship and interfaces.
Benefits	Promotion of a loosely coupled service environment by avoiding creation of coarse-grained services.
Risks	Excessive service compounding can slow down message exchange performance.
Notation	Use the "Compounded" symbol.

Exhibit 19.17   Structural Compounding Pattern Summary Table

service structure formations that are difficult to manage and support. Exhibit 19.18 identifies the three major best practices that practitioners should attend to.

Anti-Pattern Name	Best Practice
Excessive Compounding	Avoid excessive compounding of services. The charter of a service group is to augment a solution and complement a single service's capabilities by compounding a limited number of services.
Distributed Compounding	Service members of a compound formation should not be distributed across the organization and should be confined to a local implementation.
Impractical Compounding	Avoid the service compounding process if a single service can offer an adequate solution to a problem.

Exhibit 19.18   Structural Compounding Anti-Patterns

SERVICE AS PLUG-IN PATTERN.   As discussed earlier, the service compounding process simply extends a service's capabilities by collaborating with neighboring services.[3] This arrangement forms a group of service members, each of which contributes its share to solving a problem by actively participating in a message exchange with consumers. The Structural Compounding (346) pattern, discussed in the previous section, supports this partnership notion. The Service as Plug-In pattern, however, is not based on an equal contribution to a solution when it comes to exchanging messages with consumers. That is, here the plug-in entity is devised to extend a service's capabilities by offering an add-on feature, and it may not be actively involved in all communication forms with consumers.

The Service as Plug-In pattern approach is about extending the behavior of a service without the need to change its internal structural construct. This is an *external* addition that supplements a service's functionality with minimal risk to its stability. These type of extensions, known as utility or accessory services, offer fine-grained complementary operations, such as encryption of private content, universalization of text,[4] transformation of data schemas, user credential verification, user interface validations, e-mail utility, and more.

Problem.   The Service as Plug-In pattern is designed to address two fundamental challenges that typically affect the granularity level of a service and introduce unclear and, at times, unstructured internal service modules. The first is a common problem that can be found with many implementations: mixing or coupling business logic with utility-type activities, namely technical implementation. For example, a service that accepts book orders may also include a language translation utility that helps international customers interact with the service in their own language. This tightly coupled approach involving the book orders process with the language translation feature should be avoided to foster business agility and software elasticity.

The second challenge is influenced by the first: Coupling vital service capabilities with accessory-type implementations may increase the size of a service and expand its boundaries beyond an organization's acceptable best practices guidelines. Doing this contributes to the formation of coarse-grained entities that are impractical and inflexible to maintain and monitor.

Solution.   The solution to these challenges is to adapt a loosely coupled design approach by creating a service that is delegated business logic processing duties and complementing its operations with a plug-in and external service that offers utility functions. In other words, this solution is about the *structural separation* of utility functions from the main business logic and associating both implementations to a compound structure. Again, this separation-of-concerns principle requires the establishment of a utility service that should not be an integral part of a particular service implementation.

Extending the behavior of a service by compounding external capabilities should be accomplished during integration time rather than compilation time. In other words, avoid bundling service business logic with miscellaneous implementations that do not directly contribute to attaining the goals. Doing this will assist with reducing the service's executable size and enhancing its performance. Furthermore, this loosely coupled environment will allow other services to reuse these external utility services.

Example.   Exhibit 19.19 depicts three different perspectives: 3D View (a visual presentation of the involved services), Asset View (identify services' contexts), and the Service-Oriented Modeling Formal Design View. These illustrate a similar structural composition scenario to the one that is presented in the Structural Compounding (346) pattern section. They differ, however, by their contextual drivers. Here the motivation for grouping the involved services is influenced by their individual category. As is apparent, the Book Order Composite Service (CO-1) is grouped along with its two main utilities: Language Translator Utility Atomic Service (A-3) and Currency Conversion Utility Atomic Service (A-4). These are plug-in services that extend the functionality of service CO-1.

In addition, the service grouping effort is indicated by the "Compounded" symbol that is illustrated in the formal modeling diagram. Again, remember that this illustration exemplifies how a service's structural enforcement enables the compounding of service plug-ins influenced by contextual needs. Finally, observe that the indicated Architectural Traceability (on bottom) is associated with fostering a loosely coupled service environment. This explains the motivation behind the service compounding effort.

Synopsis.   Exhibit 19.20 identifies the major challenges that motivate the utilization of the Service as Plug-In pattern. As discussed, the main difficulties are associated with the creation of coarse-grained services that consist of business logic along with utility features. The solution to this

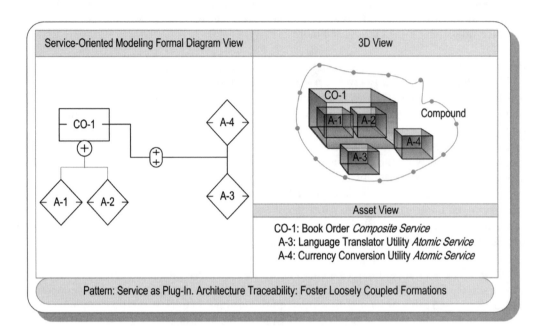

EXHIBIT 19.19   SERVICE AS PLUG-IN PATTERN EXAMPLE

Pattern Identification

Name	Service as Plug-In Pattern
Category	Structural Generalization

Problems, Solutions, and Implementations

Problem	1. The service capability boundary has been maximized and cannot be extended to provide specialized or specific features. 2. Utility functionality is tightly coupled with service logic.
Solution	Add service plug-in to provide specialty extension to a service that can be configured during integration time, and avoid augmentation of a service during compilation time.
Applicability	Apply to a service that has reached its growth limits in terms of its granularity scale yet requires structural extension to accommodate plug-in features.
Method	Utilize the service compounding approach to extend service capabilities by adding external plug-ins that can be integrated at integration time. This method advocates building autonomous and reusable plug-in services that offer utility capabilities (also known as add-on or snap-in).
Benefits	1. Promotion of a loosely coupled service environment by avoiding creation of coarse-grained services. 2. Decouple business logic from miscellaneous implementations.
Risks	1. Creation of compound formations that consist of too finely grained plug-in services. 2. Construction of plug-in services that will be underutilized.
Notation	Use the "Compounded" symbol.

EXHIBIT 19.20   SERVICE AS PLUG-IN PATTERN SUMMARY TABLE

Anti-Pattern Name	Best Practice
Fine-Grained Plug-Ins	Avoid the creation of autonomous and too finely grained plug-in services.
Underutilized Plug-Ins	Foster reusability of plug-in services.
Compilation Time Plug-Ins	A plug-in service should be autonomous and integrated during integration time rather than at compilation time.

Exhibit 19.21   Service as Plug-in Anti-Patterns

problem is clearly to separate plug-in implementations by creating external utility services that can be reused by various applications and services across the organization.

Anti-Patterns.   Remember, the plug-in category identifies services that are affiliated with utility implementations. These auxiliary entities should be decomposed from business logic, formalized as independent services, and deployed adjacent to their corresponding consuming services. Avoid too finely grained plug-in services that are impractical and offer low return on investment. Consider these best practices and their anti-patterns, which are listed in Exhibit 19.21.

CONTRACT ANALYSIS: PATTERNS AND IMPLEMENTATION

The contract analysis process should be pursued to better understand the relationship that a service maintains with its consumers. This inspection that an architect, analyst, developer, manager, or modeler should conduct is associated with studying the nature of the contracts between services and their corresponding consumers when pursuing the structural generalization process. This analysis may later lead to contract enhancement, optimization propositions, and discovery of new mechanisms to improve contact schemes. The motivation behind such an examination is driven by two chief imperatives: (1) the need to extend the scope of a solution typically triggers structural growth of a service; and (2) a service formation is also subject to extension if its consumer community has increased and thus diversified. Both motivations can influence the manner by which a contract is founded a great deal.

Another important aspect to consider is that not all the relationships between services and their associated consumers must be established by a contract. Some legacy technologies utilize wrappers because they are not advanced enough to accommodate contract bindings—the term "wrapper" pertains to adding source code or adapters to enable compatibility between new and old technologies. Furthermore, it would be impractical to institute contracts between child and parent services, for example, in a composite formation. Thus, the contract analysis effort should yield feasible recommendations as to how and in which circumstances a contract can be beneficial.

CONTRACT ANALYSIS: PATTERNS AND ANTI-PATTERNS.   The sections that follow elaborate on two major patterns that are designed to assist practitioners in establishing contracts between services and their related consumers. The first, the Contract Externalization (351) pattern, depicts the mechanisms and process for founding a contract between consumers and aggregated formation service members. It pertains to services that are an integral part of a composite service or a service cluster. The second discussed pattern, the Multiple Binding Contracts (355) pattern, provides solutions to accommodate a diversified consumer base and to satisfy its complex requirements.

CONTRACT EXTERNALIZATION PATTERN.   The structural generalization analysis discipline that is elaborated on in this chapter addresses the influence of a service's capabilities and increased functionality on its overall structure. The reader may remember that aggregation is the mechanism that enables the extension of service operations. This extension inevitably triggers alterations to the known service formations: composite, cluster, or atomic services. As anticipated, the exposure to the outside world of a fine-grained service that is aggregated into any of these structures would be drastically reduced. Because of this service isolation activity, this practice is often called service hiding.

The Contract Externalization pattern offers best practices and methods to address contract modifications in case a service is aggregated into a larger entity to help augment the functionality of the latter. In other words, modifications to contract conditions and reassignment of service-level agreements (SLAs) must take place when a service's visibility is decreased. The visibility of a service is reduced when it is isolated from the outside world or simply hidden from its consumers.

Problem. One of the major challenges with a service that is contained within another service or is part of a cluster is the effort to maintain strict security measures that can guarantee its flawless operations and execution in production. Moreover, shielding a service from the outside world, hiding it from its consumers, or reducing its visibility level comes with a cost that must be analyzed and justified. This inspection process is associated with the links that an aggregated service must maintain with its outside partners and consumers. More specifically, discontinuing contracts because of efforts to consolidate services and aggregate them in larger formations is the core of the concern.

To ensure the stability of service operations, the service-oriented discovery and analysis discipline best practices advocate that an encapsulated service, an aggregated entity, should not maintain contracts with its external trading partners and should not communicate directly with its consumers. This rule obviously introduces challenges to the design and architecture efforts. An alternative approach must be carved out to funnel messages that are sent to internal services and accommodate their response to the sending parties.

Solution. As discussed previously, a fine-grained service can be aggregated and thus hidden in one of the three major service structures: composite, cluster, and atomic. First, when it comes to aggregating a service into a composite formation, a hierarchical structure, it is advisable to establish links to the outside world through a higher authority: its parent hosting service.

Second, the same rule should be applied to a service cluster constituent. It is highly recommended that a cluster member should relinquish its contracts that have been established with corresponding consumers; these bonds should be reassigned to the cluster's "gravitation point." A cluster gravity point—discussed in detail in Chapter 12—is typically a service that acts as a traffic controller to receive and send messages on behalf of cluster members.

Finally, if an aggregation activity involves a hosting atomic service, the practitioner should apply the very same solution that is recommended for the composite formation discussed earlier. This action should be taken because ultimately an atomic formation that aggregates services is transformed into a hierarchical structure, namely a composite service.

These three solutions should adhere to the policy that prohibits direct communications between an aggregated service and the external world. At first, following such a best practice appears to be an easy task. However, a thorough examination of the contract details and its interfaces would be required. This will ensure that the channels of communication with outside consumers remain intact. That is, employ the Contract Externalization pattern to guarantee that the service isolation process will not affect the integrity of message exchange and transactions. Consider these three steps required for attaining this goal:

1. If the service is contained in a hierarchical composite structure, locate the aggregating entity (the parent service). If the service is a part of a cluster, find the gravitational point—the service that interfaces with the outside world. Either of these entities should serve as point-of-contacts for the aggregated services.
2. Remove the corresponding interfaces from the contained service and assign them to the point-of-contact service.
3. Republish the service to the organization service repository.

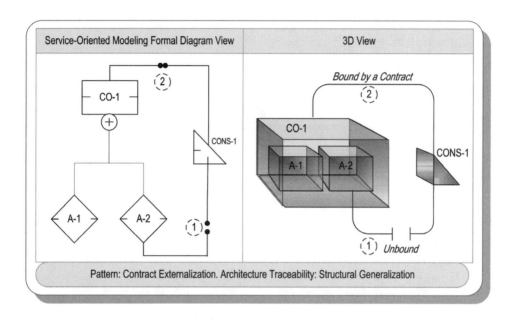

EXHIBIT 19.22   CONTRACT EXTERNALIZATION WITH COMPOSITE FORMATION PATTERN

Example.   Exhibit 19.22 illustrates the usage of the Contract Externalization pattern that depicts two different perspectives: the 3D View (far right) and the Service-Oriented Modeling Formal Diagram View (far left). The former depicts the general concept of service encapsulation and traces the sequence of the Contract Externalization event, while the formal modeling diagram uses the "Bound" and "Unbound" symbols to describe the two-step contract reassignment.

Two services and one consumer take part in this contract transition: composite service CO-1 and its aggregated atomic service A-1, and the consumer CONS-1. In the first step (marked number 1), the "Unbound" symbol denotes that the contract between the atomic service A-2 and its consumer CONS-1 has been discontinued. The second activity (identified as number 2), indicates that a contract was reestablished between the composite service CO-1 and the consumer CONS-1. This contract reassignment process attends to the policy that prohibits an internal service (child entity) from communicating with outside consumers. Instead, the contract is reassigned to the containing service CO-1 (parent).

In the same manner, the contract reassignment process takes place when a service cluster is involved. Exhibit 19.23 depicts this activity. Both apparent perspectives—the 3D View and the Service-Oriented Modeling Formal Diagram View—introduce two steps for Contract Externalization pattern completion. Both views identify the aggregating cluster CL-1 and its encompassed service members, A-1, CO-1, and A-2. Note that the first step (marked number 1) begins with contract discontinuation between services A-1 and the consumer CONS-1. In step 2 (denoted by number 2), the contract is reestablished between composite service CO-1 and consumer CONS-1. In addition, service CO-1 is regarded as the gravitation point in cluster CL-1.

Synopsis.   Exhibit 19.24 summarizes the motivation for utilizing the Contract Externalization pattern. This synopsis outlines the major problems, solutions, methods for implementation, and the accompanied risks that are affiliated with the employment of this pattern. As is apparent, the chief challenge that should be addressed is associated with the common question that architects,

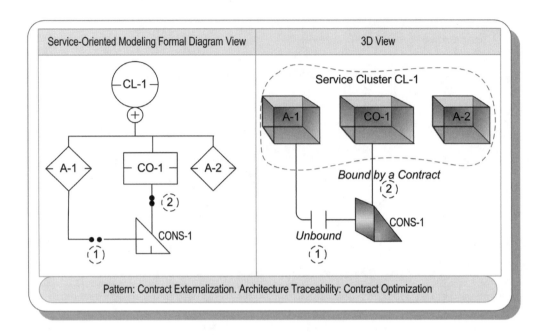

EXHIBIT 19.23   CONTRACT EXTERNALIZATION WITH CLUSTER FORMATION PATTERN

Pattern Identification	
Name	Contract Externalization Pattern
Category	Structural Generalization
Problems, Solutions, and Implementations	
Problem	How should an aggregated fine-grained service that is bound by a contract to peer services or consumers be protected and hidden from the outside world and yet continue to fulfill its contractual obligations?
Solution	A replacement contract should be established between a parent service on behalf of its corresponding child service.
Applicability	Applies to contained services in a hierarchical composite formation or to a service cluster member.
Method	The contract analysis process advocates pursuit of two steps:
	1. Terminate a contract between a contained service and its outside consumers.
	2. Reestablish the contract between the parent service and the very same consumers.
Benefits	1. Service isolation and source code hiding.
	2. Beefing up security.
Risks	Reassigning a contract or changing its terms may lead to run-time errors and inconsistencies.
Notation	Use the "Bound" and "Unbound" symbols.

EXHIBIT 19.24   CONTRACT EXTERNALIZATION PATTERN SUMMARY TABLE

Anti-Pattern Name	Best Practice
Parent/Child Contract	Avoid establishing a contract between a parent service and its corresponding child services in a composite hierarchical structure.
Hierarchy Level Contract	Steer clear of founding a contract between two child services that are positioned on the same hierarchy level in a composite service formation.
Talking to Strangers[a]	An aggregated service should not maintain contractual relationships with outside consumers. Contract obligations should be fulfilled by the outermost parent service in the composite service hierarchy.

EXHIBIT 19.25   CONTRACT EXTERNALIZATION ANTI-PATTERNS

[a]www.cmcrossroads.com/bradapp/docs/demeter-intro.html.

developers, analysts, modelers, and managers wrestle with: How do we protect and hide a service from its consumers and yet enable the fulfillment of its contractual obligations?

Anti-Patterns.   Exhibit 19.25 introduces three major Contract Externalization anti-patterns and their affiliated best practices. These are the chief principles that should guide practitioners about how to both protect a service from its consumers and still allow flawless execution of its offerings. Furthermore, the introduced anti-patterns address tenets for services hiding in a hierarchical formation. These best practices pertains to composite service structures that maintain parent/child relationships.

MULTIPLE BINDING CONTRACTS PATTERN.   The structural generalization analysis should also address the impact on contracts that are established between services and their corresponding consumers. Why should a contract model be changed in light of service growth? One of the major reasons for contract redesign is the growing diversity of consumers that a service must satisfy.

Thus the Multiple Binding Contracts pattern is devised both to tackle a growing consumer community and to respond to its rising business and technical demands. The proposed solutions should alleviate the imposed challenges of the conventional one-to-many contract style, wherein a service is bound by a single contract to multiple consumers. Therefore, multiple contracts can be founded to serve a diverse consumer base.

Problem.   The increase of a service's consumer base and the demand for widening the scope of its offered solutions are the chief causes of concern when it comes to maintaining contracts. Not only is the growing diversity of consumers in terms of their various affiliations to lines of business and organizations one of the major challenges; increases of consumers' requirements and consumption volumes are also subjects for consideration.

The chief questions that one should ask when attempting to accommodate consumer business imperatives are associated with the capability of the contract to satisfy requirements: Is the current contract general enough to facilitate consumers who are associated with multiple business practices? Is the designated contract flexible enough to enable changes to its underpinning interfaces without affecting the functionality that is provided to all consumers?

Solution.   To solve these challenges, a many-to-many contract scheme should be developed to enable consumer diversity and address their vital business or technical requirements. The term "many-to-many" contract design implies that a single service should maintain multiple contracts to satisfy multiple consumer groups that share common requirements.

Example.   The many-to-many service contract scheme is illustrated in Exhibit 19.26. The two different apparent perspectives—the 3D View (far right) and Service-Oriented Modeling Formal

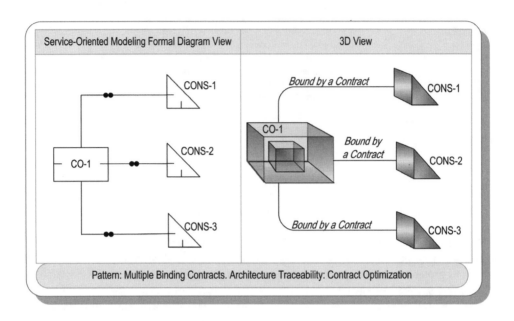

EXHIBIT 19.26   MULTIPLE BINDING CONTRACTS PATTERN EXAMPLE

Diagram View (far left)—depict a scenario that involves one composite service named CO-1 and its corresponding consumers CONS-1, CONS-2, and CONS-3. Note the use of the "Bound" symbols, which denote three binding contracts between the service and its three affiliated consumers.

Synopsis.   Exhibit 19.27 introduces a specifications summary for the Multiple Binding Contracts pattern that is designed to provide solutions and methods to accommodate a growing and diversified

Pattern Identification	
Name	Multiple Binding Contracts Pattern
Category	Structural Generalization

Problems, Solutions, and Implementations	
Problem	A service must support a growing number of consumers because of the growth of its structure and capabilities. A single contract cannot accommodate the diversity of its consumers' consumption and functionality requirements.
Solution	Establish multiple contracts for a single service to support consumer variety.
Applicability	Apply to atomic and composite services.
Method	1. Conduct a consumer segmentation analysis that can shed light on the diversity of service requestors.
	2. Group consumers by consumption requirements.
	3. Establish multiple contracts to accommodate consumption needs.
Benefits	1. Fostering loosely coupled contract binding by reducing dependencies on interfaces.
	2. Promoting software elasticity by eliminating rigid contract design.
Risks	Increasing contract count for a single service may lead to operations or interface redundancy.
Notation	Use the contract "Bound" symbol.

EXHIBIT 19.27   MULTIPLE BINDING CONTRACTS PATTERN SUMMARY TABLE

Anti-Pattern Name	Best Practice
Impractical Multiple Contract Binding	The establishment of multiple contracts for a fine-grained service is impractical.
Excessive Contract Binding	Avoid the creation of a large number of contracts for a single service.
"Many-to-One" Contract Binding	Avoid instituting multiple contracts for a single consumer that involve a single service.

EXHIBIT 19.28   MULTIPLE BINDING CONTRACTS ANTI-PATTERNS

consumer community. As was discussed earlier, the proposed solution is conducive to creating multiple contracts to increase flexibility and satisfy consumer requirements.

Anti-Patterns.   Consider the anti-patterns listed in Exhibit 19.28. These best practices are designed to guide practitioners in how to best establish multiple contracts between a single service and its diversified clients. Note that the one-to-many contract relationship is the acceptable best practice. The many-to-one approach, whereby a single service maintains multiple contracts for a single consumer, should be avoided.

DELIVERABLES

As with any software development effort, the formation of an existing service is altered. Its structure is enhanced, separated, reduced, augmented, or retired. The structural generalization process always contributes to service logical and physical growth. This growth ought to be recorded and proposed in the internal service composition diagram (discussed in Chapter 18) that depicts transformation of a service during the generalization process. Study the patterns and examples in this chapter and prepare an analysis proposition that reflects a solution to an organizational concern.

SUMMARY

- The structural generalization process is about broadening a service logical and physical formation by uniting services, augmenting service capabilities, compounding services, or aggregating services.
- The four types of analyses that facilitate the structural generalization of a service are aggregation analysis, unification analysis, compounding analysis, and contract analysis.
- The aggregation analysis process introduces mechanisms that facilitate hierarchical and Nonhierarchical Aggregation by employing patterns and anti-patterns.
- The unification analysis method advocates to merge two or more services guided by patterns and anti-patterns.
- The compounding analysis elaborates on how to group services to widen the scope of the solution.
- Finally, the contract analysis is devised to optimize and enhance the contract model that binds services and related consumers when a structural generalization is pursued.

Notes

1. Contextual service modeling is discussed in detail in Chapters 14 through 17.
2. Allen Newell, *Unified Theories of Cognition* (Cambridge, MA: Harvard University Press, 1987), p. 117.
3. Somehow like the Martin Fowler's Plugin pattern (http://martinfowler.com/eaaCatalog/plugin.html). However, the Service as Plug-In (348) pattern is utility feature added externally by a service compound member.
4. The term "text universalization" pertains to Unicode Character Encoding Model as defined by ISO/IEC 10646. For further reading, refer to http://unicode.org/reports/tr17/#CharacterEncodingModel.

CHAPTER 20

STRUCTURAL SPECIFICATION ANALYSIS PROCESS AND MODELING PATTERNS

Unlike the structural generalization practice (discussed in Chapter 19) that promotes the broadening of a service internal structure, the structural specification method advocates dissecting a service into smaller and more manageable units of analysis. Furthermore, this process introduces a set of best practices devised to facilitate *decomposition*, *retirement*, *substitution*, or *swapping* of service capabilities. These modeling operations obviously attend to the architecture best practices that encourage breaking up an overly coarse-grained service to promote loosely coupled service formations.

Structural specification is also about source code, design, and architecture refactoring. The term "refactoring" pertains to the enhancement of a service structure by analyzing first its internal formation to propose a better architecture solution and improve performance and reuse. This venture includes the utilization of modeling operations that are applied to remove impractical implementations or optimize their structures. In addition, the refactoring process may be pursued to update a service's dated capabilities and technologies or to swap aggregated services between two or more containing entities, such as composite services and service clusters.

This chapter introduces four methods and affiliated patterns that can assist practitioners with service decomposition and internal service component manipulation to optimize service capabilities:

1. **Decomposition analysis.** The decomposition analysis approach addresses how to break up a service structure into smaller components without causing major interruption to business or technical execution.
2. **Subtraction analysis.** The subtraction analysis practice is another modeling operation guide to service retirement. Following this process enables proper elimination of service components or a complete service removal from production environment.
3. **Refactoring analysis.** The refactoring analysis process is all about enhancement of service capabilities by utilizing component swapping and/or a substation to boost service reuse and the consumer base.
4. **Contract analysis.** The contract analysis practice is devised to perfect the binding relationships between services and corresponding consumer in the face of an ongoing service structural specifications effort.

The sections that follow elaborate on each of the analysis practices and introduce affiliated patterns to facilitate rapid solutions.

DECOMPOSITION ANALYSIS: PATTERNS AND IMPLEMENTATION

The decomposition process is about breaking down a service into smaller, fine-grained services that should not be retired and become autonomous entities or get aggregated into other formations. This isolation of service capabilities typically is applied to composite services or service clusters. The chief motivation for conducting decomposition analysis is driven by the practitioner's discontent over service performance, tightly coupled service internal components, problems with service maintenance, and challenges that are introduced by complex service structures. These may induce serious performance degradation in production environments and raise organizational expenditures.

When it comes to analyzing and dissecting an atomic entity, the term "decomposition" does not adequately describe the activities that a developer pursues during source code optimization or refactoring. An atomic service should also be subject to examination and source code enhancement activities. A more accurate depiction of this process, however, is *separation of operations*. Remember, an atomic service is defined as an indivisible entity that is impractical to subdivide into smaller pieces, yet a rigorous analysis should be pursued to streamline its internal construct.

STRUCTURAL DECOMPOSITION PATTERNS AND ANTI-PATTERNS. The sections that follow introduce two different flavors of service decomposition: *partial separation* and *total dissection*. The former is represented by the Selective Decomposition (360) pattern that typically is employed to reduce the scope of a service's capabilities and trim down its functionality. The total dissection approach, offered by the Total Fragmentation (365) pattern, is another service analysis mechanism that advocates a revamping of a service's internal structure. Theses two processes are designed to assist practitioners with code optimization and loosening up tightly coupled service architecture.

SELECTIVE DECOMPOSITION PATTERN. The Selective Decomposition pattern offers a formal method to separate *some* service capabilities into smaller chunks of operations. This disjointing activity does not imply that the detached functionality is to be eliminated or retired. On the contrary, the internal service components that are removed will continue to add value even after their separation. Furthermore, the breakdown effort should be performed on bulky and coarse-grained services to reduce their inefficient structure formation and trim down the constraints that a tightly coupled software entity imposes on architectural flexibility.[1]

The decomposition method that is offered by this pattern is selective. The term "selective" pertains to the approach used to separate service capabilities. Here the practitioner chooses a methodical process that allows the service formation to remain intact after the decomposition operation is performed. In other words, *some* of its operations are removed, yet its identity and *most* of its functionality is preserved. The removal process should take place in a systematic manner in which the service's internal components are extracted without damaging its overall performance. Doing this requires an orderly decomposition effort to ensure business and technical continuity.

What are the various service formations that can be decomposed? The selective approach can involve atomic and composite services and distributed service groups—namely service clusters. Can an atomic service be subject to capability separation? The rule of thumb suggests that an atomic service is an indivisible entity in its optimal configuration. But until this state has been reached, the practitioner should strive to optimize it. Thus, an atomic service should be part of the decomposition analysis to enhance its structure when appropriate. Note, when it comes to manipulation of an atomic service, the preferred term is "separation of operations" because of the different decomposition approach that is taken.

Problem. There is no defense against accumulating or piling up source code that ultimately yields bulky service formations that are not only hard to manage but also impose a serious threat to performance in a production environment. This assertion pertains to an oversized atomic service that is comprised of convoluted operations. A composite service that contains a large number of unmanaged subordinate finer-grained services is another example where design and architectural quality is at risk of being undermined. Even a cluster formation that encompasses distributed services without clear planning and strategy typically introduces risks to business execution.

But one of the greatest perils to the management of software assets is tightly coupled formations that are overly *dependent* on each other. This state challenges organizational architecture best practices and undermines business agility. The inherited side effects that emanate from the establishment of bulky service formations influence a long chain of activities during the service life cycle. This includes service integration, deployment, configuration, execution, monitoring, and management in production.

Solution. The proposed solution that the Selective Decomposition pattern offers enables architects, modelers, analysts, developers, and team leaders to examine a service structure and apply the right component separation measurements to strike the correct balance between coarse and fine-grained implementations. This solution simply suggests decomposing a large service formation into more manageable and smaller units of execution. But remember, this effort is not about dissecting or dismantling a service to the extent of identity dissipation. Here the service continues to maintain most of its processes and capabilities.

This effort obviously depends on organizational best practices and the recommended principles of service decomposition. In other words, the definition of a coarse- or fine-grained service can vary among different organizations, typically driven by what an organization conceives as a "large" or "small" service. A coarse-grained service in one organization may not be considered such in another organization. The same applies to the fine-grained service definition.

The Selective Decomposition pattern proposes four major methods for separating a service formation. The utilization of each approach depends on the involved service structure and its internal construct. Consider these service breakdown mechanisms that can help practitioners to identify the right approach for the services they analyze:

1. **Selective operation-level separation.** This method applies to atomic services that do not aggregate smaller fine-grained services. The separation is performed by extracting operations and interfaces from a service. Later the removed functionality can be added to existing services or bundled to create new services.
2. **Selective bottom-up decomposition.** This approach should be employed with composite services. The bottom-up method suggests starting from the innermost fine-grained child service and moving up to its containing entity, the parent service.
3. **Selective top-down decomposition.** The top-down approach begins with the decomposition activity from the parent entity—the containing service. This would include the removal of its encompassed child services.
4. **Selective cluster decomposition.** A cluster formation can also be a candidate for decomposition. Since it is not a hierarchical formation, the separation process for a cluster formation typically is straightforward. It simply implies that selected cluster members for separation are no longer a part of the cluster.

Example. The examples that follow illustrate the Selective Decomposition pattern's contribution to four different approaches: selective operation-level decomposition, selective bottom-up decomposition, selective top-down decomposition, and selective cluster decomposition.

Selective Operation-Level Separation Example. The simple Selective Decomposition scenario typically takes place during source code optimization, when the developer is engaged in enhancement decisions and code refactoring. This typically includes the extraction of operations and interfaces from a block of code and their relocation to a different entity. Exhibit 20.1 illustrates this idea. The Car Insurance Service source code file encompasses three major operation groups: Customer Profile Operations, Background Verification Operations, and Policy Underwriting Operations. This scenario depicts the separation of the Policy Underwriting Operations and the creation of a new dedicated source code file, named Policy Underwriting Operations.

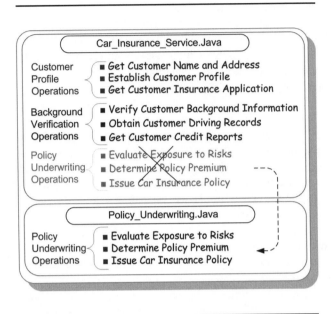

EXHIBIT 20.1 SELECTIVE OPERATION-LEVEL SEPARATION EXAMPLE

Selective Bottom-Up Decomposition Example.   The selective bottom-up approach, as illustrated in Exhibit 20.2, is best suited for decomposition operations on a composite service. This method advocates separating a service by starting at the lower level of the hierarchy and moving up toward its parent if more decomposition activities are needed. The process of decomposition is apparent in two perspectives, the 3D view (far right) and the Service-Oriented Modeling Formal Diagram View (far left). The former view is further subdivided into two windows named Problem and Solution. The Problem section depicts the starting modeling stage and Solution illustrates the final state of the

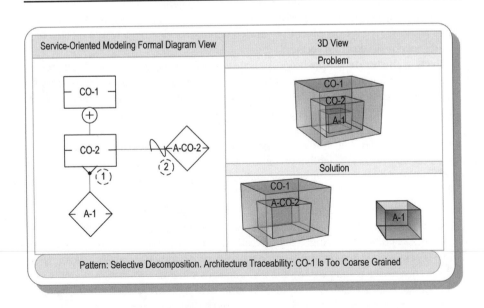

EXHIBIT 20.2 SELECTIVE BOTTOM-UP DECOMPOSITION EXAMPLE

product. It is clear that the outcome of this decomposition activity is a separated atomic service A-1 that was initially a part of composite service CO-2. Note, the service name CO-2 morphed (shown in the Solution window) into an atomic service A-CO-2 because an empty Composite Services must be transformed into an atomic service (refer to rules of decomposition in the Decomposition section in Chapter 18)

In contrast, the Service-Oriented Modeling Formal Diagram View describes the decomposition process in two steps. First it is clear that atomic service A-1 is separated from its parent composite service CO-2 by utilizing the "Decomposed" symbol (marked as step 1). The second step depicts the transformation of composite CO-2 (now empty) into the atomic service A-CO-2 by employing the "Transformed" modeling symbol. Note that the newly transformed service A-CO-2 continues to be a part of the hosting parent CO-1.

Selective Top-Down Decomposition.   Unlike the selective bottom-up decomposition method, the selective top-down decomposition approach, illustrated in Exhibit 20.3, advocates that the process of service separation should begin at a higher level and continue at lower level of the service hierarchy if needed. Here the composite Service CO-2 is extracted along with its internal atomic A-1. As depicted in the 3D view, it is apparent that the top-down method is best suited for decomposition of more than one service at a time. It is important to note that composite service CO-1, the hosting entity, is transformed into an atomic service A-CO-1 because it became an empty entity.

In the Service-Oriented Modeling Formal Diagram View, we utilize the "Decomposed" modeling symbol (marked as step 1) that denotes the breakdown of service CO-1 into two separate entities: CO-1 and CO-2. The second step (marked as 2) is performed on the hosting composite service CO-1 (since it became an empty entity) where it is transformed into an atomic service A-CO-1 by employing the "Transformed" modeling symbol.

Selective Cluster Decomposition.   Finally, the selective cluster decomposition example illustrated in Exhibit 20.4 depicts two different perspectives: the 3D View (far right) and Service-Oriented Modeling Formal Diagram View (far left). Obviously, the formal presentation view depicts the separation process of the composite service CO-1 from cluster CL-1 by employing the "Decomposed"

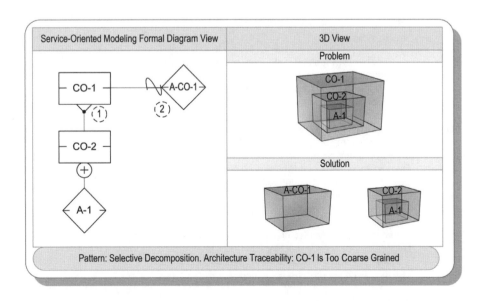

EXHIBIT 20.3   SELECTIVE TOP-DOWN DECOMPOSITION EXAMPLE

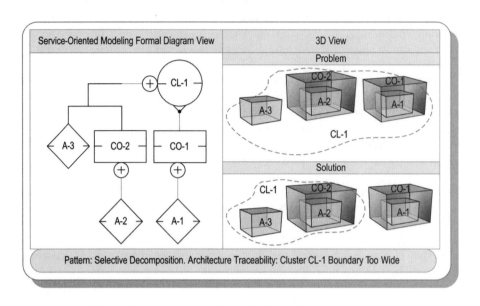

EXHIBIT 20.4   SELECTIVE DECOMPOSITION WITH SERVICE CLUSTER EXAMPLE

symbol. Note that unlike with the decomposition process that is being applied to a composite service to reduce its granularity scale and peeling off layers of its internal hierarchy, here the decomposition of the service cluster addresses the diminution of the cluster boundary and some of its functionality.

Synopsis.   The Selective Decomposition pattern's features, problems, and solutions that are introduced in Exhibit 20.5 pertain to situations that require removal of service functionality but not

Pattern Identification	
Name	Selective Decomposition Pattern
Category	Structural Specification

Problems, Solutions, and Implementations	
Problem	1. Service structure is too coarse grained or its formation boundary is too large.
	2. Service internal structure is too tightly coupled.
Solution	Trim down service capabilities by decomposing its structure.
Applicability	1. Apply to a coarse-grained composite service.
	2. Use to decompose a service cluster.
	3. Utilize to remove operations from an atomic service.
Method	Employ one or more of the introduced decomposition methods: selective operation-level separation, selective bottom-up decomposition, selective top-down decomposition, selective cluster decomposition.
Benefits	1. Fosters service loose coupling.
	2. Optimizes service granularity.
	3. Reduces tightly coupled dependencies between service components.
Risks	Decomposing a service structure introduces modifications to source code that must be thoroughly tested to avoid software execution instability.
Notation	Use the "Decomposed" symbol to denote separation of services.

EXHIBIT 20.5   SELECTIVE DECOMPOSITION PATTERN SUMMARY

Anti-Pattern Name	Best Practice
Extreme Selective Decomposition	Avoid excessive breakdown of a service that may yield smaller, too finely grained services.
Atomic Service Decomposition	Since an atomic service is not comprised of smaller fine-grained services, use the selective operation-level separation to extract functionality.
Bottom-Up or Top-Down Cluster Decomposition	Apply the selective bottom-up or top-down composite decomposition approach only to hierarchical service structures—namely, composite services. Use the selective cluster decomposition method instead to decompose a service cluster.

EXHIBIT 20.6   SELECTIVE DECOMPOSITION ANTI-PATTERNS

elimination of capabilities. This differentiation between the discontinuation of a service component and merely extracting some of its functionality is crucial to practicing this pattern. It is apparent that the Selective Decomposition process and its four major service separation approaches are devised to facilitate the preservation of operations, not to eliminate functionality.

Anti-Patterns.   The anti-patterns that are summarized in Exhibit 20.6 advocate the right usage of the Selective Decomposition pattern. These best practices should guide practitioners on how to best employ the four major service separation approaches discussed so far. As a rule of thumb, architects, developers, modelers, designers, and managers should carefully study the formation of a service that is subject to decomposition to avoid misuse of the pattern.

TOTAL FRAGMENTATION PATTERN.   Unlike the Selective Decomposition (360) pattern, which tackles partial reduction of functionality from an atomic service, composite service, or service cluster formation, the Total Fragmentation pattern is devised to accommodate an overall reorganization of a service structure. The term "reorganization" relates to analysis efforts that typically yield new services or the restructuring of an existing service. But this decomposition method advocates a general remodeling of an existing service scheme, during which the practitioner dissects a service into smaller components. In fact, the Total Fragmentation pattern advocates separating *all* service parts and analyzing their ability to offer a viable business solution. This process leads to the dissipation of the service identity because of its overall breakdown. The term "identity" is related to the service type and its attributes. Once the service is decomposed, its unique characteristics disappear as well.

Problem.   One of the most challenging tasks when it comes to analyzing a service's structure is understanding the unique contribution of each contained component. This examination typically is pursued during the architecture evaluation process, business analysis activities, and source code refactoring sessions. In fact, the driving motivation for dissecting a service formation is its coarse-grained construct that influences many aspects of its functionality and offerings. This influences on service execution may include slow performance of transaction and message exchange, difficulties with service monitoring, challenges with tightly coupled service components that depend on each other, and more.

  Another source of concern with bulky service formations is the broadened scope of their offered solutions and the large boundary of their operations. This overly grown service structure may address a wide range of concerns rather than focusing on resolving particular problems. The practitioner should meticulously analyze this service granularity scale aspect by inspecting all service structures discussed so far: atomic, composite, and service clusters.

Solution.   To alleviate these challenges, substantial measures should be taken to optimize a service structure and enhance its performance. Measures should include decomposition of service functionality, separation of its internal services, and an overall dissection of its capabilities. To understand the dependencies of a service's internal components, use the Total Fragmentation pattern designed to dismantle its structural ingredients. This exercise will assist with studying the dependencies of internal service constituents and help in carving out action items for regrouping these capabilities and proposing a more feasible solution.

The Total Fragmentation pattern should be applied to the atomic service structure, a hierarchical formation (namely a composite service), and the service cluster. Any of the three compositions can be dismembered by attending to the proposed three tenets:

1. **Atomic Service formation.** Separate groups of service operations. This separation should be performed based on their contextual affiliation and areas of expertise.
2. **Composite service structure.** Begin the fragmentation process by starting at the lowest-level child service—the finest grained—then move upward to extract the containing parents.
3. **Service cluster.** Dismantle a service cluster by extracting all cluster members.

Example.   Exhibit 20.7 illustrates the Total Fragmentation pattern process, during which all the contained services in composite service CO-1 are separated. Note that the decomposition activity (depicted in the formal modeling diagram) is denoted by the "Decomposed" symbol. In addition, the "Transformed" symbol, used twice, depicts the service structure conversion from composite to atomic formations. Consider the steps that lead to the overall breakdown of composite service CO-1:

1. In the first step, composite service CO-2 is extracted from composite service CO-1 by employing the "Decomposed" symbol.
2. Because it does not contain any internal services, composite service CO-1 is transformed to atomic service A-CO-1 utilizing the "Transformed" symbol.

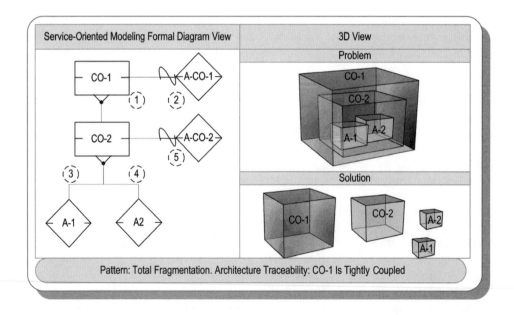

EXHIBIT 20.7   TOTAL FRAGMENTATION WITH COMPOSITE SERVICE EXAMPLE

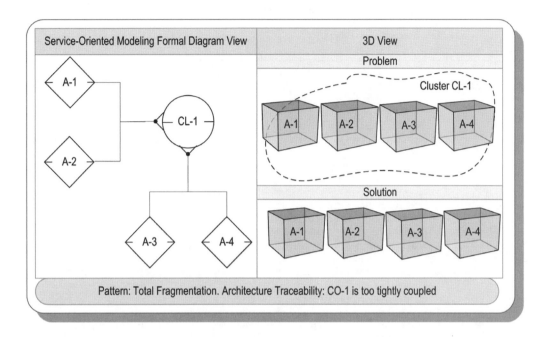

EXHIBIT 20.8 TOTAL FRAGMENTATION WITH SERVICE CLUSTER EXAMPLE

3. Atomic service A-1 is decomposed from its aggregating composite service CO-2 by employing the "Decomposed" symbol.
4. In this step, atomic service A-2 is separated from the same parent service: CO-2.
5. Since composite service CO-2 does not consist of any internal services, it is transformed to atomic service A-CO-2 by using the "Transformed" modeling symbol.

Another use of the Total Fragmentation pattern is presented by Exhibit 20.8. The scenario involves service cluster CL-1, which is dissected into four different independent atomic services: A-1, A-2, A-3, and A-4. A cluster that undergoes such radical decomposition process ceases to exist. The separated cluster members become autonomous entities that are no longer treated as associated services that must collaboratively contribute to a general cause or necessarily interact to obtain a mutual goal.

Synopsis. The Total Fragmentation pattern should be employed when a service formation introduces management and operations difficulties because of its inefficient internal architecture and design constraints and its tightly coupled foundation. The proposed solution supports an overall service dismembering and refactoring of its source code. Exhibit 20.9 summarizes these problems and solutions and identifies the involved risks.

Anti-Patterns. The Total Fragmentation anti-patterns address the aftermath of an overall composite service or service cluster decomposition. Exhibit 20.10 offers guidance in instances that require service transformation after a service's internal constituents have been removed. In addition, it is advised that practitioners who seek partial decomposition should not employ the Total Fragmentation pattern.

Pattern Identification	
Name	Total Fragmentation Pattern
Category	Structural Specification

Problems, Solutions, and Implementations	
Problem	1. Service structure is too complex.
	2. Service formation introduces operations, monitoring, and maintenance challenges.
	3. Internal service components are too tightly coupled.
Solution	An overall breakdown of the service would be required to enable rigorous analysis, design, and architecture.
Applicability	1. Apply during source code refactoring initiatives.
	2. Utilize the Total Fragmentation pattern to dissect a composite service or dismantle a service cluster that is too bulky, is underperforming, and is hard to maintain.
Method	When decomposing a composite service, follow two necessary steps:
	1. Separate the aggregated child services.
	2. Transform the "empty" composite service parent to an atomic entity.
	Services that were removed from a cluster become autonomous entities while the cluster concept ceases to exist.
	Service operation groups should be separated when applying the Total Fragmentation pattern to an atomic service.
Benefits	1. Fosters loosely coupled service environment.
	2. Provides architecture and design reevaluation opportunities.
	3. Assists with source code optimization during source code refactoring initiatives.
Risks	Overall decomposition of a service typically triggers service construction initiatives that may involve and affect a number of dependent services.
Notation	Use the "Decomposed" and "Transformed" symbols.

EXHIBIT 20.9   TOTAL FRAGMENTATION PATTERN SUMMARY TABLE

Anti-Pattern Name	Best Practice
Partial Decomposition	The Total Fragmentation pattern advocates decomposition of all service internal components. Use the Selective Decomposition pattern (360) instead if partial decomposition is required.
Empty Composite Service	A composite service that does not consist of any internal services should be transformed to atomic formation.
Empty Service Cluster	A service cluster that was dismembered should cease to exist and its former internal services should be treated as autonomous entities.

EXHIBIT 20.10   TOTAL FRAGMENTATION ANTI-PATTERNS

SUBTRACTION ANALYSIS: PATTERNS AND IMPLEMENTATION

Subtraction analysis is the process that ultimately leads to service retirement. The stage of functionality and process discontinuation indicates the demise of a service and termination of its offerings to its corresponding consumers. This action should be meticulously investigated and carefully pursued because of the risks that accompany alterations to once-offered functionality. The vacuum that service elimination leaves behind can be substantial. Not only does the disrupted relationship with former consumers require alternatives, but also the environment in which the service operates must be reengineered to accommodate its departure.

Subtraction analysis is not only about examining opportunities to retire a service. Partial elimination of functionality can also be pursued by employing the offered subtraction patterns. The term "partial" pertains to sets of operations or internal service components that are subject to deletion in an atomic service, selective removal of aggregated services contained in composite service formations, or discriminatory discontinuation of cluster service members.

Why should a service be removed from a production environment or eliminated from an architecture or design blueprint? The answers to this question are rooted in business and technical reasons that drive the motivation for service retirement. The subtraction operation calls for the departure of a service that is no longer relevant to the business. From a technological perspective, reengineering may be the chief reason for discontinuation of service operations. These drivers and more are discussed in the sections that follow on subtraction patterns and the incentives for their use.

SUBTRACTION PATTERNS AND ANTI-PATTERNS.   There are two chief subtraction patterns and corresponding anti-patterns that the architect, developer, analyst, modeler, and manager should be aware of: the Capability Subtraction (369) pattern and the Entity Elimination (372) pattern. The former addresses small-scale and selective reduction of components, functionality, and operations, while the latter tackles vital issues of complete service retirement. Either method depicts the activity of business or technical process disposal. Best practices are also offered to assist practitioners with safe discontinuation of services and to mitigate risks that can threaten the stability of business and technical environments.

CAPABILITY SUBTRACTION PATTERN.   The Capability Subtraction pattern is designed to remove business and technical functionality from an atomic or composite service or a service cluster. This extraction is intended to *permanently eliminate* service capabilities with no intention for immediate substitution. In other words, the practitioner should utilize this pattern to *retire selective* components or parts of a service formation by simply "subtracting" capabilities from the coarse-grained structure. Remember, this activity is merely a structural manipulation of a service constitution, and yet the influencing aspects are clearly contextual. The term "contextual" implies that these may be business-related imperatives or technical considerations that drive modification to a service construct, such as service functionality, specialty, or even business or technical processes.

The Capability Subtraction pattern is a powerful approach to execute the elimination of components that make up a service. But the practitioner should exercise this method with care because of the unalterable or potentially costly consequences of such activity. Substantial efforts will be required to reinstate service capabilities that have been removed with no plans for replacement. Therefore, before pursuing this process, a rigorous analysis should assess whether the cost of functionality removal outweighs the benefits.

Problem.   The manager, architect, business analyst, modeler, and developer who arrive at a decision to eliminate service's functionality or some of its components typically are concerned about the service capability to promote of the business and rectify organizational concerns. Technical considerations may also drive the employment of the Capability Subtraction pattern that advocates the removal of ineffective processes that offer negligible benefits to technological solutions.

But the reduced value of a service's offerings is not the only reason for questioning its contribution to future operations. Selective elimination of service components and capabilities can be related to software consolidation activities devised to reduce organizational expenditure. Other opportunities for partial retirement of service capabilities may be affiliated with elimination of non-crucial functionality that is too pricey to monitor and maintain. Furthermore, perhaps one of the most compelling reasons to retire some of service components is to reduce business process redundancy across the organization. This pertains to duplicate functionalities and replicated operations that typically are distributed across the enterprise.

Solution.   The proposed solution offered by the Capability Subtraction pattern involves three major service structures: atomic, composite, and cluster formations. When retiring service capabilities, the practitioner must analyze a service's internal formations and carefully remove unwanted functionality. This can be accomplished on three structural configuration levels:

1. **Source code level.** The subtraction of functionality of the source code level requires the removal of service operations and interfaces that are subject to retirement.
2. **Composite service.** This process is associated with the retirement of an aggregated child service that is structurally positioned in a composite service hierarchy.
3. **Service cluster.** Subtracting capabilities from a service cluster consists of the retirement of any cluster members, such as atomic and composite services.

Example.   The two examples in this section exemplify the process of service functionality subtraction. The first represents the challenges associated with the retirement of a service from a composite formation; the second addresses the removal of an entity from a service cluster.

Capability Subtraction from a Composite Service Example.   Exhibit 20.11 depicts a simple case of service capabilities retirement. The two perspectives that present the Capability Subtraction pattern are the 3D View (far right) and the Service-Oriented Modeling Formal Diagram View (far left). The former displays two windows: Problem and Solution. Let us first view the 3D perspective. It is apparent that the atomic service A-1 that was aggregated in the composite service CO-2 (a child service of composite service CO-1) is eliminated, and thus it does not appear in the Solution section. Note that composite service CO-2 has been transformed to atomic service A-CO-2 because it does not aggregate anymore service A-1.

This process is also shown in the formal diagram view in two steps. First, the employment of the "Subtracted" symbol (marked as step 1) conveys the retirement of atomic service A-1. The second step (marked as step 2) depicts the transformation of composite service CO-2 to atomic

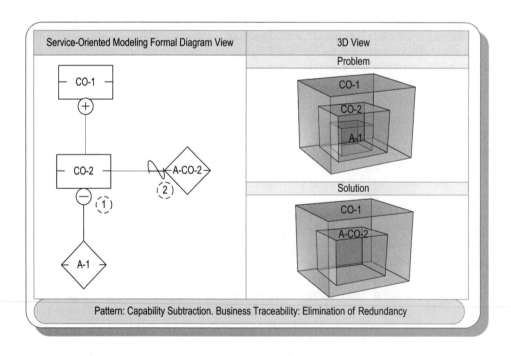

EXHIBIT 20.11   CAPABILITY SUBTRACTION FROM A COMPOSITE SERVICE

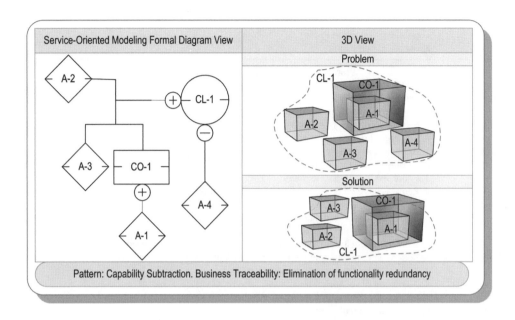

EXHIBIT 20.12   CAPABILITY SUBTRACTION FROM A SERVICE CLUSTER

Service A-CO-2. Note that the indicated business traceability is identified as elimination of service functionality redundancy. This is also the motivation for using the Capability Subtraction pattern.

Capability Subtraction from a Service Cluster Example.   Exhibit 20.12 illustrates the retirement of the atomic service A-4, a part of cluster CL-1, in two perspectives: 3D View (far right) and Service-Oriented Modeling Formal Diagram View (far left). The latter view depicts this elimination process by using the "Subtracted" symbol. This perspective also identifies the remaining aggregated services in cluster CL-1: atomic service A-2, atomic service A-3, and composite service CO-1. This is denoted by the employment of the "Aggregated" modeling symbol. Note that the motivation for the removal of atomic service A-4 is elimination of redundancy, a business traceability requirement noted on the bottom.

Synopsis.   The Capability Subtraction pattern addresses the reduction of functionality on application-level and organizational scale initiatives. The chief motivation for eliminating service offerings is source code streamlining or removal of redundant processes in an application or across the organization. Consider Exhibit 20.13, which summarizes the problems, solutions, and methods for implementation that are associated with the Capability Subtraction pattern.

Anti-Patterns.   The Capability Subtraction pattern should not be mixed with the decomposition activities. These two approaches for reduction of functionality serve different purposes. When decomposing a service, the separated components should not be removed from a production environment. However, the subtracted functionality is subject for retirement that should not be restored and executed. Furthermore, the Capability Subtraction pattern is devised to partially eliminate a service's components. For complete removal of a service or a service cluster from a production environment, employ the Entity Elimination (372) pattern. Exhibit 20.14 outlines these differences, identifies the proper use of the pattern, and provides usage alternatives.

Pattern Identification	
Name	Capability Subtraction Pattern
Category	Structural Specification

Problems, Solutions, and Implementations	
Problem	1. Service consists of redundant functionality.
	2. Service environment is comprised of duplicated business or technical processes.
	3. Service consists of unnecessary capabilities
Solution	Retire, consolidate, or eliminate partial service capabilities.
Applicability	1. Apply to source code refactoring initiatives.
	2. Employ subtraction on composite services.
	3. Retire service cluster members.
	4. Remove service operations in an atomic formation.
Method	There are three approaches to consider:
	1. Source code level reduction that involves the elimination of selected logic.
	2. Retirement of child or parent service in a composite formation.
	3. Subtraction of cluster members, such as atomic and composite services.
Benefits	1. Reduction of functionality and process redundancy.
	2. Assists with software asset consolidation.
	3. Alignment of service granularity
Risks	The capability subtraction approach may be irreversible.
Notation	Use the "Subtracted" symbol.

Exhibit 20.13   Capability Subtraction Pattern Summary Table

Anti-Pattern Name	Best Practice
Subtraction Restoration	It would be impractical to restore retired capabilities after pursuing the capability subtraction process. This initiative will be too costly.
Complete Service Retirement	It is possible to retire an entire software entity, an atomic service, a service along with its aggregated components, or a whole service cluster. The Capability Subtraction pattern, however, supports only selective elimination of service functionality. For complete abolition of service operations, employ the Entity Elimination pattern (372).
Subtraction as Decomposition	Removed service functionality is a permanent act of operation retirement. The selected subtracted components are subject to disposal. If the intention is merely to separate components, use the Selective Decomposition pattern (360) or Total Fragmentation pattern (365).

Exhibit 20.14   Capability Subtraction Anti-Patterns

ENTITY ELIMINATION PATTERN.   Unlike the Capability Subtraction (369) pattern, which addresses a selective elimination of functionality, the Entity Elimination pattern is suited for *total retirement* of a service. The term "total retirement" pertains to the discontinuation of an entire atomic service and its associated operations, removal of a composite service along with its aggregated services from a production environment, or a complete shutdown of a service cluster and its affiliated service members. This simple concept of service termination typically is motivated by business decisions that are influenced by market events, unprofitable service offerings, or costly support that does not justify further investments in an application.[2]

Technical reasons can also encourage practitioners to simply remove an implementation from a production environment or cease the development of new services. These reasons are associated with service integration challenges, unfeasible deployment efforts, complex architecture, design that may increase cost and reduce service effectiveness, and more.

Problem.   The elimination of a service from a production environment can introduce substantial risks to business stability and the continuity of a production environment. These risks typically are attributed to the relationships and dependencies that the service has been establishing, perhaps during months or years, with its corresponding consumers. The decision to entirely discontinue a certain business or technical functionality can affect the service ecosystem, disrupt consumption and information exchange activities, and affect the communications between distributed software assets. Therefore, there must be compelling reasons for entity subtraction that justify redesign, rearchitecture, and reintegration initiatives.

Consider the chief challenges that should motivate architects, developers, analysts, modelers, and managers to employ the Entity Elimination pattern:

- Substantial reduction of consumers typically triggers elimination of services.
- Design and architecture complexities contribute to halting service operations.
- Convoluted service implementation that affects its performance in production environment can spur decisions to discontinue its activities.
- Diminishing service relevancy to the business because of market trends, and changes to business strategies or business model can result in its removal from production.
- Technical reengineering initiatives may yield service ecosystem revamping efforts that recommend removal of certain services because of consolidation or architectural optimization reasons.
- Replicated services and duplication of processes can promote service retirement.

Solution.   As discussed in the previous section, the mere removal of a service from a production environment should not require a major effort. This activity is a simple shutdown that can instantly retire a service. But the implications can be vast and the risks substantial. Although the structural specification process is not about analysis and modeling of a service environment, dependencies of a candidate service for elimination on its peers and consumers should be meticulously exercised. Therefore, the proposed solution must involve several vital analysis initiatives to assess the risks and carve out a mitigation strategy to minimize damage that may be inflicted on the service ecosystem upon service subtraction. Consider a number of steps that should be exercised when employing the Entity Elimination pattern:

1. **Message route analysis.** Conduct an analysis to identify the various message paths that a candidate service for subtraction activity maintains across an organization and with its corresponding consumers.
2. **Contract terms and conditions analysis.** Study the existing contracts that a service is bound to. Identify the stipulated conditions and offerings that it is obliged to provide. Learn about the exposed interfaces and the values that a service must pass and receive from its corresponding consumers.
3. **Architecture and design constraints analysis.** Understand the service operating environment and its integration and collaboration requirements with peer services and consumers. Examine the various architecture and design constraints to uncover the risks that are involved by impending service retirement activities.
4. **Risk assessment and mitigation strategy.** Carve out an assessment and mitigation strategy to alleviate the risks involved with the removal of service from an operating environment.

Example.   Exhibit 20.15 introduces three service retirement instances, each of which represents the elimination of a distinct service structure: atomic service A-2; a service cluster, CL-1 that consists of internal service members; and a composite service CO-1 that aggregates a finer-grained service A-1 (indicated by the "Aggregated" symbol apparent in the formal modeling diagram, on the far left). The latter is also subject to removal because it is contained in its parent structure—composite service CO-1. Note that the discontinuation of the contributions of these entities is denoted by the

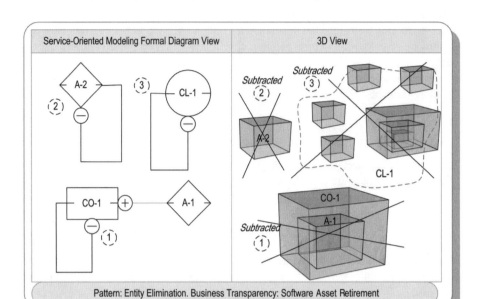

EXHIBIT 20.15   ENTITY ELIMINATION PATTERN EXAMPLE

"Subtracted" symbol. In addition, the business motivation for this action is software asset retirement, as indicated on the bottom panel.

Synopsis.   The Entity Elimination pattern is designed to address acute integration, performance, and operations risks that a service poses to its operating environment. Reduction of consumer base and poor returns on investment can also motivate practitioners to permanently retire a service and discontinue its offerings to corresponding consumers. Consider Exhibit 20.16, which summarizes

Pattern Identification	
Name	Entity Elimination Pattern
Category	Structural Specification
Problems, Solutions, and Implementations	
Problem	1. Substantial reduction of consumer scope.
	2. Operational costs outweigh the benefits and return on investment.
	3. Convoluted architecture and design models.
	4. Redundant service operations.
Solution	Service retirement.
Applicability	Applies to atomic and composite services, and service cluster members.
Method	Conduct analyses to mitigate service retirement risks: message route analysis, contract terms and conditions analysis, architecture and design constraints analysis.
Benefits	1. Reduction of architectural complexities.
	2. Decrease of process redundancy.
	3. Streamlining service integration.
Risks	Removal of a service from production may threaten stability of operations and hamper business continuity.
Notation	Use the "Subtracted" symbol.

EXHIBIT 20.16   ENTITY ELIMINATION PATTERN SUMMARY TABLE

Anti-Pattern Name	Best Practice
Partial Service Retirement	The Entity Elimination pattern should be employed to discontinue all service's components operations. Use the Capability Subtraction pattern (369) for selective removal of service functionality.
Temporary Service Retirement	The Entity Elimination pattern should be utilized when the intention is to permanently remove a service from production environment. Avoid temporary retirement of services.
Non-incremental Service Retirement	If business or technical conditions allow, the discontinuation of a service's operation should be performed incrementally to mitigate retirement risks.

EXHIBIT 20.17   ENTITY ELIMINATION ANTI-PATTERNS

the major problems and proposed solutions to these challenges. It also identifies the major benefits and risks that are involved when employing the Entity Elimination pattern.

Anti-Patterns.   Remember, service retirement is an action that is performed to permanently remove an atomic service, a composite service, or a service cluster member from a production environment. Partial or temporary eradication of service functionality should not be exercised when utilizing the Entity Elimination pattern. The best practices by which service offerings should be discontinued are outlined in Exhibit 20.17.

REFACTORING ANALYSIS: PATTERNS AND IMPLEMENTATION

During the refactoring process, the architect, developer, modeler, analyst, and manager are engaged in a series of evaluation activities designed to assess if a service's structural and contextual aspects can provide a viable solution. This activity is not only about inspecting service capabilities and their contribution to accomplishing the planned missions. The refactoring task is even more challenging: The practitioner must also optimize service source code, ensure that service implementation is modularized, and ascertain that the design and architecture indeed satisfy business requirements. These activities are often called code transformation.[3]

The term "modularized" implies that the service's internal structure is well designed and that its interfaces and operations are grouped in logical components to alleviate the challenges of source code restructuring, integration, deployment, and maintenance in production. This reorganization of software implementation should attend to best practices that advocate a number of important design principles. One of the most imperative tenets is *componentization* of service constructs and coherent grouping of functionality that properly corresponds to a service's specialty, in line with its mission and its focus on the solution.

REFACTORING ANALYSIS PATTERNS AND ANTI-PATTERNS.   Again, refactoring is the act of service logic enhancements, an optimization process that is designed to improve the efficiency of service offerings. The sections that follow introduce two major analysis patterns that address such a refactoring mission: the Capability Substitution (375) pattern and the Capability Swapping (379) pattern. The former addresses the enhancement of a service's internal structure by replacing a part of its discarded functionality with a more viable implementation. The second pattern tackles service capability exchange between two or more services to align the contextual affiliation of service operations with a service's mission and the solutions it proposes.

CAPABILITY SUBSTITUTION PATTERN.   The Capability Substitution pattern is designed to assist practitioners in applying vital changes to a service in an orderly manner, during which a component of service implementation is replaced with another. This process should be exercised with utmost care when complex service structures are involved or tightly coupled architecture introduces dependency challenges between service internal operations.

Too often practitioners replace removed functionality while analyzing a service-oriented solution. This activity is required to fill in the vacuum that was created by eliminated capabilities. Many reasons can motivate the substitution of a piece of code, including: replacement of an aggregated service that resides in a composite structure or reinstitution of an existing cluster member. These activities are critical chiefly during a service life cycle in which business processes are altered or business requirements call for the implementation of new capabilities. This substitution process can also be driven by technological trends, such as the replacement of a search engine's older version, overall redesign of message orchestration, or even alteration to a data access layer.

Problem.   One of the most challenging tasks when it comes to service redesign and the optimization of functionality is addressing the replacement of retired software components, if indeed such a remedy is required, with minimal impact to business execution. This undertaking may not only affect a service's internal constitution; the environment in which it operates and exchanges messages with its related consumers could be also subject to modifications.

To substitute service capabilities efficiently and safely and to overcome these error-prone obstacles, two major aspects of implementation must be addressed:

1. What should be the order and the various steps by which service functionality should be replaced? This concern is related to priorities and dependencies between internal service components.
2. How should the practitioner ensure business continuity during and after the substitution process?

Solution.   Undoubtedly, before substituting service capabilities, planning and analysis steps should be pursued to alleviate the risks involved with the refactoring endeavor. The practitioner should not only be familiar with the service's internal structure but also understand the ramifications of functionality replacement on the service's offerings to affiliated consumers. This may involve a thorough analysis to identify vital dependencies on peer services, an investigation of technical and architectural constraints, and even a study of the service integration scheme. Consider the five chief steps that should be pursued to guarantee a service's capability substitution success:

1. **Internal dependencies.** Identify dependencies of internal service components to assess the overall risk involved with the removal of capabilities.
2. **Comparability.** Study how comparable the substituted functionality is with the one that is to be replaced.
3. **External dependencies.** Assess the impact of internal service changes on a service's external collaboration with consumers.
4. **Service contract.** Study service contracts and understand the nature of their interaction with corresponding consumers.
5. **Planning.** Plan the proper steps for the substitution effort, and introduce an appropriate functionality replacement implementation sequence.

Example.   The three examples that are provided in this section illustrate the Capability Substitution pattern implementation. The first scenario, depicted in Exhibit 20.18, is a functionality replacement that takes place in an atomic service formation. This activity consists of two steps: (1) retirement of Customer Lookup operations group and (2) its replacement with the Account Lookup operations group.

The second example, depicted in Exhibit 20.19, illustrates two perspectives: the 3D View (far right) and the Service-Oriented Modeling Formal Diagram View (far left). Note that the defined

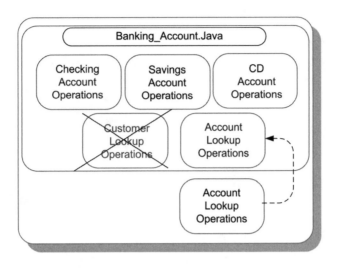

EXHIBIT 20.18   CAPABILITY SUBSTITUTION WITH ATOMIC SERVICE EXAMPLE

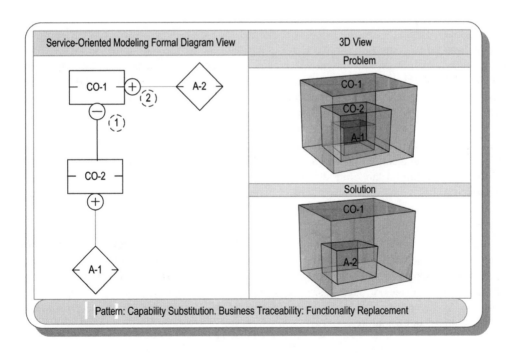

EXHIBIT 20.19   CAPABILITY SUBSTITUTION PATTERN WITH COMPOSITE SERVICE EXAMPLE

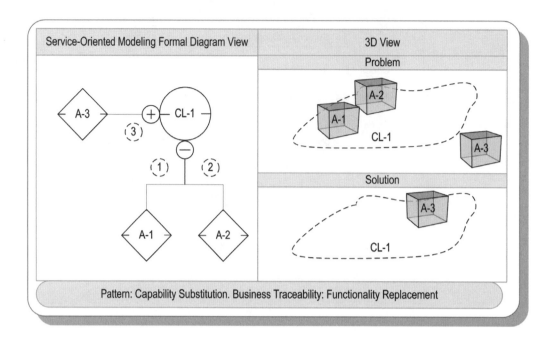

EXHIBIT 20.20　CAPABILITY SUBSTITUTION PATTERN WITH SERVICE CLUSTER EXAMPLE

mission is to retire composite service CO-2 along with its aggregated atomic service A-1 and to replace their capabilities with the atomic service A-2. These two steps take place in the parent service CO-1. Note, in the formal modeling view, the symbols that are employed to enable the substitution of this functionality are "Subtracted"[4] (step 1) and "Aggregated" in step 2. These are used in a predefined order: The former precedes the latter.

　　Finally, a distributed service group can also be subject to capability substation analysis. Exhibit 20.20 refers to the replacement of retired service members that reside in the service cluster CL-1. The eliminated entities, atomic services A-1 and A-2, are being replaced with atomic service A-3. Note in the formal modeling diagram the three steps that are taken to accomplish this task: (1) Service A-1 is removed first, next (2) A-2 is retired (using the "Subtracted" symbol[5]), followed by (3) the aggregation of service A-3 (employing the "Aggregated" symbol).

Synopsis.　The Capability Substitution pattern enables practitioners to carefully analyze and plan functionality replacement when it comes to manipulation of atomic, composite, and cluster service formations. This pattern encourages architects, developers, analysts, modelers, and managers to investigate dependencies of internal service components and to study the external implications for consumers before pursuing the substitution process. Consider Exhibit 20.21, which summarizes these challenges and solutions.

Anti-Patterns.　Remember, the Capability Substitution pattern is designed to assist practitioners in streamlining the functionality replacement process by eliminating the existing implementation and replacing it with alternate operations. This is not about decomposition or unification of services. Consider Exhibit 20.22, which introduces the anti-patterns and best practices to guide practitioners in using the Capability Substitution pattern.

Pattern Identification

Name	Capability Substitution Pattern
Category	Structural Specification

Problems, Solutions, and Implementations

Problem	Service capability is about to retire and must be replaced with a comparable or enhanced functionality.
Solution	Plan several steps to replace service functionality by ensuring minimal impact on business and technical continuity.
Applicability	Applies to replacement of capabilities in Atomic and Composite Services, and Service Clusters.
Method	1. Assess internal service modification risks.
	2. Identify service external dependencies that may be compromised.
	3. Study service contracts.
	4. Plan proper steps to address substitution of capabilities.
Benefits	Substituting functionality in a methodical manner with minimal disruption to business execution.
Risks	Capability substitution is an error-prone process that must be carefully tested and certified to avoid loss of productivity and connectivity, and business discontinuation.
Notation	Employ the "Subtracted" and "Aggregated" symbols.

Exhibit 20.21 Capability Substitution Pattern Summary Table

Anti-Pattern Name	Best Practice
Substitution by Capability Preservation	The Capability Substitution pattern is designed merely to replace a retired functionality. Use the Capability Swapping pattern (379) instead to preserve the removed components
Substitution by Unification	Avoid unification of services to accomplish substitution of functionality. Use the aggregation operation instead.
Substitution by Decomposition	Avoid using the decomposition modeling operation to replace service capabilities. Remember the decomposition process separates service capabilities that continue to operate in production. The substitution principle, however, advocates retirement of the removed capabilities.
Overall Substitution	Do not employ the Capability Substitution pattern to replace an entire service. Use the Entity Elimination (372) pattern to retire a service and then replace it with a new service.

Exhibit 20.22 Capability Substitution Anti-Patterns

CAPABILITY SWAPPING PATTERN.   The Capability Swapping pattern is rather like the Capability Substitution (375) pattern in terms of the required final goal: service functionality replacement. What is the chief difference between the two? Although the latter pattern advocates retiring the replaced capabilities, the former calls for exchanging functionalities among services. In other words, trading capabilities is essentially what the Capability Swapping pattern is about.

To better understand the "swapping" idea, imagine an Accounts Payable Composite Service that not only consists of operations that offer check issuance abilities; it also contains customer lookup functionality that should be extracted and placed in the Accounting Utility Composite Service. However, the Accounting Utility Composite Service includes accounting utility functions along with accounts payable payment history reporting capabilities that should be removed and located in the Accounts Payable Composite Service. Note that these two distinct services can trade these operation groups to better match service capabilities. In other words, the accounts payable functions should reside in the Accounts Payable Composite Service, and accounting utilities should be part of the Accounting Utility Service offerings. This matching process is often named "context matching."

Problem.   Too often services that are selected to provide a solution do not consist of capabilities that match their offered specialties. Therefore context matching is the chief challenge that the Capability Swapping pattern addresses. This pattern is devised to enhance a service's design and streamline its internal architecture.

Solution.   To alleviate these concerns the Capability Swapping pattern can be used to trade functionality between two or more service partners. This refactoring process can include several services that exchange functionality to streamline their capability offerings and their internal structure. In addition, this activity may render complicated analysis efforts that should be planned and managed with care. Consider the four chief steps that two service partners are involved with when swapping capabilities:

1. A meticulous analysis is conducted to study the functionalities of the services that are involved in the capability swapping process.
2. Some capabilities are removed from Service A.
3. The removed capabilities are added to Service B.
4. To complete this trading activity, some capabilities are extracted from Service B.
5. These capabilities are then added to Service A.

Recall that the Capability Swapping pattern can be used on the three major service formations discussed in this book: atomic, composite, and cluster structures. When it comes to capability trading that involves an atomic service, the practitioner should be concerned about exchanging operations and interfaces between services. However, with a composite formation, the traded entities are the aggregated fine-grained services that are arranged in a hierarchical formation: parent/child affiliations. Last, capability swapping between service clusters is accomplished by swapping cluster members.

Exchanging functionality can also occur between different service structures. For example, an atomic service can swap capabilities with a composite formation. In the same manner, a service cluster can trade capabilities with a composite service.

Example.   Exhibit 20.23 exemplifies the employment of the Capability Swapping pattern. The two major perspectives shown, the 3D View and the Service-Oriented Formal Modeling Diagram View, illustrate the steps taken to accomplish functionality swap between the two involved composite services: CO-1 and CO-2. In the first step, atomic service A-2 is extracted from composite service CO-1 and aggregated in the composite service CO-2 (Step 2). This swapping process concludes, in Steps 3 and 4, with the trading of atomic service A-1, which is removed from service CO-2 and added to CO-1. Note the utilization of the symbols "Decomposed" and "Aggregated," apparent in the Service-Oriented Modeling Formal Diagram View, to depict the swapping process.

Synopsis.   The Capability Swapping pattern addresses a method for functionality trading between two or more services. This exchange should be pursued to streamline the type of contribution that a service furnishes to its consumers. In other words, during the service refactoring stage, the practitioner should pursue the *contextual matching* activity, when service capabilities are analyzed to assess if they all match the service's chief specialty.

Exhibit 20.24 introduces the problem, solution, applicability, method, benefits, and risks that the Capability Swapping pattern offers.

Anti-Patterns.   Remember, the Capability Swapping pattern addresses the exchange of functionality between two or more services. This contextual refactoring is about refining service operations and focusing on clear service objectives and goals. Exhibit 20.25 introduces best practices that discuss these chief aims of the Capability Swapping pattern.

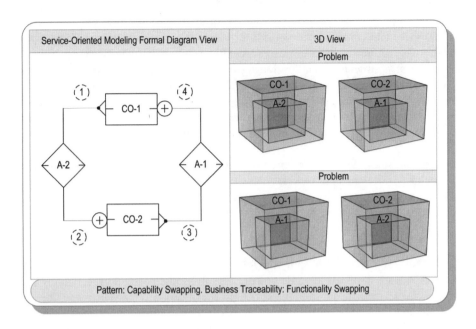

EXHIBIT 20.23 CAPABILITY SWAPPING PATTERN IMPLEMENTATION EXAMPLE

Pattern Identification	
Name	Capability Swapping Pattern
Category	Structural Specification

Problems, Solutions, and Implementations	
Problem	Two or more services that are engaged in providing a solution to a problem consist of some capabilities that do not match their individual context.
Solution	Pursue functionality exchange between services.
Applicability	Atomic, composite, and service cluster formations.
Method	The capability swapping approach advocates two major steps to accomplish capability trading: decomposition and aggregation.
Benefits	Streamlining service context by employing structural manipulation.
Risks	Significant alteration to service structure may introduce execution instability and disruption to the business.
Notation	Use the "Decomposed" and "Aggregated" symbols.

EXHIBIT 20.24 CAPABILITY SWAPPING PATTERN SUMMARY TABLE

Anti-Pattern Name	Best Practice
Swapping by Subtraction	Avoid retirement of service functionality when pursuing the capability swapping process. Instead, use the decomposition operation to extract unwanted service capabilities.
Swapping by Unification	Utilize the aggregation operation to add capabilities to service structure during the swapping process. Avoid unification to replace capabilities.
Contextual Manipulation	The Capability Swapping pattern addresses service structural manipulation that is driven by contextual matching challenges. Contextual manipulation is not the purpose of this exercise.

EXHIBIT 20.25 CAPABILITY SWAPPING ANTI-PATTERNS

CONTRACT ANALYSIS: PATTERNS AND IMPLEMENTATION

The contract analysis process conducted during the structural specification stage focuses on optimization of service and consumer relationship in terms of message exchange, consumption, and types of offerings required to satisfy consumers. This examination of service capabilities is performed because of a structural modification to a service's internal construct, during which the practitioner devises the reduction of service functionality scope. Furthermore, the contract analysis activity chiefly tackles cancellation and reinstitution of contracts that must take place after a service formation is broken up into smaller units to adhere to loose coupling principles. Service retirement and discontinuation of offerings is another reason for contract inspection and reestablishment.

In addition, source code refactoring and modification to design and architecture blueprints motivate architects, developers, modelers, analysts, and managers to reassess existing associations between services and optimize the manner by which contracts are established. This process of contract refinement and perfection entails modeling operations, such as service decomposition, contract binding and unbinding, service transformation, and service aggregation.

CONTRACT ANALYSIS: PATTERNS AND ANTI-PATTERNS.　The sections that follow discuss two major patterns that are designed to guide practitioners to handle contract cancellations and modification to service relationships during the structural specification stage. These activities typically occur after the reduction of service functionality or trimming down of service capabilities. The first pattern, the Contract Cancellation (382) pattern, introduces the chief motivations, risks, and solutions associated with discontinuing a contract. The second pattern, the Contract Internalization (384) pattern, addresses the challenges of maintaining contracts after a service decomposition or the reorganization of a service structure.

CONTRACT CANCELLATION PATTERN.　The Contract Cancellation pattern should be utilized when a contract between a service and its related consumers must be discontinued. This simple requirement typically takes place when the relationships between a service and its affiliated message exchange parties are no longer necessary. There are many reasons for cancellation of contracts. Among them are changes to business requirements or modification to technical specifications. These reasons characteristically drive alterations to service context and offerings, and encourage structural optimization efforts that influence the association of services with their consumers. The term "structural optimization" implies that the practitioner may determine to decompose a service or even retire it during the refactoring process. In these cases, clearly, contracts should be reevaluated and analyzed to identify their contribution to transaction exchanges and message delivery.

Problem.　The problems that the Contract Cancellation pattern addresses are chiefly affiliated with modifications to service operations, capabilities, and internal structure. Consider the main reasons for canceling an established contract between a service and its corresponding consumers or even with its peer services:

- **Service retirement.** Discontinuation of service offerings that may not require substitution.
- **Service decomposition.** Breaking up a service into smaller autonomous and fine-grained services typically encourages cancellation of contracts. Consumers characteristically reestablish their relationship and resume message exchange activities with these newly created services.
- **Service structural reorganization.** Refactoring of service internal formation is another aspect that can influence contract cancellation decisions.

- **Service capability reduction.** Service capability's scope is reduced and related consumers do not leverage its offerings.
- **Discontinuation of Associations.** Relationship between services and corresponding consumers are discontinued
- **Swapped Capabilities.** Service capabilities are swapped with a peer service .

Solution. Employ the Contract Cancellation pattern in a proper manner with minimum disruption to business and technology operations. The aftermath of contact discontinuation between two or more message exchange parties not only can affect the delivery of messages in a service ecosystem but also can influence overall consumption rates and performance of message exchange. But one of the most challenging tasks is to compensate for the cancellation of a contract. In other words, the immediate concern that should be tackled is the alternative to contract discontinuation. Consider the chief questions that should be asked to help address this challenge:

- Does a terminated contract necessitate substitution?
- Does a consumer require alternative consumption sources if a contract is discontinued?
- What is the influence of contract cancellation on the environment where a service and its related consumers operate?
- Should the practitioner compensate for the untied relationship between a service and a consumer?

Example. Exhibit 20.26 illustrates the Contract Cancellation pattern process. This simple example involves the atomic service A-1 and its affiliated consumer CONS-1. Note the use of the "Unbound" symbol to denote the service cancellation (in Step 1) that is apparent in the Service-Oriented Modeling Formal Diagram View (far left). In addition, the "Subtracted" symbol is used to depict service retirement (in Step 2).

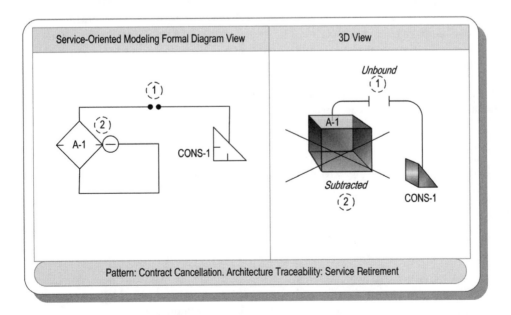

EXHIBIT 20.26 CONTRACT CANCELLATION PATTERN EXAMPLE

Pattern Identification	
Name	Contract Cancellation Pattern
Category	Structural Specification

Problems, Solutions, and Implementations	
Problem	Service capability is reduced, eliminated, or altered, while a related consumer maintains a contract relationship.
Solution	Cancellation of existing contract.
Applicability	Applies to atomic and composite services and service cluster members that are bound by contracts to related consumers.
Method	Cancellation of a contract may require capability substitution when an internal service structure is broken up or altered. Service retirement typically does not require compensation of functionality.
Benefits	1. Simplification of service contract management and contract model. 2. Reduction of consumer dependency on their providing services.
Risks	A cancellation of contract without substitution may introduce business and technical disruption. The practitioner should carefully inspect the discontinuation of contracts during the structural specification process.
Notation	Use the "Unbound" symbol.

EXHIBIT 20.27 CONTRACT CANCELLATION SUMMARY TABLE

Synopsis. As simple as it may sound, contract discontinuation may introduce serious complications to business and technical implementations. Not only will a service be retired or suspended because of certain requirements, but its consumers may be affected due to interruption to service operations. Exhibit 20.27 summarizes these problems and introduces solutions and methods to ease the negative influence on business execution.

Anti-Patterns. Remember, most instances of contract discontinuation require a rigorous analysis to determine the risks involved and agree on consumer compensation to ensure business continuity. The Contract Cancellation anti-patterns listed in Exhibit 20.28 identify best practices related to the contract terms that a practitioner must be aware of. These are associated with contract termination terms, substitution of lost capabilities, the scope of the reduction of service operations, and suspension of a contract.

Anti-Pattern Name	Best Practice
Temporary Contract Cancellation	A contract cancellation is a permanent act that should not be regarded as temporary.
Mandatory Service Substitution	Service replacement is not mandatory when a service is retired. Discontinuation of a contract, however, may require substitution of functionality to compensate for loss of capabilities when a service formation is restructured.
Permanent Contract Suspension	A suspended contract is not a permanent state of service discontinuation. This is a temporary activity that a service and a related consumer should agree on.

EXHIBIT 20.28 CONTRACT CANCELLATION ANTI-PATTERNS

CONTRACT INTERNALIZATION PATTERN. A service should not maintain direct contracts with its related consumers while it is aggregated in a composite service or a service cluster. Indirect communications with the outside world are encouraged. The term "indirect" implies that if the service is aggregated in a composite structure, the hosting service (parent) is responsible for maintaining the contracts on the aggregated service's behalf. When the service is aggregated in a cluster formation, one of the cluster members is delegated contract management responsibilities (known as the cluster gravitational point).

So how can the aggregated service continue to maintain relationships with its related consumers if it is decomposed from its hosting structure? The answer to this question is straightforward and requires a two-step solution: (1) the contract that was maintained on the service's behalf should be discontinued, and (2) once the service is completely separated, a direct contract should be established with its corresponding consumers.

Therefore employ the Contract Internalization pattern to address business continuity between former aggregated services and their related consumers.

Problem.   The structural specification process that is discussed in this chapter addresses granularity alignment and structural enhancements of service formations by reducing its capabilities. This required service structural manipulation often entails fundamental modifications to internal service design and architecture and alterations to its constituting components. To accomplish these specification analysis goals, the architect, analyst, developer, modeler, and project manager typically perform decomposition operations on bulky services to break them down into more manageable software entities. This reorganization would also require reinstatements of service contracts and the establishment of new binding contracts to accommodate these service structure optimization efforts.

Solution.   The Contract Internalization pattern should be applied when a service that was extracted from a composite or cluster formation is now an autonomous entity that must fulfill the contracts that were previously maintained on its behalf. Consider the guiding steps for employing the Contract Internalization pattern:

1. **Contract unbinding.** Discontinue an existing contract that is established on behalf of an aggregated service.
2. **Decomposition.** Separate an aggregated service from its hosting structure. This activity pertains to a service that is part of a composite service or a member of a cluster structure.
3. **Contract rebinding.** Reestablish the contract directly between the separated service and its related consumers.

Example.   The two examples in the sections that follow depict the internalization of a contract process. The activities that yield to reinstitution of a contract involve two service formations: composite and cluster structures.

Contract Internalization Example with Composite Formation.   Exhibit 20.29 illustrates the process of Contract Internalization in two different perspective windows: 3D View (far right) and the Service-Oriented Modeling Formal Diagram View (far left). This activity involves the composite service formation CO-1, its aggregated atomic service A-1, and the consumer CONS-1. Let us follow the four Contract Internalization activities that are depicted in the Service-Oriented Modeling Formal Diagram View (far left):

1. The contract between Composite Service CO-1 and the consumer CONS-1 is discontinued—denoted by the "Unbound" symbol. Remember that the parent service CO-1 handles contracts on behalf of its internal aggregated service A-1.
2. Atomic service A-1 is decomposed from its containing parent composite service CO-1— indicated by the symbol "Decomposed."
3. Composite service CO-1 is transformed to atomic service A-CO-1 since it does not contain any more any internal services.
4. Atomic service A-1 and consumer CONS-1 are re-linked by a new contract.

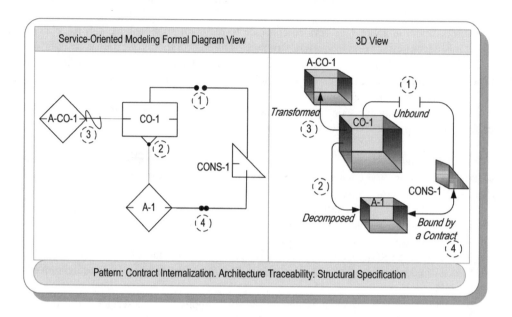

EXHIBIT 20.29 CONTRACT INTERNALIZATION PATTERN WITH COMPOSITE SERVICE EXAMPLE

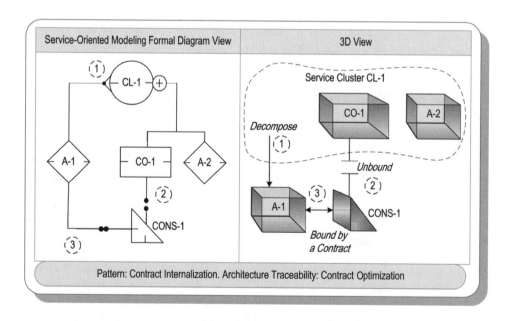

EXHIBIT 20.30 CONTRACT INTERNALIZATION PATTERN WITH SERVICE CLUSTER EXAMPLE

Contact Internalization Example with Cluster Formation. Exhibit 20.30 illustrates the utilization of the Contract Internalization pattern. The two windows encapsulate the steps that are required to pursue this process: 3D View and Service-Oriented Modeling Formal Diagram View. Let us review the necessary steps to the successful execution of Contract Internalization process:

1. Atomic service A-1 is decomposed from its encompassed cluster formation CL-1. Note the "Decomposed" symbol that denotes the separation of atomic service A-1 from its cluster formation.
2. The contract between composite service CO-1—contained in service cluster CL-1—and the consumer CONS-1 is discontinued, signified by the "Unbound" symbol. Remember, CO-1 (gravitational point) is the service that handles contracts on behalf of the CL-1 cluster members
3. A new contract is reestablished between atomic service A-1 and its corresponding consumer CONS-1 by employing the "bound" modeling symbol.

Synopsis. Two activities must take place when a service is separated from its containing composite service or extracted from a cluster formation: (1) The contract that was established and maintained on the service's behalf with its corresponding consumers must be discontinued, and (2) a new contract must be established to relink the decomposed service to its related consumers. Consider Exhibit 20.31, which identifies the problems, solutions, method for implementation, and risks involved with the employment of the Contract Internalization pattern.

Anti-Patterns. The Contract Internalization pattern applies to an aggregated service that is decomposed and must continue to maintain relationships that previously were managed by its parent service. This pattern also should be applied to a service that was separated from a service cluster, in which another service used to manage contracts on behalf of cluster members. Consider

Pattern Identification	
Name	Contract Internalization Pattern
Category	Structural Specification
Problems, Solutions, and Implementations	
Problem	A service that was extracted from a composite or cluster formation is now an autonomous entity that is publicly exposed to consumers and must fulfill the contract obligations that were previously maintained on its behalf.
Solution	Contracts that were maintained on behalf of former aggregated services should be discontinued and bound directly with the corresponding consumers.
Applicability	Applies to former aggregated services that were part of a composite service or a cluster formation.
Method	There are three major steps to accomplish contract internalization: 1. Decompose an aggregated service. 2. Discontinue the contract that was managed on behalf of the decomposed service. 3. Reinstitute the contract directly with the corresponding consumer.
Benefits	1. Ensures business and technical continuity. 2. Decomposed services that become autonomous entities are able to continue to serve consumers despite their separation from their aggregating formations.
Risks	Reinstitution of contracts may disrupt business and technical execution.
Notation	Utilize the "Bound" and "Unbound" symbols.

EXHIBIT 20.31 CONTRACT INTERNALIZATION PATTERN SUMMARY TABLE

Anti-Pattern Name	Best Practice
Preserving Contract Binding	After decomposition of a service from a composite formation, the contract that is managed on its behalf by its parent service should be unbound. This should also apply to a service that is a cluster member. Contracts that are managed on its behalf by other members should be discontinued as well. In this case no preservation of contracts should be allowed.
Contract Internalization without Decomposition	The contact internalization process must include the decomposition of a service from its containing entity.
Contract Internalization with Subtraction	Remember, a subtracted aggregated service is in fact a retired service that should be removed from production environment. Thus, use the decomposition operation to separate a service from its containing structure and then bind it by a contract to its corresponding consumers. The subtraction operation should not be employed in this case.

Exhibit 20.32 Contract Internalization Anti-Patterns

Exhibit 20.32, which presents the best practices that can guide practitioners to utilize the Contract Internalization pattern to solve these challenges.

DELIVERABLES

An internal service composition diagram (discussed in Chapter 18) should be delivered to carve an analysis proposition. This artifact should depict the reduction of service capabilities by decreasing its internal structure. Service refactoring is another view that should be presented to propose a superior structure design. The various modeling diagrams in this chapter should serve as guiding material when preparing the deliverables for the structural specification phase of the project.

SUMMARY

- The structural specification process is devised to promote loosely coupled service formations by introducing a set of best practices and modeling patterns to guide practitioners on how to safely reduce service capabilities or discontinue their execution. Service refactoring is another goal that can be attained by applying modeling operations to enhance its operations.
- The structural specification practice introduces four major analysis methods, each of which is accompanied by affiliated patterns to assist practitioners with service capability reduction or refactoring: (1) decomposition analysis, (2) subtraction analysis, (3) refactoring analysis, and (4) contract analysis.

Notes

1. Remember, the Selective Decomposition (360) pattern is about breaking up a service structure. This operation may follow a contextual specification analysis that promotes separation of concerns, depicted in Chapter 15 by the Separation of Concerns through Service Specification (252) pattern.

2. The Entity Elimination (372) pattern typically introduces great challenges to operations and configuration personnel who must remove a service with a large number of dependent consumers.

3. Martin Fowler, *Refactoring: Improving the Design of Existing Code* (Boston: Addison-Wesley, 1999), p. 14.

4. Service capability substitution can also be achieved by employing the "Decomposed" symbol that denotes separation of a component.

5. See note 4.

STRUCTURAL EXPANSION ANALYSIS PROCESS AND MODELING PATTERNS

The structural expansion practice addresses the broadening of service distribution across applications, departments, divisions, geographical locations, or partner installations. Unlike the structural generalization analysis (discussed in Chapter 19), which focuses on widening an internal service structure, the structural expansion tackles challenges attributed to deployment, integration, and interoperability efforts. This external computing landscape development is imperative when business and technical requirements call for architectural boundary expansion to enable the distribution of business offerings to a larger consumer base.

The mechanisms introduced by the three major analysis processes provided are designed to expand architecture physical limits. This mission can be fulfilled by employing network distribution patterns, utilizing service intermediaries, and centralizing contract management to enable the growth of a distributed service ecosystem. Consider the chief enabling mechanisms that can be utilized by architects, analysts, developers, modelers, and managers to promote business and technological solutions that span multiple silo implementations across the enterprise:

- **Service distribution.** The service distribution expansion approach offers five major mechanisms that can be employed to extend message exchange capabilities and increase the number of consumers across the organization or beyond: (1) network coupling, (2) circular coupling, (3) tree coupling, (4) star coupling, and (5) federation coupling. These are also message path patterns that are established to centralize service operations or to federate service deployment.
- **Service mediation.** The service mediation method advocates employing service hubs and proxy implementations to extend architecture capabilities. It includes the introduction of service intermediary, service gateway, and enterprise service bus. These mediating entities are responsible for intercepting messages, transforming data formats, interpreting network protocols, and converting security models to alleviate interoperability challenges in a distributed deployment environment.
- **Service contract.** Contracts that are instituted between a service and its corresponding consumers are subject for optimization and enhancement. To accommodate the expansion of business offerings and architecture boundaries, mediation and centralization of contract approaches are offered. These mechanisms contribute to a loosely coupled service environment and reuse of contract artifacts

The sections that follow elaborate the process of service environment expansion and offer patterns, ready-to-use solutions that can be embedded in an analysis proposition.

DISTRIBUTION ANALYSIS: PATTERNS AND IMPLEMENTATION

The distribution of software entities across an organization, lines of business, or applications is a major challenge that most practitioners struggle with. The term "distribution" means that autonomous services are deployed in different sections of the enterprise, expanding the offered functionality and broadening the scope of a solution. This collaborative effort devised to engage a group of services should be meticulously analyzed, optimized, and stylized to achieve superior transaction execution and maintain stability of message delivery.

The distribution of service activity can span multiple silo organizations and bridge the communication gaps between lines of business. This expansion of capabilities should be guided by design styles—patterns of analysis that can assist practitioners in evaluating the proposed architecture and optimizing service integration and deployment plans. Therefore, the distribution analysis process not only identifies the risks involved with certain integration configurations but also examines the business and technological benefits that are gained when pursuing architecture solutions.

DISTRIBUTION ANALYSIS PATTERNS AND ANTI-PATTERNS.   The sections that follow introduce distribution analysis patterns and anti-patterns that can guide practitioners in analyzing and proposing efficient solutions to executing and managing autonomous services in a distributed computing landscape. These enormous challenges can affect transaction performance and the cost of operations. The five patterns provided introduce coupling mechanisms that link services to a mutual cause, establishing different configuration formations that correspond to individual environment problems and production challenges:

1. Network Coupling (390)
2. Circular Coupling (394)
3. Tree Coupling (396)
4. Star Coupling (399)
5. Federated Service Coupling (402)

NETWORK COUPLING PATTERN.   The Network Coupling pattern depicts relationships that are established between distributed services across an organization or located in close proximity to resolve a problem. These participating parties, services, and even applications form *software entity groups* that are united by their mutual goal of providing a solution. Moreover, this arrangement typically is designed to overcome interoperability challenges across lines of business, connect the dots between autonomous service contributors that may span multiple business groups and partners, or offer a means of message delivery to small-scale or large-scope projects.

The phrase "means of message delivery" implies that the architect, developer, analyst, modeler, or manager proposes a relationship scheme between services based on their specialty and type of offering. But the chief challenge to be resolved is to establish *message exchange paths* that depict information flow between services and their corresponding consumers on a network to enable communication and collaboration between distributed services.

Finally, the Network Coupling pattern supports the *decentralization* of service operations notion: The flow of information is characteristically dictated by transaction exchange between distributed services with no distinguishable central point that coordinates this interaction. In addition, each participating service or consumer is allowed to fire off a message request based on individual priorities. This implies that the involved parties in the Network Coupling pattern are treated equally in terms of their contribution to a transaction execution: They are allowed to communicate directly with their corresponding collaborators and maintain their distinct schedules.

Problem.   One of the major challenges with service distribution and orchestrating message exchange between a service and its consumers is to increase reuse of processes across an organization, lines of business, and even applications. This hurdle is typically due to organizational structures and the silo operations that each group within the enterprise is executing. This independent and vertical service management not only contributes to duplication of functionality across departments and divisions, it also results in higher costs that can compromise budgets and undermine strategies.

The distribution of services that span multiple institutions or applications also increases the challenges created due to technological interoperability. Bridging heterogeneous computing environments and enhancing communications between services and consumers are other concerns that should be tackled in a distributed computing landscape. These concerns typically are attributed to geographical barriers that separate a service from its related consumer or even obstacles that arise from service and partner collaboration.

Solution.   Therefore, the Network Coupling pattern proposes to resolve challenges that are associated with the design of message routes that enable services to connect and collaborate on providing a remedy to an organizational concern. The extended solution advocates establishing, direct relationships, between services, related consumers, and peer services. These associations obviously found information routing paths and contribute to the mechanisms by which services and consumers exchange transactions. To accomplish these goals consider the three major tasks that the practitioner ought to perform:

1.   Selecting the services and consumers that must participate in a solution.
2.   Determining the message flow and routes between the collaborating entities.
3.   Analyzing the various associations of an involved service with its line of business, project, or organization.

The latter examination is vital to the execution of transactions between a service and its associated consumers because of its affiliation with an organization that not only supports its operations but also, as in a majority of cases, has been created to fulfill specific goals to promote a distinct line of business. Thus broadening the scope of a service and increasing its capability spectrum are benefits that can be gained by employing the Network Coupling pattern.

Example.   When analyzing the relationship scale between services and consumers, it is crucial to look at the dependency aspects between these message exchange parties. The practitioner should be aware of two major classes of Network Coupling approaches: tightly coupled and loosely coupled. The former identifies the relationships that a service may establish with *each* of its associated consumers and peer services that are part of the network. The loosely coupled deployment arrangement indicates that a service is linked with *some* of the participating members of the network. Consider the next two examples, discussed in the sections that follow, which depict these service coupling configurations.

Tightly Coupled Service Network Example.   Exhibit 21.1 illustrates a tightly coupled service network environment that involves six services, four of which are the atomic formations A-1, A2, A-3, and A-4. The remaining two are composite services CO-1 and CO-2. In both apparent perspectives, the 3D View and Service-Oriented Modeling Formal Diagram View, a service maintains relationships with *each* of its peer services. Note that in the formal diagram view, this is denoted by the "Coupled" symbol.

Loosely Coupled Service Network Example.   The loosely coupled service network environment illustrated in Exhibit 21.2 involves the same services depicted in the tightly coupled service network example in Exhibit 21.1. These two composite services (CO-1 and CO-2) and four atomic services, A-1, A2, A3, and A4, form a network of relationships that is less restrictive and loosely associated. That is, a service is linked to *some* of the network members. Note the use of the "Coupled" symbol in the formal diagram view to denote the coupling between the various services.

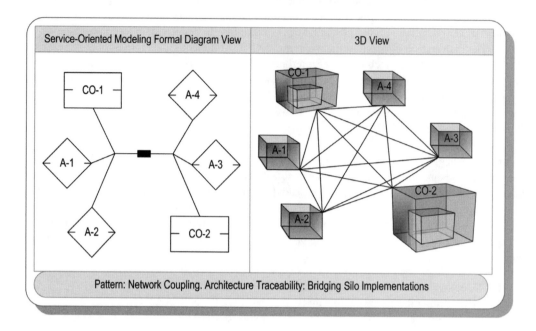

EXHIBIT 21.1   NETWORK COUPLING PATTERN: TIGHTLY COUPLED SERVICE NETWORK EXAMPLE

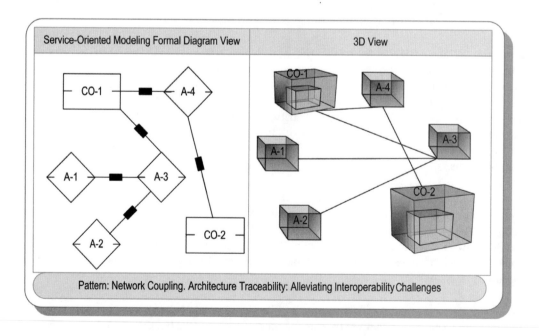

EXHIBIT 21.2   NETWORK COUPLING PATTERN: LOOSELY COUPLED SERVICE NETWORK EXAMPLE

Pattern Identification	
Name	Network Coupling Pattern
Category	Structural Expansion Analysis

Problems, Solutions, and Implementations	
Problem	1. Silo implementation challenges.
	2. Bridging technological interoperability difficulties.
	3. Low service reusability factors.
	4. Geographical barriers impose communication difficulties.
Solution	Institute a network grid of services that directly communicate and exchange messages with related consumers, avoiding a centralized service configuration.
Applicability	Involve atomic, composite, and service cluster formations that communicate and collaborate across organizations or applications.
Method	1. Selecting the services that must participate in a solution.
	2. Determining the message flow and routes between the collaborating entities.
	3. Analyzing the various associations of an involved service to determine how its capabilities can be expanded to accommodate a holistic organizational solution.
Benefits	1. Foster service reusability.
	2. Break down silo operations.
	2. Alleviate business and technological interoperability challenges.
	3. Overcome software distribution geographical barriers.
Risks	This pattern may result in an unmanaged service network that typically contributes to tightly coupled service ecosystem.
Notation	Employ the "Coupled" symbol.

Exhibit 21.3   Network Coupling Pattern Summary Table

Anti-Pattern Name	Best Practice
Organically Grown Network Links	A service network should be planned and strategized. Avoid the establishment of an ad hoc relationship between a service and its affiliated consumers, peers, and partners.
Excessive Coupling	Although the Network Coupling pattern does not restrict the amount of links between a network members, avoid excessive coupling to increase loose coupling and foster business agility.
Impractical Relationship	Reduce unnecessary dependencies between service network members.

Exhibit 21.4   Network Coupling Anti-Patterns

Synopsis.   The Network Coupling pattern links a collection of affiliated services and consumers that are designed to collaboratively execute transactions and provide common solutions to organizational concerns. These software entities typically belong to silo deployments, yet they are configured to break their organizational boundaries to contribute to holistic solutions. Consider Exhibit 21.3, which illustrates the problems, solution, applicability, methods, and risks related to the utilization of the Network Coupling pattern.

Anti-Patterns.   The Network Coupling pattern addresses the links established between network members. These constituents may be consumers, atomic services, composite services, and service clusters. One of the most significant best practices that should guide practitioners when instituting such a network of services is the reduction of unnecessary dependencies that a service may found with its corresponding message exchange parties. In other words, a significant effort should be invested in simplifying message routing and reducing unnecessary links between services, peers, and related consumers. Consider Exhibit 21.4, which identifies three chief best practices to avoid tightly coupled service associations.

CIRCULAR COUPLING PATTERN.   The Circular Coupling pattern advocates forming a ring of service relationships that link a service to two other services. The first and the last service in the circle are connected to each other. This configuration enables routing a message from a service to the next in the chain until the response is returned back to the originator. Each completed circle indicates the completion of a transaction or an activity of a transaction. Furthermore, to complete a circular path, the message must be routed through a number of mediating service members, each of which is commissioned to augment or alter the original message content. Finally, the response arrives to the originating service consisting of the requested information or including an acknowledgment that indicates transaction completion.

The Circular Coupling pattern also imposes a predetermined message path that commits the participating services to a strict discipline of information delivery. In other words, this pattern of transaction execution involves a series of service "handshakes" that commences with the originating entity and concludes at the same starting point.

Problem.   The traditional architecture solution that proposes a centralized message exchange mechanism introduces challenges to handling high-volume transaction environments. This centralization of operations is usually enabled by a message interceptor, a network traffic controller, typically implemented by locating a proxy service between the consumer and a corresponding service. The well-known Service Façade pattern[1] and the Service Locator pattern exemplify this approach. These mediating mechanisms hide service implementations from consumers and provide routing capabilities to match consumer requests with a related service offering.

But this centralized service facility that requires services and related consumers to communicate indirectly through a hub may cause management difficulties and introduces performance degradation. These challenges occur when it comes to high volume and unusual frequency of information transmission between services and their related consumers. This architectural style must be enhanced by practitioners that are responsible for flawless execution of transaction exchange.

Moreover, a centralized message mediator can be a convenient method for organizing and managing processes in an orderly manner due to the concentration of computer resources, middleware, and infrastructure. In certain configurations, the controller notion can be an effective solution for routing consumers' requests to their corresponding services. Yet employing this message centralization facility may outweigh the benefits when it comes to accommodating mission-critical applications, satisfying high-consumption requirements, and addressing unnecessary network traffic routing to an intermediary entity.

Solution.   The Circular Coupling pattern resolves the challenges of centralization of service functionality, as discussed in the Problem section, by avoiding the installation of a central hub, a message mediator to manage incoming and outgoing messages. This approach also suggests steering clear of employing a proxy service to handle mediation responsibilities, such as data formatting and data cleansing. Therefore, according to the circular approach, a transaction is managed solely by affiliated services that participate in a solution without a need for message interception or service brokering.

Furthermore, the Circular Coupling pattern fosters reduction of service dependency on a centralized routing service and eliminates the need for funneling messages through a single proxy service. This circular architecture style implies that all participating entities in a transaction bear equal responsibility when it comes to handling the delivery of messages. Thus a service that is a part of the circular motion of a transaction must be intelligent enough not only to recognize the message sender but also to direct the message to the proper participant for further processing.

Finally, this solution suggests avoiding unnecessary network traffic by directly involving the participating service partners in a transaction. Network consumption should be reduced by eliminating the mediating service role and employing a circular approach for information exchange between services. This method would also promote loose coupling and decrease dependency on auxiliary services that are not responsible for processing the message content directly.

Consider the four chief guiding and related principles for proper service analysis and use of the Circular Coupling pattern:

1. Establish a circular transaction pattern that relies on message exchange between peer services.
2. Avoid funneling messages through a central message interceptor service.
3. Reduce tightly coupled service conditions and decrease service dependency by eliminating brokering or intermediating facilities.
4. Avoid unnecessary network traffic caused by routing messages to a centralized service.

Example.   Exhibit 21.5 illustrates the Circular Coupling pattern and the relationships that are formed between the participating services. These are depicted in the two perspectives: 3D View (far right) and the Service-Oriented Modeling Formal Diagram View (far left). This simple concept is implemented by four services that share the responsibility of accepting a message and also routing it to the next service in the chain: atomic services A-1, A-2, and A-3; and composite service CO-1. Note that the association between these services—illustrated in the formal diagram view—is denoted by the "Coupled" symbol that links them together in a circular shape to enable message flow. Remember, such a configuration can connect not only atomic or composite services. A service cluster can also be a part of this scheme.

Synopsis.   The Circular Coupling pattern proposes a service distribution approach that eliminates the need for a central message dispatching mediator entity. Although the circular method does not support centralization of transaction and information exchange facilities, the practitioner is encouraged to inspect the contribution of service intermediaries to transaction execution and to assess the

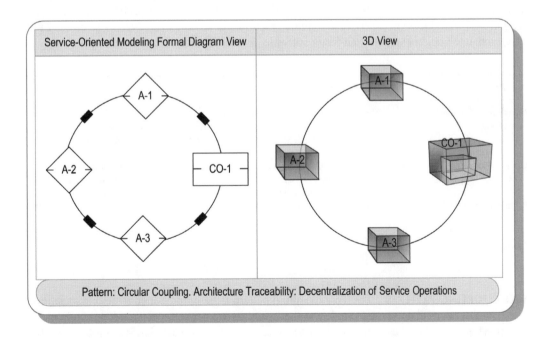

EXHIBIT 21.5   CIRCULAR COUPLING PATTERN EXAMPLE

Pattern Identification	
Name	Circular Coupling Pattern
Category	Structural Expansion Analysis

Problems, Solutions, and Implementations	
Problem	1. A service controller is unable to sustain high-volume message frequencies and consumer consumption. 2. A proposed centralized architecture increases network traffic demand.
Solution	1. Decentralize service environment and message-handling mechanisms. 2. Eliminate proxy services that offer mediation mechanisms.
Applicability	Applies to enterprise-level implementations and mission-critical applications that operate in an environment where network bandwidth is constrained.
Method	To eliminate a controller service, arrange the participating services in a circular shape that links services to each other. The message originator service should also be the entity that receives the final response.
Benefits	Elimination of central processing point and decentralization of service distribution.
Risks	The Circular Coupling pattern increases potential message processing delays and time-out conditions if the chain of services is too long.
Notation	Employ the "Coupled" symbol.

Exhibit 21.6   Circular Coupling Pattern Summary Table

overall benefit of a centralized service environment. These aspects are summarized in Exhibit 21.6, which identifies the problems that create the motivation to employ the Circular Coupling pattern and describes the corresponding implementation solutions, benefits, and risks.

Anti-Patterns.   The Circular Coupling pattern promotes the software decentralization concept by advocating the elimination of a common controller configured to accept and deliver consumers' requests and match them with their corresponding services. The anti-patterns summarized in Exhibit 21.7 introduce best practices that guide practitioners on how to analyze these circular message exchange implementations and foster software decentralization across the enterprise.

Anti-Pattern Name	Best Practice
Noncircular Message Exchange	The Circular Coupling pattern depicts the dependencies of affiliated services on each other, forming a circular formation that shapes the message exchange pattern. Thus, the circular structure is a mandatory message delivery requirement.
Circular Coupling Message Dispatcher	The Circular Coupling pattern does not support a centralized and dedicated message dispatcher. Instead, the message delivery task is designated to the member services that participate in a circular information exchange activity.
Excessive Circular Coupling	Avoid involving a large number of services in a circular coupling implementation model to reduce the risks of latency and time-out conditions.

Exhibit 21.7   Circular Coupling Anti-Patterns

TREE COUPLING PATTERN.   The Tree Coupling pattern is based on a hierarchical association of *distributed* services that are related to each other based on their contextual parent/child relationship model. This simple scheme of business or technical affiliation implies that the top-level entity in the hierarchy (parent service) operates on behalf of the low-level child services. The phrase "operated on behalf of" implies that the parent entity delivers the outside world requests to child services and responses to consumers after it has collected the corresponding replies. The reader should not confuse this arrangement with a composite formation where a parent service aggregates child services. Remember, the Tree Coupling pattern is all about arranging distributed and autonomous services in a hierarchical and logical formation to help streamline a service deployment environment. Therefore, the tree style relationship does not imply that the child services are aggregated in the parent structure.

Like the Circular Coupling (394) pattern, the Tree Coupling pattern shapes the message exchange path between a service and its peer services. This route of information passing typically is devised to modularize the relationship between distributed software entities and delegate clear roles and responsibilities to the participating services in a solution. Thus, the tree's top level is assigned to a parent service, the most coarse-grained entity, and the descending nodes are allocated to smaller fine-grained services.

Problem.   Recall that a distributed service environment is comprised of autonomous services that are deployed across organizations, configured to serve lines of business, or operating within application boundaries. The overall integration and deployment design and the manner by which they are linked can affect the message routes between services and influence transaction execution in terms of performance and consumption efficiency.

Perhaps one of the greatest problems with software distribution is to design an efficient deployment model for services that are scattered across the enterprise. Doing this includes assigning clear roles and responsibilities to the participating services in a transaction, streamlining their relationships to ease integration difficulties, and even simplifying their deployment to a production environment. Many organizations neglect to formalize these associations and allow an "organic" or "natural" linking of services, which are casually connected, often driven by individual project requirements. This ad hoc unstructured activity lacks a strategic approach to message integration and orchestration.

Another arising common challenge is to determine how to integrate coarse-grained services with fine-grained services. Should the coarse-grained entities carry more message routing responsibilities? Should the fine-grained services be subordinated to coarse-grained services? What is the most efficient method for routing messages between coarse grained and fine-grained services?

Solution.   Unstructured integration and deployment of services in a production environment motivates analyzing and restructuring service relationships and message exchange paths between peer services and their consumers. One of the most understood and easiest-to-establish patterns that can simplify a complex service integration scheme is the hierarchical coupling of services on a network.

According to this arrangement, the autonomous entities that participate in providing a solution are positioned and accessed relative to their granularity scale on the hierarchy. In other words, the message exchange routes are simply established between parent and child services to accomplish a transaction. A coarse-grained service typically assumes dominant parent responsibilities. A finer-grained service, however, operates behind the scenes and has lesser responsibilities when it comes to executing transactions. Consider the guideline outline for analyzing a distributed service environment and employing the Tree Coupling pattern:

- Identify parent/child relationships among distributed autonomous services.
- Coarse-grained entities should be considered as parent services, and finer-grained entities should be identified as subordinate services.
- Message exchange routes should be established between parent and child services.
- Service contracts should adhere to the relationships that are founded between parent and child services.

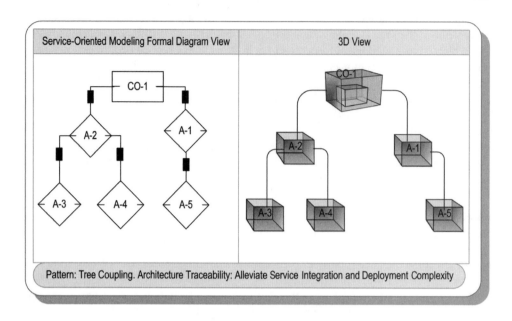

| Service-Oriented Modeling Formal Diagram View | 3D View |

Pattern: Tree Coupling. Architecture Traceability: Alleviate Service Integration and Deployment Complexity

EXHIBIT 21.8 TREE COUPLING PATTERN EXAMPLE

Example. Exhibit 21.8 illustrates the Tree Coupling pattern and the manner by which services are linked in a distributed environment. The two perspectives, 3D View and the Service-Oriented Modeling Formal Diagram View, depict hierarchical relationships in which the parent node is presented by composite service CO-1. Its immediate subordinate services are atomic services A-1 and A-2. In addition, atomic services A-3 and A-4 are the children of atomic service A-2, and atomic service A-5 is the offspring of atomic service A-1.

Remember, the Tree Coupling pattern merely addresses the relationships between distributed services on a network and is not designed to tackle the challenge of service aggregation. In the Service-Oriented Modeling Formal Diagram View these associations are denoted by the employment of the "Coupled" structural modeling symbol.

Synopsis. The Tree Coupling pattern affiliates distributed services by their business or technical contextual affiliations. Their common specialty not only provides the motivation to *structurally* group and arrange them in a hierarchical shape but also to design message exchange paths that correspond to their associations. Although this design exercise is not about contextual relationships between the participating services, the structural modeling process should be influenced by these contextual associations. Exhibit 21.9 identifies these challenges and reveals the possible solutions and methods that can guide practitioners to employ the Tree Coupling pattern.

Anti-Patterns. One of the chief challenges with analyzing and designing a distributed service environment is the establishment of hierarchical relationships between parent services and their offspring. The Tree Coupling pattern is clearly a convenient method for logically linking services, if indeed their contextual affiliation justifies such coupling. An important aspect to remember is that the offered tree structure shapes services in a hierarchical manner by which the dominating entities are parent services that hide the outside world from their child services. Therefore, the design of message routes must agree with the Tree Coupling scheme and disallow direct flow of

Pattern Identification	
Name	Tree Coupling Pattern
Category	Structural Expansion Analysis

Problems, Solutions, and Implementations	
Problem	1. Unstructured integration and deployment of services in production environment.
	2. Complex transaction message exchange routing model.
Solution	Couple services in a hierarchical model to simplify integration and deployment complexities.
Applicability	Applies to distributed atomic, composite, and service cluster formations.
Method	1. Identify parent/child relationships.
	2. Establish message routes that correspond to the parent and child services affiliations.
	3. Found service contracts that attend to relationships that are founded between parent and child services.
Benefits	Structuring a distributed service environment and establishing clear relationships between services that collaborate to provide solutions.
Risks	1. Hierarchical affiliation of services typically requires business or contextual reasoning that may not always be found in a distributed environment.
	2. Plentiful tree levels may introduce unwanted complexity to a production environment.
Notation	Employ the "Coupled" symbol.

EXHIBIT 21.9   TREE COUPLING PATTERN SUMMARY TABLE

messages to child services. Exhibit 21.10 identifies the anti-patterns and best practices that enable this arrangement on an organizational network.

Anti-Pattern Name	Best Practice
Aggregated Tree Coupling	The Tree Coupling pattern is designed to address structuring a distributed service environment. Service members of a tree coupling arrangement are not aggregated entities. The formed relationship between parent services and their offspring are merely to depict message exchange paths between the participating parties.
Excessive Tree Levels	Numerous tree levels may introduce unnecessary complexity to message exchange implementation.
Excessive Number of Service Members	Avoid a tree coupling implementation that includes a large number of service members.

EXHIBIT 21.10   TREE COUPLING ANTI-PATTERNS

STAR COUPLING PATTERN.   The Star Coupling pattern proposes a *centralized* solution for information exchange, manipulation, and prcessing. Unlike the Network Coupling (390) pattern, the Star Coupling approach advocates employing a dominant service that has control over message exchange activities and acts as a central processing unit for the inflow of data. This is typically the entity that facilitates the interaction between the distributed services and ensures proper synchronization of request/response activities. The necessity for centralizing such service operations is the chief motivation for the Star Coupling venture. Remember, the star architectural approach should not be devised merely for intercepting messages. On the contrary, this style of design advocates that the star center is a part of the solution that must participate in processing business logic, offer technical solutions, and constitute the central driving engine for service offerings.

Furthermore, the center of the star typically extends linear arms, each of which consists of related services that broaden the support for executing transactions. Obviously, this arrangement is driven by the business or technical context of the associated services. For example, the star center may be presented by the Accounting Service. Each star arm can be populated with different services that expand on accounting operations, such as Accounts Receivable Service, Accounts Payable Service, and General Ledger Service. But the chief aim is to *structurally form* a Star Coupling pattern and establish a message route model that enables efficient information trading between the participating services in this pattern.

The Star Coupling pattern can be considered for a number of deployment scenarios. One of the best-known is the *spoke-and-hub* architecture devised to connect services by a central focal point service that links participating service members. This arrangement characteristically is applied to geographically distributed service installations that must be linked to accommodate transactions. Another common use of the Star Coupling pattern is to enable transmission of information to the occupant services of the star arms. This broadcasting mission is also known as multicasting; it is the method by which the central service transmits information with no intention of getting a response from the receiving services.

Problem. The chief motivation for employing the Star Coupling pattern is rooted in inefficient *coordination* and *synchronization* of transactions that occur between peer services and their related consumers when they are organically distributed in a production environment. The term "organic" relates to unplanned or even unmanaged growth of a service landscape that keeps evolving during months or decades. Disorganized *orchestration* of business or technical processes is another cause for concern when services must collaborate and exchange messages to provide efficient solutions.

But the difficulty in controlling and harmonizing the flow of traded information between services is not the only hurdle that motivates practitioners to propose the Star Coupling configuration. Costly service management, monitoring, and securing distributed services that are scattered across an organization with no central control facility are other major challenges that should be examined and rectified if architecturally justified.

Solution. The Star Coupling pattern offers the means to address chaotic deployment and integration configurations that lead to painful service maintenance and operation support activities. The solution to centralize a production environment and create a message exchange model that enables services to collaborate and communicate efficiently to provide a proper remedy to an organizational concern is recommended. This arrangement not only offers a central point for service monitoring and operation traceability, it also provides easier means of coordinating transactions and synchronizing their activities. It is a strategic decision that managers, architects, analysts, modelers, and developers should explore and contemplate before pursuing.

Consider the guiding outline that enables the configuration of the Star Coupling pattern:

- Identify the service that can be placed in the center of the star. This entity must possess the knowledge and capabilities to enable proper coordination between the distributed services that are positioned on its arms.
- Position related services on each star's arms.
- Establish message exchange routes between the center of the star and its affiliated arms.
- Create contracts between the star members and their affiliated consumers.

Example. Exhibit 21.11 illustrates the employment of the Star Coupling pattern. The two apparent perspectives, the 3D View and the Service-Oriented Modeling Formal Diagram View, depict a total of six services that form a star formation. Atomic service A-1 is positioned in the center of the star; services A-2, A-3, A-4, CO-1, and CO-2 occupy the star arms. Note that in the formal modeling diagram (far left), the "Coupled" symbol is employed to denote the links between the various services that take part in this configuration.

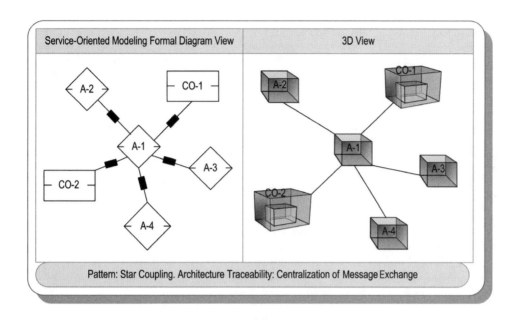

Pattern: Star Coupling. Architecture Traceability: Centralization of Message Exchange

EXHIBIT 21.11   STAR COUPLING PATTERN EXAMPLE

Synopsis.   The Star Coupling pattern offers a centralized solution for service integration and deployment. This scheme is designed to alleviate the challenges that an unstructured distributed environment introduces. The concept of centralizing control by employing a service to manage network traffic, route messages, and ensure the utmost coordination between the participating services in the star configuration is summarized in Exhibit 21.12.

Pattern Identification	
Name	Star Coupling Pattern
Category	Structural Expansion Analysis
Problems, Solutions, and Implementations	
Problem	1. The coordination of service operations and message exchange is challenging.
	2. The management, monitoring, and maintenance of distributed services is costly and difficult.
Solution	Propose a centralized service architecture that employs a service hub.
Applicability	Applies to a distributed service environment.
Method	Employ the Star Coupling pattern that consists of a centralized service that is designated to handle message routing and distribution of information to its extended arms, each of which should consist of related services that further broadens the solution.
Benefits	1. The star coupling approach characteristically benefits from high message exchange coordination capabilities.
	2. The pattern contributes to centralization of service operations.
Risks	1. The star service center can become a bottleneck.
	2. The communication between the occupants of star arms may be challenging.
	3. Failure of the central node can halt all transactions in the Star Coupling pattern (known as a single point of failure)
Notation	Utilize the "Coupled" symbol.

EXHIBIT 21.12   STAR COUPLING PATTERN SUMMARY TABLE

Anti-Pattern Name	Best Practice
Decentralized Star Formation	The Star Coupling pattern is not a decentralized architectural style; it proposes gathering services around a central controlling service that acts as a mediating hub to manage transactions and oversee message exchange activities. In addition, the central controller is designed to coordinate business events, process data, and contribute to business logic. Therefore the center of the star should be a part of the solution and not only the facilitating message exchange entity.
Overloaded Star Arms	A large number of star service members can overload the capacity of the center service node and cause operation bottlenecks.
Complex Star Formation	Avoid instituting links between services that are positioned on different star arms to reduce the complexity of message routing, integration, and deployment.

EXHIBIT 21.13 STAR COUPLING ANTI-PATTERNS

Anti-Patterns.   Overloading the consumption capacity of the central star service can obviously introduce bottlenecks to transaction execution. Establishing unnecessary links and binding contracts between the services that are positioned on different star arms should also be avoided. These best practices are summarized in Exhibit 21.13, which also defines the fundamental concept of service centralization scheme.

FEDERATED SERVICE COUPLING PATTERN.   Imagine a collection of distributed services that are "chained" to each other designed to handle transactions across an organization. These coupled services must not only coordinate the information they pass to consumers along the distribution chain, they must also offer common solutions to satisfy a diversity of consumers across the enterprise. Moreover, instead of establishing a centralized processing unit, the federation notion advocates linking distributed services that offer comparable specialties to applications, departments, divisions, and partners. This association model binds services to their peers by forming a linear structure that is used for sharing information passed from the first service node to the last in the succession.

A federated service environment typically is based on one of the two major configurations. The first type consists of "cloned" services that are connected to widen certain capabilities across an organization. For example, a number of identical (cloned) Universal Description Discovery and Integration (UDDI) repositories can be linked and deployed across the organization to enable consumers to locate services. These service *instances* typically collaborate and share information to help consumers broaden their search in a large distributed environment.

The second type does not necessarily consist of "duplicated" services. It may simply employ linked autonomous services that share common specialties; these entities may not be entirely comparable. Take a chain of composite services, each of which provides accounting functionality bases on local deployment needs. In some locations only the accounts payable module will be deployed; in others, accounts payable and general ledger will be offered. These accounting services also will be linked to enable consumers to share prior entries in the organizational accounting system.

Problem.   Sharing processes and service capabilities in a growing distributed environment that spans multiple lines of business or organizations is a challenging proposition that should be thoroughly analyzed. The service centralization model that is addressed by the Star Coupling (399) pattern may not be practical and beneficial to the diverse consumer base that operates across the enterprise. Indeed, a centralized operation may be valuable in a small environment where a limited number of services, consumers, and applications, trade transactions and propose a narrow solution scope. But what about distributed landscapes that involve numerous repositories, applications, lines of business, and even partners? What if a centralized service configuration cannot sustain the diversity of consumer requirements? How should geographical distribution of software assets be designed if the centralized serving model does not satisfy the expansion of an organizational architecture? How can a service's widening capabilities reach a broad range of consumers?

Solution.   The Federated Service Coupling pattern proposes arranging related services in a linear shape to enable the expansion of a given architecture. Each service member of this federated deployment model should be given local autonomy in the area in which it operates. The term "area" pertains to the scope and the boundary in which a service can extend its offerings. This can be a department, a division, a line-of-business, a partner's domain, or even a geographical location such as region. Obviously, either defined boundary of a service's influence limits its visibility and confines its consumer base to a predefined location in the enterprise.

Furthermore, a service that is a member of a federated deployment typically does not have oversight control on the message exchange and information sharing in the entire federation. Instead, a member is responsible for communicating with other services in the chain and sharing valuable information to assist consumers across the enterprise. Therefore, the Federated Service Coupling pattern enables individual services to stay connected, share information, and join a collaborative effort to alleviating organizational concerns.

As mentioned earlier, there are two methods for implementing a federation of services: coupling service clones and coupling related service capabilities. These approaches employ different mechanisms to promote the expansion of service capabilities across the enterprise and to connect services to a mutual cause.

Coupling Service Clones.   This method advocates creating a distributed service federation by simply duplicating a service and distributing its instances across the organization. Coupling these service replicas and deploying them to remote locations and production environments would form a federated service configuration that offers comparable functionality to diverse groups of consumers.

Coupling Related Service Capabilities.   This method is about chaining contextually associated services that offer related expertise. But these coupled entities do not necessarily provide comparable functionality. Their offerings may vary based on the local requirements of the parties that use them.

Example.   Exhibit 21.14 illustrates the coupling service clones method for establishing a Federated Service Coupling pattern. This example represents two perspectives, the 3D View (far right) and the Service-Oriented Modeling Formal Diagram View (far left). As apparent, five instances (clones) of atomic services are distributed across an organization, each of which is named A-1. The three different consumers, CONS-1, CONS-2, and CONS-3, are coupled with three instances of atomic A-1. Note that in the formal modeling diagram the "Cloned" symbol is used to denote the relationships between the replicated services. The "Coupled" symbol is also employed to illustrate the associations between the consumers and their corresponding services.

Exhibit 21.15 is another Federated Service Coupling pattern example. This scheme, however, does not employ cloned services. The participating entities are arranged according to the coupling service capabilities model, in which related services that offer diversified capabilities are chained to form a federated deployment configuration. Note the "Coupled" symbol to denote service relationships (in the Service-Oriented Formal Modeling Diagram View). This symbol also indicates that consumer CONS-1 is associated with atomic service A-4, consumer CONS-2 is related to composite service CO-1, and consumer CONS-3 is coupled with atomic service A-1.

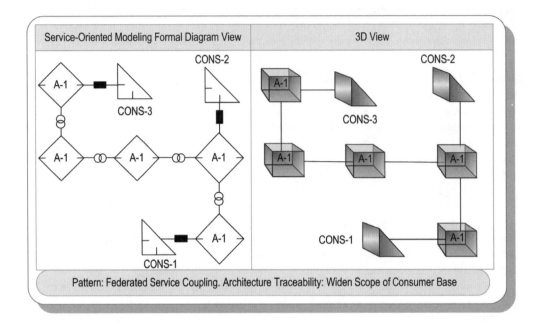

EXHIBIT 21.14 FEDERATED SERVICE COUPLING PATTERN: COUPLING SERVICE CLONES EXAMPLE

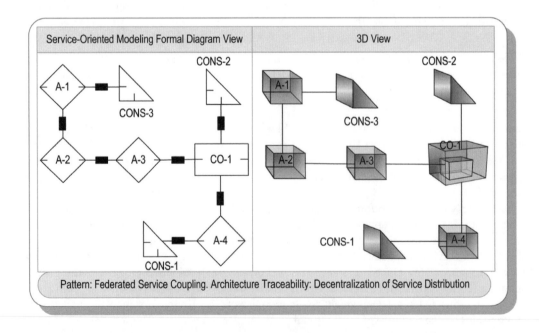

EXHIBIT 21.15 FEDERATED SERVICE COUPLING PATTERN: COUPLING SERVICE CAPABILITIES EXAMPLE

Pattern Identification	
Name	Federated Service Coupling Pattern
Category	Structural Expansion Analysis

Problems, Solutions, and Implementations	
Problem	A centralized service facility cannot facilitate the expansion of a distributed environment and limits the scope of service capabilities across applications and organizations.
Solution	A federated service environment that consists of related services that are chained to support cross-organizational business and technological initiatives.
Applicability	Applies to large distributed software environments.
Method	Employ one of the two methods to establish a federated service coupling landscape: 1. Deploy service clones that offer identical functionality. 2. Couple associated services that provide related specialties.
Benefits	Introduces decentralization of service operation to enable expansion of service capabilities across the organization and to widen the scope of their consumer base.
Risks	Interruption of information flow in the federated chain of services may preclude of sharing vital information.
Notation	For service cloning, employ the "Cloned" symbol. To denote a federation of related services, use the "Coupled" symbol.

EXHIBIT 21.16 FEDERATED SERVICE COUPLING PATTERN SUMMARY TABLE

Synopsis.   The Federated Service Coupling pattern addresses expansion of service capabilities across an organization. This method of extending service offerings to a wide range of consumers can be accomplished by cloning a service and distributing its instances or simply by positioning related services (not cloned) that share common specialties. These methods of implementation, problems, solutions, and the benefits of the Federated Service Coupling pattern are outlined in Exhibit 21.16.

Anti-Patterns.   A Federated Service Coupling implementation should be devised only for large distributed environments where information sharing is critical to the execution of transactions. The federated service model should not be employed to centralize service capabilities. Employ the Star Coupling (399) pattern instead. The vital best practices that can guide practitioners how to extend service boundaries are outlined in Exhibit 21.17.

Anti-Pattern Name	Best Practice
Centralized Federation	The Federated Service Coupling pattern does not offer a centralized solution. Use the Star Coupling (399) pattern instead.
Branched Federation	A federated service coupling configuration can be split into a few branches. To avoid the creation of centralized service operations, do not overuse this style.
Localized Federation	The Federated Service Coupling pattern should be employed in large distributed environments. Departmental or application-level implementations should not include federated service deployments.

EXHIBIT 21.17 FEDERATED SERVICE COUPLING ANTI-PATTERNS

MEDIATION ANALYSIS: PATTERNS AND IMPLEMENTATION

The mediation analysis process proposes mechanisms that enable stable and flawless execution of transactions in a distributed computing environment. The roles of the mediating software entities, the services that connect the dots, are diverse yet designed to intercept messages, process the traded information, and deliver the outputs to chosen destinations. This simple concept of brokering contributes immensely to the flow of messages across organizations and introduces a way to manipulate exchanged content on behalf of services and their corresponding consumers. Furthermore, in technological terms, mediating software entities are often referred to as brokers, hubs, interceptors, adapters, gateways, and intermediaries. Generally, these mediation responsibilities embody integration and collaboration aspects that are discussed in detail in the sections that follow.

MEDIATION ANALYSIS PATTERNS AND ANTI-PATTERNS.   The sections that follow discuss analysis and modeling patterns and anti-patterns that offer best practices to assist architects, modelers, developers, analysts, and managers in inspecting service integration solutions that take place in distributed environments. This examination should also yield an enhanced proposition that not only optimizes the collaboration between services and consumers but also fosters service reusability and reduces tightly coupled architectural conditions. Three major patterns promote best practices that advocate the employment of mediation services:

1. Enterprise Service Intermediary (406)
2. Enterprise Service Gateway (408)
3. Enterprise Service Bus (411)

ENTERPRISE SERVICE INTERMEDIARY PATTERN.   The Enterprise Service Intermediary pattern depicts a condition by which a service proxy is positioned between a service provider and a corresponding consumer. This arrangement typically is proposed to intercept messages that are exchanged in a distributed environment. Such brokering activities by a service intermediary contribute to vital message manipulation requirements, such as message transformation, protocol translation, message enrichment, security enhancements, and message routing. This process not only offloads message delivery chores from the communicating parties; it is designed to reduce their unrelated processing duties. Furthermore, the chief motivation for employing the Enerprise Service Intermediary pattern is to foster a loosely coupled service environment and decouple services by reducing their immediate dependencies on each other.

Problem.   The chief challenge that the Enterprise Service Intermediary pattern addresses is the tight coupling condition of a distributed service environment. This pertains to two major service coupling aspects: unnecessary service functionality that a service is designed to execute a large number of formed dependencies between message exchange parties.

The first aspect is related to the overwhelming and in some circumstances unnecessary mixture of duties that a service is required to execute. That is, the service capabilities are not limited to the offered service specialty or may exceed the expectation of business requirements. Any unrelated service operations characteristically hamper its execution and impose maintenance and redesign challenges. Imagine a service that not only processes car insurance claims but also is delegated protocol conversion duties and data transformation responsibilities. These additional tasks should be offloaded to streamline service design and ultimately improve its performance.

The second is associated with the distributed environment in which services operate. This aspect pertains to the overwhelming and direct dependencies that are often established between peer services and consumers: A tightly coupled condition is apparent when an excessive and needless number of contracts are founded between message exchange parties. Such an inseparable coupling effect can also occur when a vast number of message routes are designed to enable transaction exchange between the services and corresponding consumers.

Solution.   The proposed solution attacks the challenges on two fronts:

1. Decompose a service that contains unnecessary functionality and migrate its capabilities to an intermediary proxy service.

2. If the distributed environment is tightly coupled and the formed dependencies between affiliated services and their consumers are impractical, introduce service intermediaries to simplify integration complexities.

This two-step plan supports the positioning of a service intermediary that not only offloads some responsibilities of the participating entities in a message exchange but offers alternative message exchange routes and reconstitution of contracts.

Consider the examples of capabilities that can be executed by service intermediaries:

- Message transformation and validation
- Message enrichment and augmentation
- Workload management
- Message interception and filtering
- Message routing
- Message orchestration
- Security enhancement

Example. Exhibit 21.18 illustrates the Enterprise Service Intermediary pattern that is apparent in two different perspectives: 3D View (far right) and Service-Oriented Modeling Formal Diagram View (far left). These depict the intermediary atomic service A-2 and its coupled atomic services A-1 and A-3. Note that services A-1 and A-3 are linked by the proxy service A-2, indicated by the "Coupled" symbol in the formal modeling view.

Synopsis. The Enterprise Service Intermediary pattern proposes to employ a proxy service that intercepts messages that are exchanged between service providers, their peers, and consumers. This method of mediation is a fundamental mechanism that can facilitate distributed loosely coupled

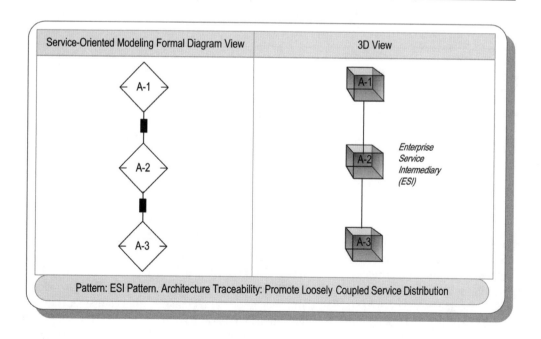

Service-Oriented Modeling Formal Diagram View	3D View
A-1	A-1
A-2	A-2 Enterprise Service Intermediary (ESI)
A-3	A-3

Pattern: ESI Pattern. Architecture Traceability: Promote Loosely Coupled Service Distribution

EXHIBIT 21.18   ENTERPRISE SERVICE INTERMEDIARY PATTERN EXAMPLE

Pattern Identification	
Name	Enterprise Service Intermediary Pattern
Category	Structural Expansion Analysis
Problems, Solutions, and Implementations	
Problem	1. Distributed service environment is tightly coupled.
	2. Service is designated duties that are not in line with its responsibilities.
Solution	Introduce an intermediary service proxy that both offloads unrelated responsibilities from services and consumers and facilitates the formation of a loosely coupled service ecosystem.
Applicability	Applies to distributed and tightly coupled service environments.
Method	1. Position an intermediary service between two or more message exchange services.
	2. Reinstitute contracts to accommodate this mediation.
Benefits	The Enterprise Service Intermediary pattern promotes loosely coupled distributed environments and fosters reusability of software assets.
Risks	Mediating services typically increase network traffic and integration efforts.
Notation	Employ the "Coupling" symbol.

EXHIBIT 21.19 ENTERPRISE SERVICE INTERMEDIARY PATTERN SUMMARY TABLE

environments. Furthermore, an intermediary entity is also designed to offload responsibilities of services and provide a common functionality that can serve a service community. Exhibit 21.19 summarizes the problems that motivate practitioners to employ service intermediaries and outlines the solutions and benefits that the Enterprise Service Intermediary pattern can contribute.

Anti-Patterns. A service intermediary typically is utilized to promote a loosely coupled distributed environment. It is employed both to intercept messages and to offer supplementary processes that service providers and consumers should not implement. In addition, excessive distribution of intermediaries should be avoided to reduce network traffic and promote integration simplicity. Exhibit 21.20 summarizes these best practices.

Anti-Pattern Name	Best Practice
Excessive Intermediary Implementation	Avoid unnecessary utilization of intermediary services to reduce integration complexity and decrease network traffic.
Data Access Layer Intermediary	A service intermediary should not provide data access layer offerings.[a]
Business Layer Intermediary	A service intermediary should not provide business layer offerings.[b]

EXHIBIT 21.20 ENTERPRISE SERVICE INTERMEDIARY ANTI-PATTERNS

[a]Refer to data access layer services (DALS) that are discussed in Chapter 8.
[b]The common business service layer is discussed in Chapter 10.

ENTERPRISE SERVICE GATEWAY PATTERN. Unlike the Enterprise Service Intermediary (406) pattern that is designed to alleviate tightly coupled service distribution, the Enterprise Service Gateway pattern addresses *interoperability* challenges in a distributed service environment. It offers an approach to tackle *technological alignment* difficulties between applications, lines of business, organizations, and business partners. The term "technological alignment" implies that an Enterprise Service Gateway pattern bridges the communication gaps between implementations that support distinct technologies, such as different operating systems, protocols, security models, data structures, networks, and more. For connecting distributed software assets, the service gateway is designed to ensure flawless message exchange activities and to guarantee stable transactions in a heterogeneous computing configuration. Consider the service gateway responsibilities outline:

- Enables seamless message exchange between applications and services that operate on different operating systems and networks.
- Transforms security models between operating systems.
- Universalizes encryption and decryption of exchanged messages.
- Preserves message integrity: converts message formats.
- Guarantees that asynchronous and synchronous calling methods are consistent between distinct environments.
- Converts protocols to preserve continuity of operations.
- Routes messages to destination services and applications.
- Aligns service contracts between distributed services that run on different technology platforms.

Problem.   One of the most challenging tasks a practitioner faces when analyzing and proposing an architecture solution for a distributed computing environment is integrating services and applications that do not necessarily share the same technologies. This unequal ground pertains to dissimilar language platforms, organizational best practices, security models, and communication protocols. Topping this list is the strategy and business model that each individual organization embraces. Linking their applications and services and enabling smooth execution of transactions is an arduous task since it typically requires costly computer resources and integration efforts.

Nowadays, this mission is somehow easier to accomplish because of the introduction of various adapters that can translate protocols or align data schemas. But the chief interoperability impediment still exists because of the considerable efforts required to customize a universal bridging solution. This software facility must not only have the knowledge of the environments that are required to interact but also must possess business intelligence and technical capabilities to enable flawless message exchange.

Solution.   The Enterprise Service Gateway pattern proposes three chief solutions to mitigate interoperability challenges: transforming, searching, and orchestrating. First, a service gateway must be intelligent enough to transform any content to be shared between services that operate in an interoperable environment. This is about the conversion of message formats, and even performing marshaling and unmarshaling of messages. Furthermore, the transformation responsibilities should also include network protocol translation, such as Transmission Control Protocol (TCP) to System Network Architecture (SNA). From a security policy perspective, conversion between security models is also a crucial requirement. For example, alignment between Mandatory Access Control (MAC) and Discretionary Access Control (DAC) security policies is often critical to the collaboration between services that run on different platforms.

Second, searching is another capability that the Enterprise Service Gateway pattern must offer. The ability to locate services or consumers in two or more distributed environments is vital for bridging their communication gaps.

Third, orchestration is another major duty that is typically designated to a gateway service. The term "orchestration" pertains to the synchronization of message exchange and business process coordination. Message delivery and routing is also affiliated with orchestration duties.

Example.   Exhibit 21.21 illustrates the Enterprise Service Gateway pattern in two different perspectives: 3D View (far right) and Service-Oriented Formal Diagram View (far left). The former

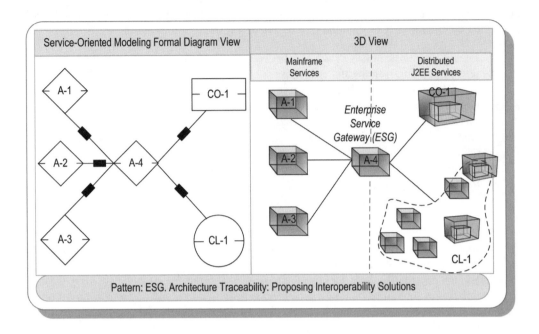

EXHIBIT 21.21 ENTERPRISE SERVICE GATEWAY PATTERN EXAMPLE

depicts two environments in which services operate and communicate: Mainframe Services and Distributed J2EE Services. In addition, atomic service A-4 is the service gateway that offers transformation, searching, and orchestration capabilities to the participating services in both environments. Atomic services A-1, A-2, and A-3 operate on the mainframe side. Conversely, composite service CO-1 and cluster CL-1 are located in the distributed J2EE environment. Note the use of the "Coupled" symbol in the formal modeling diagram view. It links all selected services to enable transactions across environment boundaries.

Synopsis. The Enterprise Service Gateway pattern is designed to reduce complexities and point-to-point message exchange between distributed services that operate in interoperable computing landscapes. The three major responsibilities of the service gateway are: (1) message and content transformation, (2) service searching, and (3) message routing and orchestration. These attributes are defined in Exhibit 21.22 along with problem definition, solutions, risks, and method of implementation.

Anti-Patterns. The Enterprise Service Gateway pattern offers a pass-through route for services that operate on different platform technologies to communicate and exchange messages. Although the service gateway is positioned midway and acts as a broker and intercepts messages, it should not be employed to carry out duties of intermediaries, as described in the Enterprise Service Intermediary (406) pattern. The chief difference between these two patterns is that the service gateway mitigates interoperability concerns by transforming protocols, data, and security models. Conversely, the service intermediary is employed to decouple a distributed environment. Exhibit 21.23 identifies the major best practices to which practitioners should be attuned.

Pattern Identification	
Name	Enterprise Service Gateway Pattern
Category	Structural Expansion Analysis

Problems, Solutions, and Implementations	
Problem	Integration challenges appear with distributed services that operate in a heterogeneous computing environment because of their distinct empowering technologies.
Solution	Introduce a gateway service that bridges the communications gaps between distributed services that operate in a diversified technological environment to enable technological alignment.
Applicability	Applies to distributed autonomous services.
Method	Three major duties should be designated to a gateway service: 1. Transformation and conversion 2. Searching 3. Message orchestration and routing
Benefits	1. Alleviating interoperability challenges. 2. Reducing service integration complexities. 3. Eliminating direct message exchange routes between distributed services.
Risks	A gateway service may become a message exchange and transaction bottleneck.
Notation	Employ the "Coupling" symbol.

EXHIBIT 21.22   ENTERPRISE SERVICE GATEWAY PATTERN SUMMARY TABLE

Anti-Pattern Name	Best Practice
Excessive Service Gateways Implementations	Avoid the employment of a large number of service gateways in a distributed environment. This redundant implementation can increase integration complexity and duplication of functionality across the enterprise.
Intermediary Service Gateway	A service gateway should not be designated to handle intermediary service responsibilities. Employ the Enterprise Service Intermediary pattern (406) instead.
Homogenous Service Gateway	There is no need for a service gateway in a homogeneous computing environment.

EXHIBIT 21.23   ENTERPRISE SERVICE GATEWAY ANTI-PATTERNS

ENTERPRISE SERVICE BUS PATTERN.   Generally, there is industry-wide confusion and perhaps misunderstanding regarding the meaning of an enterprise service bus (ESB). From a design and implementation perspective, an ESB has been defined and associated with a variety of attributes and roles that do not add to the clarity of its essence. Is it a product, pattern, architectural component, message router, broker, mediator, or hardware device? These observations obviously contribute to the ESB definition, and perhaps none is wrong. Due to technological trends and the development of new technologies, the term "ESB" has been morphing in recent years. Currently it is associated with its advanced functionality, attributes, and method of employment.[2]

The term "ESB pattern," however, addresses an old industry paradigm that is associated with asynchronous communication, message calling, and message routing. Moving away from the traditional message bus definition that was based on these core features, the ESB inherited fundamental characteristics to facilitate integration of applications and services across the enterprise. In other words, the ESB continues to connect the dots in a distributed software environment. But the list of its responsibilities has grown, and the scope of its capabilities has increased beyond the initial charter.

The ESB pattern addresses analysis, design, and architecture concerns that are related to loose coupling best practices. Asynchronous communication and message exchange are the chief aspects of its guidance. Consider the main responsibilities that are tackled by the ESB pattern:

- Asynchronous communications and message calling
- Transaction management
- Message and data transformation
- Message routing and delivering
- Service locating
- Message orchestration
- Protocol translation
- Security management
- Process choreography

Problem.   The challenge of integration is the driving motivation for resolving a painful enterprise concern: avoiding direct communications between applications and services. Rather than increasing dependencies between message exchange parties and forming tightly coupled associations between software assets across the organization, a central or federated solution is needed to efficiently manage message delivery, guarantee message distribution, enable efficient message orchestration, and tackle security challenges. Moreover, the threat of performance degradation on business execution and the increase in architecture complexity are chief concerns that must be resolved in a distributed environment. These solutions typically include bridging silo operations and enhancing communications among applications, lines of business, departments, divisions, and partners.

Solution.   The notion of the traditional ESB implementation continues to dominate recent technologies and integration strategies. The need for an advanced *bus* technology over direct message exchange mechanisms that typically yield tightly coupled distributed environments is commonly and widely accepted. Thus the ESB is a compelling solution that not only embodies the bus technology but is also a compound formation comprised of business and technical components that collaborate to offer a powerful enterprise integration solution. The business ingredients of an ESB enable process orchestration and offer a centralized business rules management facility. Conversely, the technical contribution of an ESB, as discussed, enables the message exchange parties to securely and safely trade transactions with minimum data loss and message delivery delays. Consider Exhibit 21.24, which lists examples of major technologies currently being employed by an ESB implementation.

ESB Components	Examples of Technologies
Orchestration	BEPL, JBI engine, POJO SE, Event Stream Processing (ESP), Business Rules Engine
ESB Interfaces	JMS interfaces, FTP interfaces, HTTP interfaces, e-mail interfaces, LDAP interfaces
Data Repositories, and Data Processing and Transformation	Message Encoding, XSLT, Data Integration, JAXB
Protocol Support	HTTP, TCP/IP, CORBA, RMI/IIOP, SMTP
ESB Management	ESB Console, Monitoring Dashboard for JBI and Transactions, SLA Tracking, Audit Trail

Exhibit 21.24   Enterprise Service Bus Technology Examples Table

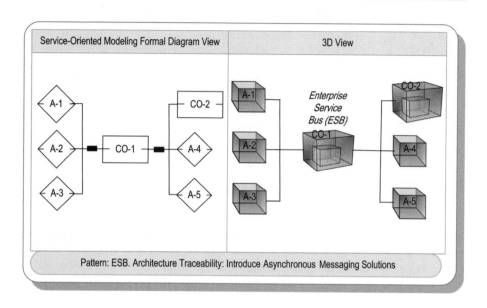

EXHIBIT 21.25   ENTERPRISE SERVICE BUS PATTERN EXAMPLE

Example.   Exhibit 21.25 illustrates the ESB pattern in two major perspectives: 3D View (far right) and Service-Oriented Modeling Formal Diagram View (far left). The composite service CO-1 represents ESB capabilities, while atomic services A-1, A-2, A-3, A-4, and A-5, and composite service CO-2 utilize its bus technology offerings. Note that in the formal modeling diagram (far left), the "Coupled" symbol is used to denote the affiliation between the subscribing services and the ESB facility.

Pattern Identification	
Name	Enterprise Service Bus Pattern
Category	Structural Expansion Analysis

Problems, Solutions, and Implementations	
Problem	1. Message delivery delays and time-out conditions.
	2. Tightly coupled architecture that relies on direct message exchange implementation.
	3. Business process synchronization and coordination challenges.
Solution	Introduce an ESB that offers three major remedies:
	1. Asynchronous message exchange mechanisms.
	2. Business integration and process orchestration capabilities.
	3. Message transformation functionality.
Applicability	Applies to a distributed and tightly coupled environment that experiences implementation delays and lack of message and business process synchronization.
Method	Centralized or federated ESB deployments should be considered in a distributed environment.
Benefits	1. Fosters loosely coupled distributed environment.
	2. Improves performance and reliability of transaction exchange.
	3. Ensures business and technical continuity.
Risks	An ESB implementation may become a single-point failure when its operations halt.
Notation	Employ the "Coupling" symbol.

EXHIBIT 21.26   ENTERPRISE SERVICE BUS PATTERN SUMMARY TABLE

Anti-Pattern Name	Best Practice
Excessive ESB Implementations	Avoid the employment of a large number of ESBs. This redundant implementation can increase integration complexity and duplication of functionality across the enterprise.
Local ESB	An Enterprise Service Bus pattern is most effective when implemented to connect applications and services across organizational boundaries and in distributed environments. Local utilization, such as application level or departmental usage, may not be practical.
Data Access Layer ESB	An ESB should not be employed to aggregate or serve data and information to applications and services; its chief charter is to intercept and persist messages. Refer to the data access services (DALS) discussion in Chapter 8.

EXHIBIT 21.27   ENTERPRISE SERVICE BUS ANTI-PATTERNS

Synopsis.   One of the major motivations for employing an ESB pattern is to ensure business and technological continuity. This not only pertains to interruptions in message exchange but guarantees nimbleness and software elasticity during integration and deployment to production environments. As indicated in Exhibit 21.26, the ESB pattern addresses integration, collaboration, and business concerns.

Anti-Patterns.   The chief motivation for employing the ESB pattern is because of its mediation capabilities and its ability to intercept messages. Asynchronous messaging is another major requirement that should drive the strategy behind ESB implementation. Employing an ESB for managing data access to organizational repositories does not justify the integration efforts involved. Furthermore, an ESB should not be considered to manage asynchronous messaging for an application or local business units that do not intend to share their processes with the rest of the organization. Exhibit 21.27 summarizes these best practices and identifies the three major ESB anti-patterns.

CONTRACT ANALYSIS: PATTERNS AND IMPLEMENTATION

Generally, the contract analysis process pursued during the service-oriented analysis and discovery life cycle phase is an essential exercise that not only validates an architecture proposition but also helps with the identification of new services. More specifically, when it comes to expanding an existing architecture and widening the scope and boundaries of a distributed environment, the contract analysis activity is imperative to optimizing service and consumer relationships and minimizing their dependencies. How can such a charter be fulfilled? Can the practitioner establish associations between message exchange parties and at the same time reduce integration complexities? Can a tightly coupled software design scheme that supports multiple contracts and binds consumers to service providers be alleviated during the contract analysis venture?

This section proposes solutions to these concerns by advocating a contract optimization approach that can assist architects, designers, modelers, analysts, developers, and managers to efficiently analyze the relationships between consumers and related services. This examination should yield a practical expansion scheme for a distributed environment, supporting either federated or simply scattered contract facilities across the enterprise.

CONTRACT ANALYSIS PATTERNS AND ANTI-PATTERNS.   In the sections that follow, two major contract patterns, the Contract Mediation (415) pattern and the Contract Hub (418) pattern, are introduced to enable the expansion of a distributed environment. The former is simply a proxy service that is assigned brokering responsibilities, by which a binding contract between a consumer and a related service is maintained. This capability reduces direct service dependencies on its corresponding service and alleviates tightly coupled architectural conditions. The Contract Mediation (415) pattern can also be employed to form a *federated* service landscape that may span multiple organizations and lines of business. The Contract Hub (418) pattern, however, addresses *centralization* of contracts in a distributed service environment. This configuration not only fosters service reuse but also eases contract enforcement, management, and monitoring challenges.

CONTRACT MEDIATION PATTERN.   The Contract Mediation pattern addresses software entity distribution and integration across applications, organizations, or lines of business. This binding effort is another mechanism that enables practitioners to expand a distributed environment by employing service mediators to connect consumers and services across boundaries of applications and organizations. More specifically, the Contract Mediation pattern advocates positioning a proxy service between a service provider and its corresponding consumers to maintain their binding contract. This intermediary service must not only ensure that the contract is executed as stipulated but also alert administrators if the service-level agreement (SLA) between the communicating parties is breached.

Obviously, the distribution of services across the enterprise is one of the major motivations for employing proxy services to fulfill the responsibilities of service and consumer contracts in an interoperable environment. Another compelling reason for employing mediating services is to enable an efficient and solid service federation that may span multiple organizations, lines of business, and business partners. As the reader may remember, the chief purpose of a service federation is to share data, transactions, and message content between the autonomous and distributed services. The information sharing may take place in heterogeneous or homogeneous computing environments.

Problem.   The establishment of direct contracts between services and their corresponding consumers and peer services typically yield dependencies that may lead to architecture complexities and service management difficulties in production. In addition, establishing contracts across applications or organizational boundaries is an approach that should be carefully examined for its practicality. In fact, contracts that span multiple business domains and applications introduce integration concerns and management hurdles because of this tightly coupled approach to binding consumers to services.

The major queries that a practitioner should ask before advising a feasible architecture proposition are: How can services and consumers maintain contracts in a distributed environment? What mechanisms can guarantee the continuity of operations when services are sponsored and owned by different stakeholders? and Is a direct contract between a service and its related consumer a practical approach for integration in a distributed environment?

Solution.   The introduction of an intermediary service that brokers message exchange activities between a service and a related consumer is a practical solution when it comes to integration of autonomous software assets in a distributed environment. This concept is discussed in the Enterprise Service Intermediary (406) pattern. The Contract Mediation pattern, however, offers solutions that address binding a consumer to a service and maintaining a contract even if these entities are geographically distributed, deployed to different production environments, or operate from a diversity of business partners' premises. Since these deployments characteristically introduce contract enforcement, monitoring, and security challenges, a contract mediator service can alleviate these concerns while allowing architecture expansion and foster business and technical agility.

Consider four logical steps for analysis and implementation of contract mediation among services, related consumers, and peer services:

1. **Untie relationship.** This activity is about discontinuation of a contract that has been established directly between a consumer and a service.
2. **Insert mediator.** Insert a proxy service between a consumer and a service to act as a contract mediator.

3. **Establish service provider/service proxy contract.** Institute a contract between the service provider and the service proxy. Previous interfaces should be preserved.
4. **Establish consumer/service proxy contract.** Institute a contract between the consumer and service proxy. Previous interfaces should be preserved.

Example.   Exhibit 21.28 illustrates the major activities that take place during the analysis and employment of the Contract Mediation pattern. The two perspectives, the 3D View (far right) and the Service-Oriented Modeling Formal Diagram View (far left), depict a step-by-step implementation scenario that inserts atomic service A-2 between consumer CONS-1 and atomic service A-1 for contract mediation. Note the use of the "Unbound" and "Bound" symbols that denote contract discontinuation and establishment, respectively (depicted in the formal modeling diagram on left).

Based on Exhibit 21.28, consider the activities, depicted in the formal modeling diagram view, that lead to the establishment of contract mediation:

1. The contract that is established between consumer CONS-1 and atomic service A-1 is discontinued by employing the "Unbound" modeling symbol.
2. A new contact is founded between atomic service A-1 and the proxy service A-2 by utilizing the "Bound" modeling symbol.
3. A new contract is introduced between consumers CONS-1 and proxy service A-2 by using the "Bound" modeling symbol.

Synopsis.   The Contract Mediation pattern is designed to address enterprise capability expansion delivered by distribution and/or federation of services across applications and organizations. This

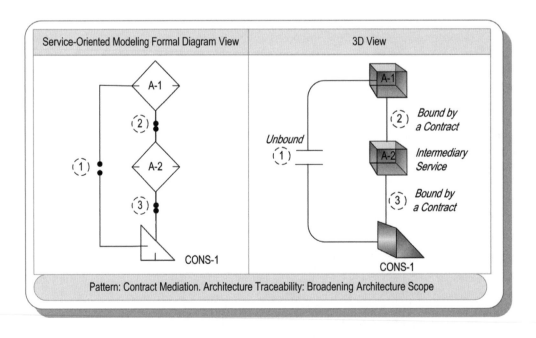

Exhibit 21.28 Contract Mediation Pattern Example

Pattern Identification	
Name	Contract Mediation Pattern
Category	Structural Expansion Analysis

Problems, Solutions, and Implementations	
Problem	1. Challenges with maintaining contract consistency in an expanded and distributed service environment.
	2. Existing contracts contribute to a tightly coupled architecture.
Solution	Establish a contract mediator service that is responsible for maintaining a stable relationship between a service provider and a related consumer.
Applicability	Applies to an expanded service deployment environment and/or federated service configuration that span multiple applications and organizations. The participating services in this venture are typically autonomous atomic, composite, or service clusters.
Method	1. A direct contract between a service and a related consumer should be terminated.
	2. A new contract between a service proxy and the service provider should be established.
	3. A new contract between a service proxy and the consumer should be founded.
Benefits	1. Enables expansion of a distributed environment.
	2. Facilitates service federation across the enterprise.
	3. Overcomes interoperability challenges.
	4. Fosters loosely coupled architecture.
Risks	Excessive usage of contract mediators may slow down message exchange execution.
Notation	Use the "Unbound" and "Bound" symbols.

EXHIBIT 21.29 CONTRACT MEDIATION PATTERN SUMMARY TABLE

vital requirement calls for contract evaluation and analysis to help optimize a distributed environment and stabilize the commitment of service providers to their consumers. The contract mediation solution advocates employing a proxy service and positioning it between message exchange parties to help execute transactions by enforcing a stipulated contract. Exhibit 21.29 outlines these challenges and introduces the solution, method, and risk that the Contract Mediation pattern is associated with.

Anti-Patterns. The Contract Mediation pattern should be employed to link a service to its related consumers by utilizing a service proxy that acts as a broker entity . This mediating service should not execute business or technical duties; it is devised merely to enforce contracts between message exchange parties. In addition, excessive implementation of the Contract Mediation pattern may contribute to contract ambiguity and redundancy of operations. Exhibit 21.30 outlines best practices.

Anti-Pattern Name	Best Practice
Business or Technical Contract Mediation Logic	Separate the service contract proxy implementation from business or technical processes. The contract mediation service should merely expose common interfaces.
Excessive Service Mediator Implementation	Avoid excessive service mediator implementations to reduce architecture complexities and contract ambiguity. At any given time there should be only one contract mediator that links a service provider to a consumer.
Tightly Coupled Contract Mediation	Contract mediation should be exercised to foster loosely coupled architecture and reduce dependencies between services and related consumers.

EXHIBIT 21.30 CONTRACT MEDIATION ANTI-PATTERNS

CONTRACT HUB PATTERN. The Contract Hub pattern is devised to facilitate contract grouping. This method addresses *centralization* of contract management in a distributed environment, where a service hub is designated the duties of both maintaining contracts between peer services and satisfying consumer requirements. Furthermore, a bank of contracts typically is structured to reduce development efforts when alterations to existing contracts are required and is designed to alleviate monitoring and contract enforcement challenges in production. This contract-handling implementation should also incorporate a centralized audit trail and alert mechanisms to enhance the control over contract fulfillment and monitoring.

The standardization of contract establishment and maintenance also fosters reuse of service capabilities and interfaces and encourages the development of a universal approach to connect services to related consumers. Institution of contract issuance and enforcement can also lead to the foundation of enterprise-wide best practices that can guide practitioners in how to discover interfaces during the analysis phase, bind consumers to service providers during design time, and efficiently monitor and control contracts in production during run-time.

Problem. Lack of contract analysis, discovery, and maintenance standards is perhaps one of the leading causes of contract maintenance operations redundancy across an organization and often results in increased expenditure when contracts must be revised or modified. Silo establishment and implementation of contracts are common because no strategic implementation of a universal approach to managing a contract life cycle has been founded. Furthermore, the decentralization of contract management obviously leads to the distribution of contracts across the organization that do not share key features, such as contract definitions, contract validation definitions, or policy definitions.

For example, any implemented Web service contract may consist of three different definitions:[3] WS-Policy definitions, WSDL definitions, and XML schema definitions. In a centralized contract facility scenario, it would be easier to share these artifacts: Multiple WSDL definitions can utilize a centralized XML schema; multiple WSDL descriptions can employ a single abstract WSDL description; multiple WSDL definitions can utilize a centralize WS-Policy.

Solution. Consumers, services, and peer services that are required to communicate and collaborate should utilize the contract hub facility to increase the reusability of contract artifacts across the organization. There are two options to establish a contract hub installation: (1) introducing a centralized contract management facility and (2) federating contract centers across the enterprise.

1. Group contracts by their business or technical affiliation. This approach calls for the classification of service capabilities and enabling access to their offerings by introducing a contract hub installation that can facilitate the dependencies and contract management between a service and corresponding consumers.
2. Simply federate contract centers across the organization. This method advocates chaining contract hubs to each other to enable resource sharing and contract artifacts.

Example. Exhibit 21.31 depicts the Contract Hub pattern and the dependencies of the involved services and the consumer. As is apparent in the two perspectives, 3D View and Service-Oriented Modeling Formal Diagram View, atomic service A-5 is the central intermediary entity that both hosts all the contracts and manages the dependencies between the message exchange parties. To demonstrate this concept, employ the "Bound" symbol, as shown in the formal modeling diagram view (far left). Note that the consumer CONS-1 communicates directly with the Contract Hub entity (A-5) and is not contractually bound to any of the atomic services (providers) A-1, A-2, A-3, and A-4.

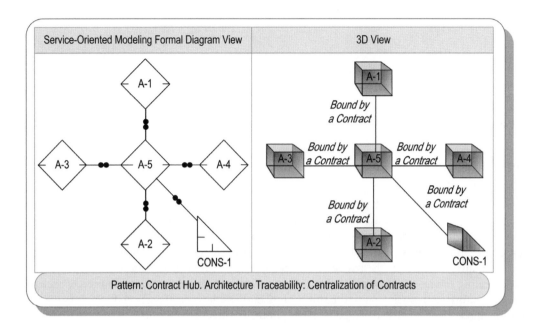

EXHIBIT 21.31   CONTRACT HUB PATTERN EXAMPLE

Pattern Identification	
Name	Contract Hub Pattern
Category	Structural Expansion Analysis
Problems, Solutions, and Implementations	
Problem	No standard approach to manage contracts and share their binding artifacts.
Solution	A contract hub should facilitate central management and monitoring of contracts between service providers and consumers.
Applicability	Applies to distributed service environment and autonomous services.
Method	Establish a centralized contract hub facility that allows design-time and run-time utilization during the service life cycle. This can be fulfilled in two major capacities:
	1. Group service contracts by their business or technical contextual affiliation.
	2. Federate contract hub facilities across the organization.
Benefits	1. Fosters reuse of contract artifacts.
	2. Encourages service reusability.
	3. Reduces service development efforts.
	4. Alleviates contract maintenance challenges.
	5. Promotes loosely coupled architecture.
Risks	A centralized contract hub may become a point of failure that should be properly scaled to avoid transaction execution interruption.
Notation	Use the "Unbound" and "Bound" symbols.

EXHIBIT 21.32   CONTRACT HUB PATTERN SUMMARY TABLE

Anti-Pattern Name	Best Practice
Contract Hub Business Logic Implementation	Avoid implementation of business logic in a contract hub.
Contract Hub Technical Utility	A contract hub is a proxy service that should be responsible for linking services to their consumers based on stipulated contracts. Technical utilities implementation should not be a part of this configuration.
Tightly Coupled Contract Hub	A contract hub should promote a loosely coupled architecture that separates consumers from their service providers by utilizing a central contract management facility.

EXHIBIT 21.33   CONTRACT HUB ANTI-PATTERNS

Synopsis.   The Contract Hub pattern addresses contract discovery, analysis, and management challenges throughout a service life cycle. This centralized solution to handling dependencies between service providers and related consumers can help minimize redundancy of service capabilities and streamline the enterprise contract maintenance process. The establishment of a contract hub installation also standardizes the manner by which an organization founds associations between the collaborating services and institutionalizes a centralized or federated scheme of message exchange between information trading parties. Exhibit 21.32 outlines these challenges and identifies the solution, methods, and benefits attributed to the use of the Contract Hub pattern.

Anti-Patterns.   The Contract Hub pattern merely tackles reuse of contract artifacts and influences the manner in which services are linked to their affiliated consumers. This facility should *not* be used as an intermediary that processes business logic or provides technical utilities for data or communication activities, such as data aggregation, data transformation, or content downloading. Consider Exhibit 21.33, which summarizes these best practices.

DELIVERABLES

A service coupling diagram is the required artifact that can illustrate the structural expansion of a distributed service environment (discussed in Chapter 18). This depiction of an expanding service ecosystem should leverage the distribution patterns offered in this chapter. Among other message path patterns, the Network Coupling (390) pattern, Tree Coupling (396) pattern, and the Federated Service Coupling (402) pattern can elaborate on the distribution approach of services. In addition, the provided mediation mechanisms, such as the Enterprise Service Gateway (408) pattern, and the Enterprise Service Bus (411) pattern can be used to illustrate the means for service integration. Finally, the Contract Mediation (415) pattern and Contract Hub (418) pattern should be embedded in the solution to perfect services relationship with their corresponding consumers, establish a service contract facility to manage contracts, and enable reuse of contract artifacts.

SUMMARY

- The structural expansion analysis and modeling process facilitates widening the boundaries of business offerings and expanding an architecture scope for a distributed service environment. This analysis and modeling process can also help practitioners face numerous challenges, including interoperability hurdles and service integrations and deployment difficulties to bridge silo implementations.
- Three distinct structural expansion analysis approaches are designed to solve challenges of an expanding distributed environment: (1) distribution analysis, (2) mediation analysis, and (3) contract analysis. Each of these methods is accompanied by solution modeling patterns that can accelerate the delivery of a analysis proposition

Notes

1. Erich Gamma, Richard Helm, Ralph Johnson, and John M. Vlissides, *Design Patterns: Elements of Reusable Object-Oriented Software* (Boston: Addison-Wesley, 1984), p. 185.

2. David Chappell defined an ESB as an entity that encapsulates integration patterns, such as validate, enrich, transform, and operate (VETRO). Refer to his book *Enterprise Service Bus* (Sepastopol, CA: O'Reilly, 2004), p. 197.

3. Thomas Erl et al., *Web Service Contract Design and Versioning for SOA* (Upper Saddle River, NJ: Prentice Hall, 2008), p. 601.

CHAPTER 22

STRUCTURAL CONTRACTION ANALYSIS PROCESS AND MODELING PATTERNS

The structural contraction process introduces best practices and modeling patterns that can assist practitioners in reducing the scope of a distributed service environment and limit an architecture expansion. This process is affiliated with efforts to narrow the spectrum of business offerings, decrease service deployments, and reduce the number of consuming parties across an organization and even beyond. Business and technological concerns call for structural reduction of service deployments, integration, and configuration because of an immeasurable number of imperatives and requirements.

Among the business reasons are reduction of commerce activities, loss of market share, alteration to business model, and change in strategies. From a technological point of view, structural contraction is often attributed to reduction of architecture complexity, improvement of an integrated service environment, and upgrading outdated technologies. Moreover, consolidation of software assets and reconciliation of service deployments are also vital to reduction of expenditure by streamlining the organizational architecture.

To fulfill these enormous challenges, a systematic method should be used to roll back an expanded business and technological landscape and alleviate risks of the structural contraction process. Removing parts of an organizational architecture or discontinuing business offerings to consumers clearly can introduce interruptions to business continuity and disruptions to technical execution. The approaches provided and their patterns are devised to lessen the structural contraction implementation concerns. Consider the approaches and study their associated patterns to help carve out an efficient analysis proposition.

- **Distribution reduction.** To achieve a successful structural contraction of a distributed service environment, the distribution contraction approach advocates trimming down on unnecessary service implementations, eliminating functionality redundancy across applications and organizations, and capitalizing on the discovery of common service capabilities to increase reuse of implementations. Reduction of service federation operations and decoupling activities can also contribute to this contraction effort.
- **Mediation rollback.** Another mechanism that can facilitate the structural contraction of services is reducing the number of mediating service facilities across applications and organizations. This can be accomplished by removing service proxies, reducing the utilization of service gateways, or even retiring the use of message buses.
- **Contract analysis.** Finally, to assist with the contraction of a distributed service environment, the contract optimization approach advocates examining the relationship between services and their consumers and perfecting the existing service contract model. Reduction of contract mediators and removal of contract hubs can contribute immensely to the structural contraction endeavor.

The sections that follow elaborate on the mechanisms to achieve a reliable and a stable distributed environment when pursuing the structural contraction process. The patterns should be leveraged to create an effective analysis proposition.

DISTRIBUTION REDUCTION ANALYSIS: PATTERNS AND IMPLEMENTATION

Contrary to the distribution expansion analysis process discussed in Chapter 21, the distribution reduction analysis approach addresses the contraction of architecture and technological configurations that span multiple applications, organizations, and lines of business. This decrease in the scope of service deployments often is required not only because a distributed computing environment is saturated with myriad applications, infrastructure, or middleware components. The necessity for controlling an environment and simplifying its complexity is often the chief motivation for trimming redundant functionality, boosting service reusability, and fostering software asset consolidation.

To optimize the process by which a distributed environment is contracted, a few approaches are provided. These best practices emphasize the elimination of duplicated operations, identification of service capability commonalities, and elimination of unnecessary services whose contribution to a business solution is negligible. These mechanisms of architectural spectrum reduction are offered by a number of analysis patterns that can be employed to examine a distributed computing landscape and propose a viable analysis proposition.

DISTRIBUTION ANALYSIS PATTERNS AND ANTI-PATTERNS.   In the sections that follow, four analysis patterns are introduced to help practitioners identify capability commonalities, assist with software asset consolidation, detect strategic and valuable software assets, and facilitate the architectural scope reduction of a distributed environment. Both the Service Cluster Intersection (424) pattern and Service Exclusion (427) pattern address the reduction of service deployments by employing clusters. Conversely, the Clipping Mask (429) pattern advocates isolating vital services from a deployment environment, abandoning the clustering approach to separate service functionality. Finally, the Federation Scope Reduction (432) pattern introduces an approach to trim down federated service formation and limit its boundaries.

SERVICE CLUSTER INTERSECTION PATTERN.   When it comes to the reduction of service functionality scope in a distributed environment, the mission is to identify what service deployments should be eliminated without any interruption to business execution and integrity of technical assets. In addition, prior to any architecture contraction activities, dependencies that have been established between services and related consumers should be carefully analyzed. This step may include examination of message exchange and orchestration of processes between entities.

To identify the candidate services that should be removed or migrated from existing architecture blueprints or even from a production environment, the practitioner is required to group services in logical formations. The Service Cluster Intersection pattern is one of the mechanisms that can help show these unnecessary or ill-fitting entities. This analysis process calls for establishing two or more service clusters and superimposing them on top of each other to *save the common services that appear in the overlapped region*. The services that are positioned in the nonoverlapping sections, however, can be used for other enterprise projects or retired, if appropriate. For example, it is apparent that in the 3D View of Exhibit 22.1, the saved services A-1 and A-2 are positioned in the intersected region that is common to clusters CL-1 and CL-2.

Problem.   One of the chief challenges with architecture contraction analysis is to assess the contribution of a service to a diversified consumer base. In particular, this analysis typically focuses on how reusable a service is, or will be, when deployed to a production environment. Furthermore, the discovery of common services across organizations or within a boundary of an application group that belongs to a department or a line of business can be an exhausting and challenging experience. The questions that a practitioner should ask before embarking on an assessment of service reusability

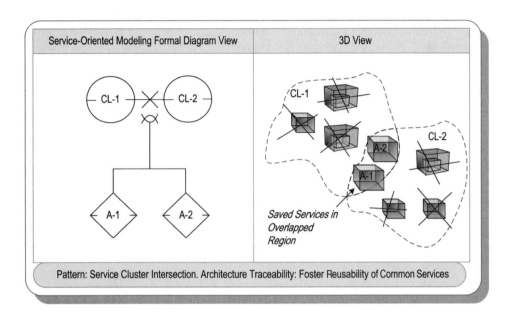

EXHIBIT 22.1   SERVICE CLUSTER INTERSECTION PATTERN EXAMPLE

are related to consumer consumption requirements and transaction collaboration needs: How many consumers are using or will be using the service offerings? What types of common services are considered necessary in a distributed environment? What is the frequency that a service will be, or is, utilized?

The discovery process of a service's viability and reusability characteristically leads to another type of software asset inventory examination: identifying the services that are *not* imperative to business execution in an organization. This analysis activity may result in enhanced architecture solutions that can restructure existing or planned service deployment schemes. Another challenge would be to determine the fate of the services that are not useful or too costly to maintain and sponsor. Should they be retired? Should they be exported to other environments where they are needed?

Solution.   To efficiently discover common services in a distributed environment and isolate those that cannot satisfy a wide range of consumer requirements, use the Service Cluster Intersection pattern. This analysis process will not only identify the proper support and funding that should be allocated to maintain vital business functionality, it will also assist practitioners in determining the destiny of services that do not play a major role in a distributed landscape. Consider the three main steps that should be pursued to employ the Service Cluster Intersection pattern successfully:

1. **Establish service clusters.** Form two or more service clusters, each of which should consist of contextually related services. This process can include services that take part in a federated deployment, autonomous services, atomic services, compound service structures, or composite services. Next, superimpose these service clusters on top of each other to form overlapping regions.
2. **Discover common services.** Services that are located in the intersected regions are obviously the most reusable entities.
3. **Identify uncommon services.** Services positioned outside of the overlapping regions are entities with lower reusability rates.

Example. Let us examine again Exhibit 22.1 that illustrates the Service Cluster Intersection pattern. The two apparent perspectives, 3D View (far right) and Service-Oriented Modeling Formal Diagram View (far left), depict a distributed environment that consists of two service groups: clusters CL-1 and CL-2. Each cluster contains internal services, and they also share two atomic services: A-1 and A-2, which are positioned in their overlapping region. The intent of this isolation exercise is both to identify common capabilities and to discover the services that are less valuable to the depicted distributed service landscape. Note the use of the "Intersected" and the "Overlapped" symbols in the formal modeling diagram (at left) to illustrate the common services that are encompassed by the two service clusters.

Synopsis. Remember, a service cluster is a logical collection of related services that collaborate in a distributed environment to achieve a certain goal and offer a solution to an organizational concern. This clustering effort not only classifies capability groups and helps clarify the overall imperatives of a distributed computing landscape; it also facilitates the discovery of common services and offers the opportunity for consolidation of functionality across the organization. Exhibit 22.2 summarizes these challenges and outlines the problem, solution, applicability, method, benefits, and risks related to the employment of the Service Cluster Intersection pattern.

Pattern Identification	
Name	Service Cluster Intersection Pattern
Category	Structural Contraction Analysis
Problems, Solutions, and Implementations	
Problem	Difficulties with identifying common and uncommon services in a distributed computing environment.
Solution	Group distributed services into two or more service clusters and discover their common capabilities and functionality.
Applicability	Applies to all distributed formations and service structures.
Method	1. Establish cluster formations.
	2. Superimpose these groups to form overlapping regions.
	3. Identify common and uncommon services.
	4. Discover service consolidation opportunities within the common services.
Benefits	1. Facilitates service consolation efforts.
	2. Fosters reusability of software assets.
Risks	Excessive service cluster formations typically yield multiple overlapping regions that may be impractical for analysis and introduce unnecessary architecture complexities.
Notation	Use the "Intersected" and the "Overlapped" symbols.

Exhibit 22.2   Service Cluster Intersection Pattern Summary Table

Anti-Pattern Name	Best Practice
Excessive Service Clustering	Avoid excessive fragmentation of a distributed service environment. This may increase architecture ambiguity and complexity.
Unrelated Service Cluster Members	A service cluster should embody services that are related by business context or specialty or by technical capability. Avoid clustering unrelated services.
Bulky Cluster Formation	A coarse-grained cluster formation that includes a large number of service members should be decomposed to avoid unnecessary dependencies and associations.

Exhibit 22.3   Service Cluster Intersection Anti-Patterns

Anti-Patterns.   The clustering process of a distributed environment should be carefully planned and crafted; its implications can influence the stability of architecture, complexity of design, and ramifications for service dependencies on peers and consumers. Therefore, attend to the best practices outlined in Exhibit 22.3.

SERVICE EXCLUSION PATTERN.   The Service Exclusion pattern tackles the reduction of functionality redundancy in a distributed environment to promote architecture contraction and reduction in scope. Like the Service Cluster Intersection (424) pattern, cluster formations are used to discover services. Their chief goal, however, is different: to identify service *consolidation* opportunities after common service capabilities have been isolated. In other words, this exercise is all about finding duplicated processes executed by services that may be candidates for elimination. This task can be fulfilled by using the same technique: creating overlapping regions by superimposing two or more service clusters. The intersected areas should be subject for analysis and assessment, and assist practitioners with decisions about service exclusion, migration, or elimination.

For example, in the 3D View illustrated in Exhibit 22.4, the overlapping region contains two atomic services, A-1 and A-2. These entities represent common or redundant functionality that should be further analyzed and help decide how to optimize the overlapping region. Again, the region that is common to two or more overlapping clusters consists of services that are candidates for retirement, consolidation, or migration.

Problem.   Too often lines of business and even distributed services and applications incorporate similar functionalities that are thought of as duplicate capabilities. These processes, executed by services, should be inspected and optimized or eliminated to foster a more efficient architecture scheme based only on necessary service capabilities rather than employing duplicated versions of a particular implementation. Common and redundant service functionality, for example, can be the

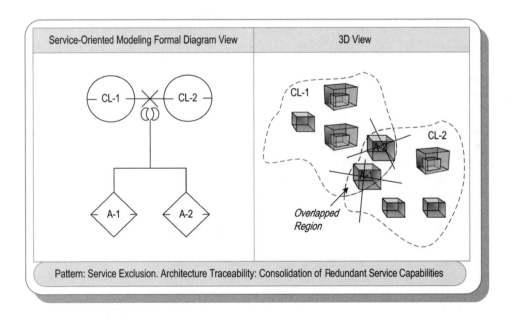

EXHIBIT 22.4   SERVICE EXCLUSION PATTERN EXAMPLE

result of a Customer Profile Service that multiple lines of business may develop to store customer information, addresses, and household details.

Another challenge that should be addressed when searching for redundant processes delivered by services is to determine the measures that should be taken to remove them from a distributed environment. Should duplicate functionality simply be eliminated or retired? Should a service that consists of redundant capabilities be migrated to another production environment? Should services that possess similar specialties be consolidated?

Solution.   Remember, a cluster is a collection of affiliated services that collaboratively provide a solution. These entities typically can be found in a distributed computing environment, installed in geographically remote locations, federated across organizations, or span multiple lines of business. To identify candidate services for consolidation or elimination across the enterprise, employ two or more service clusters, each of which should contain services that offer related specialties in their field (e.g., a group of services that provides related processes for car insurance policy issuance). Another cluster can address the workflow of a home loan approval application.

Once the clusters have been defined, the discovery process can begin. To identify commonalities and/or redundancy of service operations, simply superimpose two or more clusters to visually discover their overlapping areas of expertise. These intersected regions, the isolated common areas, should be further analyzed according to these possible scenarios:

- Consolidate common functionality.
- Eliminate redundant processes.
- Migrate duplicated service capabilities.

Example.   Exhibit 22.4 illustrates the Service Exclusion pattern and its two different areas of analysis: the overlapping region, which represents possible redundant functionality that should be further analyzed to promote the scope reduction of a distributed architecture; and the "saved" sections populated by services that seem not to share any capabilities. These are depicted in the two apparent perspectives: the 3D View and the Service-Oriented Modeling Formal Diagram View.

Note the "Intersected" and the "Excluded" symbols that are utilized in the formal modeling diagram (far left). The former denotes that the two service clusters, CL-1 and CL-2, are intersected and thus yield an overlapping region that encompasses atomic services A-1 and A-2. The "Excluded" symbol indicates that services A-1 and A-2 are isolated entities that should be subject to further analysis.

Synopsis.   The Service Exclusion pattern addresses functionality redundancy across multiple architectures, applications, and organizations. The analysis that should be pursued to discover duplicate capabilities in a distributed service landscape is vital to the reduction of architecture scope and optimization of processes in large computing configurations. These efforts should also focus on asset consolidation opportunities and on boosting reusability of services. These challenges are outlined in Exhibit 22.5. The problems, solution, method of implementation, and benefits and risks associated with the utilization of the Service Exclusion pattern are identified as well.

Anti-Patterns.   The Service Exclusion pattern enables efficient discovery of services that offer redundant capabilities by forming service cluster structures and discovering their duplicated functionalities. The goal is to isolate these services, analyze their contribution to their operating environment, and decide about service optimization, reconciliation, or elimination options. Exhibit 22.6 outlines this best practice and recommends two other guidelines related to the establishment of a service cluster.

Pattern Identification	
Name	Service Exclusion Pattern
Category	Structural Contraction Analysis

Problems, Solutions, and Implementations	
Problem	1. An organizational architecture is too large in scope.
	2. A distributed environment consists of unnecessary and redundant service capabilities.
Solution	The duplicated functionality should be identified, analyzed, and optimized to promote reduction of architecture scope.
Applicability	Applies to service cluster formations.
Method	Superimpose cluster structure to discover services. The identified entities may be consolidated, retired, or migrated.
Benefits	1. Consolidation of redundant service capabilities.
	2. Contraction of distributed architecture
Risks	Elimination, consolidation, or migration of duplicate functionality across an organization is typically a complex venture that requires multiple resources and funding. This undertaking may be difficult to achieve because of the dependencies of services on their peers and consumers.
Notation	Use the "Intersected" and "Excluded" symbols.

EXHIBIT 22.5   SERVICE EXCLUSION PATTERN SUMMARY TABLE

Anti-Pattern Name	Best Practice
Commonality Exclusion	The Service Exclusion pattern addresses the discovery of redundant functionality that is executed by distributed services. Thus, this mission is *not* to eliminate common services. On the contrary, the aim is to increase reusability of universal capabilities.
Service Elimination	The service exclusion process is preliminary not about elimination of services. This approach advocates isolating services for analysis. Once duplicated capabilities have been discovered, a decision should be made about future actions, such as service reconciliation, service migration, or service retirement.
Exclusion of Non-Overlapping Cluster Regions	The exclusion process should involve only in overlapped cluster regions. The non-overlapping areas are not the focus of this analysis.

EXHIBIT 22.6   SERVICE EXCLUSION ANTI-PATTERNS

CLIPPING MASK PATTERN.   The Clipping Mask pattern is devised to isolate service capabilities and help selecting services for analysis without employing service clusters. This examination effort advocates "slicing" a distributed environment by extracting services from various installations for inspection and modeling purposes to design a solution. The selected services that are marked for mining should be affiliated with a certain solution and goal; the services that have not been drawn out typically are entities that should not be the practitioner's focus of analysis. Moreover, architects, modelers, analysts, developers, and managers who utilize the Clipping Mask pattern should isolate services for examination and assessment purposes that are driven by new business requirements or technical specifications. This service collection may be subject to future redesign, rearchitecture, or reconstruction to satisfy the latest organizational concerns.[1]

A service that participates in this analysis can emerge from different deployment environments: a part of a composite service, a member of a service cluster, or even an autonomous entity that operates independently and serves distributed consumers. The 3D View (far right) in Exhibit 22.7, for example, illustrates the clipping mask concept. The collected services CO-1, A-1, A-2, and A-3 are "cut out" from an integrated and distributed environment that has been established to

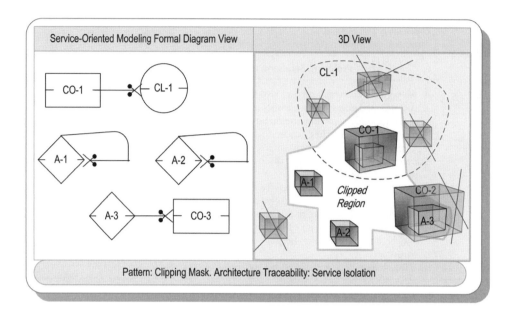

EXHIBIT 22.7 CLIPPING MASK PATTERN EXAMPLE

resolve prior organizational challenges. Note that the services that were not selected are crossed out to denote their irrelevance in the analysis process.

Problem.   How can the practitioner analyze, enhance, and reduce the scope of a distributed environment by focusing on future architecture needs and disregarding current complexities, dependencies, and constraints? How can legacy services take part in a future distributed solution while currently employed in resolving older challenges? How can a tightly coupled distributed environment be decomposed to enable efficient examination of the participating components and entities? These fundamental and common questions are often raised when a solution is being sought to improve an architectural and design proposition by incorporating legacy implementation ingredients. This challenging task is not only intrinsic to utilizing legacy applications and services, it is also imperative to combining new services and even ideas and concepts.

Solution.   The Clipping Mask pattern is an effective method for conceptually isolating services without delving into their underpinning implementation and the complexities formed by their dependencies on infrastructure, such as intermediaries, messaging, and data layer facilities. Ignoring existing contracts and relationships is another approach that should be considered. This structural exercise facilitates selection of services from different sources without getting bogged down by ownership and sponsorship considerations. This is also a method for grouping services to provide a collaborative solution by disregarding their origin and their contribution to silo organizations and applications. Therefore, the goal of this analysis process is to define a solution by involving legacy entities combined with innovative solutions.

Consider the implementation that should be considered when employing the Clipping Mask pattern:

- Study business requirements and technical specifications.
- Select services for analysis by disregarding these aspects of their implementation:
  - Structural or contextual affiliation to the extracted environment

- Architectural dependencies
- Infrastructure constraints
- Selected services can emerge from these sources:
  - Composite services
  - Service clusters
  - Autonomous services
  - Compound formations
  - Federation of services

Example.   Let us view again Exhibit 22.7 that illustrates the selection of services from an existing distributed environment. The two perspectives, the 3D View and the Service-Oriented Modeling Formal Diagram View, depict the extraction of composite service CO-1 and atomic services A-1, A-2, and A-3. Note that composite service CO-1 is also a member of service cluster CL-1, and atomic service A-3 is aggregated in composite service CO-2. In addition, the "Clipped" symbol is used in the formal modeling view (far left) to denote the withdrawal of services from their origin.

Synopsis.   The Clipping Mask pattern is designed to assist practitioners in simplifying and promoting a loosely coupled distributed environment by analyzing selected services. The main charter of this analysis is to focus on two activities: (1) promote reuse and consolidation of services; and (2) offer future solutions by employing legacy entities combined with new concepts and ideas. Exhibit 22.8 outlines these challenges and depicts the problem and solutions to help practitioners employ the Clipping Mask pattern.

Anti-Patterns.   The practitioner should employ the Clipping Mask pattern to refine a distributed environment, enhance reusability, and foster consolidation of software assets. Reusability and consolidation factors can be raised by employing legacy services for missions that differ from the

Pattern Identification	
Name	Clipping Mask Pattern
Category	Structural Contraction Analysis
Problems, Solutions, and Implementations	
Problem	1. Distributed environment scope is too large.
	2. Distributed environment is tightly coupled.
	3. Architecture model is too complex.
Solution	Isolate services from an existing distributed environment by extracting their capabilities and forming a new collaborative service group. This selection is designed to accomplish two chief tasks:
	1. Simplify an existing distributed environment for future optimization and enhancements to promote architecture contraction.
	2. Offer new solutions by employing legacy as well as new services to foster reuse and consolidation of software assets.
Applicability	Applies to a complex and tightly coupled distributed environment.
Method	Employ the clipping mask process of analysis to include two major capability sources:
	1. Legacy services and applications.
	2. New ideas and concepts and conceptual services.
Benefits	Facilitate decomposition analysis of a tightly coupled distributed environment by disregarding existing architecture complexities and dependencies barriers.
Risks	Conceptual isolation of a service typically disregards environment constraints that may introduce challenges in future implementations.
Notation	Employ the "Clipped" symbol.

Exhibit 22.8   Clipping Mask Pattern Summary Table

Anti-Pattern Name	Best Practice
Cluster Clipping Mask	The Clipping Mask pattern does not require cluster formations to define overlapping areas for service selection. Use the Service Cluster Intersection (424) pattern and the Service Exclusion (427) pattern instead.
Excessive Clipping Masks	Excessive applications of multiple clipping masks to a distributed environment may increase analysis complexities and introduce ambiguity to yielding conclusions.
Isolation for Exclusion Mask	The isolation of services that utilizes the clipping mask approach is not performed for excluding services from a distributed environment. On the contrary, this activity is pursued to refine the distribution and focus on solutions.

EXHIBIT 22.9 CLIPPING MASK ANTI-PATTERNS

original tasks that they were utilized for. The refinement of architecture takes place when services are conceptually isolated to assess their contribution to their environment. Consider Exhibit 22.9, which outlines the chief best practices that can alleviate these challenges.

FEDERATION SCOPE REDUCTION PATTERN. As the reader may remember, the term "federation" represents a distributed service formation that consists of chained services linked to each other because of their business or technical affiliation. Message exchange between the federated service constituents takes place to enhance communication and share information. Obviously, this traded content between service members can reach as far as their deployment is extended to: across lines of business, organizations, applications, and partners.[2]

To address the contraction of a distributed architecture, the Federation Scope Reduction pattern offers mechanisms to narrow the integration scale of services across the organization and trim down the range of their extended capabilities. This straightforward concept of contraction introduces opportunities for service consolidation and reduction of infrastructure that typically supports information sharing between the federation constituents. Simply by removing service members from a chain of linked services, the federated formation can be controlled, structured, and optimized to satisfy architecture contraction requirements. The term "removal" does not necessarily pertain to the retirement of a service that takes part in a federated formation. Unlinking it from the chain of services can also reduce the scope of a federation.

Problem. One of the main challenges of a growing federated configuration is the spread of services across the enterprise and the efforts that must be invested in linking them to each other to enable information sharing and flawless transaction exchange. Monitoring and maintenance of an oversized federated deployment is another concern that should be tackled during this phase of service-oriented analysis. In addition, extending the deployment model of a service federation by involving an excessive number of services can introduce challenges to controlling the information that flows from one end of the chain to the other. These chief concerns typically are affiliated to the persistence of content, performance, and consumption capabilities.

Solution. As discussed in the Federated Service Coupling (402) pattern, there are two chief ways to link services to form a federated configuration. The first approach is associated with service *coupling*, by which services that offer comparable but not identical solutions are chained to their peers to enable exchange of information and facilitate transactions. These sharing activities are designed to expand the reach of service capabilities beyond the limited boundaries of a single application or organization. The second method pertains to service *cloning*. This approach calls for distributing multiple instances of a single service across lines of business and even institutions. As expected, the relationships between service clones are also intended to strengthen the information flow between identical service operations.

Therefore, when it comes to the contraction of a federated service formation, two methods can facilitate the contraction of a federated environment by unlinking the relationships that have been established (these methods of contraction correspond to the service federation coupling and cloning mentioned earlier):

1. **Decoupling.** This approach addresses the discontinuation of a service's relationship with one or two of its immediate peers in the federation chain.
2. **Decloning.** If a federation consists of service clones, the decloning activity simply detaches a service instance from the chain by separating it from one or two of its immediate peers.

Example.   This section represents the two federation scope reduction approaches that are designed to satisfy architectural environment contraction requirements: the decoupling and decloning methods.

Decoupling Service Capabilities.   Exhibit 22.10 illustrates the Federation Scope Reduction pattern that facilitates architectural contraction by decoupling service capabilities. The two perspectives, the 3D View (far right) and the Service-Oriented Modeling Formal Diagram View (at left), depict the shortening of a service federation chain. This goal is achieved by two activities: (1) unlinking the first service in the chain, atomic service A-1, from its peer, atomic service A-2; and (2) decoupling atomic service A-4 from composite service CO-1. As a result, the service federation consists of the remaining three services: atomic service A-2, atomic service A-3, and composite service CO-1. Note the use of the "Decoupled" symbol to denote relationship discontinuation (in the formal modeling diagram view).

This decoupling process not only contracted the federated service formation, it also separated services A-1 and A-4 from the rest of the chain. Note that service A-1 will still be coupled with its corresponding consumer CONS-3, while service A-4 will continue to be bound to consumer CONS-1.

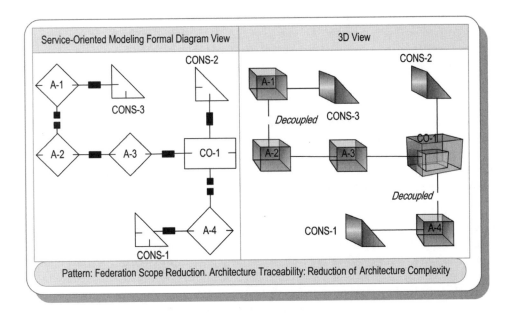

EXHIBIT 22.10   FEDERATION SCOPE REDUCTION PATTERN: DECOUPLING SERVICE CAPABILITIES EXAMPLE

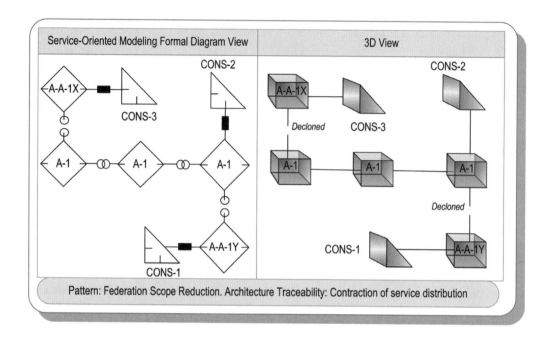

Exhibit 22.11   Federation Scope Reduction Pattern: De-Cloning Services Example

Decloning Services.   The decloning approach is designed to separate a service *instance* from a federated formation. This method is illustrated in Exhibit 22.11, which is presented by two apparent perspectives: the 3D View (far right) and the Service-Oriented Modeling Formal Diagram View (far left). Here again, the first and the last services in the chain are detached from the federation. But the method of separation is different: Atomic service A-A-1X is decloned from atomic service A-1 (the second service in the series) and atomic service A-A-1Y is decloned from atomic service A-1 (the one before the last in the series). Note the use of the "Decloned" symbols in the formal modeling diagram (at left).

Synopsis.   The Federation Scope Reduction pattern can help practitioners decrease the spectrum of a distributed environment. This architecture scale contraction is based on unlinking service members from a federation to simplify design complexity, reduce dependencies on infrastructure, and alleviate monitoring and maintenance concerns. Exhibit 22.12 outlines these challenges and identifies the core problem and proposed solutions and method of implementation.

Anti-Patterns.   A federated service formation is designed to enable its constituent services to share common information that is passed from one member to another. This configuration can be stretched over multiple applications and lines of business, and requires proper infrastructure and middleware support to sustain data transmissions. Therefore, the practitioner commissioned to reduce the scope of a federated service formation must ensure that a substantial spectrum reduction will not result in an impractical, very small-scale federation that requires extra resources to maintain. Exhibit 22.13 outlines comparable best practices that a practitioner should be aware of when reducing the scope of a federated service formation.

Pattern Identification	
Name	Federation Scope Reduction Pattern
Category	Structural Contraction Analysis

Problems, Solutions, and Implementations	
Problem	Federation of services is too large and introduces integration, infrastructure, monitoring, and maintenance challenges.
Solution	Shorten the federated service formation to satisfy architectural contraction requirements.
Applicability	Applies to a federated service formation that is subject to scope reduction.
Method	Employ one of the two methods of federation scope reduction: 1. Decouple a service from the federation chain. 2. Declone a service instance from a federation chain.
Benefits	1. Reduction of architecture complexity. 2. Decrease the scope of a federated service formation. 3. Satisfy architectural contraction requirements.
Risks	Untying service relationship is an error-prone process that should be carefully analyzed and mastered. This may include examination and discontinuation of service contracts and inspection of message paths and transaction exchange.
Notation	Use the "Decoupled" symbol to unlink autonomous services and the "Decloned" symbol to untie service instances.

EXHIBIT 22.12   FEDERATION SCOPE REDUCTION PATTERN SUMMARY TABLE

Anti-Pattern Name	Best Practice
Federation Retirement by Service Elimination	To retire a federation, all links between its service members should be untied. This activity does not necessarily remove the services from production.
Small Scale Federation	Decoupling or decloning most members of a service federation may result in a small and impractical federation formation that is supported by unnecessary infrastructure and middleware facilities.
Federation Decomposition	A federated service formation is a distributed architecture configuration that can be decoupled or decloned only. Decomposition should be applied only to breaking up bulky service structures.

EXHIBIT 22.13   FEDERATION SCOPE REDUCTION ANTI-PATTERNS

MEDIATION ROLLBACK ANALYSIS: PATTERNS AND IMPLEMENTATION

The removal of mediation services is one of the most powerful tools that can facilitate the contraction of a distributed environment. This process of mediation entity removal pertains to the reduction of an organizational distributed architecture scope and the limitations imposed on extended boundaries of service offerings. But the elimination of a service proxy does not come without substantial risks. These risks should be carefully mitigated to ensure business continuity and avoid disruptions to technical execution. What is at stake? Service mediation is about message interception and manipulation.[3] It is about conversion of protocols, messages, and security models. It is also about message integration strategies and isolation of code to protect and hide service operations.

By removing a mediating facility, we relinquish the powerful capability to centralize process orchestration. We give up on a uniform approach to monitor and trace transactions. We also allow silo organizations to take over one of the most vital platforms and keystone technological assets: messaging infrastructure. But what should motivate mediating entities removal decisions? The answer to this query is typically rooted in an organizational architecture strategic approach and best practices. These decisions are influenced by the practicality and the business and technological value that a service mediator contributes to an organization. Therefore, the final upshot of the mediation rollback analysis process is a proposition for boosting profitability, trimming down the scope of a distributed architecture environment, and reducing enterprise expenditure.

MEDIATION ROLLBACK ANALYSIS PATTERNS AND ANTI-PATTERNS.   The sections that follow depict mechanisms to reduce an organizational architectural spectrum by the removal of mediating services. Each approach introduces a unique pattern that tackles a different method to reduce service integration scope in a distributed environment. The Enterprise Service Intermediary Elimination (436) pattern is devised to remove service proxies from an integrated environment. These service brokers typically enable message interception, transformation, and routing. The Enterprise Service Gateway Elimination (438) pattern offers an approach for removing a hub that is designed to enhance interoperability challenges. The Enterprise Service Bus Elimination (441) pattern enables smooth and secure elimination of an ESB from a production environment. These discussed patterns also address the substitution of service mediator functionality in case it was eliminated from a production installation or an architecture blueprint. The anti-patterns, however, are best practices that guide practitioners how to implement the mediation rollback patterns.

ENTERPRISE SERVICE INTERMEDIARY ELIMINATION PATTERN.   The term "service intermediary" is a universal depiction of a service proxy that has mediation responsibilities. As described in the Enterprise Service Intermediary (406) pattern, this entity is designed both to intercept messages that are being exchanged between a service and its corresponding consumers and to manipulate the traded information. Obviously, there are numerous reasons to employ an intermediary entity. The chief reasons are related to enabling the expansion of a distributed environment, fostering a loosely coupled architecture, and promoting business and technology nimbleness through flexible service integration.

Conversely, when it comes to reducing the scope of an organizational architecture the Enterprise Service Intermediary Elimination pattern advocates removing intermediaries to trim the boundaries of a distributed environment and limit service capabilities across the organization. Doing this may include the removal of service proxies that are assigned duties, such as message transformation and validation, message routing, message orchestration, and security enhancements. Scaling back such vital functionality may require reassignment of these responsibilities to the communicating services and related consumers.

Why is such a practice justified? Does the removal of an intermediary yield a tightly coupled distributed environment? Does the elimination of a proxy service reduce the reusability factor of software assets? The answers to these questions are about selecting the right choice: when it comes to the reduction of architecture boundaries, the employment cost of a service intermediary may outweigh the benefits. When the integrated environment is bound to contract, service intermediaries should be analyzed for elimination.

Problem.   Although it is an effective mechanism for expanding service boundaries and promoting a loosely coupled architecture, an intermediary can also become a liability to a small-scale distributed environment. Prolonging message response time and causing timeout conditions during transaction exchange are some of the repercussions of employing service proxies. Perhaps one of the most discouraging motivations for utilizing an intermediary in a trimmed-down production environment is the cost involved for maintaining its operations.

Solution.   On a grand scale, the complete removal of service intermediaries from a distributed environment may pose serious risks to business continuity and the stability of transaction exchange activities. Remember, the elimination of a proxy service should be offset by assigning its responsibilities to the remaining services that can carry on its offered solutions; otherwise this functionality will be lost. To accomplish this transition, a gradual and *incremental* reduction of service brokers is proposed. This solution advocates decreasing architecture boundaries by controlled and safe measures, executed along with a rigorous analysis process to assess the impact of an intermediary removal. Consider the chief steps that should be pursued when employing the Enterprise Service Intermediary Elimination pattern:

1. Before moving on to the modeling activities (steps 2 to 5), study business requirements, technical specifications, contract scheme, and dependencies among the intermediary service, the service provider, and the corresponding consumers.
2. Untie the intermediary relationship with the service provider.
3. Unlink the intermediary association with the service provider's related consumers.
4. Retire the intermediary entity.
5. Couple the service provider with its corresponding consumers.

Example.   Exhibit 22.14 illustrates four major modeling activities to pursue when employing the Enterprise Service Intermediary Elimination pattern. These are depicted in the two perspectives: the 3D View (far right) and the Service-Oriented Modeling Formal Diagram View (far left). Note the use of the modeling symbols in the formal modeling diagram view: "Decoupled" to denote the disassociation of relationships, "Subtracted" to indicate service retirement, and "Coupled" to identify association establishment. Follow these necessary steps:[4]

1. Decouple atomic service A-1 (service provider) from the service intermediary atomic service A-2.
2. Decouple consumer CONS-1 from the service intermediary atomic service A-2.
3. Retire the service intermediary atomic service A-2.
4. Couple consumer CONS-with service provider A-1.

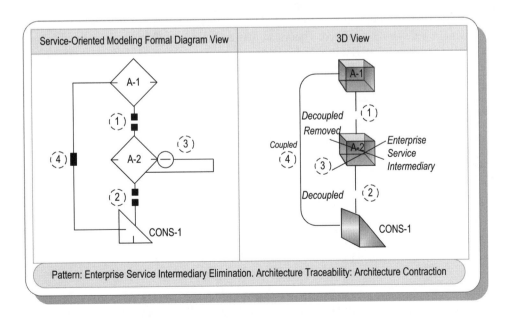

EXHIBIT 22.14   ENTERPRISE SERVICE INTERMEDIARY ELIMINATION PATTERN EXAMPLE

Pattern Identification	
Name	Enterprise Service Intermediary Elimination Pattern
Category	Structural Contraction Analysis
Problems, Solutions, and Implementations	
Problem	1. Distributed service environment is too large, difficult to maintain, and costly to support.
	2. A service intermediary is a major contributor to message exchange performance degradation.
Solution	1. Scale back deployment of service proxies.
	2. Remove a service intermediary that negatively affects consumption and message delivery.
Applicability	Applies to a distributed service environment that is sought to be contracted.
Method	These gradual four steps will be required to pursue intermediary removal from a distributed environment:
	1. Untie the service intermediary association with the service provider.
	2. Unlink the service intermediary relationship with related consumers.
	3. Eliminate the intermediary entity.
	4. Couple the service provider with its corresponding consumers.
Benefits	Contraction of distributed service environment.
Risks	Removal of intermediaries may yield tightly coupled distributed environment.
Notation	Use the "Decoupled," "Subtracted," and "Coupled" symbols.

EXHIBIT 22.15   ENTERPRISE SERVICE INTERMEDIARY ELIMINATION PATTERN SUMMARY TABLE

Synopsis.   The Enterprise Service Intermediary Elimination pattern offers a methodical process for reducing architecture scope and contracting a distributed environment. Typically it is accomplished by removing proxy services and untying their relationships with peer services and related consumers. Furthermore, this simple concept of *architecture collapse* may yield a tightly coupled integrated environment yet contribute to the reduction of service operation scope. These challenges and concerns are outlined in Exhibit 22.15, which also proposes a method of implementation and identifies the risks involved when employing service intermediaries.

Anti-Patterns.   The removal of an service intermediary typically leaves a vacuum in the distributed environment in which it has operated. This vacuum must be addressed and compensated for in order to avoid loss of capabilities. Exhibit 22.16 outlines these concerns and identifies best practices to guide practitioners with the service intermediary elimination implementation.

Anti-Pattern Name	Best Practice
One-Step Intermediary Elimination	To reduce an organizational architecture scope, pursue a gradual removal of service intermediaries to alleviate impact on business and technical continuity.
Intermediary Replacement	The service intermediary elimination process addresses the removal of one or many proxy services from a production environment or architecture blueprints. This exercise is not about replacement of an intermediary.
Lost of Intermediary Operations	Typically, the operations of a service intermediary that is retired are migrated to the service provider or related consumers. These capabilities are related to message routing, message and information transformation, and more.

EXHIBIT 22.16   ENTERPRISE SERVICE INTERMEDIARY ELIMINATION ANTI-PATTERNS

ENTERPRISE SERVICE GATEWAY ELIMINATION PATTERN.   As the reader may remember, the Enterprise Service Gateway (408) pattern discussed in Chapter 21 addresses technological alignment between two or more heterogeneous computing environments. Each installation may host distinct operating systems, language platforms, and even infrastructure and middleware facilities. To bridge these differences, this pattern advocates funneling messages through a gateway (proxy service) that enables transformation of message formats, conversion of protocols, translation between two or more security models, and more. Therefore, the main goal for employing a service gateway is to enable communications between distributed entities that reside in different environments by intercepting and converting their exchanged messages to facilitate flawless execution of transactions conducted across the enterprise.

When it comes to the architecture scope reduction and contraction of a distributed service environment, the removal of a service gateway should be considered to unlink two or more environments and limit the scope of services to their local deployment facilities. Before pursuing this proposition, a rigorous analysis must be conducted to avoid severe consequences, such as disruption to business execution or challenges to technical implementations. Obviously, the Enterprise Service Gateway Elimination pattern advocates retirement of a gateway facility only when the technical advantages are clear and the cost is justified.

Problem.   Remember, the employment of service gateways introduce challenges to the integration of services and performance of transactions that span interoperable production environments. A gateway facility typically is beneficial in large distributed installations that consist of numerous services that must exchange information through a complex network topology scheme. But for a smaller configuration that hosts a few services, a gateway may increase complexity and introduce an unnecessary layer of communication. The phrase "layer of communication" pertains to the technology and the range of products that must support the gateway's proper functionality. These may be infrastructure and middleware software enabling message exchange and orchestration or hardware that hosts application servers and repositories.

Solution.   The removal of a service gateway clearly requires preparations and detailed analysis to identify the potential impact on business and technical processes. This inspection must study the intrinsic dependencies that the collaborating services have developed on a service gateway's offerings. In addition, because of the vital mediation role that a service gateway plays, its elimination ought to be justified. Consider these five steps to pursue when employing the Enterprise Service Gateway Elimination pattern:

1. Study the service gateway functionality and technical capabilities. This may include analysis of transformation types that the gateway provides and other mediating offerings.
2. Identify the dependency of the communicating services and their corresponding consumers on the gateway implementation.
3. Untie the relationship between the gateway and its depending services and consumers.
4. If necessary, establish direct associations between the message exchange services and corresponding consumers.
5. Ensure that the removed service gateway capabilities are substituted and supported by the message exchange parties. Doing this requires adding the eliminated gateway functionalities to the collaborating services and consumers.

Example.   Exhibit 22.17 illustrates the implementation of the Enterprise Service Gateway Elimination pattern. These activities are captured in two different perspectives: the 3D View (far right) and the Service-Oriented Modeling Formal Diagram View (far left). The former depicts a heterogeneous environment that consists of two major installations: Mainframe Services and Distributed J2EE Services. Note that atomic service A-1 used to communicate with its peer composite service

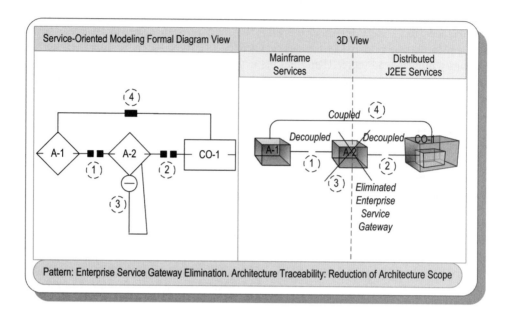

EXHIBIT 22.17 ENTERPRISE SERVICE GATEWAY ELIMINATION PATTERN EXAMPLE

CO-1 through the atomic service gateway A-2. In addition, the formal modeling diagram (at left) uses three symbols to describe the service gateway elimination activities: "Decouple" to denote discontinuation of relationship between the communicating parties with the gateway, "Subtracted" to indicate the retirement of the service gateway, and "Coupled" to identify new association between the communicating services. Consider the four steps that are depicted in this process:

1. Unlink the associations between atomic service A-1 and the atomic service gateway A-2.
2. Discontinue the relationship between composite service CO-1 and the atomic service gateway A-2.
3. Retire the atomic service gateway A-2.
4. Couple atomic service A-1 and composite service CO-1 to enable business and technical continuity.

Synopsis. Use of the Enterprise Service Gateway Elimination pattern should be considered when architecture scope reduction and distributed environment contraction is required. Removing a service gateway then should be exercised in small-scale production environments where the cost of implementation outweighs the benefits. Technical considerations, such as performance degradation and architecture complexity, should also influence such decisions. Exhibit 22.18 outlines these challenges and offers solutions and methods for implementation.

Anti-Patterns. The practitioner must ensure that the use of a service gateway is beneficial to the organizational architecture and that the investment in its establishment is justified. Once a distributed environment is reduced in scope, a service gateway is permanently removed while direct associations between the communicating services are established. These challenges and related best practices are outlined in Exhibit 22.19.

Pattern Identification

Name	Enterprise Service Gateway Elimination Pattern
Category	Structural Contraction Analysis

Problems, Solutions, and Implementations

Problem	A small-scale distributed heterogeneous environment does not justify the utilization of a service gateway because of performance degradation and infrastructure support costs.
Solution	Conduct analysis to assess the impact of the service gateway removal. If elimination is justified, compensate for the retired gateway capabilities by adding the functionalities to the communicating services.
Applicability	Elimination of a service gateway applies to a small-scale distributed environment that consists of a limited number of services.
Method	Follow three major steps:
	1. Untie the relationships between the message exchange services and consumers with the service gateway.
	2. Retire the service gateway.
	3. Establish direct associations between the communicating parties.
Benefits	Reduction of architectural scope and contraction of a distributed environment.
Risks	The elimination of a service gateway is typically a major undertaking that can cause interruption to business continuity and technical implementation because of service and supporting infrastructure dependencies.
Notation	Use the "Decoupled," "Retired," and "Coupled" symbols.

EXHIBIT 22.18   ENTERPRISE SERVICE GATEWAY ELIMINATION PATTERN SUMMARY TABLE

Anti-Pattern Name	Best Practice
No Service Gateway Substitution	The removal of a service gateway typically requires substitution of its capabilities. This compensation of functionality should replace the gateway eliminated operations
Small-Scale Service Gateway Implementation	The employment of a service gateway should be considered for large-scale distributed heterogeneous environments. Eliminate a service gateway if the costs and technical benefits are not justified.
Partial Service Gateway Utilization	Avoid partial utilization of a service gateway. This scenario pertains to usage of a gateway by some services, while others maintain direct communications with their customers.

EXHIBIT 22.19   ENTERPRISE SERVICE GATEWAY ELIMINATION ANTI-PATTERNS

ENTERPRISE SERVICE BUS ELIMINATION PATTERN.   Serving as an enterprise "spine," often named "backbone," the ESB is one of the major contributors to the expansion of a distributed integration environment. It is typically a centralized hub located between services and corresponding consumers to provide asynchronous communication capabilities. Depending on the software product manufacturer, an ESB may also incorporate vital functionality, such as process orchestration, message delivery, message transformation, security facilities, protocol transformation, asynchronous communications capabilities, and more. The ESB is an entity that connects the dots between integrated services and is designed to simplify their collaboration to provide a solution. Centralizing ESB operations is not the only configuration method that architects employ. In a large distributed environment, the ESB also can be federated to reach out to multiple organizations, connect lines of business, and bridge communication gaps between applications.

To facilitate the reduction of architecture scope and the contraction of a distributed environment, ESB removal is one of the choices that should be considered. This is addressed by the Enterprise Service Bus Elimination pattern. Note that this venture can introduce major risks to business continuity, data integrity, message orchestration functionality, service and consumer contracts, and the overall harmony of a service ecosystem. The decision to remove an ESB should be based on compelling and steadfast evidence that its contribution to business execution and technical implementation is no longer beneficial. Substantial decrease of service capabilities and slimming down an organizational architecture model are the leading reasons to remove an ESB from a production environment.

Problem. An ESB installation best suits a large-scale distributed environment that must be managed, monitored, and controlled. The cost and the efforts to maintain an ESB can be substantial because its operations typically require support of specialized infrastructure and middleware facilities. Managing the diversity of business and technical components that make up an ESB is another challenging task that must be considered prior to its incorporation in a service ecosystem. Once a computing environment has been contracted and the consumer base has been trimmed, an ESB may become a liability rather than a beneficial facility. The decrease of transaction volumes and data consumption is another indicator that justifies the removal of an ESB from production.

Solution. A rollback of an ESB is a major undertaking that must be preceded by rigorous analysis and assessment efforts to justify its pursuit. It is a strategic endeavor because of the applications, consumers, and services that may depend on its vital facilitation of message transportation. It is not a tactical process because the elimination of an ESB typically triggers modifications to the overall organizational architecture. It is critical to business execution because of the impending alterations to process orchestration and synchronization of transactions. Therefore, before employing the Enterprise Service Bus Elimination pattern, consider the chief steps that should be exercised to successfully accomplish the removal of an ESB operation and ensure stability of transactions in a distributed environment:

1. Study the integration model and dependencies of applications, services, and consumers on the ESB.
2. Assess the overall ESB removal risk that can affect business continuity and technical execution.
3. Untie communications and contracts between message exchange parties and the ESB.
4. Form direct relationships between the decoupled entities from the ESB only if necessary.

Example. To better understand the concept that is presented by the Enterprise Service Bus Elimination pattern, let us view Exhibit 22.20, which illustrates a six-step modeling process for an ESB removal. The 3D View (far right) and the Service-Oriented Modeling Formal Diagram View (far left) are the two perspectives that depict this venture. The ESB facility is presented by composite service CO-1, while atomic services A-1, A-2, A3, and composite service CO-2 are the message exchange parties that collaborate on a solution. Note the use of the modeling symbols in the formal modeling diagram (at left): "Decoupled" denotes relationship discontinuation and "Coupled" indicates establishment of new associations between the services. Follow the six steps for accomplishing the ESB elimination process:

1. Discontinue the association between atomic service A-1 and the ESB composite service CO-1.
2. Untie the relationship between composite service CO-1 (ESB) and composite service CO-2.
3. Decouple the link between atomic service A-2 and composite service CO-1 (ESB).
4. Discontinue the communication between atomic service A-3 and composite service CO-1 (ESB).
5. Found a new relationship between atomic service A-2 and A-3.
6. Establish associations between atomic service A-3 and composite service CO-2.

Synopsis. Pursue the removal of an ESB with caution. This venture should be undertaken only if a contracted distributed environment calls for reduction of mediation facilities. The elimination of

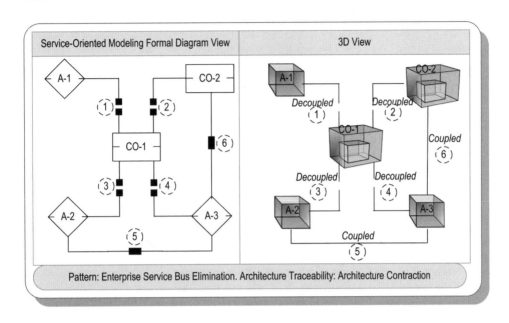

EXHIBIT 22.20   ENTERPRISE SERVICE BUS ELIMINATION PATTERN EXAMPLE

an ESB also should be considered when an organizational architecture exceeds its original boundaries or business requirements and technical specifications require reduction of services capability scope. These challenges, along with the solutions and methods of implementation, are outlined in Exhibit 22.21, which summarizes the key issues associated with the employment of the Enterprise Service Bus Elimination pattern.

Pattern Identification	
Name	Enterprise Service Bus Elimination Pattern
Category	Structural Contraction Analysis
Problems, Solutions, and Implementations	
Problem	An unnecessary ESB implementation contributes to integration complexity and unjustified support costs.
Solution	Gradually eliminate an ESB to avoid business discontinuity and technical disruptions.
Applicability	Applies to a contracted and small-scale distributed environment.
Method	To employ the Enterprise Service Bus Elimination pattern pursue three major steps:
	1. Study and analyze the risks that are associated with ESB removal.
	2. Unbind the relationships that message exchange parties maintain with the ESB.
	3. Establish direct relationship between services and corresponding consumers.
Benefits	1. Reduction of integration complexity in a small-scale distributed environment.
	2. Decrease of business sponsorship and technical support.
Risks	The removal of an ESB may:
	1. Affect business continuity and technical capabilities.
	2. Promote nonstandard messaging solutions.
Notation	Use "Decoupled" and "Coupled" symbols.

EXHIBIT 22.21   ENTERPRISE SERVICE BUS ELIMINATION PATTERN SUMMARY TABLE

Anti-Pattern Name	Best Practice
Temporary ESB Elimination	Reversing an ESB elimination process is impractical because of the major efforts that are typically invested in reconstructing message routes, process orchestration, and synchronization of transaction execution.
Nonstandard ESB Substitution	Avoid nonstandard messaging solution substitutions after the elimination of an ESB. Therefore, adhere to organizational best practices that support universal message exchange strategies.
Asynchronous to Synchronous Message Transformation	Avoid converting asynchronous to synchronous message calls between services and related consumers after the removal of an ESB.

EXHIBIT 22.22   ENTERPRISE SERVICE BUS ELIMINATION ANTI-PATTERNS

Anti-Patterns.   The Enterprise Service Bus Elimination pattern offers a radical yet powerful approach to removing an organizational messaging backbone and message transportation facility. This process should be exercised with care and should follow a rigorous analysis to rationalize such a strategic venture. The substitution of a removed ESB facility is vital to the organization as well because of the potential business disruption that can occur. The best practices that pertain to the aftermath of the ESB elimination are outlined in Exhibit 22.22.

CONTRACT ANALYSIS: PATTERNS AND IMPLEMENTATION

When decreasing the spectrum of a distributed environment and reducing the scope of an organizational architecture, the contracts between services and corresponding consumers must be analyzed and optimized as well. This inspection typically ensures a proper alignment between the trimmed-down architecture model and the service/consumer relationship. How can such an architectural transition influence the contracts between service providers and their related consuming entities? The answer to this question depends on how contracts are being managed in a distributed environment. A well-designed distributed service landscape typically employs two major mechanisms to facilitate message exchange: contract mediation and contract centralization. The removal of these contract facilities typically enables the scope reduction of enterprise architecture.

The contract mediation model assigns contract handling to a service proxy to avoid a direct relationship between a service and its related consumers. This method assists with service isolation and hiding to increase service reusability and security. The contract centralization notion offers a different approach: Contracts are managed by a central mediation authority that contributes to organizational contract management best practices and standards. Again, the elimination of these two contract management implementations typically contributes to the scope reduction of a distributed service environment and rollback of an architecture expansion. Refer to the Contract Analysis: Patterns and Implementation section in Chapter 21 to learn more about mediation and centralization of contract approaches.

CONTRACT ANALYSIS PATTERNS AND ANTI-PATTERNS.   In the sections that follow, the Contract Mediation Elimination (445) pattern and the Contract Hub Elimination (447) pattern introduce mechanisms that can be used to promote architectural scope reduction in the enterprise. The former approach addresses the elimination of a service proxy that handles contracts on behalf of a service provider and a related consumer. The latter method process tackles the removal of a centralized contract facility. It represents the diminution of contract centralization implementations and the transition to a decentralized contract management doctrine. The contract analysis anti-patterns, however, address the proper usage of introduced patterns.

CONTRACT MEDIATION ELIMINATION PATTERN. To promote agile service distribution across lines of business, organizations, and various applications, the Contract Mediation (415) pattern discussed in Chapter 21 advocates employing a service proxy designed to bind a service to its related consumers. A direct relationship, though, describes a tightly coupled architecture where contracts are customized to suit a particular association between a service and a related consumer. By employing a contract mediator entity, the relationships between a service and a related consumer are generalized. This enables a flexible expansion of the environment, increases the service's consumer base, and eases maintenance, monitoring, and contract enforcement efforts.

The Contract Mediation Elimination pattern, however, advocates removing this extra contract intermediate layer to promote the reduction of the architecture's scope, reduce the number of consumers, and limit service functionality expansion. Furthermore, trimming down contract mediators typically simplifies the relationship model among services, consumers, and partners. It also alleviates the maintenance challenges of message orchestration, message delivery, and message infrastructure. But the removal of a contract mediator characteristically encourages directly connecting a service provider to its related consumers. Doing this would negate the previously loosely coupled integrated environment and increase dependencies between message exchange parties.

Problem. Maintaining a contract mediation facility in a trimmed-down distributed environment that consists of a reduced number of services and consumers may not justify the cost and the investment in maintenance efforts. From a technological perspective, guaranteeing flawless execution of transactions that span fewer organizations may not necessitate a large investment in a infrastructure, middleware, and mediation services.

Solution. Obviously the most effective solution is to roll back some *or* all services that offer contract mediation capabilities. But this proxy service elimination proposition typically is accompanied by substantial risks to service operation stability and introduces business discontinuity. To mitigate these perils, the practitioner must ensure that the dependencies of services and corresponding consumers on the contract mediator entity are removed and properly substituted. The term "substituted" implies that a contract must be modified and directly established between a service and a consumer by disregarding proxy implementations.

A gradual and systematic approach to reducing the scope of an organizational architecture is preferred. Here the contract mediator should be eliminated in a few logical steps. These steps must not take place in a short time frame nor be performed in a single project. A number of planned initiatives would ensure the stability of a distributed environment and guarantee interruption-free execution of transactions.

Consider the four recommended steps to employ the Contract Mediation Elimination pattern successfully:

1. Study the dependencies of services and corresponding consumers on the contract mediator service.
2. Unbind the contract of a service provider with the contract mediator service.
3. Discontinue the contract that a service consumer maintains with the contract mediator service.
4. Establish a new contract between the service provider and its corresponding consumer, if applicable.

Example. Exhibit 22.23 illustrates three modeling steps to pursue when employing the Contract Mediation Elimination pattern. These are apparent in two perspectives: 3D View (far right) and Service-Oriented Modeling Formal Diagram View (far left). The contract mediation functionality that was offered by atomic service A-2 is removed and substituted by establishing a direct contract

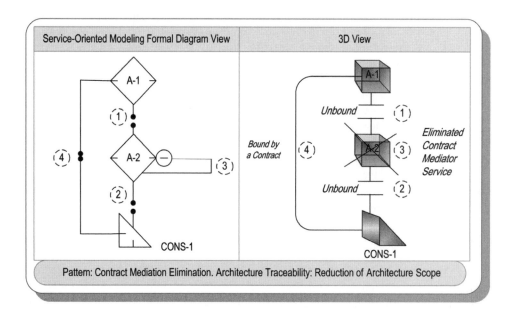

EXHIBIT 22.23   CONTRACT MEDIATION ELIMINATION PATTERN EXAMPLE

binding atomic service A-1 and its corresponding consumer CONS-1. Note that in the formal modeling diagram, three symbols are used to depict this process: "Unbound," to denote the discontinuation of a contract between a service and related consumer; "Subtracted," to indicate the retirement of the contract mediator; and "Bound," to identify the newly established contract between the message exchange parties.

Consider the four different steps that depict the progression of the contract mediator elimination:

1. Unbind the contract between service A-1 and the mediator atomic service A-2.
2. Discontinue the contract between consumer CONS-1 and the mediator atomic service A-2.
3. Retire the mediator atomic service A-2.
4. Establish a new contract between the consumer CONS-1 and mediator atomic service A-1.

Synopsis.   The Contract Mediation Elimination pattern is simply about the retirement of a contract facilitator entity that links a service provider to its related consumers and provides monitoring and contract enforcement features. Removing this functionality obviously contributes to the contraction of an architecture model and as result reduces a distributed service landscape. These challenges are outlined in Exhibit 22.24, which also indicates the affiliated risks and methods of implementation to pursue when the Contract Mediation Elimination pattern is employed.

Anti-Patterns.   A meticulous analysis effort should precede the pursuit of the Contract Mediation Elimination pattern. This examination should include the identification of dependencies between service providers and consumers on the contract mediator and its enabling infrastructure and middleware. In addition, contract substitution activity must follow the removal of the contract mediator. Exhibit 22.25 outlines the best practices that can help alleviate these challenges.

Pattern Identification	
Name	Contract Mediation Elimination Pattern
Category	Structural Contraction Analysis

Problems, Solutions, and Implementations	
Problem	1. The distributed service environment is too large in scope.
	2. The contract mediation model may be complex and costly in a decreased distributed environment.
Solution	Eliminate contract mediators to enable contraction of enterprise architecture and reduce organizational expenditure.
Applicability	Applies to a large distributed environment that employs multiple contract mediators.
Method	These major steps should be considered to remove a contract mediator:
	1. Unbind contracts that are established between message exchange parties and the contract mediator service.
	2. Retire the contract mediator.
	3. Establish a new contract between the services and related consumers.
Benefits	1. Simplify architecture and integration complexity.
	2. Facilitate the contraction of a distributed environment.
Risks	Removal of a contract mediator typically contributes to a tightly coupled distributed environment.
Notation	Employ the "Unbound," "Subtracted," and "Bound" symbols.

Exhibit 22.24 Contract Mediation Elimination Pattern Summary Table

Anti-Pattern Name	Best Practice
Reversal of Contract Mediation Elimination	The reversal of a contract mediator service removal is not practical because of the substantial efforts that are related to contract reinstitution between consumers and affiliated services.
Nonstandard Contract Handling Method	A distributed environment that supports a mix of contract binding methods, such as contract mediation services and direct contract establishment between service and consumers, is typically hard to maintain and operate because of the nonstandard contract handling approaches.
Non-Gradual Mediation Elimination	A gradual and systematic approach to eliminating a service mediator is proffered. This can be achieved by launching multiple small projects or through a succession of contract optimization initiatives.

Exhibit 22.25 Contract Mediation Elimination Anti-Patterns

CONTRACT HUB ELIMINATION PATTERN. A contract hub is simply a service broker that is assigned messaging mediation responsibilities to maintain binding relationships between service providers and consumers in a distributed environment. To optimize the design of contracts across the enterprise, the Contract Hub (418) pattern, as described in Chapter 21, addresses the generalization and reuse of contracts challenges by introducing a uniform method to managing contracts across the organization. The notion of contract centralization is established when services and consumers are linked to the Contract Hub to exchange messages and execute transactions. Beyond the connectivity aspect, the mediating hub service also enables the generalization of contract policy and schema definitions.

In contrast to the Contract Hub (418) pattern, the Contract Hub Elimination pattern reduces the scope of an organizational architecture and facilitates the reduction of a distributed service ecosystem. Moreover, the removal of the contract hub entity typically yields an array of contract substitution initiatives to compensate for the loss of the central contract management facility responsibilities, such as monitoring, security, and contract enforcement. This elimination activity often triggers the constitution of new contracts between services and corresponding consumers to ensure business continuity and technological persistency.

Problem.   In a large distributed environment, a central contract point is obviously valuable to service relationship management, monitoring, and security. This arrangement also contributes to organizational best practices and fosters a systematic method to link services to consumers and applications. A methodical approach to service maintenance is also beneficial when an advanced version of a contract is introduced. However, when reducing the scope of an organizational architecture and decreasing the consumer base of services, a contract hub may not be a necessary solution to a trimmed-down distributed environment. In addition, the architectural complexity associated with the centralized contract configuration may not be justified. Therefore, the maintenance costs may outweigh the benefits.

Solution.   Clearly, the proposed solution to resolving the impracticality of the use of a contract hub is to promote the decentralization of contract management across the organization rather than a centralized contract notion. Remember, this approach must be carefully analyzed and justified to identify the affiliated risks involved. It is a strategic and irreversible endeavor that typically requires expensive resources and funding. This is due to the dependencies of services and consumers on the contract hub that have been established over months or years. Consider the three chief steps that the practitioner should follow when employing the Contract Hub Elimination pattern:

1.   Study the dependencies of services and related consumers on the contract hub.
2.   Discontinue service and consumer contracts with the contract hub.
3.   Reestablish direct contracts between the services and related consumers, if necessary.

Example.   Exhibit 22.26 illustrates seven steps that result in the removal of a contract hub from a distributed service environment. This process is depicted in two apparent perspectives: 3D View (at right) and Service-Oriented Modeling Formal Diagram View (at left). Note the symbols that are used in the formal modeling diagram: "Unbound," to denote the discontinuation of a contract between a service or a consumer from the contract hub; "Subtracted," to indicate the retirement of the contract hub; and "Bound," to identify a new contract between the consumer and its related services. Consider the seven necessary modeling steps that depict this process:

1.   Unbind the contract between service A-1 and the contract hub atomic service A-5.
2.   Discontinue the contract between the contract hub atomic service A-5 and the atomic service A-3.
3.   Unbind the contract between atomic service A-2 and the contract hub A-5.
4.   Untie the relationship between the consumer CONS-1 and the contract hub A-5 by discontinuing their binding contract.
5.   Retire contract hub atomic service A-5.
6.   Establish a new association by a binding contract that involves consumer CONS-1 and atomic service A-2.
7.   Bind consumer CONS-1 and atomic service A-3 by a new contract.

Synopsis.   The contract hub removal process is necessary when an environment of distributed services is decreased and the centralized contract management notion does not serve its purpose. Obviously, this is a strategic pursuit that must be analyzed and rationalized before actual implementation. Exhibit 22.27 outlines these challenges and summarizes the problem, solution, applicability, method, benefits, and risks that are related to the employment of the Contract Hub Elimination pattern.

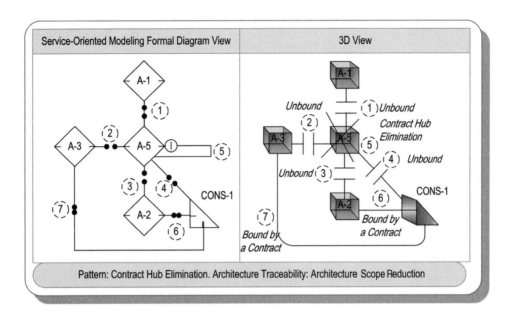

EXHIBIT 22.26   CONTRACT HUB ELIMINATION PATTERN EXAMPLE

Pattern Identification	
Name	Contract Hub Elimination Pattern
Category	Structural Contraction Analysis
Problems, Solutions, and Implementations	
Problem	1. The scope of a distributed service environment is too large.
	2. A contract hub may be impractical in a trimmed-down distributed environment.
Solution	To limit the scope of a distributed service landscape, remove the contract hub and its supporting technologies.
Applicability	Applies to a distributed environment that utilizes a centralized contract hub.
Method	Follow three simple steps to pursue the Contract Hub Elimination pattern:
	1. Study the dependencies of services and their related consumers on the contract hub.
	2. Discontinue the contracts between message exchange entities (services and consumers) and the contract hub.
	3. Establish new contracts to bind services and their corresponding services.
Benefits	1. Promotes the contraction of a distributed environment.
	2. Simplifies architecture.
Risks	1. Removal of a contract hub may yield a tightly coupled architecture.
	2. Loss of a uniform method to manage contracts and reuse of description language, policies, and schema definitions.
Notation	Employ the "Unbound," "Subtracted," and "Bound" symbols.

EXHIBIT 22.27   CONTRACT HUB ELIMINATION PATTERN SUMMARY TABLE

Anti-Pattern Name	Best Practice
Temporary Contract Hub Removal	It is impractical to reverse the elimination of a contract hub process because of the complexity involved and the costs.
Non-Gradual Contract Hub Elimination	The process of contract hub elimination should be exercised during multiple project phases to ensure a stable distributed environment.
Centralized and Decentralized Implementation Co-existence	Avoid the existence of a mix of centralized and decentralized contract handling implementations in a distributed service environment.

EXHIBIT 22.28   CONTRACT HUB ELIMINATION ANTI-PATTERNS

Anti-Patterns.   The removal of a contract hub implementation is a complex matter that requires meticulous planning and many resources to accomplish, due to the dependencies between services and their related consumers that have been established over months or even years. Therefore, a gradual and systematic contract hub elimination will limit business discontinuity and technological disruptions. These challenges and best practices are outlined in Exhibit 22.28.

DELIVERABLES

To communicate the contraction of a distributed environment, deliver a service coupling diagram (discussed in detail in Chapter 18). This artifact should leverage the structural contraction patterns that are offered in this chapter. The three major perspectives that should be apparent are reduction of the distributed environment, removal of proxy implementations, and optimization of service contracts to enable structural contraction.

SUMMARY

- The structural contraction practice offers a systematic approach for reducing the magnitude of a service distributed environment and decreasing the scale of architecture. This method also provides patterns, ready-to-use solutions that can be leveraged for creating an efficient analysis proposition. To achieve these goals, three chief methods are used: distribution contraction, mediation reduction, and contract optimization.
- The contractual contraction practice also offers three major analyses that should be pursued to satisfy business and technological contraction requirements: distribution reduction analysis, mediation rollback analysis, and contract analysis. The distribution reduction process advocates trimming down redundant service functionalities and increasing reusability of services across the organization. The mediation rollback process is devised to cut back on service proxy implementations. Finally, contract analysis is associated with efforts to optimize service contracts and revamp relationships between service providers and corresponding consumers.

Notes

1. The Clipping Mask (429) pattern can also be used to mark a service area in production for retirement.
2. Refer to Chapter 21 for establishing a service federation for expanding a distributed environment. The Federation Scope Reduction (432) pattern, however, supports decoupling of services to reduce architecture boundaries.
3. Chapter 3 introduces a mediation model for service-oriented discovery and analysis.
4. Note the as-is service modeling language feature that is devised to document past decoupling steps.

INDEX

Abstraction Loop pattern, 232, 237–240
Access control, 49–51, 55, 56, 409
Accountability, 55
Aggregated symbol, 308–311, 371, 373, 378–381
Aggregation
    analysis, 331, 332, 357
    data. *See* Data aggregation services (DAS)
    modeling operations, 45, 310, 311, 328, 329
    patterns and anti-patterns, 332–339
    structural generalization, 45, 304
Agility, 13, 17
Alexander, Christopher, 21
Alternative solution proposal, 11–13
Analysis. *See also* Analysis services, discovery of
    about, 1–3, 20
    analysis endeavor, 2–7
    analysis proposition, 1, 11–13, 15–17, 20
    approach, 5–7
    best practices model, 59, 64–68
    contextual. *See* Contextual analysis and modeling
        patterns
    defined, 2
    modeling, 15–17
    patterns, 17–20, 29. *See also* Patterns
    principles of, 13–15
    process, 2–5
    proposition, 1, 11–13, 15–17, 20, 328
    road map patterns. *See* Road map patterns for discovery
        and analysis
    solution proposition, 11–13
    traceability, 13–15
Analysis services, discovery of, 7
    attribute-driven Top-Down service discovery, 100–102,
        104
    Back-to-Front service discovery, 143
    Bottom-Up service discovery, 153, 155–157
    and business processes, 82–87
Anti-patterns (what-not-to-do), described, 17
Application level, 127, 128, 197–199
    contextual contraction, 286, 287, 289–291, 293–296
    contextual expansion, 266–268, 270, 272–274, 282
Architecture-driven Bottom-Up service discovery, 145,
    157–163
As-is modeling state, 15–17, 20
Assessment analysis, 3, 4
Asset notation, 222, 223, 228, 229
Atomic service structure
    asset notation, 223, 227–229
    contextual expansion, 265
    contextual generalization, 223, 227–231, 233, 235, 238,
        239, 242, 243
    contextual specification, 246–248, 251, 253, 255,
        257–261

service structure categorization, 193–196, 198–202,
    204
structural analysis and modeling patterns, 306, 307,
    309–314, 316–324, 329
structural contraction, 425–431, 433, 434, 437, 439,
    440, 442, 445, 446, 448
structural expansion, 391, 393, 395, 398–400, 403, 407,
    410, 413, 416–418
structural generalization, 332–334, 336–345, 347, 349,
    351–353, 356
structural specification, 360, 361, 363–381, 383–385,
    387
symbol, 223, 227
Attribute-driven Top-Down service discovery, 89–104, 124
Attributes
    core attributes, 91–93, 95, 225
    selection, 95–97
Attribution model, 89, 93–97, 100, 104
Authentication analysis, 3–5
Authorization, 55, 56

Back-to-Front service discovery, 11, 51–53, 56, 60, 62, 63,
    70, 123–144
Behavior control, 107, 110, 111
Best practices model for service-oriented discovery and
    analysis, 59–68
Binding and unbinding. *See* Service binding
Bottom-Up Contextual Contraction pattern, 291, 295–297
Bottom-Up Contextual Expansion pattern, 270, 274–276
Bottom-Up service discovery, 11, 41–45, 56, 60, 63, 70,
    145–163
Bound symbol, 308, 309, 324, 325, 387, 416–419,
    446–449
Business drivers, 64, 65, 68
Business functionality, 145–152
Business granularity, 35, 36
Business perspective, 2, 3
Business processes
    analysis, 22, 42, 43, 56
    automated, 55, 71
    and business categorization process, 207–209, 211, 212
    common business services (CBS), 165, 172–175, 180
    documentation, 71, 72, 77
    establishing, 149–151
    flow, 72, 73
    integration, 168–170, 172
    model, 78–82
    platform, 177–179
    and service abstractions, 181, 185, 187, 188
    and service discovery, 18, 71–88
    and service infrastructure, 176–179
    structure, 72, 73
Business proposition, 82–84

Business requirements, 2, 22, 28–30, 52, 55, 99, 139, 165, 166, 168, 172, 208
Business services, 38, 165, 172–175, 180, 207, 208, 211–214
Business servitization model, 38, 64, 65
Business traceability, 14, 306
Buy versus build, 66

Cache facilities, 106, 115–117, 119, 122
Canonical data model, 123, 128, 132, 136, 138, 144, 186
Capabilities, 25–27
Capability Expansion, 308, 309
Capability Reduction, 308, 309, 329
Capability Substitution pattern, 313, 375–379
Capability Subtraction pattern, 313, 369–372
Capability-Swapping pattern, 312, 375, 379–381
Categorization patterns, 17–19, 64
    service categories, establishing, 206–211, 219
    service contextual categorization, 182, 205–219
    service source categorization, 181–192
    service structure categorization, 182, 193–204
Centralization, 54, 166, 167
Chen, Peter, 124
Circular Coupling pattern and anti-patterns, 314, 390, 394–396
Circular generalization, 241
Clipped symbol, 308, 309, 323, 431
Clipping Mask pattern and anti-patterns, 323, 324, 424, 429–432
Cloned symbol, 308, 309, 326, 327, 403, 405
Cloning and decloning services. See Service Cloning and Decloning
Cluster services. See Service cluster structure
Comment symbol, 308, 310
Commercial off-the-shelf (COTS) products, 1, 14, 37, 48, 59, 66, 67, 89, 90, 103, 152, 153, 157–159, 169–171, 175–178, 189, 229
Common business services (CBS), 165, 172–175, 180
Complex event processing (CEP), 171, 177
Component Based Development and Integration Forum (CBDI), 21
Composite service structure
    asset notation, 223, 228, 229
    contextual contraction, 285, 287–290, 292, 294
    contextual expansion, 265–269, 271, 273, 275, 279–281
    contextual generalization, 223, 225, 227–233, 235, 237–240, 242–243
    contextual specification, 248, 249, 251, 253–257, 261
    service structure categorization, 193–202, 204
    structural analysis and modeling, 306–307, 309–314, 316, 318–319, 321–325, 327
    structural contraction, 425, 429, 431, 433, 439, 440, 442
    structural expansion, 391, 393, 395, 397–399, 402, 403, 410, 413, 417
    structural generalization, 339–340, 342–345, 347, 349, 351–356
    structural specification, 359–381, 384–388
    symbol, 223, 227

Compounded symbol, 308, 309, 316
Compounding
    analysis, 331, 345, 357
    modeling operations, 46, 315, 316, 328, 329, 331, 345–351
    patterns and anti-patterns, 345–351
    structural generalization, 46, 304
Concept discovery, 8, 9. See also Service concept
Conceptual data model, 123–127
Confidentiality, 55
Consolidation of services, SOA best practices, 1
Construction-time discovery, 8, 9, 20
Consumers, 303, 305–309, 312–315, 317–319, 324–326, 328
Content delivery, 106. See also User interface (UI) services
Content rendering and layout, 106, 114, 115. See also User interface (UI) services
Contextual affiliations, 196
Contextual analysis and modeling patterns, 17, 19, 221
    about, 19
    asset notation, 222, 223, 228, 229
    balanced solutions, 61, 62
    contextual analysis model, 221, 222
    contextual contraction, 19, 53, 61, 222–224, 283–301
    contextual expansion, 19, 53, 61, 222–224, 263–282
    contextual generalization, 19, 44, 45, 61, 221–243
    contextual specification, 19, 33, 34, 61, 222–224, 245–261
    modeling operations notation, 223, 224
Contextual categorization, 182, 205–219
Contextual classification model, 205–219
Contextual contraction analysis, patterns, and anti-patterns, 19, 53, 56, 61, 222–224, 283–301
Contextual coupling, 234, 236, 237, 253, 256
Contextual expansion analysis, patterns, and anti-patterns, 19, 53, 56, 61, 222–224, 263–282
Contextual Federation Contraction pattern, 291, 297–299
Contextual Federation Expansion pattern, 270, 276–278
Contextual generalization analysis, patterns, and anti-patterns, 19, 42, 44, 45, 56, 61, 221–243
Contextual integration, 264, 284
Contextual relationships, data entities, 125–127
Contextual specification analysis, patterns, and anti-patterns, 19, 33, 34, 61, 222–224, 245–261
Continuous activities, 62
Contract analysis, 34, 329, 414, 423, 444, 450
    structural contraction patterns and anti-patterns, 423, 444–450
    structural expansion patterns and anti-patterns, 389, 414–420
    structural generalization patterns and anti-patterns, 332, 351–357
    structural specification patterns and anti-patterns, 382–388
Contract binding diagram, 328
Contract Cancellation pattern, 326, 382–384
Contract Externalization pattern and anti-patterns, 326, 351–355

Contract Hub Elimination pattern and anti-patterns, 326, 444, 447–450
Contract Hub pattern and anti-patterns, 326, 414, 415, 418–420, 447
Contract Internalization pattern and anti-patterns, 326, 382, 384–388
Contract Mediation Elimination pattern and anti-patterns, 326, 445–447
Contract Mediation pattern and anti-patterns, 326, 414–417, 420
Contract optimization, 423, 450
Contracted symbol, 223, 224, 285, 293, 295, 297, 299, 301
Contraction, 41, 46, 49, 61
    contextual, 19, 53, 61, 222–224, 283–301
    distribution contraction, 423, 450
    semantic contraction, 284
    structural, 20, 54, 61, 304, 423–450
Control theory, 54
Core attributes, 91–93, 95, 225
Core knowledge, 227, 228
Core services. See "Ground zero" service
Coupled symbol, 308, 309, 313, 314, 391, 393, 395, 396, 398–401, 403, 405, 407, 408, 410, 411, 413, 437, 438, 440–443
Coupling and decoupling. See Service Coupling
Create, read, update, delete (CRUD) data functions, 51, 108, 129, 132, 177, 178
Cross-cutting concerns and activities, 22, 23, 53, 60, 62, 63, 68, 263–267, 270, 284

Data abstractions, 52, 185–188
Data access, 123, 127–133, 136, 144
Data access layer services (DALS), 128–133
Data aggregation services (DAS), 128, 133–138, 140, 141, 144
Data architecture, 128, 129
Data caching and persistence, 106. See also User interface (UI) services
Data collection, 135, 136
Data concepts, 18, 52
Data delivery, 127–129, 132, 138–141, 143, 144
Data entities, 124–129, 141, 185
Data integration, 168–170
Data mapping, 132
Data persistence, 132
Data searching, 134, 135
Data security, 123, 128, 130–132, 138–140, 144
Data services, 186
Data storage, 51–53, 129, 136–141
Data transformation, 136
Decision model, attribute-driven Top-Down service discovery, 97–100
Decision tree, 98–100, 104
Decloned symbol, 308, 309, 327, 434, 435
Decomposed symbol, 308, 311, 312, 363, 364, 366–368, 381, 385, 387
Decomposition
    analysis, 359, 360, 388
    Downward discovery and analysis, 25, 39

modeling operations, 34, 308, 311, 312, 328, 329
patterns and anti-patterns, 312, 360–368
structural specification, 34, 304
Decoupled symbol, 308, 309, 313–315, 433, 435, 437, 438, 440–443
Decoupling. See Service Coupling
Degeneralization, 245–248, 251, 252, 256
Dependency Enforcement pattern, 232, 234–237
Dependency Separation pattern, 232, 235–238
Design-time discovery, 8, 9, 20
Dijkstra, Edsger W., 33
Discovery
    about, 1–3, 20
    approach, 10, 11
    best practices model, 59, 64–68
    business and technology discovery sources, 89, 90
    discovery endeavor, 7–11
    modeling, 15–17
    patterns, 17–20, 29, 69, 70. See also Discovery patterns
    platform, 165, 177–180
    principles, 13–15
    principles of, 13–15
    process, 7–10, 90, 91
    road map patterns. See Road map patterns for discovery and analysis
    solution proposition, 11–13
Discovery patterns, 17–20, 29, 69, 70
    attribute-driven Top-Down service discovery, 89–104, 124
    Back-to-Front service discovery, 11, 51–53, 62, 63, 70, 123–144
    Bottom-Up service discovery, 11, 41–45, 56, 63, 70, 145–163
    business processes, service discovery driven by, 71–88
    Front-to-Back service discovery, 11, 50, 51, 62, 63, 70, 105–122
    Meet-in-the-Middle service discovery, 11, 59, 60, 62, 63, 70, 165–180
Distribution of services
    analysis, 329, 389, 390, 420, 423, 424
    composite service structure, 194, 196. See also Composite service structure
    contraction, 423, 450
    modeling operation, 193
    organizational zones for, 265–269
    patterns and anti-patterns, 329, 390–405
    reduction, 329, 423–435, 450
    service clusters, 194, 200, 201. See also Service cluster structure
    and service structure categorization, 195
    structural expansion, 304
Diversification of services, 181, 183
Documentation of business processes, 71, 72, 77
Domain expertise, 41, 42, 46, 47
Downward service discovery and analysis road map pattern, 22, 23, 25, 32–39, 59, 62, 63

Elasticity, 13
Enhanced solution proposal, 11, 12

Enterprise level, 127
  composite service, 198–200
  contextual contraction, 286–288, 290–293, 295, 296
  contextual expansion, 266–268, 270, 272–274, 282
Enterprise message bus, 136, 169
Enterprise Service Bus Elimination pattern and
    anti-patterns, 315, 436, 441–444
Enterprise Service Bus (ESB), 48, 66, 67, 115, 136, 169,
    171, 177, 186, 196, 199, 200, 229
Enterprise Service Bus pattern and anti-patterns, 406,
    411–414, 420
Enterprise Service Gateway Elimination pattern and
    anti-patterns, 315, 436, 438–441
Enterprise Service Gateway pattern and anti-patterns, 406,
    408–411, 420
Enterprise Service Intermediary Elimination pattern and
    anti-patterns, 315, 436–438
Enterprise Service Intermediary pattern and anti-patterns,
    406–408, 415
Entity Elimination pattern, 313, 372–375
Entity identity, 97, 98
Entity relationship diagrams (ERDs), 52, 53, 124, 126
Entity relationship discovery, 124–126
Environmental influences on service structure, 194–195,
    204
Equal-Level Contextual Contraction pattern, 291–293
Equal-Level Contextual Expansion pattern, 270–272
Event integration, 168, 170, 171
Excluded symbol, 308, 309, 322, 428, 429
Exclusion modeling operation, 321–323, 424, 426–429
Existing technologies, 11, 18
Expanded symbol, 223, 224, 265, 272, 274, 276, 278
Expansion, 41, 61
  contextual, 19, 53, 61, 222–224, 263–282
  structural, 20, 53, 54, 61, 304, 389–420

Federated Service Coupling patterns and anti-patterns,
    315, 328, 390, 402–405, 420, 432
Federation
  contextual, 276–278, 297–299
  federated service scope reduction patterns and
      anti-patterns, 315, 328, 424, 432–435
  integration services, 166–168
  and service structure categorization, 193, 200
  and structural expansion approach, 54
Federation Scope Reduction patterns and anti-patterns,
    315, 328, 424, 432–435
Format conversion, 49
Front-to-Back service discovery, 11, 50, 51, 56, 60, 62, 63,
    70, 105–122
Functionality of services, 221, 222, 224–243, 245–261,
    303

Gap analysis, 149, 150, 158, 160–163
Generalization, 22, 36, 41, 61
  contextual, 19, 44, 45, 61, 221–243
  structural, 19, 45, 46, 61, 304, 331–357
Generalized symbol, 223, 224, 228, 233, 234, 236–238,
    240, 241

Granularity assessments, 34–37, 67
Granularity levels of business processes, 72–75, 88
Graphical user interface (GUI), 50, 51, 107. See also User
    interface (UI) services
Gravity point, 201–204
Greer, Derek, 33
"Ground zero" service, 227, 229–231, 234

Hierarchical Structure Unification pattern, 318, 319,
    342–345
Horizontal processes, 23, 41, 56. See also Outward service
    discovery and analysis road map patterns; Upward
    service discovery and analysis road map patterns
Hurwitz, Adolf, 54
Hybrid service types, 211

Identity management, 55
Inception analysis, 3, 4
Information augmentation, 49, 50
Infrastructure as a service (IaaS), 191
Infrastructure-oriented services (INFOS), 165, 175–179
Integration, 41, 46–48, 54, 168–172, 284, 286–288, 291,
    293, 296, 299–301
Integration-oriented services (INTOS), 165–172
Integrity, 56
Interaction control, 107
Interface control, 107–109, 111
Internal service composition diagram, 328, 329
Interoperability model for service integration, 41, 56
Intersected symbol, 308, 309, 320–322, 426, 428, 429
Intersection modeling operation, 319–321
Inward service discovery and analysis road map pattern,
    22, 23, 25–32, 39, 59, 62, 63

Legacy systems
  and Bottom-Up service discovery, 44, 145, 146, 148,
      149, 152, 154, 156, 163
  and interoperability, 46, 48
  reuse, 60, 64, 66, 145. See also Service reuse and
      consolidation
  and service source categorization, 181, 183, 185, 188,
      189, 191, 192
  and SOA governance, 42
  and structural contraction, 430, 431
  and technological best practices, 59
Levitt, Ted, 64
Logical data model, 52, 53, 123, 127–139
Look above the box, 5, 6
Look below the box, 5, 6
Look in the box, 5, 6
Look out of the box, 5–7

Management services, 165, 167, 168, 171, 177–180
Maturity levels, 72, 76, 77, 88
Maxwell, James Clerk, 54
Mediation
  analysis, 329, 389, 405, 406, 420, 435, 436
  facilities, 165, 168, 171, 177–180
  model, 41, 48–50, 56

patterns and anti-patterns, 406–414
reduction, 423, 450
rollback analysis, 329, 423, 435–444, 450
structural expansion, 304
Meet-in-the-Middle service discovery, 11, 59, 60, 62, 63,
    68, 70, 165–180
Message delivery, 49, 50. *See also* Enterprise service bus
    (ESB)
Message integration, 168, 171
Messaging platform, 165, 176, 177, 180
Miscellaneous modeling operations and notation, 308,
    310, 329
Modeling assets, 305–307. *See also* Atomic service
    structure; Composite service structure; Service cluster
    structure
Modeling languages, 14–16, 20, 72, 178
Modeling methods, 15–17
Modeling notation, 223, 224, 228, 306–310
Modeling operations, 15, 34, 61, 67, 310
Modeling principles, 305, 306
Modeling process, 305, 306, 329
Monitoring, 49, 50, 55
Multidimension Hierarchical Aggregation pattern, 311,
    334–336
Multilevel service
    contextual contraction, 289, 290
    contextual expansion, 268, 269
Multiple Binding Contracts pattern and anti-pattern, 326,
    351, 355–357

Naming of services, 98, 100–102, 303
    and contextual generalization, 225, 226
    and contextual specification, 245, 246
Network Coupling pattern and anti-patterns, 314, 390–393,
    420
New solution proposal, 11–13
Nonhierarchical Structure Aggregation pattern, 311, 319,
    336–339, 357
Nonhierarchical Structure Unification pattern, 318,
    340–342
Nonrepudiation, 55

Objectives of service discovery process, 90, 91
Operation Numbering symbol, 308, 310
Orchestration
    and business processes, 73, 77
    and contextual contraction, 284, 285
    and gateway services, 409, 410
    and interoperability, 46
    monitoring, 55
    and Upward service discovery, 42
    workflow approach, 54, 55
Organizational zones for distribution of services,
    265–269
Out-of-the-box solutions, 15
Outward service discovery and analysis road map patterns,
    22, 23, 41, 46–56, 59, 62, 63
Overlapped symbol, 308, 309, 320–322, 426
Ownership of business processes, 72, 73, 75, 79

Partial separation service decomposition, 360
Partner level
    contextual contraction, 286, 288–295
    contextual expansion, 266–269, 271, 272, 282
Patterns
    about, 17, 18
    categorization patterns, 17–20, 181, 182. *See also*
        Categorization patterns
    contextual analysis and modeling, 17, 19, 20. *See also*
        Contextual analysis and modeling patterns
    discovery and analysis road map patterns, 15, 17–20, 29.
        See also Road map patterns for discovery and analysis
    implementation, 15, 17, 41
    as repeatable methods, 17, 69, 181, 205
    of service classification, 205
    service discovery, 69, 70. *See also* Discovery patterns
    service identification, 17, 18, 20. *See also* Service
        identification patterns
    structural analysis and modeling, 17, 19, 20. *See also*
        Structural analysis and modeling patterns
Persistence control, 106–108, 110–111, 117, 118, 122, 132
Persistence platform, 165, 177, 178, 180
Physical data model, 53, 123, 139
Physical data storage facilities, 53
Physical layer, interoperability model, 47, 48
Physical layer services (PLS), 139, 140
Platform as a service (PaaS), 191
Plug-ins, 115, 117, 316
Portal applications and technology, 109, 110, 115
Portlet technology, 109, 115
Post-proposition discovery, 8, 9, 20
Presentation layer. *See* User interface (UI) services
Principles of service-oriented discovery and analysis,
    13–15
Privacy, 55
Product specifications, 18
Project size, 1
Proposition diagrams, 328
Protocol conversion, 49
Proxy patterns, 233, 234, 243

Reduction, 245. *See also* Contextual specification analysis,
    patterns, and anti-patterns
Refactoring
    analysis, 34, 359, 375, 388
    modeling operations, 9, 329
    patterns and anti-patterns, 375–381
    structural specification, 304
Rendering technologies. *See* Content rendering and layout
Retired Symbol, 441
Retirement of service, 34, 39, 359, 372, 382
Reverse Proxy pattern, 250–252, 261
Road map patterns for discovery and analysis
    contextual analysis model, 221, 222. *See also*
        Contextual analysis and modeling patterns
    deliverables, 38, 56
    horizontal processes, 23, 41. *See also* Outward service
        discovery and analysis road map patterns; Upward
        service discovery and analysis road map patterns

Road map patterns for discovery and analysis (*Continued*)
  overview, 17, 18, 21–23, 25, 39
  service discovery process, 82, 83
  service-oriented discovery and analysis, 21
  vertical processes, 23, 39. *See also* Downward service
    discovery and analysis road map pattern; Inward
    service discovery and analysis road map pattern
Routh, Eduard John, 54
Run-time discovery, 8–10, 20

Scheduling control, 107, 110, 111
Security, 42, 44, 48–50, 55, 56, 165, 167, 168, 170, 175,
    177–180, 409
Security assertion markup language (SAML), 56
Security model translation, 49
Security technologies, 154
Selection of attributes for service discovery, 95–97
Selective bottom-up decomposition, 361–363
Selective cluster decomposition, 361, 363, 364
Selective Decomposition pattern and anti-patterns, 312,
    360–365, 368, 372
Selective operation-level separation, 361, 362
Selective top-down decomposition, 361, 363
Semantic affiliations, 19, 197, 205, 225
Semantic contraction, 284, 289, 293
Semantic layer, interoperability model, 47
Semantic reconciliation, 264
Semantic reuse, 226
Separation of Concerns through Service Specification
    pattern, 250, 252–254
Separation of operations, 360
Separation-of-concerns
  and business drivers, 65
  and contextual specification, 247, 250, 252–254, 258,
    261
  Downward service discovery and analysis, 22, 33,
    38, 62
  Front-to-Back service discovery, 107
  Meet-in-the-Middle service discovery, 176
Service, defined, 7
Service abstractions
  and contextual generalization, 222, 224–243
  and contextual specification, 245
  service source categorization, 183, 185–188
Service analysis. *See* Analysis
Service as Plug-In pattern and anti-pattern, 316, 348–351
Service Binding
  binding and unbinding, 46, 324–326, 328
  modeling notation, 308, 309, 324, 325
  modeling operation, 324–326, 329
  patterns and anti-patterns, 326, 351–357, 382–388,
    414–420, 444–450
Service brokers, 49
Service categorization. *See* Categorization patterns
Service classification, 64
Service Cloning and Decloning
  Cloned symbol, 308, 309, 326, 327
  Decloned symbol, 308, 309, 327, 434, 435
  decloning, 327, 328, 433–435

modeling operations, 326–329
patterns and anti-patterns, 279, 315, 328, 401–405, 419,
    424, 432–435
Service Cluster Intersection pattern and anti-patterns, 321,
    424–427
Service cluster structure
  asset notation, 223, 228, 229
  contextual expansion, 265, 266, 280
  contextual generalization, 223, 227, 228, 230–233,
    237–240, 242, 243
  contextual specification, 248, 249, 255–261
  service structure categorization, 193–196, 200–204
  structural analysis and modeling patterns, 307, 309, 310,
    312, 315, 318–325
  structural contraction, 424–429, 431
  structural expansion, 393, 395, 399, 410, 417
  structural generalization, 336–342, 344–346, 351–354
  structural specification, 359–361, 363–376, 378–381,
    384–388
  symbol, 223, 227, 228
Service compliance and verification process, 30, 31, 62
Service concept, 8, 9, 181, 183–187, 189, 191, 192
Service contextual categorization, 182, 205–219
Service control framework (SCF), 108–110
Service Coupling
  decoupling, 423, 433, 435, 437–439, 441–443
  diagram, 328, 419, 450
  federated, 401, 403–405
  modeling notation, 308, 309
  modeling operations, 1, 6, 9, 13, 15, 17, 313, 314, 328,
    329
  structural analysis and modeling patterns, 313–315
  structural contraction, 432
  structural expansion, 389–405
Service decloning, 308, 309, 327, 328, 433–435
Service decoupling. *See* Service Coupling
Service discovery. *See* Discovery
Service distribution. *See* Distribution of services
Service Exclusion pattern and anti-patterns, 321, 323, 424,
    427–429
Service Facade pattern, 186, 199, 202, 394, 409
Service functionality
  contextual generalization, 221, 222, 224–243
  contextual specification, 245–261
Service granularity assessment, 34–37, 67
Service identification patterns, 1, 2, 10, 11, 13, 15, 17, 18,
    20. *See also* Discovery patterns
Service integration. *See* Integration
Service intermediaries, 315, 406–408, 436–438
Service inventory management, 181, 189
Service Isolation, 308, 309, 329
Service life cycle, 1–9, 11–13, 15–18, 42–44, 56
  and service source categorization, 182, 183, 185, 189,
    191, 192
  and structural analysis and modeling, 306
Service locator pattern, 186, 394, 409
Service name. *See* Naming of services
Service operations, transforming business activities into,
    72, 84–87

Service orchestration. *See* Orchestration

Service origins, 183, 184. *See also* Categorization patterns

Service portfolio, 183, 184, 189–192, 205, 206

Service refactoring. *See* Refactoring

Service responsibilities, identifying
  and Back-to-Front service discovery, 142
  and Bottom-Up service discovery, 149
  business processes, 84–86
  Front-to-Back service discovery process, 120

Service reuse and consolidation, 1, 5–7, 9, 12, 13, 59–61, 64, 66, 67

Service sizing, 34, 67, 74. *See also* Service granularity assessment

Service source categorization, 181–192

Service source model, 183, 184

Service specialty
  contextual generalization, 221, 222, 225, 226, 230, 237, 238, 243
  contextual specification, 245, 246, 252, 255

Service Specification Loop pattern, 250, 255–258

Service structure categorization, 182, 193–204

Service subcategories, 211–219

Service transformation. *See* Transformation modeling operation

Service typing, 205. *See also* Categorization patterns

Service-oriented architecture (SOA), 1

Service-oriented conceptualization, 185. *See also* Service concept

Service-oriented discovery and analysis, 1–3, 20. *See also* Analysis; Discovery

Service-oriented discovery patterns. *See* Discovery patterns

Service-oriented governance, 42, 43

Service-Oriented Modeling Framework (SOMF), 185, 240

Servitization, 38, 64, 65, 68

Simple Hierarchical Aggregation pattern, 311, 332–334

Simple Proxy pattern, 232–234, 243

Software
  consolidation, 42, 102
  development, 21, 28, 33, 42, 43, 73
  elasticity, 25, 33, 48, 64, 171, 193
  mediating software entities, 406
  modularity and componentization, 31, 33, 64, 66
  portfolio. *See* Service portfolio
  reuse, 44, 89, 103, 171, 178, 179, 181, 187–189, 229, 230
  scalability, 37

Software as a service (SaaS), 191

Solution proposition, 11–13

Source code, 193, 197, 359–361, 365, 367, 368, 370–372, 374–376, 382

Specification
  contextual, 19, 33, 34, 38, 39, 61, 222–224, 245–261
  structural, 19, 34, 38, 39, 61, 304, 359–388
  technical specifications, 22, 25, 26, 28, 30, 31

Specified symbol, 223, 224, 246, 247, 252–254, 256, 258

Spoke-and-hub architecture, 400

Standardization of data formats, 128, 131–133

Star Coupling pattern and anti-patterns, 315, 390, 399–402

Structural aggregation, 332–339. *See also* Aggregation

Structural analysis and modeling patterns
  about, 17, 19, 20
  aggregation, 45, 310, 311, 331–339
  artifacts, 305, 317, 324, 328
  atomic service structure, 306, 307, 309–314, 316–324, 329
  balanced solutions, 61–62, 72
  benefits, 303
  binding and unbinding, 324–326
  clipping, 323, 324
  cloning and decloning, 308, 309, 326–329, 401–405
  composite service structure, 306, 307, 309–314, 316, 318, 319, 321–325, 327, 329
  compounding, 315, 316
  coupling and decoupling, 313–315
  decomposition, 34, 308, 311, 312, 328, 329, 359–368, 388
  deliverables, 328
  exclusion, 321–323
  intersection, 319–321
  modeling operations, 303–329
  modeling principles, 305, 306
  modeling process, 305, 306, 329
  overview, 17, 19, 20, 303–305
  related modeling analyses, 329–330
  service analysis proposition diagrams, 328
  service clusters, 307, 309, 310, 312, 315, 318–325, 329
  structural contraction, 20, 54, 61, 304, 423–450
  structural expansion, 20, 53, 54, 61, 304, 389–420
  structural generalization, 19, 45, 46, 61, 304, 331–357
  structural specification, 19, 34, 61, 304, 359–388
  subtraction, 312, 313
  traceability, 306, 329
  transformation, 318, 319
  transparency, 305, 306, 329
  unification, 45, 304, 316–318, 339–349

Structural Compounding analysis, patterns, and anti-patterns, 46, 316, 345–351

Structural contraction analysis, patterns, and anti-patterns, 20, 54, 56, 61, 304, 423–450

Structural expansion analysis, patterns, and anti-patterns, 20, 53, 54, 56, 61, 304, 389–420

Structural generalization analysis, patterns, and anti-patterns, 19, 42, 45, 46, 56, 61, 304, 331–357

Structural optimization, 359, 382, 385

Structural specification analysis, patterns, and anti-patterns, 19, 34, 61, 304, 359–388

Substitution of service capabilities, 34, 359

Subtracted symbol, 308, 313, 370–372, 374, 378–380, 383, 437, 438, 440, 446–449

Subtraction
  analysis, 34, 359, 368, 369, 388
  modeling operations, 312, 313, 328, 329
  patterns and anti-patterns, 369–375
  structural specification, 304

Swapping service capabilities, 34, 359

Technical services categorization, 209–211, 215–218
Technical specialties, 119, 120, 141, 142
Technical specifications, 9, 22, 25, 26, 28, 30, 31
Technological alignment and structural expansion, 389, 391, 393, 408, 409, 411, 413
Technological capabilities, 3, 28, 44, 64, 66–68, 154, 155
Technological granularity, 35, 36
Technological perspective, 3
Technological stability, 64, 67
Technological traceability, 14, 306
Technology baseline model, 153, 154
Technology-driven Bottom-Up service discovery, 145, 152–157
Thick client, 108, 114
To-be modeling state, 15, 16, 20
Top-Down Contextual Contraction pattern, 291, 293–295
Top-Down Contextual Expansion pattern, 270, 272–274
Top-Down service discovery, 10, 37, 38, 60, 62, 63, 70, 124
    attribute-driven, 89–104, 124
    business process driven, 71–88
Total dissection service decomposition, 360
Total Fragmentation pattern, 312, 319, 360, 365–368, 372
Total retirement of a service, 313, 372, 382
Traceability, 13–15, 64, 240, 306, 329, 416
Transaction management, 54
Transformation modeling operation, 306, 308–309, 318, 319, 329
Transformed symbol, 308, 309, 318, 319, 363, 366–368
Transparency, 2, 13, 14, 20, 64, 240, 305, 306, 329
Tree Coupling pattern and anti-patterns, 314, 390, 396–399, 420

Unbound symbol, 308, 309, 324, 325, 383–385, 387, 416, 417, 419, 446–449
Unification
    analysis, 45, 331, 339, 357
    modeling operations, 316–318, 328, 329, 331, 339–345

    patterns and anti-patterns, 339–345
    structural generalization, 45, 304, 339–345
Unification of Concerns through Service Specification, 250, 253–256
Unified symbol, 308, 309, 317
Upward service discovery and analysis road map patterns, 11, 22, 23, 41–46, 56, 59, 62, 63
Used-to-be modeling state, 15, 16, 20
User interface (UI) services
    content delivery services (UICDS), 50, 51, 106, 111–114, 122
    content rendering services (UICRS), 50, 51, 106, 114–117, 122
    control services (UICS), 50, 106–111, 122
    and service discovery, 18
    user interface (UI), 50, 105
    value services (UIVS), 50, 51, 106, 117, 118, 122

Verification analysis, 3–5
Vertical processes, 23, 39, 41
    Downward road map patterns. See Downward service discovery and analysis road map pattern
    Inward road map patterns. See Inward service discovery and analysis road map pattern
Veryard, Richard, 21
View and behavior control, 106. See also User interface (UI) services
Virtual data layer services (VDLS), 128, 136–138
Virtual entities, 181, 183, 188, 191, 192
Virtualization, 14, 20, 28, 52, 64, 66, 136–138, 165, 170, 175, 177, 178, 180

Web 2.0, 109, 110
Web Services for Remote Portlets (WSRPs), 115
Widgets, 106–111, 116
Workflow, 54, 73

Zachman Framework, 77